Sunset

Recipe Annual

2002 EDITION

Strawberry-Nectarine Almond Tart (page 91)

By the Editors of Sunset Magazine
and Sunset Books

Sunset Publishing Corporation ■ **Menlo Park, California**

SUNSET BOOKS

VP, General Manager
Richard A. Smeby

VP, Editorial Director
Bob Doyle

Production Director
Lory Day

Director of Operations
Rosann Sutherland

Art Director
Vasken Guiragossian

STAFF FOR THIS BOOK
Managing Editor
Cornelia Fogle

Production Coordinator
Eligio Hernandez

SUNSET PUBLISHING CORPORATION

Senior Vice President
Kevin Lynch

VP, Publisher
Christopher D. Kevorkian

VP, Administration and Marketing
Lorinda Reichert

VP, Editor-in-Chief, Sunset Magazine
Katie Tamony

Consumer Marketing Director
Christina Olsen

Managing Editor/ sunset.com Editor
Carol Hoffman

Art Director
James H. McCann

Senior Editor, Food & Entertaining
Jerry Anne Di Vecchio

Associate Art Directors
Dennis W. Leong
Keith Whitney

JAMES CARRIER; FOOD STYLING: BASIL FRIEDMAN

Our Favorite Roast Chicken (page 37)

This book marks the 15th edition of the *Sunset Recipe Annual*, a collection of the recipes and food articles from the past year's issues of *Sunset Magazine*.

Again this year our writers roamed the West to discover fresh ways to prepare favorite foods, including cracked crab and roast chicken, classic stews and strawberry desserts, hearty salads and traditional fruit pies. Innovative Western chefs and readers shared their special recipes.

We joined accomplished cooks as they entertained, ranging from an intimate Northwest summer supper in the garden featuring the late-summer harvest to an all-American neighborhood barbecue. Our food year ended with a cornucopia of Thanksgiving dishes and a magnificent Western Christmas feast—and the winning recipes from our holiday cookie contest.

We're proud of this year's collection, and we hope you enjoy it.

First printing November 2001
Copyright © 2001 Sunset Publishing Corporation, Menlo Park, CA 94025. First edition. All rights reserved, including the right of reproduction in whole or in part in any form.

ISBN 0-376-02709-6 (hardcover)
ISBN 0-376-02710-X (softcover)
ISSN 0896-2170
Printed in the United States

Cover: Broiled salmon with corn relish (page 17). Cover design: Vasken Guiragossian. Photographer: James Carrier.

Back cover photographer: James Carrier (3).

Material in this book originally appeared in the 2001 issues of *Sunset Magazine*. All of the recipes were developed and tested in the *Sunset* test kitchens. If you have comments or suggestions, please let us hear from you. Write us at Sunset Books, Cookbook Editorial, 80 Willow Road, Menlo Park, CA 94025.

Contents

A Letter from Sunset

DEAR READER,

As time moves on change, which is inevitable, brings new opportunities as well as landmark events. This Recipe Annual marks a turning point in my own life.

After 42 truly wonderful years of researching, reporting, and savoring the food and wines of the West (and the rest of the world), I am leaving my position as Sunset Magazine's Senior Food Editor. It's been a dream job and I've loved every minute of it, but I'm ready to relax, enjoy time with my three little grandsons, and even remodel my own well-worn kitchen. But this is not farewell. I'm still writing my Food Guide column.

Who'll be running things? A skilled team headed by Sunset veterans Sara Schneider and Linda Anusasananan with expert support.

What, you may ask, does all this mean to you? Certainly, you can count on an ongoing flow of interesting, reliable recipes and exciting as well as practical ideas for entertaining.

Kitchen Cabinet, a regular feature since 1929, will continue to present recipes contributed by you that have earned a stamp of approval from your own families and friends. These recipes, like all others, go through rigorous testing and are then double-checked by meticulous retesters in our test kitchens. Our objective, always: the best results, the simplest steps, and the fewest dirty dishes. To share ideas or ask questions, write *Food Department, Sunset Magazine, 80 Willow Road, Menlo Park, CA 94025*; e-mail us at recipes@sunset.com, or telephone our reader-service at (800) 321-0372.

Other ongoing features include The Quick Cook (for occasions when time matters most); The Low-Fat Cook (where calories and flavor count equally); and The Wine Guide (to help you choose quality wines, with the "steal of the month" that's an exceptional value).

As usual, the Recipe Annual presents each article, and all the recipes published in every issue of the magazine, arranged by month. January leads off with 21 easy, healthful suppers using international flavors—interpreted with supermarket-available ingredients—to produce wholesome, delicious, intelligently balanced meals.

Nostalgia-laden favorites appear as we revisit classic dishes, adapting them to contemporary concerns about nutrition, time, ingredients, and equipment. Some examples: Perfect Roast Chicken (page 36), Crêpe Craze (page 42), Grand Old Pot Pies (page 58), renowned salads with historical Western pedigrees (page 110), recipes from popular pie parlors (page 156), *croque monsieur* (page 184), and *blanquette*

The writing team, left to right: Elaine Johnson (senior writer), Jerry Anne Di Vecchio (senior food editor), Sara Schneider (senior editor), Charity Ferreira (food writer), Paula Freschet (contributing writer), Linda Lau Anusasananan (senior writer).

The support team, front row, left to right: Allene Russell (retester), Jean Strain (retester), Dorothy Decker (retester), Jennifer Chaney (photo editor, food), Angela Brassinga (retester), Bernadette Hart (test kitchen manager, editorial services), Marlene Kawahata (retester), Laura Berner (retester); back row: Dennis W. Leong (associate art director), James Carrier (staff photographer), Wendy Connors (retester), Sarah Epstein (retester), Keith Whitney (associate art director), Linda Tebben (retester), Eligio Hernandez (editorial services).

TERREMCE MCCARTHY

de veau (page 234). If you feel like splurging, learn how to deal with fresh foie gras (page 259).

To take advantage of fresh ingredients at the height of their season, January satisfies A Craving for Crab (page 20), as Dungeness crab boats bring in their largest hauls. Honor prime berry season with seven great berry desserts (page 90). As summer comes on, work cool wonders with fresh mint (page 116) and use juicy limes (page 138) for piquant flavor enhancement.

For a touch of exotica, investigate artichoke-like cardoon (page 64); try desserts sparked with mustard (page 65); use falafel mix for crisp coatings and fast flavoring (page 102); savor easy Turkish kebabs (page 126); and freeze low-fat Mexican-style popsicles (page 149).

Throughout the year, you'll find menus for entertaining. At Easter, enjoy A Spring Lamb Feast from Portugal (page 74). In May, celebrate Cinco de Mayo with festive red and green rice dishes (page 98), or let the children take charge of a family brunch for Mother's Day (page 94). For the Fourth of July, throw a Colorado-style all-American barbecue (page 132). In September's relaxed Indian-summer weather, try a Portland Summer Supper party (page 178). For Thanksgiving, choose among the bountiful selection of ideas for turkey and all the trimmings (page 212). And bake winners from our cookie recipe contest (page 246) for a supply of treats throughout the winter holidays.

We also bring you a tree-trimming buffet from New Mexico (page 240), a Christmas Eve crab feed from the California coast (page 242), and to top it all off, a magnificent Western Christmas feast (page 244).

It's been a grand year of shared experiences, great food, and friendly company. Keep in touch! We have adventures to come.

Jerry Di Vecchio

Jerry Di Vecchio
Senior Editor, Food and Entertaining

TO USE OUR NUTRITIONAL INFORMATION

The most current data from the USDA is used for our recipes: calorie count; fat calories; grams of protein, total and saturated fat, carbohydrates, and fiber; and milligrams of sodium and cholesterol.

This analysis is usually given for a single serving, based on the largest number of servings listed. Or it's for a specific amount, such as per tablespoon (for sauces); or by unit, as per cookie.

Optional ingredients are not included, nor are those for which no specific amount is stated (salt added to taste, for example). If an ingredient is listed with an alternative, calculations are based on the first choice listed. Likewise, if a range is given for the amount of an ingredient (such as ½ to 1 cup milk), values are figured on the first, lower amount.

Recipes using broth are calculated on the sodium content of salt-free broth, homemade or canned. If you use canned salted chicken broth, the sodium content will be higher.

Entrées for 21 easy weeknight suppers prove that delicious food can be quick, light, and healthy (see page 8).

January

quick, light & healthy

weeknight wisdom

Eat right, eat well—delicious meals that strike a balance
in the face of diet extremes

By Linda Lau Anusasananan • Photographs by James Carrier • Food styling by Susan Devaty

Science and fashion——unusual bedfellows—meet in our culture of dieting. Trimming trends, usually claiming solid scientific support, cycle in and out of favor almost as fast as the seasons. One year complex carbohydrates reign; the next year protein dominates weight-conscious menus and carbs are the enemy.

Two principles, however, have survived this confusing roller-coaster ride of fad diets: balance and moderation. Dr. Barbara Schneeman, professor of nutrition at the University of California at Davis and assistant administrator for human nutrition for the USDA agricultural research service, affirms these basics: A healthy diet includes moderate portions of foods from all five major groups in the USDA food pyramid. The largest number of calories you consume should come from the base of the pyramid, the complex carbohydrates (breads, cereals, rice, and pasta). Add to that generous amounts of vegetables and

fruits and moderate amounts of dairy products (milk, yogurt, and cheese) and proteins (meats, poultry, fish, dry beans, eggs, and nuts). Indulge in fats and sweets sparingly.

The secret to maintaining this balance over the long haul is to avoid letting moderation turn into monotony. With a little imagination, as in the ideas we offer here, weeknight meals can be highly varied without being time-consuming. They can also draw from all the food groups—and even veer toward high-protein or high-carb preferences—and still weigh in at less than 30 percent calories from fat, the amount recommended by the USDA and the U.S. Department of Health and Human Services.

The simple accompaniments suggested in the recipe notes turn each dish into an appealing, well-rounded meal. Consider this collection both blueprint and inspiration for a nutritious diet to last a lifetime.

Vietnamese Skewered Pork and Onions

Vietnamese Skewered Pork and Onions

PREP AND COOK TIME: About 45 minutes

NOTES: Serve with thinly sliced cucumbers marinated in seasoned rice vinegar.

MAKES: 4 servings

- 1 **pork tenderloin** (1 lb.)
- 3 **green onions** (3 oz. total)
- ¼ cup **soy sauce**
- 2 tablespoons **honey**
- 2 cloves **garlic,** peeled and pressed or chopped
- 1 teaspoon **pepper**
- 1½ cups **long-grain white rice**
- 3 tablespoons **orange marmalade**
- 3 tablespoons **rice vinegar**
- 12 **green-** or red-**leaf lettuce** leaves (3 oz. total), rinsed and crisped

1. Trim and discard fat from tenderloin. Rinse meat and pat dry. Cut crosswise into ½-inch-thick slices and place in a heavy plastic food bag.

2. Rinse onions and trim and discard ends. From white ends, roughly slice enough onions to make ⅓ cup; cut remaining green tops into 1½-inch lengths and set aside. In a blender or food processor, whirl roughly sliced onions, soy sauce, honey, garlic, and pepper until smooth. Pour marinade over pork and seal bag; turn to mix well. Let stand 10 to 15 minutes.

3. Meanwhile, in a 2- to 3-quart pan, combine rice and 2¾ cups water. Bring to a boil over high heat and cook until most of the water is absorbed, 7 to 10 minutes. Reduce heat to low, cover, and simmer until rice is tender to bite, 10 to 15 minutes longer.

4. While rice cooks, lift pork from marinade; reserve marinade. Thread equal portions of meat onto 4 metal skewers (8 to 10 in.) so slices lie flat, with 1 reserved green onion piece perpendicular to skewer between each 2 meat slices.

5. Set skewers in a single layer on a rack in a foil-lined 10- by 15-inch broiler pan; broil 3 inches from heat, turning once, until pork is browned on both sides and no longer pink in the center (cut to test), 6 to 8 minutes total.

6. In a 1- to 2-quart pan over high heat, bring reserved marinade, any pan juices, marmalade, and vinegar to a boil. Pour into a bowl.

7. Serve skewers with lettuce leaves, rice, and marmalade-vinegar sauce. Place a spoonful of rice and a piece of meat on a lettuce leaf, drizzle with sauce to taste, and wrap up to eat.

Per serving: 468 cal., 7.9% (37 cal.) from fat; 28 g protein; 4.1 g fat (1.4 g sat.); 78 g carbo (1.4 g fiber); 1,097 mg sodium; 68 mg chol.

Polenta with Sausage and Greens

PREP AND COOK TIME: About 20 minutes

NOTES: Look for mustard greens washed and cut into pieces in the produce

Polenta with Sausage and Greens

Sautéed Chicken with Artichokes

Top equally with sausage–mustard green mixture. Sprinkle with cheese and add salt and pepper to taste.

Per serving: 481 cal., 19% (90 cal.) from fat; 29 g protein; 10 g fat (1.8 g sat.); 68 g carbo (7.7 g fiber); 579 mg sodium; 57 mg chol.

Sautéed Chicken with Artichokes

PREP AND COOK TIME: About 35 minutes

NOTES: Accompany with hot cooked capellini (angel hair) pasta and a green salad with slivers of fresh fennel.

MAKES: 4 servings

- 4 **boned, skinned chicken breast halves** (5 to 6 oz. each)
  Salt and **pepper**
- 1 teaspoon **olive oil**
- ⅔ cup fat-skimmed **chicken broth**
- 1 can (13¾ oz.) **artichoke hearts**, rinsed and drained
- ¼ cup **pitted niçoise** or Spanish-style **olives**
- 2 tablespoons drained **capers**
- 1 tablespoon **lemon juice**
- ½ teaspoon **dried oregano leaves**
- 2 tablespoons chopped **parsley**
  Lemon wedges

1. Rinse chicken and pat dry. Sprinkle lightly all over with salt and pepper. Place each breast half between sheets of plastic wrap; with a flat mallet or rolling pin, gently and evenly pound chicken to ¼ inch thick. Peel off plastic wrap.

2. Pour oil into an 11- to 12-inch nonstick frying pan over high heat, tilting to coat bottom. When oil is hot, add chicken in a single layer, without crowding. When edges begin to turn white, turn pieces and cook until no longer pink in the center (cut to test), 3 to 4 minutes total. As chicken is cooked, transfer to a platter and keep warm; repeat to cook remaining breasts.

3. Add broth, artichoke hearts, olives, capers, lemon juice, and oregano to pan; stir, scraping browned bits free, until mixture boils. Stir in parsley. Spoon sauce evenly over chicken. Add more salt and pepper to taste. Garnish with lemon wedges.

Per serving: 223 cal., 24% (54 cal.) from fat; 35 g protein; 6 g fat (1 g sat.); 5.7 g carbo (1.3 g fiber); 402 mg sodium; 83 mg chol.

Mexican Pocket Bread Tostadas

PREP AND COOK TIME: About 20 minutes

NOTES: Strips of grilled chicken or beef, available in supermarket meat

section of a well-stocked supermarket. If they aren't available, rinse whole mustard greens well and drain; cut into 2-inch pieces. Serve polenta with cherry tomato halves lightly dressed with an herb vinaigrette.

MAKES: 4 servings

- 3 cups fat-skimmed **chicken broth**
- 2 cups **nonfat milk**
- 1 cup **polenta** or yellow cornmeal
- ½ teaspoon **olive oil**
- ½ pound **hot Italian turkey sausages,** casings discarded
- 2 or 3 cloves **garlic,** peeled and chopped
- ¼ teaspoon **hot chili flakes** (optional)
- 4 quarts **washed and cut mustard greens** (1 lb.; see notes)

- ½ cup **shredded light** or regular **Italian blend cheese** or shaved parmesan cheese
  Salt and **pepper**

1. In a 3- to 4-quart pan, mix broth, milk, and polenta. Stir over high heat until boiling; reduce heat to low and stir often until polenta is smooth to taste, 12 to 15 minutes. If polenta is thicker than desired, stir in 2 to 4 tablespoons water.

2. Meanwhile, pour oil into a 5- to 6-quart nonstick pan over high heat, tilting to coat bottom. When oil is hot, add sausages and break apart with a spoon. Add garlic and chili flakes; stir often until meat is browned and crumbled, about 4 minutes. Add mustard greens and stir often until wilted, about 2 minutes.

3. Spoon polenta equally into 4 bowls.

sections, add low-fat protein to this quick take on a tostada.

MAKES: 4 servings

- 4 **pocket breads** (6 to 6½ in.)
- 1 can (16 oz.) **nonfat refried beans**
- 6 ounces **sliced grilled chicken breast** or sliced grilled tender beef steak (see notes)
- ½ cup chopped **red onion**
- 1 can (7 oz.) **diced green chilies**
- 1 cup (¼ lb.) **shredded light** or regular **Mexican blend cheese** or shredded reduced-fat cheddar cheese
- 3 cups **finely shredded cabbage**
- ½ cup **fresh cilantro** leaves
  About ¾ cup **tomato salsa**
  Salt and **pepper**

1. Arrange pocket breads slightly apart on a 14- by 17-inch baking sheet. Spread ¼ of the beans evenly on each round.

2. Top beans equally with chicken, onion, chilies, and cheese.

3. Bake in a 425° regular or convection oven until pocket breads are crisp and cheese is melted, about 8 minutes (6 minutes in a convection oven). Transfer each round to a plate. Mound cabbage equally on rounds and top with cilantro. Serve tostadas with salsa and salt and pepper to add to taste.

Per serving: 487 cal., 14% (68 cal.) from fat; 32 g protein; 7.6 g fat (3.7 g sat.); 74 g carbo (8 g fiber); 2,078 mg sodium; 38 mg chol.

Italian Meatballs with Spaghetti

PREP AND COOK TIME: About 45 minutes
NOTES: If desired, omit red wine in sauce and add ⅓ cup more beef broth in step 4. Serve meatballs and spaghetti with a crisp green salad.

MAKES: 4 servings

- 1 pound **ground lean beef** (7% or less fat)
- 2 cups finely chopped **onions** (¾ lb.)
- 1 **large egg** white
- 3 tablespoons **fine dried bread crumbs**
- 1 tablespoon minced **garlic**
  About ½ teaspoon **salt**
  About ¼ teaspoon **pepper**
- 1 can (28 oz.) **tomato purée**
- ⅓ cup **dry red wine** (see notes)
- ⅓ cup fat-skimmed **beef broth**
- 1 teaspoon **dried basil**
- 1 teaspoon **sugar**

- ¾ pound **dried spaghetti**
  About ¼ cup **shredded parmesan cheese**
- 2 tablespoons chopped **parsley**

1. In a covered 5- to 6-quart pan over high heat, bring 2½ to 3 quarts water to a boil.

2. In a bowl, mix beef, ½ cup onions, egg white, bread crumbs, ½ tablespoon garlic, ½ teaspoon salt, and ¼ teaspoon pepper. Shape mixture into 12 equal balls (about 1¾ in. each).

3. Place meatballs in a single layer, without crowding, in an 11- to 12-inch nonstick frying pan over high heat; turn as needed to brown on all sides, about 5 minutes total per batch. As meatballs are browned, transfer to a plate with a slotted spoon.

4. Add remaining 1½ cups onions and ½ tablespoon garlic to frying pan; stir often until onions begin to brown, about 5 minutes. Add tomato purée, wine, broth, basil, and sugar; stir until boiling.

5. Add browned meatballs to sauce; when sauce boils, cover, reduce heat, and simmer, stirring occasionally, until meatballs are no longer pink in the center (cut to test), 8 to 10 minutes.

6. Meanwhile, add spaghetti to boiling water and cook until barely tender to bite, 7 to 9 minutes; drain well.

7. Mound spaghetti in a wide bowl. Pour meatballs and sauce over pasta. Sprinkle with ¼ cup cheese and parsley; serve with salt, pepper, and additional cheese to add to taste.

Per serving: 670 cal., 16% (108 cal.) from fat; 42 g protein; 12 g fat (4.3 g sat.); 97 g carbo (8.2 g fiber); 1,318 mg sodium; 69 mg chol.

Halibut and Potatoes with Cilantro Sauce

PREP AND COOK TIME: About 40 minutes
NOTES: Serve with hot cooked green beans.

MAKES: 4 servings

- 12 **red thin-skinned potatoes** (1½ in. wide, 1 lb. total), scrubbed
- 1½ cups fat-skimmed **chicken broth**
- ½ cup **dry white wine**
- 1 tablespoon minced **garlic**
- 1½ pounds **boned, skinned halibut** or other firm white-flesh fish
- 1 tablespoon **cornstarch**
- ½ cup chopped **fresh cilantro**
  Salt and **white pepper**

1. In a 5- to 6-quart pan over high heat, bring potatoes, broth, wine, and garlic

to a boil. Cover, reduce heat, and simmer 15 minutes.

2. Meanwhile, rinse fish and cut into 4 equal pieces. Add to pan and return broth mixture to a boil over high heat; cover, reduce heat, and simmer just until fish is opaque but still moist-looking in center of thickest part (cut to test) and potatoes are tender when pierced, 10 to 12 minutes. With a slotted spatula, lift fish and potatoes from broth and arrange equally on plates; keep warm.

3. In a small bowl, mix cornstarch with 1 tablespoon water until smooth. Add to broth mixture over high heat and stir until mixture boils, about 1 minute. Stir in cilantro and add salt and pepper to taste. Spoon sauce equally over fish.

Per serving: 322 cal., 13% (42 cal.) from fat; 39 g protein; 4.7 g fat (0.8 g sat.); 24 g carbo (2 g fiber); 143 mg sodium; 56 mg chol.

Shortcut Hungarian Goulash

PREP AND COOK TIME: About 40 minutes
NOTES: Begin the meal with coleslaw.

MAKES: 6 servings

- 1 **onion** (½ lb.)
- 2 **red** or green **bell peppers** or 1 of each (1 lb. total)
- 2 **Roma tomatoes** (½ lb. total)
- 1 teaspoon **salad oil**
- 2 tablespoons **Hungarian** or regular **paprika**
- 1 teaspoon **caraway seed**
- 1 cup fat-skimmed **beef broth**
- 1 pound **dried egg noodles**
- 1 package (about 2 lb.) **cooked boned beef pot roast with gravy**
  Chopped **parsley** (optional)

1. In a 5- to 6-quart covered pan over high heat, bring 2½ to 3 quarts water to a boil.

2. Peel and thinly slice onion. Rinse, stem, and seed peppers; slice length-wise into ¼-inch-wide strips. Rinse and core tomatoes; cut each lengthwise into 6 wedges.

3. In a 12-inch nonstick frying pan or a 5- to 6-quart nonstick pan over high heat, stir onion and bell peppers in oil until limp, about 5 minutes. Add paprika and caraway seed; stir. Add tomatoes and broth; stir until boiling.

4. Add noodles to boiling water and cook until barely tender to bite, about 5 minutes; drain.

5. Meanwhile, discard any solidified fat from pot roast and sauce. Scrape sauce from meat and mix with vegetables in frying pan. Cut beef across the grain into ¼-inch-thick slices. Put slices in

simmer, stirring occasionally, until reduced to ½ cup, 7 to 9 minutes. Cover pan and remove from heat; let stand 5 to 10 minutes. Taste, and add salt and more vinegar if desired. Pour sauce through a fine strainer into a bowl.

3. Meanwhile, rinse fish, pat dry, and cut into 4 equal portions. Rub fish all over with olive oil and sprinkle lightly with salt. Set a 10- to 12-inch nonstick frying pan (with ovenproof handle) over high heat. When pan is hot, add fish and turn as needed to brown on both sides, 2 to 3 minutes total. Sprinkle pepper evenly over fish.

4. Put pan with fish in a 400° oven; bake until fish is opaque but still moist-looking in center of thickest part (cut to test), 5 to 7 minutes.

5. Transfer fish to rimmed plates. Spoon sauce evenly around fish and sprinkle with chives.

Per serving: 171 cal., 30% (51 cal.) from fat; 23 g protein; 5.7 g fat (1.4 g sat.); 5.5 g carbo (0 g fiber); 116 mg sodium; 44 mg chol.

Moroccan Beef Stew with Couscous

PREP AND COOK TIME: About 35 minutes
NOTES: Serve with a salad of shredded carrots dressed with lemon juice, olive oil, salt, and pepper.
MAKES: 6 servings

  1 **onion** (¾ lb.), peeled and chopped
  1 teaspoon **salad oil**
 1½ teaspoons **ground cumin**
 1½ teaspoons **ground coriander**
  ¼ to ½ teaspoon **cayenne**
  ¼ teaspoon **ground dried turmeric**
  2 cans (14½ oz. each) **diced tomatoes**
  1 package (about 2 lb.) **cooked boned beef pot roast with gravy**
  3 cups fat-skimmed **chicken broth**
  2 cups **couscous**
  ¼ cup chopped **fresh mint** leaves

1. In a 12-inch nonstick frying pan or a 5- to 6-quart pan over medium-high heat, frequently stir onion in oil until limp, 4 to 5 minutes.

2. Add cumin, coriander, cayenne, and turmeric and stir until fragrant, about 30 seconds. Add tomatoes and their juice; bring to a boil over high heat, stirring often.

3. Discard any solidified fat from beef and sauce. Scrape sauce from meat into pan. Cut beef into ¾-inch cubes and add to pan. Cover, reduce heat to low, and simmer until meat is hot, 5 to 7 minutes.

4. Meanwhile, in a 2- to 3-quart pan

Peppered Swordfish with Cardamom-Carrot Sauce

pan; cover, reduce heat, and simmer until beef is hot, 5 to 6 minutes.

6. Pour hot noodles onto a rimmed platter. With a wide, slotted spatula, lift beef from pan and mound on noodles. Spoon vegetables and sauce around and over beef. Sprinkle with parsley.

Per serving: 557 cal., 18% (99 cal.) from fat; 46 g protein; 11 g fat (3.5 g sat.); 68 g carbo (4.2 g fiber); 503 mg sodium; 157 mg chol.

Peppered Swordfish with Cardamom-Carrot Sauce

PREP AND COOK TIME: About 35 minutes
NOTES: Chef Hubert Keller of Fleur de Lys restaurant in San Francisco demonstrated this imaginative dish last year at the Winter Wine Escape at the Mauna Kea Resort in Hawaii. Serve with sautéed spinach and roasted fingerling potatoes.
MAKES: 4 servings

  1 teaspoon **cardamom pods**
  ¾ cup **refrigerated carrot juice**
     About 1½ teaspoons **rice vinegar**
  1 teaspoon **cornstarch**
  ½ teaspoon **sugar**
     Salt
  1 pound **boned, skinned swordfish** or halibut
  1 teaspoon **olive oil**
  ¼ teaspoon **coarse-ground pepper**
  1 tablespoon minced **fresh chives** (optional)

1. Crush cardamom pods; remove black seed.

2. In a 1- to 1½-quart pan, mix cardamom seed, carrot juice, 1½ teaspoons vinegar, cornstarch, and sugar until well blended. Stir over high heat until mixture boils; reduce heat to low and

over high heat, bring broth to a boil. Stir in couscous, cover pan, and remove from heat; let stand until broth is absorbed and couscous is tender to bite, about 5 minutes. Pour couscous into a wide bowl. Spoon stew over couscous and sprinkle with mint.

Per serving: 519 cal., 14% (73 cal.) from fat; 47 g protein; 8.1 g fat (2.9 g sat.); 63 g carbo (4.2 g fiber); 740 mg sodium; 85 mg chol.

Braised Chicken in Coconut Milk

PREP AND COOK TIME: About 45 minutes
NOTES: Laxmi Hiremath of San Ramon, California, braises chicken breasts in spiced coconut milk for a rich-tasting dish that has a surprisingly moderate amount of fat. Serve with hot cooked rice and a salad of thinly sliced cucumbers and onions dressed with lemon juice, salt, and pepper.
MAKES: 4 servings

- 2 teaspoons **ground coriander**
- 1 teaspoon **ground cumin**
- 1/2 teaspoon **cayenne**
- 1/4 teaspoon **ground dried turmeric**
- 2 tablespoons **white wine vinegar**
- 4 **boned, skinned chicken breast halves** (5 to 6 oz. each)
- 1 teaspoon **salad oil**
- 1 cup thinly sliced **onion**
- 2 tablespoons minced **garlic**
- 1 tablespoon minced **fresh ginger**
- 1 can (14 oz.) **reduced-fat coconut milk**
  About 1/2 teaspoon **salt**
  Thin **red** or green **bell pepper** rings (optional)

1. In a small bowl, mix coriander, cumin, cayenne, turmeric, and vinegar until smooth.
2. Rinse chicken and pat dry. Rub spice mixture all over breast halves.
3. Pour oil into a 10- to 12-inch nonstick frying pan over high heat, swirling to coat bottom. When oil is hot, add chicken and turn as needed to brown on both sides, 4 to 5 minutes total. Transfer to a rimmed plate.
4. Add onion, garlic, and ginger to pan; stir often until onion is lightly browned, 2 to 3 minutes. Add coconut milk and 1/2 teaspoon salt; stir often until mixture boils. Add chicken and any accumulated juices, reduce heat, and simmer uncovered, turning pieces once, until no longer pink in center of thickest part (cut to test), 10 to 12 minutes total. Transfer chicken to a rimmed platter.
5. Turn heat to high and boil sauce

until reduced to 1 1/2 cups, about 4 minutes. Spoon evenly over chicken. Add more salt to taste, and garnish with pepper rings if desired.

Per serving: 253 cal., 30% (76 cal.) from fat; 35 g protein; 8.4 g fat (3.9 g sat.); 10 g carbo (0.8 g fiber); 411 mg sodium; 82 mg chol.

Braised Chicken with Vegetables

PREP AND COOK TIME: About 45 minutes
NOTES: Clean, refreshing flavors characterize this simple stew from Nicole Perzik of Los Angeles. Start with a salad of shredded celery root or beets dressed with lemon juice, olive oil, salt, and pepper. Serve with a baguette.
MAKES: 4 servings

- 1 **onion** (6 oz.)
- 4 stalks **celery** (1/2 lb. total)
- 4 **Roma tomatoes** (3/4 lb. total)
- 4 **boned, skinned chicken breast halves** (5 to 6 oz. each)
  Salt and **pepper**
- 1 teaspoon **olive oil**
- 1 cup fat-skimmed **chicken broth**
- 1/2 teaspoon **dried thyme**

1. Peel onion and cut lengthwise into 8 wedges. Rinse celery and tomatoes. Trim and discard ends of celery and cut into 3-inch lengths (reserve leaves for garnish); core tomatoes and cut in half lengthwise.
2. Rinse chicken and pat dry. Sprinkle lightly all over with salt and pepper.
3. Pour oil into a 10- to 12-inch nonstick frying pan over high heat, tilting to coat bottom. When oil is hot, add chicken and turn as needed to brown lightly on both sides, 4 to 5 minutes total. Transfer to a rimmed plate.
4. Add onion, celery, and tomatoes to pan; turn vegetables occasionally until lightly browned, 3 to 5 minutes total. Return chicken and any accumulated juices to pan and add broth and thyme. Cover, reduce heat to low, and simmer until chicken is no longer pink in center of thickest part (cut to test), 6 to 8 minutes.
5. Transfer breast halves to wide, shallow bowls; ladle vegetables and broth around chicken. Add more salt and pepper to taste. Garnish with celery leaves.

Per serving: 215 cal., 15% (33 cal.) from fat; 35 g protein; 3.7 g fat (0.9 g sat.); 9.8 g carbo (2.6 g fiber); 177 mg sodium; 83 mg chol.

Pork Tenderloin with Prunes

PREP AND COOK TIME: About 35 minutes
NOTES: Nicole Perzik uses evaporated

low-fat milk instead of cream in this fruit sauce to impart richness without extra calories. For an extra-lean sauce, omit the evaporated milk and add another 1/4 cup fat-skimmed chicken broth in step 4. Serve the pork with tiny red thin-skinned potatoes and hot cooked broccoli.
MAKES: 4 servings

- 1 **pork tenderloin** (about 1 lb.)
- 1/2 teaspoon **salad oil**
- 2 tablespoons **Dijon mustard**
- 1/2 cup **dry white wine**
- 1/2 cup fat-skimmed **chicken broth**
- 1/2 cup **pitted prunes**
- 1/4 cup **evaporated low-fat milk**
- 1 teaspoon **cornstarch**
  Salt and **pepper**

1. Trim and discard fat from tenderloin. Rinse meat and pat dry.
2. Pour oil into a 10- to 12-inch nonstick frying pan (with ovenproof handle) over high heat, tilting pan to coat bottom. When oil is hot, add tenderloin and turn as needed to brown on all sides, about 4 minutes total. Remove from heat and spread mustard evenly all over meat.
3. Put pan with pork in a 400° regular or convection oven; bake until a thermometer inserted in center of thickest part of meat reaches 155°, 18 to 25 minutes. Transfer tenderloin to a rimmed platter and let stand 5 minutes.
4. While pork stands, add wine, broth, and prunes to unwashed frying pan. Stirring to release browned bits, boil over high heat for 1 minute. With a slotted spoon, lift prunes from pan and arrange around pork. Mix evaporated milk and cornstarch until smooth; add to pan and stir until sauce boils. Add salt and pepper to taste. Pour into a small bowl.
5. Cut pork diagonally into 1/2-inch-thick slices. Serve with sauce and salt and pepper to add to taste.

Per serving: 223 cal., 18% (41 cal.) from fat; 24 g protein; 4.6 g fat (1.4 g sat.); 15 g carbo (1.4 g fiber); 265 mg sodium; 71 mg chol.

Portabella Steaks with Mustard-Shallot Sauce

PREP AND COOK TIME: About 30 minutes
NOTES: Serve with mashed potatoes and a spinach salad dressed with a low-fat vinaigrette.
MAKES: 4 servings

- 1/3 pound **watercress** (3 cups)
- 4 **portabella mushroom caps** (about 5 in. wide, 1 to 1 1/4 lb. total)

1 tablespoon **olive oil**

4 teaspoons **Worcestershire**

    Salt and **pepper**

½ cup chopped **shallots**

3 tablespoons **balsamic vinegar**

¾ teaspoon **dried tarragon**

½ teaspoon **cornstarch**

1 cup **evaporated low-fat milk**

2 tablespoons **Dijon mustard**

1. Rinse and drain watercress; pluck off tender sprigs (you should have 1½ to 2 cups). Chop enough of the remaining watercress (including stems) to make ¼ cup; save leftovers for other uses or discard.

2. Trim off and discard any mushroom stems to make ends flush with interior of caps; rinse caps and pat dry. In a small bowl, mix olive oil and 1 table- spoon Worcestershire. Rub mixture evenly over smooth sides of mush- room caps. Sprinkle both sides lightly with salt and pepper. Lay caps, gill side down, on a rack in a 10- by 15-inch broiler or baking pan.

3. Broil about 4 inches from heat until juice starts to drip from mushroom caps, 4 to 5 minutes. Turn caps over and broil until juice in caps bubbles and mushrooms are flexible, 5 to 7 minutes longer.

4. Meanwhile, combine shallots, vine- gar, and tarragon in an 8- to 10-inch frying pan; boil over high heat, stir- ring often, until all the liquid has evaporated, about 1 minute. In an- other small bowl, mix cornstarch with 2 tablespoons water until smooth; whisk in milk, mustard, and remain- ing 1 teaspoon Worcestershire. Add to shallot mixture and stir until boiling.

Add salt and pepper to taste.

5. Transfer mushroom caps to dinner plates. Tuck watercress sprigs along- side caps. Spoon sauce equally over mushrooms and sprinkle with chopped watercress.

Per serving: 142 cal., 29% (41 cal.) from fat; 8.4 g protein; 4.6 g fat (0.5 g sat.); 17 g carbo (2.6 g fiber); 330 mg sodium; 10 mg chol.

Sweet-and-Sour Chicken-Apricot Skewers

PREP AND COOK TIME: About 45 minutes

NOTES: Serve with hot cooked cous- cous and a spinach salad with currants and toasted pine nuts.

MAKES: 4 servings

½ cup **apricot jam**

1½ tablespoons **soy sauce**

½ teaspoon **dried basil**

¼ teaspoon **cayenne**

2 **lemons** (5 oz. each)

1 pound **boned, skinned chicken breast halves**

    About ½ cup **dried apricots**

    Salt and **pepper**

1. In a small microwave-safe bowl, heat jam in a microwave oven at full power (100%) until melted, 30 to 45 seconds. Stir in soy sauce, basil, and cayenne.

2. Rinse lemons and cut crosswise into ⅛-inch-thick slices. Discard ends and any seeds.

3. Rinse chicken and pat dry; cut into 1-inch pieces.

4. Thread 2 pieces of chicken onto an 8- to 10-inch-long skewer. Fold 1 lemon slice around 1 dried apricot and thread onto skewer through both sides of lemon slice. Repeat to fill 4 skewers equally. Set skewers on a rack in a foil- lined 10- by 13-inch broiler pan. Brush jam mixture generously all over chicken and fruit.

5. Broil about 4 inches from heat, turning once, until chicken is no longer pink in the center (cut to test), 8 to 10 minutes total. If desired, set pan over high heat, add any remaining jam mixture, and stir, scraping up browned bits, until boiling; pour into a small bowl and serve with meat. Add salt and pepper to taste.

Per serving: 279 cal., 5.7% (16 cal.) from fat; 28 g protein; 1.8 g fat (0.4 g sat.); 44 g carbo (5 g fiber); 479 mg sodium; 66 mg chol.

Pronto Beef Chili

PREP AND COOK TIME: About 25 minutes

NOTES: Serve chili with hot cooked black beans or pinto beans and warm corn tortillas; accompany with a

Sweet-and-Sour Chicken-Apricot Skewers

Pork Chops with Cumin and Orange

sliced-orange and -onion salad dressed with seasoned rice vinegar.

MAKES: 6 servings

- 1 **onion** (½ lb.), peeled and chopped
- 2 cloves **garlic,** peeled and pressed or minced
- 1 teaspoon **cumin seed**
- 1 can (19 oz.) **red enchilada sauce** (also called red chili sauce)
- 1 package (about 2 lb.) **cooked boned beef pot roast with gravy**

  Reduced-fat sour cream

  Thinly sliced **green onions** (including tops)

1. In a 10- to 12-inch nonstick frying pan over medium-high heat, stir onion, garlic, and cumin seed until onion is limp, about 5 minutes. Add enchilada sauce and stir until simmering.

2. Discard any solidified fat from beef and sauce. Scrape sauce from meat and stir into enchilada sauce mixture. Cut beef into ¾-inch cubes and add to pan; cover, reduce heat to medium-low, and simmer, stirring occasionally, until beef is hot, **5 to 8 minutes.**

3. Spoon chili into bowls. Serve with sour cream and green onions to add to taste.

Per serving: 322 cal., 19% (61 cal.) from fat; 36 g protein; 6.8 g fat (2.7 g sat.); 30 g carbo (0.6 g fiber); 1,672 mg sodium; 85 mg chol.

Pork Chops with Cumin and Orange

PREP AND COOK TIME: About 35 minutes

NOTES: Accompany with thinly sliced

cucumbers dressed with seasoned rice vinegar and chopped fresh mint.

MAKES: 4 servings

- 4 **center-cut loin pork chops** (each about ¾ in. thick and 6 oz.)
- ¾ teaspoon **cumin seed**
- ¾ teaspoon **coarse-ground pepper**

  Salt
- 2⅓ cups fat-skimmed **chicken broth**
- 1½ cups **couscous**
- 1 **orange** (½ lb.)

1. Trim and discard fat from chops; wipe chops with a damp towel. Press cumin seed and pepper equally onto both sides of chops. Sprinkle lightly with salt. Place each chop between sheets of plastic wrap; with a flat mallet or rolling pin, gently pound meat to

¼ inch thick, pounding as close to the bone as possible.

2. In a 2- to 3-quart pan over high heat, bring 2 cups broth to a boil. Stir in couscous, cover tightly, and remove from heat; let stand until broth is absorbed and couscous is tender to bite, about 5 minutes.

3. Meanwhile, set a 10- to 12-inch nonstick frying pan over high heat. When pan is hot, add chops, without crowding, in a single layer, and turn as needed to brown on both sides, 3 to 4 minutes total. As chops are cooked, transfer to a rimmed plate.

4. Meanwhile, rinse orange; cut in half lengthwise, then cut 1 half crosswise into thin slices, discarding seeds. Cut remaining orange half into 4 wedges.

5. Return all chops and any accumulated juices to pan. Add sliced orange and ⅓ cup broth; cover and simmer over low heat until meat is no longer pink in the center (cut to test), about 4 minutes.

6. Spoon couscous equally onto plates. Arrange chops and orange slices alongside; drizzle pan juices evenly over meat. Accompany with orange wedges to squeeze over pork. Add salt to taste.

Per serving: 448 cal., 14% (63 cal.) from fat; 35 g protein; 7 g fat (2.4 g sat.); 58 g carbo (2.4 g fiber); 142 mg sodium; 72 mg chol.

Broiled Salmon with Corn Relish

PREP AND COOK TIME: About 25 minutes

NOTES: Serve with sliced tomatoes lightly dressed with balsamic vinegar.

MAKES: 4 servings

- 1 cup **polenta**
- 3½ cups fat-skimmed **chicken broth**
- 1 pound **boned salmon fillet with skin** (maximum 1 in. thick)
- **Salt** and **pepper**
- 1 cup **frozen corn kernels**, thawed
- 1 jar (2 oz.) **diced pimientos**, drained
- ⅓ cup chopped **red onion**
- 3 tablespoons **lime juice**
- 1 tablespoon chopped **fresh mint**

1. In a 5- to 6-quart pan, combine polenta and broth. Stir over high heat until mixture boils, then reduce heat and simmer, stirring often, until polenta is smooth to taste, about 15 minutes.

2. Meanwhile, rinse fish and pat dry; cut into 4 equal pieces. Sprinkle lightly all over with salt and pepper. Lay salmon skin side up in a lightly oiled 10- by 15-inch pan.

3. Broil about 4 inches from heat for 4 minutes. With a wide spatula, turn salmon over and broil until fish is opaque but still moist-looking in center of thickest part (cut to test), 3 to 4 minutes longer.

4. Meanwhile, in a small bowl, mix corn, pimientos, onion, lime juice, and mint.

5. Spoon polenta equally onto plates. Add a piece of salmon to each and garnish with corn relish. Add more salt and pepper to taste.

Per serving: 536 cal., 22% (117 cal.) from fat; 37 g protein; 13 g fat (2.5 g sat.); 65 g carbo (8.2 g fiber); 139 mg sodium; 67 mg chol.

Kung Pao Shrimp

PREP AND COOK TIME: About 35 minutes

NOTES: Begin the meal with a soup made of chicken broth seasoned with fresh ginger and simmered with green onions, sliced mushrooms, and spinach leaves.

MAKES: 4 servings

- 1½ cups **long-grain white rice**
- ¾ cup fat-skimmed **chicken broth**
- 2 tablespoons **soy sauce**
- 2 tablespoons **white wine vinegar**
- 1 tablespoon **cornstarch**
- 1½ teaspoons **sugar**
- ½ teaspoon **hot chili flakes**
- ¼ teaspoon **salt**
- 1 pound **broccoli florets**, rinsed and cut into 1-inch-wide pieces
- 1 teaspoon **salad oil**
- 1 tablespoon minced **fresh ginger**
- 2 teaspoons minced **garlic**
- 1 pound (41 to 50 per lb.) **shelled, deveined shrimp**

Broiled Salmon with Corn Relish

Kung Pao Shrimp

¼ cup chopped **roasted, salted peanuts**

1. In a 2- to 3-quart pan, combine rice and 2¾ cups water. Bring to a boil over high heat and cook until most of the water is absorbed, 7 to 10 minutes. Turn heat to low, cover, and cook until rice is tender to bite, 10 to 15 minutes longer. Spoon rice into a bowl.

2. Meanwhile, in a small bowl, mix broth, soy sauce, vinegar, cornstarch, sugar, chili flakes, and salt until smooth.

3. In a 12-inch nonstick frying pan or a 14-inch wok over high heat, combine broccoli and ½ cup water. When boiling, cover, reduce heat to medium, and simmer, stirring occasionally, until broccoli is bright green and just tender when pierced, 4 to 7 minutes. Pour into a colander to drain.

4. Add oil, ginger, and garlic to pan; stir over high heat until garlic begins to brown, 30 to 45 seconds. Add shrimp and stir until opaque but still moist-looking in center of thickest part (cut to test), 3 to 4 minutes. Stir in broccoli.

5. Stir cornstarch mixture and add to pan. Stir until sauce boils. Pour shrimp into a bowl and sprinkle with peanuts. Serve with cooked rice.

Per serving: 492 cal., 16% (80 cal.) from fat; 35 g protein; 8.9 g fat (1.5 g sat.); 68 g carbo (4.7 g fiber); 932 mg sodium; 173 mg chol.

Leek and Potato Frittata

PREP AND COOK TIME: About 25 minutes
NOTES: Serve with sliced tomatoes sprinkled with salt and freshly ground pepper.
MAKES: 4 servings

- 1 pound **leeks**
- ½ pound **red thin-skinned potatoes**
- 1 teaspoon **olive oil**
- 1 teaspoon **dried thyme**
- 3 **large eggs**
- 3 **large egg** whites
  About ½ teaspoon **salt**
  About ¼ teaspoon **pepper**
- ⅓ cup **shredded Italian blend cheese** or shredded parmesan cheese
- 1 tablespoon chopped **parsley** (optional)
- 4 slices (1 oz. each) **French bread,** toasted

1. Trim and discard root ends and tough tops from leeks; peel 1 layer off each leek. Cut leeks in half lengthwise and hold each half under cool running water, flipping to remove grit between layers. Thinly slice crosswise (you should have about 3 cups). Scrub potatoes and cut into ⅓-inch chunks.

2. In a 10- to 12-inch nonstick frying pan (with ovenproof handle), combine leeks, potatoes, olive oil, thyme, and 1 cup water. Bring to a boil over high heat; cover pan, reduce heat to medium, and simmer, stirring occasionally, until potatoes are tender when pierced, 6 to 8 minutes. If any liquid remains in pan, uncover and simmer, stirring often, until evaporated. Spread vegetable mixture level in pan.

3. Meanwhile, in a bowl, beat eggs, egg whites, ½ teaspoon salt, ¼ teaspoon pepper, and 1 tablespoon water to

blend. Pour egg mixture over vegetables in pan. As edges begin to set, lift with a spatula and tilt pan to let uncooked egg mixture flow underneath. Cook until eggs are firm but still moist on top, 2 to 4 minutes.

4. Remove from heat and sprinkle with cheese. Broil about 6 inches from heat until cheese is melted, 1 to 2 minutes. Sprinkle with parsley. Slide frittata onto a plate; cut into wedges. Add salt and pepper to taste. Serve with toast.

Per serving: 257 cal., 25% (64 cal.) from fat; 15 g protein; 7.1 g fat (2.2 g sat.); 33 g carbo (2.3 g fiber); 485 mg sodium; 163 mg chol.

Warm Turkey Picadillo Spinach Salad

PREP AND COOK TIME: About 40 minutes
NOTES: Serve this salad with hot cooked rice or baked tortilla chips.
MAKES: 4 servings

- ⅓ cup **pine nuts** or slivered almonds
- 1 **onion** (½ lb.), peeled and chopped
- 2 cloves **garlic,** peeled and pressed or minced
- 1 pound **ground turkey breast**
- ⅓ cup **raisins**
- 2 tablespoons **chili powder**
- ¼ teaspoon **ground cinnamon**
- ½ cup **orange juice**
- ¼ cup **dry sherry** or orange juice
- 2 tablespoons **cider vinegar**
  Salt and **pepper**
- 2 quarts **baby spinach leaves** (½ lb.), rinsed and drained
- 1 cup **cherry tomatoes,** rinsed, stemmed, and halved

1. In a 10- to 12-inch nonstick frying pan over medium heat, stir or shake nuts until lightly browned, about 5 minutes. Pour from pan.

2. Add onion and garlic to pan and stir over medium-high heat until onion begins to brown, about 5 minutes. Add ground turkey and stir often, breaking up with spoon, until browned and crumbled, about 5 minutes.

3. Add raisins, chili powder, and cinnamon; stir until spices are fragrant, about 30 seconds. Add orange juice, sherry, and vinegar; bring to a boil. Add salt and pepper to taste.

4. Mound spinach leaves in a wide salad bowl. Pour hot turkey mixture onto spinach. Sprinkle with pine nuts and top with tomatoes. Lift with 2 large spoons to mix.

Per serving: 323 cal., 21% (68 cal.) from fat; 34 g protein; 7.6 g fat (1.2 g sat.); 30 g carbo (7.8 g fiber); 208 mg sodium; 70 mg chol.

Tofu and Pea Curry

PREP AND COOK TIME: About 40 minutes
NOTES: Accompany with sliced cucumbers, tomatoes, and onions dressed with lemon juice, salt, and pepper.
MAKES: 4 servings

- 1½ cups **long-grain white rice**
- 14 to 16 ounces **reduced-fat firm tofu**
- 1 **onion** (6 oz.), peeled and chopped
- 1 tablespoon chopped **fresh ginger**
- 2 cloves **garlic,** peeled and pressed or minced
- 1 teaspoon **salad oil**
- 1 tablespoon **curry powder**
- 1 teaspoon **ground coriander**
- ¼ teaspoon **cayenne**
- 2 cups **vegetable broth**
- 1 package (10 oz.) **frozen petite peas**
- 1½ tablespoons **cornstarch**
  Salt and **pepper**
- 2 tablespoons chopped **fresh cilantro**
  Plain nonfat yogurt

1. In a 2- to 3-quart pan, combine rice and 2¾ cups water. Bring to a boil over high heat and cook until most of the water is absorbed, 7 to 10 minutes. Turn heat to low, cover, and cook until rice is tender to bite, 10 to 15 minutes longer.

2. Meanwhile, rinse tofu; cut into ½-inch cubes and put in a colander to drain.

3. In a 10- to 12-inch nonstick frying pan over medium-high heat, stir onion, ginger, and garlic in oil until onion begins to brown, 3 to 5 minutes. Add curry powder, coriander, and cayenne and stir until fragrant, about 30 seconds.

4. Add broth and stir often until boiling. Whack pea carton on a flat surface to separate peas. Pour peas into pan and add tofu. Reduce heat to low, cover, and simmer, stirring occasionally, until tofu is hot, 6 to 8 minutes. Mix cornstarch and 2 tablespoons water. Add to pan and stir over high heat until boiling. Add salt and pepper to taste.

5. Pour curry into a bowl and sprinkle with cilantro. Mound hot rice in another bowl to accompany curry. Serve with yogurt to add to taste.

Per serving: 454 cal., 8.1% (37 cal.) from fat; 23 g protein; 4.1 g fat (0.3 g sat.); 80 g carbo (9.3 g fiber); 137 mg sodium; 0 mg chol. ◆

Cracked and messy or shelled
and mannerly, crab gives our region a reason to feast

a *craving* for
crab

My sister was coming for a midwinter visit, intent on cramming all the essential San Francisco Bay Area experiences into her stay. Of course, the subject of the ultimate meal came up. "I think we should get bushels of fresh-cooked crab and some sourdough bread and have a grand feast," she suggested. To a landlocked Kansan, getting her fill of Dungeness crab was the California quintessence.

Her timing was excellent. By January the official commercial Dungeness crab–fishing season is under way from Alaska to the central coast of California. And while Dungeness is the most widely available crab in the West, king crab from Alaska—primarily cooked and frozen—is also broadly distributed.

With little more than lemon juice or melted butter, basic cracked crab—Dungeness or Alaska king—makes a quick, irresistible meal. And it takes only a few more minutes to turn in-the-shell crab into cioppino (far left) or to glaze it with a tangy tamarind sauce. But there is a *neat* side to crab as well, shelled and made into dishes both satisfying and sophisticated: crab cakes, risotto, and crab and caviar parfaits. See the box on page 23 for tips on procuring the sweet meat from a seafood counter or plucking out your own at home.

By Andrew Baker • Photographs by James Carrier • Food styling by Basil Friedman

Quick Crab Cioppino

PREP AND COOK TIME: **About 25 minutes**
NOTES: **Serve with thick slices of crusty bread to sop up the juices.**
MAKES: **4 servings**

- 2 tablespoons **olive oil**
- 1 **onion** (about ½ lb.), peeled and chopped
- 2 cloves **garlic,** peeled and minced
- 3 cups fat-skimmed **chicken broth**
- 1 cup **dry white wine**
- ⅓ cup **tomato paste**
- 2 tablespoons chopped **fresh basil** leaves or dried basil
- 1 tablespoon chopped **fresh oregano** leaves or dried oregano
- 2 teaspoons **fresh thyme** leaves or dried thyme
    Salt and **pepper**
- 2 cooked **Dungeness crabs** (about 2 lb. each), cleaned and cracked (see box, page 23)
    Fresh basil sprigs (optional)

1. Pour olive oil into a 5- to 6-quart pan over medium-high heat. When hot, add onion and garlic and stir often until limp, 3 to 4 minutes. Add broth, wine, tomato paste, basil, oregano, and thyme; stir often until boiling. Reduce heat and simmer, stirring occasionally, to blend flavors, about 10 minutes. Add salt and pepper to taste.

2. Add crabs and simmer, occasionally stirring

gently, until hot, about 5 minutes.

3. Ladle crabs and broth mixture into wide bowls and garnish with basil sprigs.

Per serving: 279 cal., 29% (81 cal.) from fat; 30 g protein; 9 g fat (1.2 g sat.); 9.8 g carbo (1.9 g fiber); 535 mg sodium; 109 mg chol.

Creamy Crab and Caviar Parfaits

PREP TIME: **About 25 minutes**

NOTES: **Assemble through step 2 up to 4 hours ahead; cover and chill airtight. Garnish with cucumber and chives just before serving. If using salmon caviar, rinse with cold water and drain; use cold.**

MAKES: **4 servings**

½ cup finely chopped **celery**

½ cup finely chopped **English cucumber**

¼ cup minced **fresh chives**

½ pound **shelled cooked crab** (1 cup; see box, page 23)

Creamy wasabi dressing (recipe follows)

½ cup **tobiko** caviar or salmon **caviar** (see notes)

4 or 8 very thin slices **English cucumber**

Fresh chive spears, rinsed

1. In a bowl, mix celery, chopped cucumber, and minced chives.

2. Spoon 2 tablespoons crab into each of 4 tall, stemmed glasses (about 8 oz. each); divide half the celery mixture, half the creamy wasabi dressing, and half the caviar among glasses. Repeat, ending with caviar.

3. Garnish parfaits with cucumber slices and chive spears.

Per serving: 274 cal., 69% (189 cal.) from fat; 20 g protein; 21 g fat (3.6 g sat.); 3.5 g carbo (0.6 g fiber); 738 mg sodium; 259 mg chol.

Creamy wasabi dressing. In a bowl, mix ¼ cup **mayonnaise**, ¼ cup **sour cream**, ½ teaspoon grated **lemon** peel, 1 teaspoon **lemon juice**, and 1½ to 2 teaspoons **prepared wasabi** to taste. Makes about ½ cup.

Per tablespoon: 65 cal., 97% (63 cal.) from fat; 0.3 g protein; 7 g fat (1.7 g sat.); 0.6 g carbo (0 g fiber); 43 mg sodium; 7.2 mg chol.

Crab-wise Seafood Cakes

PREP AND COOK TIME: **About 50 minutes**

NOTES: **Cooking teacher and cookbook author Heidi Haughy Cusick, who coordinates Mendocino Crab and Wine Days on California's North Coast, developed**

DUNGENESS 101

These sought-after West Coast crustaceans don't yield their sweet meat easily. Cooking, cleaning, cracking, and shelling crab is a chore. Fortunately, the experts behind the seafood counter are willing to help: They almost always sell freshly cooked crabs, and they're willing to clean and crack them for no extra charge. They also offer shelled cooked crab, for a (sometimes hefty) price. If you want to keep the cost down—or simply want the satisfaction of conquering the beasts and filling your kitchen with the briny smell as they simmer away in a big pot on the stove—buy them live and take it from the top at home. Here's how.

■ How to cook crab

1. Keep live crabs loosely covered in the refrigerator up to 12 hours. Grasp crabs carefully from the rear end, between the legs, and put in a pan to make sure they fit, with 3 to 4 inches of clearance below pan rim. Remove crabs and fill pan with enough water to cover crabs by 2 to 3 inches. Cover pan and bring water to a boil over high heat.

2. One at a time, grasp crabs as described above and plunge them headfirst into the boiling water; if you have too much water, ladle out excess and discard. Cover pan and start timing. When water resumes boiling, reduce heat to a simmer. Cook 1½- to 2½-pound crabs 15 minutes, 3-pound crabs about 20 minutes.

3. Drain crabs; to be able to handle quickly, rinse briefly with cool water.

■ How to clean, crack, and shell crab

1. Pull off and discard triangular flap from belly side.

2. Turn crab belly side down; pulling from the rear end, lift off back shell. Drain and discard liquid from shell. If desired, scoop soft, golden crab butter and white crab fat from shell into a small bowl to eat by the spoonful with crab or to stir into a dipping sauce. If using back shell for garnish, break bony section (mouth) from front end of shell and discard. Rinse shell well and drain.

3. On the body section, pull off and discard reddish membrane that covers the center (if it hasn't come off with the back) and any loose pieces. Scoop out any remaining golden butter and add to bowl. Pull off and discard long, spongy gills from sides of body. Rinse body well with cool water.

4. Twist legs and claws from body. Using a nutcracker or wood mallet, crack the shell of each leg and claw section. With a knife, cut the body into quarters.

5. Break apart legs and claws; using your fingers, a small fork, a pick, or a crab leg tip, remove meat. Pull body sections apart and dig out pockets of meat. Discard shells. *One cooked, cleaned 1¾- to 2-pound crab (with back shell) yields 7½ to 8 ounces (1⅓ to 1½ cups) of meat; heavier crabs do not always have more meat.*

Above, citrus chutney adds sweet heat to creative crab cakes. At left, crunchy caviar and cucumber, tender crab, and pungent wasabi dressing offer a glassful of contrasts.

this recipe for times when local crab is not available and other crab is expensive. When local Dungeness *are* readily available, you can increase the shelled cooked crab to 1 pound (2 cups) and omit the shrimp and rockfish.

MAKES: **4 main-dish servings**

- 1 **large egg**
- ⅓ pound **shelled cooked crab** (about ⅔ cup; see box, at left)
- ⅓ pound **uncooked shelled, deveined shrimp,** rinsed and coarsely chopped
- ⅓ pound **skinned, boned rockfish,** rinsed and coarsely chopped
- ½ cup **fine dried bread crumbs**
- ⅓ cup thinly sliced **green onions** (including tops)
- ⅓ cup finely chopped **red bell pepper**
- ¼ cup fat-skimmed **chicken broth**
- 1 teaspoon **dry mustard**
- 1 tablespoon **salad oil**
  Mandarin chutney (recipe follows)
  Salt and **pepper**

1. In a large bowl, beat egg to blend. Add crab, shrimp, rockfish, bread crumbs, green onions, bell pepper, broth, and mustard. Gently shape mixture into 8 equal patties about 3 inches wide and ¾ inch thick; set slightly apart on a sheet of waxed paper or foil.

2. Pour ½ tablespoon oil into a 10- to 12-inch nonstick frying pan over medium-high heat. When hot, add half the crab cakes and cook, turning once, until cakes are browned on both sides and seafood in center of thickest part is opaque but still moist-looking (cut to test), 6 to 8 minutes total. As cakes are cooked, transfer to an ovenproof platter and keep warm in a 200° oven. Add remaining ½ tablespoon oil to pan and cook remaining cakes.

3. Serve crab cakes with mandarin chutney and salt and pepper to add to taste.

Per serving: 224 cal., 30% (67 cal.) from fat; 26 g protein; 7.4 g fat (1.3 g sat.); 11 g carbo (0.9 g fiber); 321 mg sodium; 161 mg chol.

Mandarin chutney. With a sharp knife, cut off and discard peel and outer membrane from 2 **mandarin oranges** or tangerines (about ½ lb. total). Hold fruit over a bowl and cut between fruit and inner membranes to release segments into bowl; squeeze juice from membranes into bowl, then discard membranes. In a 1- to 1½-quart pan over high heat, stir 1 tablespoon minced **garlic** and 1 tablespoon minced **fresh jalapeño chili** in ½ teaspoon **salad oil** until garlic and chili begin to sizzle, about 1 minute. Add ½ cup **mango chutney,** 2 tablespoons **rice vinegar,** ⅛ teaspoon **hot chili flakes,** and mandarin segments and their juice. Stir until boiling, then reduce heat and simmer, stirring often, until mixture is reduced to ½ cup, 8 to 10 minutes. Serve hot or warm. Makes about ½ cup.

Per tablespoon: 74 cal., 3.6% (2.7 cal.) from fat; 0.2 g protein; 0.3 g fat (0 g sat.); 17 g carbo (0.5 g fiber); 170 mg sodium; 0 mg chol.

Cracked Crab with Tamarind Sauce

PREP AND COOK TIME: About 30 minutes

NOTES: Tamarind is sold in many forms. The concentrate, not to be confused with paste or pulp, is a thick liquid created from the pulp, with the seeds and other solids strained out. It's available in Asian food stores. If you can't find it, in step 2 substitute 1 can (6 oz.) tomato paste and ¼ cup lime juice mixed with 1 cup fat-skimmed chicken broth.

MAKES: 4 servings

¼ cup **salad oil**

½ cup thinly sliced **shallots**

1¼ cups **tamarind concentrate** (see notes)

½ cup **honey**

¼ cup **reduced-sodium soy sauce**

1 tablespoon minced **garlic**

1 tablespoon minced **fresh ginger**

1½ teaspoons **hot chili flakes**

2 cooked **Dungeness crabs** (about 2 lb. each), cleaned and cracked (see box, page 23)

1 tablespoon minced **fresh cilantro**

1. Pour oil into a 14-inch wok or a 5- to 6-quart pan over high heat. When it's hot, add shallots and stir often until well browned and crisp, 1 to 2 minutes. With a slotted spoon, transfer shallots to paper towels to drain.

2. To wok, add tamarind concentrate, honey, soy sauce, garlic, ginger, and chili flakes. Bring to a boil and stir often until mixture is reduced to 1 cup, about 5 minutes. Add crab and stir until coated with sauce and hot, about 5 minutes.

3. Pour crab onto a rimmed platter. Sprinkle with shallots and cilantro.

Crisp shallots and a sticky tamarind glaze make cracked crab a multinapkin treat.
LOWER RIGHT: Delicate Japanese chawan mushi savory custard.

Per serving: 430 cal., 33% (144 cal.) from fat; 25 g protein; 16 g fat (2 g sat.); 50 g carbo (2.3 g fiber); 1,246 mg sodium; 109 mg chol.

Crab and Mushroom Risotto

PREP AND COOK TIME: About 1 hour

NOTES: This dish is an indulgent treat with or without the beef marrow.

MAKES: 4 servings

8 **beef marrow bones** (each 3 to 4 in. long, 6 lb. total), optional

½ pound **mushrooms**

2 tablespoons **butter** or margarine

1 cup **medium-grain white rice** such as arborio or pearl

¼ cup thinly sliced **green onions** (including tops)

3½ cups fat-skimmed **chicken broth**

1 cup **dry white wine**

¼ cup **brandy**

1 pound **shelled cooked crab** (2 cups; see box, page 23)

¼ cup minced **parsley** or fresh chives

1. Place marrow bones in a single layer in a 3-quart shallow casserole (about 9 by 13 in.). Bake in a 450° regular or convection oven until bones are lightly browned and marrow is very soft when pierced, 25 to 35 minutes. When bones are cool enough to handle, in about 30 minutes, lift 1 bone at a time and tilt at an angle; use a chopstick, marrow spoon, or long, slender knife to release marrow, and shake it into a bowl. Keep warm.

2. Meanwhile, trim and discard discolored stem ends from mushrooms. Rinse mushrooms and thinly slice.

3. In a 3- to 4-quart pan over high heat, stir mushrooms in butter until well browned, 8 to 10 minutes. Add rice and green onions; stir until rice is opaque and onions are limp, about 3

minutes. Add 3 cups broth, wine, and brandy; bring to a boil, reduce heat, and simmer, stirring often, until liquid is absorbed and rice is tender to bite, about 20 minutes.

4. Stir in remaining ½ cup broth, then add crab and mix gently.

5. Spoon risotto into wide bowls. Top equally with marrow, cut into chunks. Sprinkle with parsley.

Per serving without marrow: 429 cal., 17% (75 cal.) from fat; 35 g protein; 8.3 g fat (3.9 g sat.); 42 g carbo (1.7 g fiber); 449 mg sodium; 129 mg chol.

King Crab with Lemon Grass–Ginger Butter and Roasted Potatoes

PREP AND COOK TIME: **About 1 hour**

NOTES: Jack Amon, chef at the Marx Bros. Café in Anchorage, serves Alaska king crab with a simple butter sauce and hearty potatoes. If you buy the crab legs thawed, you can have the fishmonger crack them for you, or use a nutcracker or wood mallet to crack the shell along each section of crab legs. Cracked Dungeness crab is also delicious brushed with the lemon grass–ginger butter, then broiled (step 4).

MAKES: **5 or 6 servings**

1¾ pounds **red thin-skinned potatoes** (each 2 to 2½ in. wide)

Lemon grass–ginger butter (recipe follows; see notes)

2 tablespoons **grated parmesan cheese**

2 tablespoons minced **shallot** or onion

1 tablespoon minced **parsley**

1 teaspoon minced **garlic**

5 pounds thawed **frozen cooked Alaska king crab legs,** cracked (see notes)

1 tablespoon minced **fresh basil** leaves or 1 teaspoon dried basil

1. Scrub potatoes; cut each in half across widest dimension and brush cut sides with lemon grass–ginger butter, about 1 tablespoon total. Set potatoes cut side up in a shallow 3-quart casserole (about 9 by 13 in.).

2. Bake in a 400° regular or convection oven for 20 minutes. Turn potatoes cut side down and bake until well browned and tender when pierced, 20 to 30 minutes longer.

3. Meanwhile, in a small bowl, mix parmesan cheese, shallot, parsley, and garlic. When potatoes are done, sprinkle mixture evenly over them. Cover and keep warm.

4. Arrange crab legs in a single layer in an 11- by 17-inch pan. Brush with lemon grass–ginger butter, using about 2 tablespoons total. Broil 4 to 6 inches from heat until meat is hot in center of thickest part of leg (cut where cracked to test), 8 to 10 minutes.

5. Transfer crab legs to a platter, arrange potatoes around them, and sprinkle with the minced fresh basil. Serve with the remaining lemon grass–ginger butter to add to taste.

Per serving: 381 cal., 23% (86 cal.) from fat; 46 g protein; 9.6 g fat (4 g sat.); 25 g carbo (2.3 g fiber); 687 mg sodium; 228 mg chol.

Lemon grass–ginger butter. Trim and discard tough tops and root ends from 4 stalks **fresh lemon grass** (about ¼ lb.

total). Remove and discard tough outer layers. With the flat side of a knife, crush tender inner stalks; cut crushed stalks into 2-inch pieces. In a 1½- to 2-quart pan over high heat, combine lemon grass pieces, 1 cup (½ lb.) **butter** or margarine, ¼ cup minced **fresh ginger,** and 4 teaspoons minced **garlic.** When butter is melted, turn heat to low and stir often until flavors are blended, 15 to 20 minutes. With a slotted spoon, lift out and discard lemon grass. Use butter hot. If making up to 1 day ahead, let cool, cover, and chill; reheat to serve. Makes about ¾ cup.

Per tablespoon: 139 cal., 97% (135 cal.) from fat; 0.3 g protein; 15 g fat (9.6 g sat.); 0.7 g carbo (0.1 g fiber); 157 mg sodium; 41 mg chol.

Crab Chawan Mushi

PREP AND COOK TIME: **About 40 minutes**

NOTES: Classically, this Japanese custard is made with clams. *Dashi-no-moto* (powdered soup base made from fish, mushrooms, and seaweed) is sold in Asian markets or well-stocked grocery stores. Reconstitute as directed on package for noodle soup; cool slightly.

MAKES: **4 first-course servings**

4 **large eggs**

3 tablespoons **dry sherry**

2 teaspoons **soy sauce**

1 teaspoon **sugar**

½ teaspoon **salt**

1⅓ cups warm prepared **dashi-no-moto** (see notes) or fat-skimmed chicken broth

6 ounces **shelled cooked crab** (¾ cup; see box, page 23)

2 tablespoons thinly sliced **green onion** (including tops)

1 teaspoon minced **fresh ginger**

1. In a bowl, beat eggs to blend with sherry, soy sauce, sugar, and salt. Whisk in dashi, then stir in crab, green onion, and ginger.

2. Pour egg mixture equally into 4 custard cups or ramekins (8-oz. size). Cover cups tightly with foil.

3. Pour 1 inch of water into a 5- to 6-quart pan (about 10 in. wide and 4 in. deep); set a rack in pan over water. Bring to a boil over high heat; reduce heat to a simmer and set custard cups slightly apart on rack. Cover pan and simmer until custards barely jiggle in the center when cups are gently shaken (lift foil to check), 8 to 10 minutes.

Per serving: 151 cal., 34% (52 cal.) from fat; 18 g protein; 5.8 g fat (1.6 g sat.); 2.7 g carbo (0.1 g fiber); 669 mg sodium; 255 mg chol. ◆

food guide

By Jerry Anne Di Vecchio

Pasta stacks up

Layering lasagna the easy way

■ My fondest memories of lasagna take me back to Bologna. Surely, in this scholarly Italian city—home to one of Europe's oldest universities—the pasta that separates the layers of brick red, mellow meat sauce is the thinnest to be found in all of Italy. It's also often green from spinach, which, to my mind, contributes more color than flavor. It's the contrast between the delicate density of the pasta and the creamy béchamel and subtle meat sauce that pushes Bologna's lasagna to the top of the class.

At home, instead of making pasta, I have settled for thick, ripply dried lasagna, which doesn't quite stack up. But a recently introduced oven-ready dried lasagna (page 27) meets Bolognese standards with ease.

Lazy Lasagna Bolognese

PREP AND COOK TIME: About 2¼ hours
NOTES: Prepare béchamel sauce while meat sauce simmers. Assemble lasagna (through step 4) up to 1 day ahead, cover, and chill; bake about 50 minutes.
MAKES: 8 servings

- ½ pound **mushrooms**
- 1 **onion** (½ lb.), peeled and chopped
- 2 tablespoons **olive oil**
- 1 cup finely chopped **parsley**
- 1 pound **ground beef chuck**
- ½ pound **mild Italian sausages**, casings removed
- ½ teaspoon **dried thyme**
- 2 tablespoons **balsamic vinegar**
- 1 can (6 oz.) **tomato paste**
- 1 can (8 oz.) **tomato sauce**
- 2 cups fat-skimmed **chicken broth**
  Béchamel sauce (recipe follows)
- 1 box (9 oz.) **oven-ready dried lasagna**

About 1¼ cups **shredded parmesan cheese** (about 5 oz.)

¼ teaspoon **ground nutmeg**

1. Rinse mushrooms; trim off and discard discolored stem ends. Thinly slice mushrooms. In a 5- to 6-quart pan, combine mushrooms, onion, and olive oil. Cover and stir often over medium-high heat until mushrooms are juicy, about 4 minutes. Uncover, add parsley, and stir often over high heat until vegetables are lightly browned, 5 to 8 minutes. Pour mixture into a bowl.

2. Add beef and sausages to pan. Over high heat, crumble meats with a spoon and stir often until well browned, 10 to 15 minutes; discard fat. Add mushroom mixture, thyme, vinegar, tomato paste, tomato sauce, and broth; stir until boiling. Reduce heat and simmer, stirring often, until most of the liquid has evaporated, about 30 minutes.

3. Spoon 1 cup béchamel sauce into a shallow 9- by 13-inch casserole (3 qt.) and spread evenly over bottom. Arrange ¼ of the pasta evenly over

béchamel sauce to cover as much of the casserole bottom as possible.

4. Spoon ⅓ of the meat sauce over pasta in casserole and spread level. Drizzle meat sauce with about ½ cup béchamel and sprinkle with about ¼ cup cheese. Cover cheese with another ¼ of the pasta and top with another ⅓ of the meat sauce, ½ cup béchamel, and ¼ cup cheese. Arrange a third layer of pasta over cheese and cover with remaining meat sauce, ½ cup béchamel, and ¼ cup cheese. Cover with the last ¼ of the pasta and spread remaining béchamel over pasta to moisten evenly; sprinkle with remaining cheese and the nutmeg. Cover pan tightly with foil.

5. Bake in a 350° regular or convection oven until sauce is bubbling vigorously and pasta edges are beginning to brown (lift a corner of foil to check), about 40 minutes.

6. Let stand about 10 minutes; cut into rectangles and serve with a wide spatula.

Per serving: 533 cal., 42% (225 cal.) from fat; 35 g protein; 25 g fat (10 g sat.); 43 g carbo (3.9 g fiber); 988 mg sodium; 71 mg chol.

Sunshine sugars

■ Last spring, a busload of Swedish food editors, including my old friend Astrid Abrahamsson, stopped by for a visit on their annual research and recreation expedition, and we cooked lunch together at *Sunset.*

They went wild over our thick beef steaks, which we grilled, and the fruit, which they cut up and moistened with orange and lemon juices. The final touch was a new twist for me: lime sugar—grated peel (enough to add color as well as flavor) mixed with sugar.

Citrus sugars can also be made with lemon, orange, or grapefruit. All are long-lasting, with even more uses than cinnamon sugar. They add a wonderful aromatic dimension as well as taste to any fresh fruit. I also sprinkle them over plain yogurt or onto toast (they're particularly tasty on raisin toast). Citrus sugars also make great flavorings for whipped cream.

Citrus Sugar

In a small bowl, mix ½ cup **granulated sugar** with 1 to 1½ teaspoons grated **citrus** peel (1 lime, 1 lemon, 1 orange, or part of a grapefruit), crushing with the back of a spoon to release flavor. Serve, or seal airtight and store at room temperature until flavor fades, up to 1 month. Makes about ½ cup.

Per teaspoon: 16 cal., 0% (0 cal.) from fat; 0 g protein; 0 g fat; 4.2 g carbo (0 g fiber); 0 mg sodium; 0 mg chol.

JAMES CARRIER

E. SPENCER TOY

Béchamel Sauce

PREP AND COOK TIME: About 25 minutes

MAKES: 4 cups

- 1 **onion** (6 oz.), peeled and finely chopped
- 1 tablespoon **butter** or olive oil
- ½ teaspoon **ground nutmeg**
- ¼ cup **all-purpose flour**
- 2½ cups **low-fat milk**
- 2 cups fat-skimmed **chicken broth**

1. In a 5- to 6-quart pan over medium-high heat, frequently stir onion in butter until lightly browned, about 5 minutes. Add nutmeg and flour; stir until lightly browned, about 2 minutes.

2. Remove from heat and whisk in milk and broth. Stir over high heat until boiling; reduce heat and boil gently, stirring often, until sauce is reduced to 4 cups, about 10 minutes. Use hot or cold.

Per ½ cup: 76 cal., 28% (21 cal.) from fat; 5.1 g protein; 2.3 g fat (1.4 g sat.); 8.3 g carbo (0.4 g fiber); 72 mg sodium; 6.9 mg chol.

Fresh from a box

■ Ho hum! Another no-boil, just-bake lasagna pasta. Is this news? I was a doubter until the Barilla folks dropped by and turned their product into a layered casserole anchored by pasta thin and tender enough to pass for fresh-made.

A 9-ounce box of the Barilla OvenReady Lasagna is just the right amount for four layers of pasta separated by a total of 8 to 10 cups of sauce and cheese in a shallow 3-quart casserole (9 by 13 in.).

However, to provide adequate moisture for the dried oven-ready pasta to rehydrate as it bakes, add ½ to 1 cup more liquid, such as meat or vegetable broth, to the lasagna sauce you ordinarily use—purchased or homemade. Also, be sure the top layer of pasta is evenly coated with some of the sauce.

Seal the casserole with foil to keep the moisture in as the lasagna is baking, then uncover the container if you want more browning. The pasta will be cooked by the time the sauce is bubbling vigorously, usually in 40 to 50 minutes.

Barilla OvenReady Lasagna is sold in many supermarkets, including most major chains, alongside other dried pasta products.

Hopi on hominy

■ Juanita Tiger Kavena's firsthand knowledge about foods of the Hopi people—particularly those using indigenous plants and substances—make her book *Hopi Cookery* (University of Arizona Press, Tucson, 1980; $14.95; 800/426-3797) both an excellent reference and a practical cookbook. Though not Hopi-born herself (she is Native American), Kavena, a home economist and former cooperative extension agent, was adopted into the tribe and has been married to Hopi Wilmer Kavena for more than 50 years. And for much of that time she has devoted herself to learning why the basic Hopi diet has served its people so well. In her book, she describes how many regional ingredients, found in the wild or cultivated, contribute to the nutritional balance as well as the character of traditional dishes. Corn, for example, is at the heart of the nutrition matrix; it's also a mystical part of the culture.

On the Hopi reservation, I met with Kavena and Dale McFarland, regional general manager for Aramark at Mesa Verde National Park. For lunch, we enjoyed a version of Hopi hominy and lamb stew with a companion dish of grilled fresh green chilies, one of

Kavena's favorite combinations. As we dined, Kavena lamented that making hominy from dried corn, a method she includes in her book, is one of many traditional processes and secrets being lost to progress and packaged foods. But she conceded to the reality that most cooks will start with canned hominy to make this very easy, slowly simmered stew. It's just right for a chilly evening—humble but satisfying.

Instead of serving fresh green chilies alongside, as Kavena does, I've taken the liberty of adding canned green chilies to simmer with the chunks of lamb.

Hopi Hominy and Lamb Stew

PREP AND COOK TIME: About 2¼ hours

NOTES: If making up to 2 days ahead, cool and chill airtight; reheat, stirring often.

MAKES: 4 servings

- 1½ pounds fat-trimmed **boned lamb shoulder**
- 2 cans (1 lb. each) **hominy,** drained
- 3 cups fat-skimmed **chicken broth**
- 1 can (7 oz.) **whole green chilies,** torn into wide strips
  Salt and **pepper**

1. Rinse lamb and cut into 1-inch chunks. Put meat in a 5- to 6-quart pan and add hominy, broth, and chilies.

2. Bring to a boil over high heat, cover, reduce heat, and simmer until meat is very tender when pierced, 1¾ to 2 hours. Skim fat from pan and discard. Season stew to taste with salt and pepper; ladle into bowls.

Per serving: 447 cal., 28% (126 cal.) from fat; 43 g protein; 14 g fat (4.4 g sat.); 35 g carbo (6.2 g fiber); 955 mg sodium; 112 mg chol.

BELOW: E. SPENCER TOY (2)   JAMES CARRIER

Books for more than cooks

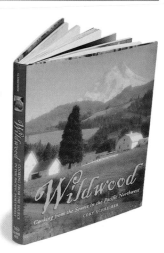

■ Two fine Northwest chefs have recently published books of their own recipes—Portland's Cory Schreiber and Seattle's Tom Douglas. But I wouldn't call either publication just a cookbook. Both men are ardent fans of the superb foods produced in the Northwest, and their books are filled to the brim with fascinating details about these foods—their sources, harvesting, and quality.

Schreiber was born in Oregon, traveled afar, then returned to Portland; his story starts with his family's roots in the restaurant business. Douglas, on the other hand, transported himself in his youth from Delaware to Seattle, liked what he saw, and stayed. Their books offer a bridge between their kitchens and yours.

Wildwood: Cooking from the Source in the Pacific Northwest, by Cory Schreiber (Ten Speed Press, Berkeley, 2000; $39.95; 800/841-2665). *Tom Douglas' Seattle Kitchen,* by Tom Douglas, with Denis Kelly, Shelley Lance, and Duskie Estes (Morrow Cookbooks, New York, January 2001; $30; 800/331-3761). ◆

The Wine Guide

By Karen MacNeil-Fife

The big steal

■ Is $20 too much to spend on a bottle of Chardonnay for a week-night dinner? How about $100 for a bottle of top-rated Cabernet or Bordeaux to drink on your birthday? Of course, there's no one right answer here. One thing, however, we probably all agree on: There's nothing like finding a good wine at a bargain-basement price.

To find out whether such wines are available on a regular basis, I tasted 70 wines in two categories: jug wines (inexpensive generic blends) and just plain inexpensive wines. The jug wines came in 1.5-liter bottles and ranged in price from $5.99 to $11.99. The others were in regular 750-milliliter bottles and cost $4 to $8 each—my personal definition of inexpensive. Here's what I found out.

1. Very good, very cheap wines do exist, but they are definitely in the minority on the inexpensive-wine shelves. Most of the wines I tasted had weak, washed-out flavors, and many were downright dank.

2. Color doesn't matter. Inexpensive white wines aren't any better

RICK MARIANI

than rosés or reds, and vice versa.

3. No single state or country seems to have a lock on producing good cheap wines. I tasted wines from California, Washington, France, Italy, Australia, South Africa, Chile, and even one from Morocco; no country did better or worse than any other.

4. You also can't rely completely on a particular brand. Just because a producer's inexpensive Chardonnay is pretty good doesn't mean its inexpensive Merlot will be too. (Conversely, you shouldn't write a brand off after tasting just one of its wines; another

variety might be much better.)

5. At very low prices, don't expect unique varietal flavors. Merlot, Zinfandel, and Cabernet Sauvignon don't taste that different from one another; they taste like basic red wine. Similarly, Sauvignon Blancs and Chardonnays taste like basic white wine.

6. If you're looking for real personality, concentration, and varietal flavor, you generally have to spend a little more. For the sake of comparison, I tasted Fetzer Vineyard's 1997 Valley Oaks Cabernet Sauvignon and Beaulieu Vineyard's 1997 Coastal Zinfandel, at $19.99 for a 1.5-liter bottle and $10 for a 750-milliliter bottle, respectively. The extra few dollars were well worth the higher quality both wines offered.

In the end, there's no good-cheap-wine magic. The producer's goal when making superinexpensive wines is to minimize cost. The top vineyards, best equipment, and most talented winemakers may not be part of the picture. Still, by choosing carefully, you can find some dependable wines for times when meatloaf and a video will do just fine. As they say, life's too short to drink bad wine.

REAL DEALS

For each wine, I've noted the size of bottle I bought, but you may be able to find them in different sizes.

WHITES AND ROSÉS

■ **Columbia "Cellarmaster's Reserve" Riesling 1999 (Columbia Valley, WA),** $7 (750 ml.). Apricots, honey, oranges, and cream—a delicious Riesling with just a bit of sweetness.

■ **Inglenook Chablis nonvintage (California),** $6.99 (1.5 l.). Fresh and melony—delightful and stunningly well priced.

■ **Inglenook French Colombard nonvintage (California),** $7.99 (1.5 l.). Dry, crisp, and slightly spicy, with thirst-quenching herbal notes. A real bargain.

■ **Pepperwood Grove Viognier 1999 (California),** $7 (750 ml.). On par with Viogniers that go for three times the price. Very floral and loaded with honeysuckle, melon, and litchi flavors.

■ **Sutter Home Chardonnay 1999 (California),** $5.99 (750 ml.). Simple, with light apple notes and good body.

■ **Sutter Home White Zinfandel 1999 (California),** $5 (750 ml.).

Slightly sweet, but good acidity provides a refreshing counterpoint. Pleasant spicy strawberry flavors.

REDS

■ **Glen Ellen Reserve Merlot 1997 (California),** $6.99 (750 ml.). Juicy and soft, with a touch of vanilla.

■ **Heritage Vineyards Cabernet Sauvignon 1998 (California),** $11.99 (1.5 l. Very dry, with basic red berry flavors and a hint of vanilla.

■ **Nathanson Creek Zinfandel nonvintage (California),** $4.29 (750 ml.). A simple, juicy wine at a price that's hard to pass up.

■ **Rosemount Grenache-Shiraz 2000 (Southeastern Australia),** $7.99 (750 ml.). Packed with juicy boysenberry fruit. A real steal at the price.

■ **Santa Rita 120 Merlot 1999 (Lontue Valley, Chile),** $6.29 (750 ml.). Smoky and sharp, with bold eucalyptus-like flavors.

■ **Vendange Zinfandel nonvintage (California),** $4.49 (750 ml.). Simple but good, with ripe cherrylike flavors and a nice, soft mouth-feel. ◆

Sugar-dusted gingersnaps—crisp or chewy—get their kick from three forms of ginger (from front to back): Ground, fresh, and candied in syrup.

A bold hand with ginger

There are more reasons than ever to love this zesty rhizome

By Elaine Johnson • Photographs by Craig Maxwell

Hot and cool, invigorating yet soothing, ginger dances on the palate. For millennia, cooks worldwide have taken advantage of the seasoning's affinity for both sweet and savory foods. Ginger was a precious commodity in the time of Confucius and as valuable as salt and pepper in the Middle Ages.

Today this tropical rhizome is playing to audiences in the New World. While a timid teaspoon once sufficed for most Western cooks, now we measure fresh ginger by the handful, ground ginger by the tablespoon. And we have more choices than ever. Crystallized and pickled ginger, ginger juice, and other convenient forms are emigrating from Asian and specialty food shops to mainstream supermarkets. Look for them in the Asian foods or baking section. (The various forms of ginger are described in "Ginger Jargon," page 31.)

Here are a handful of recipes packed with the lively flavor.

Ultimate Gingersnaps

PREP AND COOK TIME: About 1½ hours, plus at least 1¼ hours to chill

NOTES: This triple-ginger recipe comes from Royal Pacific Foods (see "Ginger Jargon," page 31). Candied ginger in syrup is sold in 9½- to 10½-ounce jars. These cookies will be chewy; for crisper cookies, bake 3 to 5 minutes longer.

High-altitude note: At a mile high, decrease brown sugar to ¾ cup, increase flour to 2½ cups, and decrease baking soda to 1½ teaspoons.

MAKES: About 30 cookies

- ½ cup drained chunks **candied ginger in syrup,** plus ¼ cup syrup
- ¼ cup **light molasses**
- 1½ tablespoons chopped **fresh ginger**
- 2 teaspoons **ground ginger**
- 1 cup firmly packed **dark brown sugar**
    About ¾ cup (⅜ lb.) **butter** or margarine, at room temperature
- 1 **large egg**
- 2¼ cups **all-purpose flour**
- 2 teaspoons **baking soda**
- ½ teaspoon **salt**
- ¼ cup **granulated sugar**

1. In a blender, whirl candied ginger and syrup, molasses, fresh ginger, and ground ginger until smooth. Scrape into a large bowl. Add brown sugar and ¾ cup butter, and beat with a mixer at medium speed until well blended. Add egg and beat until blended.

2. In another bowl, mix flour, baking soda, and salt. Add to ginger mixture and stir, then beat until blended. Cover dough with plastic wrap and chill until firm to touch, about 1¼ hours in the freezer or 4 hours in the refrigerator.

3. Pour granulated sugar into a small bowl. Shape dough, 2 tablespoons at a time, into 1½-inch balls and roll in sugar to coat. Set balls 2 inches apart on buttered 12- by 15-inch baking sheets.

4. Bake 2 pans at a time in a 325° oven until cookie edges spring back when lightly pressed but centers are still soft, 15 to 18 minutes; switch pan positions halfway through baking. Let cookies stand 1 minute on pans, then transfer with a wide spatula to racks to cool. Serve, or store airtight up to 3 weeks; freeze to store longer.

Per cookie: 144 cal., 31% (44 cal.) from fat; 1.2 g protein; 4.9 g fat (3 g sat.); 25 g carbo (0.4 g fiber); 193 mg sodium; 20 mg chol.

Sherried Carrots with Ginger

PREP AND COOK TIME: About 20 minutes

MAKES: 4 servings

- 1⅔ pounds **carrots** (maximum ½ to ¾ in. wide)
- 2 tablespoons **butter** or margarine
- ½ cup chopped **crystallized ginger** or ginger chips
    About 3 tablespoons **dry sherry**
- 1 teaspoon minced **parsley**
    Salt and **pepper**

1. Peel carrots, trim ends, and rinse. Melt butter in a 12- to 14-inch frying pan over medium-high heat. Add carrots in a single layer and turn as needed until browned, 8 to 10 minutes.

2. Add ginger, 3 tablespoons sherry, and 3 tablespoons water; mix, cover, reduce heat, and simmer until carrots are tender-crisp to bite, about 5 minutes. Stir in parsley and season to taste with salt and pepper.

3. Arrange carrots on a platter and scrape ginger mixture evenly over them. Add more sherry to taste.

Per serving: 244 cal., 23% (55 cal.) from fat; 1.8 g protein; 6.1 g fat (3.6 g sat.); 44 g carbo (6.5 g fiber); 143 mg sodium; 16 mg chol.

Bacon-Ginger Sandwiches

PREP AND COOK TIME: About 10 minutes

MAKES: 2 servings

- 6 slices **bacon** (6 oz. total)
- 2 tablespoons **mayonnaise**
- 4 slices **dense pumpernickel bread** or whole-wheat bread (about 6 oz. total), lightly toasted
- ⅔ cup lightly packed **salad mix,** rinsed and crisped
- ¼ to ½ cup drained **sliced pickled ginger**

1. In a 10- to 12-inch frying pan over medium-high heat, brown bacon, turning slices once or twice, about 5 minutes total. Transfer to towels to drain; discard fat in pan.

2. Spread mayonnaise on 1 side of each toast slice. Mound salad mix equally on mayonnaise on 2 slices. Lay 3 slices of bacon on each mound of salad mix and cover evenly with pickled ginger. Lay remaining toast, mayonnaise side down, on top. Cut each sandwich in half.

Per serving: 519 cal., 43% (225 cal.) from fat; 15 g protein; 25 g fat (6.1 g sat.); 57 g carbo (5.5 g fiber); 1,167 mg sodium; 28 mg chol.

Ginger Short Ribs

PREP AND COOK TIME: About 3¼ hours

NOTES: Have the ribs sawed into pieces at the market. Serve ribs and juices with hot cooked jasmine rice.

MAKES: 4 to 5 servings

- About 6 ounces **fresh ginger**
- 4 to 4½ pounds **lean beef short ribs,** fat trimmed, cut into 3- to 4-inch pieces (see notes)
- 2 cups finely chopped **onions**

- 1 cup finely chopped **pineapple,** fresh or canned unsweetened, drained
- About ⅓ cup **soy sauce**
- ¼ cup thinly sliced **fresh mint** leaves
- **Mint sprigs**

1. Peel ginger and cut into matchsticks ⅛ to ¼ inch thick and 2 to 3 inches long (you should have 1⅓ cups).

2. Rinse ribs, drain, and lay in a single layer in a 12- by 16-inch casserole at least 2 inches deep (5 to 6 qt.). Evenly distribute ginger, onions, and pineapple over and around meat. Mix 1 cup water with ⅓ cup soy sauce and add to casserole. Cover tightly with foil.

3. Bake in a 375° oven until meat is very tender when pierced, 2¾ to 3 hours; halfway through baking, turn ribs in sauce and, if necessary, add water to bring liquid level up to ¾ inch.

4. Uncover ribs and bake until browned, about 10 minutes. Skim fat from juices and discard. Scatter sliced mint over meat; garnish with mint sprigs. Add soy sauce to taste.

Per serving: 331 cal., 44% (144 cal.) from fat; 31 g protein; 16 g fat (6.5 g sat.); 16 g carbo (2.3 g fiber); 1,191 mg sodium; 88 mg chol.

Ginger Lemonade

PREP TIME: About 5 minutes

MAKES: 2 servings

In a 1-quart pitcher or glass measure, stir ¼ cup **lemon juice,** 4 teaspoons **sugar,** and 1 teaspoon **ginger juice** until sugar is dissolved. Add 2 cups **sparkling water.** Pour through a fine strainer into **ice**-filled glasses. If desired, add more sugar to taste.

Per serving: 39 cal., 2.3% (0.9 cal.) from fat; 0.1 g protein; 0.1 g fat (0 g sat.); 10 g carbo (0 g fiber); 6.5 mg sodium; 0 mg chol.

Slivers of fresh ginger turn soft and golden when oven-braised with beef short ribs and pineapple.

Fresh. The most flavorful ginger choice—slightly hot on the palate and refreshing, with citrus overtones. Look for smooth, heavy *hands,* as the knobs of the rhizome are called. As ginger loses its freshness, it shrivels and may mold. Store unwrapped in the refrigerator. Peel off the papery skin with a vegetable peeler or small, sharp knife, then slice or mince the fibrous flesh. Excellent in relishes, soups, curries, and meat and fish dishes.

Candied in syrup. Chunks of ginger cooked in syrup. Young, very tender pieces prepared this way are called stem ginger. Chop the chunks and add to baked goods, fruit salads, or carrot soup. Drizzle the syrup into tea or mix into salad dressings.

Crystallized. Drained candied ginger rolled in sugar. Should be moist and tender. Store airtight. Cook with vegetables such as carrots; sprinkle on cereal and waffles; use in salads and desserts; stir into cookies, scones, and ice cream; nibble as candy.

Chips. Chopped crystallized ginger. Use in the same way.

Ground. Pulverized dried ginger. Pungent and earthy. Use in baking, in curries—anywhere you want a hit of spicy heat.

Juice. The essence of ginger in handy bottled form. Hot, earthy—a little goes a long way. Splash into fruit juice, carrot juice, and tea, or over grilled fish. Once opened, keeps up to two months in the refrigerator.

Pickled. Sweet-sour, hot, and slightly salty. Made from young ginger, it may be a natural ivory color or dyed red, in paper-thin slices or matchsticks. Great with sushi (it's also called sushi ginger), salads, and sandwiches.

A good source for prepared ginger products is Royal Pacific Foods in Monterey, California. *(800) 551-5284 or www.gingerpeople.com.* ◆

Kitchen Cabinet

Readers' recipes tested in Sunset's kitchens

By Andrew Baker

Vegetable-Pilaf Stacks

Nancee Melin, Tucson

"Eye appeal enhances the meal," says Nancee Melin. These vegetable and rice stacks are an example of the fun vertical foods she likes to create. Assemble them through step 4 up to 1 day ahead and chill airtight; bake as directed in step 5.

PREP AND COOK TIME: About 1½ hours

MAKES: 4 servings

- 1 package (6 oz.) **seasoned precooked dried white rice**
- 2 **onions** (about 1 lb. total), peeled and sliced
- 1 tablespoon **butter** or margarine
- ¾ pound **broccoli florets** (about 1 qt.)
- **Salad oil**
- 1 jar (about 13 oz.) **canned peeled roasted red peppers**, drained and chopped
- ½ cup **cherry tomatoes**, rinsed
- **Parsley sprigs**
- **Salt** and fresh-ground **pepper**

1. In a 2- to 3-quart pan, cook rice as directed on package.

2. Meanwhile, in a 10- to 12-inch frying pan over medium-high heat, stir onions in butter until limp and just beginning to brown, about 4 minutes. Pour into a bowl.

3. Add broccoli and ¼ cup water to pan. Bring to a boil over high heat; cover, reduce heat, and simmer until broccoli is barely tender when pierced, about 5 minutes. Drain.

4. Remove labels from 4 empty food cans (about 2¾ in. wide and 4¼ in. tall; 14-oz. to 1-lb. size), each with 1 end removed; wash cans with soap, and dry. Rub interiors of cans lightly with oil and set, open end up and slightly apart, in a 10- by 15-inch pan. Spoon 2 tablespoons hot cooked rice into each can and press down with a spoon to compact and make level. Spoon ½ cup broccoli onto rice in each can, then ¼ cup onions and 1½ tablespoons roasted peppers, spreading each level. Continue to layer all ingredients, packing down with a spoon to compact layers as you add each, ending with rice.

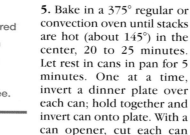

Bright, simple ingredients layered and baked in an empty food can make a jaunty vegetarian entrée.

5. Bake in a 375° regular or convection oven until stacks are hot (about 145°) in the center, 20 to 25 minutes. Let rest in cans in pan for 5 minutes. One at a time, invert a dinner plate over each can; hold together and invert can onto plate. With a can opener, cut each can end free; press end down lightly and lift up can to release vegetable-pilaf stack. Lift off can and can end. Garnish plates with cherry tomatoes and parsley. Add salt and pepper to taste.

Per serving: 285 cal., 20% (58 cal.) from fat; 8.7 g protein; 6.4 g fat (2.3 g sat.); 53 g carbo (6.1 g fiber); 755 mg sodium; 7.8 mg chol.

Walnut Shortbread Cookies

Lisa Sarenduc, Santa Fe

In the process of typing up all the recipes she had collected on scraps of paper during the last 40 years, Lisa Sarenduc realized these maple-flavored shortbread cookies were one of her best creations. Granulated maple sugar—which "makes a significant difference"—is available in well-stocked supermarkets and in natural-food stores. If you can't find it, substitute ⅔ cup regular granulated sugar and add ½ teaspoon maple extract.

PREP AND COOK TIME: About 40 minutes

MAKES: About 30

- 1 cup **chopped walnuts**
- 2 cups **all-purpose flour**
- ⅔ cup **granulated maple sugar** (see notes)
- ¼ teaspoon **baking powder**
- ¼ teaspoon **salt**
- 1 cup (½ lb.) **butter** or margarine, cut into chunks
- ½ teaspoon **almond extract**

JAMES CARRIER

1. In a food processor, whirl walnuts until finely chopped. Add flour, maple sugar, baking powder, and salt; whirl to mix. Add butter and almond extract; whirl just until dough holds together. (Or whirl nuts in a blender until finely chopped, or finely chop nuts with a knife, and place in a large bowl. Add flour, maple sugar, baking powder, and salt, and stir to combine. Add butter and almond extract, and rub with your fingers until fine crumbs form. Pat dough into a ball.)

2. Shape dough into 1½-inch balls and set 2 inches apart on 14- by 17-inch baking sheets. With the bottom of a glass or your palm, flatten balls to about ½ inch thick.

3. Bake in a 325° oven until cookies are golden, 23 to 25 minutes (about 30 minutes in a 300° convection oven); if baking more than 1 sheet at a time, switch pan positions halfway through baking. With a spatula, transfer cookies to a rack to cool. Serve warm or at room temperature. Store cool cookies airtight up to 3 days; freeze to store longer.

Per cookie: 122 cal., 64% (78 cal.) from fat; 1.5 g protein; 8.7 g fat (4.1 g sat.); 10 g carbo (0.4 g fiber); 86 mg sodium; 17 mg chol.

Italian Sausage and Cabbage

Elena Conboy, Westminster, California

This heartwarming dish came from a new member of Elena Conboy's family—her daughter-in-law, Elane Conboy.

PREP AND COOK TIME: About 40 minutes

MAKES: 4 servings

- 2 tablespoons **butter** or margarine
- 2 tablespoons **olive oil**
- 1 pound **hot** or mild **Italian sausages**, casings removed
- 1 head **cabbage** (about 2 lb.), rinsed and thinly sliced
- ¼ cup fat-skimmed **chicken broth**
- ½ cup minced **parsley**
  Salt and **pepper**

1. In a 5- to 6-quart pan over medium-high heat, combine butter and oil. Add sausages and break apart with a spoon; stir often until lightly browned, about 5 minutes. Add cabbage, broth, and parsley, and bring to a boil. Reduce heat, cover, and simmer, stirring occasionally, until cabbage is tender to bite, about 30 minutes.

2. Spoon sausage and cabbage mixture into bowls. Add salt and pepper to taste.

Per serving: 562 cal., 77% (432 cal.) from fat; 20 g protein; 48 g fat (17 g sat.); 13 g carbo (5.8 g fiber); 937 mg sodium; 102 mg chol. ◆

Caffeine castles

Great coffeehouses in Arizona and New Mexico

By Jeanie Puleston Fleming with Nora Burba Trulsson

■ In many areas, more and more small coffeehouses are getting "Starbucked" out of existence. But in Arizona and New Mexico, some are thriving, in part because they are unique and locally owned, they roast their own beans, and they offer such goodies as coffee-related gear and fresh pastries. So set out on some chilly winter day, drop in, and warm up with a steaming cup of joe.

ARIZONA. A Flagstaff favorite, **Macy's European Coffeehouse** (14 S. Beaver St.; 520/774-2243) has long been known for its fresh-roasted coffee and bohemian atmosphere, each helping make it a popular hangout for Northern Arizona University students and faculty alike. Along with the espresso, try the bakery items or vegetarian offerings.

In Tucson, it's **Coffee Etc.** (6091 N. Oracle Rd.; 520/544-8588). Craving a cappuccino at 3 A.M.? This place never closes, offering a full breakfast-to-dinner menu.

NEW MEXICO. The roaster fires up five times a week at **Double Rainbow Bakery Cafés** in Albuquerque (3416 Central Ave. NE; 505/255-6633), where you can watch the action behind glass; also check out the fruit tarts and quiches. Nearby, at **Satellite Toys & Coffee** (3513 Central NE; 256-0345), java is served alongside an impressive selection of imported windup toys, coffee-related accessories, and old-fashioned hard candy in barrels. Or try **Whiting Coffee Co.** (3700 Osuna Rd. NE; 344-9144), where Norm Whiting roasts beans in the back and the tiny front room is crammed with beans, brews, and coffee paraphernalia.

Susan Ohori is a Santa Fe pioneer of bean wrangling, having set up her roaster nearly 20 years ago. At **Ohori's Coffee, Tea & Chocolate** (507 Old Santa Fe Trail; 505/988-7026), don't miss her powerful dark roast or the Earl Grey tea with a touch of lavender. Worth seeking out is **Las Chivas Coffee Roaster** (7 Avenida Vista Grande, 466-1010; or 3003C S. St. Francis Dr., 995-0099) full of teapots, hand-painted mugs, and enticing coffee aromas.

In Taos, the **Bean** (1033 Paseo del Pueblo Sur; 505/758-5123) offers hearty breakfasts, lunches, and opinions: Owner and roaster Peter Miceli says double espresso shots are "the only way to go" for cappuccinos and lattes. We couldn't agree more. ◆

Crêpes continue to delight: For dessert, top chocolate-hazelnut soufflé crêpe with vanilla ice cream (recipe on page 45).

CRAIG MAXWELL

February

the *perfect* roast

chicken

Think big, crisp, and gloriously browned when you want a bird that reigns supreme at the table

By Sara Schneider • Photographs by James Carrier • Food styling by Basil Friedman

Size matters. Position doesn't. That's what a palate-weary *Sunset* panel decided after blind-tasting more than 50 chickens. The objective: to settle the argument about the best way to roast a bird.

The panel came to other critical conclusions as well, as we put the core methods to the test: What's the ideal oven temperature to produce a chicken that is beautifully browned and crisp and still yields succulent breast and thigh meat? Is the breast really juicier if roasted downward—even part of the time? Does rubbing the chicken with fat before roasting achieve anything? Is the skin more or less crisp when basted? And—perhaps the most controversial question of all—are free-range, organic chickens any more flavorful than their standard commercially reared cousins?

We fired up our ovens (even this was eye-opening, as we compared their performances) for a series of side-by-side tests to learn exactly what techniques do and don't work. Here's what the scoring revealed; see page 40 for more detailed tips on achieving the best results at home.

■ **Oven temperature.** A constant 425° oven—regular or convection—produced the crispest, most richly browned skin and juiciest breast and thigh meat. (At 500°, the chicken browned well, but it also spewed a prodigious amount of fat and smoke—more than you may want in your kitchen.) Starting at a very high temperature, then lowering it, also yielded brown, crisp skin, but the minimal difference doesn't warrant the step.

■ **Chicken position.** Starting the bird breast down, then turning it over to brown, didn't keep the meat any moister. Nor did rotating the chicken from side to side. And in both cases, the skin wasn't as nicely colored.

(Continued on page 38)

Our Favorite Roast Chicken

PREP AND COOK TIME: 1½ to 2 hours

NOTES: Consider this basic recipe a blank palette on which to layer flavors—herbs under the skin and in the body cavity, other seasonings with the salt and pepper over the skin, or embellishments to the pan juices afterward.

MAKES: 6 to 8 servings

Root vegetables fill pan beneath orange-thyme roast chicken, absorbing vibrant flavor from the drippings.

1 **chicken** (6 to 8 lb.)

Salt and **pepper**

1. Remove giblets from chicken and reserve for other uses. Pull off and discard lumps of fat. Rinse bird well inside and out; pat dry.

2. Sprinkle chicken lightly with salt and pepper. If desired, fold wing tips under first joint. Set bird breast up on a V-shaped rack in an 11- by 17-inch pan.

3. Roast in a 425° regular or convection oven until a thermometer inserted through thickest part of breast to bone reaches 170°, or 180° through thickest part of thigh at joint, 1¼ to 1¾ hours. If drippings start to smoke, tilt pan, skim fat and discard; then add about ¼ cup water.

4. Insert a carving fork into body cavity, piercing carcass; lift bird and tilt to drain juices into pan. Set chicken on a rimmed platter and let rest in a warm place about 15 minutes.

5. Meanwhile, skim and discard fat from pan. Stir juices to release browned bits and pour through a fine strainer, if desired, into a small bowl. Carve chicken and serve with juices. Add salt and pepper to taste.

Per serving: 392 cal., 55% (216 cal.) from fat; 42 g protein; 24 g fat (6.6 g sat.); 0 g carbo; 128 mg sodium; 134 mg chol.

- **Rubbing with fat.** Smearing the bird with butter or oil before roasting made the skin slightly crisper but had no flavor impact.
- **Basting.** Spooning the pan drippings over the chicken as it roasted made the skin less crisp and, again, added nothing to the meat flavor.
- **Free or not.** In the most telling taste tests of all, standard commercially reared chickens edged out free-range birds for best flavor. So let your environmental convictions be your guide. The bottom line: Proper roasting makes any bird delectable.
- **Size.** Big chickens—often labeled roasters (generally 6 to 8 lb., occasionally up to 10 lb., but less than 12 weeks old)—have deeper, richer, and more complex fla-

ROASTING CHART

WEIGHT	OVEN TEMP. (REGULAR OR CONVECTION)	COOKING TIME
3½ to 6 lb.	425°	50 minutes to 1¼ hours
6 to 8 lb.	425°	1¼ to 1¾ hours
8 to 10 lb.	425°	1½ to 2 hours

vor than smaller ones. Of course, young chickens (also called broilers and fryers; under 6 lb. and about seven weeks old) can be roasted. But by the time the skin is an appealing color, the breast meat of smaller birds is cooked past its prime. A roaster, however, reaches perfection inside and out at the same time.

In fact, everything a roast chicken does well, it does best when bigger. It makes a more dramatic presentation, it accommodates more people, and it provides leftovers for sandwiches, soups, salads, pastas, or just plain nibbles. Best of all, there's time to cook other ingredients in the pan along with the roasting bird, as we've done in the recipes that follow, to create grand chicken dinners.

Orange-Thyme Roast Chicken with Root Vegetables

PREP AND COOK TIME: 1¾ to 2½ hours
MAKES: 6 to 8 servings

- 1 **chicken** (6 to 8 lb.)
- 2 **oranges** (about ½ lb. each), rinsed
- 3 tablespoons chopped **fresh thyme** leaves
- 6 to 8 **thyme sprigs**, rinsed
- 1½ pounds **shallots** (each about 1½ in. wide), peeled
- 3 pounds **red thin-skinned potatoes** (each about 2½ in. wide), scrubbed and dried
- 1½ pounds **baby carrots** (max. ¾ in. thick), rinsed and peeled, or baby-cut peeled carrots
- 1 tablespoon **olive oil**
  Salt and **pepper**
- ½ cup **dry sherry**
- 1 cup fat-skimmed **chicken broth**
- ½ cup **whipping cream**

1. Remove giblets from chicken and reserve for other uses. Pull off and discard lumps of fat. Rinse bird well inside and out; pat dry. If desired, fold wing tips under first joint. Set bird breast up on a V-shaped rack in an 11- by 17-inch pan.

2. Grate 2 tablespoons peel from oranges. Cut oranges in half crosswise and ream juice; you need at least ⅔ cup. In a small bowl, mix grated peel and thyme leaves. Starting at the neck, gently ease your fingers under chicken skin to loosen it over breast. Push 3 tablespoons orange peel–thyme mixture under skin and spread evenly over breast. Place 2 orange halves (discard remainder), 4 thyme sprigs, and 2 shal-

lots in body cavity.

3. In a bowl, mix remaining shallots, the potatoes, and carrots with olive oil. Distribute vegetables around chicken in pan. Pour ⅓ cup orange juice over chicken. Sprinkle chicken lightly with salt and pepper.

4. Roast in a 425° regular or convection oven until vegetables are well browned and tender when pierced and a thermometer inserted through thickest part of breast to bone reaches 170°, or 180° through thickest part of thigh at joint, 1¼ to 1¾ hours. After about 30 minutes, turn vegetables with a wide spatula. If pan juices start to scorch, pour about ¼ cup water around edge of pan and stir to scrape drippings free, mixing with vegetables.

5. Insert a carving fork into the body cavity, piercing carcass; lift bird and tilt to drain juices into pan. Set chicken on a rimmed platter. With a slotted spoon, lift vegetables from pan and arrange around chicken. Let rest in a warm place about 15 minutes.

6. Meanwhile, skim and discard fat from pan. Add sherry, broth, cream, and remaining orange peel–thyme mixture and orange juice. Stir often over high heat, scraping browned bits free, until reduced to 1 cup, 8 to 10 minutes. Add salt and pepper to taste. Pour through a fine strainer into a small pitcher or bowl.

7. Garnish platter with remaining thyme sprigs. Carve chicken and serve with vegetables and sherry-cream sauce. Add salt and pepper to taste.

Per serving: 713 cal., 38% (270 cal.) from fat; 50 g protein; 30 g fat (9.7 g sat.); 55 g carbo (3.6 g fiber); 210 mg sodium; 150 mg chol.

Soy-Ginger Roast Chicken with Shiitake Mushrooms

PREP AND COOK TIME: 2¼ to 2¾ hours, plus at least 4 hours to brine

NOTES: Brining the chicken with soy sauce and brown sugar produces deep mahogany skin and aromatic meat. Mirin, a sweet rice wine, and hoisin are available in well-stocked supermarkets and in Asian grocery stores. Serve chicken and mushrooms with hot rice cooked with coconut milk.

MAKES: 6 to 8 servings

- 1¼ cups **soy sauce**
- 1 cup firmly packed **brown sugar**
- ½ cup coarsely chopped **fresh ginger**
- 10 cloves **garlic**, peeled and crushed
- 1 **chicken** (6 to 8 lb.)
- ½ cup chopped **fresh cilantro**
- ¼ cup **cilantro sprigs**, rinsed
  Salt and **pepper**
- 1 cup fat-skimmed **chicken broth**
- ¼ cup **rice vinegar**
- ¼ cup **mirin** (see notes) or sake
- 1 tablespoon **prepared hoisin sauce**
- 1 tablespoon **Asian** (toasted) **sesame oil**
- 2 pounds **fresh shiitake mushrooms** (2-in. caps)
- 1 pound **green onions**

1. In a 10- to 12-quart pan, combine 1 cup soy sauce, brown sugar, ¼ cup ginger, 6 cloves garlic, and 4 quarts water; mix well.

2. Remove giblets from chicken and reserve for other uses. Pull off and discard lumps of fat. Rinse bird well inside

Shiitake mushrooms, roasted with ginger and soy sauce, surround bird.

10. Sprinkle mushroom mixture with remaining ¹/₂ cup chopped green onion tops. Carve chicken and serve with vegetables and pan juices. Add salt and pepper to taste.

Per serving: 508 cal., 44% (225 cal.) from fat; 47 g protein; 25 g fat (6.8 g sat.); 20 g carbo (2.7 g fiber); 703 mg sodium; 134 mg chol.

Roast Chicken Cacciatore

PREP AND COOK TIME: 1³/₄ to 2¹/₄ hours

NOTES: Instead of braising the ingredients for chicken cacciatore, we roast them here to intensify their natural sweetness. Serve the meat and vegetables with hot cooked polenta.

MAKES: 6 to 8 servings

- 1 **chicken** (6 to 8 lb.)
- ¹/₄ cup chopped **fresh rosemary** leaves
- ¹/₂ cup chopped **fresh basil** leaves
- 14 cloves **garlic**, peeled
- 6 **rosemary sprigs**, rinsed
  About 1 teaspoon **salt**
  About ¹/₄ teaspoon **pepper**
- 2 **red bell peppers** (about 1¹/₂ lb. total)
- 2 **yellow bell peppers** (about 1¹/₂ lb. total)
- 2 **onions** (about 1 lb. total)
- 8 **Roma tomatoes** (about 2 lb. total)
- 2 tablespoons **olive oil**
- ¹/₃ cup **salt-cured black** or calamata **olives**
- ¹/₄ cup **balsamic vinegar**
- ¹/₂ cup **dry red wine**
- 1 cup fat-skimmed **chicken broth**

1. Remove giblets from chicken and reserve for other uses. Pull off and discard lumps of fat. Rinse bird well inside and out; pat dry. If desired, fold wing tips under first joint. Set bird breast up on a V-shaped rack in an 11-by 17-inch pan.

2. In a small bowl, mix chopped rosemary and basil. Starting at the neck, gently ease your fingers under skin to loosen it over breast. Push ¹/₃ of the rosemary-basil mixture under skin and spread evenly over breast. Place 6 garlic cloves and 3 rosemary sprigs in body cavity. Sprinkle chicken lightly with salt and pepper.

3. Rinse, stem, and seed red and yellow bell peppers; cut into ¹/₃-inch-wide strips. Peel onions and cut each into 6 wedges. Rinse and core tomatoes; cut in half lengthwise. Distribute peppers, onions, and remaining garlic around chicken in

and out; pierce skin all over with a fork. Lay chicken breast down in brine; cover and chill at least 4 or up to 12 hours, turning bird several times.

3. Discard brine and rinse chicken thoroughly under cold running water, rubbing gently; pat dry. If desired, fold wing tips under first joint. Set bird breast up on a V-shaped rack in an 11-by 17-inch pan.

4. Starting at the neck, gently ease your fingers under skin to loosen it over breast. Push ¹/₄ cup chopped cilantro under skin and spread evenly over breast. Place cilantro sprigs in body cavity; add 2 tablespoons ginger and remaining 4 cloves garlic. Sprinkle chicken lightly with salt and pepper.

5. Roast in a 425° regular or convection oven for 30 minutes.

6. Meanwhile, in a large bowl, mix remaining ¹/₄ cup soy sauce, 2 tablespoons ginger, and ¹/₄ cup chopped cilantro with broth, vinegar, mirin, hoisin, and sesame oil. Rinse and drain shiitake mushrooms; trim and discard stems. Rinse and drain green onions;

trim and discard ends. Cut off green tops and chop; also chop white bottoms. Mix mushrooms, chopped white parts of onions, and all but ¹/₂ cup chopped green tops with soy mixture. Lift out with a slotted spoon and distribute around chicken in pan; reserve soy mixture.

7. Continue to roast chicken, turning vegetables with a wide spatula after about 20 minutes, until a thermometer inserted through thickest part of breast to bone reaches 170°, or 180° through thickest part of thigh at joint, ³/₄ to 1¹/₄ hours longer.

8. Insert a carving fork into body cavity, piercing carcass; lift bird and tilt to drain juices into pan. Set chicken on a rimmed platter. With a slotted spoon, arrange vegetables around chicken. Let rest in a warm place about 15 minutes.

9. Meanwhile, skim and discard fat from pan. Add reserved soy mixture and stir often over high heat, scraping browned bits free, until reduced to ³/₄ cup, about 10 to 12 minutes. Pour through a fine strainer into a small pitcher or bowl.

pan; spread level. Set tomatoes, cut side up, on pepper mixture and sprinkle vegetables with another ⅓ of the herb mixture, 1 teaspoon salt, and ¼ teaspoon pepper; drizzle with olive oil.

4. Roast in a 425° regular or convection oven until vegetables begin to brown and a thermometer inserted through thickest part of breast to bone reaches 170°, or 180° through thickest part of thigh at joint, 1¼ to 1¾ hours.

5. Insert a carving fork into chicken cavity, piercing carcass. Lift bird and tilt to drain juices into pan. Set chicken on a

Roasting concentrates flavors of tomatoes, peppers, and onions for chicken cacciatore.

rimmed platter; let rest in a warm place about 15 minutes. With a slotted spoon, transfer vegetables to a shallow bowl; sprinkle with olives and keep warm.

6. Skim and discard fat from pan; add vinegar, wine, broth, and remaining herb mixture. Stir often over high heat, scraping browned bits free, until reduced to ¾ cup, 6 to 8 minutes. Pour through a fine strainer into a small pitcher or bowl.

7. Garnish platter with remaining rosemary sprigs. Carve chicken and serve with vegetables. Add pan juices and salt and pepper to taste.

Per serving: 537 cal., 49% (261 cal.) from fat; 46 g protein; 29 g fat (7.3 g sat.); 22 g carbo (4.9 g fiber); 546 mg sodium; 134 mg chol.

ROASTING TIPS

- **Don't truss.** Tying the chicken legs together blocks heat from penetrating the interior of the thighs, which are the slowest parts of the bird to cook.

- **Use a V-shaped rack.** Elevating the chicken allows the heat to circulate and brown evenly—otherwise, the bird back stays pale and unappealing.

- **Double-check your oven temperature.** In the on-and-off pattern to maintain heat, some ovens cycle at more extreme ranges than others. Some also lose heat faster when the oven door is opened. Each of the six ovens in *Sunset's* test kitchen produced slightly different results. If a chicken roasts significantly slower or faster than suggested in the Roasting Chart (page 38), you may want to check the accuracy of your oven with a reliable oven thermometer and adjust the thermostat or have your oven serviced.

- **Use a cooking thermometer.** The best way to determine doneness is to use a thermometer. It can be a quick-read thermometer or one that heats with the bird.

- **Position the thermometer carefully.** A chicken isn't the same temperature all over when it's cooked. For the breast, insert the thermometer through the thickest part of the meat to the bone; for the thighs, insert the thermometer parallel to the thighbone through the meat to the hip joint (shown at right). The

chicken is done when the breast temperature reaches 170° and the thigh temperature is 180°.

Unfortunately, the critical parts of a chicken don't always cook at proportional rates, so the breast may not be 170° at the precise moment the thigh meat reaches 180°. It depends on the heat distribution in the oven and the shape of the respective body parts (after all, birds, male or female, aren't shaped the same). Fortunately, chickens are forgiving when roasted at the ideal oven heat—both breast and thigh meat will be moist within a reasonable range of temperatures.

- **Ignore the color of the juices.** Conventional wisdom has it that a chicken is done when the juices at the thigh joint run clear. This is an old wives' tale. The color of the juices in any part of the bird is not a good indication of whether it's done. In the body cavity, the juices are usually pink; at the thigh joint, they are not always clear, even at 180° when the meat is cooked.

- **Don't panic at red thigh meat.** It's almost always a little pink when you first cut into the joint, even when overcooked. However, if the thigh has reached 180°, the meat will lose its rosy tint very quickly on contact with the air.

- **Don't trust the wiggle test.** Moving a leg to see how loose it is in the socket isn't a reliable test of the bird's doneness—but it clearly indicates overcooking. If the skin is nice and crisp, it will hinder movement; furthermore, judging mobility is too subjective to be trustworthy.

- **Let the chicken rest.** We found a dramatic difference in the moistness of the meat—especially in the breast—between birds carved immediately and those allowed to rest (uncovered, to keep the skin crisp) about 15 minutes. If sliced hot from the oven, juices drain out and leave the meat dry. When birds rest a spell, the juices stay put. ◆

The Quick Cook

Fish bundle, glamorized with chives, awaits a final accessory—shallot wine sauce.

Good for your sole food

■ Like the little black dress that accessorizes up or down for the occasion, sole is the fish that adjusts for style. Delicately flavored and unassertive, it provides an elegant foundation for simple to complex seasonings.

Fish notes: All sole are members of the flounder family. You'll find the largest variety at a fish market. Choices may include petrale, English, sand, and Rex sole, starry flounder, and sand dabs (usually whole). Boned sole fillets vary considerably in size—from 2 to 8 ounces, depending upon the variety. Some fillets are skinned, others aren't, as the skin is very thin and tender. To make these dishes, choose thin fillets; thicker pieces will take a bit longer to cook.

Asparagus Sole Rolls

PREP AND COOK TIME: About 30 minutes
MAKES: 4 servings

- 1 pound **asparagus** (½ in. thick)
- 1½ pounds **boned sole fillets** (4 to 12, about ¼ in. thick and 2 to 3 in. wide—cut wide pieces in half lengthwise; see "Fish notes," above)
- **Wine sauce** (recipe follows)
- **Salt** and **pepper**

1. Rinse asparagus; snap off and discard tough ends. In a 10- to 12-inch frying pan over high heat, bring ½ inch water to a boil. Add asparagus and simmer, stirring occasionally, until barely tender when pierced, about 2 minutes; drain.

2. Meanwhile, rinse sole and lay pieces flat (if unskinned, skin up). Align an equal portion of asparagus, tips in same direction, at 1 end and across the narrow width of each fillet; roll fillet to enclose asparagus. Set sole, seam down, in a buttered, shallow 2½- to 3-quart casserole. Cover tightly with foil.

3. Bake in a 425° regular or convection oven until fish is opaque but moist-looking in center of thickest part (cut to test), 12 to 16 minutes.

4. Spoon wine sauce over fish and season to taste with salt and pepper.

Per serving: 248 cal., 36% (89 cal.) from fat; 35 g protein; 9.9 g fat (5.3 g sat.); 4.5 g carbo (0.9 g fiber); 221 mg sodium; 102 mg chol.

Wine sauce. In a 10- to 12-inch frying pan over medium-high heat, frequently stir 2 tablespoons *each* **butter** or margarine and minced **shallots** until golden, about 3 minutes. Add ¾ cup **dry white wine.** Boil on high heat, stirring occasionally, until reduced to ¼ cup, 5 to 7 minutes. Use hot or warm. ◆

Tapenade Sole Bundles

PREP AND COOK TIME: About 30 minutes
MAKES: 4 servings

Follow directions for **asparagus sole rolls** (preceding), but omit asparagus. Instead, spread fillets equally with **canned olive tapenade** (¼ cup total) and roll to enclose. To **wine sauce** (preceding), with wine add 2 tablespoons chopped **canned roasted red pepper.** Garnish portions with chopped **parsley.**

Per serving: 274 cal., 46% (126 cal.) from fat; 32 g protein; 14 g fat (5.2 g sat.); 1.6 g carbo (0.1 g fiber); 617 mg sodium; 102 mg chol.

Vodka-Pepper Stuffed Sole

PREP AND COOK TIME: About 30 minutes
NOTES: Mickey Strang of McKinleyville, California, contributes this recipe.
MAKES: 4 servings

In a bowl, combine 1½ cups coarse, fresh **sourdough bread** crumbs, ½ teaspoon fresh-ground **pepper,** 1 teaspoon grated **lemon** peel, and 2 tablespoons *each* **vodka, lemon juice,** chopped **green onion,** and chopped **parsley.**

Follow directions for **asparagus sole rolls** (at left), but omit asparagus. Instead, cover fillets equally with bread mixture and roll to enclose.

For **wine sauce** (see above), use ½ cup wine and add ¼ cup **vodka;** when simmering, ignite (not beneath an exhaust fan or flammable items) and shake pan until flame dies. Pour over fish and garnish with chopped **parsley.**

Per serving: 330 cal., 27% (90 cal.) from fat; 34 g protein; 10 g fat (5.4 g sat.); 12 g carbo (0.7 g fiber); 335 mg sodium; 102 mg chol. ◆

THE BASICS

Thin crêpes, made with a batter about the consistency of whipping cream, are tender and delicate. When the egg whites are whipped and folded into a very similar batter, they contribute volume and texture that makes the crêpes puffy and thicker (page 45).

The size of a crêpe is determined by the pan in which it cooks. For best results, the pan must be flat on the bottom and the batter swirled to the edge. Traditional crêpe pans, which come in many sizes, have angled, shallow sides that give the crêpe a neat round shape. A regular frying pan with curved sides also works—and those with nonstick finishes are easiest to use—but the crêpes are not always as perfectly round. To determine diameter, measure across the bottom of the inverted pan.

Thin Crêpes

PREP AND COOK TIME: About 20 minutes

NOTES: If making up to 3 days ahead, stack crêpes, wrap airtight, and chill; freeze to store longer. If you place a sheet of waxed paper on top of each crêpe as you stack them, the crêpes can be easily separated when cold. Otherwise, to avoid tearing, let the stack warm to room temperature or heat briefly in a microwave before separating.

MAKES: 15 (6-in.), 12 (7-in.), 8 (8-in.) crêpes

crêpe craze

These classics, whether thick or thin, savory or sweet, continue to delight

By Linda Lau Anusasananan • Photographs by Craig Maxwell

■ The beguiling simplicity of crêpes is the secret of their lasting popularity. It's a rare kitchen that doesn't yield the basic ingredients of eggs, milk, and flour. Most pantries have a suitable pan in which to make them. True, it may take a few tries to perfect your cooking technique, but to some it's child's play—I've watched a young friend barely old enough to write turn them out by the stack.

Crêpes are delectable sweet or savory; they take on endless guises and roles. On the streets of Paris, they become an elegant snack when brushed with butter and jam or chestnut purée and splashed with a little liqueur. The same or similar combinations make an exceptional breakfast. With only a few more flavors, these little cakes become the grand dame of dessert: crêpes

Warm crêpes ooze soft brie cheese and sweet, spicy chutney; toasted pecans add a crunchy bite.

suzette. Wrapped around something as modest as melting cheese, crêpes are a lovely way to start a meal; wrapped around a more substantial filling, they become the meal.

But not all crêpes are thin. The same ingredients also produce puffy versions. In this collection of dishes, you'll find crêpes, thick and thin, for occasions superlative to simple.

Brie and Chutney Crêpe Triangles

PREP AND COOKING TIME: About 40 minutes

NOTES: If making up to 1 day ahead, cover and chill; bake uncovered. Serve these sweet-savory crêpes for breakfast, as a light lunch with salad, or as a first course at dinner.

MAKES: 4 first-course servings

- 16 to 24 **pecan halves**
- 1 tablespoon melted **butter** or margarine
- 8 **thin crêpes** (7 or 8 in., page 42)
- 1 cup **Major Grey chutney**
- ¾ pound **firm-ripe brie cheese**

- 3 **large eggs**
- ⅔ cup **all-purpose flour**
- 1 cup **milk**

  About 2 tablespoons melted **butter** or margarine

1. In a blender or food processor, whirl the eggs, flour, and milk until batter is smooth; scrape container as needed.

2. Use a crêpe pan or regular or nonstick frying pan with a bottom that measures 6 to 8 inches across. Set pan

on medium-high heat; when hot, brush bottom with butter (as needed or for flavor, in a nonstick pan).

3. At once pour a measured amount of batter into the hot pan and tilt to coat bottom: For each crêpe, use 2½ to 3 tablespoons for a 6- to 7-inch pan, 3½ to 4 tablespoons for an 8-inch pan. If heat is correct, crêpe sets at once, forming tiny bubbles (don't worry if there are a few holes—if they are large, fill with a drizzle of batter). If pan is too cool, the batter does not bubble; increase heat slightly. Cook

crêpe until edge is lightly browned and surface looks dry, 30 to 60 seconds.

4. Run a wide metal spatula under crêpe edge to make sure it is loose in the pan. Turn crêpe over with the spatula and brown lightly on bottom, 5 to 10 seconds. Tip pan over onto a flat plate to release crêpe. Repeat to cook remaining batter, stacking crêpes on the first.

Per 6-inch crêpe: 59 cal., 47% (28 cal.) from fat; 2.4 g protein; 3.1 g fat (1.6 g sat.); 5.1 g carbo (0.2 g fiber); 36 mg sodium; 49 mg chol.

1. In a small bowl, mix pecans with butter.

2. Lay crêpes on a counter in a single layer, pale side up. Spread each crêpe with about 2 tablespoons chutney. Thinly slice cheese, including rind, and cut into about 1-inch lengths. Distribute cheese evenly over crêpes. Gently fold each crêpe in half over filling, then in half again to make a triangle. Set filled crêpe triangles slightly apart on a 12- by 15-inch baking sheet. Lay 2 or 3 pecan halves on each crêpe.

3. Bake in a 400° regular oven or 375° convection oven until cheese melts and nuts are lightly toasted, 6 to 9 minutes. With a wide spatula, transfer crêpes to plates.

Per serving: 723 cal., 46% (333 cal.) from fat; 24 g protein; 37 g fat (6 g sat.); 70 g carbo (0.6 g fiber); 1,335 mg sodium; 215 mg chol.

Crêpes Milanese

PREP AND COOK TIME: About 15 minutes
NOTES: To increase servings, fill additional ramekins with more of the same ingredients.
MAKES: 2 main-dish servings

- 2 **thin crêpes** (8 in., page 42)
- 2 thin slices **prosciutto** (about ¼ oz. each)
- 2 **large eggs**
- 6 to 8 **asparagus** spears (⅓ to ½ lb. total), rinsed and tough ends snapped off
- 2 to 3 tablespoons **shredded parmesan cheese**
  Salt and **pepper**

1. Gently fit each crêpe, dark side up, into a buttered shallow ramekin (about 4- by 6-in. oval or 4- to 5-in. round); edges will extend over rim. Lay 1 slice prosciutto smoothly over each crêpe. Crack an egg; holding close to prosciutto, pull shell apart to let egg flow gently into 1 ramekin. Repeat step for second ramekin. Set ramekins in a 10- by 15-inch pan.

2. Bake in 375° regular or convection oven just until egg yolk is softly set, 8 to 10 minutes.

3. Meanwhile, in a 10- to 12-inch frying pan over high heat, bring about 1 inch water to a boil. Add asparagus and cook just until barely tender when pierced, 4 to 6 minutes. Drain.

4. Divide asparagus equally between ramekins, laying spears beside eggs. Sprinkle with cheese, and add salt and pepper to taste.

Per serving: 242 cal., 52% (126 cal.) from fat; 17 g protein; 14 g fat (6 g sat.); 13 g carbo (0.9 g fiber); 377 mg sodium; 315 mg chol.

Fontina, Spinach, and Onion Crêpes

PREP AND COOK TIME: About 50 minutes
NOTES: If making up to 1 day ahead, cover and chill; bake uncovered.
MAKES: 4 main-dish servings

- About 1 tablespoon **butter** or margarine
- 2 **onions** (1 lb. total), peeled and thinly sliced
- 1 teaspoon **caraway seed**
- 1 package (10 oz.) **frozen chopped spinach**, thawed
- 3 cups shredded **fontina cheese** (¾ lb.)
  Salt
- 8 **thin crêpes** (6 or 7 in., page 42)

1. In a 5- to 6-quart pan over medium heat, combine 1 tablespoon butter, onions, caraway, and ½ cup water. Cover and stir occasionally until onions are very limp, 10 to 15 minutes (add a few more tablespoons water if liquid evaporates before onions are ready), then uncover and stir often until liquid evaporates. Remove from heat.

2. Squeeze excess liquid from spinach. Mix spinach with onions. Add 2½ cups of the cheese and salt to taste; mix well.

3. Lay crêpes slightly apart on a counter, pale side up. Spoon equal amounts of spinach filling down center of crêpes; roll to enclose.

4. Set filled crêpes, seams down and side by side, in a buttered shallow 3-quart casserole (9 by 13 in.).

5. Bake in a 375° regular oven or 350° convection oven until hot in center, 15 to 20 minutes. Sprinkle remaining cheese in a band down center of crêpes. Return to oven and bake until cheese melts, about 3 minutes. With a wide spatula, transfer crêpes to plates. Add salt to taste.

Per serving: 532 cal., 61% (324 cal.) from fat; 30 g protein; 36 g fat (21 g sat.); 23 g carbo (3.6 g fiber); 838 mg sodium; 204 mg chol.

Crêpes Suzette

PREP AND COOK TIME: About 30 minutes
NOTES: For a good show, prepare this French classic at the table in an attractive frying pan over a tabletop burner or in a chafing dish with canned fuel. If your tabletop heat is not sufficient to melt the sugar in just a few minutes, complete step 3 on the kitchen range, then finish the dish in front of guests.
MAKES: 6 dessert servings

- 12 **thin crêpes** (6 or 7 in., page 42)
- 2 teaspoons grated **orange** peel
- 1 teaspoon grated **lemon** peel
- ½ cup **orange** juice
- 1 tablespoon **lemon** juice
- 6 tablespoons **sugar**
- ¼ cup (⅛ lb.) **butter** or margarine
- ¼ cup **orange-flavor liqueur** such as Grand Marnier or curaçao
- ¼ cup **cognac**, brandy, or more orange-flavor liqueur
  Vanilla ice cream (optional)

1. Fold crêpes in half, pale surfaces inside, and lay, overlapping, on a plate.

2. In a bowl, mix orange and lemon peel with orange and lemon juice.

3. In a 10- to 12-inch frying pan or chafing dish over high heat, melt sugar, shaking pan often, until it turns amber, about 2 minutes. Reduce heat to low and add juice mixture all at once; sugar hardens. Stir until sugar dissolves. Add butter and stir until melted.

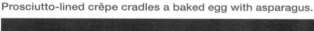
Prosciutto-lined crêpe cradles a baked egg with asparagus.

4. With 2 large spoons and working quickly, lay 1 folded crêpe at a time in sauce, turn over, fold crêpe again to make a triangle, and push to a side of the pan. Repeat to moisten and fold each crêpe, overlapping as needed to fit in pan.

5. Pour liqueur and cognac over crêpes; when liqueurs are slightly warm, about 30 seconds, ignite (not beneath an exhaust fan or flammable items). Shake pan or spoon sauce over crêpes until flame dies. Let simmer 1 or 2 minutes, then spoon crêpes and sauce onto plates. Accompany with ice cream.

Per serving: 284 cal., 44% (126 cal.) from fat; 5.1 g protein; 14 g fat (8 g sat.); 30 g carbo (1.1 g fiber); 152 mg sodium; 118 mg chol.

Soufflé Crêpes

PREP AND COOK TIME: About 30 minutes
NOTES: The first crêpes tend to be thicker and require slightly more batter to fill pan; as batter stands, it thins and spreads more readily. To store, see notes for thin crêpes (page 42).
MAKES: 8 (7-in.) or 6 (8-in.) crêpes

- 4 **large eggs,** separated
- ¼ teaspoon **cream of tartar**
- 1 tablespoon **sugar**
- 1¼ cups **milk** or half-and-half (light cream)
- ½ cup **all-purpose flour**
- ¼ teaspoon **baking powder**
  About 2 tablespoons melted **butter** or margarine

1. In a bowl with mixer on high speed, beat egg whites and cream of tartar until they form a thick foam. Continue to beat, gradually adding sugar until whites hold stiff moist peaks.

2. In a blender, whirl egg yolks, milk, flour, and baking powder until smooth; scrape container as needed. Pour into whipped whites; fold gently until mixture is thoroughly blended.

3. Use a crêpe pan or regular or non-stick frying pan with a bottom that measures 7 to 8 inches across. Set pan on medium heat; when hot, brush bottom with butter (as needed or for flavor, in a nonstick pan). Pour ½ to ⅔ cup batter into pan all at once, and with the back of a spoon spread to cover pan bottom evenly. Cook until crêpe is golden brown on both sides, turning once with a wide spatula, 1½ to 2½ minutes total.

4. Invert crêpe onto a flat plate; cover with a sheet of plastic wrap. Repeat to cook and stack remaining crêpes (it gets thinner as it stands; stir often), tilting pan to coat bottom evenly.

Soufflé crêpe packet with chocolate-hazelnut filling is topped with vanilla ice cream.

Per 7-in. crêpe: 121 cal., 50% (60 cal.) from fat; 5.2 g protein; 6.7 g fat (3.4 g sat.); 9.7 g carbo (0.2 g fiber); 95 mg sodium; 119 mg chol.

Chocolate-Hazelnut Soufflé Crêpes

PREP AND COOK TIME: About 50 minutes
NOTES: If making up to 1 day ahead, prepare through step 6. Cover filled crêpes and reserved sauce separately and chill. Unwrap crêpes to bake.
MAKES: 6 dessert servings

- ½ cup **hazelnuts**
- 3 tablespoons **hazelnut-flavor liqueur** such as Frangelico
- ¾ cup **whipping cream**
- 6 ounces **semisweet chocolate,** chopped
- 4 **large egg whites**
- ¼ teaspoon **cream of tartar**
- 3 tablespoons **granulated sugar**
- 6 **soufflé crêpes** (8 in., at left)
  Powdered sugar
  Vanilla ice cream (optional)

1. In a 350° regular or convection oven, bake nuts in an 8- or 9-inch-wide pan until lightly browned under skin, about 15 minutes. Pour onto a towel; fold towel to enclose nuts and rub packet between your hands to remove as much brown nut skin as possible. Let cool. Lift nuts from towel, leaving skins behind. Whirl nuts in a food processor or blender with liqueur until a smooth paste forms; scrape container sides as needed.

2. In a 1- to 2-quart pan over high heat, stir whipping cream until boiling. Remove from heat; add chocolate and stir until sauce is smooth. Measure ¼ cup

chocolate sauce into a microwave-safe bowl; set aside for garnish. Add hazelnut-liqueur paste to chocolate sauce in pan, nest in ice water, and stir until well mixed. Stir often until mixture cools to room temperature, 3 to 4 minutes.

3. In a deep bowl with mixer on high speed, beat egg whites and cream of tartar until they form a thick foam. Continue to beat, gradually adding granulated sugar and until whites hold distinct peaks.

4. Stir about ¼ of the whipped whites into the chocolate-hazelnut mixture. Scrape chocolate-hazelnut mixture into bowl with remaining whites and fold gently until blended.

5. Lay crêpes on a counter, pale sides up and slightly apart. Mound equal portions of chocolate-hazelnut mixture in the center of crêpes and quickly fold all crêpe sides over filling to enclose, making packets 3 to 3½ inches square. Lay packets seam side down.

6. Butter 6 shallow ramekins (5- to 6-in.-wide rounds or 4- by 6-in. ovals) and lay 1 filled crêpe, seam down, in each dish. Or arrange crêpes slightly apart in a buttered 10- by 15-inch pan.

7. Bake in 400° regular oven or 375° convection oven until centers barely jiggle when lightly touched, 10 to 15 minutes. If reserved chocolate sauce in bowl has solidified, warm in a microwave oven on full power (100%) for about ½ minute, stirring once or twice.

8. Serve dessert in ramekins or use a wide spatula to transfer to plates. Sift powdered sugar over crêpes. Top with ice cream and chocolate sauce.

Per serving: 472 cal., 61% (288 cal.) from fat; 11 g protein; 32 g fat (15 g sat.); 39 g carbo (2.7 g fiber); 158 mg sodium; 156 mg chol. ◆

food guide

By Jerry Anne Di Vecchio • Photographs by James Carrier

Paris and onions

Formidable together when flavor's at steak

Despite France's complex contributions to the world of cuisine, humble onion soup—as served in Paris's old Les Halles neighborhood—is one of its most famous dishes. If you think the impact is slight, consider where California dip would be without a packet of dried French onion soup mix.

The essence of this exalted flavor is nothing more than onions cooked until limp and lightly browned to bring out their natural sweetness. And herein lies the not-so-secret element of culinary whiz Sally McArthur's sumptuous rib eye steak at Seattle's Metropolitan Grill. The onions, cloaked in a delicate cheese sauce, are mounded on a hunk of meat, then finished under the broiler with an additional glaze of cheese. A final touch of broth mingles with the juices as you carve the steak, restating the onion soup connection. Certainly, you could grill the steak, as McArthur does, but browning the meat in a pan, then finishing it in the oven, makes cool-season sense.

French Onion Rib Eye Steak

PREP AND COOK TIME: About 25 minutes

NOTES: You can prepare the French onions up to 1 day ahead or start them just before the steak.

MAKES: 4 servings

- 1 **fat-trimmed beef rib eye steak** (cut 2 in. thick, 1¼ to 1½ lb.)
- ½ teaspoon *each* **kosher** or coarse **salt, cracked pepper, dried onion flakes,** and **dried garlic flakes**
- 1 teaspoon **olive oil**
  French onions (recipe follows)
- ½ cup shredded **gruyère** or Swiss **cheese**
- ½ cup fat-skimmed **beef broth**

1. Rinse beef steak and pat dry. Pat salt, pepper, onion flakes, and garlic flakes evenly onto meat.

2. Pour olive oil into an 8- to 10-inch ovenproof nonstick frying pan over high heat; tilt to coat pan bottom. When hot, add steak and brown on both sides, about 4 minutes total. Supporting meat with tongs, tip steak onto its edge and rotate to brown lightly, about 2 minutes total. As fat in pan accumulates, wipe out with paper towels.

3. Put pan with steak in a 400° regular or convection oven and bake until meat is done to your taste (cut to test), 8 to 12 minutes for rare or about 25 minutes for well done.

4. Turn oven heat to broil. Remove pan and wipe out fat with a paper towel. Mound French onions onto meat and sprinkle with cheese. Broil in pan about 6 inches from heat until cheese is bubbling and beginning to brown, 3 to 4 minutes. Remove pan from oven and pour broth around meat, stirring to release browned bits.

5. Leave meat in pan or use a wide spatula to transfer steak and onions to a warm rimmed platter (pour juices around meat). To serve, cut meat and onions into 4 equal portions; set each on a rimmed plate and spoon juices around meat.

Per serving: 302 cal., 51% (153 cal.) from fat; 33 g protein; 17 g fat (7.4 g sat.); 0.6 g carbo (0.1 g fiber); 329 mg sodium; 99 mg chol.

French onions. Peel and thinly slice 1 **onion** (½ lb.). In a 10- to 12-inch frying pan, combine onion, 2 tablespoons **butter** or margarine, and 1 teaspoon **sugar.** Stir often over medium-high heat until onion is limp and lightly browned, 12 to 15 minutes. Add 1½ teaspoons **all-purpose flour** and mix well. Remove pan from heat; stir in ¼ cup **milk** and ½ cup fat-skimmed **beef broth.** Stir over high heat until boiling; continue stirring until liquid is almost evaporated and mixture doesn't flow when scraped from pan bottom, 4 to 5 minutes. Remove from heat. Add ½ cup shredded **gruyère cheese** and 2 tablespoons grated **parmesan cheese;** stir until melted. Season to taste with **salt** and **pepper.** Use hot. If making up to 1 day ahead, let cool, then cover and chill; reheat in a microwave-safe bowl in a microwave oven at full power (100%) for about 1 minute. Makes 1 cup.

Per serving: 162 cal., 67% (108 cal.) from fat; 72 g protein; 12 g fat (7 g sat.); 7.5 g carbo (0.9 g fiber); 171 mg sodium; 35 mg chol.

A winter's salad

■ In my Germanic grandfather's household, potatoes were a staple, and salads made of them were often served warm. This has several advantages: You don't have to wait for the potatoes to cool, seasonings soak in more effectively, and in the winter, when picnic fare seems out of step, warm potato salad makes a welcome menu addition. Watercress, a cool-weather green, adds a bright bite to this mellow dish.

Warm Potato-Watercress Salad

PREP AND COOK TIME: About 45 minutes

NOTES: If making salad up to 6 hours ahead, don't mix in the watercress; cover salad and chill. Add the chopped watercress and the leaves just before serving.

MAKES: 6 servings

- 4 or 5 **Yukon gold** or other thin-skinned **potatoes** (6 to 8 oz. each, about 2 lb. total)
- 1/4 pound **watercress**
- 1/2 cup finely chopped **shallots**
- 1/2 cup **white wine vinegar**
- 2 tablespoons **coarse-ground mustard**
- 1 teaspoon **sugar**
- 1/2 teaspoon **dried tarragon**

  About 1/2 cup **sour cream** or reduced-fat sour cream

  Salt
- 1/4 cup fat-skimmed **chicken broth** (optional)

1. Scrub potatoes and put in a 3- to 4-quart pan. Add enough water to barely cover potatoes and bring to a boil over high heat.

Cover, reduce heat, and simmer until potatoes are tender when pierced, about 40 minutes.

2. Meanwhile, rinse watercress, drain, and discard discolored or bruised leaves and stems. Pinch off 1 to 2 cups leaves, wrap in a towel, enclose in a plastic bag, and chill. Finely chop remaining watercress, including stems.

3. In a 1- to 2-quart pan, combine shallots, vinegar, mustard, sugar, and tarragon. Bring to a boil over high heat; reduce heat and simmer, stirring occasionally, about 1 minute. Remove from heat.

4. Drain cooked potatoes; when just cool enough to touch, in 10 to 15 minutes, pull off skins and discard. Cut potatoes into 1/2-inch chunks and put in a bowl. Stir in shallot mixture. Add 1/2 cup sour cream and chopped watercress; mix, and season to taste with salt. For a more moist salad, add additional sour cream or up to 1/4 cup broth and mix gently.

5. Scrape salad into a serving bowl and garnish with chilled watercress leaves.

Per serving: 182 cal., 21% (38 cal.) from fat; 3.9 g protein; 4.2 g fat (2.5 g sat.); 32 g carbo (2.6 g fiber); 84 mg sodium; 8.4 mg chol.

Meat juices and broth make the sauce for steak topped by onions glazed with cheese.

Grinding impact

■ Of late, a number of spice companies have been covering their jars with lids that grind. You twist as you dispense the contents, grinding the herbs and spices to release the freshest flavor. As a longtime advocate of fresh grinding, I view this as a step forward in good taste. And the concept is spreading. On a recent whirlwind tour of spice production around the world, hosted by Spice Islands, I even came across jars of black peppercorns topped with grinding lids in India. Closer to home, several companies are packaging spices, herbs, and salts this way; many offer blends, and some have citrus zests or flowers. They include Melissa's My Grinder (800/588-0151 or www.melissas.com for sources) and the Elements of Spice (800/451-7647 or www.elements-of-spice.com). You may pay a small premium for the grinder, but it will usually last long enough for you to refill the jar several times.

Have a ball with pancakes

■ Cooks who collect tools—particularly Scandinavian cooks— probably have an *aebleskiver* (aw-*bluh*-skeever) pan, or monk's pan. Easy to identify, it looks like the offspring of a marriage between a heavy frying pan and a muffin tin. It's decorative enough to hang on the wall. I first learned about the pan from a Danish friend, so I called the pancakes made in them "Danish." But both the pancakes and the pan are at home anywhere in Scandinavia. When my daughter was small, she liked me to entertain her friends at breakfast by making these ball-shaped cakes. Now I do the same for my grandsons, Henry and Jack—or for my weekend guests who linger in the kitchen to keep me company. Why make pancakes as balls? Just because you can, once you have an aebleskiver pan (easy to find at cookware stores).

Danish Pancake Balls (Aebleskiver)

PREP AND COOK TIME: 35 to 40 minutes

NOTES: Serve the warm pancake balls with butter and jam or dusted with powdered sugar. To make filled aebleskiver, add about ½ teaspoon jam to the batter in each cup just before you make the first turn. Serve the pancake balls as they are cooked, or keep warm in a napkin-lined basket until all are ready. The batter can also be cooked on a lightly buttered griddle over medium heat to make light, tender pancakes. For mile-high baking, reduce the baking powder to 2½ teaspoons.

MAKES: 12 or 13 pancake balls

1¼ cups **all-purpose flour**

3 tablespoons **sugar**

2¾ teaspoons **baking powder**

¼ teaspoon **ground cardamom** or ground cinnamon

¼ teaspoon **salt**

1 **large egg**

1 cup **milk**

About 2 tablespoons melted **butter** or margarine

1. In a bowl, mix flour with sugar, baking powder, cardamom, and salt. In a small bowl, beat egg to blend with milk and 2 tablespoons butter. Add liquids to dry ingredients and stir until evenly moistened.

2. Place an aebleskiver pan over medium-low heat. When pan is hot

enough to make a drop of water dance, brush pancake cups lightly with melted butter and fill each to slightly below the rim with batter **(A)**.

3. In about 1½ minutes, thin crusts will form on bottoms of balls (centers will still be wet); pierce the crust with a slender wood skewer and gently pull shell to rotate the pancake ball until about half the cooked portion is above the cup rim and uncooked batter flows down into cup **(B)**. Cook until crust on bottom of ball is again firm enough to pierce, about another minute, then rotate ball with skewer until the ridge formed as the pancake first cooked is on top. Cook, turning occasionally with skewer, until balls are evenly browned and no longer moist in the center, another 10 to 12 minutes. Check by piercing center of last pancake ball added to pan with skewer **(C)**—it should come out clean—or by

breaking the ball open slightly; if balls start to get too brown, turn heat to low until they are cooked in the center. Lift cooked balls from pan and serve hot (see notes). Repeat to cook remaining batter.

Per pancake ball: 88 cal., 30% (26 cal.) from fat; 2.3 g protein; 2.9 g fat (1.6 g sat.); 13 g carbo (0.3 g fiber); 180 mg sodium; 24 mg chol.

Boxed aebleskiver. When sisters Janet Pendergrass and Linda Strand were growing up, their mother often treated the family to an aebleskiver breakfast. As adults, they decided this tradition shouldn't be lost, so they created a kit containing the pan, a mix, and preserves. (They also sell the mix separately.) Purchase at or order from Your NorthWest stores (888/ 252-0699 or www.yournw.com); the kit costs $26.95, the mix is $4.95, plus shipping. ◆

The Wine Guide

By Karen MacNeil-Fife

JANCIS ROBINSON:

A wine expert for us

■ Jancis Robinson is arguably the most influential wine expert in the world today. Robinson, who lives in London with her husband, Nick Lander, and three children, has racked up every top wine award there is. A prolific writer and broadcaster, she produced and hosted the 10-part television series *Jancis Robinson's Wine Course,* which has aired on both PBS and the BBC, and edited the opus *Oxford Companion to Wine.*

Recently, Robinson was in California to promote *The Oxford Companion to the Wines of North America,* for which she was consulting editor and Bruce Cass was editor. I couldn't pass up the opportunity to talk with her about her success and American wine.

KMF: *How did a college math and philosophy major— and an active mother—become one of the world's leading authorities on wine?*

JR: First, I'm married to a saint. Because my husband writes about food and restaurants, he's always at home, so I've been able to go off on trips to wine regions around the world. Second, I've come to realize that I'm a workaholic. If someone gives me a challenge, I just seem to take it up.

KMF: *When you were starting out, was there ever a point when you were intimidated—when you felt that wine was just too complex to master?*

JR (with a laugh): Not at all. When you start out learning about something, you don't actually realize how complex it is. I was so naive that after about a year I thought, "Well, now I've got it—I understand wine." Only now do I realize how little I know and how many exciting things there still are to learn.

KMF: *Generally speaking, Europeans are, well, chauvinistic about European wines. What do you think about American wines?*

JR: I honestly believe that America is making some wines that are as good as the best anywhere in the world. But I'm concerned that many American wine producers don't try very hard to make good inexpensive ones.

KMF: *In general, I agree. But you may be interested to know that last month I went on a mission to find delicious inexpensive wines, and you* can *find them [for Karen MacNeil-Fife's list of steals, see* Sunset's *website], you just have to hunt. And speaking of American wine—inexpensive or expensive—do you think there's a particular American wine character?*

JR: Yes. They're about directness, fruitiness, ripeness. They're ready to drink this instant.

KMF: *What makes wine so captivating to you? Why spend a lifetime learning about it?*

JR: Well, first, it tastes good (and very important, it makes food taste good). It has just the right amount of alcohol. It's not like spirits that can knock you over or beer that can make you feel full. But there's also the fact that wine is about stories, about people, and about culture. It's tied to the history of mankind.

KMF: *Finally, what advice would you give someone who wanted to learn more about wine and fit it into their life a bit more?*

JR: I think the most important thing is to find a friendly retailer—someone you trust and like. Tell them you're curious about wine, and then let them be responsible for bringing out new and delicious things for you to taste.

The Oxford Companion to the Wines of North America (Oxford University Press, New York, 2000; $45; 800/451-7556), a comprehensive encyclopedia, includes introductory essays by many well-known wine experts, including two by Robinson.

WESTERN PICKS

Jancis Robinson follows American wine quite closely. Here are four producers she thinks are among the very best, and my brief descriptions of the wineries.

■**Araujo Estate Wines,** Napa Valley. Specializes in Cabernet Sauvignon but also makes Sauvignon Blanc. Its Eisele Vineyard Cabernet ($125) is sensational. Says Robinson, "Araujo wines have a real expression of place."

■**Harlan Estate,** Napa Valley. Makes only top-flight Cabernet Sauvignon blend. Tiny production means the wine is expensive ($175) and hard to come by. Robinson says, "Harlan Estate's Cabernet gives Pomerol [Bordeaux] a run for its money."

■**Kistler Vineyards,** Russian River Valley, CA. The tiny winery specializes in rich, complex Chardonnays—approximately 11 from different vineyards ($50 to $65). The most famous of these are Dutton Ranch and Cuvée Cathleen. "Kistler's Chardonnays have regularly trumped white Burgundies at my dinner table," reports Robinson.

■**Ridge Vineyards,** Santa Cruz Mountains, CA. Specializes in vineyard-designated Zinfandels and a stellar Cabernet blend called Monte Bello ($120). According to Robinson, "Ridge has a great track record." ◆

MATT PRINCE

Inn-spiration
A make-it-yourself menu from great inns around the West

At a fine inn, it seems foolish to ever leave the premises, what with a picture-perfect setting, luxurious accommodations, pampering service, and meals that can rival four-star restaurant food. ❧ Our search for the best places to get away turned up some stellar dishes. Sample them in this indulgent dinner for eight, as a whole or in selected parts. If you can't actually leave home, you can at least bring the flavors of a luxurious holiday to your dining room.

— *Linda Lau Anusasananan*

Innkeeper's Mussel Chowder

PREP AND COOK TIME: About 1¼ hours

NOTES: This creamy mussel chowder debuted in 1981 on the first menu at Shelburne Inn's Shoalwater Restaurant in Seaview, Washington. If making it up to 1 day ahead, cool, cover, and chill; reheat to serve.

MAKES: 8 to 10 first-course servings

- 5 pounds **mussels in shells**
- 1 cup **dry white wine** or water
- 1 pound **thin-skinned potatoes**
- 1 **onion** (½ lb.)
- 1 stalk **celery** (3 oz.)
- 2 tablespoons **butter** or margarine
- 2 teaspoons **curry powder**
- 1½ teaspoons **dried basil**
- 1 can (28 oz.) **tomato sauce**
- 2 cups **whipping cream**
  Salt and **pepper**

1. Scrub mussels in cool water and pull off beards; discard any whose shells don't close when tapped. In an 8- to 10-quart pan, combine mussels and wine; bring to a boil over high heat. Cover and simmer over medium heat until mussels open, 5 to 8 minutes. Pour into a colander set in a large bowl to collect juices. Let mussels stand until cool enough to touch.

2. Meanwhile, peel potatoes and cut into ½-inch cubes. Peel and chop onion. Rinse celery and cut into ½-inch pieces.

3. In the pan used for mussels, melt butter over medium heat. Add onion and celery; stir often until onion is limp, 6 to 8 minutes. Add curry powder and basil; stir until spices become more fragrant, about 30 seconds.

4. Pour mussel juices from bowl into pan. Add tomato sauce, cream, and potatoes. Turn heat to high; when mixture is boiling, cover, reduce heat to low, and simmer, stirring occasionally,

until flavors are well blended, about 30 minutes.

5. Meanwhile, remove mussels from shells; discard shells.

6. Add mussels to soup; cover and simmer just until mussels are hot, 3 to 5 minutes. Add salt and pepper to taste. Ladle into bowls.

Per serving: 285 cal., 60% (171 cal.) from fat; 11 g protein; 19 g fat (11 g sat.); 19 g carbo (2.5 g fiber); 721 mg sodium; 78 mg chol.

Apple-Mint Salad

PREP AND COOK TIME: About 15 minutes

NOTES: Chef Eric Skokan at Gold Lake Mountain Resort and Spa in Ward, Colorado, serves this simple dish as a palate cleanser. Here it's a fresh interlude between the soup and the pork. Prepare through step 2 up to 3 hours ahead; cover and chill.

MAKES: 8 servings

- 6 tablespoons **lemon juice**
- 2 **Granny Smith apples** (1 lb. total)
- ⅓ cup **orange juice**

- Innkeeper's Mussel Chowder*
- Apple-Mint Salad*
- Chardonnay
- Peppered Pork Tenderloin with Cranberry-Onion Compote*
- Sugar Snap Peas Snow Peas
- Potato Risotto*
- Pinot Noir
- Chocolate Tart with Nut Crust*
- Coffee

*Recipe provided

Star billing goes to the main course of peppered pork tenderloin with cranberry compote and herb-infused potato risotto.

JAMES CARRIER

- 2 tablespoons **salad oil**
- ⅓ cup finely slivered **fresh mint** leaves
  Salt
- 8 **butter lettuce** leaves, rinsed and crisped
  Fresh mint sprigs

1. In a 4- to 5-quart bowl, mix lemon juice with 1 quart water. Rinse apples, cut in half, and core; thinly slice lengthwise, then cut slices into matchstick-size slivers. As apples are cut, immerse in lemon water.

2. Drain apples thoroughly in a colander; return to bowl. Add orange juice and oil, and mix gently.

3. Just before serving, add mint leaves. Mix gently and add salt to taste. Place a lettuce leaf on each of 8 salad plates. Spoon apple salad equally onto lettuce leaves; garnish with mint sprigs.

Per serving: 68 cal., 47% (32 cal.) from fat; 0.4 g protein; 3.6 g fat (0.5 g sat.); 9.5 g carbo (1.5 g fiber); 1.7 mg sodium; 0 mg chol.

Peppered Pork Tenderloin with Cranberry-Onion Compote

PREP AND COOK TIME: About 1 hour

NOTES: Chef Stephen Smith of Albion River Inn in Albion, California, created this dish.

MAKES: 8 servings

2 fat-trimmed **pork tenderloins** (1 lb. each)

2 tablespoons **coarse-ground pepper**

4 teaspoons **salad oil**

1 **red onion** (6 oz.), peeled and chopped

1 cup **dried sweetened cranberries**

⅓ cup **raspberry vinegar**

⅓ cup fat-skimmed **chicken broth**

1 tablespoon **sugar**

⅓ cup **butter** or margarine

Salt

1. Rinse pork and pat dry; roll in pepper to coat evenly.

2. Set an 11- to 12-inch frying pan with ovenproof handle over high heat. When pan is hot, add 1 tablespoon oil and swirl to coat bottom. Add pork (cut tenderloins crosswise to fit pan if necessary) and turn as needed to brown on all sides, 5 to 7 minutes total.

3. Set pan in a 400° regular or convection oven; bake until a thermometer inserted in center of thickest part of meat reaches 155°, 20 to 30 minutes. Remove from oven and let meat stand in a warm place about 5 minutes.

4. Meanwhile, in a 1- to 1½-quart pan over high heat, stir onion in remaining 1 teaspoon oil until limp, about 5 minutes. Add cranberries, vinegar, broth, and sugar; stir occasionally until liquid is reduced to about 2 tablespoons, about 7 minutes. Reduce heat to low. Add butter and stir until melted and incorporated into sauce.

5. Cut meat on the diagonal across the grain into ¼-inch-thick slices; arrange on 8 plates. Spoon sauce equally over and around meat. Add salt to taste.

Per serving: 292 cal., 43% (126 cal.) from fat; 25 g protein; 14 g fat (6.7 g sat.); 16 g carbo (1.6 g fiber); 130 mg sodium; 88 mg chol.

Potato Risotto

PREP AND COOK TIME: About 1 hour

NOTES: At Restaurant 301 in the Hotel Carter in Eureka, California, Mark

Save room for a chocolate tart with a walnut and pine nut crust.

JAMES CARRIER

Carter makes an interesting herb-scented "risotto" out of diced potatoes instead of rice. Prepare through step 3 up to 2 hours ahead; cover and let stand at room temperature. Reheat and continue.

MAKES: 6 to 8 servings

2 pounds **Yukon gold potatoes**

2 tablespoons **butter** or margarine

1 tablespoon minced **shallots**

1 teaspoon minced **garlic**

1 tablespoon minced **fresh thyme** leaves or 1 teaspoon dried thyme

1 teaspoon minced **fresh rosemary** leaves or ½ teaspoon chopped dried rosemary

1½ cups fat-skimmed **chicken** or vegetable **broth**

½ cup **whipping cream**

Salt and **pepper**

1. Peel potatoes and cut into ¼-inch cubes; put in a large bowl and cover with water.

2. In a 5- to 6-quart pan over medium heat, melt butter. Add shallots and garlic and stir until shallots are limp, about 1 minute.

3. Drain potatoes and add to pan, along with thyme and rosemary. Stir often until potatoes appear slightly translucent, about 8 minutes.

4. Add broth and stir often until potatoes are tender to bite and have absorbed most of the liquid, 12 to 15 minutes. Add cream and stir often until almost all is absorbed, 2 to 4 minutes. Add salt and pepper to taste.

Per serving: 160 cal., 43% (69 cal.) from fat; 3.9 g protein; 7.7 g fat (4.7 g sat.); 19 g carbo (1.8 g fiber); 57 mg sodium; 24 mg chol.

Chocolate Tart with Nut Crust

PREP AND COOK TIME: About 50 minutes

NOTES: John Johnson, chef and owner of Rancho de San Juan in Española, New Mexico, serves this very rich chocolate-nut tart with softly whipped cream. If making up to 1 day ahead, cover and chill. To serve, let warm to room temperature, about 1 hour.

MAKES: 8 to 10 servings

1 cup **chopped walnuts**

1 cup **pine nuts**

½ cup plus 3 tablespoons **sugar**

½ cup (¼ lb.) **butter** or margarine

9 ounces **bittersweet** or semisweet **chocolate**

6 **large egg** yolks

1 teaspoon **cognac** or brandy

½ teaspoon **almond extract**

Unsweetened cocoa powder

1. In a food processor, whirl walnuts, pine nuts, and ½ cup sugar until nuts are coarsely ground. Pour into a 9-inch tart pan with removable rim. In a 2-cup glass measure, melt ¼ cup butter in a microwave oven at full power (100%), 20 to 30 seconds. Add melted butter to nut mixture and rub in with your fingers to blend. Press mixture evenly over bottom and up sides of pan. Set pan on a foil-lined 12- by 15-inch baking sheet.

2. Bake in a 325° regular or convection oven until crust begins to brown around edges, 20 to 30 minutes.

3. Meanwhile, chop half the chocolate into ½-inch chunks and set aside. Finely chop remaining chocolate.

4. In the glass measure, combine remaining ¼ cup butter, cut into small pieces, with finely chopped chocolate. Heat in a microwave oven at half power (50%) until chocolate is soft, 30 to 45 seconds. Stir until mixture is smooth.

5. In a bowl with a mixer on high speed, beat egg yolks, remaining 3 tablespoons sugar, cognac, and almond extract until mixture turns pale yellow, about 3 minutes. Add chocolate-butter mixture and beat to blend. Stir in coarsely chopped chocolate. Scrape into warm nut crust.

6. Bake in a 325° regular or convection oven until filling barely jiggles when pan is gently shaken, about 15 minutes. Set on a rack until warm or cool.

7. To serve, remove rim; dust tart lightly with cocoa and cut into wedges.

Per serving: 448 cal., 72% (324 cal.) from fat; 8.7 g protein; 36 g fat (13 g sat.); 32 g carbo (2.8 g fiber); 100 mg sodium; 152 mg chol. ◆

Kitchen Cabinet

Readers' recipes tested in *Sunset's* kitchens

By Andrew Baker

South African Beef Curry

Nancy Sephton,
Kensington, California

When Nancy Sephton lived in South Africa in the '50s, lamb curry was as ubiquitous there as hamburgers and hot dogs are in the United States. On a return visit a number of years later, she came across the curry made with beef, which has become a favorite with her family.

PREP AND COOK TIME: About 3 hours

MAKES: 6 to 8 servings

- 3 pounds **boned, fat-trimmed beef chuck**
- 2 **onions** (1 lb. total), peeled and chopped
- ¼ cup **curry powder**
- 2 tablespoons **mustard seed**
- 1 tablespoon minced **garlic**
- 1 teaspoon **ground dried turmeric**
- 2 cups fat-skimmed **beef broth**
- 1¼ pounds **Roma tomatoes**, rinsed, cored, and chopped
- 2 tablespoons minced **fresh jalapeño chilies**
- 2 tablespoons minced **fresh ginger**
- 1 **firm-ripe banana** (about 5 oz.), peeled and thinly sliced

  About ½ cup **mango chutney**

  About ⅓ cup **sweetened shredded dried coconut**

  Cucumber yogurt sauce (recipe follows)

  About 6 cups hot cooked **rice**

  Salt

1. Rinse beef, pat dry, and cut into 1-inch chunks. In a 5- to 6-quart pan, combine beef, onions, and 1 cup water. Cover and bring to a boil over high heat; reduce heat and simmer 30 minutes. Uncover, turn heat to high, and stir often until liquid evaporates and meat and onions are lightly browned, 5 to 7 minutes. Spoon out and discard any fat.

Beef curry goes well with chutney, yogurt sauce, and bananas.

2. Add to pan the curry powder, mustard seed, garlic, and turmeric; stir until spices are more fragrant, about 1 minute. Add broth, tomatoes, chilies, and ginger; stir to free browned bits. Return to a boil, cover, reduce heat, and simmer until meat is very tender when pierced, 2 to 2½ hours.

3. Put banana, chutney, coconut, and cucumber yogurt sauce each in separate small bowls.

4. Ladle beef curry over rice on plates. Add banana, chutney, coconut, cucumber yogurt sauce, and salt to taste.

Per serving: 559 cal., 26% (144 cal.) from fat; 40 g protein; 16 g fat (5.8 g sat.); 63 g carbo (4 g fiber); 337 mg sodium; 111 mg chol.

Cucumber yogurt sauce. In a small bowl, mix 1 cup **plain low-fat yogurt**, ¾ cup chopped **English cucumber**, 1 teaspoon minced **fresh ginger**, 1 teaspoon minced **garlic**, and **salt** to taste. Makes about 1½ cups.

Per tablespoon: 6.7 cal., 27% (1.8 cal.) from fat; 0.5 g protein; 0.2 g fat (0.1 g sat.); 0.8 g carbo (0 g fiber); 6.6 mg sodium; 0.6 mg chol.

Whole-wheat Muffins

Karen Johnson McWilliams,
Joplin, Montana

Karen Johnson McWilliams was away at graduate school when she got engaged, so her mother threw a wedding shower back home in Joplin, Montana, without her. Friends brought special family recipes, which mom mailed to the bride and groom. This recipe remains one of Karen's favorites.

PREP AND COOK TIME: About 25 minutes

MAKES: 12 muffins

- ¼ cup (⅛ lb.) **butter** or margarine
- 1 cup firmly packed **brown sugar**
- 1 cup **milk**
- ¼ cup **plain nonfat yogurt**
- 1 **large egg**
- ½ teaspoon **vanilla**
- 2 cups **whole-wheat flour**
- 1 teaspoon **baking soda**
- 1 cup chopped **pecans**

1. In a large bowl with a mixer, beat butter and sugar until very well mixed and no lumps remain. Add milk, yogurt, egg, and vanilla; beat just until blended. Add flour, soda, and pecans; stir until mixture is evenly moistened.

2. Spoon batter equally into 12 buttered or paper-lined muffin cups (2½ to 2¾ in. wide).

3. Bake in a 425° regular or convection oven until muffins just begin to pull from pan sides and spring back in the center when lightly pressed, about 15 minutes.

4. Cool muffins in pan about 5 minutes, then invert onto a rack and turn rounded side up. Serve hot, warm, or cool. If making up to 1 day ahead, wrap cool muffins airtight and store at room temperature; freeze to store longer. To reheat, seal in foil and bake in a 350° regular or convection oven about 10 minutes.

Per muffin: 262 cal., 41% (108 cal.) from fat; 4.9 g protein; 12 g fat (4.2 g sat.); 35 g carbo (3.1 g fiber); 183 mg sodium; 34 mg chol.

Apple-Yam Soup

Bettigene Reiswig, Port Orford, Oregon

As a vegetarian, Bettigene Reiswig finds the ingredients she prefers to eat and cook with are well suited to thick, hearty, satisfying soups. She uses vegetable broth for this mixture, but suggests chicken broth for others who prefer its richer flavor.

PREP AND COOK TIME: About 45 minutes

MAKES: About 6 cups; 4 servings

- ½ cup thinly sliced **celery**
- 1 cup chopped **onion**
- 2 teaspoons **salad oil**
- 3 cups diced (½ in.) peeled **yams** (1 lb. total)
- 2 cups diced (½ in.) peeled, cored **Granny Smith apples** (8 to 9 oz. total)
- 3 cups fat-skimmed **chicken** or vegetable **broth**

  Plain low-fat yogurt or sour cream

  Salt and **pepper**

1. In a 3- to 4-quart pan over high heat, frequently stir celery and onion in oil until lightly browned, about 5 minutes. Add yams, apples, and broth; bring to a boil, cover, reduce heat, and simmer until yams are tender when pierced, about 15 minutes.

2. With a slotted spoon, transfer vegetables and apples to a blender or food processor; whirl until smooth, adding enough cooking liquid to purée easily. Pour purée back into pan and stir over medium-high heat just until steaming, 2 to 3 minutes.

3. Ladle soup into wide bowls. Add yogurt, salt, and pepper to taste.

Per serving: 228 cal., 11% (24 cal.) from fat; 8.4 g protein; 2.7 g fat (0.4 g sat.); 44 g carbo (6.5 g fiber); 81 mg sodium; 0 mg chol.

Roasted Squash with Spinach and Gruyère

Rosemary La Puma, San Francisco

When Rosemary La Puma's nutritionist encouraged her to include three to five vegetables a day in her menus, she turned to roasting, in addition to other basic preparation techniques, because it's so easy. And La Puma likes roasted squash as a natural bowl for one more vegetable, spinach.

PREP AND COOK TIME: About 45 minutes

MAKES: 4 servings

- 2 **acorn squash** (about 1 lb. each)
- 1 package (10 oz.) **frozen chopped spinach,** thawed
- 1 cup shredded **gruyère cheese** (about 4 oz.)
- ¼ cup **chopped walnuts**

  Salt and fresh-ground **pepper**

1. Rinse squash and cut each in half lengthwise; scoop out and discard seeds. Place squash halves, cut side down, in a 10- by 15-inch pan.

2. Bake in a 400° regular or convection oven until squash is just tender when pierced, 25 to 30 minutes.

3. Meanwhile, squeeze moisture from spinach. In a bowl, mix spinach, ¾ cup cheese, and walnuts. Season to taste with salt and pepper.

4. With tongs or a spatula, turn squash halves over and spoon spinach mixture equally into cavities. Sprinkle equally with remaining ¼ cup cheese. Return squash to oven and bake until cheese melts and filling is hot in the center, 15 to 20 minutes.

Per serving: 251 cal., 50% (126 cal.) from fat; 13 g protein; 14 g fat (5.8 g sat.); 22 g carbo (7.9 g fiber); 154 mg sodium; 31 mg chol. ◆

Tequila time

Try the trendy spirit in a pie; or spike a sauce for barbecued spareribs

By Elaine Johnson

Tequila has become a tony tipple, with premium bottles crowding the shelves behind bars and along liquor store aisles. To be called tequila, the product must contain at least 51 percent blue agave juice. But that's where simple definitions end. Generally, premium tequilas are made from 100 percent blue agave juice, but not always; price is an indication.

There are four varieties of tequila. *Plata* (silver, also called *blanco,* or white) and *oro* (gold, which may have caramel coloring or sweetener added) are typically unaged; silver has the cleaner agave flavor. *Reposado* (literally, peaceful) has aged a minimum of three months in oak barrels. *Añejo* (aged) has spent a minimum of one year on oak. The more time a tequila spends on oak, the more complex and woodsy its flavor—and the more expensive it usually is—so premium versions tend to fall into the last two categories. But you can find premium silver tequilas too.

Regardless of its age or agave content, tequila isn't just for margaritas (or shots); it adds an intriguing nip to many dishes, from entrées to desserts. And though the nuances of premium brands do come through in cooking, the following recipes also work well with a silver or gold tequila.

Frozen Margarita Pie

PREP AND COOK TIME: About 25 minutes, plus 3 hours to freeze

NOTES: Use a silver tequila.

MAKES: 8 servings

- 1½ cups (3½ oz.) lightly packed **white marshmallows**
- ⅔ cup **half-and-half** (light cream)
- 1 teaspoon grated **lime** peel
- ¼ cup **lime juice**
- ¼ cup **tequila** (see notes)
- 20 **thin chocolate wafer cookies** (about 2 in. wide; 5 oz. total)
- 2 tablespoons melted **butter** or margarine
- 1 cup **whipping cream**
- 1½ tablespoons **sugar**

Frozen margarita pie: Cocktail flavors in a dark chocolate crust, with a twist of lime.

JAMES CARRIER

1. In a 3- to 4-quart pan over medium heat, stir marshmallows with half-and-half until melted, about 5 minutes.

2. Nest pan in ice water; stir often until cool, about 3 minutes. Add lime peel, lime juice, and tequila; stir occasionally until cold, 8 to 10 minutes.

3. In a food processor, whirl cookies until finely ground. Add butter and whirl until mixed. Press cookie mixture evenly over bottom and halfway up sides of a 9-inch cake pan with removable rim.

4. In a bowl with a mixer on high speed, whip cream with sugar until it holds soft peaks. Fold in marshmallow mixture, blending well.

5. Pour filling into crust and spread level. Freeze until firm to touch in the center, about 1 hour, then wrap airtight and freeze until solid, at least 2 hours longer or up to 2 weeks.

6. Unwrap pie, run a thin knife between crust and pan rim, and remove rim. Set dessert on a flat plate. Let stand at room temperature about 10 minutes to soften slightly, then cut into wedges.

Per serving: 284 cal., 54% (153 cal.) from fat; 2.7 g protein; 17 g fat (9.6 g sat.); 28 g carbo (0.6 g fiber); 158 mg sodium; 49 mg chol.

Classic Margarita Rocks

PREP TIME: About 5 minutes

MAKES: 2 servings

If desired, rub rims of 2 glasses (8 oz. each) with 1 **lime** wedge. Put **coarse salt** in a shallow dish; dip glass rims into salt. Put ¾ cup **ice cubes** in each glass. In a pitcher, mix ¼ cup *each* **tequila, orange liqueur,** and **lime juice.** Pour equally into glasses. Garnish with lime wedges.

Per serving: 164 cal., 0.5% (0.9 cal.) from fat; 0.1 g protein; 0.1 g fat (0 g sat.); 11 g carbo (0 g fiber); 4.9 mg sodium; 0 mg chol.

Tequila Barbecued Spareribs

PREP AND COOK TIME: About 1¼ hours

MAKES: 4 servings

3 pounds **pork spareribs,** fat trimmed

1 cup **tequila barbecue sauce** (recipe follows)

Salt

1. Rinse ribs and pat dry. Arrange in a single layer in an 11- by 17-inch pan. Add ¾ cup water; cover tightly with foil.

2. Bake in a 425° oven until meat is tender when pierced, 40 to 45 minutes. Lift ribs out. Skim and discard fat and save juices for other uses, or discard.

3. Place ribs on a barbecue grill over a solid bed of medium coals or medium heat on a gas grill (you can hold your hand at grill level only 4 to 5 seconds); close lid on gas grill. Cook, turning as needed, until ribs are browned on both sides, about 10 minutes total.

4. Set aside ¼ cup of the sauce. Baste tops of ribs with about half the remaining sauce; turn over and brown, 4 to 5 minutes. Baste other sides of ribs with remaining sauce; turn over and brown, 4 to 5 minutes.

5. Transfer to a board; cut between ribs and serve with reserved ¼ cup sauce to add to taste. Add salt to taste.

Per serving: 721 cal., 51% (369 cal.) from fat; 40 g protein; 41 g fat (15 g sat.); 29 g carbo (1 g fiber); 311 mg sodium; 161 mg chol.

Tequila barbecue sauce. In a 4- to 5-quart pan, combine 1 can (12 oz.) **frozen pineapple juice concentrate,** 1 can (6 oz.) **tomato paste,** 1 cup **tequila,** ¼ cup **lemon juice,** 2 tablespoons **distilled white vinegar,** 1 tablespoon minced **garlic,** and 1 tablespoon minced **canned chipotle chili in adobo sauce** (including sauce) or 1 teaspoon hot sauce. Bring to a boil over medium-high heat and stir often until reduced to 2 cups, about 20 minutes. Use sauce, chill airtight up to 2 weeks, or freeze. Makes 2 cups.

Per ¼ cup: 194 cal., 1.4% (2.7 cal.) from fat; 1.6 g protein; 0.3 g fat (0 g sat.); 29 g carbo (1 g fiber); 188 mg sodium; 0 mg chol. ◆

Over easy on the central California coast

Beach breakfasts at these eateries are simple, satisfying, and served with a whiff of salt air

By Lisa Taggart

Not much will get me out of bed on a winter weekend morning. But the prospect of eggs poached just right with house potatoes and a steaming mug of coffee might open one eye. Add to that the luxury of strolling on the beach when it's empty save for the birds, and I'll push aside that cozy comforter.

What is it about surf and sand that excites the appetite? It's inexplicable: All I know is that food just tastes better after a walk by the ocean. Perhaps it's because my cravings are simpler. A nonfat double decaf and an entrée topped with hollandaise doesn't seem right at the continent's edge. The beach is about the basics. When we head out for an early morning of good eating, my husband says, "We're not getting anything foofy."

We found seven breakfast joints in the San Francisco Bay area where you can gaze at the sea over a short stack or a plate of eggs and potatoes. There's nothing too fancy about these places. But the food is hearty, servings are generous, and the tab won't bust your budget. And there's no better way to start your day than to take your coffee with a little saltwater.

■ **PACIFICA: Nick's Seashore Restaurant.** The scalloped, powder blue booths and carved wood fish hanging on the walls give this Pacifica standard the ambience of an aquarium. Outside the fishbowl, surfers work Rockaway Beach's famous waves. From inside, you can watch their tricks without the chill, sampling old-fashioned eye-openers such as steak and eggs or corned beef hash. *9 A.M.–10 P.M. Mon-Fri, 8 A.M.–11 P.M. Sat-Sun; breakfast until 1 daily. 100 Rockaway Beach Ave.; (650) 359-3900.*

■ **POINT REYES: Drakes Beach Cafe.** The menu is short and the cafe tiny here near the tip of Point Reyes, but the food is tasty and cooked up right in front of you. You can get an omelet with oysters harvested just down the road or a generous stack of pancakes with blackberries. From the cafe's cozy interior, watch the waves crash onto the spot where Sir Francis Drake and his crew may have landed in 1579. Or use the telescope to gaze at points afar and look for whales. Outdoor tables are great when the wind and fog aren't too heavy. *10–6 Thu-Mon; breakfast all day. Visitor center at Drakes Beach (off Sir Francis Drake Blvd., follow signs to Drakes Beach); (415) 669-1297.*

■ **SAN FRANCISCO: Louis'.** The orange- and green-dotted faux brick linoleum is the tip-off that this is a San Francisco old-timer, overlooking Seal Rocks and the Sutro Baths—and, later, its ruins—since 1937. Though tour buses pack 'em in at the Cliff House just down the road, this is where the locals come. The coffee is weak and plentiful, the omelets layered with American cheese, and the servers frazzled but friendly. Add stupendous views to the menu, and you've got the quintessential beach breakfast. Stick to old standbys like pancakes or scrambled eggs. *6:30– 4:30 Mon-Fri, 6:30–6 Sat-Sun; eggs all day, pancakes until 12, waffles until 2:30 daily. 902 Pt. Lobos Ave.; (415) 387-6330.*

■ **SAN FRANCISCO: Pier 23 Cafe.** Though the restaurant draws a foot-stomping dance crowd at night, mornings on the back deck overlooking San Francisco's waterfront have the recuperative lassitude of a frat house on a Sunday. Tasty brunch choices here include spicy chilaquiles and artichoke frittata. *11:30–3, 6–10 Mon-Fri (music 10–2); brunch 10–3 Sat-Sun. Pier 23 on the Embarcadero; (415) 362-5125.*

■ **SANTA CRUZ: Aldo's Harbor Restaurant.** From the deck's wood chairs, you can watch boats entering and exiting Santa Cruz Harbor, as well as beachgoers heading out over the dunes. You may have to shoo the shorebirds from your tofu scramble (it is, after all, Santa Cruz), fierce pesto omelets, and spicy house potatoes—but the fight, like the salt air, just makes the meal more satisfying. *7–4 Mon-Fri, 7–5 Sat-Sun; breakfast until 1 daily. 616 Atlantic Ave.; (831) 426-3736.*

■ **STINSON BEACH: Parkside Café.** Okay, so you can't actually see the ocean from this cafe's back patio. Still, it's only a short stroll from the water's edge, and it's worth the amble just to sink a fork into the cafe's cheddar cheese, tomato, and bacon scramble, or to munch the sweet, crumbly coffee cake. Go early: The cafe can get crowded on weekends. *7:30–2 daily; breakfast all day. 43 Arenal Ave.; (415) 868-1272.*

■ **TIBURON: Sweden House.** Locals squeeze onto the tiny back deck of this downtown Tiburon spot, as much for the postcard views across the bay to San Francisco as for the limpa, a slightly sweet, orange-flavored Swedish rye bread. Perfectly fluffy omelets and house potatoes are other good menu options, or choose from the wide selection of pastries. *8–5 Mon-Fri, 8–6 Sat-Sun; breakfast until 3 daily. 35 Main St.; (415) 435-9767. ◆*

Blueberries, suspended in the tart filling, add a fresh twist to popular lemon squares (recipe on page 70).

JAMES CARRIER

March

grand old pot pies

Blanketing a heartwarming stew with a flaky brown crust is a great idea whose time has come…again

By Linda Lau Anusasananan • Photographs by James Carrier • Food styling by Karen Shinto

■ A pot pie is a simple equation: stew plus pastry. However, the sum is greater than its parts—a hearty stew capped with handsome pastry is all dressed up for a party.

For the savory base, choose a classic stew like chicken or beef, or go zany with an inverted pizza. Cap it traditionally or stretch the definition of a crust—purchased pastry or dough can top a pot pie almost instantly.

We've done all of the above in the recipes that follow. And to make each of our pies easy-entertaining fare, we've built in a plan for preparing the elements one day and baking them the next. With a green salad, a little wine, and ice cream sundaes, you can present a beautiful Sunday supper with little more work than it takes to turn out an ordinary weeknight meal.

Chicken Pot Pie

PREP AND COOK TIME: About 1 hour

NOTES: Prepare through step 4 up to 1 day ahead; chill uncovered until egg coating on crusts is dry, about 15 minutes, then cover airtight and chill.

MAKES: 6 servings

- ½ pound **red thin-skinned potatoes** (1½ in. wide)
- ½ pound **carrots**
- ½ pound **green beans**
- 3 cups fat-skimmed **chicken broth**
- 1 tablespoon **dried herbes de Provence** or 1½ teaspoons *each* dried thyme and crumbled dried rosemary
- 3½ tablespoons **cornstarch**
- ½ cup **whipping cream** or fat-skimmed chicken broth
- 3 cups bite-size pieces **skinned cooked chicken**
  Salt and **pepper**
- 1 package (10 oz.) **frozen puff pastry shells**, thawed
- 1 tablespoon beaten **egg**

1. Scrub potatoes and cut into quarters. Peel carrots, and trim and discard ends; cut carrots diagonally into ¼-inch-thick slices. Rinse beans, and trim and discard ends; cut beans into 1½-inch lengths.

2. In a covered 5- to 6-quart pan over high heat, bring potatoes, carrots, broth, and herbs to a boil. Reduce heat and simmer until carrots are almost tender when pierced, about 5 minutes. Add beans; cover and simmer until all the vegetables are tender when pierced, 3 to 5 minutes longer.

3. In a small bowl, mix cornstarch and cream. Add to vegetable mixture and stir until boiling, about 2 minutes. Remove from heat and stir in chicken. Add salt and pepper to taste. Spoon equally into 6 round soufflé dishes or ramekins (1-cup size; 3½ to 4½ in. wide). Let cool to room temperature, about 35 minutes.

4. Meanwhile, on a lightly floured board, roll each puff pastry shell into a round about 1 inch wider than the diameter of soufflé dishes. Brush egg around edge of each pastry in a border about ½ inch wide. Invert a pastry onto each dish, egg side down, and press edges firmly against sides of dish. Brush egg lightly over pastry tops and sides. Set dishes at least 1 inch apart in a 10- by 15-inch pan.

5. Bake in a 400° regular or convection oven until pastry is richly browned, 15 to 25 minutes.

Per serving: 548 cal., 49% (270 cal.) from fat; 30 g protein; 30 g fat (7.9 g sat.); 39 g carbo (3.2 g fiber); 243 mg sodium; 95 mg chol.

Southwest Cheese Puff Beef Pot Pie

PREP AND COOK TIME: About 50 minutes

NOTES: Prepare through step 6 up to 1 day ahead. Cover stew and chill; store cool pastry airtight at room temperature. Reheat stew, covered, over low heat until steaming, 10 to 15 minutes. Reheat pastry, uncovered, in a 350° regular or convection oven until warm and crisp, about 5 minutes.

MAKES: 8 servings

- 1 **frozen puff pastry sheet** (half of a 17.3-oz. package), thawed
- 2 tablespoons **milk**
- ⅓ cup **shredded cheddar cheese**
- 3 **zucchini** (1 lb. total)
- 1 **onion** (½ lb.)
- 2 to 4 **canned chipotle chilies** (or ½ to ¾ teaspoon cayenne)
- 1 teaspoon **cumin seed**
- 1 teaspoon **olive oil**
- 2 cans (14½ oz. each) **stewed tomatoes with Mexican seasonings** (or canned tomatoes and 1 teaspoon *each* ground cumin and dried oregano leaves)
- 1 can (14½ oz.) **yellow hominy**, rinsed and drained
- 1 package (about 2 lb.) **cooked boned beef pot roast with gravy**

Dig through a flaky, golden crust to scoop out chunks of chicken, potatoes, and carrots in a creamy herb sauce.

Cheese-flecked puff pastry crowns a stovetop beef-and-chili stew.

2 tablespoons **cornstarch**

Salt and **pepper**

1. Unfold pastry on a lightly floured board. If necessary, roll out or cut pastry to fit snugly inside top of a shallow 3-quart casserole (9 by 13 in.). Transfer pastry to a 12- by 15-inch nonstick baking sheet. Cut through pastry in several places to make a decorative pattern. Brush lightly with milk and sprinkle evenly with cheese. Cover with plastic wrap and freeze.

2. Rinse zucchini, and trim and discard ends; cut into ³⁄₄-inch chunks. Peel onion and cut into ³⁄₄-inch chunks. Discard chipotle chili stems; if desired for less heat, also remove veins and seeds. Chop chilies.

3. Uncover pastry and bake in a 425° regular or convection oven until golden brown, 10 to 15 minutes.

4. Meanwhile, in a 5- to 6-quart pan over high heat, frequently stir zucchini, onion, and cumin in olive oil until vegetables are lightly browned, 7 to 9 minutes. Add tomatoes, including juice, and hominy; bring to a boil.

5. Discard any fat from pot roast and

sauce. Scrape gravy from beef and reserve. Cut beef into ³⁄₄-inch chunks.

6. Add beef and gravy to pan and mix; cover and bring to a boil. Reduce heat to low and simmer, stirring occasionally, until beef is hot, 7 to 9 minutes. Add chilies to taste. In a small bowl, mix cornstarch and 3 tablespoons water. Add to pan and stir until boiling.

7. Pour hot mixture into a warmed shallow casserole. Set hot pastry on filling. Use a large spoon to break through pastry and scoop out portions. Add salt and pepper to taste.

Per serving: 488 cal., 44% (216 cal.) from fat; 27 g protein; 24 g fat (6.9 g sat.); 38 g carbo (4.3 g fiber); 1,142 mg sodium; 66 mg chol.

Turkey, Onion, and Apple Pot Pie

PREP AND COOK TIME: About 1½ hours
NOTES: Prepare through step 5 up to 1 day ahead; cover and chill. Bake chilled pot pie 60 to 65 minutes.
MAKES: 6 to 8 servings

2	**onions** (1 lb. total)
2	**Golden Delicious apples** (1 lb. total)
1	or 2 **yams** (1 lb. total)
1	tablespoon **butter** or margarine
1½	pounds **ground turkey** or turkey sausage patties
2	teaspoons **dried rubbed sage**
1½	teaspoons **caraway seed**
1⅓	cups fat-skimmed **chicken broth**
⅔	cup **dry sherry** or apple juice
3	tablespoons **cornstarch**
	Salt and **pepper**
	Cream cheese pastry (recipe follows) or 1 refrigerated pastry for a single-crust 9-inch pie, at room temperature
1	tablespoon **whipping cream** or beaten egg

1. Peel onions and thinly slice crosswise. Peel and core apples; thinly slice crosswise. Peel yams; cut in half lengthwise, then thinly slice crosswise.

2. Melt butter in a 5- to 6-quart pan

Turkey-apple filling, spiked with sherry, peeks through cutouts in pastry.

Turn pizza upside down: Familiar ingredients bubble beneath twisted breadsticks.

over high heat. Crumble turkey into pan; stir often until no longer pink, about 4 minutes.

3. Add onions, apples, yams, sage, and caraway seed; cover and cook over medium heat, stirring occasionally, for 10 minutes. Uncover, turn heat to high, and stir often until liquid is evaporated and onions begin to brown, about 5 minutes.

4. In a small bowl, mix broth, sherry, and cornstarch. Add to turkey mixture and stir until it boils and thickens. Remove from heat and add salt and pepper to taste. Let cool to room temperature, stirring occasionally, 30 to 40 minutes. Spoon mixture into a shallow, round 1½- to 2-quart casserole or a 10-inch pie pan that holds at least 6 cups.

5. On a lightly floured board, roll cream cheese pastry (or unfold and roll refrigerated pastry) into a round about 2 inches wider than the diameter of the casserole or pie pan. Center pastry over filling; trim edges to overhang rim about 1 inch. Fold overhang under pastry flush with rim. Flute pastry firmly against casserole or pan rim and slash top decoratively. If desired, reroll pastry scraps, cut into decorative shapes, and lay on top of pie.

6. Set pie on a foil-lined 12- by 15-inch baking sheet. Brush top with cream.

7. Bake in a 375° regular or convection oven until pastry is well browned and filling is bubbling, 35 to 45 minutes. If crust rim darkens excessively before center browns, fold foil from sheet up to cover rim loosely. Spoon pastry and filling from casserole to serve.

Per serving: 492 cal., 46% (225 cal.) from fat; 21 g protein; 25 g fat (13 g sat.); 46 g carbo (4.5 g fiber); 266 mg sodium; 137 mg chol.

Cream Cheese Pastry

PREP TIME: About 5 minutes

NOTES: If making up to 1 day ahead, wrap dough airtight and chill.

MAKES: Single 9- or 10-inch crust

In a food processor or bowl, combine 1⅓ cups **all-purpose flour;** ½ cup (¼ lb.) **butter** or margarine, cut into chunks; and 1 package (3 oz.) **cream cheese,** cut into chunks. Whirl or rub in with your fingers until coarse crumbs form. Add 1 **large egg** yolk; whirl or stir with a fork until dough holds together. Pat into a flat disk about 8 inches wide.

Per serving: 222 cal., 65% (144 cal.) from fat; 3.4 g protein; 16 g fat (9.7 g sat.); 16 g carbo (0.6 g fiber); 150 mg sodium; 69 mg chol.

Topsy-turvy Pizza Pot Pie

PREP AND COOK TIME: About 1 hour

NOTES: Prepare through step 2 up to 1 day ahead; cover and chill.

MAKES: 6 servings

- ½ pound **mushrooms**
- 1 **onion** (½ lb.)
- 2 **red bell peppers** (1 lb. total)
- 2 cloves **garlic**
- 1 pound **hot** or mild **Italian sausages,** casings removed
- 1 jar (27 oz.) **marinara** or other spaghetti **sauce**
  Salt and **pepper**
- 1 cup **shredded mozzarella cheese**
- 1 package (11 oz.) **refrigerated soft breadsticks**
- 1 tablespoon **olive oil**
- 2 tablespoons **grated parmesan cheese**

1. Rinse mushrooms, and trim and discard discolored stem ends; thinly slice mushrooms. Peel onion and thinly slice. Rinse, stem, seed, and thinly slice bell peppers. Peel and mince garlic.

2. Crumble sausages into a 5- to 6-quart pan over high heat; stir until no longer pink, 4 to 6 minutes. Add mushrooms, onion, bell peppers, and garlic; stir until vegetables begin to brown, about 15 minutes. Remove from heat and stir in marinara sauce; add salt and pepper to taste. Scrape into a shallow, round 1½-quart casserole or 9- to 10-inch pie pan that holds at least 6 cups. Sprinkle evenly with mozzarella.

3. Separate breadstick dough into individual strips. Gently twist each strip and stretch it to fit from rim to rim over filling (if necessary, pinch ends of strips together to make longer or cut to fit), laying half the strips about 1 inch apart over pie in 1 direction and half at right angles on top of the first. If desired, weave strips over and under each other in a lattice pattern. Fold excess under and press ends against rim.

4. Brush dough strips lightly with oil. Sprinkle pie evenly with parmesan cheese. Set pie on a foil-lined 12- by 15-inch baking sheet.

5. Bake in a 400° regular oven or a 375° convection oven until crust is browned and filling is bubbling, 20 to 30 minutes. If edges brown too rapidly, fold foil from baking sheet up to cover pie rim loosely.

Per serving: 606 cal., 55% (333 cal.) from fat; 23 g protein; 37 g fat (13 g sat.); 47 g carbo (4.7 g fiber); 1,811 mg sodium; 74 mg chol. ◆

food guide

By Jerry Anne Di Vecchio • Photographs by James Carrier

Spicy secrets

Masala magic in good taste

■ As Indian restaurants have multiplied in the West, the flavors they present are becoming an everyday passion. The pressure's on to find ways to create popular dishes quickly and easily at home. For the purist, it's a challenge—there's no escaping a long list of spices to be found, ground, and toasted. For the realist, one authentic abbreviation is *garam masala* (roughly, "warm-flavored mixture"), an Indian-style spice blend that is increasingly available in supermarkets. Each brand—like each region and cook in India—has its own palette of ingredients. Most I've sampled bear aromatic evidence of cinnamon, cloves, and cumin, which Indians describe as "warm" spices and use in savory dishes.

One garam masala–reliant dish I've become very fond of is butter chicken. It's mild enough for the timid and sufficiently intriguing for the curious. When I asked my friend Ranjan Dey, a chef who hails from Calcutta, for the recipe, his litany of spices included extensive grinding. I tried his way first, got the gist, put more faith in the garam masala, and got butter chicken on the table in half an hour. You might do it in less.

Indian Butter Chicken

PREP AND COOK TIME: About 30 minutes

NOTES: If you can't find garam masala (see preceding), use these seasonings: ½ teaspoon ground cumin, ½ teaspoon paprika, ¼ teaspoon ground cinnamon, ¼ teaspoon cayenne, ¼ teaspoon cracked dried bay leaves, and ⅛ teaspoon ground cloves. Sprinkle chopped fresh cilantro onto individual portions of butter chicken, if you like.

MAKES: 5 or 6 servings

- 1 **onion** (½ lb.), peeled and chopped
- 2 tablespoons chopped **fresh ginger**
- 1 **fresh jalapeño chili** (about 1 oz.), rinsed, stemmed, seeded, and chopped
- 1 tablespoon **salad oil**
- 2 teaspoons **garam masala** (see notes)
- 1 can (6 oz.) **tomato paste**
- 2 cups fat-skimmed **chicken broth**
- ½ cup **whipping cream**
- 1½ pounds **boned, skinned chicken breasts**, rinsed and cut into ¾-inch chunks
- ½ teaspoon **coarse-ground black pepper**
- **Salt**
- ¼ cup (⅛ lb.) **butter** or margarine
- 6 cups hot cooked **white basmati rice**
  Lime wedges

1. In a 5- to 6-quart pan, combine onion, ginger, chili, and oil. Stir often over high heat until onion is lightly browned, 3 to 5 minutes. Stir in garam masala. Scrape mixture into a blender; add tomato paste and chicken broth. Whirl until very smooth. Pour mixture back into pan, add cream, and bring to a gentle boil over high heat (mixture is inclined to spatter). Reduce heat and simmer, stirring often, until reduced to 3 cups, about 5 minutes. Pour sauce into a bowl. Rinse and dry pan.

2. Mix chicken with pepper and sprinkle lightly with salt. Set pan over high heat; add 1 tablespoon butter and the chicken. Stir until chicken is no longer pink on the surface, 2 to 3 minutes. Add the sauce and simmer over medium heat, stirring often, until chicken is no longer pink in the center (cut to test), 3 to 4 minutes. Cut remaining 3 tablespoons butter into chunks and stir into sauce until melted.

3. Spoon chicken and sauce onto rice. Add salt to taste. Squeeze lime juice over portions.

Per serving: 529 cal., 32% (171 cal.) from fat; 37 g protein; 19 g fat (9.5 g sat.); 57 g carbo (2.4 g fiber); 439 mg sodium; 109 mg chol.

From a traveler's notebook

■ Ireland's green beauty may leave a more lasting impression than its cuisine on some. But frequent visitors Charlotte and Stanley Fisher (Stanley was once a local lad) have high praise for the meals they enjoyed in the south coast city of Kinsale, County Cork, corroborating its local reputation as a gourmet capital. Charlotte, who appreciates an easy recipe that works well, passed along this Kinsale version of soda bread. It's made with whole-wheat flour, which another Irish buff friend of mine declared makes it brown bread. I'm sure such a fine point of semantics can be settled calmly over a foamy pint with a warm wedge of this hearty bread and a nice hunk of cheese.

Kinsale's Irish Soda Bread

PREP AND COOK TIME: 45 to 50 minutes

NOTES: If making bread up to 1 day ahead, cool, wrap airtight, and store at room temperature. To serve warm, unwrap and reheat on a baking sheet in a 325° oven for 10 to 15 minutes.

MAKES: About 2 pounds; 8 to 10 servings

2½ cups **whole-wheat flour**

About ½ cup **all-purpose flour**

1 teaspoon **baking soda**

¾ teaspoon **salt**

2 cups **buttermilk**

About ⅓ cup **salad oil**

2 tablespoons **light molasses** or corn syrup

1. In a bowl, mix whole-wheat flour, ½ cup all-purpose flour, soda, and salt. Add buttermilk, ⅓ cup oil, and molasses; stir until well moistened.

2. Rub a 9-inch cake pan with oil, then dust with all-purpose flour. Scrape the bread batter into the pan and spread level.

3. Bake in a 400° regular or convection oven until bread is well browned and just begins to pull from pan sides, 35 to 45 minutes. Let cool in pan at least 5 minutes. Cut loaf into wedges in pan or invert from pan, turn over, and cut into wedges.

Per serving: 225 cal., 35% (78 cal.) from fat; 6.4 g protein; 8.7 g fat (1.3 g sat.); 32 g carbo (4 g fiber); 355 mg sodium; 2 mg chol.

New look for mozzarella

■ A talent for making prizewinning fresh mozzarella cheese (which in various shapes is also called ovaline, bocconcini, and ciliegine) has prompted the merger of two California companies: Mozzarella Fresca of Benicia and ItalCheese of Gardena. As I toured the Gardena plant recently, I got a good look at—and taste of—one of their freshest ideas: mozzarella packed alongside marinated vegetables to mix together to make insalatas. The salads are perfect for a first course or light meal. The refrigerated cheeses and vegetables (roasted red peppers, artichokes, roasted tomatoes, and calamata olives, in various combinations) are packed separately to preserve their texture and flavor integrity until you open the pouches and mix them together. The packs (18 to 21 oz.; 4 to 5 first-course servings) cost from $4.99 to $5.99; you'll find them, labeled ItalCheese, with specialty cheeses in many supermarkets, particularly those that focus on natural foods. For a source near you, call (707) 746-6818.

Cabbage with relish

■ When I was *Sunset's* bureau chief in Los Angeles, a number of El Salvadoran restaurants near the office were our favorite lunch spots because *pupusas* (a tacolike packet of filled and grilled masa dough) outshone the local sandwiches. At each table there was a jar of *curtido,* a crunchy, piquant relish of cabbage cured briefly in a salt-and-vinegar brine. You ladled out the relish to munch along with your warm, crusty pupusas or to eat in more generous portions as a salad.

Curtido is easy to make at home, and this would be a good month to expand its international role: Serve it as a companion for corned beef on St. Patrick's Day. In fact, it's great on a corned beef sandwich any time of year.

Red Cabbage Curtido

PREP TIME: About 10 minutes, plus at least 4 hours to chill
NOTES: Curtido stays fresh and crisp up to 1 week; store airtight in the refrigerator.
MAKES: Drained, 3 to 3½ cups

- ⅓ cup **white vinegar**
- 1 teaspoon **salt**
- ½ teaspoon **dried oregano**
- 1 **fresh jalapeño chili** (about 1 oz.), rinsed, stemmed, seeded, and minced
- 3 cups shredded **red cabbage**
- 1 **carrot** (¼ lb.), peeled and shredded
- ⅓ cup chopped **onion**

1. In a bowl or jar (at least 4 cup), mix vinegar, salt, oregano, chili, and 1¾ cups water. Combine cabbage, carrot, and onion; add to bowl and push mixture down into liquid.
2. Cover and chill 4 hours or up to 1 week; mix occasionally to keep vegetables immersed in liquid.
3. To serve, lift out relish with a slotted spoon and drain.

Per ½ cup: 20 cal., 4.5% (0.9 cal.) from fat; 0.7 g protein; 0.1 g fat (0 g sat.); 4.8 g carbo (1.2 g fiber); 342 mg sodium; 0 mg chol.

Renaissance vegetable

■ If you've read Food Guide over the years, you've met my Italian mother-in-law, who lived on an artichoke ranch and cooked from the garden. Her culinary heritage was grounded in Tuscany. So was her garden, where cardoons (in Italian, *cardoni;* in French, *cardons*) flourished. Cardoons, which look like overgrown celery bunches, are a close relative of the artichoke, but it's the large stalks, not the thistlelike flower buds, that are edible. The plants grow in the cool season wherever artichokes do; you'll find them now in markets that feature Mediterranean vegetables.

Cardoons are sadly ignored these days, except by a shrinking number of cooks who know how to deal with them. I've read recipes so complicated that a novice would be discouraged. But my mother-in-law's approach was straightforward: She went to the garden and cut a few broad, silvery stalks. Back in the kitchen, she rinsed the individual stalks and trimmed off the leaves and any discolored sections. Then, with a sharp knife (a peeler tends to clog), she cut the coarse, stringy fibers off the stalk backs, discarded any pithy portions, and cut the vegetable into large pieces or ½-inch dice.

Cardoons, like artichokes, discolor when cut and taste bitter when raw. Cooking solves both problems. My mother-in-law had two approaches.

For both, she dropped the trimmed cardoons into a generous amount of boiling water. Then she either simmered them until creamy to bite (30 to 40 minutes) or boiled them just until tender-crisp (about 15 minutes), drained them, and finished simmering the vegetable in broth with seasonings such as peppercorns, fennel seed, and coriander seed.

For a hot dish, sizzle cooked cardoons in butter or olive oil (with or without garlic and onions); boil with a little whipping cream to glaze, then sprinkle with parmesan cheese; add to stews; or dip large pieces in batter and fry for fritters (my mother-in-law's favorite treatment). ◆

Sweet heat

Mustard adds a hint of intrigue to familiar desserts

By Linda Lau Anusasananan

The chefs' competition at the annual Napa Valley Mustard Festival produces some ingenious dishes. As a past judge, I've tasted mustard in almost every possible application. In my book one of the most creative was apple pie: I loved the pungent kick under the sharp cheddar streusel.

Mustard and sweet foods—especially fruit—have actually enjoyed a long and synergetic relationship (although some notable fellow judges were slightly less enthusiastic about the pie than I was). If you like contrasts, you'll find these desserts downright intriguing. And if you're a mustard fan, check out the festival in Napa, held annually in February and March. For information, call (707) 938-1133 or go to www.mustardfestival.org.

Custard apple tart delivers a pleasant mustard bite.

JAMES CARRIER

Apple Tart with Mustard Custard and Cheese Streusel

PREP AND COOK TIME: About 2 hours, plus 1½ hours to cool

NOTES: Pastry chef Les Carmona of the Lodge at Sonoma, in Sonoma, California, uses yellow hot dog mustard in this tart. Bake the pastry before making filling. If making tart up to 1 day ahead, cool, cover, and chill. Bring to room temperature or heat in a 350° oven for about 20 minutes before serving.

MAKES: 8 to 10 servings

- ½ cup (¼ lb.) **butter** or margarine
- ⅔ cup **sugar**
- 2½ tablespoons **all-purpose flour**
- 1½ teaspoons **dry mustard**
- 2 tablespoons **prepared mustard** (see notes)
- 1 **large egg**
- 4 cups coarsely chopped peeled **Golden Delicious apples** (about 1¾ lb.)
- **Butter pastry** (recipe follows)
- **Cheese streusel** (recipe follows)

1. In a 1- to 1½-quart pan over medium heat, melt butter and stir often until golden brown, 5 to 7 minutes. Remove from heat.

2. Meanwhile, in a bowl, with a mixer on medium speed, beat sugar, flour, and dry mustard until well blended. Beat in prepared mustard and egg. Add hot butter in a thin, steady stream, beating until mixture is cool, 2 to 3 minutes. Gently stir in apples.

3. Spoon apple mixture into warm baked butter pastry and spread level. Sprinkle cheese streusel evenly over filling. Set tart on a foil-lined 12- by 15-inch baking sheet.

4. Bake in a 350° regular or convection oven until streusel is golden brown, 45 to 55 minutes. If tart edges brown excessively, drape lightly with foil. Cool on a rack about 1½ hours. Remove pan rim. Cut tart into wedges.

Per serving: 534 cal., 46% (243 cal.) from fat; 6 g protein; 27 g fat (16 g sat.); 70 g carbo (1.7 g fiber); 323 mg sodium; 111 mg chol.

Butter pastry. In a food processor or a bowl, whirl or stir 1⅓ cups **all-purpose flour** and ¼ cup sugar to blend. Add ½ cup (¼ lb.) **butter** or margarine, cut into chunks, and whirl or rub in with your fingers until fine crumbs form. Add 1 **large egg** yolk; whirl until dough is blended and comes together, or mix with a fork until blended, then press into a ball. Press pastry evenly over bottom and up sides of a 10½-inch tart pan with removable rim. Bake in a 350° regular or convection oven until golden, 15 to 20 minutes.

Per serving: 167 cal., 53% (89 cal.) from fat; 2.1 g protein; 9.9 g fat (5.9 g sat.); 18 g carbo (0.4 g fiber); 95 mg sodium; 46 mg chol.

Cheese streusel. In a food processor or bowl, whirl or stir 1 cup **all-purpose flour,** ½ cup **granulated sugar,** and ½ cup firmly packed **brown sugar** until blended. Add ¼ cup (⅛ lb.) **butter** or margarine, cut into chunks, and ½ cup shredded **sharp cheddar cheese;** whirl or cut in with a pastry blender until fine crumbs form.

Per serving: 191 cal., 32% (61 cal.) from fat; 2.8 g protein; 6.8 g fat (4.2 g sat.); 30 g carbo (0.3 g fiber); 89 mg sodium; 19 mg chol.

Honey-Mustard Cream

PREP AND COOK TIME: About 25 minutes, plus about 3 hours to chill

NOTES: Mustard adds an intriguing hot bite to this cool, creamy dessert.

MAKES: 6 servings

- 1 envelope (¼ oz.) **unflavored gelatin**
- 2 tablespoons **dry mustard**
- 1 teaspoon grated **orange** peel
- ⅔ cup **honey**
- 1½ cups **plain nonfat yogurt**
- 1 cup **whipping cream**
- 1 teaspoon **vanilla**
- Thin **orange** slices

1. In a 1½- to 2-quart pan, mix gelatin and mustard. Stir in ½ cup cold water and the grated orange peel. Let stand about 5 minutes, then stir over high heat until boiling, about 2 minutes. Remove from heat.

2. Whisk in honey, yogurt, cream, and vanilla until smooth. Pour mixture equally into 6 custard cups or soufflé dishes (6-oz. size). Chill until firm, about 3 hours.

3. Garnish desserts with orange slices and serve; or cover airtight and chill up to 1 day, then garnish.

Per serving: 278 cal., 42% (117 cal.) from fat; 5.7 g protein; 13 g fat (7.8 g sat.); 37 g carbo (0 g fiber); 61 mg sodium; 45 mg chol. ◆

The Wine Guide

By Karen MacNeil-Fife

Wine bests

■ This month we bring you some vinous superlatives. After all, wine is one of the best things about the West.

Best winemaker

Steve Edmunds. Once a Berkeley hippie-intellectual, a postman, and a poet-musician, Edmunds found his true calling in life when he scraped together enough money to found Edmunds St. John. From this winery, located in a nondescript Berkeley warehouse, come the very best Syrahs and other Rhône wines made in the West. Edmunds, shy and soulful, uses no fancy equipment or razzle-dazzle techniques, just lightning-rod instincts for finding stellar vineyards, then coaxing from them sensational grapes that will become even more sensational wines. *(510) 981-1510.*

Best trend

Relatively inexpensive **Chardonnays** that don't have huge oak flavors. (What's the point of buying a wine that tastes like a 2-by-4?) A number of Washington wineries in particular are coming out with Chardonnays that are anything but oak monsters. Try Bookwalter (about $10) or Hogue (about $9).

Best advice

Try wines you don't know. After all, the best way to learn nothing about wine is to continue to drink what you know you already like.

Best rambling

Santa Barbara County. Just 2½ hours north of Los Angeles, serene rolling hills and vast vine-covered mesas compose the Santa Maria and Santa Ynez Valleys. This is wine country at its most gorgeous (and least tourist-ridden). Best of all, in the last

There's no better lure than bubbles, and no more effective ones than Roederer Estate's.

five years, Santa Barbara County has experienced nothing short of a wine revolution. Dozens upon dozens of sensational wines are now being made here, and the wineries, B&Bs, spas, and good local restaurants make wandering a pleasure. Don't miss tasting at Zaca Mesa, Cambria, and Byron. The Santa Barbara County Vintners' Association can provide you with maps and a complete list of wineries. *(800) 218-0881.*

Best seduction wine

I know Valentine's Day is over, but a good seduction wine should come in handy more than once a year. Our vote: **Roederer Estate Brut** (about $20) from California's Anderson Valley—sleek and sophisticated with a fine, tingling bead of bubbles, yet creamy enough to be thoroughly hedonistic.

Best wine getaway

The **Yosemite Vintners' Holidays** program at the **Ahwahnee** hotel in Yosemite National Park. Hike in the snow-draped forest, then return to a blazing fire and glasses of some of the Golden State's best wines. This fall will be the 20th year the Ahwahnee has invited renowned California vintners—

more than 20 this time—to pour and talk about their wines. Seminars are capped by a banquet (and more great wines) in the historic hotel's candlelit dining room. Runs from about Thanksgiving through mid-December; reserve early. *(559) 253-2001.*

Best up-and-coming sommelier

Rajat Parr, wine director at the **Fifth Floor** restaurant in San Francisco. Born in Calcutta, India, 28-year-old Parr was introduced to wine in England by his uncle, who had an extensive cellar. Later, Parr attended the Culinary Institute of America in Hyde Park, New York, with the goal of becoming a chef. But after the institute's wine classes proved irresistible, he went on to study wine intensely on his own and eventually landed a job with supersommelier Larry Stone at San Francisco's Rubicon. Says Stone, "When it comes to wine-tasting skills, Rajat is astonishing." *Fifth Floor, in the Hotel Palomar, 12 Fourth St.; (415) 348-1555.*

A fine restaurant deserves a great sommelier. Rajat Parr and Fifth Floor make a good match.

Bank on finding the bottle you want at San Diego's premier wine shop.

Best shop

The **Wine Bank** in the historic Gaslamp Quarter of San Diego. Wine shops often have all the charm of a cardboard box. Not this one. Once a drugstore with a vault, it's now divided into 10 cozy rooms, one for Rhône wines, one for champagnes, one for Italian wines, and so forth. Meandering from room to room, you don't quite realize that the 4,000-square-foot store carries "a couple hundred thousand wines," according to wine buyer Terry Hudson. Absolutely everything you could ever want to drink is here, but the shop's forte is hard-to-find wines. So the next time you read about a terrific wine but can't find it where you live, call the Wine Bank; they can probably send it to you. If you're a lucky local, you can also attend special tastings every Wednesday, Friday, and Saturday evening ($10 to $20 per seminar). *363 Fifth Ave; (800) 940-9463 or (619) 234-7487.*

Best tasting (open to the public)

The **ZAP**—Zinfandel Advocates & Producers—tastings are held in five or six cities each winter through spring. The grandest of the events is in January in San Francisco, where more than 7,000 wine lovers show up to taste virtually every Zinfandel made (more than 350), in an atmosphere of madcap fun. Tastings will also be held this year in Austin, Texas (April 23); Scottsdale, Arizona (April 25); Las Vegas (April 26); and Folsom, California (June 9). *(530) 274-4900.*

Best wine from an unlikely place

Callaghan Syrah (about $22), from Cochise County on a 4,200-foot-high plateau in southeast Arizona, land once roamed by Apache warriors. Young (and restless) owner and winemaker Kent Callaghan is an undiscovered talent. His production is small, but any wine he makes is worth seeking out the next time you're in Arizona. *(520) 455-5322.* ◆

Raise a glass to Arizona wine (make it Callaghan Syrah).

Say cheese

Tasting and touring at Northern California's artisan cheese factories

By Lora J. Finnegan

Cindy Callahan never set out to be a cheese maker. In the 1980s her family bought a home in the Sonoma County countryside, and, she says, they "got a few sheep to mow the pasture grasses." The sheep multiplied, so the Callahans started milking them and ultimately began making sheep's milk cheeses. Thus was born the Bellwether Farms cheese company. "If we'd gotten a lawn mower back then, we wouldn't be cheese makers today," Callahan says with a laugh.

Today, Bellwether Farms is one of a number of small, independent cheese makers that have popped up in Northern California in recent years. Scattered between Sonoma and Crescent City, producers like these are designated as artisan cheese factories by the American Cheese Society because they are small and use traditional methods—with most work done by hand. A few allow you to buy products on-site and take tours to watch the cheese-making process.

One thing they have in common: All consider cheese making an art. At Loleta Cheese Company, co-owner Carol Laffranchi explains, "Unlike the big computer-controlled factories, at ours, cheese makers look, feel, and smell each batch, because each is unique."

Most of these manufacturers use milk produced by animals fed on pasture grasses (instead of commercially produced grains from the feed store).

Like winemakers discussing *terroir* (soil and site, and their effects on the flavors of grapes used to make wine), these artisans contend that their product also gains nuances of flavor from the land on which the animals graze. "What we have here is the Napa Valley of pasture grasses," notes Laffranchi, "and it produces a more flavorful milk and better-quality cheese."

Take a tour and you'll discover that the process includes a fair amount of backbreaking labor. Ignazio Vella of Sonoma's Vella Cheese Company, sums it up, "Unlike winemaking, there's no romance to making cheese—just hard work." He adds, "But I'm 72 years old and it hasn't hurt me a bit." Neither has it hurt the delicious final product, most would agree.

The cheeseries listed here have both on-site sales and either public tours or viewing windows. If you can't pay a visit but want to try some artisan cheeses, the cheeseries will let you order products either by mail or on-line.

Greater Bay Area

■ **Bellwether Farms.** Drive through the creaking metal gate (close it behind you), up the rutted country lane past a hillside dotted with cows and sheep, and head up to the old red barn. You're at Bellwether Farms, where the drive in is half the fun. The rest comes when you meet members of the Callahan family, who make 11 types of cheese, including five from sheep's milk and six from cow's milk. Most popular are crème fraîche (cultured cream), crescenza (a buttery, soft-ripened cheese), and ricotta. On tours you'll get a quick course on artisan cheese making as you walk through the small, pristine facility and aging rooms.
WHERE: 9999 Valley Ford Rd., Petaluma.
SALES/TOURS: By appointment.
CONTACT: (888) 527-8606, (707) 763-0993, or www.bellwethercheese.com.

■ **Cowgirl Creamery.** At the Cowgirl Creamery in Point Reyes Station, specialties such as fromage blanc (tangy, soft, and spreadable) and fresh clabbered cottage cheese are made from organic milk. The sales case holds at least 60 types. Among the most popular varieties here are Mt. Tam (a triple-cream, mold-ripened type) and Humboldt Fog (a mild goat's milk cheese with a layer of decorative ash). As for the company logo—a rider on a rearing horse—cheese maker Sue Conley says, "Hey, we're in the Wild West and proud of it."
WHERE: 80 Fourth St. (in Tomales Bay Foods), Point Reyes Station.
SALES/TOURS: Sales 10–6 Wed-Sun. Watch cheese making 10–1 Wed-Fri.
CONTACT: (415) 663-9335, 663-8153, or www.cowgirlcreamery.com.

■ **Joe Matos Cheese Factory.** In Santa Rosa, this family-run operation bears the distinctive stamp of its Old World owner, Joe Matos. Originally from the Portuguese Azores Islands, Matos makes only one cheese: St. George, a smooth, cheddarlike cheese from his homeland. Daughter Sylvia and wife, Mary, guide tours.
WHERE: 3669 Llano Rd., Santa Rosa.
SALES/TOURS: By appointment.
CONTACT: (707) 584-5283.

■ **Marin French Cheese Co.** When new owners took over recently, they added a few varieties but kept the same family-run atmosphere. French-style cheese has been made here since 1865. The company's famous for brie and camembert, but don't miss the breakfast cheese, flavored bries (pesto, jalapeño, tomato-basil), Schloss (pungent and nutty), and garlic quark (thick and creamy). This is a picture-perfect spot for a spring picnic, set at the base of a hillside next to a pond. In the sales room, you can sample and buy cheeses as well as purchase bread, picnic foods, and wine.
WHERE: 7500 Red Hill Rd., Petaluma.
SALES/TOURS: Sales and picnicking 9–5 daily. Tours 10–4 daily.
CONTACT: (800) 292-6001, (707) 762-6001, or www.sfnet.net/cheesefactory.

■ **Sonoma Cheese Factory.** Founded in 1931 by Celso Viviani, Sonoma Cheese Factory is run today by his son Pete and grandson, David. It's the busiest spot on the historic Sonoma plaza, selling a wide range of specialty foods, picnic items, and wines. Fifteen types of cheeses are produced, including the mainstay Sonoma jack (in eight flavors), a dry jack called ParmaJack (a hard cheese for grating), and teleme.
WHERE: 2 Spain St., Sonoma.
SALES/TOURS: Sales 8:30–5:30 daily (until 6 Sat-Sun). Watch cheese making through windows (Mon-Fri) or catch a short slide show on the process.
CONTACT: (800) 535-2855, (707) 996-1931, or www.sonomacheese.com.

■ **Vella Cheese Company.** In this handsome 1904 stone building, once a brewery, you can see every step of the process. Tours begin in a warm, damp room where men roll 13-pound bags of curds into what will become, after drying, 10-pound cheese wheels. The trip ends in an aging room stacked with 13,000 wheels coated with pepper, vegetable oil, and cocoa. Vella Cheese Company makes three types of cheese—asiago, cheddar, and Monterey jack; the nutty-tasting dry jack is peerless.
WHERE: 315 Second St. E, Sonoma.
SALES/TOURS: Sales 9–6 Mon-Sat, 10–5 Sun. Tours by appointment.
CONTACT: (800) 848-0505, (707) 938-3232, or www.vellacheese.com.

North Coast

■ **Loleta Cheese Company.** Almost 20 years ago, the Laffranchi family moved into a 1935 redwood lumber-yard building (they lived upstairs) to create an artisan cheese factory. Today they make about 20 cow's milk types, the most popular a golden, creamy Monterey jack; other standouts include old-fashioned (milled) cheddar and a smoked salmon–flavored Monterey jack.
WHERE: 252 Loleta Dr., Loleta.
SALES/TOURS: Sales 9–5 daily. Watch cheese making though tall windows.
CONTACT: (800) 995-0453 or (707) 733-5470.

■ **Rumiano Cheese Co.** Founded in 1921, the company is now run by the third generation of Rumianos. One of the larger artisan operations, it produces about 20 types of cheese, from flavored cheddars to Monterey jack and mozzarellas. The Rumianos are proudest of their dry Monterey jack. Among the more unusual cheeses are the raw milk cheddar and jack.
WHERE: 511 Ninth St., Crescent City.
SALES/TOURS: Sales 8–5 Mon-Fri. View the process (Mon-Fri) through large windows.
CONTACT: (707) 465-1535 or www.rumianocheese.com. ◆

The Low-Fat Cook

Healthy choices for the active lifestyle
By Paula Freschet

Showtime snacks

■ What makes a good movie better? For some it's a really big theater screen, digital sound, and hot buttered popcorn—or other nutritionally challenged junk food. For me it's renting a film, getting cozy at home, and snacking smart. The obvious choices are healthy vegetables like carrots, celery, and cherry tomatoes. But is there a wholesome way to satisfy the craving for munchy, crunchy, and salty snacks with a kick? Such treats are surprisingly simple to make with lentils and rice. You cook the grains first in a boldly seasoned liquid to soften them, season some more, then bake until crisp. Flavor with the lively spice blends suggested (now available in supermarkets), make your own mix, or experiment with other blends.

Another source: Japanese food markets, where you'll find low-fat savory rice crackers and low-fat roasted green peas. You'll also find the peas that, laced with wasabi (Japanese horseradish), pack a significant wallop.

Spiced Lentil Crunch

PREP AND COOK TIME: About 25 minutes

NOTES: Garam masala, an Indian spice blend, is available in well-stocked supermarkets and Indian grocery stores. If you can't find the blend, use this mixture: Stir together ³/₄ teaspoon *each* ground coriander and ground cumin; ¹/₄ teaspoon onion salt; and ¹/₈ teaspoon *each* pepper, cayenne, and garlic salt.

MAKES: About 1 cup

1 cup **dried Red Chief** (decorticated) **lentils**

Movie crunchies: Spicy rice and lentils, roasted peas.

JAMES CARRIER

4 cups **vegetable** or fat-skimmed chicken **broth**

About 2¹/₂ teaspoons **garam masala** (see notes)

2 teaspoons **salad oil**

Salt

1. Sort lentils and discard debris. Rinse lentils, drain, and put in a 2- to 3-quart pan. Add broth and 1 teaspoon garam masala. Bring to a boil over high heat. Stir, and when boil resumes, reduce heat to a gentle simmer; stir occasionally, until lentils are barely tender to bite, about 5 minutes. Pour into a strainer over a bowl and drain well; reserve broth for other uses or discard. Mix 1¹/₂ teaspoons garam masala with lentils.

2. Rub 2 baking pans (each 10 by 15 in.) evenly with oil. Divide lentils equally between pans and spread into a level layer.

3. Bake in a 375° regular or convection oven until lentils are lightly toasted and crisp to bite, 10 to 12 minutes, stirring occasionally. Let cool in pan about 10 minutes. Lentils may soften when cool; if so, return to oven and stir occasionally until they are again crisp to bite.

4. Pour lentils into a serving bowl. Add more garam masala and salt to taste. Serve, or store airtight up to 2 weeks.

Per tablespoon: 55 cal., 11% (6.3 cal.) from fat; 5.4 g protein; 0.7 g fat (0.1 g sat.); 6.9 g carbo (1.4 g fiber); 50 mg sodium; 0 mg chol.

Crisp "Dirty" Rice

PREP AND COOK TIME: About 45 minutes

NOTES: Cajun spice blends are available in well-stocked supermarkets and specialty food stores. If unavailable, mix and use 1 teaspoon chili powder; ¹/₄ teaspoon *each* dried oregano, garlic salt, and paprika; and ¹/₈ teaspoon *each* cayenne and onion powder.

MAKES: About 1¹/₂ cups

1 cup **long-grain white rice**

4 cups **vegetable** or fat-skimmed chicken **broth**

About 2 teaspoons **Cajun spice blend** (see notes)

2 teaspoons **salad oil**

Salt

1. Pour rice into a fine strainer and rinse well with cool water. In a 2- to 3-quart pan over high heat, bring broth and 1 teaspoon Cajun spice blend to a boil. Stir in rice; when boil resumes, reduce heat and simmer until rice is barely tender to bite, 10 to 12 minutes. Pour into a strainer over a bowl and drain well; reserve broth for other uses or discard. Mix 1 teaspoon Cajun spice blend with rice.

2. Rub 2 baking pans (each 10 by 15 in.) evenly with oil. Divide rice equally between pans and spread into a level layer.

3. Bake in a 375° regular or convection oven until rice is lightly toasted and crisp to bite, 10 to 13 minutes, stirring occasionally. Let cool in pan about 10 minutes. Rice may soften when cool; if so, return to oven and stir occasionally until grains are again crisp to bite.

4. Pour rice into a serving bowl. Add more Cajun spice blend and salt to taste. Serve, or store airtight up to 2 weeks.

Per tablespoon: 38 cal., 12% (4.5 cal.) from fat; 0.7 g protein; 0.5 g fat (0.1 g sat.); 7.4 g carbo (0.1 g fiber); 28 mg sodium; 0 mg chol. ◆

Kitchen Cabinet

Readers' recipes tested in Sunset's kitchens

By Andrew Baker • Photographs by James Carrier

Blueberry-Lemon Squares

Sergeff Suomi,
Taos, New Mexico

Suomi, a major fan of lemon squares, says this is her favorite recipe, handed down from her grandmother. However, she has added blueberries to please her husband. It's a delicious solution.

PREP AND COOK TIME: About 50 minutes

MAKES: 24 squares

2¼ cups **all-purpose flour**

About ½ cup **powdered sugar**

1 cup (½ lb.) **butter** or margarine

4 **large eggs**

1 cup **granulated sugar**

1 teaspoon grated **lemon peel**

⅓ cup **lemon juice**

½ teaspoon **baking powder**

⅛ teaspoon **salt**

1½ cups **blueberries,** fresh and rinsed or frozen

1. In a food processor or a bowl, whirl or stir flour and ½ cup powdered sugar until blended. Add butter and whirl or rub in with your fingers until dough holds together when squeezed. Press evenly over the bottom of a 9- by 13-inch pan.

2. Bake in a 350° regular or convection oven until crust is golden brown, 20 to 25 minutes.

3. Meanwhile, in a bowl with a mixer on medium speed or a whisk, beat eggs to blend with granulated sugar, lemon peel, lemon juice, baking powder, and salt. Stir in blueberries.

4. Pour egg mixture into pan over warm crust. Return to oven and bake until filling no longer jiggles when pan is gently shaken, 20 to 25 minutes. Sprinkle lightly with powdered sugar and let cool at least 15 minutes. Serve warm or cool. If making up to 1 day ahead, wrap airtight when cool and

Blueberries, suspended in the tart filling, add a fresh twist to popular lemon squares.

chill. Cut into about 2-inch squares and lift out with a spatula.

Per square: 171 cal., 45% (77 cal.) from fat; 2.4 g protein; 8.6 g fat (5 g sat.); 21 g carbo (0.5 g fiber); 113 mg sodium; 56 mg chol.

Fruit and Nut Breakfast Tabbouleh

Betty Ray, Vancouver, Washington

When out of couscous and other ingredients to make her special version of tabbouleh, Ray turned to bulgur wheat and dried fruits. The results are a wholesome cooked cereal mixture, good hot or cold, that makes a splendid breakfast dish served plain, with milk, or with vanilla-flavor yogurt.

PREP AND COOK TIME: About 20 minutes

MAKES: 4 cups; 3 or 4 servings

1 can (about 8 oz.) **crushed pineapple**

About ½ cup **cranberry juice blend**

½ teaspoon **ground cinnamon**

¼ teaspoon **ground nutmeg**

½ cup **bulgur wheat**

1 cup chopped peeled **Golden Delicious apples**

2 teaspoons **lemon juice**

2 tablespoons *each* **dried sweetened cranberries, dried currants,** and **chopped dates**

¼ cup **chopped pecans**

1. Drain juice from pineapple into a glass measure; pour pineapple into a large bowl. To pineapple juice add enough cranberry juice blend to make 1 cup; pour into a 1- to 1½-quart pan and add cinnamon and nutmeg. Bring to a boil over high heat; add bulgur. Stir, cover, reduce heat, and simmer until juices are absorbed, about 15 minutes.

2. Add to pineapple the apples, lemon juice, cranberries, currants, dates, and pecans; mix. Add warm bulgur and mix.

3. Serve hot, warm, or cool; if making up to 1 day ahead, cover when cool and chill.

Per serving: 214 cal., 21% (46 cal.) from fat; 3.2 g protein; 5.1 g fat (0.4 g sat.); 43 g carbo (5.3 g fiber); 5.4 mg sodium; 0 mg chol.

Yanka's Ukrainian Meatball-Spinach Soup

Gloria Mann, Los Angeles

An old family recipe, this spinach soup comes from the Ukraine, and Mann recommends that you serve it with warm, crusty French bread.

PREP AND COOK TIME: 50 to 60 minutes.

MAKES: 2½ quarts; 4 to 6 servings

2 **large eggs**

⅔ cup **long-grain white rice**

1 pound **ground lean beef** or ground lean turkey (or ½ of each)

½ cup finely chopped **onion**

½ teaspoon grated **lemon** peel

2 tablespoons **lemon juice**

½ teaspoon **dried oregano**

About ¼ teaspoon **salt**

About ⅛ teaspoon **pepper**

About ¼ cup **all-purpose flour**

1½ quarts fat-skimmed **chicken broth**

3 quarts **spinach leaves** (about 1 lb.), rinsed and drained

1. In a bowl, beat 1 egg to blend. Add rice, beef, onion, lemon peel, lemon juice, oregano, ¼ teaspoon salt, and ⅛ teaspoon pepper; mix well.

2. Put flour on a rimmed plate. Shape meat mixture into 1-inch balls, rolling each in flour as formed; shake off excess. Set balls slightly apart on a sheet of waxed paper.

3. In a 5- to 6-quart pan over high heat, bring broth to a boil. Add meatballs, reduce heat, and simmer just until no longer pink in the center (cut to test), about 15 minutes.

4. Add spinach leaves and stir gently until wilted, about 5 minutes. In a small bowl, beat with a fork remaining egg to blend. Pour into soup, stirring. Ladle soup into wide bowls. Add salt and pepper to taste.

Per serving: 594 cal., 39% (234 cal.) from fat; 41 g protein; 26 g fat (10 g sat.); 47 g carbo (7.5 g fiber); 583 mg sodium; 191 mg chol.

Turkey Chili Burritos

Christine Datian, Las Vegas

Ground turkey is a light alternative for ground beef chuck that Datian uses in these simple main-dish burritos. If making the filling up to 1 day ahead, cover and chill, then reheat to continue.

PREP AND COOK TIME: About 40 minutes

MAKES: 6 servings

1 pound **ground lean turkey**

1 tablespoon minced **garlic**

1 teaspoon **salad oil**

1 **green bell pepper** (about ½ lb.), rinsed, stemmed, seeded, and chopped

1 **red onion** (about ½ lb.), peeled and finely chopped

1¼ cups **tomato salsa**

1 **firm-ripe tomato** (½ lb.), rinsed, cored, and chopped

1 can (4 oz.) **diced green chilies**

½ cup chopped **fresh cilantro**

1½ tablespoons chopped **pimiento-stuffed Spanish-style olives**

1 teaspoon **chili powder**

1 teaspoon **ground cumin**

½ teaspoon **pepper**

6 **flour tortillas** (10 in.)

1 cup **shredded jack cheese** (about 4 oz.)

4 cups shredded **iceberg lettuce**

Salt

1. In a 10- to 12-inch nonstick frying pan over high heat, stir turkey, garlic, oil, bell pepper, and onion, breaking meat apart with a spoon, until juices evaporate and turkey is lightly browned, about 15 minutes.

2. Add ½ cup tomato salsa, the chopped tomato, green chilies, cilantro, olives, chili powder, ground cumin, and pepper. Stir often until the flavors are blended, about 10 minutes. Pour mixture into a bowl.

3. Meanwhile, stack flour tortillas and seal in foil. Bake in a 350° oven until hot in center (open packet to check), about 10 minutes. Put remaining tomato salsa, cheese, and lettuce in separate bowls.

4. To assemble each burrito, spoon ⅙ of the turkey mixture down the center of each tortilla, leaving about 2 inches bare at 1 end. Top equally with salsa, cheese, lettuce, and salt to taste. Fold bottom, then sides of tortilla over filling to enclose. Hold to eat.

Per serving: 422 cal., 34% (144 cal.) from fat; 24 g protein; 16 g fat (5.2 g sat.); 45 g carbo (4.2 g fiber); 956 mg sodium; 73 mg chol.

Beets Sumac

Roxanne Chan, Albany, California

Tangy sumac, a dried sour berry in the Middle Eastern seasoning blend called *zahtar,* is what Chan uses to give zing to this beet salad, but lemon juice is an effective alternate. Look for ground sumac in the spice section of a specialty food store. Black sesame seed, found in Asian markets, is striking visually in this dish, or you can use toasted white sesame seed.

PREP AND COOK TIME: About 20 minutes

MAKES: 2½ cups; 4 servings

1 teaspoon **white** or black **sesame seed** (see notes)

1 can (15 oz.) **sliced beets,** drained and chopped

¼ cup **low-fat plain yogurt**

2 tablespoons finely chopped **red onion**

1 teaspoon **ground sumac** (see notes) or 1 tablespoon lemon juice

½ teaspoon **fresh thyme** leaves or dried thyme

4 large **butter lettuce** leaves, rinsed and crisped

Salt and fresh-ground **pepper**

1. In a 6- to 8-inch frying pan over medium-high heat, stir or shake white sesame seed until golden, 4 to 5 minutes (don't toast black sesame seed). Pour into a small bowl.

2. To sesame seed, add beets, yogurt, onion, sumac, and thyme; mix.

3. Arrange a lettuce leaf on each plate and mound beet salad equally onto leaves. Add salt and pepper to taste.

Per serving: 38 cal., 17% (6.3 cal.) from fat; 1.7 g protein; 0.7 g fat (0.2 g sat.); 7.4 g carbo (1.4 g fiber); 175 mg sodium; 0.8 mg chol. ◆

Middle Eastern seasonings flavor this beet salad.

It's prime season for avocados; show off and savor them in this piquant sandwich and other recipes beginning on page 78.

April

Portuguese flavors resonate in this Easter dinner: Garlic and herbs coat the lamb; mint dusts the asparagus.

Spring lamb feast

A simple, fresh Easter menu from the vineyards of Portugal

By Linda Lau Anusasananan • Photographs by James Carrier • Food styling by Christine Masterson

■ On the steep hills of the port-producing Douro River Valley in northern Portugal, the seven siblings of the Viseu family tend the vineyards their great-grandfather bought in 1820. "The Quinta de Santa Eufémia represents our roots," explains Bernardo Viseu. And as they manage the estate, they nurture those ancestral roots, gathering in the vineyards on weekends and holidays for hearty family feasts.

I shared one such festive meal with the clan in the winery overlooking their vines. The menu, bursting with the greens of spring and anchored by a leg of lamb, would be ideal for Easter dinner. As with most Por-tuguese food, the familiar ingredients and flavors—fresh vegetables and tender lamb, embellished very simply with garlic, herbs, and olive oil—are easy to embrace and produce. The golden flan, kissed with port, melts in your mouth.

Products from Portugal, such as cheese and wine, give the menu authenticity but aren't essential. The imported cheeses are available in some specialty food stores; Joe Matos Cheese Factory in Santa Rosa, California, makes a Portuguese-style cheese (to order, call 707/584-5283). Port is widely available here, of course; see page 85 for a discussion of this signature Portuguese wine.

Salted Roasted Almonds

PREP AND COOK TIME: About 15 minutes

NOTES: If making up to 2 days ahead, store airtight at room temperature.

MAKES: About 2 cups; 8 servings

- 2 cups **blanched almonds** (³⁄₄ lb.)
- 1 tablespoon **extra-virgin olive oil**
  About ¼ teaspoon **kosher** or regular **salt**

1. In a 9- by 13-inch pan, mix almonds with oil.

2. Bake in a 350° regular or convection oven until nuts are golden, 12 to 14 minutes, stirring once about halfway through. Add salt to taste. Let cool completely.

Per serving: 264 cal., 82% (216 cal.) from fat; 8.7 g protein; 24 g fat (2.4 g sat.); 7.9 g carbo (4.8 g fiber); 49 mg sodium; 0 mg chol.

Garbanzo and Watercress Soup

PREP AND COOK TIME: About 45 minutes

NOTES: Bright green watercress adds a peppery bite to this simple garbanzo soup. For a vegetarian dish, use vegetable broth. Prepare through step 4 up to 1 day ahead; cover garbanzo mixture and watercress separately and chill. Reheat garbanzo mixture and continue.

MAKES: About 3 quarts; 8 servings

- 1 **onion** (³⁄₄ lb.)
- 2 **carrots** (½ lb. total)
- 4 cloves **garlic**
- 1 teaspoon **extra-virgin olive oil**
- 4 cans (15 oz. each) **reduced-sodium garbanzos**
- 2 quarts fat-skimmed **chicken** or vegetable **broth**
- ¼ pound **watercress**
  Salt and **pepper**

1. Peel and chop onion, carrots, and garlic. In a 4- to 5-quart nonstick pan over high heat, stir vegetables in olive oil until onion is limp, 4 to 5 minutes.

2. Drain and rinse garbanzos. Add garbanzos and broth to pan. Cover and bring to a boil; reduce heat to low and simmer until carrots are tender when pierced, 5 to 7 minutes.

3. Meanwhile, remove and discard any yellow or wilted leaves from watercress; rinse and drain watercress. Pluck off about 2 cups tender sprigs (about 3 in. long). Chop enough remaining watercress, including stems, to make about ½ cup; reserve remainder for another use or discard.

4. Working in batches, whirl all but 4½ cups garbanzo mixture in a blender until smooth, holding lid down with a

MENU

Portuguese Easter Dinner

Salted Roasted Almonds*

Cheeses: *Queijo da Serra* (or Brie), *Serpa* (or a fresh sheep's-milk cheese), and *Queijo da Ilha* (or white cheddar)

White or Tawny Port

Garbanzo and Watercress Soup*

Butter Lettuce and Cilantro Salad*

Portuguese Dry White Wine or Sauvignon Blanc

Roast Leg of Lamb with Herbs*

Mint-dusted Asparagus*

Pilaf with Peppers*

Crusty Country Bread

Portuguese Red Wine or Pinot Noir

Citrus-scented Port Flan*

Tawny or Ruby Port

Espresso

*Recipe provided

Start with a rustic soup of garbanzos and carrots flecked with watercress.

towel. Return purée to pan with remaining garbanzo mixture.

5. Stir often over high heat until boiling; add watercress sprigs and chopped watercress and stir until wilted, about 30 seconds. Add salt and pepper to taste. Ladle soup into bowls.

Per serving: 201 cal., 14% (29 cal.) from fat; 19 g protein; 3.2 g fat (0.1 g sat.); 36 g carbo (13 g fiber); 470 mg sodium; 0 mg chol.

Butter Lettuce and Cilantro Salad

PREP TIME: About 15 minutes
NOTES: Rinse and crisp lettuce up to 1 day ahead.
MAKES: 8 servings

- ¼ cup **extra-virgin olive oil**
- 2 tablespoons **lemon juice**
- 1 clove **garlic,** peeled and pressed or minced
- 3 quarts bite-size pieces rinsed and crisped **butter lettuce** (about 1 lb.)
- 1½ cups **cherry tomatoes,** rinsed, stemmed, and halved
- ⅓ cup chopped **fresh cilantro**

  Salt and **pepper**

1. In a large bowl, mix oil, lemon juice, and garlic.

2. Add lettuce, tomatoes, and cilantro; mix salad gently. Add salt and pepper to taste.

Per serving: 73 cal., 89% (65 cal.) from fat; 0.9 g protein; 7.2 g fat (1 g sat.); 2.6 g carbo (0.8 g fiber); 5.5 mg sodium; 0 mg chol.

Roast Leg of Lamb with Herbs

PREP AND COOK TIME: About 2 hours
NOTES: Prepare through step 2 up to 1 day ahead; cover lamb and chill.
MAKES: 8 servings

- 1 **leg of lamb** (5 to 6 lb.)
- 3 tablespoons **dry white wine** or lemon juice
- 2 tablespoons chopped **parsley**
- 2 tablespoons chopped **fresh mint** leaves
- 2 tablespoons **olive oil**
- 1 tablespoon minced **garlic**
- 1 teaspoon **paprika**
- ½ teaspoon crushed or crumbled **dried bay leaves**

  About ½ teaspoon **pepper**

  Salt

1. Rinse lamb and pat dry; trim off and discard excess surface fat.

2. In a small bowl, mix wine, parsley, mint, olive oil, garlic, paprika, bay leaves, and ½ teaspoon pepper. Rub all over lamb.

3. Set lamb on a rack in an 11- by 17-inch pan. Roast in a 375° regular or convection oven until a thermometer inserted through thickest part of meat to the bone registers 140° for medium-rare, about 1½ hours, or 150° for medium, about 1¾ hours. If drippings begin to burn, pour water into pan, ¼ cup at a time, as needed.

4. Transfer lamb to a rimmed board or platter and, keeping it warm, let stand 10 to 15 minutes. Slice meat from the bone to serve. Add salt and pepper to taste.

Per serving: 279 cal., 39% (108 cal.) from fat; 39 g protein; 12 g fat (4 g sat.); 0.9 g carbo (0.2 g fiber); 94 mg sodium; 121 mg chol.

Mint-dusted Asparagus

PREP AND COOK TIME: About 15 minutes
NOTES: Serve hot or at room temperature. If making up to 1 day ahead and serving cool, prepare through step 3; cover and chill. Let come to room temperature, then continue with step 4, mixing with remaining ingredients right in chilling container.
MAKES: 8 servings

- 3 pounds **asparagus**
- ¼ cup chopped **fresh mint** leaves
- 2 tablespoons **extra-virgin olive oil**
- 1 tablespoon **lemon juice**
- 1 tablespoon minced **garlic**

  Salt and **pepper**

1. In a 5- to 6-quart pan over high heat, bring about 1½ quarts water to a boil.

2. Meanwhile, rinse asparagus and snap off and discard tough stem ends.

3. Add asparagus to boiling water; cover and cook until barely tender to bite, 3 to 4 minutes. Drain. To serve at room temperature, immerse asparagus at once in ice water until cool; drain.

4. Return hot or cool asparagus to unwashed pan. Add mint, olive oil, lemon juice, garlic, and salt and pepper to taste; mix gently. Pour into a serving dish.

Per serving: 63 cal., 54% (34 cal.) from fat; 4.3 g protein; 3.8 g fat (0.6 g sat.); 5.8 g carbo (1.6 g fiber); 4.2 mg sodium; 0 mg chol.

Preparation countdown

■ **Up to 2 days ahead:**
Roast almonds and bake flan.

■ **Up to 1 day ahead:** Make soup, rinse and crisp lettuce for salad, season lamb, and cook asparagus (if serving at room temperature).

■ **2 hours ahead:** Roast lamb.

■ **45 minutes ahead:** Cook pilaf.

■ **15 minutes ahead:** Reheat soup, dress asparagus, and make salad.

■ **10 minutes before dessert:**
Unmold flan and slice berries.

Port marks the finish—twice: in a citrus-flavored flan and in a glass to sip.

Pilaf with Peppers

PREP AND COOK TIME: **About 45 minutes**
MAKES: **8 servings**

1 **onion** (½ lb.), peeled and chopped

½ cup chopped **prosciutto** (3¼ oz.) or cooked ham

2 cloves **garlic,** peeled and pressed or minced

¼ cup **olive oil**

2½ cups **long-grain white rice**

3⅓ cups fat-skimmed **chicken broth**

½ cup chopped **canned peeled roasted red peppers**

1 tablespoon chopped **parsley** (optional)

1. In a 4- to 5-quart nonstick pan over medium-high heat, stir onion, prosciutto, and garlic in olive oil until onion is limp, 4 to 5 minutes. Add rice and stir until it begins to turn opaque, about 2 minutes.

2. Add broth and red peppers and bring to a boil; reduce heat to low, cover, and simmer until rice is tender to bite, 15 to 20 minutes. Scoop into a bowl. Sprinkle with parsley if desired.

Per serving: 325 cal., 24% (79 cal.) from fat; 11 g protein; 8.8 g fat (1.4 g sat.); 50 g carbo (1.1 g fiber); 264 mg sodium; 9.3 mg chol.

Citrus-scented Port Flan

PREP AND COOK TIME: **About 1 hour, plus at least 13½ hours to chill**
NOTES: The flan from the Shoalwater Restaurant in Seaview, Washington (we added a little port), ends this Portuguese meal perfectly. Prepare through step 6 at least 1 or up to 2 days ahead.

MAKES: **8 servings**

1⅔ cups **sugar**

1 **orange** (about ½ lb.)

1 **lemon** (about 5 oz.)

2 cups **milk** or half-and-half (light cream)

2 cups **whipping cream**

12 **large egg** yolks

¼ cup **tawny port**

½ cup sliced **strawberries** (optional)

1. In a 10- to 12-inch frying pan over high heat, tilt and shake ⅔ cup sugar often until it liquefies and turns amber, 3 to 5 minutes. At once, pour into a 10-inch pie

pan (at least 6-cup capacity). Quickly tilt pan to spread syrup over bottom; it doesn't need to cover completely.

2. Rinse orange and lemon; with a vegetable peeler, pare off colored parts of orange and lemon peel in thin strips. In unwashed frying pan, mix peel and remaining 1 cup sugar, pressing peel with a wooden spoon to release oils.

3. Add milk and cream to citrus-sugar mixture. Set over medium-high heat and stir occasionally until steaming (do not boil). Cover pan and remove from heat; let stand 10 to 15 minutes.

4. Meanwhile, in a bowl, beat egg yolks and port to blend. Pour hot milk mixture through a fine strainer into a 1-quart glass measure; discard peel. Gradually whisk milk mixture into egg yolk mixture until blended.

5. Set caramel-lined pie pan in a slightly larger baking pan about 2 inches deep. Pour custard mixture over caramel. Carefully transfer both pans to a 350° regular or convection oven. Pour about 1 inch boiling water into outer pan.

6. Bake until center of custard barely jiggles when pie pan is gently shaken, 40 to 45 minutes. Lift custard from hot water and chill until cold, about 1½ hours; cover and chill at least 12 hours or up to 2 days.

7. Run a knife between flan and pan edge. Invert a large rimmed platter over flan; holding pan and platter tightly together, invert and let flan and syrup slip out. Lift off pan.

8. Cut flan into wedges and use a pie server to transfer to plates. Spoon syrup equally over portions; garnish with sliced strawberries, if desired.

Per serving: 468 cal., 54% (252 cal.) from fat; 7.5 g protein; 28 g fat (15 g sat.); 48 g carbo (0.1 g fiber); 62 mg sodium; 394 mg chol. ◆

Avocado green

Once a favorite shade,
always a prized crop—
avocado stars in satisfyingly
simple dishes

By Linda Lau Anusasananan
Photographs by James Carrier

On the steep hills of Ladera Ranch in Ojai, California, avocado grower Roger Essick points out the pear-shaped fruit hidden under glossy, dark green leaves. They are almost ready to be picked. To Essick, a 30-year veteran of the trade, these greenish black, pebbly skinned Hass avocados—the variety most commonly available in the market—represent gold. For consumers, they take a lot of gold to come by.

There are good reasons why avocados fetch premium prices. Though the fruit doesn't ripen completely on the tree, it needs to hang there until it acquires a certain oil content—generally a full year. (At that age most Hass avocados weigh 8 to 12 ounces.) Then the fruit is handpicked, which is no mean feat considering the pitch of the slopes and the 20- to 30-foot height of the trees.

Prime season for these precious ovals is now through August. Markets should be full, and prices the year's lowest. But don't eat the avocados before their time. To optimize their but-

Fresh, colorful ingredients turn into brightly seasoned guacamole.

tery texture, make sure they're ripe: Store Hass avocados at room temperature until they give slightly when gently pressed (don't squeeze hard—they bruise easily) and have turned an even, dark green. Once they're ripe, pop them in the refrigerator.

A perfectly firm-ripe avocado is outstanding with fruit, as an edible bowl for crab salad, on a steak or sandwich, or in a shrimp cocktail or spicy soup. Once it slips past the firm-ripe stage, enjoy its creamy goodness in everyone's favorite chip dip: guacamole.

To pit an avocado: Cut the fruit in half lengthwise around pit; pull halves apart. Insert the tip of a paring knife into the tip of the pit and carefully pry pit out.

All-time Favorite Guacamole

PREP TIME: About 15 minutes

NOTES: Serve with tortilla chips or crisp raw vegetables.

MAKES: About 1½ cups; 4 servings

- 1 **ripe avocado** (¾ lb.)
- ⅓ cup chopped **firm-ripe tomato**
- 2 tablespoons minced **shallots** or onion, rinsed and drained
- 1 tablespoon **lime juice**
- 1 tablespoon chopped **fresh cilantro**
- 1 clove **garlic,** peeled and pressed or minced

- 2 to 3 teaspoons minced **fresh jalapeño chili**
  Salt

1. Pit and peel avocado. Place in a bowl.
2. Add tomato, shallots, lime juice, cilantro, and garlic. With a potato masher, coarsely mash mixture. Add chili and salt to taste, and mix.

Per serving: 112 cal., 79% (88 cal.) from fat; 1.6 g protein; 9.8 g fat (1.6 g sat.); 6.8 g carbo (1.5 g fiber); 9.2 mg sodium; 0 mg chol.

Avocado-Shrimp Cocktail

PREP TIME: About 15 minutes

NOTES: In Mexico, saltine crackers are often served with seafood cocktails like this.

MAKES: 4 to 6 servings

- 1 can (11½ oz.) **tomato and chili cocktail** (bloody Mary) **mix**
- ⅓ cup **tequila**
- 3 tablespoons **lime juice**
- ⅓ cup finely chopped **onion**, rinsed and drained
- ⅓ cup chopped **fresh cilantro**
- 2 to 3 teaspoons minced **fresh jalapeño chili**
- 2 **firm-ripe avocados** (1 to 1¼ lb. total)
- ¾ pound **shelled cooked shrimp** (50 to 70 per lb.), rinsed
  Kosher or regular **salt**
  Lime wedges
  Tortilla chips or saltine crackers (see notes)

1. In a bowl, stir together tomato and chili cocktail mix, tequila, lime juice, onion, cilantro, and 2 teaspoons chili.

2. Pit and peel avocados; cut into ½-inch cubes. Add avocados and shrimp to cocktail mixture. Mix gently and add salt and more chili to taste.

3. If desired, rub rims of 4 to 6 margarita or martini glasses with a lime wedge. Immediately dip into a dish filled with ¼ inch kosher salt.

4. Spoon avocado-shrimp cocktail equally into glasses. Garnish with lime wedges and serve with tortilla chips.

Per serving: 196 cal., 42% (83 cal.) from fat; 13 g protein; 9.2 g fat (1.5 g sat.); 8.1 g carbo (1.3 g fiber); 367 mg sodium; 111 mg chol.

Spicy Broth with Avocado

PREP AND COOK TIME: About 25 minutes

MAKES: About 1 quart; 4 servings

- 1 or 2 **fresh jalapeño chilies** (about ¾ oz. each)
- 1 quart fat-skimmed **chicken** or vegetable **broth**
- 2 strips (½ by 3 in.) **lime peel** (green part only)
- 1 **firm-ripe avocado** (¾ lb.)
- ⅔ cup diced **Roma tomatoes** (optional)
- 2 tablespoons **lime juice**

Avocado glorifies a tequila-spiked shrimp cocktail.

- 2 tablespoons **fresh cilantro** leaves
  Salt

1. Rinse chilies and cut in half lengthwise. Place 2 chili halves, broth, and lime peel in a 3- to 4-quart pan over high heat; bring to a boil, cover, reduce heat to low, and simmer 5 minutes. Taste broth and, if desired, add more chili and simmer, covered, 5 minutes longer.

2. Meanwhile, pit and peel avocado. Cut lengthwise into thin slices or into ½-inch cubes. Arrange equal portions of avocado and tomatoes in each of 4 wide, shallow bowls.

3. With a slotted spoon, lift chili and lime peel from broth and discard. Stir lime juice into broth. Gently ladle broth around avocado and tomatoes in bowls. Sprinkle with cilantro leaves. Add salt to taste.

Per serving: 142 cal., 62% (88 cal.) from fat; 9.4 g protein; 9.8 g fat (1.6 g sat.); 6 g carbo (1.4 g fiber); 83 mg sodium; 0 mg chol.

Crab Salad in Avocado Boats

PREP TIME: About 15 minutes

MAKES: 4 servings

- ¼ cup **sour cream**
- ½ teaspoon grated **lemon** peel
- 2 tablespoons **lemon juice**

- 6 ounces **shelled cooked crab**
- 2 tablespoons finely chopped **fresh chives** or thinly sliced green onion
- 2 tablespoons minced **red bell pepper**
  Salt and **pepper**
- 2 **firm-ripe avocados** (¾ lb. each)
- 4 **canned anchovy fillets**, drained (optional)
  Lemon wedges
  Whole **fresh chives**

1. In a bowl, mix sour cream, lemon peel, and 1 tablespoon lemon juice. Gently stir in crab, chopped chives, and bell pepper. Add salt and pepper to taste.

2. Cut avocados in half lengthwise; remove pits. Brush all cut surfaces of the avocados with remaining 1 tablespoon lemon juice.

3. Set each avocado half, cut side up, on a salad plate; if necessary, cut a strip off the bottom of each, through peel, to balance. Mound crab salad equally in cavities. Garnish with anchovy fillets, lemon wedges, and whole chives. Add more salt and pepper to taste.

Per serving: 280 cal., 74% (207 cal.) from fat; 12 g protein; 23 g fat (5 g sat.); 11 g carbo (2.6 g fiber); 141 mg sodium; 49 mg chol.

Guacamole on the Half Shell

PREP TIME: About 5 minutes

NOTES: Eligio Hernández of Mountain View, California, often ate this make-it-yourself guacamole for a casual lunch or snack in Mexico, where he grew up. Its simple presentation also makes it a stunning first course for a meal.

MAKES: 2 servings

- 1 **firm-ripe avocado** (½ lb.)
- 2 tablespoons **tomato salsa** or ½ to 1 teaspoon hot sauce
- 1 **lime** (2 oz.), rinsed and cut in half
- 4 to 6 warm **corn tortillas** (6 in.) or 2 to 3 cups (2 to 3 oz.) tortilla chips
  Salt

1. Cut avocado in half lengthwise; remove pit. Set each half, cut side up, on a salad plate. Spoon 1 tablespoon salsa into each cavity. Set lime halves and tortillas alongside.

2. To eat, squeeze lime halves over avocado and sprinkle with salt to taste. With a fork or a spoon, mash avocado slightly with salsa in peel, then spoon mixture onto tortillas.

Per serving: 254 cal., 50% (126 cal.) from fat; 4.6 g protein; 14 g fat (2.2 g sat.); 32 g carbo (4.3 g fiber); 194 mg sodium; 0 mg chol.

Simple, succulent combo: skirt steak capped with green chilies, jack cheese, and avocado.

Chili-Cheese Steak with Avocado

PREP AND COOK TIME: About 20 minutes

MAKES: 4 servings

- 1 pound fat-trimmed **skirt steak**
- 1 teaspoon **olive oil**
- ¼ cup **tequila**
- 1 tablespoon **red wine vinegar**
- 1 can (7 oz.) **whole green chilies,** drained
- ¼ pound **jack cheese,** thinly sliced
- 1 **firm-ripe avocado** (10 to 12 oz.)
  Salt and **pepper**

1. Rinse steak and pat dry. Cut into 4 equal pieces.

2. Set an 11- to 12-inch frying pan with ovenproof handle over high heat; when pan is hot, add oil and tilt to coat pan bottom. Add steak and cook, turning pieces once, until browned on both sides but still rare in the center (cut to test), 6 to 7 minutes total. Remove from heat and add tequila and vinegar to pan. Light with a match (not under an exhaust fan or any flammable materials)

and shake pan until flames subside.

3. Lay chilies equally on steaks; top with cheese slices. Broil 4 inches from heat just until cheese is melted, 1 to 2 minutes.

4. Meanwhile, pit, peel, and thickly slice avocado.

5. Transfer steaks to plates. Spoon any pan juices around meat. Arrange avocado equally on portions. Add salt and pepper to taste.

Per serving: 425 cal., 55% (234 cal.) from fat; 31 g protein; 26 g fat (10 g sat.); 7.2 g carbo (1.6 g fiber); 543 mg sodium; 87 mg chol.

Avocado and Grapefruit Salad with Mint Dressing

PREP TIME: About 45 minutes

MAKES: 4 servings

- 2 **red** or pink **grapefruit** (¾ lb. each)
- 2 tablespoons **lemon juice**
- 1 tablespoon chopped **fresh mint** leaves
- 1 tablespoon minced **shallot**
- 1 teaspoon **honey**
- 2 **firm-ripe avocados** (10 to 12 oz. each)
- 4 **frisée** or butter lettuce **leaves,** rinsed and crisped
- ⅓ cup finely chopped **radishes**
  Salt and **pepper**

1. Cut peel and white membrane from grapefruit. Working over a strainer set over a bowl, cut between inner membranes and fruit to release segments into strainer. Squeeze juice

from membranes into bowl (discard membranes); you need about ¼ cup juice (reserve any remainder for other uses).

2. Add lemon juice, mint, shallot, and honey to grapefruit juice, and mix.

3. Peel and pit avocados; cut lengthwise into ½-inch-thick slices. Set a frisée leaf on each of 4 salad or dinner plates and arrange equal portions of grapefruit segments and avocado slices on top. Sprinkle with chopped radishes.

4. Spoon dressing evenly over salads. Add salt and pepper to taste.

Per serving: 206 cal., 70% (144 cal.) from fat; 2.8 g protein; 16 g fat (2.6 g sat.); 17 g carbo (3 g fiber); 16 mg sodium; 0 mg chol.

Avocado, Red Onion, and Prosciutto Sandwiches

PREP AND COOK TIME: About 40 minutes

NOTES: Make pickled onions (step 1) up to 1 day ahead; cover and chill.

MAKES: 2 servings

- 1 tablespoon **sugar**
- ¼ cup **red wine vinegar**
- 1 cup thinly sliced **red onion**
- 1 tablespoon **mayonnaise**
- 2 slices (4 to 4½ in. square) **whole wheat bread,** toasted
- 4 slices **prosciutto** (2 oz. total)
- 1 **firm-ripe avocado** (½ lb.), pitted, peeled, and thickly sliced
  Salt and **pepper**

1. In a 1- to 2-quart pan over high heat, bring 1 cup water and the sugar to a boil. Add vinegar and onions, and stir occasionally until boiling again. Remove from heat and let cool, about 30 minutes.

2. Meanwhile, spread mayonnaise on toast and set each slice, mayonnaise side up, on a plate. Arrange half the prosciutto, then half the avocado, on each slice of toast.

3. Drain onions well and mound half on each open-faced sandwich. Sprinkle with salt and pepper. Eat with a knife and fork.

Per serving: 359 cal., 60% (216 cal.) from fat; 14 g protein; 24 g fat (4.1 g sat.); 29 g carbo (4.9 g fiber); 729 mg sodium; 27 mg chol. ◆

Pile piquant pickled onions on an avocado and prosciutto sandwich.

The Quick Cook

Entrées in 30 minutes or less
By Linda Lau Anusasananan

Lower the heat on fish

■ Delicate fish flourishes when treated gently. Chef Brian Streeter at Cakebread Cellars in Napa Valley retains moisture in salmon by roasting it at a low temperature. Surprisingly, less heat doesn't mean significantly more time in the oven. In about 15 minutes, the fish is cooked through and meltingly succulent. That's just enough time to prepare a few ingredients that turn salmon into a spectacular meal.

Roast Salmon with Coriander Couscous

PREP AND COOK TIME: About 30 minutes

MAKES: 4 servings

1½	pounds **boned salmon fillet**
2	tablespoons **olive oil**
½	cup chopped **onion**
½	cup chopped **red bell pepper**
1½	cups fat-skimmed **chicken** or vegetable **broth**
1	cup **couscous**
1	teaspoon **coriander seed**
¾	cup **orange juice**
3	tablespoons **seasoned rice vinegar**
1	teaspoon **ground coriander**
6	cups **baby spinach leaves** (about 9 oz.), rinsed and crisped
	Orange wedges (optional)
	Salt and **pepper**

1. Rinse fish and pat dry; cut into 4 equal pieces. Rub fish all over with 1 tablespoon olive oil and set pieces, skin down and slightly apart, in a 10- by 15-inch baking pan.
2. Bake in a 300° regular or convection oven until fish is barely opaque but still moist-looking in center of thickest part (cut to test), 14 to 16 minutes.
3. Meanwhile, in a 1½- to 2-quart nonstick pan over medium-high heat, stir onion and red pepper in remaining 1 tablespoon olive oil until onion is limp, 3 to 5 minutes. Add broth, cous-

cous, and coriander seed; bring to a boil over high heat. Cover pan and remove from heat; let stand until liquid is absorbed, about 5 minutes.
4. In a large bowl, mix orange juice, vinegar, and ground coriander. Gently stir ½ cup of the juice mixture into cooked couscous. Add spinach to bowl and mix to coat.
5. With tongs or a slotted spoon, lift spinach from bowl and divide equally among 4 dinner plates. Mound couscous on spinach. Slide a wide spatula between fish and skin and lift fillet pieces off skin; set 1 on each mound of couscous. Drizzle remaining juice mixture in bowl over fish. Serve with orange wedges to squeeze over salmon. Add salt and pepper to taste.

Per serving: 609 cal., 35% (216 cal.) from fat; 43 g protein; 24 g fat (4.4 g sat.); 53 g carbo (6 g fiber); 471 mg sodium; 94 mg chol.

Roast Salmon in Lemon-Ginger Broth

PREP AND COOK TIME: About 30 minutes

MAKES: 4 servings

12	**red thin-skinned potatoes** (1½ in. wide, 1 lb. total), scrubbed
3	cups fat-skimmed **chicken broth**
6	slices (quarter-size) peeled **fresh ginger**
3	strips (½ by 3 in.) **lemon** peel (yellow part only)
1½	pounds **boned salmon fillet**
1	tablespoon **olive oil**
1	head **napa cabbage** (1 lb.)
1	cup **frozen petite peas**
	Lemon wedges
	Salt and **pepper**

1. In a covered 5- to 6-quart pan over high heat, bring potatoes, broth,

Roasted at a low temperature, salmon remains succulent and moist. Serve it on spiced couscous and baby spinach.

ginger, and lemon peel to a boil. Reduce heat to low and simmer until potatoes are almost tender when pierced, 12 to 15 minutes.
2. Meanwhile, rinse fish and pat dry; cut into 4 equal pieces. Rub fish all over with olive oil and place pieces, skin down and slightly apart, in a 10- by 15-inch baking pan.
3. Bake in a 300° regular or convection oven until fish is barely opaque but still moist-looking in center of thickest part (cut to test), 14 to 16 minutes.
4. Rinse cabbage and cut lengthwise into quarters. When potatoes are almost tender, set cabbage on top of potatoes. Cover, turn heat to medium, and steam until cabbage is tender when pierced, about 5 minutes. With a slotted spoon, lift out cabbage and potatoes and arrange equally in 4 wide bowls. Slide a wide spatula between fish and skin and lift fillet pieces off skin; arrange 1 piece of fish alongside vegetables in each bowl.
5. With a slotted spoon, remove and discard lemon peel and ginger from broth. Stir in peas and bring to a boil over high heat. Ladle broth and peas equally over fish and vegetables. Offer lemon wedges to squeeze over portions. Add salt and pepper to taste. ◆

Per serving: 492 cal., 38% (189 cal.) from fat; 44 g protein; 21 g fat (4 g sat.); 30 g carbo (5.9 g fiber); 232 mg sodium; 94 mg chol. ◆

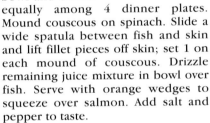

food guide

By Jerry Anne Di Vecchio • Photographs by James Carrier

Coquettish ways with eggs

No need to trifle with truffles

FOOD STYLIST: BASIL FRIEDMAN

In my 40-year-old copy of *Larousse Gastronomique,* by Prosper Montagné, there is no hint of culinary trendiness, just plenty of charming French food chauvinisms. The description of eggs *en cocotte* (cooked in individual dishes) is particularly amusing: "Eggs en cocotte are easily digestible, except if ... served with a heavy garnish such as foie gras, truffles, mushrooms, etc." Fortunately, my neighbor during my yearly sojourn in Provence, Hervé Poron (who owns the Ets Plantin truffle factory), is unaware of this hazard, or blatantly ignores it. The eggs en cocotte that he served one balmy evening as the first course for dinner were very, very heavily garnished with truffles and buried in cream, with a mantle of cheese. Montagné's advice fell on deaf ears. I've reprised the pleasure of that first course much more economically with mushrooms—and a spoonful of couscous under the egg to soak up the abundant sauce.

Veiled by layers of cream and cheese, a golden egg bakes to perfection on a tender bed of mushrooms and couscous.

Eggs en Cocotte with Couscous

PREP AND COOK TIME: About 40 minutes

NOTES: The diameter of the ramekins makes this dish work; if the baking dish is wider than suggested, the cream won't well up over the eggs.

MAKES: 6 first-course servings

- ½ pound **mushrooms**
- 1 tablespoon **butter** or margarine
- ½ cup fat-skimmed **chicken broth**
- ½ cup **couscous**
  Salt
- ¾ cup **whipping cream**
- 6 **large eggs**
- ¾ cup shredded **fontina** or gruyère **cheese**
  Fresh-grated **nutmeg**

1. Rinse mushrooms; trim and discard discolored stem ends. With a knife or in a food processor, finely chop mushrooms. Put mushrooms and butter in a 10- to 12-inch frying pan over medium-high heat. Cover and stir occasionally until juicy, about 3 minutes. Uncover and stir often over high heat until mushrooms are lightly browned, about 15 minutes.

2. Add broth and couscous to mushrooms; stir, cover, and remove from heat. Let stand 10 minutes. Stir couscous and season to taste with salt. Use hot or cool. If making up to 2 hours ahead, cover and let stand at room temperature; stir with a fork before using. Spoon couscous mixture equally into 6 ramekins (2¾ to 3 in. wide, 1¾ to 2 in. deep).

3. In a bowl with a mixer on high speed, whip cream until it holds soft peaks. Spoon cream equally into ramekins. Break 1 egg onto cream in each ramekin, then sprinkle equally with cheese. Sprinkle nutmeg lightly over cheese. Set ramekins slightly apart in a rimmed pan (9 by 13 or 10 by 15 in.).

4. Bake in 450° regular or convection oven until yolks are softly set (press gently with tip of a spoon to test), 8 to 10 minutes, or until firm, 12 to 14 minutes. Serve with spoons. Add salt to taste.

Per serving: 304 cal., 62% (189 cal.) from fat; 14 g protein; 21 g fat (11 g sat.); 15 g carbo (1 g fiber); 215 mg sodium; 267 mg chol.

Cooking from the heart

■ In St. Helena, California, the old hatchery beside the railroad has been Terra restaurant for more than a decade. And I've enjoyed many a finely crafted, robust dish within the mellowed stone walls of this tranquil setting. Now, a new, handsomely illustrated cookbook, *Terra: Cooking from the Heart of Napa Valley* (Ten Speed Press, Berkeley, 2000; $40.00; 800/841-2665), by chef-owners Hiro Sone and Lissa Doumani, features highlights of the restaurant's menu, which reflects an interesting blend of their family trees. Sone, who grew up in Japan, was trained in classic French and Italian cuisines. Doumani, who was reared in a California winemaking family, has a Lebanese heritage. The couple, who met working in the kitchen of Los Angeles's legendary Spago, merged their talents to open Terra. If dishes with clear, friendly flavors—like grilled spice-rubbed pork chops with pickled onions, or fromage blanc tart with caramelized pears—appeal to your taste, so will this book.

Pounded thin and flat between sheets of plastic wrap, pork tenderloin becomes an exceptionally tender steak to season with Mexican flavors and sear quickly.

Flat-out flavor

■ Pork tenderloin is a wonderful cut—easy to find, quick to cook, lean, and boneless. Usually the tenderloin is treated like a little roast or cut into small chops. But it also makes a great steak if you pound it thin, a process that takes only a minute or two (and enhances the meat's tenderness to boot). In effect, the tenderloin becomes a big slab of scaloppine, which you can sauté in butter and serve with a squeeze of lemon juice and a scattering of capers. Or you can season the meat as they do in Jalisco, Mexico, with a tangy *adobo* rub of paprika, herbs, and vinegar.

Jalisco-style Pork Steak

PREP AND COOK TIME: About 20 minutes
NOTES: Don't be concerned if the frying pan looks a bit small; when the meat hits the heat, it shrinks almost at once.
MAKES: 3 or 4 servings

  1 **pork tenderloin** (¾ to 1 lb.)
  1 tablespoon **paprika**
  1 tablespoon **red wine vinegar**
  1 teaspoon minced **garlic**
  ½ teaspoon **ground cumin**
  ½ teaspoon **dried oregano**
     About ½ teaspoon **salt**
  1 to 2 teaspoons **olive** or salad **oil**
     Lime wedges

1. Rinse pork; trim and discard any fat. Place meat between sheets of plastic wrap. With a flat mallet, pound until meat is an even ¼ inch thick (above right).
2. In a small bowl, mix paprika, vinegar, garlic, cumin, oregano, and ½ teaspoon

salt. Uncover meat and rub seasoning mixture evenly over both sides.
3. Add enough oil to a 10- to 12-inch frying pan over high heat to coat pan bottom when swirled. When pan is hot, add meat and cook until edges turn white, about 2 minutes. Turn meat and brown other side, about 2 minutes. Continue to turn for even color until pork is no longer pink in the center (cut to test), about 8 minutes total. Cut into serving pieces. Add salt and lime juice to taste.

Per serving: 120 cal., 33% (39 cal.) from fat; 18 g protein; 4.3 g fat (1.2 g sat.); 1.6 g carbo (0 g fiber); 333 mg sodium; 55 mg chol.

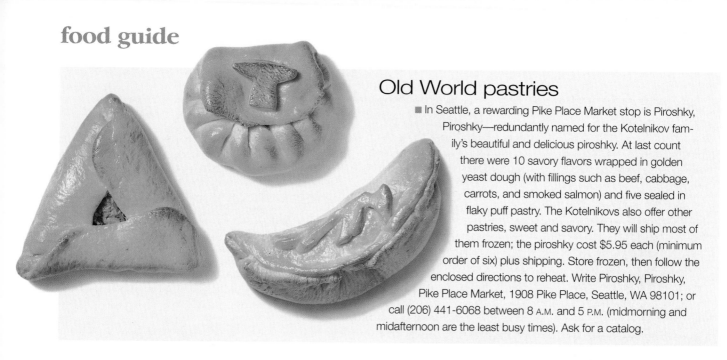

Old World pastries

■ In Seattle, a rewarding Pike Place Market stop is Piroshky, Piroshky—redundantly named for the Kotelnikov family's beautiful and delicious piroshky. At last count there were 10 savory flavors wrapped in golden yeast dough (with fillings such as beef, cabbage, carrots, and smoked salmon) and five sealed in flaky puff pastry. The Kotelnikovs also offer other pastries, sweet and savory. They will ship most of them frozen; the piroshky cost $5.95 each (minimum order of six) plus shipping. Store frozen, then follow the enclosed directions to reheat. Write Piroshky, Piroshky, Pike Place Market, 1908 Pike Place, Seattle, WA 98101; or call (206) 441-6068 between 8 A.M. and 5 P.M. (midmorning and midafternoon are the least busy times). Ask for a catalog.

Tropical stacks

■ Mashing bananas and mixing them into pancake batter make less flavor impact than you'd expect. But if you add slices of banana to the uncooked side of a pancake, then turn it over and brown the batter around the heating fruit, each bite is loaded with pure banana taste. This is the way they flip the pancakes for breakfast at 5 Spot in Seattle. Open through dinner, this casual, comfortable establishment works its way around the United States by region, with changing menu themes and walls lined with local artists' images of the destination of the moment.

5 Spot Banana Pancakes

PREP AND COOK TIME: About 30 minutes

NOTES: If desired, sprinkle about 1 teaspoon chopped pecans on each pancake after adding banana slices. Serve pancakes with butter and warm maple syrup or a dusting of cinnamon-sugar.

MAKES: 12 pancakes; 4 to 6 servings

   ¾ cup **all-purpose flour**

   6 tablespoons **whole-wheat flour**

1¼ teaspoons **baking powder**

   ¾ teaspoon **baking soda**

1½ teaspoons **sugar**

   ¼ teaspoon **salt**

   1 **large egg**

1½ cups **buttermilk**

   About 3 tablespoons melted **butter** or margarine

   2 **ripe bananas** (¾ to 1 lb. total), peeled and thinly sliced

1. In a bowl, mix all-purpose flour, whole-wheat flour, baking powder, baking soda, sugar, and salt.

2. In another bowl, whisk to blend eggs, buttermilk, and 3 tablespoons butter. Add to dry ingredients and stir just until batter is evenly moistened.

3. Ladle batter, ¼ cup at a time, onto a lightly buttered medium-hot (350°) griddle or lightly buttered 10- to 12-inch nonstick frying pan (or use 2 pans at the same time) over medium heat. Scatter 3 to 5 banana slices onto each pancake and cook until edges of the cake look dry, 3 to 4 minutes. Turn with a wide spatula and cook until browned on the bottom, 3 or 4 minutes longer.

4. Serve pancakes immediately, or place in a single layer on baking sheets and keep warm in a 200° regular or convection oven until all are cooked.

Per serving: 209 cal., 33% (68 cal.) from fat; 6.1 g protein; 7.6 g fat (4.3 g sat.); 30 g carbo (2 g fiber); 488 mg sodium; 53 mg chol. ◆

The Wine Guide

By Karen MacNeil-Fife

JAMES CARRIER

The age of port

■ Like programming a VCR, port seems simple enough—until you really get into it. In fact, port is one of the world's most intricate and painstakingly handcrafted beverages. But this shouldn't make any of us wary. Just the opposite—port deserves our attention precisely because it is intellectually fascinating and tastes like nothing else in the world.

Port is a lusciously sweet wine from Portugal that has about 10 percent of its original natural sugar and is fortified to about 20 percent alcohol. Port-style wines are made in many places. Some sensational ones are coming out of Australia; California produces a few good ones too. But to truly understand port, the best place to begin is with the real McCoy.

Multiple grapes indigenous to Portugal are used to make port. Further complicating the picture, the wine is made in 10 radically different styles. Here are the five main ones.

Ruby port

This is a blend of young wines from different years, each of which has been in barrels or tanks for two to three years on its own. It's bottled and sold without any further aging. The grapes used in ruby port are just decent; still, the wine can be tasty, and the price is right.

Vintage character port

This is a confusing term, for these juicy ports don't come from a single vintage and many don't resemble vintage ports (see below) at all. A better name for them would be super rubies. Made up of good but not great wines that have spent on average four to six years in barrels, vintage character ports are relatively inexpensive.

Late-bottled vintage port

LBVs do come from single vintages that have been aged in the barrel for four to six years. Bold and fruity, most of these delicious ports are ready to drink upon release, and cost about half as much as vintage ports.

Aged tawny port

Usually designated on the label as 10-, 20-, 30-, or more-than-40-year-old aged tawnies, these refined and elegant ports are among the best loved, both as aperitifs and as after-dinner drinks. Aged tawny ports are blends of high-quality wines from several years, left in the barrel until they take on nutty, brown sugar, and vanilla flavors and a soft, silky texture. Long barrel aging also changes their color from deep ruby red to—well, tawny. The designation "10-year-old" and so on means the age of the *flavor* of the wine, if you will. In other words, a 10-year-old tawny tastes like it's made up of wines that are about 10 years old.

Vintage port

No port is more sought after—or as expensive. Vintage port is made by firms only in very good years, when they "declare" a vintage. All of the grapes in the blend come from that vintage, and only from top vineyards. For the second half of the 20th century, the great vintage port years have been 1997, '95, '94, '92, '91, '85, '83, '80, '77, '75, '70, '66, '63, '60, '58, and '55.

Vintage ports are aged for two years in the barrel to round off their powerful edges, then for many years in the bottle. As the wine slowly matures, it becomes more refined, its flavors integrated (although even very young, bold vintage ports can be lip-smackingly delicious). To maintain the intensity and richness of the wine, it is neither fined nor filtered; it therefore throws a great deal of sediment and must be decanted. ◆

FOUR STAR PORTS

■ **Quady Starboard Batch 88**, nonvintage (California), $18. Don't be fooled by the play on words—Quady makes the finest port-style wines in California. This one is in the tawny style.

■ **Ramos-Pinto Late Bottled Vintage Port** (Portugal), $16. Ramos-Pinto makes some of the richest, raciest LBVs around, with torrents of plum, spice, and mocha flavors.

■ **W. & J. Graham's 20 Year Old Tawny Port** (Portugal), $47. Hauntingly delicious flavors of roasted nuts, brown sugar, exotic spices, and crème brûlée. The finish is so long, it might make your toes curl.

■ **Taylor Fladgate & Yeatman Vintage Port** (Portugal), about $80 for the 1997. Taylor's vintage ports are expensive; they're also powerful, edgy, and cloaked with a dense curtain of tannin when young, but sensationally elegant, sophisticated, and rich with 15 or more years of aging. Buy the oldest vintage you can find and afford.

STEAL OF THE MONTH

■ **Smith Woodhouse Lodge Reserve Vintage Character Port**, $15. Surrender—it's the only logical reaction to a port so voluptuous, plump, and syrupy. Chocolate, toffee, mocha, and baked cherry flavors ooze from the glass. — KAREN MacNEIL-FIFE

Kitchen Cabinet
Readers' recipes tested in *Sunset's* kitchens
By Andrew Baker

Tender dumplings steam in simmering turkey-and-mushroom stew.

JAMES CARRIER (2)

Garlic Turkey and Dumplings

Donna Enz, Snohomish, Washington

To temper the heat in this comforting dish, Enz recommends seeding and deveining the jalapeño chilies before mincing. If you don't want to take time to peel the garlic, purchase peeled fresh garlic cloves.

PREP AND COOK TIME: About 2 hours

MAKES: 4 servings

- 1½ pounds **turkey thighs** (2 or 3)
- 2 tablespoons **butter** or margarine
- 2 heads **garlic** (about 7 oz. total)
- 3 cups thinly **sliced mushrooms** (about ½ lb.)
- ¾ cup thinly sliced **celery**
- 3 tablespoons minced **fresh jalapeño chilies**
- 3½ cups fat-skimmed **chicken broth**
- 1 cup **dry white wine**
- ¾ cup minced **fresh cilantro**
- 1 cup **all-purpose flour**
- 2 teaspoons **baking soda**
  About ½ teaspoon **salt**
- 1 **large egg,** beaten to blend
- 5 tablespoons **milk**

1. Pull off and discard turkey skin; rinse thighs and pat dry.
2. In a 4- to 5-quart nonstick pan over medium-high heat, melt butter. Add turkey thighs in a single layer and turn often until browned on all sides, 4 to 5 minutes total. Transfer turkey to a rimmed plate.
3. Meanwhile, peel garlic cloves. Add to butter in pan; stir often until lightly browned, 2 to 3 minutes. Add mushrooms, celery, and chilies; stir often until vegetables are lightly browned, 8 to 10 minutes. Add turkey and any accumulated juices, broth, and wine. Bring to a boil; cover, reduce heat, and simmer until turkey is very tender when pierced, 1¼ to 1½ hours. Remove from heat and return turkey to rimmed plate. When turkey is cool enough to handle, pull meat from bones, tearing it into bite-size pieces; discard bones. Return meat to pan and stir in ½ cup minced cilantro.
4. Meanwhile, in a bowl, mix flour, baking soda, and ½ teaspoon salt. Add egg and milk; stir with a fork just until dough is evenly moistened and holds together.
5. Return turkey mixture to high heat; when boiling, reduce heat to simmering. Gently drop 2-tablespoon scoops of dough into pan in a single layer. Cover and simmer, without stirring, until dumplings are no longer moist in the center of the thickest part (cut to test), about 10 minutes.
6. Spoon turkey and dumplings into wide bowls. Sprinkle evenly with remaining ¼ cup minced cilantro. Add salt to taste.

Per serving: 433 cal., 25% (108 cal.) from fat; 37 g protein; 12 g fat (5.8 g sat.); 44 g carbo (3.1 g fiber); 1,181 mg sodium; 145 mg chol.

Tarragon Chicken Salad with Grapes

Dominique Faber, Salt Lake City

When Faber became a stay-at-home mom, lunch out was a thing of the past. Her solution is to invite friends over and serve this salad, which she invented to use some of her favorite ingredients.

PREP TIME: 10 to 15 minutes

MAKES: 4 servings

- ⅔ cup **reduced-fat** or regular **mayonnaise**
- 2 tablespoons **sour cream**
- 1 tablespoon **dried tarragon**
- 2 teaspoons **lemon juice**
- 4 cups shredded skinned cooked **chicken**
- 1 cup **red seedless grapes,** rinsed and halved
- 1 **Granny Smith apple** (about ½ lb.), rinsed, cored, and chopped
- 1 quart bite-size pieces rinsed and crisped **red-leaf lettuce** (about 7 oz.)
  Salt and fresh-ground **pepper**

1. In a large bowl, mix mayonnaise, sour cream, tarragon, and lemon juice. Add chicken, grapes, and apple. Mix gently.
2. Mound lettuce equally on dinner plates. Spoon chicken salad equally onto lettuce. Add salt and pepper to taste.

Per serving: 457 cal., 41% (189 cal.) from fat; 42 g protein; 21 g fat (5.2 g sat.); 25 g carbo (2.2 g fiber); 452 mg sodium; 128 mg chol.

Veracruz Jicama Caesar Salad

Betty Jean Nichols, Eugene, Oregon

Tijuana may be the birthplace of Caesar salad, but it's become such a classic that variations have evolved everywhere. Among Nichols's innovations are jicama for cool crunch and corn chips instead of toasted croutons for crispness.

PREP TIME: About 25 minutes

MAKES: 6 servings

- ⅓ cup **olive oil**
- ⅓ cup **grated parmesan cheese**

Jicama
and corn chips
add crunch to Caesar salad.

- ¼ cup **lime juice**
- 2 tablespoons minced **fresh cilantro**
- 1 tablespoon minced **garlic**
- 1 teaspoon **anchovy paste**
- ¼ teaspoon **pepper**
- 6 cups bite-size pieces **Romaine lettuce** (about ¾ lb.)
- 3 cups matchstick-size sticks peeled **jicama** (about 10 oz.)
- 3 cups **corn chips**
- ¾ pound **firm-ripe tomatoes,** rinsed, cored, and chopped

  Salt and **pepper**

1. In a large bowl, mix olive oil, parmesan cheese, lime juice, cilantro, garlic, anchovy paste, and pepper.

2. Add lettuce, jicama, and 2 cups corn chips; mix gently.

3. Spoon salad equally onto dinner plates; garnish with tomatoes and remaining corn chips. Add salt and pepper to taste.

Per serving: 299 cal., 63% (189 cal.) from fat; 5.3 g protein; 21 g fat (3.5 g sat.); 24 g carbo (5.6 g fiber); 287 mg sodium; 3.7 mg chol.

Lemon–Cream Cheese Strudel

Laura Klesper, Encinitas, California

Klesper reports that her husband got hooked on cream cheese strudel during a trip to Germany and Austria. When he requested a reproduction of the dessert at home, she came up with this surprisingly easy variation.

PREP AND COOK TIME: About 1 hour

MAKES: 6 to 8 servings

- 1 sheet (half of a 17-oz. package) **frozen puff pastry,** thawed
- 2 packages (8 oz. each) **cream cheese**
- 1 **large egg**
- ½ cup **powdered sugar**
- 1 teaspoon grated **lemon** peel
- 1 tablespoon **lemon juice**
- 1 tablespoon **granulated sugar**

1. Unfold pastry on a lightly floured board. With a floured rolling pin, roll pastry into a neat 10- by 14-inch rectangle.

2. In a bowl, with a mixer, beat cream cheese, egg, powdered sugar, lemon peel, and lemon juice until well blended.

3. Spoon cream cheese mixture down center of longest dimension of pastry to within 1 inch of each end; spread evenly to make a 4-inch-wide band. Fold 1 long pastry edge over filling; brush top of edge with water. Fold remaining edge over filling, overlapping opposite side of pastry. Pinch pastry ends to seal. With 2 wide spatulas, gently lift the roll and lay, seam down, on a lightly buttered 14- by 17-inch baking sheet. With a sharp knife, make shallow slashes at 1-inch intervals across the pastry. Sprinkle pastry evenly with granulated sugar.

4. Bake in a 400° regular or convection oven until strudel is deep golden brown, 25 to 30 minutes. Let cool on pan at least 5 minutes. Serve warm or cool. Cut into 6 to 8 equal slices and transfer to plates.

Per serving: 419 cal., 69% (288 cal.) from fat; 7.5 g protein; 32 g fat (14 g sat.); 26 g carbo (0.6 g fiber); 252 mg sodium; 89 mg chol. ◆

New takes on tea

Sip in style at these unusual Bay Area teahouses

By Lolly Winston

"The Americans can send a man into space but they can't make a decent cup of tea," lamented Frank McCourt's Irish mother, Angela, in McCourt's memoir 'Tis. Maybe it's taken a while, but we have gotten better at brewing tea over the years, and now teahouses all over the country—including the San Francosco Bay area—offer quality brews along with creative finger foods. Afternoon tea at finer hotels is always a treat, but it's also fun to visit smaller teahouses, which offer their own interpretations of taking tea. Here are a few favorites.

Every Saturday afternoon, bird owners from around the Bay Area gather at the **Imperial Tea Court** in San Francisco's Chinatown to honor an ancient tradition: drinking tea and displaying their birds. More than 200 types of tea are available. Teas are served in the traditional Chinese *gai-wan* (small covered teacups). *Closed Tue. 1411 Powell St. at Broadway, San Francisco; (415) 788-6080.*

Sink into a wicker chair in the indoor parlor while sipping a cup of chai, or nibble a crumpet in the small, rose-filled garden at **Chai of Larkspur.** *Closed Mon–Tue. 25 Ward St., Larkspur; (415) 945-7161.*

Lovejoy's Antiques and Tea Room in San Francisco is noteworthy both for its tea and its food: Sandwiches are made to order, and heavenly scones and comfort foods are whipped up by an Irish baker. With its endearing grandma's-garage-sale ambience of antique sofas and chairs and mismatched china, silver, and

trivets, this place is utterly without airs. *Closed Mon. 1351 Church St., San Francisco; (415) 648-5895.*

At **NFusion** in Berkeley, you get "tea with a twist": concoctions made of fruit juice, chocolate, ginseng, honey, and other ingredients, served hot, cold, or as a frothy shake. *Closed Sun– Mon. 2068 University Ave., Berkeley; (510) 704-0882.*

The owners of **Tea Time** in Palo Alto take their trade so seriously they offer tea classes, where tea nuts sniff, swirl, sip, and learn about brews from around the globe. This is also a nice place to sit and savor tea, served with à la carte tea sandwiches and baked goods. *Closed Sun. 542 Ramona St., Palo Alto; (650) 328-2877.*

In Mountain View, **Lucy's Tea House** is a Taiwanese-influenced teahouse serving teas alongside sandwiches, rice plates, and desserts like jasmine tea ice cream. *Closed Sun. Back of 180 Castro St., Mountain View; (650) 969-6365.* ◆

Perfect for a picnic: Bright colors make this rice salad an inviting choice for an alfresco meal (recipe on page 103).

May

Swirls of jam-glazed strawberries and nectarines cover an almond filling spread over a buttery crust.

berry sweet endings

Seven grand desserts celebrate spring's reddest, ripest fruit

By Elaine Johnson • Photographs by James Carrier • Food styling by Basil Friedman

I am old-fashioned—and a bit stubborn—when it comes to strawberries. I know that modern agriculture and global commerce have made strawberries available even in mid-December, and those berries are fairly red and have decent enough flavor. But I also know that more thrilling fare is coming. So I wait—until April and May, when local fields are pumping out fruit, the price drops, and at last the strawberries are deep red, tender, and intensely sweet. These are *real* strawberries. And I'm willing to forgo the wannabes all year for them. • To capture strawberries' peak-season flavor, first choose smooth, bright red ones with fresh-looking green caps. Then use them as soon as possible. If you need to hold the berries a day or two, chill them in their boxes, loosely covered with plastic wrap. Wash with caps attached just before using, then hull. For best flavor, serve raw berries at room temperature.

The secret ingredient to our shortcake's tender texture is whipping cream in the dough.

Strawberry-Nectarine Almond Tart

PREP AND COOK TIME: About 1¼ hours

MAKES: 10 servings

- 1⅓ cups **all-purpose flour**
- 6 tablespoons **sugar**
- ½ cup (¼ lb.) plus 1 tablespoon **butter** or margarine
- 1 **large egg,** separated
- ½ cup packed **almond paste,** broken into chunks
- 2¼ cups sliced **firm-ripe nectarines** (¼ in. thick; ¾ lb.)
- 1½ cups sliced **strawberries** (¼ in. thick)
- ⅓ cup **strawberry jam**

1. In a food processor or bowl, combine flour and ¼ cup sugar. Add ½ cup butter, cut into chunks. Whirl or rub in with your fingers until fine crumbs form. Add egg yolk; whirl or mix with a fork until dough holds together. Firmly pat into a ball.

2. Press dough evenly over bottom and up sides of a 10- to 11-inch tart pan with removable rim.

3. Bake in a 300° regular or convection oven until golden, 25 to 30 minutes.

4. Meanwhile, in food processor (no need to wash) or a bowl with a mixer on medium-high speed, whirl or beat remaining 2 tablespoons sugar, 1 tablespoon butter, egg white, and almond paste until smooth. Gently spread over bottom of tart crust.

5. Return to oven and bake until crust is deep golden brown and almond paste mixture feels dry to touch, about 15 minutes. Let cool on a rack.

6. Arrange nectarines on almond filling in concentric circles around outside of tart, strawberries in the middle.

7. Heat jam in a microwave-safe bowl in a microwave oven on full power (100%) until melted, about 1 minute, stirring after 30 seconds. Brush evenly over fruit.

8. Chill until jam is set, about 1 hour, or chill airtight up to 6 hours. Remove pan rim and cut tart into wedges.

Per serving: 288 cal., 44% (126 cal.) from fat; 4.3 g protein; 14 g fat (6.9 g sat.); 38 g carbo (1.7 g fiber); 118 mg sodium; 49 mg chol.

Melt-away Strawberry Shortcakes

PREP AND COOK TIME: About 45 minutes

NOTES: Prepare shortcakes through step 4 up to 1 day ahead; let cool completely, then store airtight at room temperature.

MAKES: 6 servings

- About 1½ cups **all-purpose flour**
- About 7 tablespoons **sugar**
- 1 tablespoon **baking powder**
- ¼ teaspoon **salt**
- ⅓ cup (⅙ lb.) **butter** or margarine, in chunks
- 1½ cups **whipping cream**
- 1 quart sliced **strawberries** (¼ in. thick)
- ½ teaspoon **vanilla**

1. In a bowl, mix 1½ cups flour, ¼ cup sugar, baking powder, and salt. Add butter and cut in with a pastry blender or rub in with your fingers until fine crumbs form. Add ¾ cup cream and stir with a fork until dough holds together.

2. On a lightly floured board, knead

dough just until smooth, 3 or 4 turns. Coat board with more flour and roll dough into a 4- by 8-inch rectangle. With a floured knife or fluted cutter, cut into 6 equal rectangles. Space rectangles 2 inches apart on a 12- by 15-inch baking sheet. Sprinkle evenly with 1 teaspoon sugar.

3. Bake in a 375° regular or 350° convection oven until shortcakes are deep golden brown, 20 to 25 minutes. Let cool on sheet at least 15 minutes.

4. As shortcakes bake, in a bowl, gently mix strawberries with 2 tablespoons sugar. In another bowl, with a mixer on medium-high speed, whip remaining ¾ cup cream, 1 tablespoon sugar, and vanilla until mixture holds soft mounds; cover and chill.

5. With a serrated knife, split shortcakes in half horizontally. Set bottoms cut side up on plates. Mound strawberries and whipped cream on bottoms. Set tops cut side down on fruit and cream.

Per serving: 472 cal., 55% (261 cal.) from fat; 5.4 g protein; 29 g fat (18 g sat.); 49 g carbo (3.5 g fiber); 464 mg sodium; 94 mg chol.

Strawberry–Sour Cream Ice Cream

PREP AND COOK TIME: About 1 hour

MAKES: About 1 quart

2½ cups **strawberries,** rinsed

1 cup **sugar**

1 cup **sour cream**

1½ cups **half-and-half** (light cream)

2 teaspoons **vanilla**

¼ teaspoon **almond extract**

Strawberry ice cream, tangy with sour cream, draws a smile.

Classic soda takes a twist with a splash of raspberry vinegar. Sliced berries and strawberry ice cream complete the treat.

1. Hull strawberries and place in a 3- to 4-quart pan. Coarsely mash with a potato masher. Add ½ cup sugar and stir occasionally over medium-high heat until mixture begins to bubble, 2 to 3 minutes.

2. Nest pan in a bowl of ice water and stir often until cold, 5 to 10 minutes. Remove pan from ice water.

3. Add remaining ½ cup sugar, sour cream, half-and-half, vanilla, and almond extract to berries; stir until blended (mixture will be streaked).

4. Pour into an ice cream maker (1½-qt. or larger capacity). Freeze according to manufacturer's directions until mixture is softly frozen, dasher is hard to turn, or machine stops.

5. Spoon out and serve softly frozen or, to scoop, freeze airtight about 3 hours; store airtight in the freezer up to 1 week.

Per ½ cup: 235 cal., 42% (99 cal.) from fat; 2.5 g protein; 11 g fat (7 g sat.); 32 g carbo (1.2 g fiber); 34 mg sodium; 29 mg chol.

Strawberry-Raspberry Soda

PREP TIME: About 10 minutes

MAKES: 1 serving

In a tall glass (at least 16 oz.), layer scoops of firm **strawberry–sour cream ice cream** (1 cup total; recipe precedes) and ⅓ cup sliced **strawberries** (¼ in. thick). In a 1-cup measure, mix 2 teaspoons *each* **sugar** and **raspberry vinegar** until sugar is dissolved. Add ¾ cup chilled **club soda.** Pour mixture over ice cream in glass. Serve with a spoon and straw.

Per serving: 518 cal., 40% (207 cal.) from fat; 5.3 g protein; 23 g fat (14 g sat.); 75 g carbo (3.8 g fiber); 107 mg sodium; 59 mg chol.

Strawberry Streusel Sundaes

PREP AND COOK TIME: About 15 minutes

NOTES: This recipe is adapted from a creation by Leslie Revsin, a chef for Driscoll's berry growers in Watsonville, California from 1993 to 2000. The strawberry–sour cream ice cream must be frozen at least 3 hours to be firm enough to scoop.

MAKES: 6 servings

1 quart **strawberry–sour cream ice cream** (recipe at left; see notes)

⅓ cup **coarsely chopped pecans**

¼ cup (⅛ lb.) **butter** or margarine

¼ cup firmly packed **brown sugar**

2½ cups quartered **strawberries**

Gingersnap cookies (optional)

1. Scoop firm ice cream into bowls (1- to 1½-cup size). Place in freezer.

2. In a 2- to 3-quart pan over medium heat, stir pecans in butter until golden beneath skins, 3 to 5 minutes. Add brown sugar and stir until incorporated into butter, about 30 seconds. Remove from heat and gently stir in strawberries.

3. Spoon berry mixture equally over ice cream in bowls. Serve with gingersnaps.

Per serving: 476 cal., 51% (243 cal.) from fat; 4.3 g protein; 27 g fat (15 g sat.); 57 g carbo (3.7 g fiber); 131 mg sodium; 61 mg chol.

Strawberry-Rhubarb Pie

PREP AND COOK TIME: About 1¼ hours

MAKES: 8 to 10 servings

About 2¼ cups **all-purpose flour**

About ¾ cup **sugar**

¼ teaspoon **salt**

¾ cup (⅜ lb.) **butter** or margarine

2 cups sliced **strawberries** (½ in. thick)

2 cups sliced **rhubarb** (½ in. thick; about ⅔ lb.)

½ teaspoon **ground cardamom**

1. In a food processor or a bowl, combine 2 cups flour, ¼ cup sugar, and salt. Cut all but 2 teaspoons butter into small pieces and add to flour mixture. Whirl or rub in with your fingers until fine crumbs form. Add ¼ cup water; whirl or stir with a fork just until dough holds together. Pat into a smooth 5-inch round. Wrap airtight and freeze until slightly firm, about 15 minutes.

2. Meanwhile, in a bowl, gently mix strawberries, rhubarb, ½ cup sugar, 3 tablespoons flour, and cardamom.

3. On a lightly floured board, roll dough into a 14-inch round. Slide onto a 14- by 17-inch baking sheet; if dough tears, press back together.

4. Stir berry mixture; spoon evenly onto pastry, leaving a 3-inch border. Fold dough border over edges of fruit, tucking to incorporate excess pastry.

Fold a free-form pastry over strawberries and rhubarb for a grand rustic pie.

5. Melt remaining 2 teaspoons butter in a microwave-safe bowl in a microwave oven at full power (100%), about 15 seconds. Brush pastry rim with butter and sprinkle with 1 teaspoon sugar.

6. Bake in a 375° regular or 350° convection oven until pastry is browned and fruit bubbling, 40 to 45 minutes.

7. Let cool at least 30 minutes. Slide a long metal spatula under pastry to release. Slide pie onto a platter. Serve warm or cool. Cut into wedges.

Per serving: 302 cal., 42% (126 cal.) from fat; 3.5 g protein; 14 g fat (8.8 g sat.); 40 g carbo (1.6 g fiber); 202 mg sodium; 38 mg chol.

Berry–Muscat Wine Goblets

PREP AND COOK TIME: About 30 minutes, plus at least 1 hour to chill

NOTES: Use a plain sweet Muscat wine such as Bonny Doon Vineyard's Vin de Glacière, or an Orange Muscat wine such as Quady Winery's Essensia.

MAKES: 4 servings

1 cup **white grape juice**

1 envelope **unflavored gelatin**

2 tablespoons **sugar**

1 cup **Muscat dessert wine** (see notes)

1½ cups sliced **strawberries** (¼ in. thick)

⅓ cup **blueberries**, rinsed

1. In a 2- to 3-quart pan, mix grape juice, gelatin, and sugar. Stir over medium heat until gelatin and sugar are dissolved, 3 to 4 minutes.

2. Remove from heat and add wine. Nest pan in a bowl of ice water and stir often until mixture is cold and mounds slightly on a spoon, about 20 minutes.

3. Remove pan from ice water and stir in strawberries and blueberries.

4. Spoon mixture equally into 1- to 1½-cup wineglasses. Chill airtight until gelatin mixture is firm to touch, at least 1 hour or up to 1 day.

Per serving: 186 cal., 1.2% (2.3 cal.) from fat; 1.9 g protein; 0.3 g fat (0 g sat.); 29 g carbo (1.8 g fiber); 15 mg sodium; 0 mg chol. ◆

Close dinner on a light note with berries suspended in jelled sweet Muscat wine.

Erin and Sarah Robinson push squares of cooking parchment into tiny flowerpots, then drop an easy-to-mix cornmeal batter inside. The muffins, dotted with green onions, puff to a golden brown in the oven. Meanwhile, Dad helps slice oranges, glaze bacon with maple syrup, and bake a spinach and artichoke custard.

a brunch for Mom

There's a muffin in every pot—and a beautiful custard on the table—for Mother's Day

By Linda Lau Anusasananan • Photographs by James Carrier • Food styling by Basil Friedman

■ Sure, Mom would love to go out for brunch on Mother's Day. But consider the gratification she would feel sitting down to a meal that Dad and the kids had produced themselves. Her heart would positively melt at the sight of little fingers extracting warm corn muffins from flowerpots, or slightly older hands pulling a warm spinach and artichoke custard and maple-glazed bacon from the oven.

Those muffins—and a wonderfully moist sour cream cake—take on a fresh, whimsical shape when you bake them in clean, new, unglazed terra-cotta flowerpots. Just line the pots with cooking parchment (sold in supermarkets near waxed paper), and both muffins and cake pop out with ease.

The muffins, and the rest of our simple menu, are designed to tickle the kids and be realistic for Dad—cooking expert or kitchen rookie—to tackle as supervisor. Every dish can be started, or prepared completely, up to a day ahead of time. And the menu serves eight, so you can invite Grandpa and Grandma to see the children turn into minichefs, and Mom into queen for a day.

MENU

- Green Onion Corn Muffins in Flowerpots*
- Spinach and Artichoke Cheese Custard*
- Maple-candied Bacon*
- Cardamom Sour Cream Cake in a Flowerpot*
- Blueberries with Oranges*
- Sparkling Apple Cider
- Orange Juice
- Tea or Coffee

*Recipe provided

Green Onion Corn Muffins in Flowerpots

PREP AND COOK TIME: About 50 minutes

NOTES: If making up to 1 day ahead, remove muffins from pots after step 5 and cool on racks, then wrap airtight and store at room temperature. To reheat, set muffins slightly apart in a baking pan, cover loosely with foil, and bake in a 350° oven just until warm, 7 to 10 minutes. Return muffins to pots to serve. Offer butter with muffins. You may also bake the muffins in 8 muffin cups (2½-in. diameter), either well buttered or lined with paper baking cups.

MAKES: 8 muffins

- 8   **unglazed terra-cotta pots** (2½ to 2¾ in. tall and 2¼ to 2½ in. wide, about ½-cup capacity)
- 8   pieces (7½ in. square) **cooking parchment**
- 1   cup **all-purpose flour**
- ⅔   cup **yellow cornmeal**
- 2   teaspoons **baking powder**
- ½   teaspoon **baking soda**
- ½   teaspoon **salt**
- 2   **large eggs**
- ¼   cup **sugar**
- 1   cup **plain nonfat yogurt**
- ½   cup thinly sliced **green onions**
- ¼   cup melted **butter** or margarine
- ¼   teaspoon **caraway seed** (optional)

1. Wash pots with soap and water, and dry well. Line pots with cooking parchment: Gently push center of a square into each pot; bend parchment edges outward slightly over edges of pots.

2. In a small bowl, mix flour, cornmeal, baking powder, baking soda, and salt.

3. In another bowl, beat eggs and sugar until well blended. Add flour mixture, yogurt, onions, and melted butter; stir just until batter is evenly moistened.

4. Spoon batter equally into lined pots, filling pots almost to the top. Sprinkle with caraway seed. Set pots slightly apart in a 9- by 13-inch baking pan.

5. Bake muffins in a 400° regular or 375° convection oven until tops are lightly browned and centers are firm to touch, 18 to 20 minutes. Let muffins cool in pots 5 to 10 minutes.

6. Serve warm, or invert pots to remove muffins and lay on their sides on racks to cool. Serve muffins in parchment liners.

Per muffin: 211 cal., 32% (67 cal.) from fat; 5.9 g protein; 7.4 g fat (4 g sat.); 30 g carbo (1.2 g fiber); 443 mg sodium; 69 mg chol.

Spinach and Artichoke Cheese Custard

PREP AND COOK TIME: About 1¼ hours

NOTES: To thaw frozen vegetables quickly, place in a colander and run hot water over them. Prepare custard through step 3 up to 1 day ahead and chill airtight; uncover and continue with step 4 (bake 10 to 15 minutes longer).

MAKES: 8 to 12 servings

- 10   **large eggs**
- 2   cups **small-curd low-fat cottage cheese**
- 2   cups **shredded jack cheese** (½ lb.)
- ½   cup **grated parmesan cheese** (2½ oz.)
-    About ½ teaspoon **salt**
- ¼   teaspoon **ground nutmeg**
- 1   package (8 oz.) **frozen artichoke hearts,** thawed (see notes), or 1 can (13¼ oz.) quartered artichoke hearts, drained
- 1   package (10 oz.) **frozen chopped spinach,** thawed

1. In a large bowl, whisk eggs, cottage cheese, 1 cup jack cheese, parmesan cheese, ½ teaspoon salt, and nutmeg until well blended.

2. Coarsely chop artichoke hearts. With your hands, squeeze as much liquid as possible from spinach. Stir artichokes and spinach into egg mixture.

3. Spread mixture level in a buttered shallow, rectangular 2½- to 3-quart casserole. Sprinkle remaining 1 cup jack cheese evenly over the top.

4. Bake in a 350° regular or convection oven until custard is firm to touch in the center, 25 to 40 minutes. Let stand about 10 minutes, then cut into portions. Add more salt to taste.

Per serving: 201 cal., 54% (108 cal.) from fat; 18 g protein; 12 g fat (6.1 g sat.); 4.6 g carbo (1.9 g fiber); 530 mg sodium; 203 mg chol.

Maple-candied Bacon

PREP AND COOK TIME: About 1 hour

NOTES: Young children need adult supervision when spooning fat from pan. Prepare bacon through step 3 up to 1 day ahead; cool, cover, and chill. Uncover and bake in a 350° oven until browned, 15 to 20 minutes. Let stand at room temperature up to 1 hour.

MAKES: 8 servings

- 16   pieces **thick-sliced bacon** (1¼ lb.)
- ½   cup **maple syrup**

1. Line two 10- by 15-inch baking pans with foil. Lay bacon slices side by side on foil.

2. Bake in a 350° regular or convection oven until bacon edges begin to curl, 10 to 15 minutes. Remove pan from oven. Set a rack inside pan against bacon to hold in place; tilt pan slightly and spoon off and discard fat (see notes).

3. Pour syrup evenly over bacon.

4. Return to oven and bake until bacon is deep golden brown, 10 to 15 minutes longer.

5. With tongs or a wide spatula, lift bacon from pan and set in a single layer on a rack over paper towels. If bacon sticks to pan, return to oven just until maple glaze softens, then remove from pan immediately. Let cool until crisp, about 5 minutes.

Per serving: 140 cal., 63% (88 cal.) from fat; 6 g protein; 9.8 g fat (3.5 g sat.); 6.7 g carbo (0 g fiber); 318 mg sodium; 17 mg chol.

Cardamom Sour Cream Cake in a Flowerpot

PREP AND COOK TIME: About 2¼ hours, plus 1½ hours to cool

NOTES: Cake may also be baked in a 9- by 5-inch loaf pan that holds at least 8 cups; instead of lining pan with parchment, rub with butter and dust with

Crown brunch with a tender cardamom-scented cake baked in a large flowerpot.

flour. Bake in a 325° regular or 300° convection oven until a long wooden skewer inserted in center comes out clean, 1¼ to 1½ hours. If making cake up to 1 day ahead, cool, wrap airtight, and store at room temperature.

MAKES: 8 to 12 servings

> 1 **unglazed terra-cotta pot** (5 in. tall and 6 in. wide)
>
> 1 piece (about 15 in. square) **cooking parchment**
>
> ¾ cup (6 oz.) **butter** or margarine, at room temperature
>
> 1¼ cups **sugar**
>
> 3 **large eggs**
>
> 1 cup **sour cream**
>
> 2½ cups **all-purpose flour**
>
> 1 cup **golden raisins**
>
> 1½ teaspoons **baking powder**
>
> ½ teaspoon **baking soda**
>
> ½ teaspoon **ground cardamom**
>
> 3 tablespoons **sliced almonds**

1. Wash pot with soap and water and dry well. Line pot with cooking parchment: Push center of parchment into pot, then press outward to fit contours of pot; bend parchment edges outward over edges of pot.

2. In a bowl, with a mixer on high speed, beat butter and sugar until fluffy. Add eggs and beat until well blended. Turn mixer to medium and beat in sour cream.

3. In another bowl, mix flour, raisins, baking powder, baking soda, and cardamom. Add to butter mixture and beat on medium speed until well blended. Scrape batter into parchment-lined pot. Sprinkle almonds evenly over the top.

4. Set cake in the lower third (but preferably not on bottom level) of a 300° regular or convection oven. If you must set pot on the bottom level to fit, place on an inverted shallow baking pan to lift cake slightly so

bottom doesn't get too brown. If parchment touches top of oven, fold down farther over pot edges. Bake until a long wooden skewer inserted in center of cake comes out clean, 1½ to 1¾ hours.

5. Cool cake in pot on a rack for 15 to 20 minutes, then lift from pot and set upright on rack. Cool at least 1½ hours longer. For presentation, return cake to pot. To serve, lift cake from pot, peel off parchment, and cut into wedges.

Per serving: 382 cal., 42% (162 cal.) from fat; 5.7 g protein; 18 g fat (10 g sat.); 52 g carbo (1.4 g fiber); 258 mg sodium; 93 mg chol.

Blueberries with Oranges

PREP TIME: About 20 minutes

NOTES: Young children need adult supervision to cut the oranges. You can also substitute purchased refrigerated orange segments or canned mandarin orange segments. If preparing the fruit up to 2 hours ahead, cover and chill.

MAKES: 8 servings

> 4 **oranges** (about 2½ lb. total)
>
> 2 to 3 cups **blueberries,** rinsed and drained

1. With a small, sharp knife, cut ends off oranges, down to flesh. Set each orange on 1 cut end on a board. Following contour of fruit, cut off wide strips of peel and white membrane from top to bottom, deep enough to reveal orange flesh. Cut oranges crosswise into ½-inch-thick slices.

2. Arrange the orange slices and the blueberries in random layers in a wide, shallow bowl.

Per serving: 69 cal., 5.2% (3.6 cal.) from fat; 1 g protein; 0.4 g fat (0 g sat.); 17 g carbo (3.3 g fiber); 2.2 mg sodium; 0 mg chol. ◆

- Up to 1 day ahead:
  Bake muffins, **mix** custard, **prebake** bacon, and **bake** cake.

- Up to 2 hours ahead:
  Prepare blueberries with oranges.

- About 1 hour ahead:
  Bake precooked bacon.

- About 40 minutes ahead:
  Bake custard.

- About 10 minutes ahead:
  Reheat muffins, and **make** tea or coffee.

JAMES CARRIER. FOOD STYLING: BASIL FRIEDMAN

Simple vegetable-chili mixtures flavor two styles of Mexican rice.

Two-tone rice

For Cinco de Mayo, color it red, green—or both

By Elaine Johnson

At the Border Grill restaurants in Santa Monica and Las Vegas, tacos arrive with a two-tone accompaniment—moist and mild red rice and boldly flavored green rice. To achieve these colors, chefs Mary Sue Milliken and Susan Feniger cook rice with the elements of red and green salsa: tomatoes, onions, and a touch of jalapeño for the red, and a vibrant blend of poblano chilies, cilantro, and tomatillos for the green.

These contrasting versions of Mexican rice would make great additions to a Cinco de Mayo buffet, perhaps with your favorite fajitas. But they both taste so good, you may simply decide to wrap them with black beans in tortillas and call it a meal.

Red Rice

PREP AND COOK TIME: 35 to 40 minutes

MAKES: 5½ cups; 6 to 8 servings

- ¾ cup minced **onion**
- 1 teaspoon minced **garlic**
- 2 tablespoons **salad oil**
- 1½ cups **long-grain white rice**
- 2 tablespoons minced **fresh jalapeño chilies**
- 1¼ cups fat-skimmed **chicken broth** or water
- 1 can (about 15 oz.) **diced tomatoes**

  About ½ teaspoon **salt**

1. In a 2- to 3-quart pan over medium heat, frequently stir onion and garlic in oil until vegetables are limp and beginning to brown, 5 to 8 minutes. Add rice and chilies; stir often until rice is opaque, 2 to 3 minutes.

2. Stir in broth, tomatoes (including juice), and ½ teaspoon salt. Bring to a boil over high heat, cover, reduce heat, and simmer until rice is tender to bite, 18 to 20 minutes.

3. Stir with a fork to distribute tomatoes evenly, and add more salt to taste. Mound rice on a platter.

Per serving: 180 cal., 19% (34 cal.) from fat; 4.4 g protein; 3.8 g fat (0.5 g sat.); 32 g carbo (1 g fiber); 246 mg sodium; 0 mg chol.

Green Rice

PREP AND COOK TIME: About 50 minutes

NOTES: The fresh poblano chilies add quite a bit of heat; for milder rice—or for a shortcut—substitute 1 can (7 oz.) diced green chilies and skip step 1. If making the green salsa (through step 2) up to 1 day ahead, chill airtight.

MAKES: 5½ cups; 6 to 8 servings

- ½ pound **fresh poblano chilies** (about 2), rinsed and dried (see notes)
- ¾ cup coarsely chopped **romaine lettuce leaves**
- ¾ cup coarsely chopped **fresh cilantro**
- ⅓ cup coarsely chopped **fresh tomatillos** or drained canned tomatillos
- 2 tablespoons coarsely chopped **green onions**
- 2 cloves **garlic**, peeled

  About 2 cups fat-skimmed **chicken broth** or water
- 1½ cups **long-grain white rice**
- 2 tablespoons **salad oil**

  About ½ teaspoon **salt**

1. Place chilies in a 10- by 15-inch baking pan. Broil 2 to 3 inches from heat, turning occasionally, until charred all over, about 15 minutes. Let stand until cool enough to handle. Pull off and discard skins, stems, and seeds.

2. In a blender or food processor, whirl roasted chilies, lettuce, cilantro, tomatillos, green onions, and garlic until smooth. Pour the purée into a 1-quart glass measure and add enough broth to make 3 cups.

3. In a 2- to 3-quart pan over medium-high heat, frequently stir rice in oil until opaque, 3 to 4 minutes.

4. Stir in chili mixture and ½ teaspoon salt. Bring to a boil over high heat; cover, reduce heat, and simmer until rice is tender to bite, 18 to 20 minutes.

5. Stir with a fork, and add more salt to taste. Mound rice on a platter.

Per serving: 174 cal., 19% (33 cal.) from fat; 4.1 g protein; 3.7 g fat (0.5 g sat.); 31 g carbo (0.9 g fiber); 159 mg sodium; 0 mg chol. ◆

food guide

By Jerry Anne Di Vecchio

Noodling around
International accord on dinner in a bowl

■ As I've trekked through intriguing cities in Asia, such as Hong Kong, Kyoto, and Bangkok, I've noticed that the best-value restaurants feature noodles. They also offer great dining adventure—there's no end to the kinds of noodles and presentations. After innumerable noodle houses, I've acquired a hunger for the savory-sour-salty balance of this hearty soup.

To simplify cooking it at home, I've shifted my shopping from Asian markets to supermarkets, substituting sour pickles for salted mustard greens, ground turkey for ground pork, and fettuccine for Asian noodles. But should this soup turn up in a Thai noodle shop, my guess is that few would discern it was plain old home cooking.

JAMES CARRIER; FOOD STYLING: BASIL FRIEDMAN

Green Onion Noodle Soup

PREP AND COOK TIME: About 30 minutes

MAKES: 4 main-dish servings

- 2 tablespoons **sesame seed**
- 2 teaspoons **salad oil**
- ½ pound **ground lean turkey** or ground lean pork
- ¼ cup finely chopped **sour pickles** (cornichons or dills)
  Peanut sauce (recipe follows)
- 6 cups fat-skimmed **chicken broth**
- 1 package (8 to 9 oz.) **fresh fettuccine**
- 2 cups chopped **green onions** (including green tops)
- ¼ cup finely chopped **roasted, salted peanuts**
  Thin **green onion** slivers, including tops (optional)

1. In a 5- to 6-quart pan over medium-high heat, stir sesame seed until lightly toasted, 6 to 8 minutes. Pour into a small bowl and set aside.

2. Add oil and ground turkey to pan; stir over high heat until meat is crumbled and lightly browned, about 5 minutes.

3. Mix pickles and peanut sauce with meat; add broth and cover pan. When mixture is boiling, uncover, add fettuccine, and stir to separate pasta; when boil resumes, reduce heat and simmer until pasta is tender to bite, about 3 minutes total.

4. Stir in chopped green onions. Ladle soup into bowls; sprinkle with sesame seed, peanuts, and green onion slivers. Eat with chopsticks or a fork and spoon.

Per serving: 620 cal., 45% (279 cal.) from fat; 36 g protein; 31 g fat (5 g sat.); 51 g carbo (4.5 g fiber); 1,227 mg sodium; 83 mg chol.

Peanut sauce: In a bowl, stir to blend 3 tablespoons *each* **peanut butter, soy sauce, Asian** (toasted) **sesame oil,** and **sugar;** 2 tablespoons **rice vinegar;** and 1 teaspoon (or to taste) **hot chili flakes.**

E. SPENCER TOY

Passion for a good cause

■ As a breast cancer survivor, I was invited to participate in the creation of a cookbook to benefit the Susan G. Komen Breast Cancer Foundation. Uncle Ben's sponsored the production of *A Passion for Good Food* (Uncle Ben's, 2000; $19.90), a lovely little volume that has nearly four dozen recipes (most are beautifully photographed) from 16 high-profile culinary professionals who have been touched by this form of cancer—including three acquaintances of mine. Preceding her recipes, each woman simply and openly shares the story of how she dealt with the cancer. To order the book, go to www.unclebens.com, click on Gourmet Shop, then Uncle Ben's Products, and finally, Cookware & Accessories.

MAY1   99

The heat's on beef ceviche

■ David Reinbold, former chef at Seattle's Hotel Edgewater, served this hearty, refreshing salad. He attributes the recipe to Micronesia, where it is made with raw beef "cooked" with citrus juice just as seafood ceviches are. I've adapted the idea for food-safety-conscious kitchens by pouring boiling broth over the beef to arrest bacterial activity while keeping the dish's cultural orientation. Reinbold also adds a Northwest slant by using sweet Walla Walla onions in the salad—a fine international merger.

JAMES CARRIER (2), FOOD STYLING: BASIL FRIEDMAN (2)

Walla Walla Beef Salad

PREP AND COOK TIME: About 30 minutes, plus 1 hour to chill

NOTES: For a more colorful salad, use a sweet red onion. Serve with toasted pocket bread.

MAKES: 4 main-dish, 8 appetizer servings

- ¾ pound **fat-trimmed beef tenderloin** or other tender beef steak
- 3 cups fat-skimmed **beef** or chicken **broth** or water
- ¾ cup **lime juice**
- 3 tablespoons **lemon juice**
- 1 **Walla Walla** or other sweet **onion** (½ lb.), peeled and cut lengthwise into thin slivers
  About 1 tablespoon **hot chili flakes**
  About ¾ teaspoon **kosher** or coarse **salt**
- 2 **pink** or ruby **grapefruit** (1 lb. each)
  About 4 cups **watercress sprigs**, rinsed and crisped
  Asian fish sauce (*nuoc mam* or *nam pla*)

1. Cut beef into matchstick-size strips about ¹⁄₁₆ inch thick and no more than 2 inches long; put into a large bowl. In a 4- to 5-quart pan over high heat, bring broth to a boil. Pour over beef and stir. For rare beef, drain at once; for medium, let stand 5 minutes, then drain (save broth for other uses).

2. In bowl, mix meat with lime juice, lemon juice, and onion; add chili flakes and salt to taste. Cover and chill until cold, at least 1 hour or up to 6 hours, stirring occasionally.

3. Meanwhile, working over a bowl, with a small, sharp knife, cut off and discard peel and white membrane from grapefruit. Cut between fruit segments and inner membranes to release fruit into bowl. Squeeze juice from membranes into bowl; discard membranes.

4. With a slotted spoon, lift beef mixture from bowl and mound equally on plates. Lift grapefruit segments from juice and arrange equally alongside; reserve juice for other uses. Add equal portions of watercress. Spoon beef marinade over fruit and greens. Add fish sauce or more salt to taste.

Per main-dish serving: 213 cal., 31% (66 cal.) from fat; 21 g protein; 7.3 g fat (2.6 g sat.); 18 g carbo (2.6 g fiber); 356 mg sodium; 53 mg chol.

Sweet leaves from Paraguay

■ A gardener friend told me about a curious annual that originated in South America—an herb called *Stevia rebaudiana* (also "sweet leaf" and "sweet herb of Paraguay"), with intensely sweet, tender green leaves that grow on woody stems. I've noticed stevia at nurseries and in specialty produce catalogs. To use stevia, think of it as a sweet green. Try the leaves sprinkled into fruit salads with strawberries or bush berries (blues, blacks, and raspberries), oranges, peaches, and pineapple. Or, as a pleasant surprise to go with a cup of tea, lay the leaves on open-faced sandwiches of thin white bread spread with cream cheese. To make a pale green, sweet liquid to flavor regular or herbal tea, combine 1 tablespoon chopped stevia leaves with 1 cup water in a microwave-safe bowl. Heat in a microwave oven on full power (100%) until mixture has boiled about 1 minute. Cover and let cool. Pour liquid through a fine strainer into a jar; discard leaves. To store, cover and chill. For suggestions on how to use stevia, read Rita DePuydt's *Baking with Stevia: Recipes for the Sweet Leaf* (Sun Coast Enterprises, Oak View, CA 1997; $12.95; 805/645-5309). For fresh plants, contact Melissa's produce (800/588-0151 or www.melissas.com).

Paring pineapple

■ Of the various tools made for extracting the flesh of a pineapple from its shell quickly, the all-plastic, easy-to-clean, Dutch-made Vacu Vin corer is the first I've encountered that is very easy to use and empties the shell without piercing it. You first cut off the pineapple top to expose the fruit, then twist the tool down into the fruit to cut it into one long, uniformly thick spiral. The Vacu Vin base supports the spiral as you lift it from the shell. Just pop the handle free and slide the fruit from the corer's stem. Drain the juice from the shell (if you want to use the shell, cut the tough core out with a grapefruit knife). Slice the fruit any way you like and fill the shell with a drink, dessert, or salad. You'll find this pineapple corer in many cookware stores; it comes with one or three coring units, each geared to specific fruit sizes.

A cool milkshake makes a perfect filling for a pineapple shell. For harvest-sweet flavor, try this one with the new Del Monte Hawaii Gold pineapple. Sure, the shell container is just for fun—a few tall glasses can do the same job, but they fall short when it comes to conviviality.

Tool supports spiral-cut pineapple as it's lifted from the shell.

Pineapple Shake

PREP TIME: About 10 minutes

NOTES: A 3¾-pound pineapple yields about 3 cups of fruit. When you core and cut it, save the juice.

MAKES: 4 servings

- About 3 cups **pineapple** chunks with any juice (see notes)
- 2 tablespoons finely chopped peeled **fresh ginger**
- 1 pint **vanilla ice cream**
- ½ cup **rum** (optional)

Put pineapple, any juice, and ginger in a blender or food processor. Whirl until fruit is coarsely puréed. Add scoops of ice cream and whirl until smooth. Add rum and whirl to blend.

Fill a fresh pineapple shell or tall glasses with milkshake; add straws for sipping. Refill pineapple shell as needed with remaining shake.

Per serving: 192 cal., 36% (70 cal.) from fat; 2.8 g protein; 7.8 g fat (4.5 g sat.); 30 g carbo (1.5 g fiber); 54 mg sodium; 29 mg chol.

JAMES CARRIER (3), FOOD STYLING: BASIL FRIEDMAN (3)

Rocky Mountain rainbows

■ Janice Henning and Tim Elenteny of Denver's Beehive Restaurant focus on regionally produced fruits, vegetables, cheeses, meats, and fish to give their menu a rich sense of place. Recently, they put together a special event for me, and among the Rocky Mountain treats was this very simple and flavorful smoked-trout rillettes. Rillettes may be French at heart and traditionally made from shredded slow-cooked meats, but there is nothing fishy about this updated version.

Beehive Smoked-Trout Rillettes

PREP TIME: **About 15 minutes**

NOTES: For an appetizer, spoon the trout rillettes (or pipe through a pastry bag with a plain, round tip at least ½ in. wide) in about 1-tablespoon mounds onto the concave side of Belgian endive leaves; garnish with capers. Or use the rillettes as a sandwich spread. If making up to 2 days ahead, cover and chill.

MAKES: About 1 cup; 6 to 8 appetizer servings

- 1 **boned smoked trout** (about 6 oz.)
- 1 tablespoon chopped **shallot**
- 1 tablespoon drained **capers**
- 1 tablespoon packed **parsley** sprigs, rinsed
- ½ cup **crème fraîche** or sour cream
- 1 to 2 teaspoons **lemon juice**

Pull off and discard trout skin; break fish into chunks. In a food processor, whirl trout, shallot, capers, and parsley until finely minced (or finely mince with a knife). Stir in crème fraîche and lemon juice to taste.

Per tablespoon: 42 cal., 74% (31 cal.) from fat; 2.4 g protein; 3.4 g fat (1.8 g sat.); 0.4 g carbo (0 g fiber); 116 mg sodium; 7.8 mg chol. ◆

The Quick Cook

Entrées and appetizers in 30 minutes or less

By Jerry Anne Di Vecchio

Falafel flavors in main dishes

■ Mixes are designed to help the busy cook, but sometimes the basic purpose of a mix is not its most useful application. A prime example is falafel. The mix, made of garbanzo flour seasoned robustly with cumin, onion, garlic, and parsley, is sold with pilafs and the like at the supermarket. The package tells you how to make basic falafel balls. But the mix is also a very fast way to add a zesty, crunchy coating to baked chicken wings and sausage balls, or to retain juiciness in burgers made with lean turkey or beef.

Falafel-crusted Chicken Drumettes

PREP AND COOK TIME: About 30 minutes

MAKES: 12 to 14 pieces; 6 or 7 appetizer, 3 or 4 main-dish servings

- 2 pounds **chicken drumettes** (shoulder-wing joint)

  About ¾ cup **dried falafel mix**

  Salt

1. Rinse chicken drumettes. Put falafel mix in a heavy plastic food bag. Add 5 or 6 drumettes to bag at a time, shake well, lift out, and lay slightly apart in an oiled 10- by 15-inch pan.

2. Bake in a 475° oven for 10 minutes. Turn drumettes over and bake until lightly browned and meat at bone in thickest part is no longer pink (cut to test), about 15 minutes longer. Add salt to taste.

Per appetizer serving: 225 cal., 40% (90 cal.) from fat; 23 g protein; 10 g fat (2.4 g sat.); 11 g carbo (3 g fiber); 259 mg sodium; 73 mg chol.

Sausage Falafel Balls

PREP AND COOK TIME: About 15 minutes

NOTES: Serve with plain yogurt or tahini (sesame seed sauce) mixed with lemon juice to taste; thin with broth or water to dipping consistency. For an appetizer, dip balls in yogurt or tahini

Seasonings are built into the falafel coating on crisp, oven-roasted chicken drumettes.

JAMES CARRIER

sauce; for a main dish, spoon the sauce over the hot meat.

MAKES: 8 appetizer, 4 main-dish servings

- 1 pound **bulk pork sausage**

  About ¾ cup **dried falafel mix**

  Salt

1. In a bowl, combine sausage, ½ cup falafel mix, and ½ cup water; mix well. Put remaining ¼ cup falafel mix in a small bowl. Scoop meat (mixture is soft) into 1-tablespoon portions and drop into falafel mix; roll to coat. Place balls slightly apart on an oiled 10- by 15-inch pan.

2. Bake in a 500° oven for 5 minutes; turn balls (or shake pan) and continue to bake until lightly browned and no longer pink in the center (cut to test), about 5 minutes longer. Add salt to taste.

Per appetizer serving: 212 cal., 68% (144 cal.) from fat; 8.5 g protein; 16 g fat (5.5 g sat.); 8.3 g carbo (2.3 g fiber); 497 mg sodium; 30 mg chol.

Succulent Turkey Burgers

PREP AND COOK TIME: 15 to 20 minutes

NOTES: Serve the burgers on hamburger buns with your favorite trimmings or with a green salad.

MAKES: 4 servings

- 1 pound **ground lean turkey**
- ½ cup **dried falafel mix**
- 2 teaspoons **salad oil**

  Salt

1. In a bowl, combine turkey, falafel mix, and ½ cup water; mix well. Shape meat into 4 equal patties, each about ¾ inch thick.

2. Set a 10- to 12-inch nonstick frying pan over high heat; add oil and tilt pan to coat bottom. When pan is hot, reduce heat to medium-high and add the turkey patties. Cook until browned on the bottom, 4 to 5 minutes; turn with a wide spatula and cook until browned on the other side, 4 to 5 minutes. Continue to turn for even browning until meat is no longer pink in the center (cut to test), about 4 minutes longer. Season to taste with salt.

Per serving: 296 cal., 55% (162 cal.) from fat; 24 g protein; 18 g fat (3.5 g sat.); 11 g carbo (3 g fiber); 273 mg sodium; 70 mg chol.

Spiced Beef Burgers

PREP AND COOK TIME: 15 to 20 minutes

NOTES: Serve burgers on hamburger buns with your favorite trimmings or with a green salad.

MAKES: 4 servings

- 1 pound **ground lean beef**
- ¾ cup **dried falafel mix**
- 2 teaspoons **olive** or salad **oil**

  Salt

1. In a bowl, combine beef, falafel mix, and ¾ cup water; mix well. Shape meat into 4 equal patties, each about ¾ inch thick.

2. Set a 10- to 12-inch nonstick frying pan over high heat; add oil and tilt pan to coat bottom. When pan is hot, reduce heat to medium-high and add the beef patties. Cook until browned on the bottom, 4 to 5 minutes; turn with a wide spatula and cook until browned on the other side, 4 to 5 minutes. Continue to turn for even browning until meat is no longer pink in the center (cut to test), about 4 minutes longer. Season to taste with salt.

Per serving: 372 cal., 56% (207 cal.) from fat; 25 g protein; 23 g fat (8.1 g sat.); 16 g carbo (4.5 g fiber); 348 mg sodium; 77 mg chol. ◆

Bay Area picnics

Grab lunch—and a pal—and
head to these scenic nosh spots

By Lisa Taggart

Here's a recipe for spring's best meal: Start with two glasses of chilled wine. Add a delectable salad and a stellar view. Toss in the luxury of privacy, a sprinkling of wildflowers, and many lungfuls of fresh spring air. Mix and enjoy.

It's a no-fail recipe, so pack up your basket and hit the trail. These picnic areas near San Francisco are enough off the beaten track to provide quiet, but the hikes aren't so long you can't tote a bottle of wine and lunch for two.

■ **CORTE MADERA AND MILL VALLEY/MARIN COUNTY** Camino Alto Open Space Preserve. In the hills between Corte Madera and Mill Valley, you'll find postcard views of San Francisco. Trails aren't labeled; head up the short, somewhat steep hill on the south side for the best view. **WHERE:** Park at turnouts along Corte Madera Ave. (which becomes Camino Alto) near fire road access gates. **DISTANCE:** About 2 miles round trip. **CONTACT:** (415) 499-6387.

■ **RICHMOND/CONTRA COSTA COUNTY** Pt. Pinole. Hike beside San Pablo Bay, catching views of Mt. Tamalpais. Picnic along Marsh Trail on your way out to the fishing pier at the point's end. It can get windy here, so bundle up. **WHERE:** Off Giant Hwy., 4 miles north of downtown Richmond. **DISTANCE:** 1¼ miles one way. **CONTACT:** (510) 635-0135.

■ **SAN FRANCISCO BAY** Angel Island State Park. Take Perimeter Road around the island, stopping for a

(Continued on next page)

JAMES CARRIER

Bright colors make this salad a visually pleasing alfresco meal.

Comestible rewards

Any hike—ambitious or trifling—makes you feel virtuous. You deserve to consume something indulgent on the other end. What you pack can be as tantalizing as the setting if you forage at a good local deli. Here's a tangy rice salad to anchor your picnic. Pair it with a chilled bottle of Pinot Grigio Trentino.

Rice Salad with Ham and Tomatoes

PREP AND COOK TIME: About 30 minutes

NOTES: To make a vegetarian salad, substitute provolone for the ham and cook the rice with water. If making salad up to 2 days ahead, chill airtight. Transport salad in an insulated bag or serve within 2 hours.

MAKES: 3 quarts; 8 to 10 servings

- 2 quarts fat-skimmed **chicken broth** or water

- 2 cups **arborio rice** or medium-grain white rice such as pearl

- 1 pound **thin-sliced cooked ham** (see notes)

- 3 cups **cherry tomatoes** (1 in. or smaller)

- 1 cup lightly packed **fresh basil** leaves

- ⅔ cup drained **capers**

- 2 cloves **garlic**

- 3 tablespoons **extra-virgin olive oil**

  Salt

  Fresh-ground **pepper**

  Basil sprigs, rinsed (optional)

1. In a 5- to 6-quart pan over high heat, bring broth and rice to a boil. Reduce heat and simmer, stirring occasionally, until rice is just tender to bite, 13 to 15 minutes. Drain rice; reserve broth for other uses, or discard. Pour rice into a shallow 11- by 17-inch pan and spread level. Let cool, stirring occasionally, about 20 minutes.

2. Meanwhile, stack ham slices and cut into strips ¼ inch wide and 1 inch long. Rinse and drain tomatoes, basil, and capers. Cut tomatoes in half and basil leaves into slivers; peel and mince garlic.

3. In a large bowl, mix ham, tomatoes, basil slivers, capers, garlic, and olive oil. Add cool rice, mix gently, and season to taste with salt and pepper. Garnish with basil sprigs.

Per serving: 281 cal., 28% (79 cal.) from fat; 20 g protein; 8.8 g fat (2 g sat.); 30 g carbo (3.3 g fiber); 1,151 mg sodium; 27 mg chol.

— Sara Schneider

picnic along the way. Or climb up 781-foot Mt. Livermore for a picnic spot with the island's best view. WHERE: San Francisco Bay, east of Tiburon. Ferries run from Alameda, San Francisco, Tiburon, and Vallejo. (For more about ferries, see "Playing hooky by ferry," page 48.) DISTANCE: Perimeter Rd., 5 miles. FYI: Consult the return ferry schedule before you set out. CONTACT: (415) 435-1915.

■ SAN GERONIMO/MARIN COUNTY Roy's Redwoods Open Space Pre-

serve. In spring this secluded meadow is covered in wildflowers, and Roy's Redwoods Loop Trail is peaceful and shady. For views of the San Geronimo Valley, take an out-and-back hike on Dickson Ridge Fire Road, then settle down in the meadow for a feast. WHERE: Off Nicasio Valley Rd., San Geronimo (west Marin). DISTANCE: Loop trail about 2½ miles. CONTACT: (415) 499-6387.

■ SANTA CRUZ COUNTY Castle Rock State Park. In the hills above

Santa Cruz, the trails in Castle Rock provide gorgeous vistas of the Santa Cruz Mountains. Summit Meadows Trail has scenic stopping points and benches with views. WHERE: Main entrance off Skyline Blvd., 3 miles south of State 9. Or park at the turnout off State 9, about a mile west of the intersection with Skyline. DISTANCE: Summit Meadows Trail bench and view point about ⅓ mile from State 9 turnout. CONTACT: (408) 867-2952. ◆

The other Washington wines

Make a wine-tasting detour to Oregon's Washington County

By Karl Samson

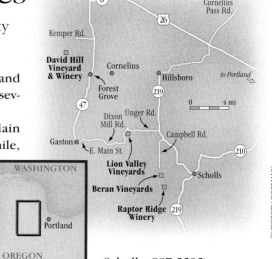

Did you know that Oregon makes excellent Washington wines? That's right. In Oregon's Washington County, out to the west of Portland among the high-tech companies of Silicon Forest, new wineries are springing up everywhere. If your travels take you to Portland, it's worth a day's detour to sample some Washington County vintages.

Start your tour by heading west on U.S. 26, with a stop for breakfast at Sweet Oregon Grill (Cornelius Pass Rd. and West Union Rd., just north of the highway outside Hillsboro; 503/614-8747), a retro-style eatery housed in a historic barn.

Back on U.S. 26, continue west to State 6. From State 6, head south on State 47, then turn right on Kemper Road, left on Thatcher Road, and right on David Hill Road. Watch for the David Hill Vineyard & Winery sign (46350 N.W. David Hill Rd., Forest Grove; 992-8545).

From David Hill, head south to Gaston. The highlight here is 24 Brix (108 Mill St.; 985-3434), which

serves gourmet sandwiches and doubles as a tasting room for several small wineries.

From Gaston, take East Main Street (S.W. Gaston Rd.) 1 mile, turn left on Hardebeck Road, then make a quick right onto Dixon Mill Road. At the end, turn right onto Unger Road, which will bring you to Lion Valley Vineyards (weekends only; 35040 S.W. Unger Rd., Cornelius; 628-5458), known for its Pinot Noirs.

If all this wine tasting makes you drowsy, take heart: There's espresso nearby. In the community of Scholls at State 219 and State 210, you'll find the South Store Cafe (628-1904), a former country store.

Not far from the South Store Cafe are two small wineries (call ahead for tasting appointments). Beran Vineyards (30088 S.W. Egger Rd., Hillsboro; 628-1298) produces only Pinot Noir; nearby is Raptor Ridge Winery (29090 S.W. Wildhaven Lane,

Scholls; 887-5595).

Finally, stop for dinner at the Hillsboro Pub & Grill (118 E. Main St., Hillsboro; 640-4579), where contemporary American fare is paired with local wines. The restaurant's owner also operates Main Street Wine (132 E. Main St., Hillsboro; 381-5778) and a website (www.wines2u.com), both of which specialize in Washington County wines.

WHERE: About 15 miles west of downtown Portland.

FYI: Pick up a "Wineries of Washington County, Oregon" brochure at most area wineries or at the visitors bureau (800/537-3149, 503/644-5555, or www.wcva.org). ◆

The Low-Fat Cook
Healthy choices for the active lifestyle
By Andrew Baker

Saucy ravioli

■ The quest to curtail fat when saucing ravioli generally ends with the tomato. And it's a fine choice—but only one. Legumes and vegetables yield many hearty yet lean options when cooked with herbs and spices, then puréed.

Use mild cheese-filled ravioli or tortellini as a neutral foil for these unique sauces. Both pastas come in several shapes, sizes, and colors; smaller pockets tend to hold their shapes best during cooking. And the sauces are smoother if puréed in a blender rather than a food processor.

Rich-tasting ravioli is sauced with yellow split peas.

Ravioli with Split Pea Sauce

PREP AND COOK TIME: About 1¼ hours

NOTES: Hema Kundargi of Cupertino, California, uses traditional flavors from her native India in this creative sauce.

MAKES: 4 servings

- 1 quart fat-skimmed **chicken broth**
- 1⅓ cups **dried yellow split peas**
- 2 packages (9 oz. each) **cheese-filled ravioli** or tortellini
- 3 **dried hot chilies** (2 in. long)
- ½ teaspoon **olive** or salad **oil**
- 2 teaspoons minced **garlic**
- 1 teaspoon **cumin seed**
- 1 quart **baby spinach leaves** (about ¼ lb.), rinsed
- ½ cup **red cherry tomatoes** (about 1 in.), rinsed and halved
- ½ teaspoon **turmeric**
  Salt and fresh-ground **pepper**

1. In a 3- to 4-quart pan over high heat, bring broth and split peas to a boil; cover, reduce heat, and simmer until peas fall apart, about 50 minutes.
2. In a 5- to 6-quart pan over high heat, bring 2 quarts water to a boil; add ravioli. Stir occasionally until pasta is tender to bite, 4 to 6 minutes; drain.
3. Meanwhile, transfer split pea mixture to a blender or food processor; whirl until smooth.
4. Remove and discard stems from chilies; shake out and discard seeds. Wipe the 3- to 4-quart pan dry. Add chilies, oil, garlic, and cumin; stir over medium-high heat until garlic is lightly browned, about 1 minute.
5. Pour split pea purée into pan with chili mixture. Add spinach, tomatoes, and turmeric; stir just until steaming.
6. Add drained ravioli to sauce and mix gently. Spoon equally into wide bowls. Add salt and pepper to taste.

Per serving: 714 cal., 20% (144 cal.) from fat; 46 g protein; 16 g fat (7.5 g sat.); 97 g carbo (8.9 g fiber); 625 mg sodium; 110 mg chol.

Ravioli with Green Pea Pesto

PREP AND COOK TIME: About 30 minutes

MAKES: 4 servings

- 2 packages (9 oz. each) **cheese-filled ravioli** or tortellini
- 2½ cups **frozen petite peas,** thawed
- 2 cups fat-skimmed **chicken broth**
- 2¼ cups lightly packed **fresh basil** leaves, rinsed
- 1 cup lightly packed **fresh mint** leaves, rinsed
- 2 tablespoons **pine nuts**
- ½ teaspoon **olive** or salad **oil**
- 1 teaspoon minced **garlic**
  Salt and fresh-ground **pepper**

1. In a 5- to 6-quart pan over high heat, bring 2 quarts water to a boil; add ravioli. Stir occasionally until pasta is tender to bite, 4 to 6 minutes; drain.
2. Meanwhile, in a blender or food processor, purée peas, broth, 2 cups basil leaves, and mint leaves.
3. In a 3- to 4-quart pan over medium-high heat, stir or shake pine nuts until lightly browned, 3 to 4 minutes. Pour from pan.
4. Add oil and garlic to pan; stir just until garlic begins to brown, 30 seconds to 1 minute. Add pea mixture and stir until steaming.
5. Add drained ravioli to sauce and mix gently. Spoon equally into wide bowls.
6. Cut remaining basil leaves into slivers and scatter over portions. Sprinkle with pine nuts. Add salt and pepper to taste.

Per serving: 572 cal., 30% (171 cal.) from fat; 33 g protein; 19 g fat (7.8 g sat.); 69 g carbo (12 g fiber); 633 mg sodium; 110 mg chol.

Ravioli with Salsa Verde

PREP AND COOK TIME: About 30 minutes

MAKES: 4 servings

- 1 pound **tomatillos**
- ¾ pound **fresh poblano** (also called pasilla) **chilies,** rinsed
- 1 **onion** (½ lb.), peeled
- 3 cloves **garlic,** unpeeled
- 1 cup fat-skimmed **chicken broth**
- ½ cup **fresh cilantro,** rinsed
- 2 packages (9 oz. each) **cheese-filled ravioli**
- ¼ cup finely chopped **tomato**
  Salt

1. Remove and discard husks from tomatillos; rinse tomatillos well. Cut chilies in half lengthwise; remove and discard stems, seeds, and veins. Cut onion crosswise into 1-inch slices. Arrange tomatillos, chilies (cut sides down), onion, and garlic in a single layer in a 10- by 15-inch pan.
2. Broil 4 to 6 inches from heat until vegetables are well browned, 15 to 20 minutes. When garlic is cool, peel.
3. Transfer vegetables and any liquid to a blender or food processor. Add broth and cilantro; whirl until smooth.
4. Pour chili mixture into a 3- to 4-quart pan over medium heat; stir occasionally until steaming.
5. Meanwhile, in a 5- to 6-quart pan over high heat, bring 2 quarts water to a boil; add ravioli. Stir occasionally until pasta is tender to bite, 4 to 6 minutes; drain.
6. Add ravioli to the chili mixture and stir gently. Spoon equally into wide bowls. Garnish with tomato and add salt to taste.

Per serving: 512 cal., 26% (135 cal.) from fat; 26 g protein; 15 g fat (7.4 g sat.); 68 g carbo (4.9 g fiber); 511 mg sodium; 110 mg chol. ◆

Kitchen Cabinet

Readers' recipes tested in *Sunset's* kitchens

By Paula Freschet

Baby artichokes and tender chunks of lamb soak up spices as they cook.

Lamb and Artichoke Spring Stew

Kathryn M. Walker, Cupertino, California

Kathryn Walker is fond of artichokes and her father loves lamb, so she harmonizes their favorite ingredients in this hearty main dish.

PREP AND COOK TIME: About 2 hours

MAKES: 4 servings

- 1 tablespoon **olive oil**
- 2 cloves **garlic,** minced or pressed
- 1 **onion** (about ½ lb.), peeled and chopped
- 1 **carrot** (about ¼ lb.), peeled and thinly sliced
- 2 stalks **celery** (about 6 oz. total), rinsed and thinly sliced
- 1 pound **fat-trimmed, boned lamb shoulder,** cut into 1-inch chunks
- ½ cup fat-skimmed **chicken broth**
- 1 can (14½ oz.) **diced tomatoes**
- ⅓ cup **dry red wine**
- ½ teaspoon **fennel seed**
- ¼ teaspoon **dried rubbed sage**
- 12 **baby artichokes** (1½ in. wide) or 1 package (8 oz.) frozen artichoke hearts, thawed

- 1 tablespoon **vinegar**
- 8 **thin-skinned potatoes** (about 1½ in. wide), scrubbed and cut into quarters

   About ¼ cup chopped **parsley**

   Salt and **pepper**

1. In a 4- to 5-quart pan, combine oil, garlic, onion, carrot, and celery. Stir often over high heat until vegetables begin to brown, 6 to 8 minutes. Pour from pan into a bowl.

2. To pan, add lamb and broth; cover and bring to a boil on high heat. Reduce heat and boil gently for 10 minutes. Uncover, turn heat to high, and stir often until juices evaporate, drippings are very browned, and meat is lightly browned, 8 to 10 minutes. Return browned vegetables to pan.

3. Add tomatoes with their liquid, wine, fennel seed, and sage; stir to free browned bits. Bring to a boil, then reduce heat, cover, and simmer for 40 minutes; stir occasionally.

4. Meanwhile, rinse fresh artichokes, drain, and break off outer coarse leaves down to the very tender inner yellow ones (easily pierced with your fingernail). Cut off thorny artichoke tips, peel coarse fibers from bottoms, and cut artichokes in half lengthwise. In a bowl, mix with 2 cups water and vinegar; drain. If using frozen artichokes, omit water and vinegar.

5. Add artichokes and potatoes to lamb mixture. Cover and simmer until potatoes and lamb are very tender when pierced, about 30 minutes longer; stir occasionally. Pour into a bowl, sprinkle with parsley, and season to taste with salt and pepper.

Per serving: 359 cal., 30% (108 cal.) from fat; 29 g protein; 12 g fat (3.3 g sat.); 36 g carbo (8.4 g fiber); 340 mg sodium; 75 mg chol.

Sticky Bun French Toast

Diane and Jim Peiker, Denver

At Castle Marne, the bed-and-breakfast operated by Diane and Jim Peiker, this baked French toast with a sticky bun topping is very popular with the guests. It's also very easy to make. You can start it the night before and have it ready to bake in the morning.

PREP AND COOK TIME: About 1 hour, plus at least 8 hours to chill

MAKES: 5 to 6 servings

   About ¼ cup (⅛ lb.) **butter** or margarine

- 1 **sourdough baguette** (8 oz.), cut diagonally in 1-inch-thick slices
- 5 **large eggs**
- 1 cup **half-and-half** (light cream)
- 1 cup **milk**
- ¼ teaspoon **ground nutmeg**
- 1 teaspoon **ground cinnamon**
- 1 teaspoon **vanilla**
- ½ cup firmly packed **brown sugar**
- 1 tablespoon **light corn syrup**
- ½ cup chopped **pecans** or walnuts

1. Lightly butter a 9- by 13-inch pan. Lay baguette slices on a cut side in a single layer in pan, squeezing if needed to make them fit. In a blender or in a bowl with a whisk, whirl or beat eggs, half-and-half, milk, nutmeg, cinnamon, and vanilla to blend well. Pour egg mixture over bread to moisten evenly. Cover and refrigerate at least 8 or up to 24 hours.

2. In a 1- to 2-quart pan over medium heat, stir ¼ cup butter with brown sugar, corn syrup, and pecans until butter melts. Uncover bread mixture and spread slices evenly with the butter mixture, using all of it.

3. Bake, uncovered, in a 350° oven until topping is browned and bubbly, about 45 minutes. Scoop portions into bowls.

Per serving: 461 cal., 51% (234 cal.) from fat; 12 g protein; 26 g fat (11 g sat.); 46 g carbo (1.6 g fiber); 418 mg sodium; 221 mg chol.

Asparagus, Potato, and Papaya Salad with Green Onion Dressing

Christine Datian, Las Vegas

Christine Datian and Bill Hodson, her business associate, created this lavish salad as the main course for lunch or dinner.

PREP AND COOK TIME: About 40 minutes

MAKES: 4 main-dish servings

- 1 pound **asparagus,** rinsed
- 1 pound **thin-skinned red potatoes** (about 1½ in. wide), scrubbed
- 1 **firm-ripe papaya** (about 1 lb.), peeled and seeded
- 4 cups **salad mix** (about 4 oz.), rinsed and crisped
- ½ cup **calamata olives,** pitted

   Green onion dressing (recipe follows)

   Salt

Green onion dressing complements this handsome vegetable and fruit salad.

1. Snap off and discard tough asparagus ends. In a 3- to 4-quart pan over high heat, bring 2 quarts water to a boil. Add asparagus; cook until barely tender when pierced, 3 to 5 minutes. With tongs, lift out asparagus and immerse in ice water. When cool, about 3 minutes, lift out and drain.

2. Meanwhile, add potatoes to boiling water. Cover and simmer over medium heat until they are just tender when pierced in thickest part, 20 to 30 minutes. Drain potatoes and immerse in ice water. When cool, about 10 minutes, drain and cut into halves. Cut papaya lengthwise into ¼-inch-thick slices.

3. Line a platter with salad mix. Arrange asparagus, potatoes, papaya, and olives on greens. Add dressing and salt to taste to individual portions.

Per serving: 296 cal., 23% (45 cal.) from fat; 6.5 g protein; 12 g fat (1.4 g sat.); 46 g carbo (5.4 g fiber); 807 mg sodium; 0 mg chol.

Green onion dressing. Rinse and trim ends from 8 **green onions;** cut into 2-inch pieces (including tops). In a food processor or blender, purée the onions, ¼ cup **seasoned rice vinegar,** 2 tablespoons each **dry white wine, Dijon mustard, salad oil,** chopped **parsley,** chopped **fresh mint** leaves, and chopped **fresh basil** leaves until smooth. Stir in **white pepper** to taste. Scrape into a small bowl; if making up to 1 day ahead, cover and chill. Makes about 1 cup.

Per tablespoon: 24 cal., 63% (15 cal.) from fat; 0.2 g protein; 1.7 g fat (0.2 g sat.); 1.4 g carbo (0.3 g fiber); 121 mg sodium; 0 mg chol.

Risotto with Peas and Mushrooms

Russell Ito, San Mateo, California

Russell Ito says he cooks for fun because it's a relaxing diversion from the intensity of his work. Therefore, he's willing to take extra steps like making vegetable broth for the risotto, using fresh pea pods and mushroom trimmings. But canned broth works equally well for cooks who have to get meals together on a tight schedule.

PREP AND COOK TIME: About 45 minutes

MAKES: 4 servings

- ½ pound **mushrooms,** a mixture (at least 2 kinds and any combination) of chanterelle, common, portabella, and shiitake
- 1 tablespoon **olive oil**
- 1 clove **garlic,** minced or pressed
- 1 **onion** (about 6 oz.), peeled and chopped
- 1½ cups **white arborio** or pearl (medium-grain) **rice**
- 4 to 5 cups **vegetable broth**
- 1 cup **shelled fresh** or frozen petite **peas**
- 1 tablespoon **butter** or margarine
- ⅓ cup grated **parmesan cheese**
  Salt and **pepper**

1. Trim and discard any grit or soil and discolored stem ends from mushrooms (trim and discard shiitake stems). Immerse mushrooms in cool water, swishing gently to rinse well, then quickly lift out and drain. Thinly slice mushrooms.

2. In a 3- to 4-quart pan over medium-high heat, combine oil, garlic, onion, and mushrooms. Stir often until vegetables just begin to brown, about 6 minutes. Add rice and stir until some of the grains are opaque, about 2 minutes.

3. Add 4 cups broth to pan; when it boils, reduce heat to medium or medium-low and simmer, stirring often, until rice is just tender to bite, 15 to 20 minutes. Add peas and butter and stir often until peas are tender to bite, 2 to 5 minutes. For a creamier risotto, add more broth until mixture is desired consistency and boiling. Stir in half the cheese. Season risotto to taste with salt and pepper, pour into a bowl, and sprinkle with remaining cheese.

Per serving: 412 cal., 22% (90 cal.) from fat; 12 g protein; 10 g fat (3.8 g sat.); 68 g carbo (7.4 g fiber); 257 mg sodium; 14 mg chol.

Chocolate Amaretto Cheesecake

Valerie M. Corpuz, Wilmington, California

The dairy-fresh tang of neufchâtel and cottage cheese balances the rich chocolate flavor—mostly from cocoa—in this smooth cheesecake.

PREP AND COOK TIME: About 1 hour, plus 2 hours to cool

MAKES: 10 to 12 servings

- 20 **thin chocolate wafer cookies** (about 2 in. wide; 5 oz. total)
- 2 tablespoons melted **butter** or margarine
- 1½ packages (8 oz. size, 12 oz. total) **neufchâtel** (light cream) **cheese** or cream cheese
- 1 cup **small-curd low-fat cottage cheese**
- 1 **large egg**
- ¾ cup **sugar**
- 6 tablespoons **unsweetened cocoa**
- ¼ cup **all-purpose flour**
- 1 teaspoon **vanilla**
- ¼ teaspoon **salt**
- ¼ cup **almond-flavor liqueur** (such as amaretto) or ¼ teaspoon almond extract
- 2 tablespoons **miniature** (or coarsely chopped regular) **semisweet chocolate chips**

1. In a food processor, whirl cookies until finely ground. Add butter and whirl until mixed. Press cookie mixture evenly over bottom and ¾ inch up the side of a removable-rim 8-inch cheesecake or cake pan (at least 1½ in. deep).

2. In a food processor or in bowl with a mixer, whirl or beat until smooth the neufchâtel, cottage cheese, egg, sugar, cocoa, flour, vanilla, salt, and almond liqueur. Stir in chocolate chips. Scrape mixture into chocolate crust.

3. Bake cheesecake in a 350° regular or convection oven until filling looks dry at rim of the cake and is firm in the center when pan is gently shaken, 30 to 40 minutes.

4. Run a thin-bladed knife between cake and pan rim. Refrigerate cake, uncovered, until cool, at least 2 hours. Serve, or if making up to 2 days ahead, wrap airtight and chill. Remove pan rim and cut cake into wedges.

Per serving: 241 cal., 45% (108 cal.) from fat; 7.3 g protein; 12 g fat (6.5 g sat.); 29 g carbo (1.2 g fiber); 331 mg sodium; 45 mg chol. ◆

Savory skewers cooked on the grill: Tangy apricot sauce tops a turkey-beef kebab (recipes on page 126).

JAMES CARRIER

108

June

SEVEN MAIN-DISH SALADS THAT *STILL* RULE THE WEST

hail, Caesar...
& Louis & Victor

By Elaine Johnson • Photographs by James Carrier
Food styling by Karen Shinto

Italy perfected pasta. France transformed sauces. The American West taught the world how to make a grand salad. • In the early days of the last century, as more and more people populated the West, inspiration was right outside the kitchen door in one form or another: fields of greens stretching under sunny skies, seafood just plucked from the ocean, orchards dotted with lemons, a year-round supply of fresh herbs—in many regions, all of the above. • Some of the world's best-known salads were born then. A few came to the fore through a famous person, place, or event, and those legends live on. Others rose to fame more obscurely, shared from one home kitchen to the next. • Today these classic salads are in as fine a form as ever: Our choice of fresh ingredients just keeps getting better. We've learned to use seasonings with a bolder hand. And we expect our dishes to be as pleasing to look at as they are to eat. • A whole meal of salad—it's a natural here. We salute the cooks—both famous and unknown—behind the concept.

Caesar

Tijuana, Mexico, July 4, 1924, Caesar's Place: As the restaurant fills with holiday diners, Italian-born chef and restaurant owner Caesar Cardini runs short on ingredients for the day's salad. He improvises with what's on hand: romaine leaves, parmesan cheese, olive oil, lemon juice, a raw egg, Worcestershire (anchovies came later), and croutons. The salad's a hit with the Hollywood set who frequent Cardini's restaurant, and they take their reverence for Caesar back home.

Served plain or topped with everything from grilled chicken to fried ginger, the salad has become a hallmark of California cuisine. Here we return Caesar to its simple roots, but build it on a grand scale as befits a legend. To alleviate concerns about bacteria, we've eliminated the raw egg; a quick buzz in the blender emulsifies the classic components into a creamy dressing.

Stacked Caesar Salad with Parmesan Rafts

PREP AND COOK TIME: About 1 hour

NOTES: This salad is dramatic when made with whole inner romaine lettuce leaves (often sold as "romaine hearts"), but you can substitute 4 quarts bite-size pieces of romaine; in step 5, arrange the parmesan curls on top of the mixed salad. To make the curls, pull a vegetable peeler across the block of cheese.

MAKES: 4 to 6 main-dish servings

1 **sourdough baguette** (about 2 in. wide; 8 to 12 oz.)
About ¾ cup **extra-virgin olive oil**
1⅓ cups finely shredded **parmesan cheese** (about ¼ lb.)
⅓ cup **lemon juice**
9 canned **anchovy fillets,** drained
4 teaspoons minced **garlic**
¾ teaspoon fresh-ground **pepper**
About ½ teaspoon **salt**
4 quarts **tender inner romaine lettuce leaves** (max. 8 in. long, 1⅓ lb. total; see notes), rinsed and crisped
1 cup **parmesan cheese** curls (each about 3 in. long and 1 in. wide, 3 oz. total; see notes)

Dressed to thrill: Tender romaine leaves and crisp parmesan croutons stack up to a grand Caesar salad.

1. To make parmesan rafts, cut baguette into diagonal slices ¼ inch thick and 4 to 6 inches long. Lightly brush both sides of each slice with olive oil, using 3 to 4 tablespoons total. Arrange in a single layer in 2 shallow 12- by 17-inch baking pans.

2. Bake in a 325° regular or convection oven for 5 minutes. Sprinkle slices evenly with 1 cup shredded parmesan. Bake until cheese is melted and bread is golden, 10 to 12 minutes longer.

3. In a blender or food processor, whirl 9 tablespoons olive oil, ⅓ cup shredded parmesan, lemon juice, anchovies, garlic, pepper, and ½ teaspoon salt until smooth.

4. Place lettuce in a large bowl and parmesan rafts in another. Drizzle ⅔ of the dressing over lettuce and remaining ⅓ over rafts. Mix rafts to coat with dressing; with your hands or two spoons, gently lift and mix lettuce to coat.

5. Divide ⅓ of the lettuce equally among

dinner plates, arranging all leaves on each plate in the same direction. Arrange ⅓ of the parmesan rafts equally on top, at right angles to leaves, and add ⅓ of the parmesan curls. Repeat to layer remaining lettuce, rafts, and curls. Season salads to taste with more salt.

Per serving: 521 cal., 67% (351 cal.) from fat; 20 g protein; 39 g fat (10 g sat.); 25 g carbo (2.8 g fiber); 1,234 mg sodium; 28 mg chol.

- **To rinse and crisp salad greens,** immerse in water and swish gently to remove any grit, then drain or spin dry. Wrap in paper towels and enclose in a plastic bag. Chill until crisp, at least 30 minutes or up to 1 day.

- **To cut fine shreds of iceberg lettuce,** first cut head in half through core; cut out and discard core. Cut each half in half again lengthwise, then place each quarter on 1 cut side and slice thinly lengthwise from the other cut side.

- **To cut fine shreds of other lettuce leaves,** such as romaine, stack a few leaves at a time, roll lengthwise into a cylinder, and slice thinly crosswise.

- **The highest-quality ingredients** make the best salads: Use flavorful extra-virgin olive oil and top-quality parmesan cheese or other cheeses (shred or crumble just before using).

Crab Louis

Whoever Louis (or Louie) was—no one's quite sure—the Hotel St. Francis in San Francisco was serving his addictive combination of Dungeness crab, iceberg lettuce, and chili-mayo dressing in 1910.

The greens in our updated version reflect the broader choices now available. And zesty salsa and smoky chipotle chilies replace the chili sauce for a more interesting interplay of flavors. But a little mountain of sweet, fresh crab—a far dearer component now than a century ago—still crowns the dish.

Deviled Crab Louis

PREP TIME: About 1¼ hours

NOTES: You can shred the lettuce up to 1 day ahead; chill airtight.

MAKES: 4 main-dish servings

- 8 **romaine** or iceberg **lettuce** leaves (10 in. long), rinsed and crisped
- 1 head **Belgian endive** (white or red; 3 oz.), leaves separated, rinsed, and crisped
- 2 quarts finely shredded **romaine** or iceberg **lettuce** (use half romaine and half iceberg or all 1 kind)
- ¼ cup chopped **parsley**
  Deviled Louis dressing (recipe follows)
- 1 pound **shelled cooked crab**
- 2 **firm-ripe tomatoes** (¾ lb. total), rinsed, cored, and each cut into 8 wedges
- 2 hard-cooked **large eggs,** shelled and each cut into 4 wedges

- 2 tablespoons chopped **fresh chives**
  Whole **fresh chives**
  Salt and **pepper**
  Lemon wedges

1. Line dinner plates or wide bowls equally with whole lettuce leaves, then Belgian endive leaves.

2. In a large bowl, combine shredded lettuce and parsley. Add ⅔ cup deviled Louis dressing and mix gently. Divide equally among lettuce-lined plates.

3. Remove and discard any bits of shell from crab. Mound crab in center of shredded lettuce mixture; arrange tomato and egg wedges around edges. Sprinkle salads with chopped chives and garnish with whole chives. Offer remaining dressing, salt and pepper, and lemon wedges to season salads to taste.

Per serving: 610 cal., 72% (441 cal.) from fat; 30 g protein; 49 g fat (7.6 g sat.); 14 g carbo (3.9 g fiber); 904 mg sodium; 252 mg chol.

Deviled Louis dressing. In a blender or food processor, whirl ½ cup **tomato salsa** (medium to hot) and 1 to 2 teaspoons drained **canned chipotle chilies** (depending on desired heat) until smooth. Pour into a bowl and stir in 1 cup **mayonnaise,** 3 tablespoons **lemon juice,** and 1½ teaspoons **sugar.** Serve, or chill airtight up to 1 week. Makes 1¾ cups.

Per tablespoon: 59 cal., 95% (56 cal.) from fat; 0.1 g protein; 6.2 g fat (0.9 g sat.); 0.8 g carbo (0 g fiber); 77 mg sodium; 4.6 mg chol.

Celery Victor

With a red fez set rakishly atop his head and a persona larger than life, chef Victor Hirtzler—native of Strasbourg, France, former taster

for Czar Nicholas II, and once chef to King Carlos I of Portugal—reigned over the Hotel St. Francis in San Francisco from 1904 to 1926. Among the astonishingly varied, European-inspired creations Hirtzler named after himself, celery Victor (circa 1910) may be the most enduring. The simple and delicious poached vegetable dish hails from the days before raw greens defined a salad. We've added shrimp for substance and capers for spark.

Shrimp Celery Victor

PREP AND COOK TIME: About 30 minutes, plus at least 2½ hours to chill

NOTES: Many supermarkets sell tender hearts of celery, but if they aren't available, pull off large outer stalks from regular bunches and save for other uses; use tender inner stalks.

MAKES: 6 main-dish servings

- 3 **celery hearts** (each about 2½ in. wide, ½ to ¾ lb.; see notes)
- 3½ cups fat-skimmed **chicken broth**
- ⅓ cup **extra-virgin olive oil**
- ⅓ cup **tarragon-flavor** or plain white wine **vinegar**
- 1¼ pounds (30 to 35 per lb.) **shelled, deveined shrimp,** rinsed and drained
- 12 **canned anchovy fillets** (about 1½ oz. total), drained
- 2 tablespoons drained **capers**
- 1 quart lightly packed **watercress** sprigs (about 4 oz.), rinsed and crisped
  Salt and **pepper**

1. Trim and discard tough stem ends from celery hearts, keeping stalks attached to bases; trim and discard tops to make stalks about 8 inches long. Rinse and drain celery hearts. With a vegetable peeler, pare coarse strings from outer stalk backs. Cut each heart in half lengthwise; tie each half tightly around center with cotton string.

2. Combine celery and broth in a 5- to 6-quart pan (at least 10 in. wide). Bring to a boil over high heat; cover, reduce heat, and simmer until celery is tender when pierced, 12 to 15 minutes, turning bundles over halfway through cooking.

3. Combine olive oil and vinegar in a 1-gallon heavy plastic food bag. With tongs, transfer celery from broth to bag. Set upright and let cool.

4. Meanwhile, add shrimp to broth; bring to a simmer over high heat, then reduce heat and simmer, uncovered, just until shrimp are opaque but still moist-looking in center of thickest part (cut to test), 30 seconds to 1 minute. With a slotted spoon, lift shrimp from broth and add to plastic bag with celery (save broth for other uses or discard). Let cool, about 30 minutes, then press bag to seal. Turn bag to coat celery and shrimp with dressing. Chill until cold, at least 2 hours or up to 1 day, turning bag occasionally.

5. Lift celery from dressing; remove and discard strings, and place a bundle on each dinner plate. With a slotted spoon, lift shrimp from dressing and mound beside celery.

6. Crisscross 2 anchovy fillets on each portion, then sprinkle with capers. Tuck watercress around celery and shrimp. Spoon remaining dressing from bag over salads, and add salt and pepper to taste.

Per serving: 235 cal., 57% (135 cal.) from fat; 23 g protein; 15 g fat (2.2 g sat.); 3.6 g carbo (1 g fiber); 570 mg sodium; 148 mg chol.

Cobb

Late one night in the 1920s, a hungry Bob Cobb, manager of Hollywood's Brown Derby, wandered into the kitchen and created what would become the restaurant's signature salad—from leftovers. Pals Jack Warner, Sid Grauman, Wilson Mizner, and Gene Fowler liked the looks of the greens topped with chopped chicken, Roquefort cheese, and vegetables and soon began requesting it. The Cobb became an official menu item in 1929.

The original restaurant (that conspicuous Bunyan-size domed hat) is now closed. But the salad appears on the Hollywood Brown Derby menus at the MGM Grand in Las Vegas, the MGM Grand Detroit Casino, and Disney-MGM Studios near Orlando.

Cobb Salad

PREP AND COOK TIME: About 1½ hours
NOTES: Apple wood–smoked bacon adds especially rich flavor to this salad. Use leftover cooked chicken or buy roast chicken from a deli. Choose a

BETTMAN/CORBIS

pungent blue cheese such as Oregon blue, Roquefort, or gorgonzola.

MAKES: 4 to 6 main-dish servings

- 1 pound **sliced bacon** (see notes), coarsely chopped
- ⅓ cup **extra-virgin olive oil**
- ¼ cup **tarragon-flavor vinegar**
- 1 tablespoon **Dijon mustard**
- 1 tablespoon minced **shallot**
  About ½ teaspoon fresh-ground **pepper**
  About ¼ teaspoon **salt**
- 1 quart lightly packed **watercress** sprigs (4 oz.), rinsed and crisped
- 5 quarts finely shredded **lettuce** (use half butter lettuce and half iceberg or all iceberg)
- 2 **firm-ripe tomatoes** (⅔ lb. total), rinsed, cored, and chopped
- 1½ cups thinly sliced skinned **cooked chicken** (7 oz.; see notes)

Classic Cobb salad (above) hails from Hollywood's famed Brown Derby restaurant (left).

- ⅔ cup crumbled **blue cheese** (3 oz.; see notes)
- 2 hard-cooked **large eggs,** shelled and chopped
- 1 **firm-ripe avocado** (½ lb.), halved, pitted, peeled, and thinly sliced crosswise

1. In a 10- to 12-inch frying pan over medium-high heat, stir bacon often until browned and crisp, 10 to 15 minutes; spoon out and discard fat in pan as it accumulates. With a slotted spoon, transfer bacon to towels to drain; discard remaining fat in pan.

2. In a 1-cup glass measure or small bowl, mix olive oil, vinegar, mustard, shallot, ½ teaspoon pepper, and ¼ teaspoon salt.

3. Set aside 4 to 6 watercress sprigs; coarsely chop remaining sprigs. In a large bowl, combine chopped watercress and lettuce. Add all but 2 tablespoons dressing and mix gently to coat.

4. Arrange equal portions of lettuce mixture in wide, shallow bowls. On each, in pie-shaped wedges, arrange equal portions of bacon, tomatoes, chicken, blue cheese, eggs, and avocado.

5. Spoon remaining dressing evenly over toppings. Garnish salads with reserved watercress sprigs. Add salt and pepper to taste.

Per serving: 458 cal., 71% (324 cal.) from fat; 25 g protein; 36 g fat (10 g sat.); 12 g carbo (3.5 g fiber); 768 mg sodium; 129 mg chol.

Green Goddess

In 1923 a play opened in San Francisco: *The Green Goddess,* starring well-known British actor George Arliss. To celebrate the play's success, a dinner party was held at the grand Palace Hotel, for which executive chef Philip Roemer created a special salad dressing to gild artichoke bottoms filled with shrimp, chicken, or crab. In keeping with the era's tastes, it incorporated just a whiff of green herbs and anchovies, and plenty of mayonnaise.

In keeping with modern tastes, Peter DeMarais, current executive chef of the Palace Hotel (and whose great-grandfather was also a chef there), uses herbs with a bold hand in his dressing.

Green Goddess Salad

PREP TIME: About 45 minutes

NOTES: Chef DeMarais uses reduced-fat sour cream to make a tangy dressing; regular mayonnaise produces a mellower blend. Chervil gives the dressing a subtle licorice flavor; if it's unavailable, delete it and increase tarragon leaves to 1 cup.

MAKES: 6 main-dish servings

- 1 head **iceberg lettuce** (1 lb.), rinsed and drained
- 1 head **radicchio** (⅓ lb.), rinsed and drained
- 1 can (15 oz.) **artichoke bottoms,** drained
- 1¼ pounds **shelled cooked tiny shrimp,** rinsed and drained
- 1½ cups **cherry** or pear-shaped **tomatoes** (red, yellow, or a combination), rinsed, stemmed, and halved if larger than 1 inch

  Green Goddess dressing (recipe follows)

  Paper-thin **red onion** rings

  Fresh tarragon sprigs

  Breadsticks

  Salt and **pepper**

1. Cut iceberg lettuce lengthwise through core into 6 equal wedges. Also cut radicchio lengthwise into 6 equal

ROBERT HOLMES/CORBIS

wedges. Rinse and drain greens. Arrange 1 lettuce and 1 radicchio wedge on each dinner plate.

2. Place 1 artichoke bottom, cup side up, beside lettuce on each plate; reserve any extra for other uses. Mound shrimp equally in artichokes on plates, letting shrimp spill over edges. Arrange tomatoes alongside.

3. Spoon about half the Green Goddess dressing equally over salads. Garnish with onion rings, tarragon sprigs, and breadsticks. Offer remaining dressing and salt and pepper to add to taste.

Per serving: 446 cal., 63% (279 cal.) from fat; 27 g protein; 31 g fat (4.8 g sat.); 15 g carbo (3.7 g fiber); 944 mg sodium; 210 mg chol.

Green Goddess dressing. In a blender or food processor, combine 1 cup **regular mayonnaise** or reduced-fat sour cream (see notes); 5 cups lightly packed **spinach leaves** (6 oz.), rinsed and drained; 1 cup lightly packed **parsley,** rinsed and drained; ½ cup lightly packed **fresh tarragon** leaves, rinsed and drained; ½ cup lightly packed **fresh chervil,** rinsed and drained (or more tarragon; see notes); 1 tablespoon **lemon juice;** 1 tablespoon chopped **shallot;** and 1 can (2 oz.) **anchovies,** drained. Whirl until very smooth. Serve, or chill airtight up to 1 week. Makes 2 cups.

Per tablespoon: 56 cal., 89% (50 cal.) from fat; 0.8 g protein; 5.6 g fat (0.8 g sat.); 0.9 g carbo (0.3 g fiber); 96 mg sodium; 4.8 mg chol.

Decades of diners at San Francisco's Palace Hotel (left) have spooned its addictive Green Goddess dressing over salads (above).

Chinese Chicken

Historians point an uncertain finger to California for the first public appearance of Chinese chicken salad. Chef Lee of the New Moon Cafe (now the New Moon Restaurant), which opened in Los Angeles in 1950, claims to have brought the recipe from Hong Kong. And in San Francisco in the early 1960s, Cecilia Chiang served Chinese chicken salad at the Mandarin.

Sunset's first recipe for Chinese chicken salad, published in 1970, came from Ming's of Palo Alto. Former owner Dan Lee reports that the restaurant started serving the top-selling dish sometime between 1958 and 1960. "We based it on a Chinese dish called finger-shredded chicken," he recalls.

We've rolled all our favorite components together: a hot mustard hit like Ming's, crunch from crisp cabbage and carrots with the iceberg, puffy fried bean thread noodles, thicker chow mein noodles, nuts—and the convenience of bagged salad mixes.

Four-Crunch Chinese Chicken Salad

PREP AND COOK TIME: About 1 hour

NOTES: The Asian ingredients are available in most supermarkets. If Asian salad mix is unavailable, use a combination of shredded iceberg lettuce, butter lettuce, cabbage, and carrots (2 quarts total), plus 1 cup canned chow mein noodles. A 2½-pound cooked chicken yields about 4 cups shredded meat. Up to 1 day ahead, shred the chicken, make the dressing (chill both airtight), and fry the noodles (store airtight at room temperature).

MAKES: 6 main-dish servings

¼ cup **dry mustard**

½ cup **seasoned rice vinegar**

¼ cup **soy sauce**

2 tablespoons **Asian** (toasted) **sesame oil**

½ teaspoon **Chinese five spice**

Salad oil

2½ ounces **dried bean thread noodles** (*saifun*)

4 cups shredded skinned **cooked chicken** (see notes)

2 packages (10 oz. each) **Asian salad mix with chow mein noodles** (see notes)

1 cup coarsely chopped **fresh cilantro**

1 cup finely chopped **roasted, salted almonds** or cashews

1. In a small bowl, stir mustard and ¼ cup water until smooth. Let stand 10 minutes. Stir in vinegar, soy sauce, sesame oil, and Chinese five spice.

2. Pour 1½ inches salad oil into a 12- to 14-inch wok or 5- to 6-quart pan over medium-high heat. When oil reaches 375° (a bean thread noodle dropped in expands at once), adjust heat to maintain temperature.

3. Meanwhile, inside a large paper bag, pull bean thread noodles apart. Drop a handful of noodles into hot oil; noodles should puff and expand immediately. With a wire strainer or slotted spoon, push noodles down into oil. When they stop crackling, in about 10 seconds, turn entire mass over and cook until crackling stops, a few seconds longer. Lift noodles out and drain on towels. Repeat to cook remaining noodles.

4. Line a wide, shallow bowl (at least 8 qt.) or dinner plates with noodles.

5. In a large bowl, gently mix chicken, salad mix with chow mein noodles (reserve dressing for other uses), cilantro, and almonds with mustard dressing. Spoon salad over bean thread noodles and serve immediately (noodles soften as they stand).

Per serving: 704 cal., 66% (468 cal.) from fat; 35 g protein; 52 g fat (7.1 g sat.); 26 g carbo (5.4 g fiber); 1,386 mg sodium; 83 mg chol.

Taco Salad

As Mexican food became part of mainstream Western dining, creative cooks began transferring elements of popular dishes like tacos to salad form. *Sunset* introduced the concept in 1954 with Mexican tostadas— "open-face sandwiches [that] serve as salads." By the 1970s, taco salad had grabbed the West's imagination, and during that decade we published nearly a dozen versions. It's been a perennial favorite.

Taco Salad with Tortilla Whiskers

PREP AND COOK TIME: About 50 minutes
NOTES: Up to 1 day ahead, shred lettuce (chill airtight) and make tortilla whiskers (store airtight at room temperature).

MAKES: 4 to 6 main-dish servings

3 **corn tortillas** (about 6 in. wide)

1½ tablespoons **olive oil**

About ¾ teaspoon **salt**

¾ teaspoon **chili powder**

¾ pound **boneless tender beef steak** such as top loin, fat trimmed, rinsed, and dried

1 tablespoon **distilled white vinegar**

½ teaspoon **ground cumin**

¼ teaspoon **ground cinnamon**

3 quarts finely shredded **romaine lettuce**

1 can (about 15 oz.) **reduced-sodium** or regular **black beans**, rinsed and drained

1 cup **shredded sharp cheddar cheese** (4 oz.)

1¼ cups **guacamole** (recipe follows)

½ cup **reduced-fat** or regular **sour cream**

¼ cup sliced **green onions**

2 cups **fresh tomato salsa**

1. Stack tortillas and cut into ⅛- to ¼-inch-wide strips. In a 12- by 17-inch baking pan, mix strips with 1 tablespoon olive oil, ¾ teaspoon salt, and chili powder.

2. Bake tortilla strips in a 425° regular or convection oven, stirring occasionally, until crisp, 5 to 8 minutes. Pour out of pan and let cool.

3. Meanwhile, cut steak across the grain into ¼-inch-thick slices. Stack a few slices at a time and cut into strips about ¼ inch wide and 3 to 4 inches long. In a small bowl, mix vinegar, cumin, and cinnamon.

4. Place a 10- to 12-inch nonstick frying pan over high heat. When hot, add remaining ½ tablespoon oil and quickly swirl to coat bottom. Add beef at once and stir just until browned on the surface and still pink in the center (cut to test), about 1 minute. Add vinegar mixture and stir just until liquid is evaporated, about 1 minute.

5. Mound lettuce in the center of a large, shallow bowl. Surround with tortilla whiskers. Layer beans, cheese, then steak evenly over lettuce. Top with guacamole and sour cream and sprinkle with green onions. Gently spoon salad onto plates; serve with salsa.

Per serving: 426 cal., 53% (225 cal.) from fat; 27 g protein; 25 g fat (8 g sat.); 30 g carbo (7.2 g fiber); 1,100 mg sodium; 60 mg chol.

Guacamole. Pit and peel 2 ripe **avocados** (1 lb. total). In a bowl, using a fork, coarsely mash avocados with 1 tablespoon *each* **lime juice** and chopped **fresh cilantro** and 1 teaspoon minced **garlic**. Add **salt** and **cayenne** to taste. Serve, or chill airtight up to 2 hours. Makes 1¼ cups.

Per tablespoon: 27 cal., 85% (23 cal.) from fat; 0.3 g protein; 2.6 g fat (0.4 g sat.); 1.3 g carbo (0.3 g fiber); 1.8 mg sodium; 0 mg chol. ◆

Crisp tortilla whiskers surround seasoned steak, black beans, and guacamole in an old favorite.

In mint condition

A familiar green herb livens up
beautiful dishes for spring

Fresh mint
makes a julep
the coolest
sip of all.

■ Parsley, sage, rosemary, and thyme might have inspired a catchy tune, but mint evokes visions of riches. As herbs go, it consorts with better-heeled companions than most—bourbon and sugar in frosty silver glasses on hot derby days, bittersweet chocolate over plump scoops of Italian gelato. But just as mint can cover more territory than you'd expect in your garden, it can reach far beyond predictable flavor matches in your kitchen. We've freshly minted a few other culinary couples— lobster and mango, scallops and peas, lamb and parmesan cheese—for entrées rich in fresh flavor.

By Paula Freschet • Photographs by James Carrier • Food styling by Karen Shinto

Classic Mint Julep

PREP TIME: About 5 minutes

MAKES: 1 serving

- 1 **lemon,** rinsed

  About 2 teaspoons **sugar**

- 5 **fresh mint** sprigs (3 to 5 in.), rinsed and drained

  About 1½ cups **crushed** or shaved **ice**

- ¼ cup **bourbon**

  About 2 tablespoons **club soda**

Roasted tomatoes and seared scallops bask in a mint green broth.

1. With a vegetable peeler or a sharp knife, pare a 2-inch strip of peel (yellow part only) from the lemon, then cut into long, thin shreds. Cut lemon in half and rub 1 cut side on the rim of a glass (10 to 12 oz.) to moisten; save lemon for other uses. Pour 2 teaspoons sugar on a small plate and dip moist glass rim in it to coat evenly, then pour sugar into glass.

2. Add 4 mint sprigs to glass. With a wood spoon, crush mint sprigs with sugar to bruise the leaves and release the herb's flavor. Fill glass with ice. Add bourbon, then fill to rim with club soda. Let stand until glass is frosty, about 2 minutes. Garnish with lemon peel and remaining mint sprig. Sip julep through a straw, adding more sugar to taste.

Per serving: 182 cal., 1% (1.8 cal.) from fat; 0.8 g protein; 0.2 g fat (0 g sat.); 11 g carbo (1.6 g fiber); 14 mg sodium; 0 mg chol.

Seared Scallops in Mint Broth with Peas and Roasted Tomatoes

PREP AND COOK TIME: About 1¼ hours

NOTES: Assembling this dish is easy if you handle the steps in this order: While the tomatoes roast, purée the broth mixture, but for best color, don't heat it until you brown the scallops. As soon as the scallops are cooked, start the wine sauce in the frying pan, then fill the bowls as it cooks.

MAKES: 4 servings

- 4 **Roma tomatoes** (3 to 4 oz. each)

  Salt, pepper, and **sugar**

- 1 cup firmly packed **fresh mint** leaves, rinsed and drained

- 1 tablespoon **olive oil**

- 2¼ cups fat-skimmed **chicken broth**

- 2 cups **frozen petite peas,** thawed

  Fresh mint sprigs, rinsed and drained

- 1 pound **scallops** (each 1½ to 2 in. wide)

- 1 tablespoon **butter** or margarine

- ¼ cup **dry white wine**

1. Rinse tomatoes, cut in half lengthwise, and place, cut sides up, in a 9-inch-wide pan. Sprinkle lightly with salt, pepper, and sugar. Finely chop enough of the mint leaves to make 2 tablespoons; mix with ½ tablespoon olive oil. Pat mixture onto cut sides of tomatoes. Drizzle evenly with remaining ½ tablespoon oil. Bake in a 400° regular or convection oven until browned on top, about 1 hour. (If pan juices begin to blacken, add a few tablespoons water to pan.)

2. Meanwhile, measure 2 cups broth. In a blender or food processor, whirl peas, remaining mint leaves, and as much of the broth as needed to process until very smooth. Pour into a 2- to 3-quart pan and add remainder of the 2 cups broth.

3. Rinse and drain scallops; pat dry. Sprinkle lightly with salt and pepper. Set a 10- to 12-inch nonstick frying pan over medium-high heat and add butter; when it's just beginning to turn brown, lay scallops, flat side down, in pan. Cook until well browned, about 2 minutes; turn to brown other sides well, and cook until scallops are opaque but still moist-looking in center (cut to test), 2 to 3 minutes longer. Meanwhile, bring pea-mint broth to a simmer over high heat, about 4 minutes. Transfer scallops equally to wide, shallow soup bowls.

4. Add remaining ¼ cup broth and the wine to frying pan; turn heat to high and stir often to free browned bits until reduced to about ⅓ cup, 2 to 4 minutes.

5. Set 2 tomato halves on scallops in each bowl, pour hot pea-mint broth equally around scallops. Drizzle wine sauce over tomatoes, and garnish bowls with mint sprigs.

Per serving: 297 cal., 25% (75 cal.) from fat; 31 g protein; 8.3 g fat (2.6 g sat.); 24 g carbo (11 g fiber); 408 mg sodium; 45 mg chol.

Parmesan-Herb Lamb Chops with Mint Aioli

PREP AND COOK TIME: 25 to 30 minutes

NOTES: *Panko,* the coarse dried bread crumbs that give these lamb chops a crunchy coating, are sold in Japanese food markets and in the Asian food sections of well-stocked supermarkets. Stored airtight, they keep for months.

MAKES: 4 servings

2 tablespoons **white wine vinegar**

1 teaspoon **Dijon mustard**

1 clove **garlic,** peeled and minced or pressed

¼ teaspoon **coarse-ground pepper**

¾ cup **panko** (see notes) or other fine dried bread crumbs

1½ tablespoons **grated parmesan cheese**

2 tablespoons chopped **fresh mint** leaves

8 **lamb rib chops** (each about ¾ in. thick, 2 lb. total)

2 tablespoons melted **butter** or margarine

Mint aioli (recipe follows)

Salt

1. In a shallow bowl, mix vinegar, mustard, garlic, and pepper. In another shallow bowl, stir together panko, cheese, and mint.

2. Trim excess fat from lamb and discard. Rinse chops and pat dry. One at a time, turn chops in vinegar mixture to coat well; lift out and press firmly in panko mixture, turning to coat all sides. Place chops slightly apart in a lightly oiled 10- by 15-inch pan; drizzle evenly with butter.

3. Bake in a 500° regular or convection oven until coating is browned and meat is medium-rare (pink) in center of thickest part (cut to test), 10 to 14 minutes, turning once after 5 minutes. Serve with mint aioli and season to taste with salt.

Per serving: 300 cal., 54% (162 cal.) from fat; 23 g protein; 18 g fat (7.8 g sat.); 8.4 g carbo (0.6 g fiber); 221 mg sodium; 87 mg chol.

Mint aioli. In a small bowl, mix ½ cup **mayonnaise,** 2 tablespoons finely chopped **fresh mint** leaves, 1 tablespoon minced **garlic,** and 1½ teaspoons **white wine vinegar.** Add **salt** to taste. If making up to 1 day ahead, cover and chill. Makes ½ cup.

Per tablespoon: 101 cal., 98% (99 cal.) from fat; 0.3 g protein; 11 g fat (1.6 g sat.); 0.9 g carbo (0.1 g fiber); 79 mg sodium; 8.1 mg chol.

Mango-Mint Lobster Rolls

PREP AND COOK TIME: 45 to 50 minutes

NOTES: Edible rice paper wrappers are sold in Asian food markets and some well-stocked supermarkets. To make a dazzling main-dish salad, eliminate the rice paper and increase salad mix to 6 cups. Mound the salad mix on plates, top with lobster, mango, onion, mint, and cucumbers, then drizzle with the mint-lime dipping sauce.

MAKES: 4 servings

1 **spiny** or rock **lobster tail** (about 12 oz.), thawed if frozen

1 **firm-ripe mango** (about 1 lb.)

1 piece **English cucumber** (5 in. long, 6 oz.), rinsed

¼ cup slivered **red onion**

⅓ cup **fresh mint** leaves, rinsed and drained

12 rounds **edible rice paper wrappers** (also called dried egg roll or dried spring roll wrappers; about 8 in.)

Mint goes into a crunchy coating for lamb chops, in a classic flavor pairing.

Sweet mango, mint, and lobster are wrapped with cucumber in delicate rice paper.

Mint Gelato with Bittersweet Chocolate Sauce

PREP AND COOK TIME: About 1 hour

NOTES: Garnish servings with fresh mint sprigs if desired.

MAKES: About 1 quart; 4 to 6 servings

- 3 cups **milk**
- ¾ cup **sugar**
- ½ cup chopped **fresh mint** leaves
- 1 thin strip **lemon** peel (about 2 in., yellow part only)
- 1 piece **vanilla bean** (2 to 3 in.), slit open lengthwise, or 1 teaspoon vanilla
- 6 **large egg** yolks
- 4 ounces **bittersweet** or semisweet **chocolate**, finely chopped
- ½ cup **whipping cream** or half-and-half (light cream)

1. In a 3- to 4-quart pan, combine milk, sugar, chopped mint, lemon peel, and vanilla bean (if using extract, add in step 3). Stir over medium heat just until sugar is dissolved, 1 to 2 minutes.

2. In a bowl, beat egg yolks to blend. Whisk in warm milk mixture; return to pan. Stir over medium-low heat, scraping pan with a spatula, until custard coats the back of a spoon in a thin layer, 10 to 12 minutes (don't boil).

3. Pour mixture through a fine strainer into a large bowl; discard lemon peel and mint. Rinse vanilla bean, let dry, and reserve for other uses (if using vanilla extract, stir into strained custard). Nest bowl in ice water and stir mixture often until cold, 20 to 30 minutes. Or cover and chill until cold, at least 2 hours, or up to 2 days.

4. Meanwhile, in a microwave-safe container, combine chocolate and cream. Heat in a microwave oven at full power (100%), stirring every 30 seconds, until chocolate is soft, about 1½ minutes total. Stir until smooth.

5. Pour custard mixture into an ice cream maker (1-qt. or larger capacity). Freeze according to manufacturer's directions until mixture is firm enough to scoop, dasher is hard to turn, or machine stops, 25 to 30 minutes.

6. Scoop softly frozen gelato into bowls, or for firmer gelato, freeze at least 1½ hours or up to 1 week. Spoon chocolate sauce over gelato (if desired, warm sauce in microwave oven at full power for 30 seconds, then stir).

Per serving: 385 cal., 51% (198 cal.) from fat; 8.7 g protein; 22 g fat (11 g sat.); 42 g carbo (0.7 g fiber); 75 mg sodium; 252 mg chol. ◆

- 3 cups **salad mix** (about 3 oz.), rinsed and crisped

  Mint-lime dipping sauce (recipe follows)

1. In a 4- to 5-quart pan over high heat, bring about 2 quarts water to a boil. Add lobster; when boil resumes, reduce heat and simmer until meat is opaque but still moist-looking in center of thickest part (cut to test), about 10 minutes. Drain lobster, then immerse in ice water until cool to touch, about 5 minutes; drain again.

2. Meanwhile, cut pit and peel from mango and discard; cut fruit into small chunks. Cut cucumber lengthwise into thin slices; stack slices and cut stack lengthwise to make ⅜-inch-wide sticks.

3. With scissors, snip underside of lobster shell free from back shell and lift off. Pull out lobster tail; discard shell. If vein is present, pull out and discard. Coarsely chop meat and put into a bowl. Add mango, onion, and mint; mix gently.

4. Shape 2 rolls at a time: Immerse 1 rice paper round in a large bowl of hot tap water, lift out, drain briefly, and lay on a counter. Let stand until paper is soft and pliable, about 30 seconds. Repeat to moisten another rice paper round and lay on counter.

5. Working quickly, spoon about ¹⁄₁₂ of the filling down the center of each wrapper, leaving 1 inch of the wrapper bare at both ends. Lay ¹⁄₁₂ of the cucumber sticks parallel to the filling and mound ½ cup salad mix on top.

6. Fold the 1-inch ends of each wrapper over filling, then, holding filling in place with your fingers, roll wrapper snugly around it. Press wrapper edges to seal; if edges are too dry to stick, moisten with a little more hot water. Set each roll, seam down, on a platter and cover airtight with plastic wrap.

7. Repeat steps 4 through 6 to fill remaining rice paper wrappers (replace water in bowl as needed to keep hot).

8. If making rolls up to 3 hours ahead, chill. Uncover rolls and cut each in half diagonally; if desired, stand rolls upright, cut ends up. Dip into mint-lime sauce to eat.

Per serving: 293 cal., 2% (4.5 cal.) from fat; 14 g protein; 0.5 g fat (0.1 g sat.); 59 g carbo (3.2 g fiber); 184 mg sodium; 32 mg chol.

Mint-lime dipping sauce. In a small bowl, mix ¼ cup **lime juice**; ¼ cup **seasoned rice vinegar**; 2 tablespoons finely chopped **fresh mint** leaves; ½ to 1 rinsed **fresh red** or green **jalapeño chili** (1-oz. size), minced; and 1 tablespoon *each* **Asian fish sauce** (*nuoc mam* or *nam pla*), minced **shallot**, and minced **garlic**. If making up to 1 day ahead, cover and chill. Makes ⅔ cup.

Per tablespoon: 12 cal., 15% (1.8 cal.) from fat; 0.4 g protein; 0.2 g fat (0 g sat.); 2.4 g carbo (0.1 g fiber); 180 mg sodium; 0 mg chol.

Wrap mint ice cream with chocolate; layer strawberry or peach with oatmeal cookies.

KEVIN CANDLAND; FOOD STYLING: BASIL FRIEDMAN

The coolest sandwiches

Homemade cookies layered with ice cream bring chills of delight

By Elaine Johnson

One of the happiest sounds of my childhood summers was the jingling strain of the ice cream truck, faint and far off at first, then getting louder and nearer. By the time the little white vehicle reached the bottom of our hill, a swarm of neighborhood kids had converged—barefoot, dimes clutched in hands—to buy their favorite treats: Nutty Buddies, Push-Ups, and those wonderfully squishy vanilla ice cream sandwiches made with slightly cardboardy chocolate cookies.

My taste for ice cream sandwiches has grown up, as I have. It turns out that making them at home is as fun as buying them from the ice cream vendor. And homemade versions are several notches higher on the gourmet ladder. They can be customized with favorite flavors to boot—slabs of crunchy oatmeal cookies packed with peach or strawberry ice cream, chewy brownies layered with coffee or mint–chocolate chip ice cream (I dunk the works in melted chocolate).

Full-fat ice cream freezes the hardest, producing the neatest, easiest-to-handle bundles; lower-fat ice cream makes sandwiches that are softer and a little less tidy, but still perfectly delicious.

Crunchy Ice Cream–Cookie Sandwiches

PREP AND COOK TIME: About 1$\frac{1}{2}$ hours, plus at least 3 hours to freeze

NOTES: Buy ice cream in cardboard cartons, not plastic tubs (you need to be able to snip the cartons and peel them off, then quickly slice the ice cream). It's easiest to use ice cream in rectangular cartons, but round ones will work.

MAKES: 9 sandwiches

About $\frac{1}{3}$ cup **butter** or margarine

$\frac{1}{2}$ cup firmly packed **brown sugar**

$\frac{1}{4}$ cup **dark corn syrup**

1 teaspoon **vanilla**

$\frac{1}{4}$ teaspoon **salt**

2 cups **quick-cooking rolled oats**

$\frac{1}{2}$ cup **sweetened shredded dried coconut** or sliced almonds

1 quart **strawberry** or peach **ice cream**

1. Lightly butter a 10- by 15-inch rimmed baking pan. Line pan with a 15- by 20-inch piece of cooking parchment, spreading it smooth (edges will stick up above pan rim). Butter and flour parchment.

2. In a 2- to 3-quart pan over medium-high heat, melt $\frac{1}{3}$ cup butter, stirring often, about 2 minutes. Remove from heat and add sugar, corn syrup, vanilla, and salt; stir until smooth. Add oats and coconut; mix until evenly blended. Scatter oat mixture in lined pan; with a long metal spatula, spread mixture level.

3. Bake in a 375° regular or convection oven until cookie is browned at edges and bubbling all over, about 10 minutes. Let cool just until cookie begins to firm but is still warm, about 2 minutes (if too cool, cookies will crack when cut). Invert a 12- by 15-inch baking sheet over pan; holding pan and sheet together, carefully invert cookie onto sheet. Cut into 18 rectangles 2$\frac{1}{2}$ by 3$\frac{1}{3}$ inches. Let cool.

4. Return 9 of the cookies, smooth side up, to lined pan, setting them side by side in a single layer to make a snug rectangle in half the pan.

5. With scissors, snip through opposite sides of ice cream carton from top to bottom; peel carton from ice cream and discard. Working quickly, place ice cream on a board (if round, trim off 1 side and lay on flat side). With a long, heavy knife, cut crosswise into $\frac{1}{2}$-inch-thick slices. Set slices side by side over cookies in pan; fill in any bare spots with ice cream scraps to cover completely, and trim off any excess. Freeze remaining ice cream for other uses. Cover ice cream with remaining 9 cookies, matching the orientation of bottom cookies. Wrap pan airtight and freeze until ice cream is firm, at least 3 hours.

6. Lift ice cream sandwiches on parchment from pan and transfer to a board. Cut between cookies; trim sandwich edges with a knife, if desired. Serve, or wrap sandwiches individually airtight and freeze up to 2 weeks.

Per sandwich: 338 cal., 40% (135 cal.) from fat; 5 g protein; 15 g fat (5.8 g sat.); 49 g carbo (2.1 g fiber); 202 mg sodium; 36 mg chol.

Mocha Brownie Ice Cream Stacks

PREP AND COOK TIME: About 1¾ hours, plus at least 3½ hours to freeze

MAKES: 12 stacks

    About ¼ cup (⅛ lb.) **butter** or margarine

    About ½ cup **all-purpose flour**

1 ounce **unsweetened chocolate**

½ cup **sugar**

2 teaspoons finely ground **coffee**

1 teaspoon **vanilla**

1 **large egg**

1 quart **coffee ice cream**

2 packages (12 oz. each) **semisweet chocolate chips**

6 tablespoons **solid vegetable shortening**

1. Butter and flour 12 muffin cups, each about 2½ inches wide.

2. In a 1- to 2-quart pan over medium-low heat, stir ¼ cup butter and the unsweetened chocolate often until melted and smooth, 5 to 6 minutes. Remove from heat and stir in sugar, ground coffee, vanilla, and egg. Add ½ cup flour and mix until smooth. Spoon batter equally into muffin cups (about 3½ teaspoons per cup).

3. Bake in a 350° regular or convection oven just until brownie edges spring back when lightly pressed, 6 to 8 minutes. Loosen brownies from pans with a knife and tip out onto a rack. Let cool completely, about 20 minutes.

4. Line unwashed muffin cups with 6-inch squares of plastic wrap, letting edges extend above cup rims. Return brownies to cups.

5. Scoop a ¼-cup portion of ice cream onto each brownie. (If ice cream is too hard to scoop, warm—1 carton at a time, if using more than 1—in a micro-

Cover cookies with ice cream, then the ice cream with more cookies, and freeze.

Scoop ice cream onto brownies, freeze until hard, then dunk in chocolate.

wave oven at half power (50%) just until slightly softened, checking every 10 seconds.) With the bottom of a glass, press ice cream in each cup down to form a firm, even layer. Wrap pans airtight and freeze until ice cream is firm, at least 3 hours.

6. Lift brownie stacks in plastic from muffin cups; pull off plastic wrap and discard. Place stacks slightly apart on a 12- by 15-inch baking sheet and put back in freezer.

7. Pour 1 inch of water into the bottom of a double boiler or into a 3- to 4-quart pan; bring to a boil over high heat, then reduce heat to a simmer. Combine chocolate chips and shortening in top of double boiler or a metal bowl or pan that fits snugly in pan with water; set over simmering water (bottom of bowl shouldn't touch water). Stir mixture occasionally just until chocolate is soft, 3 to 5 minutes. Remove from double boiler and stir until chocolate is melted and mixture is smooth. If hotter than 95° to 100°, continue stirring often until cooled to this range. Replace simmering water in bottom of double boiler or in other pan with very hot tap water. Set chocolate mixture over hot water (top container should sit on, or just above, water), not over heat.

8. Working quickly with 2 forks, lower 1 brownie stack at a time into chocolate and turn to coat all sides. Lift stack out and return, flat side down, to chilled pan (don't move stack once it touches frozen pan, or chocolate will stick to pan and peel off ice cream; if this happens, patch with melted chocolate). Reserve extra chocolate mixture for other uses. Freeze stacks until ice cream is firm, at least 30 minutes.

9. Dab any ice cream drips off stacks with a paper towel. Serve stacks, or wrap individually airtight and freeze up to 2 weeks.

Per stack: 506 cal., 57% (288 cal.) from fat; 6.3 g protein; 32 g fat (16 g sat.); 53 g carbo (0.5 g fiber); 94 mg sodium; 111 mg chol.

Brownie–Mint Ice Cream Stacks

Follow directions for **mocha brownie ice cream stacks** (preceding), but omit ground coffee and instead of coffee ice cream, use mint–chocolate chip. If desired, use 1½ pounds **mint-flavor chocolate** instead of chocolate chips. Makes 12 stacks.

Per sandwich: 438 cal., 55% (243 cal.) from fat; 4.9 g protein; 27 g fat (15 g sat.); 50 g carbo (0.5 g fiber); 79 mg sodium; 48 mg chol. ◆

The Wine Guide

By Karen MacNeil-Fife

Salad solutions

■ Remember the old chestnut "white wine with fish; red wine with meat"? Besides being too dogmatic, that so-called rule implies that wine is meant for only fish and meat. But what about vegetables? What about bountiful salads?

As I scanned the recipes for main-course classics (page 110), I started thinking about how, after pairing salads and wine for almost 20 years, I not only choose wines I've discovered work well, but I also instinctively tweak my salad ingredients to maximize the match. Here's what I've found on both sides of the equation.

• With green salads, think "green" wines. The wine with just about the greenest flavors in the world is Sauvignon Blanc (also called Fumé Blanc), which has a sassy, bold, herbal tilt. For a lighter green note, go with Pinot Grigio.

• High-acid salad ingredients (goat cheese, tomatoes, citrus fruits) pair best with high-acid wines like Sauvignon Blanc, Riesling, sparkling wines, and Champagne.

• Salty and pungent ingredients like anchovies present fewer partnering problems than you'd expect, as long as the wine is very fruity and possibly even a tad sweet to offset the saltiness. With a classic Caesar, for example, one of the best choices is a California or Washington State Riesling. Chinese chicken salad needs a fruity wine as a counterpoint to its soy sauce.

JAMES CARRIER

• You can improve the wine compatibility of any salad by adding or increasing protein (meat, seafood, eggs, and cheese). That's why a Cobb salad, with its roast chicken, bacon, eggs, and blue cheese, works effortlessly with many wines, especially those in the fruity, low-tannin range, like a Beaujolais.

• Certain "bridge" ingredients can connect the flavors in a salad with those in a wine. My favorites are roasted nuts (especially hazelnuts and walnuts), avocados, aged gouda or dry jack cheese, and mayonnaise.

• There are also bridge techniques—adding grilled vegetables rather than uncooked ones, and roasted garlic instead of raw.

• Since bold vinegars make wines taste harsh, use softer vinegars in dressings. Balsamic is the softest of

SALAD GREATS

Most good wines for salad have two things in common: They're not very oaky (which eliminates most Chardonnays), and they're not very tannic (which takes care of many Merlots and Cabernet Sauvignons). Here are some of my favorites.

■ **Delamotte Brut nonvintage (Champagne), $30.** Cold Champagne on a warm summer night turns a salad into a feast. Delamotte has all the finesse, balance, and personality you could hope for.

■ **Château Carbonnieux Bordeaux Blanc 1998 (Pessac-Leognan, France), $28.** This wine isn't cheap, but it's sensational with salads. Minerally and sharp, with pinpoint freshness, it has a shower of lemon drops, hints of honey, and a wonderful touch of pear.

■ **Chateau Souverain Sauvignon Blanc 1999 (Alexander Valley, CA), $12.** With wonderful aromas and flavors reminiscent of snow peas, grass, herbs, and green figs, this Sauvignon is as zesty and crisp as a salad itself.

■ **Zenato Pinot Grigio 2000 (Veneto, Italy), $10.** Gertrude Stein's infamous quip about Oakland, California ("there is no there there"), could be applied to many Pinot Grigios as well. Not this one. Floral and creamy, it's laced with light peach, almond, and herbal notes.

all, but aged sherry vinegar is also fabulous. Or consider a substitute for the vinegar (or at least part of it): orange juice, lemon juice, or even the wine you plan to drink (if it's white).

• Finally, dress salads with the very best extra-virgin olive oil you can find and afford. As European winemakers (many of whom also produce olive oil) have always known, supple, peppery, citrusy olive oil is one of the greatest partners wine has ever had. ◆

food guide

By Jerry Anne Di Vecchio

Meal out of the blue

■ In Arizona and New Mexico, corn is grown in many colors, including red, white, and blue. The blue variety, finely ground into meal, is a ubiquitous ingredient in Southwest native foods. Blue cornmeal is put to work in tortillas and chips, plus a host of other intriguing, lesser-known dishes, such as Hopi paper bread.

With its pleasant parched flavor and slightly crunchy texture, blue cornmeal has also gained popularity in recent years in everyday non-native foods like pancakes and waffles. Near Santa Fe, where I often visit for the cultural contrasts of opera and rodeo, I came across these thick, platter-size blue cornmeal pancakes, as light and tender as any I've eaten. You can find blue cornmeal in natural-food stores and most well-stocked supermarkets throughout the West.

JAMES CARRIER; FOOD STYLING: BASIL FRIEDMAN

Blue Corn Pancakes

PREP AND COOK TIME: **15 to 20 minutes**
NOTES: Serve these pancakes with butter and warm maple syrup.
MAKES: 6 pancakes; 6 servings

1 cup **all-purpose flour**

1 cup **blue cornmeal**

1¼ teaspoons **baking powder**

¾ teaspoon **baking soda**

1½ teaspoons **sugar**

½ teaspoon **salt**

1 **large egg**

1½ cups **buttermilk**

Butter or salad oil

1. In a large bowl, mix flour, blue cornmeal, baking powder, baking soda, sugar, and salt.

2. Add egg and buttermilk. Whisk until batter is well moistened and there are no lumps.

3. Place a nonstick griddle or a 10- to 12-inch nonstick frying pan over medium heat (350°). When griddle is hot, adjust heat to maintain temperature; coat griddle lightly with

butter and spoon batter in ½-cup portions onto it. Cook until pancakes are browned on the bottom and edges begin to look dry, about 2 minutes; turn with a wide spatula and brown other sides, 1½ to 2 minutes longer.

4. Serve pancakes as cooked, or arrange in a single layer on 1 or 2 baking sheets (12 by 15 in. each) and keep warm in a 150° oven up to 15 minutes.

Per serving: 213 cal., 14% (29 cal.) from fat; 7.2 g protein; 3.2 g fat (1.5 g sat.); 38 g carbo (1.8 g fiber); 541 mg sodium; 41 mg chol.

Recycled, refurbished, and refueled

NEW SERVICE

■ According to the Barbecue Industry Association, 85 percent of households in this country have barbecues, and 60 percent of them are fueled by propane gas. But not only do propane gas tanks need refilling now and then at qualified service facilities, they also tend to get rusty and worn out by the elements. Blue Rhino now offers a fresh solution to both problems. At any of its 26,000 locations nationwide (including major home-supply chains like Home Depot and Orchard Supply Hardware), you can swap your empty, worn, even old gas tank for a full, clean, refurbished, safety-inspected one, for just $2 to $3 more than a standard refill costs. What's more, Blue Rhino tanks have a simple label device that shows when they contain less than enough fuel for two hours of grilling (the absence of an indicator is known to lead to major crises, when the flames die out under half-cooked steaks). To locate a Blue Rhino tank exchange near you, go to www.bluerhino.com and enter your zip code, or call (800) 258-7466. Be sure to specify whether you need a threaded or quick-coupling valve (gas grills vary).

food guide

Surefire success with chicken

■ Ask a food professional what he or she cooks at home to elicit rave reviews, and the answer is both predictable and surprising—rarely is the recipe complicated, although it may have professional flair. Christine Keff, chef-owner of Seattle's Flying Fish and Fandango restaurants, confirms these patterns with her favorite home recipe for chicken thighs. She applies her Flying Fish know-how to Southeast Asian ingredients (all of which are readily available in the supermarket), marinating the meat and making a chili glaze well ahead of time. The thighs, boned so they soak up more flavor from the coconut marinade and cook more quickly, sizzle away on the grill at the last minute, then are finished off with the tangy, sticky glaze.

Larry Peter's holy cow

■ No breed of cow has a more ardent proponent than the Jersey does in Larry Peter. Jerseys fell out of favor, he says, because they don't produce as much milk as Holsteins. But the milk the gentle brown cows do give is proportionately higher in butterfat and protein. In Peter's opinion, it's ideal for making cheeses, which he does at Spring Hill Farm in Petaluma, California.

Peter's cheeses range from fresh and delicate to complex and developed, including cheddars, jacks, and several proprietary creations: Breeze, similar to but slightly firmer than a white-coated brie; a soft Italian much like teleme; golden, buttery Giana, similar to Italy's taleggio; and pale yellow, smooth, mild Old World Portuguese, like a cheese Peter grew up with. Spring Hill Jersey Cheeses are sold in natural-food stores, such as Whole Foods, and in other specialty food and cheese shops in the West. They can also be ordered from Spring Hill Jersey Cheese, 4235 Spring Hill Rd., Petaluma, CA 94952; call (707) 762-3446 or e-mail springhillcheese@yahoo.com.

Ginger-marinated chicken thighs are set off by a sweet-and-sour glaze—chef-inspired simple home cooking.

Sticky Coconut Chicken

PREP AND COOK TIME: About 30 minutes, plus at least 1 hour to marinate

MAKES: 6 to 8 servings

6 to 8 **boned, skinned chicken thighs** (1¼ to 1½ lb. total)

¾ cup **canned coconut milk** (stir before measuring)

1 tablespoon minced **fresh ginger**

1 teaspoon fresh-ground **pepper**

1 teaspoon **hot chili flakes**

Chili glaze (recipe follows)

4 or 5 **green onions**, ends trimmed, cut lengthwise into thin slivers (including tops)

1. Rinse chicken and pat dry. In a large bowl, mix coconut milk, ginger, pepper, and hot chili flakes. Add chicken and mix; cover airtight and chill at least 1 hour or up to 1 day.

2. Lift chicken from bowl, reserving marinade; pull thighs open and lay flat on a lightly oiled barbecue grill over a solid bed of hot coals or high heat on a gas grill (you can hold your hand at grill level only 2 to 3 seconds); close lid on gas grill. Cook, turning thighs as needed to brown on both sides, until meat is no longer pink in center of thickest part (cut to test), 10 to 12 minutes, basting frequently with remaining marinade (use it all).

3. Transfer thighs to a warm platter and pour the chili glaze evenly over meat; garnish platter with green onions.

Per serving: 147 cal., 48% (71 cal.) from fat; 17 g protein; 7.9 g fat (4.9 g sat.); 1.5 g carbo (0.3 g fiber); 77 mg sodium; 71 mg chol.

Chili glaze. In a 2- to 3-quart pan, combine ¾ cup **rice vinegar**, ½ cup **sugar**, 3 tablespoons **soy sauce**, and 1 teaspoon **hot chili flakes**. Bring to a boil over high heat and cook until mixture is reduced to ½ cup, 8 to 10 minutes. Use hot. If making glaze up to 1 week ahead, cover and chill; reheat before serving. Makes ½ cup.

Per tablespoon: 53 cal., 0% (0 cal.) from fat; 0.4 g protein; 0 g fat; 0.4 g carbo (0.1 g fiber); 386 mg sodium; 0 mg chol.

A plum-sweet tart

■ Heat makes a delicious impact on any red or purple plum. The skin blossoms with floral aromatics and develops a significant tang that seeps into the fruit as it softens while cooking. And when plum slices are neatly arranged on a thin layer of quickly prepared, firm-textured cake batter, they settle in as they bake, each pale to rosy fruit segment framed by a dark rim. The result is a simply beautiful summer dessert.

Plum Portrait Tart

PREP AND COOK TIME: 1¼ hours

NOTES: Top dessert wedges with slightly sweetened whipped cream, crème fraîche or sour cream, or vanilla ice cream.

MAKES: 8 to 10 servings

About ½ cup (¼ lb.) **butter** or margarine

½ cup plus 2 tablespoons **granulated sugar**

1 teaspoon grated **orange** peel

½ teaspoon **almond extract**

¼ teaspoon **salt**

3 **large eggs**

About 1 cup **all-purpose flour**

1 to 1¼ pounds **firm-ripe red-** or purple-**skinned plums**

1 to 2 tablespoons **powdered sugar**

1. Cut ½ cup butter into small pieces and put in a bowl. Add ½ cup granulated sugar and stir to combine, then beat with a mixer on high speed until well blended, about 2 minutes. Add orange peel, almond extract, salt, and eggs. Stir to mix, then beat on high speed until well blended and smooth, 3 to 4 minutes. Add 1 cup flour and stir to mix, then beat on high speed to blend.

2. Butter and flour an 11- to 11½-inch tart pan with removable bottom. Scrape batter into pan and spread level.

3. Rinse plums, cut in half, and pit; cut fruit into ¼-inch-thick slices. Overlap all the slices on batter; sprinkle with remaining 2 tablespoons granulated sugar.

4. Bake on the middle rack of a 375° regular or convection oven until batter that pops up around fruit is lightly browned and tart begins to pull away from pan sides, 35 to 45 minutes. Let cool about 10 minutes. Dust with powdered sugar (on the cut fruit, the sugar melts quickly).

5. Remove pan rim (if tart sticks, use a small knife to release it from the rim) and set on a plate. Serve hot, warm, or cool.

Per serving: 231 cal., 43% (99 cal.) from fat; 3.7 g protein; 11 g fat (6.5 g sat.); 29 g carbo (1.2 g fiber); 174 mg sodium; 90 mg chol.

Here's the rub

■ With all due respect to Shakespeare, "the rub" represents more than irony. In culinary terms, it's a seasoning mix like the one used at Tony's Meats & Specialty Foods in Littleton, Colorado. Mick Rosacci, who oversees the flavorful preparations at his family's two premium stores, recommends rubbing it onto a beef roast or steaks, then barbecuing or oven-roasting them.

Chipotle-Pepper Rub

PREP AND COOK TIME: About 5 minutes

NOTES: If making up to 1 week ahead, store airtight at room temperature.

MAKES: About ⅓ cup, enough for a 4- to 5- pound beef roast

3 **dried chipotle chilies** (each about 2 in. long)

2 tablespoons **black peppercorns**

1 tablespoon **pink peppercorns**

1 tablespoon **coarse salt,** such as sea salt or kosher salt

1 tablespoon **cumin seed**

Heat chipotles in a microwave oven at full power (100%) until they puff and smell slightly toasted, 15 to 30 seconds. Trim and discard stems. Slit chilies open; discard seeds and veins. Coarsely chop chilies. In a food processor or spice grinder, combine chilies, black peppercorns, pink peppercorns, salt, and cumin seed. Whirl until finely ground.

Per teaspoon: 5.5 cal., 33% (1.8 cal.) from fat; 0.2 g protein; 0.2 g fat (0 g sat.); 1.1 g carbo (0.4 g fiber); 277 mg sodium; 0 mg chol. ◆

The Quick Cook

Entrées for meals in 30 minutes or less

By Andrew Baker

Savory skewers

■ In Turkey, fast food often comes in the form of kebabs—skewered meats cooked on the grill. Almost any meat will do, even those that are ground. And if you blend a bold-flavored ground meat, like beef, with a milder choice, like turkey (the bird, not the country), the result is a fresh balance in taste—lightness from one side, more character from the other. You can get the same effect by combining lamb and chicken. These blended ground meats, seasoned and mixed with bread crumbs to retain juiciness, stand well on their own. But they are equally agreeable when brushed and served with easy sauces made of tomato, fruit, or herbs.

Tangy apricot sauce tops a turkey-beef kebab.

Turkey-Beef Kebabs

PREP AND COOK TIME: About 20 minutes

MAKES: 4 servings

- ½ pound **ground lean turkey**
- ½ pound **ground lean beef**
- 6 tablespoons **fine dried bread crumbs**
- 2 tablespoons minced **onion**
- 1 **large egg** yolk

  About ¼ teaspoon **salt**
- ⅛ teaspoon **pepper**

  Sauce (optional; choices follow)

1. In a bowl, mix turkey, beef, bread crumbs, onion, egg yolk, ¼ teaspoon salt, and pepper.
2. Divide meat mixture into 4 equal portions. Pat each portion around a metal skewer (flat ones are easiest to handle) to form a log 1 inch thick and 7 to 8 inches long.
3. Lay skewers on a lightly oiled barbecue grill over a solid bed of hot coals or high heat on a gas grill (you can hold your hand at grill level only 2

to 3 seconds); close lid on gas grill. Rotating skewers to brown meat evenly, cook until kebabs are no longer pink in center (cut to test), 7 to 10 minutes. If desired, about 1 minute before meat is done, brush lightly with the sauce of your choice.

Per serving: 247 cal., 47% (117 cal.) from fat; 22 g protein; 13 g fat (4.4 g sat.); 7.9 g carbo (0.5 g fiber); 317 mg sodium; 130 mg chol.

Chicken-Lamb Kebabs

Follow directions for **turkey-beef kebabs,** preceding, but use **ground chicken** instead of turkey and **ground lean lamb** instead of beef.

Per serving: 232 cal., 43% (99 cal.) from fat; 23 g protein; 11 g fat (3.4 g sat.); 7.9 g carbo (0.5 g fiber); 313 mg sodium; 139 mg chol.

Sauces

Golden Apricot Sauce

PREP AND COOK TIME: About 5 minutes

NOTES: If making up to 1 week ahead, cover and chill.

MAKES: ½ cup

- ½ cup **rice vinegar**
- ¼ cup **dried apricots**
- 3 tablespoons **sugar**

1. In a microwave-safe bowl, combine vinegar, apricots, and sugar. Heat in a microwave oven at full power (100%) until vinegar is boiling, about 3 minutes.
2. Pour mixture into a blender or food

processor and whirl until smooth. Scrape into a small bowl. Serve warm or cool.

Per tablespoon: 28 cal., 0% (0 cal.) from fat; 0.1 g protein; 0 g fat; 7.2 g carbo (0.3 g fiber); 0.4 mg sodium; 0 mg chol.

Orange-Ginger Catsup

PREP AND COOK TIME: About 5 minutes

NOTES: If making up to 1 week ahead, cover and chill.

MAKES: About ⅔ cup

- ½ cup **catsup**
- ¼ teaspoon grated **orange peel**
- 2 tablespoons **orange juice**
- ½ teaspoon minced **fresh ginger**
- ¼ teaspoon fresh-ground **pepper**

1. In a microwave-safe bowl, combine catsup, orange peel, orange juice, ginger, and pepper. Cover loosely with plastic wrap.
2. Heat in a microwave oven at full power (100%) until mixture is bubbling, stirring once or twice, about 1 minute total. Scrape into a small bowl to serve.

Per tablespoon: 18 cal., 5% (0.9 cal.) from fat; 0.2 g protein; 0.1 g fat (0 g sat.); 4.6 g carbo (0.3 g fiber); 178 mg sodium; 0 mg chol.

Herb Vinaigrette

PREP TIME: About 5 minutes

NOTES: If making up to 2 days ahead, cover and chill.

MAKES: About 6 tablespoons

- ¼ cup **sherry vinegar**
- 1½ tablespoons **olive oil**
- 1 tablespoon minced **parsley**
- 1 teaspoon **ground cumin**
- ½ teaspoon **dried oregano**
- ½ teaspoon **hot chili flakes**

  Salt

In a bowl, whisk together vinegar, oil, parsley, cumin, oregano, and chili flakes. Add salt to taste.

Per tablespoon: 34 cal., 94% (32 cal.) from fat; 0.1 g protein; 3.5 g fat (0.5 g sat.); 0.9 g carbo (0.1 g fiber); 1 mg sodium; 0 mg chol. ◆

Frank Sinatra ate here

These classic Los Angeles eateries have withstood the test of time

By Norman Kolpas

In a city and an era always on the lookout for the next new thing, any place that endures for more than a decade seems a historic survivor. The ever-fickle nature of the restaurant business makes it even harder to find a place with any sort of staying power.

Yet a select few Los Angeles dining establishments have withstood the test of time, thanks to noteworthy food, service, ambience, or all of the above. The following restaurants, which range in age from 82 to a relatively youthful 37 years, offer the chance to savor what life in Southern California was like way back in—well, another century.

The **Musso & Frank Grill,** affectionately known as Musso's, opened in 1919, when Hollywood was not yet on the map. Still a favorite hangout for deal makers and wannabes, it works its spell with a comfortably faded atmosphere and a menu that, though printed daily, seems eternal. The steaks, chops, and chicken potpies are still as tasty as ever. *11–11 Tue–Sat. 6667 Hollywood Blvd., Hollywood; (323) 467-7788.*

Gone are the days of elegant railroad dining, but at the **Pacific Dining Car,** they live on. In the original section, you almost expect to hear the clickety-clack of iron wheels on railroad tracks. Original owners Fred and Lovey Cook built the railroad dining car replica to distinguish their new steak house; that structure endures in the entrance and front dining area of the much-expanded restaurant. This dining classic still enjoys a stellar reputation for its USDA prime beef, a wine list lauded by *Wine Spectator,* and excellent service. *Open 24 hours daily. 1310 W. Sixth St., Los Angeles; (213) 483-6000.*

Ask Los Angeles Mayor Richard Riordan why he bought stock in the **Original Pantry** back in 1980, and he might well cite bad service at the top of his list. The first time he ate there, his waiter insulted him. "I came from New York City and sort of missed that out here," he chuckles. Though some customers might object to the sometimes brusque manner of the staff in this bare-bones, linoleum-floored joint, since 1924 they've been queuing up for huge portions of bargain-priced food—macaroni and cheese, lamb curry, prime rib, and steaks—all from the menu scribbled on a wall-mounted blackboard. "I still eat there about three times a week," says the mayor—and he's not alone. *Open 24 hours daily. 877 S. Figueroa St., Los Angeles; (213) 972-9279.*

Lawrence Frank all but dispensed with menus when he opened **Lawry's the Prime Rib** on the block known as Restaurant Row in 1938. Sure, evening guests arriving in the stately dining room were and still are welcomed with printed lists. But those are to explain the various sizes of cuts sliced from the huge, succulent beef roasts that carvers wheel from table to table in gleaming metal carts. Service remains downright theatrical: Order a salad and watch as your server spins a giant metal bowl on a bed of ice while pouring dressing from a sauceboat held high above. *5–10 Mon–Fri (until 11 Fri), 4:30–11 Sat, 4–10 Sun. 100 N. La Cienega Blvd., Beverly Hills; (310) 652-2827.*

A more subdued atmosphere reigns at the **Polo Lounge,** decorated in the signature greens and pinks of the establishment it has served since 1941, the Beverly Hills Hotel. Once a hangout of Frank Sinatra and the Rat Pack, this landmark retains a classic Tinseltown air. Though some things have changed—the cuisine, for example, improved considerably when executive chef Katsuo Sugiura (a.k.a. Chef Suki) introduced his East-West fusion menu in 1997—almost everyone occupying its secluded booths still looks like an old-time producer or agent. Midday, the pretty, palm-fringed patio fills with Beverly Hills ladies who lunch. *7 A.M.–1 A.M. daily. 9641 Sunset Blvd., Beverly Hills; (310) 276-2251.*

Taylor's Steak House has been serving meat lovers since 1953. With its cozy booths and dim lighting, it's the perfect spot for an old-fashioned rendezvous. The house specialty is the culotte steak, a 2-inch-thick cut from the end of the top sirloin. *11:30–10 Mon–Fri, 4–10 Sat–Sun (until 10:30 Sat). 3361 W. Eighth St., Los Angeles; (213) 382-8449.*

Relative youngster though it is, **Dan Tana's,** opened in 1964 by none other than Dan Tana, feels like as much of an L.A. bastion as any of its older peers. Credit that to a menu, prepared for the last 31 years by chef Mate Mustac, that offers definitive renditions of such classics as Caesar salad, mozzarella marinara, linguini with clams, and New York steak. Each night, show-biz regulars fill the red leather booths beneath hanging Chianti bottles in the little yellow bungalow just south of the Sunset Strip. *5 P.M.–2 A.M. daily. 9071 Santa Monica Blvd., West Hollywood; (310) 275-9444.* ◆

Kitchen Cabinet

Readers' recipes tested in *Sunset's* kitchens

By Paula Freschet

Sweet and Sticky Oven-Barbecued Pork Back Ribs

Mary Lou Nuffer, Orange, California

These ribs have been served for the annual luau fellowship dinner of Mary Lou Nuffer's church for at least the last 30 years. She gives Evelyn Smith credit for the original recipe. Even though this is barbecue season, the ribs are easier to bake than grill because the sticky sauce is inclined to burn.

PREP AND COOK TIME: About 1½ hours, plus 2 hours to marinate

MAKES: 5 or 6 servings

- ¾ cup **soy sauce**
- ¾ cup **orange marmalade**
- ½ cup **pineapple juice**
- ¼ cup **honey**
- 3 cloves **garlic,** peeled and minced or pressed
- 2 tablespoons minced **fresh ginger**
- 1 tablespoon **lemon juice**
- 2 teaspoons chopped **fresh rosemary** leaves or crumbled dried rosemary
- ¼ teaspoon **pepper**
- 4 to 5 pounds **pork back ribs,** fat trimmed

1. In a bowl, mix soy sauce, orange marmalade, pineapple juice, honey, garlic, ginger, lemon juice, rosemary, and pepper.

2. Rinse ribs, pat dry, and place half in each of 2 plastic food bags (1-gal. size). Pour half the soy sauce mixture into each bag; seal bags, turn to coat ribs with marinade, and set in a large bowl. Chill at least 2 hours or up to 1 day, turning occasionally.

3. Line a rimmed pan (11 by 17 in. or 12 by 15 in.) with foil (the drippings char). Set a rack in pan. Lift ribs from marinade and arrange in a single layer, edges curving down, on rack. Pour marinade into a bowl.

4. Bake ribs in a 350° regular or convection oven, basting with marinade every 20 minutes for the first hour, until meat is well browned and pulls easily from bones, about 1¼ hours total. Transfer ribs to a platter

Honey-sweet, ginger-laced glaze conquers restraint and decorum. Stack napkins high to manage the mess.

and cut apart between bones.

Per serving: 716 cal., 54% (389 cal.) from fat; 38 g protein; 43 g fat (16 g sat.); 45 g carbo (0.2 g fiber); 2,219 mg sodium; 172 mg chol.

Black Bean–Mango Salsa

Tami J. Harmon, Yuma, Arizona

Tami Harmon first tried this salsa on her honeymoon in Hawaii. When she asked for the recipe, the restaurant presented it to her with best wishes. Serve the salsa with tortilla chips; spooned over grilled fish such as swordfish, sea bass, or halibut; or simply as a salad.

PREP TIME: About 15 minutes

MAKES: About 4 cups

- 1 can (15 oz.) **black beans,** rinsed and drained
- 1 cup diced **firm-ripe mango**
- 1 **Roma tomato** (about ¼ lb.), rinsed, cored, and coarsely chopped
- ½ cup *each* diced **orange** and **yellow bell pepper** (or all 1 color)
- ¼ cup finely diced **onion**
- 1 tablespoon minced **fresh jalapeño chili**
- 1 tablespoon chopped **fresh cilantro**
- 1 clove **garlic,** peeled and minced
- 2 tablespoons **lime juice**
- 1 tablespoon **red wine vinegar**

  Salt and **pepper**

In a bowl, mix beans, mango, tomato, bell peppers, onion, jalapeño, cilantro, garlic, lime juice, and vinegar. Add salt and pepper to taste. Serve, or cover and chill up to 1 day.

Per ¼ cup: 26 cal., 6.9% (1.8 cal.) from fat; 1.2 g protein; 0.2 g fat (0 g sat.); 5.3 g carbo (1.1 g fiber); 44 mg sodium; 0 mg chol.

Roasted Vegetable Pasta Primavera

A. Ferber, Denver

A vegetarian, A. Ferber finds it no challenge to create pasta dishes to suit her tastes. This is one that received rave reviews at a large family gathering.

PREP AND COOK TIME: About 50 minutes

MAKES: 4 servings

- 2 tablespoons **olive oil**
- 1 **red bell pepper** (about ½ lb.), rinsed, stemmed, seeded, and cut into ¾-inch-wide strips
- 1 **onion** (½ lb.), peeled and sliced ½ inch thick
- 2 **Roma tomatoes** (¼ lb. each), rinsed and cut into quarters
- ½ pound **green beans,** rinsed, ends trimmed
- 6 cloves **garlic,** peeled and cut into quarters
- ½ cup **dried tomatoes** (5 oz. total), cut into ¼-inch-wide strips
- 2 tablespoons **pine nuts**
- 9 ounces **fresh linguine**

  About ¾ cup **shredded parmesan cheese**

  Salt

1. In an 11- by 17-inch pan, mix oil with bell pepper, onion, and fresh tomatoes.

2. Bake in a 425° regular or convection oven for 15 minutes. Add beans and garlic, mix, and bake until tomatoes are soft and well browned around edges, 25 to 30 minutes longer.

3. Meanwhile, in a small bowl, pour ½ cup boiling water over dried tomatoes. Let stand, stirring occasionally, until tomatoes are soft, about 20 minutes.

4. Also, in an 8- to 10-inch frying pan over medium heat, shake pine nuts frequently until pale gold, 1 to 2 minutes; pour from pan.

5. When vegetables are almost done, bring about 3 quarts water to a boil in a 5- to 6-quart pan over high heat.

6. When vegetables are done, add dried tomatoes and their soaking liquid to the pan. Stir to release browned bits in pan and keep mixture warm. At the same time, add the linguine to the boiling water and cook until pasta is barely tender to bite, 4 to 5 minutes. Drain pasta and pour into roasting pan; mix well, lifting with 2 forks. Add pine nuts and ½ cup cheese, mix, and spoon pasta into wide bowls. Add more cheese and salt to taste.

Per serving: 507 cal., 27% (135 cal.) from fat; 24 g protein; 15 g fat (4.4 g sat.); 72 g carbo (12 g fiber); 343 mg sodium; 58 mg chol.

Southwest Grilled Shrimp Salad

Margaret Pache, Mesa, Arizona

To complement the Southwest flavor orientation of this refreshing grilled shrimp salad, Margaret Pache suggests a garnish of chopped pecans. This may not sound regional, but in fact, pecan production flourishes in Arizona.

PREP AND COOK TIME: About 1 hour

MAKES: 4 main-dish servings

- 1 pound (16 to 20 per lb.) **shelled, deveined shrimp,** rinsed
- ¼ cup **seasoned rice vinegar**
- ¼ cup **tequila**
- 2 tablespoons **orange-flavor liqueur** or orange juice
- 3 tablespoons **salad oil**

- 1 tablespoon minced **fresh jalapeño chili**
- 1 clove **garlic,** peeled and minced or pressed
- ¼ cup minced **green onions** (including tops)
- ½ teaspoon **ground cumin**
- ⅛ teaspoon **cayenne**
- 1 **orange** (¾ lb.)
- 2 **firm-ripe avocados** (about ½ lb. each)
- 2 quarts **salad mix** (½ lb.), rinsed and crisped
  Chili-orange dressing (recipe follows)
  Salt

1. In a bowl, mix shrimp, vinegar, tequila, liqueur, oil, jalapeño, garlic, green onions, cumin, and cayenne. Cover and chill 30 minutes or up to 1 day, mixing occasionally.

2. Meanwhile, cut peel and white membrane from orange. Working over a bowl to catch juice, cut between fruit and inner membranes to release segments into bowl. Squeeze juice from membranes into bowl; discard membranes and peel.

3. Pit, peel, and slice avocados; add to oranges and mix gently.

4. Drain shrimp, reserving marinade. Thread shrimp onto flat metal skewers. Lay skewered shrimp on a barbecue grill over very hot coals or very high heat on a gas grill (you can hold your hand at grill level only 1 to 2 seconds); close lid on gas grill. Cook shrimp, turning once and brushing frequently with marinade for the first 2 to 3 minutes, until bright pink and opaque but still moist-looking in center of thickest part (cut to test), 4 to 5 minutes total.

5. Mound salad mix equally on dinner plates. Push hot shrimp from skewers. Arrange shrimp, orange segments, and avocados equally on salad mix; moisten equally with chili-orange dressing, and add salt to taste.

Top swordfish with colorful tropical salsa for a quick, spectacular entrée.

Per serving: 436 cal., 56% (243 cal.) from fat; 26 g protein; 27 g fat (3.9 g sat.); 24 g carbo (3.9 g fiber); 641 mg sodium; 173 mg chol.

Chili-orange dressing. In a small bowl, mix ¼ cup **seasoned rice vinegar,** 2 tablespoons *each* **salad oil** and **orange juice,** 2 teaspoons minced **fresh jalapeño chili,** and 1 clove **garlic,** minced. Makes ½ cup.

Per tablespoon: 39 cal., 79% (31 cal.) from fat; 0.1 g protein; 3.4 g fat (0.4 g sat.); 2.1 g carbo (0 g fiber); 149 mg sodium; 0 mg chol.

Apricots with Brandy, Lemon, and Honey

Kathleen Moretto, Stockton, California

When a friend dropped by with a box of ripe apricots on a very hot day, Kathleen Moretto ruled out turning the fruit into pies or jams in favor of a cooler cooking medium: her microwave oven. She plumped the apricots with brandy, lemon, and honey, then spooned the luxurious mixture over ice cream to make an ideal summer dessert.

PREP AND COOK TIME: **15 to 20 minutes**

MAKES: 4 or 5 servings

- 8 to 10 **ripe apricots** (about 1 lb. total), rinsed, drained, halved, and pitted
- ¼ cup **golden raisins**
- ½ cup firmly packed **brown sugar**
- ¼ cup **brandy**
- 2 tablespoons **lemon juice**
- 2 tablespoons **honey**
- 1 tablespoon **butter** or margarine, cut into small pieces
  About 1 quart **vanilla ice cream**

1. Place apricots, cut side up, in a microwave-safe 9- or 10-inch pie pan or shallow round casserole. Sprinkle apricots with raisins and brown sugar.

2. In a 2-cup glass measure, combine brandy, lemon juice, honey, and butter. Heat in a microwave oven on full power (100%) until butter is melted, about 30 seconds. Stir and pour evenly over apricots.

3. Cover apricots and heat in a microwave oven at full power until juices are bubbling and fruit is hot, about 5 minutes; let stand about 5 minutes.

4. Meanwhile, scoop the ice cream into bowls. Ladle fruit and juices over ice cream.

Per serving: 434 cal., 29% (126 cal.) from fat; 5.2 g protein; 14 g fat (8.6 g sat.); 69 g carbo (1.5 g fiber); 120 mg sodium; 53 mg chol. ◆

Celebrate the Fourth of July with a neighborhod barbecue—burgers, salads, and a grand pie. Article begins on page 132.

July

PAUL BOUSQUET (2)

All-American barbecue

A neighborhood
comes together for
the Fourth of July

I t's the kind of spread that conquers restraint: big, juicy burgers with your favorite fixings, fresh corn on the cob, smoky baked beans. Kids clamber to see the edible American flag (with stripes made of hot dogs). Volunteers handle the grilling, and a line forms as fast as you can say "cheese." • Such a scene—full of old-fashioned, small-town camaraderie—is an annual highlight for five Boulder families. For eight years now, the Heyman-McConnells and their friends have been celebrating the Fourth with a neighborhood block party. "Even though this party's on a grand scale," says Jane McConnell, whose home is the base of operations, "we've got it down to a system. One night before the party, we meet to set it all up, and it all comes together seamlessly." • We've acquired recipes, ideas, and tips from the Boulder gang (adding a few of our own) to create a menu that can work for a gathering of two or three families or for an entire block party. The dishes serve about 10 people; scale the quantities or number of dishes up or down, divvy up the cooking, and make an old-fashioned feast your new tradition.

By Amy McConnell with Paula Freschet • Food photographs by James Carrier

Chips, Dips, and Salsas

Classic Western Burgers*
with Special Slaw*

Hot Dogs and Buns

Grilled Corn on the Cob

Quick Baked Beans with Smoked Bacon*

Greens with Chèvre and Berries*

Artichoke, Fennel, and Tomato Salad*

Jane's Famous Dilled Potato Salad*

Sliced Watermelon

Old Glory Cherry-Blueberry Pie*

Mile-High Banana Cream Pie*

Fire-Engine Red
Cranberry-Raspberry Spritzer*

Sodas, Beer, and Wine

Recipes provided

all-american barbecue

Classic Western Burgers

PREP AND COOK TIME: About 1⅓ hours

NOTES: To make bread crumbs, whirl about 2 slices of fresh bread, torn into pieces, in a food processor or blender. The special slaw builds an array of condiments right into this burger. If desired, however, offer a condiment bar of your favorites: lettuce, avocados, tomatoes, pickles, mayo, mustard, and catsup.

MAKES: 10 servings

- 10 slices **thick-cut bacon** (about ¾ lb. total)
- 2 **large eggs**
- ⅔ cup **milk**
- 1 **onion** (about 8 oz.), peeled and minced
- 2 teaspoons minced **garlic**

  About 1¼ teaspoons **salt**

  About ½ teaspoon **pepper**
- 3 pounds **ground lean** (about 7% fat) **beef**
- 1 cup soft **bread crumbs** (see notes)
- 10 slices **red onion** (each ¼ in. thick and 3 to 4 in. wide)
- 10 slices (about 4 by 4 in.) **extra-sharp white** or yellow **cheddar cheese** (about 5 oz. total)
- 10 **hamburger buns** (each about 4 in. wide; 3 oz.), split in half

  Special slaw (recipe follows)

1. In a 10- to 12-inch frying pan over medium-high heat, cook bacon, in batches if necessary, turning occasionally, until browned on both sides and crisp, 8 to 10 minutes. With tongs, transfer to paper towels to drain. When cool, break each slice in half.

2. Meanwhile, in a large bowl, beat eggs, milk, onion, garlic, 1¼ teaspoons salt, and ½ teaspoon pepper to blend. Add beef and bread crumbs and mix gently. Form into 10 equal patties, each about 4½ inches wide.

3. Brush onion slices lightly on both sides with bacon fat in pan. Discard remaining fat.

4. Lay patties and onion slices on a barbecue grill over a solid bed of hot coals or high heat on a gas grill (you can hold your hand at grill level only 2 to 3 seconds); close lid on gas grill. Cook, turning meat and onions once to brown on both sides, until a thermometer inserted in center of thickest part of meat registers 160° (no longer

Greens with chèvre and berries

pink in center), 6 to 8 minutes total.

5. About 2 minutes before patties are done, top each with a slice of cheese. Also lay bun halves, cut side down, on grill and toast 1 to 2 minutes.

6. Set bun bottoms on a platter or plates. With a wide spatula, transfer patties to bun bottoms. Top each with a grilled onion slice, 2 pieces of bacon, and a spoonful of special slaw. Add salt and pepper to taste. Cover with bun tops.

Per serving: 718 cal., 40% (288 cal.) from fat; 46 g protein; 32 g fat (12 g sat.); 60 g carbo (4.8 g fiber); 1,317 mg sodium; 152 mg chol.

Special Slaw

PREP TIME: About 45 minutes

NOTES: With a medley of flavors reminiscent of Thousand Island dressing, this slaw is just as good on its own as it is smothering the classic Western burger (preceding). If making up to 1 day ahead, cover and chill.

MAKES: 10 servings

- ½ cup **plain nonfat yogurt**
- ¼ cup **mayonnaise**
- 3 tablespoons **sweet pickle relish**
- 2 tablespoons **tomato-based chili sauce** (for seafood cocktails)
- 1 tablespoon **coarse-grain Dijon mustard**
- 10 cups finely shredded **green cabbage**
- 2 cups finely shredded **carrots**
- ¾ cup diced (¼ in.) **red bell pepper**
- ½ cup thinly sliced **green onions**, including tops

  Salt and **pepper**

1. In a large bowl, mix yogurt, mayonnaise, pickle relish, chili sauce, and mustard.

2. Add cabbage, carrots, bell pepper,

Artichoke, fennel, and tricolor tomato salad

Greens with Chèvre and Berries

PREP TIME: About 1 hour

NOTES: Basil-flavor olive oil is available in well-stocked supermarkets and specialty food shops. If making vinaigrette (step 1) up to 2 hours ahead, cover and let stand at room temperature.

MAKES: 10 servings

- ⅔ cup **dried cranberries**
- 2 tablespoons chopped **dried apricots**
- 6 tablespoons **rice vinegar**
- ¼ cup **basil-flavor** or plain **extra-virgin olive oil**
- 4 quarts **salad mix** (about 12 oz.), rinsed and crisped
- 4 ounces fresh **chèvre** (goat) **cheese,** coarsely crumbled
- 1 cup **blueberries,** rinsed and drained

   Salt and **pepper**

1. In a 2-cup glass measure or small microwave-safe bowl, combine 2 tablespoons cranberries, apricots, and vinegar. Heat in a microwave oven at full power (100%) until steaming, about 1 minute. Let stand at room temperature or chill until cool.

2. In a blender or food processor, whirl fruit mixture until smooth. Pour purée back into glass measure; add oil and whisk to blend.

3. Put greens in a wide, shallow bowl. Add ⅔ of the vinaigrette and mix gently to coat. Scatter cheese, blueberries, and remaining cranberries evenly over greens. Drizzle with remaining vinaigrette. Add salt and pepper to taste.

Per serving: 133 cal., 62% (82 cal.) from fat; 3 g protein; 9.1 g fat (3.1 g sat.); 11 g carbo (1.3 g fiber); 67 mg sodium; 9 mg chol.

Artichoke, Fennel, and Tricolor Tomato Salad

PREP TIME: About 30 minutes

NOTES: If making up to 4 hours ahead, don't add basil; cover and chill. Add basil just before serving, and mix gently.

MAKES: 10 servings

- 2 jars (6½ oz. each) **marinated artichoke hearts,** drained (reserve marinade)
- 2 tablespoons **balsamic vinegar**
- 1 tablespoon **Dijon mustard**
- 1 teaspoon minced **garlic**

and green onions; mix well. Season to taste with salt and pepper.

Per serving: 87 cal., 47% (41 cal.) from fat; 2 g protein; 4.6 g fat (0.7 g sat.); 10 g carbo (2.6 g fiber); 168 mg sodium; 3.5 mg chol.

Quick Baked Beans with Smoked Bacon

PREP AND COOK TIME: About 1 hour

NOTES: If assembling through step 2 up to 1 day ahead, cover and chill; bake chilled beans about 50 minutes.

MAKES: 10 servings

- 6 ounces **thin-sliced apple wood–smoked** or regular **bacon** (about 6 slices), cut into ¾-inch pieces
- 2 **onions** (about 1 lb. total), peeled and chopped
- 3 cans (28 oz. each) **Boston-style baked beans**
- ½ cup **catsup**
- 2 tablespoons firmly packed **brown sugar**
- 1 tablespoon **dry mustard**

1. In a 5- to 6-quart pan over medium-high heat, stir bacon often until browned and crisp, 6 to 8 minutes. With a slotted spoon, transfer to paper towels to drain. Discard all but 1½ tablespoons fat in pan.

2. Add onions to pan and stir often until they begin to brown and stick to bottom of pan, 7 to 9 minutes. Add beans and their liquid, catsup, brown sugar, dry mustard, and cooked bacon; mix well. Pour into a shallow 3-quart casserole.

3. Bake, uncovered, in a 350° regular or convection oven until beans are bubbling in the center, 30 to 40 minutes. Serve hot.

Per serving: 316 cal., 19% (59 cal.) from fat; 15 g protein; 6.6 g fat (2.3 g sat.); 56 g carbo (14 g fiber); 1,278 mg sodium; 22 mg chol.

1 head **fennel** (about 3 in. wide)

6 cups **cherry tomatoes** (use a mix of red, yellow, and orange, each about ¾ in. wide), rinsed and drained

1 cup **pitted calamata olives**

1 cup lightly packed rinsed **fresh basil** leaves (¾ to 1½ in. long)

½ cup slivered **red onion**

Fresh-ground **pepper**

1. In a wide, shallow bowl, whisk ¼ cup artichoke marinade (discard remainder or save for other uses), vinegar, mustard, and garlic.

2. Rinse and drain fennel. Cut off and save a few feathery green leaves for garnish. Trim off and discard remaining stalks, root end, and any bruised areas. Cut head in half lengthwise across widest dimension, then cut each half crosswise into paper-thin slivers.

3. Add fennel, tomatoes, olives, basil, onion, and artichoke hearts to dressing in bowl. Mix gently to coat. Garnish salad with reserved fennel leaves. Add pepper to taste.

Per serving: 107 cal., 56% (60 cal.) from fat; 2.2 g protein; 6.7 g fat (0.9 g sat.); 11 g carbo (4.1 g fiber); 493 mg sodium; 0 mg chol.

Jane's Famous Dilled Potato Salad

PREP AND COOK TIME: About 2 hours, plus at least 2 hours to chill

NOTES: If making up to 1 day ahead, cover and chill.

MAKES: 10 servings

4½ pounds **Yukon Gold** or other thin-skinned white **potatoes** (each about 2½ in. wide), scrubbed

2½ cups chopped **celery**

1 cup **mayonnaise**

⅔ cup **cider vinegar**

½ cup finely chopped **red onion**

⅓ cup **sweet pickle relish**

3 hard-cooked **large eggs,** shelled and chopped

⅔ cup chopped **parsley**

⅓ cup chopped **fresh dill**

Salt and **pepper**

Fresh dill sprigs

1. In a 6- to 8-quart pan, combine potatoes and 4 quarts water. Cover and bring to a boil over high heat. Reduce

heat and simmer until potatoes are tender when pierced, 25 to 30 minutes. Drain and let stand until cool enough to touch, about 15 minutes.

2. Meanwhile, in a large bowl, mix celery, mayonnaise, vinegar, onion, and pickle relish. Peel warm potatoes, cut into 1-inch chunks, and add to dressing; mix gently. Let stand at room temperature or chill until cool.

3. Add eggs, parsley, and chopped dill; mix gently and season to taste with salt and pepper. Cover and chill until cold, at least 2 hours. Garnish with dill sprigs.

Per serving: 365 cal., 47% (171 cal.) from fat; 6.1 g protein; 19 g fat (3.1 g sat.); 44 g carbo (3.5 g fiber); 237 mg sodium; 77 mg chol.

Old Glory Cherry-Blueberry Pie

PREP AND COOK TIME: About 1¾ hours, plus at least 3 hours to cool

NOTES: If using fresh cherries, buy about 1¾ pound; if using frozen, you'll need about 1½ packages, 16 ounces each.

MAKES: 8 to 10 servings

5 cups **fresh sweet, dark cherries,** rinsed and pitted, or frozen pitted cherries (see notes)

3 tablespoons **lemon juice**

1½ cups **fresh blueberries,** rinsed and drained, or frozen blueberries

1 cup **sugar**

¼ cup **cornstarch**

Flag pastry (recipe follows)

2 teaspoons **butter** or margarine, cut into small pieces

Vanilla ice cream (optional)

1. In a large bowl, mix cherries with 2 tablespoons lemon juice. In a smaller bowl, mix blueberries with remaining 1 tablespoon lemon juice. Combine sugar and cornstarch; gently stir 1 cup of the mixture into cherries and ¼ cup into blueberries.

2. Spoon cherry mixture over ¾ of the pastry in pan, leaving 1 quadrant free. Spoon blueberry mixture into unfilled area. Scatter butter evenly over fruit.

3. Top filling with stars and stripes as directed for flag pastry. Set pie in a foil-lined 13- by 17-inch baking pan.

4. Bake on the bottom rack of a 400° regular or convection oven until fruit is bubbling in the center and pastry is well browned, about 1 hour. If pastry

edges brown too quickly (check after 40 minutes), cover loosely with foil.

5. Let pie cool on a rack at least 3 hours; let stand at room temperature up to 8 hours. Cut into wedges and serve with ice cream, if desired.

Per serving: 387 cal., 37% (144 cal.) from fat; 3.8 g protein; 16 g fat (6.9 g sat.); 59 g carbo (2.3 g fiber); 197 mg sodium; 21 mg chol.

Flag Pastry

1. In a bowl, mix 2 cups **all-purpose flour** and ½ teaspoon **salt.** Add 6 tablespoons cold **butter** or margarine, cut into chunks, and 6 tablespoons cold **solid vegetable shortening,** cut into chunks. With a pastry blender or your fingers, cut in fats or rub in with your fingers until mixture forms pea-size pieces.

2. Sprinkle 4 tablespoons cold **water** over mixture and stir with a fork just until evenly moistened. Gently squeeze about ¼ cup of the dough into a ball; if it won't hold together, crumble lump back into bowl and sprinkle with more water, 1 tablespoon at a time; stir with a fork until evenly moistened.

3. With lightly floured hands, gently squeeze dough into a ball. Divide in half and pat each half into a 4-inch-wide round. Lay 1 round on a lightly floured surface. With a flour-coated rolling pin, roll firmly but gently in short strokes from center of dough outward to form a 12-inch-wide round. If edges split, push back toward center to make relatively smooth. Occasionally lift dough and dust underneath with flour to prevent sticking.

4. Fold dough round in half, lift gently without stretching, and lay folded edge across the middle of a 9-inch pie pan. Unfold pastry and ease into pan without stretching. Trim dough ¾ inch beyond pan rim.

5. Fill as directed for Old Glory cherry-blueberry pie (preceding).

6. On lightly floured board, roll remaining pastry dough into a 10-inch round. With a pastry wheel or a sharp knife, cut 6 strips (¾ in. wide) across center of round. Place filled crust in front of you with blueberry quadrant at the upper left. Lay the longest pastry strip across pie with 1 edge adjacent to bottom of blueberry quadrant, then evenly space remaining strips across pie parallel to first strip. Cut away portions of strips over blueberry filling. With a 1½-inch star-shaped cookie cutter, cut 6 stars from remaining pastry; arrange over blueberry filling.

Old Glory cherry-blueberry pie

blend. Stir about ½ cup of the hot milk mixture into yolks, then stir mixture back into pan. Return pan to medium-low heat and stir until mixture just begins to bubble, about 2 minutes. Remove from heat and stir in butter and 1 teaspoon vanilla.

3. Peel bananas. Slice half into chocolate pastry, covering bottom evenly. Pour half the warm custard evenly over bananas. Repeat to layer remaining bananas and custard. Cover surface of custard with plastic wrap. Chill until cold, at least 2 hours.

4. In a bowl, with a mixer on high speed, beat whipping cream and remaining 2 tablespoons sugar and 1 teaspoon vanilla until mixture holds soft peaks. Mound on pie and swirl to cover decoratively. Top with chocolate curls, if desired.

Chocolate pastry. In a food processor or a bowl, combine 1 cup **all-purpose flour**, ¼ cup **sugar**, 3 tablespoons **unsweetened cocoa**, and ¼ teaspoon **salt**; whirl or mix to blend. Add ½ cup (¼ lb.) **butter** or margarine, cut into chunks; whirl or rub in with your fingers until fine crumbs form. Add 1 **large egg** yolk and ½ teaspoon **vanilla**; whirl or mix with a fork until blended. Pour mixture into a 9-inch pie pan and press evenly over bottom and up sides to edge of rim. Bake in a 350° regular or convection oven just until crust is slightly darker around edges, 18 to 20 minutes. Let cool on a rack at least 1 hour.

Per serving: 421 cal., 51% (216 cal.) from fat; 5.8 g protein; 24 g fat (14 g sat.); 48 g carbo (1.4 g fiber); 272 mg sodium; 172 mg chol.

Fire-Engine Red Cranberry-Raspberry Spritzer

PREP TIME: About 10 minutes

NOTES: If you prefer a spritzer on the sweet side, use lemon-lime soda; add mineral water or soda just before serving. For an adult version, add 3 to 4 tablespoons vodka—or if you're adventurous, Campari—to each glass.

MAKES: 10 servings

In a 3- to 3½-quart glass pitcher, mix 5 cups **refrigerated** or canned **cranberry-raspberry juice blend** and ⅔ cup **grenadine**. Pour in 5 cups chilled **lemon-flavor mineral water** or lemon-lime soda (see notes) and add 1 **lemon** (about 5 oz.), rinsed and thinly sliced (ends discarded). Pour into tall, ice-filled glasses (at least 12 oz.).

Per serving: 111 cal., 1.6% (1.8 cal.) from fat; 0.3 g protein; 0.2 g fat (0 g sat.); 28 g carbo (0.7 g fiber); 4.2 mg sodium; 0 mg chol. ◆

---

7. Fold edge of bottom crust over ends of strips, flush with pan rim. Flute decoratively.

Per serving: 226 cal., 60% (135 cal.) from fat; 2.8 g protein; 15 g fat (6.3 g sat.); 20 g carbo (0.7 g fiber); 187 mg sodium; 19 mg chol.

Mile-High Banana Cream Pie

PREP AND COOK TIME: About 1¼ hours, plus at least 1 hour to cool crust

NOTES: To make the chocolate curls, pull a vegetable peeler or sharp knife lengthwise down the side of a semisweet chocolate bar at room temperature. Or as an alternative to the curls, sprinkle pie with unsweetened cocoa. You can bake chocolate pastry up to 1 day before filling it; cover and let stand at room temperature. If making pie through step 3 up to 4 hours ahead, cover and chill. Top with whipped cream and chocolate curls just before serving.

MAKES: 8 to 10 servings

> ¾ cup plus 2 tablespoons **sugar**
> ⅓ cup **cornstarch**
> ¼ teaspoon **salt**
> 2¼ cups **milk**
> 4 **large egg** yolks
> 2 tablespoons **butter** or margarine
> 2 teaspoons **vanilla**
> 3 ripe **bananas** (about 6 oz. each)
> **Chocolate pastry** (recipe follows)
> 1 cup **whipping cream**
> **Chocolate curls** (optional; see notes)

1. In a 1½- to 2-quart pan, combine ¾ cup sugar, cornstarch, and salt. Add milk and whisk to blend. Whisk over medium heat until mixture boils and thickens, taking care not to scorch. Remove from heat.

2. In a small bowl, beat egg yolks to

the flavor of lime

This tart green citrus works magic, course after course

By Andrew Baker • Photographs by James Carrier
Food Styling by Basil Friedman

Pale but intense lime curd is topped with coconut-flavored whipped cream. Salsa-spiked, herb-flecked broth (right) is ladled around crisp tortilla strips, avocado and lime slices, and more salsa.

■ A squeeze of lime juice is vital to many classic dishes. It's the kick in a margarita, the spark that ignites many curries, and the tart foil to sweetness in a host of desserts. Conveniently, for such an indispensable ingredient, limes are available year-round. Most of those in Western markets are the Persian variety—large, bright green, and highly acidic. They keep up to two weeks if you seal them with a sprinkle of water in a plastic bag and store them in the warmest part of your refrigerator. • We've flavored dishes for every course of the meal with this exquisitely mouth-puckering citrus. In some cases we've used a light hand, in others a generous one, but in each dish we've given the sour fruit some creamy or sweet ballast—avocado, honey, sugar, or coconut milk.

Arizona Tortilla Soup

PREP AND COOK TIME: About 1 hour

NOTES: This soup comes from Donna Nordin, chef-owner of Café Terra Cotta in Tucson and Scottsdale, Arizona. Make the salsa while the soup boils.

MAKES: 6 servings

- 4 **corn tortillas** (6 to 7 in.)
- 3 tablespoons **salad oil**
- 1 **onion** (4 to 5 oz.), peeled and finely chopped
- 1 teaspoon minced or pressed **garlic**
- 1 **dried bay leaf**
- 1/2 teaspoon **dried oregano**
- 1/2 teaspoon **black peppercorns**
- 1/2 teaspoon **hot chili flakes**
- 8 cups fat-skimmed **chicken broth**

    Salsa fresca (recipe follows)
- 1 **ripe** or firm-ripe **avocado** (about 8 oz.)
- 1 **lime** (about 3 oz.)
- 3/4 cup **shredded jack cheese**

    Salt and **pepper**

1. Stack tortillas and cut into 1-inch-wide strips. Pour oil into a 5- to 6-quart pan over high heat. When oil is hot, add tortilla strips and stir often until crisp and lightly browned, 2 to 3 minutes. Remove from heat and, with a slotted spoon, transfer tortilla strips to towels to drain.

2. Add onion and garlic to pan. Stir often over medium-high heat until onion is limp, 3 to 4 minutes. Add bay leaf, oregano, peppercorns, chili flakes, and broth. Bring to a boil over high heat and boil until reduced to about 6 cups, 20 to 25 minutes.

3. Meanwhile, whirl half the salsa fresca in a blender until coarsely puréed. Pit, peel, and thinly slice the avocado. Rinse lime and cut crosswise into thin slices; discard ends.

4. In wide soup bowls (at least 1 1/2-cup size), arrange equal portions of tortilla strips, remaining salsa, avocado slices, lime slices, and jack cheese.

5. Pour puréed salsa into hot soup, season to taste with salt and pepper, and ladle equally around tortilla strips and garnishes in bowls.

Per serving: 274 cal., 53% (144 cal.) from fat; 17 g protein; 16 g fat (4.1 g sat.); 18 g carbo (2.8 g fiber); 215 mg sodium; 15 mg chol.

Salsa Fresca

PREP TIME: **About 15 minutes**

MAKES: **About 2¼ cups**

- 1 pound **ripe** or firm-ripe **tomatoes**
- 1 **fresh jalapeño** or Fresno **chili**
- ¼ cup finely chopped **onion**
- ¼ cup chopped **fresh cilantro**

  About 3 tablespoons **lime juice**

  Salt and **pepper**

Rinse and core tomatoes and cut into about ¼-inch dice; put the tomatoes with their juices into a bowl. Rinse and stem the jalapeño; shake out seeds and cut out the veins. Finely chop the chili. Add it to the bowl, along with the onion, cilantro, and 3 tablespoons lime juice. Stir gently to mix, and add more lime juice and salt and pepper to taste.

Per tablespoon: 3.3 cal., 0% (0 cal.) from fat; 0.1 g protein; 0 g fat; 0.7 g carbo (0.2 g fiber); 1.3 mg sodium; 0 mg chol.

Ginger-Lime Beef Stir-fry

PREP AND COOK TIME: **About 30 minutes**

NOTES: Serve with hot cooked rice or spoon mixture onto crisp salad greens.

MAKES: **4 servings**

- 1 **red bell pepper** (about ½ lb.)
- 1 pound **boned beef top sirloin,** fat trimmed
- ½ teaspoon **salad oil**

(Continued on page 140)

Beef sirloin and red bell peppers get a bite from ginger and lime sauce.

1/3 cup **lime juice**

2 tablespoons **honey**

2 tablespoons **hoisin sauce**

2 teaspoons **soy sauce**

2 tablespoons minced **fresh ginger**

1/2 teaspoon **hot chili flakes**

1/4 cup minced **fresh cilantro**

1. Rinse, stem, and seed bell pepper; trim out and discard white veins. Cut pepper into strips about 1/4 inch wide and 2 inches long.

2. Rinse beef and pat dry. Cut across the grain into 1/16- to 1/8-inch-thick slices, then cut slices into bite-size pieces.

3. Pour oil into a 10- to 12-inch nonstick frying pan over high heat. When oil is hot, add bell pepper and stir just until tender-crisp to bite, about 3 minutes. Pour from pan into a bowl.

4. Add beef to pan and stir just until no longer pink, about 2 minutes. With a slotted spoon, transfer meat to bowl with pepper.

5. To meat juices in pan, add lime juice, honey, hoisin sauce, soy sauce, ginger, and chili flakes. Boil over high heat, stirring often, until mixture is reduced to about 1/3 cup, 5 to 6 minutes. Pour beef and bell pepper back into pan and stir until hot, about 30 seconds.

6. Spoon beef stir-fry onto plates and sprinkle with cilantro.

Per serving: 229 cal., 22% (51 cal.) from fat; 25 g protein; 5.7 g fat (1.8 g sat.); 18 g carbo (0.9 g fiber); 400 mg sodium; 69 mg chol.

Lime Tarts with Coconut Cream

PREP AND COOK TIME: About 1 1/4 hours, plus at least 1 hour to chill lime curd

NOTES: Tarts can be assembled in 10 minutes if you bake butter crusts and make lime curd ahead—up to 1 day for crusts, 3 days for curd.

MAKES: 6 servings

1/3 cup **sweetened shredded** or flaked **dried coconut**

2/3 cup **whipping cream**

1/3 cup **canned coconut milk** (stir before measuring)

2 to 3 tablespoons **powdered sugar**

Butter crusts (recipe follows)

Lime curd (recipe follows)

1. In an 8- to 10-inch frying pan over medium-high heat, stir coconut until lightly browned, 1 to 2 minutes; pour into a small bowl. Cover and let stand at room temperature up to 2 hours.

2. In another bowl, combine whipping cream, coconut milk, and powdered sugar. Beat with a mixer on high speed until coconut cream holds soft mounds. Cover and chill up to 2 hours. Whip to blend before using.

3. Remove pan rims from crusts, and set each crust on a dessert plate. Fill crusts equally with lime curd. Top each tart with equal portions of coconut cream and sprinkle with coconut.

Per serving: 749 cal., 58% (432 cal.) from fat; 9.9 g protein; 48 g fat (29 g sat.); 73 g carbo (1.3 g fiber); 389 mg sodium; 325 mg chol.

Butter Crusts

PREP AND COOK TIME: About 35 minutes

MAKES: 6 tart crusts (each 4 1/2 in. wide)

1 1/3 cups **all-purpose flour**

1/4 cup **sugar**

1/2 cup (1/4 lb.) **butter** or margarine, cut into small pieces

1 **large egg** yolk

1. In a food processor or bowl, combine flour and sugar. Add butter; whirl or rub in with your fingers until fine crumbs form. Add yolk; whirl or mix with a fork until dough holds together. Pat into ball.

2. Divide dough into 6 equal portions. Firmly and evenly press each one over bottom and up sides of a 4 1/2-inch tart pan with removable rim. Set pans slightly apart on a 14- by 17-inch baking sheet.

3. Bake in a 300° regular or convection oven until pale gold, 15 to 25 minutes; let cool at least 15 minutes. If making up to 1 day ahead, cool completely, wrap airtight, and store at room temperature.

Per crust: 279 cal., 52% (144 cal.) from fat; 3.5 g protein; 16 g fat (9.9 g sat.); 30 g carbo (0.7 g fiber); 158 mg sodium; 77 mg chol.

Lime Curd

PREP AND COOK TIME: About 50 minutes, plus at least 1 hour to chill

NOTES: This curd is delicious spread on shortbread or slices of pound cake, or served as a sauce over ice cream.

MAKES: About 2 1/2 cups

About 1 1/4 pounds **limes**, rinsed

1 cup **sugar**

5 **large eggs**

1/2 cup (1/4 lb.) **butter** or margarine, cut into chunks

1. With a vegetable peeler, pare green part of peel from 4 limes. Put peel and sugar in a food processor and whirl until peel is very finely chopped; let stand, covered, 30 minutes or up to 6 hours. Ream juice from limes. Measure 1 cup; save remainder for other uses.

2. Add the 1 cup lime juice to sugar mixture in food processor; whirl until sugar dissolves. Pour mixture through a fine strainer into a 2- to 3-quart pan, pressing liquid from peel; discard peel. Add eggs and whisk to blend; add butter.

3. Stir over medium-low heat until mixture thickly coats a metal spoon, about 15 minutes. Scrape into a bowl, cover, and chill until cold, at least 1 hour, or up to 3 days. Stir before using.

Per tablespoon: 51 cal., 51% (26 cal.) from fat; 0.8 g protein; 2.9 g fat (1.6 g sat.); 5.7 g carbo (0 g fiber); 31 mg sodium; 33 mg chol. ◆

food guide

By Jerry Anne Di Vecchio • Photographs by James Carrier

Denver flavors

Road food redux

During the long, see-America-first car trips of my youth, when truck stop cafes provided the best—and often the only—fare for travelers, I first encountered the Denver omelet, an egg mixture with bell peppers, onions, and ham. On more recent trips to the mile-high city in the heat of summer, my son-in-law's flourishing vegetable garden has inspired me to recapitulate those flavors in this simple main-dish pasta. The imprint of the old Denver omelet is visible, despite quite a few contemporary shifts: Pasta replaces the eggs, sautéed slivers of mellow green poblano chilies edge out the bell peppers, and the ham becomes crisp-baked bacon.

FOOD STYLING: BASIL FRIEDMAN

Denver Pasta Supper

PREP AND COOK TIME: About 1 hour

NOTES: If you have only 1 oven, cook the bacon first, then roast the tomatoes.

MAKES: 4 servings

  8 **Roma tomatoes** (3 to 4 oz. each, about 1¾ lb. total)
     About 1½ tablespoons **olive oil**
  ½ pound **poblano** (also called pasilla) **chilies**
  1 **onion** (½ lb.)
  ¾ pound **dried rigatoni pasta** or large elbow macaroni
  1 to 1½ cups fat-skimmed **chicken broth**
  ½ cup **whipping cream**
  ½ to 1 cup **shredded parmesan cheese**
     Salt and fresh-ground **pepper**
     Baked bacon (optional; directions follow)

1. Rinse and core tomatoes; cut in half lengthwise, rub lightly all over with olive oil, and lay cut side up in a single layer in a 10- by 15-inch pan.

2. Bake tomatoes in a 450° regular or convection oven until edges begin to brown, 25 to 35 minutes.

3. Meanwhile, rinse, stem, and seed poblano chilies; cut lengthwise into ¹⁄₁₆- to ⅛-inch-wide strips. Peel and chop onion. In a 5- to 6-quart pan, combine chilies, onion, and 1 tablespoon olive oil. Stir often over medium-high heat until

chilies are limp and beginning to brown, 10 to 15 minutes.

4. When tomatoes are done, push to 1 side of the pan. Scrape chili mixture into empty section; keep warm in a 150° oven.

5. In the 5- to 6-quart pan, bring 3 quarts water to a boil over high heat; add pasta. When boil resumes, reduce heat and boil gently until pasta is tender to bite, 6 to 10 minutes.

6. Drain pasta and return to pan. Set over high heat and immediately add 1 cup broth and the whipping cream; stir until boiling. For moister pasta, add more broth as desired (it soaks in quickly). Remove from heat and stir in chili mixture. Add ¼ cup cheese, and mix. Pour pasta mixture into a wide serving bowl, sprinkle with ¼ cup cheese, and arrange roasted tomatoes on top. Spoon onto plates. Add more cheese, salt, and pepper to taste. Accompany with baked bacon.

Per serving: 586 cal., 31% (180 cal.) from fat; 22 g protein; 20 g fat (9.1 g sat.); 82 g carbo (5.8 g fiber); 283 mg sodium; 43 mg chol.

Baked bacon. Arrange 1 pound **thick-sliced bacon** in a single layer in a 10- by 15-inch rimmed pan. Bake in a 375° regular or convection oven until browned, 17 to 25 minutes, turning slices over after 10 minutes. Transfer bacon to towels to drain; discard fat in pan. Serve warm or at room temperature. Makes 4 or 5 servings.

Per serving: 146 cal., 80% (117 cal.) from fat; 7.7 g protein; 13 g fat (4.4 g sat.); 0.2 g carbo (0 g fiber); 405 mg sodium; 22 mg chol.

Never-fall soufflés

■ Victor Scargle, chef at San Francisco's Grand Café, offers up these puffy, golden polenta soufflés as a hearty first course. Paired with a salad, they make a handsome, satisfying entrée for lunch or a simple supper. Although moist and light, the soufflés are more like spoon bread than the classic puffer. This deviation is a blessing because, unlike a temperamental true soufflé, which demands careful timing, these polenta soufflés endure. You can even bake them ahead, then reheat.

Polenta Soufflé and Salad

PREP AND COOK TIME: **About 55 minutes**

NOTES: You can also bake these soufflés in 12 muffin cups (2½ in. wide, ⅓-cup capacity); butter the cups and dust lightly with grated parmesan cheese (¼ cup total), then fill cups, mounding batter slightly. Bake as directed (step 5). Ease the baked soufflés free with a thin knife, tip them out of the pan, and serve hot (3 per serving). If making up to 1 day ahead, let cool (in soufflé dishes or out of muffin cups); reheat several at a time in a microwave oven on full power (100%) until steaming, ½ to 1 minute for each batch.

MAKES: 4 servings

　　　About ¼ cup (⅛ lb.) **butter** or margarine
　2　tablespoons **grated parmesan cheese**
　2　cups **milk**
　½　cup **polenta**
　　　About ¾ teaspoon **salt**
　4　**large eggs,** separated
1½　teaspoons **baking powder**
　　　About 8 cups rinsed, crisped **butter lettuce** leaves
　　　Mushroom dressing (recipe follows)
　　　Cambozola fondue (recipe follows)
　2　tablespoons chopped **fresh chives**

1. Butter 4 soufflé dishes (1¼- to 1½-cup size) and dust with the parmesan cheese.

2. In a 3- to 4-quart pan, mix milk with polenta and ¾ teaspoon salt; add ¼ cup butter, cut into chunks. Stir over medium-high heat until mixture boils, then reduce heat to medium and stir until polenta is thick enough to hold a clean path for a few seconds when spoon is drawn across bottom of pan, 8 to 10 minutes; remove from heat.

3. Meanwhile, in a large bowl, with a mixer on high speed, whip egg whites until they hold distinct, moist peaks.

4. Stir baking powder into polenta, then add egg yolks and stir to mix well. Add about ¼ of the egg whites and stir to mix. Fold polenta mixture into remaining egg whites. Spoon batter equally into soufflé dishes. Set dishes slightly

apart in a shallow 10- by 15-inch pan.

5. Bake in 375° regular or convection oven until soufflés are well browned, 30 to 40 minutes. Set each on a plate and mound lettuce leaves beside the dish. Spoon warm mushroom dressing equally onto lettuce. Spoon cambozola fondue equally over soufflés and salads; sprinkle with chives. Add salt to taste.

Per serving: 700 cal., 59% (414 cal.) from fat; 31 g protein; 46 g fat (26 g sat.); 42 g carbo (5.7 g fiber); 2,035 mg sodium; 320 mg chol.

Mushroom dressing. Rinse ¾ pound **mushrooms;** trim and discard discolored stem ends, and thinly slice mushrooms. In a 10- to 12-inch frying pan over high heat, frequently stir mushrooms; 1 tablespoon *each* **butter** or margarine, **olive oil,** and minced **shallot;** and 1 teaspoon minced **garlic** until mushrooms are lightly browned, 6 to 8 minutes. Add 2 tablespoons **port** and ¾ cup **condensed beef broth;** stir often until liquid is evaporated, about 4 minutes. Add **salt** to taste. Use hot. If making up to 1 day ahead, cover and chill; reheat to serve. Makes 4 servings.

Per serving: 96 cal., 61% (59 cal.) from fat; 3 g protein; 6.6 g fat (2.3 g sat.); 5.8 g carbo (1.1 g fiber); 341 mg sodium; 7.8 mg chol.

Cambozola fondue. In a microwave-safe container, combine 2 tablespoons fat-skimmed **chicken broth** and 1 cup firmly packed **cambozola cheese** (about ½ lb.), cut into chunks. Heat in a microwave oven on full power (100%), stirring occasionally, until cheese is melted, 1 to 2 minutes. Rub mixture through a strainer into a bowl; discard residue. Use hot. If making up to 1 day ahead, cover and chill; reheat in microwave oven. Makes about 1 cup.

Per ¼ cup: 201 cal., 81% (162 cal.) from fat; 12 g protein; 18 g fat (12 g sat.); 0 g carbo (0 g fiber); 783 mg sodium; 50 mg chol.

All-new bubble machine

■ My morning simply doesn't start well without a big mug filled with equal portions of espresso and hot, foamy milk. It's so important that for a long time I put up with the spurting and spattering of the steam jet on my espresso machine. When the plunger devices that force bubbles into hot milk came along, I was an immediate convert. Now, I've found an even more effective tool: the Froth Au Lait. It heats the milk while frothing it with a whisk. You just set the pitcher on the motor base, add the milk, put the cover in place, and push the button; the machine shuts off automatically in about 3 minutes.

Curiously, the finest, thickest, and most stable milk froth is made with nonfat milk (1 cup becomes about 4 cups), but low-fat (1%) and reduced-fat (2%) also make richly textured foams. Whole milk gets somewhat frothy, but cream doesn't foam up.

Hot milk froth has many uses beyond coffee drinks. We flavored it with chocolate drink powders, malted milk powder, and flavored syrups to make luxuriously thick beverages. Try the hot sundae that follows.
Froth Au Lait: $49.95; (866) 376-8437 or www.frothaulait.com.

Warm Raspberry Sundae Floats

PREP AND COOK TIME: About 5 minutes

NOTES: Flan mix is found in supermarkets near gelatin dessert mixes. If desired, drizzle floats with the caramel sauce in the flan package.

MAKES: 2 servings

- 1 cup **raspberries,** rinsed and drained
- 3 tablespoons **raspberry** (or other berry) **syrup**

  About 2 cups **nonfat vanilla frozen yogurt**
- 1 cup **nonfat milk**
- 2 tablespoons **flan mix powder** (see notes)

1. Divide raspberries between 2 deep bowls (2½- to 3-cup size). Add 1 tablespoon raspberry syrup to each and slightly mash fruit. Scoop equal portions of frozen yogurt onto berries.

2. Pour milk into a Froth Au Lait container and turn motor on. When the froth has formed and the container feels warm to touch, open hatch in lid and pour flan mix powder and remaining 1 tablespoon raspberry syrup into milk. When mixture is well blended or motor turns off, quickly pour and scrape the hot foamy liquid equally over berries and frozen yogurt. If you don't have a Froth Au Lait, use a blender (foam will be thinner): First pour milk into a glass measuring cup and heat in a microwave oven on full power (100%) until steaming, about 2 minutes. Pour into blender and add flan mix powder and remaining 1 tablespoon raspberry syrup; cover and whirl on high speed until frothy, about 10 seconds. Pour into bowls.

Per serving: 414 cal., 1.3% (54 cal.) from fat; 8.7 g protein; 0.6 g fat (0.2 g sat.); 93 g carbo (2.9 g fiber); 158 mg sodium; 2.5 mg chol. ◆

The Wine Guide

By Karen MacNeil-Fife

Tickled pink

■If you and I were having dinner right now in some small cafe in Provence, you know what we'd probably be drinking? A chilled, crisp rosé. For the French—as well as the Spanish, the Portuguese, and the Italians—summer is the season for snappy, fruity wines. And this usually means dry rosés, not white wines, because rosés possess the best of two worlds: They are refreshing like whites, but have a deeper character close to reds. In fact, dry rosé is a bonus summertime drink for red *and* white wine drinkers: It gives the former something a little more thirst-quenching, the latter a little more fruit.

Both traits are virtues when you add dinner to the equation. Rosés have enough of both acidity and bold fruitiness to be extremely flexible with food. One reason they're so ubiquitous around the Mediterranean this time of year is that they're a perfect match for salads as well as grilled foods liberally seasoned with olive oil, garlic, herbs, and spices.

Alas, despite all this (and seemingly countless Peter Mayle novels), we Americans are only on the brink of drinking pink. But I sense a greater spirit of vinous experimentation afoot. Recently I walked into the prestigious wine department of Dean & DeLuca gourmet market in the Napa Valley, and there within easy reach was a long row of pink wines, just waiting to be taken home with a round of creamy, ripe French cheese to begin a summer's evening.

It may come as a surprise to learn that those rosés aren't easy to make. Well, good ones aren't, anyway—there are some that taste dank and watery, as though the winemaker decided to turn a batch of lackluster leftover grapes into a cheap sip that looked a lot prettier than it tasted. Great rosés, on the other hand, require all the care, patience, skill, and good grapes that any other great wine takes.

There are actually several ways to make high-quality rosés, all of which revolve around a central theme: The winemaker crushes red grapes, but instead of letting the juice ferment on the skins, separates it off after it's lightly tinted pink. (Remember, making a custard sounds easy, too, but every good cook knows better.)

At first glance, it might seem as if white Zinfandels and rosés are the same thing. They are not. The process of making the two is essentially the same, but they don't taste alike. Count on white Zins to be sweeter, softer, and less concentrated. While dry rosés have a centuries-long history in the Old World, white Zinfandel was invented in 1972 by the large California winery Sutter Home, which had the brainstorm of making a soft, light, slightly sweet pinkish white wine using red Zinfandel grapes. Today

THINKING PINK

■**Ca' del Solo Freisa (Frizzante) 1999 (Monterey County),** $16. This fizzy—but not quite sparkling—wine made from the Italian grape Freisa is crisp and sassy. Low in alcohol (5.8 percent—standard wines are around 13 percent), it's great as an aperitif. Or just hop in the hammock with a good novel and a bottle of this.

■**Mumm Cuvée Napa Blanc de Noirs nonvintage (Napa Valley),** $18. The palest pink, this sparkler has a rush of citrus and strawberries, in perfect balance.

■**Domaine Tempier Bandol Rosé 1999 (Provence, France),** $23. Boldly fruity, this rosé, based on Mourvèdre and Grenache grapes, has aromas and flavors right out of a Vincent van Gogh painting: warm earth, haystacks, citrus trees, and dried wild herbs.

■**McDowell Grenache Rosé Reserve 1999 (Mendocino),** $9. Fresh and spicy, with subtle strawberry and watermelon notes.

■**Trefethen SIN (Summer In Napa) 1999 (Napa Valley),** $12. Terrific— bold and sassy, with just a touch of raspberry and vanilla. The back label says it all: "Kick off your shoes."

■**Zaca Mesa Z Gris 2000 (Santa Barbara County),** $9. A basketful of fruit (strawberries figure prominently) and a hint of sweetness conjure up images of carnivals; a long, spicy finish makes you take this Rhône blend more seriously.

white Zinfandel is very popular, but considered something of a "beginners' wine" by connoisseurs.

Not so dry rosés. There are numerous still rosés, but don't forget about sparkling ones. They're sensational in summer: You get all the personality of a rosé plus the thirst-quenching action of bubbles. Some rosé sparklers are labeled as such, but there are also sparklers called blanc de noirs.

These are made with all red grapes (Pinot Noir), but they aren't as deeply pink-colored as other rosés; in fact, a blanc de noirs usually has just the faintest touch of color.

So, this weekend, fire up the grill, put on some French (or Italian) music, sit out on the deck, and open a chilled rosé. Sure, it's not the same as being on the Riviera, but it's pretty wonderful all the same. ◆

Driving the berry trail

In July, these rural routes are among the sweetest roads in the West

Midsummer marks the peak of the berry harvest in the West. In many rural areas, family farmers sell freshly picked berries at roadside stands, and some invite you into the fields to pick your own. Here are several U-pick berry farms in Washington and central California where you can experience the pleasure of picking your own dessert.

■ **Tualco Valley, Washington—** Berry farmer Kurt Biderbost quite admires the efficiency of the supermarket-bound strawberries grown in a certain state to the south. "You can eat the berries," he says pleasantly, "and then keep eating when you come to the flat, because the cardboard won't taste any different.

The berry industry can easily ignore Biderbost's elbow. His pipsqueak plot in the Tualco Valley east of Seattle has all of 4 acres of strawberries and raspberries. But can *we* afford to disregard the product—berries that recall the fresh bounty of the family farm?

Farms like Biderbost's are endangered, along with the berries they produce. You can see incipient sub-urbanization even here, 20 miles from Seattle, as real estate signs sprout along State 203 from Monroe to Fall City—the berry trail. The percentage of land devoted to agriculture is steadily shrinking, but it isn't too late to reacquaint ourselves with what we're in danger of losing.

That's as in hands-on reacquaintance. Biderbost's farm, like several others, offers a U-pick option. Take a cardboard flat, forage through the fields, and cart home a personal harvest for 60 to 75 cents a pound, a third of the supermarket price at the peak of the season. But price isn't the reason for doing it. Nor is it the flavor, even though these strawberries and raspberries are so obviously superior to the supermarket variety that they're like a species from another planet. It's the sense of connection to the land—something from which we're almost perfectly estranged today.

"A lot of parents bring their kids out here just to experience something other than picking up food at the grocery store," says Nancy Harvold, who oversees 19 acres of U-pick berry fields just outside the town of Carnation.

Strawberries and raspberries offer the perfect introduction to farm work. The harvest is labor-intensive and demands a bit of quickly acquired expertise (pick them too green or overripe and you're wasting time and your joints). But finding a perfect berry in a tangle of leaves and stems is like discovering a miniature treasure: The color will shame a Ferrari, and the plump, moist feel can only be described as sensual. The berries' seductiveness is fortunate, because these varieties don't last long: Eat them within two days, or freeze them.

State 203, though not Washington's only berry trail, is the perfect summer drive. The Cascades, often snow-mantled into berry season, poke over the hills to the east; the Snoqualmie River scribbles through a forest to the northwest. There may be transient thoughts of hiking boots and canoes. But after the first taste of freshly picked berries, you'll decide they can wait. —*Lawrence W. Cheek*

■ **Pajaro Valley, California**—This month, in the rich valley surrounding Watsonville, all kinds of berry plants are busily transforming sunshine into edible sweetness. And here's the absolute best way to appreciate these summer delicacies: Pick them yourself.

Getting lost among the rows as you search for ripe treats hidden behind the leaves somehow adds to a berry's flavor. Gathering the berries yourself—and getting your own fingers stained with berry juices—also ensures you get the pick of the crop.

Several farms around Watsonville, about 10 miles south of Santa Cruz, open up their fields of boysenberries, blackberries, olallieberries, raspberries, and strawberries to visitors wanting to work a little for dessert.

With its coastal fog and mild climate, Watsonville is the perfect place to grow berry crops, says Vince Gizdich, a third-generation fruit farmer

California planner

WHERE: Watsonville is about 10 miles southeast of Santa Cruz. Most of the farms are east of downtown. It's best to bring your own containers for picking. Berry ripeness varies with the weather, so call ahead to find out which fields are open.

For general area information, contact **Pajaro Valley Chamber of Commerce,** 444 Main St., Watsonville; 831/724-3900 or www.pvchamber.com.

BERRY FARMS: Emile Agaccio Farms has chesterberries (a kind of blackberry) and raspberries for picking, and a gift shop. *8:30–7 daily. 4 Casserly Rd., Watsonville; 831/728-2009.*

Gizdich Ranch offers U-pick boysenberries, olallieberries, raspberries, and strawberries, and a gift shop, pie stand, and deli. Two new varieties of blackberries this year are Black Butte and Triple Crown. *8–5 daily (raspberry fields 8–12). 55 Peckham Rd., Watsonville; 831/722-1056.*

EVENT: Celebrate the regional bounty at the area's Strawberry Festival, Main and Peck St., Watsonville, with strawberry treats, including a strawberry pie–eating contest, plus live bands and food and craft booths. *12–5 Aug 4–5 in 2001, 55 Peckham Rd., Watsonville, 831/728-6183.*

at the Gizdich Ranch. "Our summers don't get very hot, which is great. If you can grow a fruit over a period of time, you get good quality. The fruit ripens slowly, so it's very juicy and very large.

This month, you'll find sweet blackberries and raspberries, and if you get out soon, there will still be some olallieberries—the berry of choice for Debbie Fort, whose family has been growing fruit at Emile Agaccio Farms since the early 1950s. "It's my favorite jam, my favorite cobbler, one of my favorite pies," says Fort. "I guess olallie would have to be my overall favorite."

These same berries fetch high prices at the grocery store—even in season. Going directly to the farm and plucking the berries yourself is more fun, and costs a lot less. "The savings are two- or threefold," says Gizdich; at his ranch, the berries cost approximately $1.29 per pound.

The joy of discovering the perfect berry, over and over again, can leave you with more fruit than you know what to do with. Of course, jams, cobblers, and pies all put berries to good use, and plenty of berry recipe books are on sale at Gizdich's and Fort's farms. Growers are quick to offer other suggestions. Says Fort: "You can make a berry slushy with ice. Or put them over ice cream. Or serve them chopped over sponge cake."

"So many berries, so little time," was what I was thinking during a morning that yielded a $4 flat with enough berries for two pies and plenty left over to give friends. And I've never felt quite so enthusiastic about fruit.

If you need a solid meal before heading home to bake, you can picnic in the orchard with homemade lemonade and sandwiches from the Gizdich Ranch Pie Shop/Deli.

But be sure to leave room for those berries. —*Lisa Taggart* ◆

Butterflied chicken marinated in lemon and herbs browns beautifully under the weight of bricks.

FOOD STYLING: JULIE SMITH (2)
KEVIN CANDLAND (2)

Brick chicks

For crisp, juicy birds, grilling is a weighty proposition

By Linda Lau Anusasananan

Many Italian menus these days offer a catchy-sounding item: "brick-grilled chicken." This translates into whole chicken, cut open and flattened, marinated, and then grilled under a weight. It's an old technique, designed to produce juicy meat and rich brown skin.

But is it a gimmick, an attempt to make basic grilled chicken sound intriguing? Our restaurant research revealed that in some trendy eateries, it is—the weight seems to have very little effect on the bird. In others, however, it seemed a truly effective method; the grilled chicken was moist and succulent.

In our test kitchen, we unearthed the secret to successful brick-grilling: The weight must be heavy enough. Four bricks suffice, and they work well because they're flat and compact. When you lay the split-open chickens skin down on the grill and then set a roasting pan filled with the bricks on top, the weight flattens the fowl to steaklike thickness for quick, even browning—there's no time for the meat to dry out. One turn, to brown the birds on the other side,

sans weight, and they emerge—juicy, crisp, and handsomely ridged with grill marks.

And what's good for a chick is good for a bird of any size. We brick-grilled Cornish hens—even quail—with mouthwatering results.

Brick-Grilled Chicken

PREP AND COOK TIME: About 35 minutes for quail, 45 minutes for Cornish hens and chickens, plus at least 30 minutes to marinate

NOTES: Instead of bricks, you can use cast-iron pans (20 to 25 lb. total) to flatten birds. Weights work best if equally sized and evenly distributed.

MAKES: 4 servings

- 2 **chickens** (about 3 lb. each), 4 Cornish hens (about $1^3/4$ lb. each), or 8 quail ($4^1/2$ to 6 oz. each)
- $^1/4$ cup **lemon juice**
- $^1/4$ cup chopped **parsley**
  About 3 tablespoons **olive oil**
- 3 tablespoons minced **garlic**
- 1 teaspoon **dried basil**
- 1 teaspoon **dried oregano**
- $^1/2$ teaspoon **coarse-ground pepper**
- $^1/2$ teaspoon **hot chili flakes**
  About $^1/2$ teaspoon **salt**
  Lemon wedges

1. Remove neck and giblets from chickens, hens, or quail if present; reserve for another use or discard. Pull off and discard any lumps of fat from birds. With poultry shears or kitchen scissors, cut along one side of backbone on each bird,

cutting back completely in two; for chickens, cut along other side of backbones as well and discard backbones. Rinse birds well and pat dry. Pull birds open and set skin side up on a flat surface; with your hand, press birds to flatten.

2. In a 9- by 13-inch baking dish, mix lemon juice, parsley, olive oil, garlic, basil, oregano, pepper, chili flakes, and $^1/2$ teaspoon salt. Rub mixture all over birds. Place in dish, overlapping and stacking as needed. Cover and chill at least 30 minutes or up to 1 day.

3. Set birds, skin side down and side by side, on a 12- by 17-inch section of an oiled barbecue grill over a solid bed of medium coals or medium heat on a gas grill (you can hold your hand at grill level only 4 to 5 seconds). Set a 12- by 17-inch roasting pan, right side up, on birds. Distribute 4 clean bricks (5 to 6 lb. each) evenly in pan (see notes).

4. Cover grill and cook until skin is well browned (lift pan to check), about 20 minutes for chickens, 18 minutes for hens, and 12 to 15 minutes for quail. Remove weighted pan and, with a wide spatula, turn birds over. Cover grill and cook without weighted pan until meat at thigh bones is no longer pink (cut to test), 5 to 10 minutes longer for chickens and hens, 2 to 5 minutes for quail.

5. Transfer birds, skin up, to a platter. With a knife or poultry shears, cut chickens into quarters and hens into halves if desired. Serve with lemon wedges to squeeze over birds. Add salt to taste.

Per serving of chicken: 771 cal., 54% (414 cal.) from fat; 82 g protein; 46 g fat (12 g sat.); 2.3 g carbo (0.2 g fiber); 392 mg sodium; 264 mg chol. ◆

The Quick Cook

Meals in 30 minutes or less
By Linda Lau Anusasananan

Thin, coconut-flavored crêpe holds tiny shrimp and crisp bean sprouts.

World wraps

■ At first glance, Vietnamese "sizzling" or "happy" pancakes look like giant omelets. In fact, they're crêpes whose golden color comes from turmeric, not eggs. Filled with shrimp and bean sprouts, the crisp crêpes are perfect for a light meal; season them with fish sauce, chili, and lime. Without the filling, the crêpes make a unique appetizer.

Rice flour (finely ground rice) gives the crêpes their interesting texture, which varies according to how finely the grain was ground. Most rice flours from Asia are as silky as baby powder; they produce a very thin, crisp crêpe. Slightly coarser, grittier flours make thicker pancakes. Don't use sweet or glutinous rice flour. Look for rice flour in natural-food stores and in Asian or Latino food markets.

Crackle Crêpes with Shrimp

PREP AND COOK TIME: About 30 minutes

NOTES: If using Asian rice flour, use 2 tablespoons less water in step 1. To serve crêpes Vietnamese style, arrange a few leaves of red leaf lettuce and some mint sprigs alongside; cut off chunks of the crêpe, place in a piece of lettuce, add a few mint leaves and a spoonful of seasoned fish sauce, and wrap in the lettuce to eat. Serve with hot cooked rice and a light soup for supper.

MAKES: 3 main-dish servings

- ½ cup **rice flour** (see notes)
- ¼ cup **cornstarch**
- ½ teaspoon **ground dried turmeric**
- ¼ cup **canned coconut milk**
- 2 tablespoons thinly sliced **green onion,** including tops
- 1 tablespoon **salad oil**
- ½ pound **bean sprouts** (1 quart), rinsed and crisped
- 6 ounces **shelled cooked tiny shrimp,** rinsed and drained
- **Seasoned fish sauce** (recipe follows)

1. In a bowl, mix rice flour, cornstarch, and turmeric. Add 1 cup water (see notes) and the coconut milk, and whisk to blend. Stir in green onion.

2. Set a 12-inch nonstick frying pan (about 10 inches across bottom) over high heat. When pan is hot, add 1 teaspoon oil and tilt to coat bottom.

3. Stir rice flour batter to blend. Pour ½ cup batter into pan all at once and tilt pan to cover entire bottom evenly.

4. Distribute ⅓ of the bean sprouts and ⅓ of the shrimp evenly over half the crêpe. Cook, uncovered, until crêpe is browned and crisp on the bottom, 7 to 10 minutes. Fold plain side over filled side, then slide crêpe onto an oven-proof plate. Keep warm in a 200° regular or convection oven up to 25 minutes. Repeat to cook 2 more crêpes. Add seasoned fish sauce to taste.

Per serving: 296 cal., 29% (87 cal.) from fat; 16 g protein; 9.7 g fat (4.4 g sat.); 36 g carbo (1.7 g fiber); 136 mg sodium; 111 mg chol.

Seasoned Fish Sauce

PREP TIME: About 4 minutes

NOTES: Look for Asian fish sauce and chili paste in a well-stocked supermarket or an Asian grocery store.

MAKES: ½ cup

Stir together ¼ cup **water,** 2 tablespoons **Asian fish sauce** (*nuoc mam* or *nam pla*), 1 tablespoon **sugar,** 1 tablespoon **lime juice,** 1 teaspoon minced **garlic,** and ¼ teaspoon **Asian red chili paste** or hot chili flakes.

Per tablespoon: 17 cal., 26% (4.5 cal.) from fat; 0.7 g protein; 0.5 g fat (0.1 g sat.); 2.6 g carbo (0 g fiber); 150 mg sodium; 0 mg chol.

Golden Rice Crisps

PREP AND COOK TIME: About 30 minutes

NOTES: If making up to 1 day ahead, cool and store airtight. If crêpes soften, bake, uncovered, in a 350° regular or convection oven until crisp again, 5 to 10 minutes.

MAKES: 3 to 6 appetizer servings

1. Follow steps 1 through 3 for **crackle crêpes with shrimp** (preceding).

2. Cook until crêpe is browned and crisp on the bottom, 3 to 5 minutes. With a wide spatula, transfer to a 14- by 17-inch baking sheet. Repeat to cook 2 more crêpes, adding in a single layer to sheet as cooked (use 2 sheets).

3. Bake in a 350° regular or convection oven until crêpes are crisp, 8 to 12 minutes. Transfer to racks to cool.

4. Break off pieces and dip into **seasoned fish sauce** (preceding) to eat.

Per serving: 108 cal., 38% (41 cal.) from fat; 1 g protein; 4.5 g fat (2.1 g sat.); 16 g carbo (0.4 g fiber); 2.1 mg sodium; 0 mg chol. ◆

The Low-Fat Cook

Healthy choices for the active lifestyle

By Elaine Johnson

Fresh fruit pops are one easy step beyond homemade juice bars.

JAMES CARRIER; FOOD STYLING: DIANE SCOTT GSELL

Popsicles, Mexican style

■ At Mexican markets throughout the West, freezer cases full of familiar shapes but not-so-familiar flavors tempt young (and young-at-heart) shoppers. They're *paletas* (little shovels, in Spanish), frozen treats that take ordinary juice bars to imaginative heights. Some are creamy, made with sweet tropical fruits and berries. Others are icy, flavored with tart fruits or even cucumber and chili (watch out—the latter pack some heat). All are refreshingly low-fat and a cinch to whip up at home.

Mexican Paletas

PREP TIME: 10 to 20 minutes, plus at least 3 hours to freeze

NOTES: The paletas that contain milk are slightly creamy; the others are icy. Use frozen fruit bar molds with a ¼- to ⅓-cup capacity; they're sold in many cookware and hardware stores and through some cookware catalogs.

MAKES: 6 paletas

1. Pour **paletas mixture** (choices follow) equally into 6 juice bar molds (see notes). Attach covers. Insert sticks, leaving 1½ to 2 inches of each exposed. Freeze paletas upright until firm, at least 3 hours or up to 2 weeks.

2. Hold each mold up to the rim under warm running water just until paletas are released from sides of molds, 5 to 15 seconds. Remove covers and pull out paletas.

Banana paletas. In a 2-cup glass measure, combine 1 cup **milk,** ¾ cup smoothly mashed **ripe banana,** 1 teaspoon **vanilla,** and ¼ cup **sugar;** stir until sugar is dissolved (mixture is no longer grainy to taste).

Per paleta: 85 cal., 16% (14 cal.) from fat; 1.6 g protein; 1.5 g fat (0.9 g sat.); 17 g carbo (0.5 g fiber); 20 mg sodium; 5.7 mg chol.

Blackberry paletas. In a blender, whirl 2½ cups rinsed, drained **black-berries** until smooth. Push through a strainer into a 2-cup glass measure; discard residue. Add 1 cup **milk** and 6 tablespoons **sugar** to berry purée; stir until sugar is dissolved.

Per paleta: 104 cal., 13% (14 cal.) from fat; 1.8 g protein; 1.6 g fat (0.8 g sat.); 22 g carbo (0 g fiber); 20 mg sodium; 5.7 mg chol.

Cucumber-chili paletas. In a blender, combine 3 cups 1-inch chunks peeled, seeded **cucumber** (1½ lb.); ⅔ cup **sugar;** ⅓ cup **lemon juice;** and 1 rinsed, stemmed **jalapeño chili** (1 to 1½ oz.; remove seeds and veins for less heat). Whirl until smooth. Push mixture through a fine strainer set over a 2-cup glass measure; discard residue.

Per paleta: 100 cal., 0.9% (0.9 cal.) from fat; 0.5 g protein; 0.1 g fat (0 g sat.); 26 g carbo (0.4 g fiber); 7.5 mg sodium; 0 mg chol.

Mango paletas. In a blender, combine 2½ cups 1-inch chunks **mangoes** (from 1½ lb. fruit), ¼ cup **sugar,** and 3 tablespoons **lime juice;** whirl until smooth.

Per paleta: 85 cal., 2.1% (1.8 cal.) from fat; 0.4 g protein; 0.2 g fat (0.1 g sat.); 22 g carbo (0.8 g fiber); 2.9 mg sodium; 0 mg chol.

Piña colada paletas. In a blender, combine 1 cup **milk,** ½ cup 1-inch chunks **fresh** or canned **pineapple,** ⅓ cup **sugar,** 1 teaspoon **vanilla,** and ½ teaspoon **coconut extract;** whirl until smooth.

Per paleta: 76 cal., 17% (13 cal.) from fat; 1.4 g protein; 1.4 g fat (0.8 g sat.); 15 g carbo (0.2 g fiber); 20 mg sodium; 5.7 mg chol.

Sour orange paletas. In a 2-cup glass measure, combine 1⅓ cups **orange juice,** ⅓ cup **lime juice,** and ¼ cup **sugar;** stir until sugar is dissolved.

Per paleta: 60 cal., 1.5% (0.9 cal.) from fat; 0.4 g protein; 0.1 g fat (0 g sat.); 15 g carbo (0.1 g fiber); 2.8 mg sodium; 0 mg chol.

Strawberry paletas. In a blender, whirl 3¾ cups rinsed, hulled **straw-berries** until smooth. Push through a fine strainer into a 2-cup glass measure; discard residue. Add ⅓ cup **sugar** and 1 tablespoon **lemon juice** to berry purée; stir until sugar is dissolved.

Per paleta: 72 cal., 5% (3.6 cal.) from fat; 0.6 g protein; 0.4 g fat (0 g sat.); 18 g carbo (2.5 g fiber); 1.6 mg sodium; 0 mg chol. ◆

Gazpacho takes on a new color with yellow bell peppers. Grapes, tomatoes, cucumber, and almonds add interesting crunch.

JAMES CARRIER; FOOD STYLING: BASIL FRIEDMAN

Cool bowlfuls

Soups for the heat of summer

By Andrew Baker

From new-wave, no-cook golden gazpacho to a classic, snowy vichyssoise, an easy and elegant way to temper a sizzler of a day is to serve a cool soup. For lunch, each of these vegetable-intense soups makes a satisfying main course to serve with crisp breadsticks or dainty sandwiches. For the first course of a dinner party, they are even more appealing because they can be made ahead of time.

Note: To quick-chill soups, nest soup-filled pan in ice water and stir often until soup is cool, 15 to 20 minutes.

Golden Gazpacho

PREP TIME: About 25 minutes

MAKES: 4 servings

- 2 **yellow bell peppers** (about 1 lb. total)
- 1 cup chilled fat-skimmed **chicken broth** or vegetable broth
- ½ cup chilled **sour cream**
- 2 tablespoons **lemon juice**
- ⅔ cup **seedless green grapes**, rinsed and cut in half
- ⅔ cup **cherry tomatoes** (¾ to 1 in.

wide), stemmed, rinsed, and cut into halves or quarters
- ⅔ cup diced **English cucumber**
- ¼ cup coarsely chopped **salted roasted almonds**
- 2 tablespoons minced **fresh cilantro**
- 2 tablespoons minced **fresh mint** leaves
  Salt and fresh-ground **pepper**

1. Rinse, stem, seed, and coarsely chop bell peppers.
2. In a blender, combine peppers,

---

broth, sour cream, and lemon juice. Whirl until smooth. If making up to 1 day ahead, cover and chill.

3. Ladle soup into wide bowls. Onto the centers, spoon equal portions of grapes, tomatoes, cucumber, almonds, cilantro, and mint. Add salt and pepper to taste.

Per serving: 184 cal., 59% (108 cal.) from fat; 6.4 g protein; 12 g fat (4.4 g sat.); 16 g carbo (3.7 g fiber); 117 mg sodium; 13 mg chol.

Classic Vichyssoise

PREP AND COOK TIME: About 40 minutes if quick-chilled

MAKES: 4 servings

- 1 pound **thin-skinned potatoes**
- ½ cup chopped **onion**
- 2¾ to 3 cups fat-skimmed **chicken broth**
- 3 tablespoons **dry sherry**
- 1 cup **half-and-half** (light cream)
- ¼ pound **sliced bacon,** chopped
- 3 tablespoons minced **fresh chives**
  Salt and fresh-ground **pepper**

1. Rinse and peel potatoes; cut into ½-inch chunks.
2. In a 2- to 3-quart pan over high heat, combine potatoes, onion, 2¾ cups broth, and sherry. Bring to a boil, reduce heat, cover, and simmer until the potatoes mash easily, about 20 minutes.
3. In a blender or food processor, whirl potato mixture until smooth. Return to pan and add half-and-half. Quick-chill soup (see note at left), or cover and refrigerate until cold, at least 1 hour or up to 1 day. Stir in more broth if a thinner consistency is desired.
4. Meanwhile, in an 8- to 10-inch frying pan over high heat, stir bacon frequently until crisp, 4 to 5 minutes. With a slotted spoon, transfer bacon to towels to drain. Discard pan drippings.
5. Ladle soup into wide bowls. Sprinkle equally with bacon and chives. Add salt and pepper to taste.

Per serving: 253 cal., 39% (99 cal.) from fat; 12 g protein; 11 g fat (5.7 g sat.); 23 g carbo (2.1 g fiber); 212 mg sodium; 29 mg chol.

Red Pepper Purée with Smoked Trout

PREP AND COOK TIME: About 40 minutes if quick-chilled

MAKES: 4 servings

- 1 pound **thin-skinned potatoes**
- ½ cup chopped **onion**
- 3 cups fat-skimmed **chicken broth**
- ¾ cup **canned peeled roasted red peppers**

1 cup **half-and-half** (light cream)

2 **oranges** (about ½ lb. each)

1 hard-cooked **large egg**

¼ pound **boned, skinned smoked trout**

3 tablespoons minced **fresh chives**

Salt and fresh-ground **pepper**

1. Rinse and peel potatoes; cut into ½-inch chunks.

2. In a 2- to 3-quart pan over high heat, combine potatoes, onion, broth, and red peppers. Bring to a boil, reduce heat, cover, and simmer until potatoes mash easily, about 20 minutes.

3. In a blender or food processor, whirl potato mixture until smooth. Return to pan and add half-and-half. Quick-chill soup (see note on page 150), or cover and refrigerate until cold, at least 1 hour or up to 1 day.

4. Meanwhile, with a sharp knife, cut peel and white membrane from oranges. Working over a bowl, cut between inner membranes and fruit to release segments into bowl; discard peel and membrane.

5. Shell egg and shred or finely chop. Break trout into flakes.

6. Ladle soup into wide bowls. Garnish equally with orange segments and trout; sprinkle egg and chives on top. Add salt and pepper to taste.

Per serving: 317 cal., 34% (108 cal.) from fat; 19 g protein; 12 g fat (5.4 g sat.); 35 g carbo (4.3 g fiber); 449 mg sodium; 83 mg chol.

Ginger-Lemon Salad Soup

PREP AND COOK TIME: About 40 minutes if quick-chilled

NOTES: Serve with chopsticks and a spoon, or a fork and spoon.

MAKES: 4 servings

2 stalks (each 12 to 15 in.) **fresh lemon grass**

¼ cup minced **fresh ginger**

1 quart fat-skimmed **chicken broth** or vegetable broth

2 ounces **dried thin rice noodles** (*mai fun* or rice sticks)

⅔ cup long, thin **carrot** shreds

⅔ cup long, thin **daikon** shreds

2 tablespoons **fresh cilantro** leaves

2 tablespoons slivered **fresh mint** leaves

Asian fish sauce (*nuoc mam* or *nam pla*) or salt

1. Rinse lemon grass; trim and discard stem ends and leaves, and pull off and discard coarse outer layer. Cut stalks into ½-inch pieces.

2. In a 2- to 3-quart pan over high heat, combine lemon grass, ginger, and broth. Bring to a boil, cover, reduce heat, and simmer for 20 minutes. Quick-chill soup (see note on page 150), or cover and refrigerate until cold, at least 1 hour or up to 1 day.

3. Meanwhile, in a 1- to 1½-quart pan, bring 2 cups water to a boil. Add rice noodles and stir to separate. Cook until tender to bite, about 3 minutes. Pour into a fine strainer over the sink and rinse with cold water until cool, about 1 minute. With scissors, cut noodles in 2 or 3 places to make smaller pieces.

4. In a bowl, mix noodles, carrot, and daikon.

5. Pour broth mixture through a fine strainer into four wide bowls; discard residue. Mound noodle mixture equally in centers of bowls. Scatter cilantro and mint on top. Add fish sauce to taste.

Per serving: 102 cal., 0.9% (0.9 cal.) from fat; 8.5 g protein; 0.1 g fat (0 g sat.); 16 g carbo (0.8 g fiber); 111 mg sodium; 0 mg chol. ◆

Burgers on the beach

From Encinitas to Lompoc, our guide to Southern California's best beachside burgers

■ Nothing tastes better than a burger at the beach. Food scientists have probably attempted the research—brine plus sand plus languorous sun-smashed laze equals a sensual riot and an all-beef hunger that logic can't explain. Here are a few of our favorites.

Padaro Beach Grill, Carpinteria. Feast on a ⅓-pound burger accompanied by a pound of fries. The grill is set on an acre of grassy fields, with toys and a sandbox for the kids, 50 yards from the Pacific. *3765 Santa Claus Lane (take Santa Claus Lane exit off U.S. 101); (805) 566-0566.*

Boll Weevil Restaurant, Encinitas. Try standing up after downing the Big Daddy—a 1-pound burger, accompanied by a tray heaped with garnishes ranging from hot chilies to the house special sauce, an institution since 1965. *277 El Camino Real; (760) 942-1368.*

Good Stuff, Hermosa Beach. Great burgers—the avocado bacon cheeseburger is a favorite—and great gawking. Eat on the patio, a coin toss from the beach, and watch the human tide jog, roll, ride, and preen along the Strand. *1286 the Strand, near the Hermosa Pier; (310) 374-2334.*

Ruby's Diner, Huntington Beach. At the end of the Huntington Beach Pier, watch surfers wave-dance while you opt for one of 60 burger variations. Wash it down with an Oreo Cookie Fantasy shake. *1 Main St.; (714) 969-7829.*

Jalama Beach Store & Grill, **Jalama Beach County Park.** The Jalama Burger is one of the few hamburgers immortalized on a T-shirt, and it amply justifies the distinction. The burger consists of ¼ pound of 90 percent lean ground sirloin, but Kathy Eittreim isn't giving away the contents of her secret sauce. *Exit State 1 at Lompoc (one hour north of Santa Barbara); take Jalama Rd. 14 miles to Jalama Beach County Park; (805) 736-5027.*

Chief's Burgers & Brew, Solana Beach. A local hangout—Solana Beach's version of *Cheers*—with surf videos and big screen sports. The Super Chief is a double cheeseburger named after the old Santa Fe train. *124 Lomas Santa Fe Dr., across the street from the Amtrak station; (858) 755-2599.* — Ken McAlpine ◆

Kitchen Cabinet

Readers' recipes tested in *Sunset's* kitchens

By Paula Freschet

Grilled Salmon with Blackberry-Cabernet Coulis

Krista Painter and Amy French, Seattle

Classmates in culinary school, Krista Painter and Amy French are also friends who cook together for fun. At Pike Place Market, when the bounty of summer is at its peak, they snap up the freshest blackberries and salmon to make this festive dish.

PREP AND COOK TIME: About 50 minutes

NOTES: The berry sauce should be nicely balanced between sweet and tart; judge the amount of sugar to add by the sweetness of the fruit.

MAKES: 6 servings

- 1 cup **Cabernet Sauvignon** or other dry red wine
- 2½ cups **blackberries,** rinsed and drained
- 2 tablespoons minced **shallots**
- 2 tablespoons minced **fresh ginger**
- 2 to 3 tablespoons **sugar**
- 1 tablespoon **butter** or margarine
- 6 **salmon steaks** (1 in. thick, 6 to 7 oz. each)

  Salt and **pepper**

1. In a food processor or blender, combine wine and 2 cups berries; whirl until puréed. Rub berry mixture through a fine strainer into a 1½- to 2-quart pan; discard residue. Add shallots, ginger, and 2 tablespoons sugar. Bring berry mixture to a boil over high heat, and stir often until reduced to 1 cup, about 10 minutes. Remove from heat, and stir in butter and more sugar to taste (see notes).

2. Rinse salmon and pat dry. Coil belly strips of fish into center of steaks and secure each portion with a small skewer (such as the kind used for trussing turkeys).

3. Lay salmon on an oiled grill over a solid bed of hot coals or high heat on a gas grill (you can hold your hand at grill level only 2 to 3 seconds); close lid on gas grill. Cook fish, turning once, until opaque but still moist-looking in center of thickest part (cut to test), 7 to 10 minutes.

4. Set a salmon steak on each of 6

Fresh blackberry and ginger sauce dresses up grilled salmon steaks.

warm plates (remove skewers if desired). Spoon berry coulis (if cool, stir over high heat until warm, about 1 minute) equally over steaks. Garnish with remaining ½ cup whole berries; add salt and pepper to taste.

Per serving: 344 cal., 47% (162 cal.) from fat; 30 g protein; 18 g fat (4.5 g sat.); 13 g carbo (2.7 g fiber); 110 mg sodium; 93 mg chol.

Corn Chowder with Red Peppers and Pancetta

Betty Jean Nichols, Eugene, OR

In Oregon during the summer, Betty Jean Nichols says, "There are some chilly days when my family wants something hot and hearty." She offers this warming vegetable chowder.

PREP AND COOK TIME: About 1 hour

MAKES: 6 servings

- 5 ears **corn** (7 to 8 in.)
- ¼ pound **sliced pancetta** or sliced bacon, diced
- 1 cup chopped **onion**
- 2 cups diced **red thin-skinned potatoes** (about ¾ lb.), scrubbed
- 1 jar (about 7 oz.) **roasted red peppers,** drained and chopped
- 6 cups fat-skimmed **chicken broth**

- 2 **oregano sprigs** (about 3 in.), rinsed, or ¾ teaspoon dried oregano
- ½ cup **whipping cream**

  Salt and fresh-ground **pepper**

1. Husk corn, discard husks and silks, and rinse ears. With a sharp knife, cut corn kernels from cobs into a bowl.

2. In a 5- to 6-quart pan over medium-high heat, frequently stir pancetta until lightly browned and crisp, 5 to 7 minutes. With a slotted spoon, transfer pancetta to towels to drain.

3. Add onions to pan; stir frequently until they're just beginning to brown, 3 to 5 minutes. Add corn, potatoes, peppers, broth, and oregano. Bring to a boil over high heat, stirring often. Reduce heat, cover, and simmer, stirring occasionally, until potatoes mash easily when pressed, about 15 minutes. Discard oregano sprigs.

4. In a blender, whirl about ⅓ of the soup mixture (use a towel to hold down blender lid) until smooth. Pour purée back into pan with remaining soup. Add cream and stir until soup is hot, about 1 minute. Add salt and pepper to taste.

5. Ladle the soup into bowls; top equally with cooked pancetta.

Per serving: 373 cal., 46% (171 cal.) from fat; 16 g protein; 19 g fat (8.1 g sat.); 40 g carbo (5.7 g fiber); 279 mg sodium; 35 mg chol.

Artichoke and Red Pepper Bruschetta

Lynn Lloyd, Mt. Shasta, CA

In an effort to duplicate the topping on a bruschetta she liked at a restaurant, Lynn Lloyd came up with this flavorful appetizer.

PREP AND COOK TIME: About 40 minutes

MAKES: 3 dozen appetizers

- 1 **red bell pepper** (about ½ lb.), rinsed, stemmed, seeded, and finely chopped
- 1 **red onion** (about 6 oz.), peeled and finely chopped
- 1 clove **garlic,** peeled and minced or pressed
- 1 tablespoon **olive oil**

1 can (14 oz.) **artichoke hearts**, drained and finely chopped

¼ cup minced **parsley**

¼ cup finely chopped **pimiento-stuffed Spanish-style green olives**

2 teaspoons **lemon juice**

Salt and **pepper**

36 diagonally cut slices (¼ in. thick) **sourdough baguette** (about 1 slender 8-oz. loaf)

½ cup grated **asiago** or parmesan **cheese**

1. In a 10- to 12-inch nonstick frying pan over medium-high heat, frequently stir bell pepper, onion, and garlic in oil until vegetables begin to brown, 8 to 10 minutes. Add artichokes, parsley, olives, and lemon juice, mixing well. Remove from heat. Season to taste with salt and pepper. If making up to 1 day ahead, cover and chill.

2. Arrange baguette slices in a single layer on a 12- by 15-inch baking sheet. Broil 4 to 6 inches from heat until toasted on 1 side, about 1 minute. Remove from oven and turn slices over.

3. Spoon artichoke mixture equally on untoasted side of baguette slices; spread level. Sprinkle with cheese.

4. Broil 4 to 6 inches from heat until cheese begins to melt and topping is hot, about 1 minute.

Melt asiago cheese over a layer of bell peppers, artichokes, and olives for lively bruschetta.

Per serving: 34 cal., 29% (9.9 cal.) from fat; 1.3 g protein; 1.1 g fat (0.4 g sat.); 4.5 g carbo (0.4 g fiber); 80 mg sodium; 1.1 mg chol.

Grilled Eggplant–Pesto Sandwich

Jean Dillon, Grand Junction, CO

Inspired by a trip to the local farmers' market, Jean Dillon used a variety of fresh produce plus some bacon to create this new version of a grand old standby, the BLT.

PREP AND COOK TIME: About 30 minutes

MAKES: 4 servings

4 **Asian eggplants** (about 5 oz. each), rinsed

2 tablespoons **olive oil**

Salt and **pepper**

8 slices **bacon** (about ½ lb. total)

1 **slender baguette** (8 oz.)

¼ cup **pesto**, homemade or purchased

2 **Roma tomatoes** (about 3 oz. each), rinsed, cored, and thinly sliced

¼ pound **thin-sliced jack cheese**

2 cups **arugula** (about ⅛ lb.), rinsed and crisped

1. Trim and discard eggplant stems. Cut each eggplant lengthwise into ¼-inch-thick slices. Brush slices on each side lightly with olive oil.

2. Lay eggplant on a barbecue grill over a solid bed of hot coals or high heat on a gas grill (you can hold your hand at grill level only 2 to 3 seconds); close lid on gas grill. Cook, turning as needed, until eggplant is browned on both sides and soft when pressed, 6 to 8 minutes. Sprinkle lightly with salt and pepper; transfer to a platter.

3. In a 10- to 12-inch frying pan over medium heat, cook bacon until browned and crisp, about 8 minutes, turning slices as needed. Drain bacon on towels and discard fat in pan.

4. Cut baguette in half lengthwise. Spread pesto onto cut sides of baguette. Lay eggplant slices on bottom half of baguette and cover with bacon, tomatoes, cheese, and arugula. Set top half of baguette in place and, pressing sandwich firmly together, cut into 4 equal portions with a serrated knife. Add salt and pepper to taste.

Per serving: 538 cal., 55% (297 cal.) from fat; 20 g protein; 33 g fat (10 g sat.); 42 g carbo (4.4 g fiber); 874 mg sodium; 46 mg chol.

Cherry-Chocolate Strudel

Jane Shapton, Portland

If chocolate-covered cherries are a confection favorite, this dessert will suit your tastes. Jane Shapton suggests topping warm slices of this crisp, easy-to-make strudel with cool whipped cream and dark shavings of semisweet chocolate.

PREP AND COOK TIME: About 50 minutes

MAKES: 6 servings

⅓ cup **vanilla cookie crumbs**

1 cup **Bing** or other dark, sweet **cherries**, rinsed and pitted (or use frozen pitted cherries)

⅓ cup **dried sweet cherries**

⅓ cup **slivered almonds**

⅓ cup **semisweet chocolate chips**

¼ cup **sugar**

½ teaspoon **ground cinnamon**

1 tablespoon **kirsch** (optional)

6 sheets **filo dough** (about 12 by 18 in.)

¼ cup (⅛ lb.) **butter** or margarine, melted

Powdered sugar (optional)

1. In a bowl, gently mix cookie crumbs, fresh cherries, dried cherries, almonds, chocolate chips, sugar, cinnamon, and kirsch.

2. Lay 1 filo sheet flat (cover remaining filo with plastic wrap to prevent drying) and brush lightly with butter. Cover with another filo sheet and brush lightly with more butter. Repeat to stack remaining filo.

3. Spread cherry-chocolate filling in a 3-inch-wide band along 1 long edge of the dough, 2 inches in from edge and the ends. Fold long edge, then the ends of dough over filling. Gently roll the filled side of dough forward to form a compact cylinder, ending seam side down.

4. Gently transfer the strudel roll, seam down, to a buttered 12- by 15-inch baking sheet. Brush top of roll with remaining melted butter.

5. Bake on the center rack in a 375° regular or convection oven until golden brown, 15 to 25 minutes. Using 2 wide spatulas, transfer strudel to a platter. Sprinkle lightly with powdered sugar, if desired. Cut into 1½-inch-wide slices and serve warm.

Per serving: 303 cal., 48% (144 cal.) from fat; 3.8 g protein; 16 g fat (7.2 g sat.); 39 g carbo (0.7 g fiber); 188 mg sodium; 22 mg chol. ◆

Scaled-down and spiced-up, little roasts cooked outdoors on the grill make for easy summer dinners (see page 166).

August

pies à la road

Western cafes offer wedges well worth a special trip—and recipes to make at home

FOOD STYLING: DIANE SCOTT GSELL

ERIC O'CONNELL

Kathy Knapp offers two capital creations from New Mexico's Pie-O-Neer Cafe. At left, lattice-topped raspberry-rhubarb, cream cheese–filled fresh peach, and sugar-sprinkled apple-lemon pies wait for lucky diners.

Some people travel in search of enlightenment. Others seek cultural enrichment. The wisest set their sights on a great piece of pie. On the highways and backroads of the West, there are pie stops worth a special trip, places where culinary kings and queens reign over empires of flaky crusts and luscious fillings. Their kingdoms are modest: eateries strategically positioned near summer travel destinations. But their subjects are loyal, and their treasures mighty. ■ For those of us consigned to our own realms this summer, six of these expert bakers offer peerless pies to make at home. This is enlightenment and enrichment enough.

By Elaine Johnson • Food photographs by James Carrier

Rolling in dough

**Pie-O-Neer Cafe,
Pie Town, New Mexico**

■ In a place called Pie Town, you'd expect to find great pie. But when Kathy Knapp drove the 150 miles from Albuquerque to Pie Town, population 75, there were no pies.

The town's name and reputation date back to the '20s, when a gold miner started baking pies to supplement his income. Eventually, however, the population dwindled, and with the people went the pies.

So in 1994, Knapp, with the help of family and community, put the pie back in Pie Town, serving up her grandmother's recipes—including one for pinto bean pie (it tastes like pumpkin—Knapp promises).

Closed Mon. Milepost 59 on U.S. 60, Pie Town; (505) 772-2900.

Pie-O-Neer Coconut Cream Meringue Pie

PREP AND COOK TIME: About 1 hour, plus at least 3 hours to cool

NOTES: Prepare *Sunset's* Favorite Pie Pastry or the Sunglow Pie Pastry (recipes on page 162), or use 1 refrigerated pastry (half of a 15-oz. package) and follow steps 5 and 6 of the *Sunset* recipe to line pie pan.

MAKES: 8 servings

Pastry for a 9-inch single-crust pie (see notes)

1 cup **sweetened flaked dried coconut**

1⅓ cups **sugar**

¼ cup plus 1½ teaspoons **cornstarch**

2¼ cups **whole milk**

3 **large eggs,** separated

1 teaspoon **vanilla**

¼ teaspoon **cream of tartar**

⅛ teaspoon **salt**

1. With a fork, prick bottom and sides of unbaked pastry in pan at about 1-inch intervals. Bake in a 375° regular or convection oven until golden, 15 to 20 minutes. Let cool on a rack.

2. Scatter coconut over bottom of pastry.

3. In a 2- to 3-quart pan, mix 1 cup sugar, ¼ cup cornstarch, milk, and egg yolks until well blended. Stir over medium-high heat until mixture boils and thickens, 10 to 15 minutes. Remove from heat and stir in vanilla. Pour over coconut in crust.

4. In a small bowl, mix remaining ⅓ cup sugar and 1½ teaspoons cornstarch.

5. In a deep bowl, with a mixer on high speed (use whisk attachment if available), beat egg whites, cream of tartar, and salt until very foamy. Add sugar-starch mixture, 1 tablespoon every 30 seconds, and continue to beat until meringue holds stiff, glossy peaks.

6. Spoon meringue onto hot pie filling. With a spatula, spread meringue evenly to rim of pie shell.

7. Bake in a 325° regular or convection oven until meringue is lightly browned, 15 to 20 minutes.

8. Let pie cool on a rack about 3 hours. Cut into wedges and serve, or invert a large bowl over pie (it shouldn't touch meringue) and chill up to 1 day.

Per serving: 399 cal., 36% (144 cal.) from fat; 6.6 g protein; 16 g fat (8.5 g sat.); 57 g carbo (1.1 g fiber); 234 mg sodium; 101 mg chol.

A wedge of old-fashioned coconut cream pie topped with meringue is hard to resist.

Slice of history

**The Eatery Restaurant,
Skagit River Resort,
Rockport, Washington**

■ "My dad's mother came here in 1888. She was paddled up the river by the Indians," Tootsie Clark recounts. "She ran a roadhouse above Marble Mount [near the entrance to North Cascades National Park]."

The resort includes a string of cabins, a bed-and-breakfast, and a restaurant, where Clark still holds court with her homestyle cooking. Which of her pies is most popular? Clark hesitates: "Well, the pecan goes over very well. People seem to like the wild blackberry too. We also do rhubarb-strawberry, and lemon, and I make my own mincemeat out of elk meat...."

58439 State 20, Rockport; (800) 273-2606.

The Eatery Pecan Pie

PREP AND COOK TIME: About 1¼ hours, plus at least 1½ hours to cool

NOTES: Prepare *Sunset's* Favorite Pie Pastry or the Sunglow Pie Pastry (recipes on page 162), or use 1 refrigerated pastry (half of a 15-oz. package) and follow steps 5 and 6 of the *Sunset* recipe to line pie pan. Serve pie with sweetened whipped cream flavored with bourbon and nutmeg.

MAKES: 8 servings

- 3 **large eggs**
- ⅔ cup **sugar**
- 1 cup **dark corn syrup**
- ⅓ cup melted **butter** or margarine
- ½ teaspoon **salt**
- 1 cup **pecan halves**

  Pastry for a 9-inch single-crust pie (see notes)

1. In a large bowl, with a mixer on medium-high speed or with a spoon, beat eggs, sugar, corn syrup, butter, and salt until well blended. Stir in pecans. Scrape mixture into unbaked pastry in pan.

2. Bake on bottom rack of a 375° regular oven or 350° convection oven until center jiggles only slightly when pan is gently shaken, 40 to 50 minutes. If crust browns too quickly (check after 35 minutes), cover pie loosely with foil.

3. Let pie cool on a rack at least 1½ hours. Cut into wedges and serve, or chill airtight up to 1 day.

Per serving: 503 cal., 50% (252 cal.) from fat; 5.1 g protein; 28 g fat (9.9 g sat.); 63 g carbo (1.3 g fiber); 425 mg sodium; 112 mg chol.

Tootsie Clark tempts pie lovers.

The upper crust
Rock Creek Lakes Resort, near Bishop, California

■ "We're going for pie in the sky," declare bicyclists as they set out on the 50-mile round-trip, 3,000-foot climb up the canyon from State 203, near Mammoth Lakes, to Rock Creek Lakes Resort. At the top, the reward for both athletes and mere mortals is a piece of one of Sue King's pies—especially her fruit ones: rhubarb, peach, boysenberry, pear with cheddar streusel, and Dutch apple. King has been perfecting the art of pie baking since 1979, when she and her husband, Jim, bought the resort. Describing her kitchen as "a walk-in closet with plumbing," she warns that her production is limited: "Everything is from scratch. We only sell pies by the slice, and we sell out early most days."

1 Rock Creek Rd.; (760) 935-4311.

Sue King shares her wares with bicyclists who've made it to the top, geographically and gustatorily.

Rock Creek Lake Fresh Peach Pie

PREP AND COOK TIME: About 1¼ hours, plus at least 3 hours to chill

NOTES: Prepare *Sunset's* Favorite Pie Pastry or the Sunglow Pie Pastry (recipes on page 162), or use 1 refrigerated pastry (half of a 15-oz. package) and follow steps 5 and 6 of the *Sunset* recipe to line pan. Serve pie with sweetened whipped cream flavored with grated orange peel.

MAKES: 8 servings

- **Pastry** for a 9-inch single-crust pie (see notes)
- 1 package (8 oz.) **cream cheese,** at room temperature
- 1¼ cups **sugar**
- 6½ cups sliced peeled **firm-ripe peaches** (about 4 lb.)
- ¾ cup **orange juice**
- ¼ cup **cornstarch**
- ¼ cup **lemon juice**

1. With a fork, prick bottom and sides of unbaked pastry in pan at about 1-inch intervals. Bake in a 375° regular or convection oven until golden, 15 to 20 minutes; let cool on a rack.

2. Meanwhile, in a bowl, mix cream cheese and ½ cup sugar until smooth. Spread evenly over bottom of cool pastry.

3. In a blender or food processor, whirl 1 cup sliced peaches, remaining ¾ cup sugar, orange juice, and cornstarch until smooth. Pour into a 3- to 4-quart pan; stir over medium-high heat until mixture boils and thickens, about 4 minutes. Remove from heat and stir in lemon juice.

4. Add remaining 5½ cups peaches to hot peach glaze and mix to coat slices. Let cool until tepid, about 25 minutes, then scrape onto cream cheese mixture in crust.

5. Chill, uncovered, until firm enough to cut, at least 3 hours. Cut into wedges and serve, or invert a large bowl over pie (it shouldn't touch fruit) and chill up to 1 day.

Per serving: 459 cal., 37% (171 cal.) from fat; 5.2 g protein; 19 g fat (10 g sat.); 70 g carbo (3.3 g fiber); 202 mg sodium; 43 mg chol.

Just like Mom's

Mom's Pies, Vida, Oregon

■ Bertha Nyseth is the second mom to have produced pies for Mom's Pies, 45 miles east of Eugene on State 126. The quirky restaurant has specialized in pies since World War II. Of the battalion that Nyseth turns out daily now, berries get the most requests: berry medley (a trio of blackberry, blueberry, and raspberry), red and blue (raspberry-blueberry), black and blue (blackberry-blueberry), apple-raspberry, raspberry-rhubarb, strawberry-rhubarb, raspberry-cherry—you get the picture.

49647 McKenzie River Hwy., Vida; (541) 822-3891.

Mom's Raspberry-Rhubarb Pie

PREP AND COOK TIME: About 1¾ hours, plus at least 2 hours to cool

NOTES: Prepare *Sunset's* Favorite Pie Pastry or the Sunglow Pie Pastry (recipes on page 162), or use 1 package (15 oz.) refrigerated pastry and follow steps 5 and 6 of the *Sunset* recipe to line pan, weave lattice top, and flute edges. Instead of using a lattice crust, you can make a regular double-crust pie, as served at Mom's Pies.

MAKES: 8 servings

- 1⅓ cups **sugar**
- ¼ cup **cornstarch**
- 3½ cups **raspberries,** rinsed and drained
- 3½ cups ¾-inch lengths **rhubarb** (about 1 lb.)
- **Pastry** for a 9-inch lattice-top pie (see notes)
- 1 **large egg** yolk

1. In a bowl, mix sugar and cornstarch. Add raspberries and rhubarb and gently mix to coat.
2. Scrape mixture into unbaked bottom crust in pan. Cover with lattice top and flute edges (see notes). Line a 12-inch pizza pan or a 10- by 15-inch baking pan with foil (to catch drips) and set pie on foil.
3. Bake on bottom rack of a 375° regular oven or 350° convection oven for 30 minutes. Meanwhile, in a small bowl, beat egg yolk with 2 teaspoons water to blend. Brush lattice top and crust edges lightly with yolk mixture

(save extra for other uses or discard). Continue baking until filling bubbles in the center, 40 to 50 minutes longer in regular oven, about 1 hour and 40 minutes in convection. If crust browns too quickly (check 10 minutes after brushing with egg yolk mixture), cover pie loosely with foil.

4. Let pie cool on a rack at least 2 hours. Serve, or chill airtight up to 1 day.

Per serving: 327 cal., 28% (90 cal.) from fat; 3 g protein; 10 g fat (4.1 g sat.); 58 g carbo (3 g fiber); 120 mg sodium; 38 mg chol.

Pie queen

Sunglow Family Restaurant, Bicknell, Utah

■ The Pie Queen of Wayne County—that's what they called Cula Ekker, who turned out mysterious and magnificent creations for more than 25 years at the former Sunglow Cafe in central Utah, near the gateway to Capitol Reef National Park. Pinto bean pie. Sweet pickle pie. Buttermilk pie. Oatmeal pie. More traditional fruit pies too. Ekker still visits what's now named the Sunglow Family Restaurant regularly to make sure the recipes—faithfully reproduced by new owner Patty Krause—meet her standards.

Was it hard to follow in Ekker's footsteps? "At first I thought, 'I'll never get this,'" Krause remembers. "But Cula came every day at first and

Berry good

Longhorn Restaurant, Rock River, Wyoming

■ Way out on the Wyoming prairie, a little bit north of Laramie along Interstate 30, the Longhorn Restaurant in Rock River is a pie lover's oasis par excellence. Chef Chris Martin whips up the pies of your dreams: pecan, sour cream–cherry, and a four-berry pie that tastes like all the Rocky Mountains' sweetest berries pirouetting in a crust for your enjoyment.

Amazingly, Martin has only been seriously baking pies since he moved to Rock River from Arizona in 1995. "I play around with different recipes until I find one I really like," he says. "Then I modify it until I'm satisfied with it. That's how this berry pie came about."

Closed Sun. 362 N. Fourth St., Rock River; (307) 378-2567.

Longhorn Restaurant Four-Berry Pie

PREP AND COOK TIME: About 1½ hours, plus at least 3 hours to cool

NOTES: Prepare *Sunset's* Favorite Pie Pastry or the Sunglow Pie Pastry (recipe on page 162), or use 1 package (15-oz.) refrigerated pastry and follow steps 5 and 6 of the *Sunset* recipe to line pan, position top crust, and flute edges.

MAKES: 8 servings

- 1 cup **sugar**
- ¼ cup **cornstarch**
- 2 tablespoons **butter** or margarine, melted and cooled
- 5 cups **mixed fresh berries** (1¼ cups *each* blackberries, blueberries, raspberries, and ¼-inch-thick slices of strawberries), rinsed and drained
- **Pastry** for a 9-inch double-crust pie (see notes)

1. In a bowl, mix sugar, cornstarch, and butter. Gently stir in berries.

2. Scrape berry mixture into unbaked bottom crust in pan. Cover with top crust and flute edges (see notes). Line a 12-inch pizza pan or a 10- by 15-inch baking pan with foil (to catch drips) and set pie on foil.

3. Bake on bottom rack of a 375° regular oven or 350° convection oven until filling bubbles in center (check through cutout or slits), 45 to 55 minutes in regular oven, about 1½ hours in convection. If crust browns too quickly (check after 40 minutes), cover pie loosely with foil.

4. Let pie cool on a rack at least 3 hours. Cut into wedges and serve, or chill airtight up to 1 day.

Per serving: 453 cal., 44% (198 cal.) from fat; 4 g protein; 22 g fat (9.6 g sat.); 62 g carbo (3.9 g fiber); 263 mg sodium; 31 mg chol.

STEPHEN COLLECTOR

Chris Martin provides a sweet interlude to a trip across Wyoming. At left: his four-berry wonder disappears fast.

---

helped me. Four years later, I guess I've perfected it. What makes the pies especially good is the crust. Lard is the secret"(see page 162).

Closed Sun. 91 E. Main St., Bicknell; (435) 425-3701.

Sunglow Apple-Lemon Pie

PREP AND COOK TIME: About 1¾ hours, plus at least 1½ hours to cool

NOTES: Prepare *Sunset's* Favorite Pie Pastry or the Sunglow Pie Pastry (recipes on page 162), or use 1 package (15 oz.) refrigerated pastry and follow steps 5 and 6 of the *Sunset* recipe to line pan, position top crust, and flute edges.

MAKES: 8 servings

- ¾ cup plus 1 tablespoon **sugar**
- 3 tablespoons **quick-cooking tapioca**
- 2 tablespoons **butter** or margarine, melted and cooled
- 1 teaspoon **lemon extract**
- 2¼ pounds **Newtown Pippin apples** (about 4)
- **Pastry** for a 9-inch double-crust pie (see notes)
- 1 **large egg** yolk

1. In a bowl, mix ¾ cup sugar, tapioca, butter, and lemon extract. Peel and core apples; slice (¼ in. thick) into sugar mixture and mix to coat (you should have 8 cups apple mixture).

2. Scrape apple mixture into unbaked bottom crust in pan. Cover with top crust and flute edges (see notes).

3. Bake on bottom rack of a 375° regular or convection oven for 30 minutes. Meanwhile, in a small bowl, beat egg yolk with 2 teaspoons water to blend. Brush pie lightly with yolk mixture (save extra for other uses or discard), then sprinkle with remaining tablespoon sugar. Continue baking until filling bubbles in center (check through cutout or slits), 25 to 30 minutes longer. If crust browns too quickly (check 10 minutes after brushing with egg), cover pie loosely with foil.

4. Let pie cool on a rack at least 1½ hours. Cut into wedges and serve, or chill airtight up to 1 day.

Per serving: 465 cal., 43% (198 cal.) from fat; 3.8 g protein; 22 g fat (9.8 g sat.); 64 g carbo (2.9 g fiber); 279 mg sodium; 58 mg chol.

A perfect crust

■ Tender, flaky, rich—a great crust makes a great pie. You know one when you see one—but how to recreate such a masterpiece at home?

Some of our pie masters revealed a pet ingredient or technique, but others confessed to the simplest formulas: "Our pie dough is Crisco, flour, and salt," says Lysa Sangermano, co-owner of Mom's Pies. "Not real complicated, but when you have a woman who has made pies for 20 years, it becomes second nature." And therein lies the truth: A good crust is part art, part science.

So what's a beginning pie baker to do? After putting *Sunset's* recipe testers through a battery of formulas and refinements, we settled on two fine crusts you can rely on. One combines butter and shortening for flavor and texture balance. The other relies on lard for exceptional flakiness. Even inexperienced bakers had good luck with both.

Sunset's Favorite Pie Pastry

PREP TIME: About 20 minutes

MAKES: 8 servings

For a 9-inch single-crust pie

About 1 cup **all-purpose flour**

¼ teaspoon **salt**

3 tablespoons cold **butter** or margarine, cut into chunks

3 tablespoons cold **solid vegetable shortening,** cut into chunks

For a 9-inch double-crust or lattice-top pie

About 2 cups **all-purpose flour**

½ teaspoon **salt**

6 tablespoons cold **butter** or margarine, cut into chunks

6 tablespoons cold **solid vegetable shortening,** cut into chunks

1. In a bowl, mix 1 cup flour and the salt (for single crust) or 2 cups flour and the salt (for double crust). Add butter and shortening and, with a pastry blender or your fingers, cut in the fats or rub in with your fingers until the largest pieces are pea-size.

2. Sprinkle 3 tablespoons water (for single crust) or 6 tablespoons water (for double crust) over flour mixture. Stir with a fork just until evenly moistened. Gently squeeze about ¼ cup of the dough into a ball; if it won't hold together, crumble lump back into bowl and sprinkle with more water, 1 tablespoon at a time; stir with a fork until evenly moistened.

3. With lightly floured hands, gently squeeze dough into a ball. For double crust, divide in half and shape each half into a ball. Pat dough into a smooth 4-inch-wide round (2 rounds for double crust). Wrap dough in plastic wrap and chill until slightly firm, 15 to 30 minutes.

4. Lay dough (1 round for double crust) on a lightly floured surface. With a floured rolling pin, roll gently and evenly in short strokes from center of dough outward to form a 12-inch-wide round. If edges split while rolling, push them back toward center to make round relatively smooth. Occasionally slide a long metal spatula under dough and lift, dusting flour beneath to prevent sticking.

5. Fold the dough round in half, lift it gently without stretching, and lay the folded edge across the middle of a 9-inch pie pan. Unfold and ease dough into pan without stretching. With scissors, trim dough edge evenly ¾ inch beyond pan rim.

6. *For a single-crust pie:* Fold dough edge under itself, flush with pan rim. To flute, press down with your thumb and first finger on dough rim to make indentations; at the same time, press against dough edge with 1 finger of your other hand, pushing it between your fingers on the rim. Repeat indentations side by side around rim. Bake or fill crust as recipe directs.

For a double-crust pie: Fill bottom crust as recipe directs. Roll second ball of dough as directed in step 4 into an 11-inch-wide round. If desired, make a decorative cutout in dough's center. Fold as directed in step 5, center on filling, and unfold. Trim edge flush with dough in pan. Fold dough edges under, flush with pan rim. Flute as directed for single-crust pie. If dough has no cutout, with a small, sharp knife, cut several 2- to 3-inch slits in top pastry to let steam escape.

For a lattice-top pie:
Fill bottom crust as recipe directs. Roll second ball of dough as described in step 4, shaping it as close as you can into a 10-inch square. With a knife or fluted cutter, cut dough into ¾-inch-wide strips. Arrange half the strips over pie filling about 1 inch apart. One at a time, weave remaining strips perpendicular to and over and under every other strip in the first set (lifting first strips as needed) into a lattice pattern. Trim edges flush with dough in pan. Fold dough edges under, flush with pan rim. Flute as directed for single-crust pie.

Per serving for a single-crust pie: 137 cal., 61% (84 cal.) from fat; 1.7 g protein; 9.3 g fat (3.9 g sat.); 12 g carbo (0.4 g fiber); 116 mg sodium; 12 mg chol.

Sunglow Pie Pastry

Follow directions for **Sunset's Favorite Pie Pastry** (preceding), but instead of butter and solid vegetable shortening use 6 tablespoons **lard** (for single-crust pie) or ¾ cup lard (for double-crust pie). In step 2, instead of the 3 tablespoons water for a single-crust pie, use a mixture of 1 tablespoon beaten **egg,** 1 teaspoon **distilled white vinegar,** and 2 tablespoons **water;** or for a double-crust pie, use a mixture of 2 tablespoons beaten egg, 2 teaspoons vinegar, and ¼ cup water.

Per serving for a single-crust pie: 146 cal., 62% (90 cal.) from fat; 1.8 g protein; 10 g fat (3.8 g sat.); 12 g carbo (0.4 g fiber); 74 mg sodium; 17 mg chol. ◆

Patty Krause meets Cula Ekker's Sunglow standards.

EDWARD McCAIN

food guide
By Jerry Anne Di Vecchio

Mix it up

A lively salad of many textures from the Land of Enchantment

■ Helen Evans Brown, who wrote *Sunset's* Adventures in Food feature during the 1950s and '60s, taught me that texture could add as much variation as seasonings to a dish. And in Helen's day, salads, where texture is a core issue, were often made entirely of chopped ingredients, including the greens.

Today, these dense chopped salads are making a comeback as an interesting alternative to mixed green salads. Recently I enjoyed this hearty, handsome version in New Mexico.

New Mexico Chopped Salad

PREP AND COOK TIME: About 50 minutes

NOTES: To cook corn, put kernels in a microwave-safe bowl and heat in a microwave oven on full power (100%) until steaming, about 2 minutes. Let cool.

MAKES: 8 servings

- 2 **ears corn** (each about 7 in. long), husks and silks removed, rinsed
- 2 **poblano** (also called pasilla) **chilies** (½ lb. total), rinsed, stemmed, and seeded
- 1 **red bell pepper** (½ lb.), rinsed, stemmed, and seeded
- 1 **cucumber** (¾ lb.), rinsed, peeled, and seeded
- 1 cup chopped **green onions** (including tops)
- 1 cup diced (¼ in.) **jicama**
- 1 can (about 15 oz.) **black beans**, rinsed and drained
- 2 **firm-ripe avocados** (about 1 lb. total)
- ½ cup **lime juice**

  About 1 teaspoon **hot chili flakes**

  Salt

  Green desert dressing (recipe follows)

  Cornbread croutons (recipe follows)

KEVIN CANDLAND; FOOD STYLING: BASIL FRIEDMAN

1. Cut corn kernels from cobs; discard cobs. Taste corn. If it's tender, use raw; if it's starchy, cook as directed in notes. Put in a large bowl.

2. Cut chilies, bell pepper, and cucumber into ¼-inch dice; add to bowl, along with green onions, jicama, and beans.

3. Cut avocados in half; pit and peel them. Cut 3 halves into ¼-inch dice; reserve remaining half for dressing. Add diced avocado, lime juice, and 1 teaspoon chili flakes to bowl and mix gently. Add salt to taste.

4. Mound salad equally in wide, shallow bowls. Pile croutons alongside and spoon dressing over the top (or serve on the side). Sprinkle with more chili flakes to taste.

Per serving: 417 cal., 39% (162 cal.) from fat; 9.9 g protein; 18 g fat (3.3 g sat.); 59 g carbo (6.7 g fiber); 651 mg sodium; 34 mg chol.

Green desert dressing. In a blender or food processor, whirl 1 peeled avocado half (see New Mexico chopped salad, preceding), ¾ cup **sour cream**, ¼ cup **reduced-fat** or regular **mayonnaise**, ½ cup coarsely chopped **fresh cilantro,** ½ cup coarsely chopped **parsley,** ¼ cup chopped **green onions** (including tops), and 1 can (2 oz.) **flat anchovy fillets** with oil until smooth. Makes about 1¾ cup.

Cornbread croutons. Prepare 1 box (about 13 oz.) **cornbread mix** as directed, or use your favorite cornbread recipe; bake in an 8-inch square pan. Let cool about 10 minutes, then invert onto a rack to cool. Cut into 1-inch cubes. Spread 3 tablespoons **olive** or salad **oil** in a rimmed 10- by 15-inch pan. Add cornbread and turn to coat lightly with oil. Bake in a 375° regular or convection oven, turning occasionally, until evenly browned, 15 to 20 minutes. Let cool at least 10 minutes. Use warm or cool.

for the grill

Volumes of advice

Jamie Purviance, who brought us *Weber's Art of the Grill,* has turned out another volume full of barbecue expertise from the master of barbecue manufacturers, Weber-Stephen Products. A paperback, *Weber's Big Book of Grilling* (Chronicle Books, San Francisco, 2001; $22.95; 800/722-6657) has more than 365 recipes, covering appetizers to desserts. When the coals cool down after you've cooked the Rocky Mountain salmon below, take a cue from the book and use the embers to grill some fresh peaches for dessert. Add a puréed raspberry sauce and sweetened whipped cream flavored with grated lemon peel.

Glazed grilled peaches. Rinse 6 **firm-ripe peaches** (6 oz. each); cut each in half and pit. In a 9- to 10-inch frying pan over medium-high heat, melt 6 tablespoons **butter** or margarine; add ¼ cup **sugar** and stir until well blended. Remove pan from heat, set peaches in butter mixture, and turn them to coat evenly.

Lay peaches, cut side down, on a barbecue grill over a solid bed of medium coals or medium heat on a gas grill (you can hold your hand at grill level only 4 to 5 seconds); close lid on gas grill. Cook until peaches are hot and lightly browned on the bottom. Brush tops with more butter mixture, then turn fruit over and brush cooked sides with mixture. Cook until peaches are warm but still hold their shape, 6 to 10 minutes total. Makes 6 servings.

Per serving: 189 cal., 57% (108 cal.) from fat; 1 g protein; 12 g fat (7.2 g sat.); 23 g carbo (2.1 g fiber); 117 mg sodium; 31 mg chol.

Mile-high fish

■ At the two Tony's Meats & Specialty Foods in Littleton, Colorado, the cases are laden with foods judiciously seasoned and ready to cook. Mick Rosacci (Tony's son), who oversees the development of these preparations, shares this locally popular recipe for barbecued salmon.

Rocky Mountain Salmon

PREP AND COOK TIME: About 40 minutes, plus at least 1 hour to marinate

NOTES: Instead of a fillet, you can use salmon steaks. If marinating salmon (through step 2) up to 1 day ahead, chill airtight. If time is short, use the marinade as a sauce instead; heat and spoon over cooked salmon.

MAKES: 6 servings

¼ cup firmly packed **brown sugar**

2 tablespoons **dry white wine**

2 tablespoons **soy sauce**

2 tablespoons **butter** or margarine

1 tablespoon **lemon juice**

1 **salmon fillet with skin** (about 2 lb.; see notes)

1. In a microwave-safe 9- by 13-inch baking dish, combine brown sugar, wine, soy sauce, butter, and lemon juice. Heat in a microwave oven at full power (100%) until boiling, about 2 minutes, stirring several times. Let cool 10 to 15 minutes.

2. Rinse salmon, pat dry, and lay skin side up in sugar-soy marinade. Cover and chill at least 1 hour or up to 1 day.

3. Lift salmon from marinade, drain (reserve marinade), and lay skin side down on a sheet of heavy foil. Trim foil to outline of fish.

4. Transfer fish on foil to a grill over a solid bed of hot coals or high heat on a gas grill (you can hold your hand at grill level only 2 to 3 seconds). Cover barbecue; open vents for charcoal.

Cook until salmon is opaque but still moist-looking in center of thickest part (cut to test), or 140° on a thermometer, 20 to 25 minutes. With 2 wide spatulas, transfer fish to a platter.

5. Return marinade to microwave oven and heat at full power until boiling, 1 to 2 minutes, stirring several times. Pour into a small bowl.

6. Cut fish into portions, lift from skin onto plates, and add marinade to taste.

Per serving: 338 cal., 51% (171 cal.) from fat; 29 g protein; 19 g fat (5.5 g sat.); 9.6 g carbo (0 g fiber); 471 mg sodium; 95 mg chol.

KEVIN CANDLAND; FOOD STYLING: BASIL FRIEDMAN; ABOVE : E. SPENCER TOY

Relish it

■ During MasterChef USA's Chefs' Challenge on television, the tension of timing a meal keeps both contestants and audience on edge. When I joined the judging team, Kathy Urbano of Monroe, Washington, minimized the pressure by pairing barbecued steak with this very easy fresh tomato and chipotle marmalade. It would make a great hamburger relish as well.

Tomato–Chipotle Chili Marmalade

PREP AND COOK TIME: About 15 minutes

MAKES: About 1¼ cups

- 1 pound **ripe** or firm-ripe **tomatoes**
- ¼ cup firmly packed **brown sugar**
- 3 tablespoons **cider** or red wine **vinegar**
- 1 tablespoon chopped drained **canned chipotle chilies**
- **Salt**

1. Immerse tomatoes in boiling water for about 10 seconds; lift out. Pull off skins and cut out cores and discard. Cut tomatoes in half and squeeze juice into a 2- to 3-quart pan. Chop tomatoes into ¼-inch pieces; add to pan, along with brown sugar, vinegar, and chilies.

2. Boil over high heat, stirring often, until tomatoes begin to fall apart and almost all the liquid has evaporated, about 5 minutes. Let cool. Add salt to taste. Serve, or cover and chill up to 2 weeks.

Per ¼ cup: 63 cal., 5.7% (3.6 cal.) from fat; 0.7 g protein; 0.4 g fat (0 g sat.); 16 g carbo (1.1 g fiber); 38 mg sodium; 0 mg chol.

KEVIN CANDLAND; FOOD STYLING: BASIL FRIEDMAN

WINE GUIDE By Karen MacNeil-Fife

Uncorking a new trend

■ The reassuring *thwock* of a cork being pulled from a wine bottle has been music to the ears of wine lovers for about three centuries. Now it seems the wine industry might be changing its tune. Almost all the producers of the prestigious Rieslings coming out of Australia's Clare Valley have started topping their bottles with screw caps instead of corks. Why the change?

Recent rumor had it that the world was running out of cork. Not true. More than enough cork is produced each year—mostly in Portugal—to meet world demand.

JAMES CARRIER

No, the driving force behind screw caps (Stelvins, as the most common are called) is a flaw in cork itself. Although on one hand, it's a fairly miraculous product—almost impermeable to air and water, resistant to rot, and elastic enough to be compressed into the neck of a wine bottle—cork is susceptible to a contamination known as cork taint, which causes some wines to develop a musty aroma akin to wet cardboard. Drinking a "corked" wine isn't harmful, but it's very unpleasant and frustrating, especially when you paid $25 for that Chardonnay now languishing in the fridge. Needless to say, the Chardonnay's producer isn't happy either, since you now associate his or her wines with wet cardboard. Some experts put the value of ruined wine at $10 billion annually.

There appears to be only one real cure for "corkedness": Don't use corks. Many producers have tried synthetic cork look-alikes. But some of these smell pretty bad themselves and are nearly impossible to get out of the bottle.

Then one local producer took a radical step: PlumpJack Winery in the Napa Valley released half of its 1997 and 1998 reserve Cabernet Sauvignons in bottles with screw caps (priced at $135) and the remainder in bottles with traditional corks ($125). Guess which people preferred? Yes, the screw caps. And the buzz is that several top California producers are considering following PlumpJack and the Australians and going with Stelvins.

WINES FROM DOWN UNDER

Corks and caps aside, Australia has become an exciting wine region.

■ **Grosset Polish Hill Riesling 2000 (Clare Valley)**, $26. A crisp, sassy white, packed with mineral and peach flavors and easy to drink—just unscrew the cap!

■ **Tahbilk Marsanne 2000 (Nagambie Lakes)**, $12. A fresh white wine, with hints of honey and crisp apples.

■ **Jasper Hill "Georgia's Paddock" Shiraz 1999 (Heathcote, Victoria)**, $60. A dense, lush, mouth-filling red.

■ **Penfolds Old Vine Shiraz/Grenache/ Mourvèdre 1998 (Barossa Valley)**, $19. Velvet-textured and as fruity as a boysenberry pie. ◆

little roast,
big taste

By Paula Freschet • Photographs by James Carrier • Food styling by Susan Devaty

■ The word *roast* conjures images of grand holiday dinners following loving but lengthy watches in the kitchen tracking the slowly rising internal temperature of behemoth pieces of meat. But adjust the size and the setting, and a roast can bring manageable flair to a summer dinner party.

Many small cuts of meat take well to dry heat: boned turkey breast and thighs, lamb loin, and pork tenderloin, for instance. We've stuffed and seasoned these variously with cheeses, herbs, and spices, and tied them into roasts—steps that in every case can be done a day ahead of time. And when you put the heat to them outdoors—that is, pop them on the grill—they make great warm-weather fare.

Scaled-down, spiced-up cuts make for *easy* summer dinners

Spiced Lamb Loin with Grilled Ratatouille

PREP AND COOK TIME: About 45 minutes
NOTES: Have the butcher bone a lamb loin (1¾ to 2 lb.; make sure you don't get a tenderloin) and roll and tie it to make a roast about 8 inches long and 2½ inches wide. You can prepare roast (through step 2) up to 1 day ahead; cover and chill. Grill chilled roast 50 to 60 minutes.
MAKES: 4 servings

- 1 **fat-trimmed lamb loin,** boned, rolled, and tied (about 1 lb. boned; see notes)
- ½ cup **olive oil**
- 2 tablespoons chopped **shallots**
- 1 tablespoon chopped **garlic**
- 1½ tablespoons **fresh thyme** leaves or 1½ teaspoons dried thyme
- ½ teaspoon grated **lemon** peel
- 1 tablespoon **lemon juice**
- 2 teaspoons **Dijon mustard**
- ½ teaspoon **ground cumin**
- ¼ teaspoon **ground allspice**
- ¼ teaspoon **ground cinnamon**
- ⅛ teaspoon **cayenne**

Grilled ratatouille (recipe follows)
Fresh thyme sprigs (optional), rinsed
Salt and **pepper**

1. Rinse and dry lamb.
2. In a blender, combine olive oil, shallots, garlic, thyme leaves, lemon peel and juice, mustard, cumin, allspice, cinnamon, and cayenne; whirl until coarsely puréed. Brush ¼ cup spiced oil all over lamb; save remaining for grilled ratatouille (recipe follows).
3. Prepare barbecue for indirect heat according to instructions in box, page 168. Cook lamb loin until a thermometer inserted in center of thickest part reaches 135° for medium-rare, 25 to 30 minutes, or until it's as done as you like.
4. Transfer roast to a platter and, keeping it warm, let rest 5 to 10 minutes. Surround with grilled ratatouille, and garnish with thyme sprigs if desired. Cut roast into thin slices and add salt and pepper to taste.

Per serving: 248 cal., 54% (135 cal.) from fat; 26 g protein; 15 g fat (3.9 g sat.); 1 g carbo (0.1 g fiber); 87 mg sodium; 81 mg chol.

Grilled ratatouille. Rinse, stem, and seed 1 **yellow bell pepper** (about 6 oz.); cut into 1½-inch pieces. Rinse 2 **zucchini** (3 to 4 oz. each) and trim and discard ends; cut zucchini crosswise into ¾-inch-thick rounds. Rinse 2 **Asian eggplants** (4 oz. each) and trim and discard ends; cut egg-

A lamb loin coated with a profusion of spices makes an aromatic roast to grill with summer vegetables.

plants crosswise into ³⁄₄-inch-thick rounds. Rinse and stem 2 cups **cherry tomatoes** (about 1¼ in. wide, about ³⁄₄ lb. total). Thread vegetables onto thin metal skewers at least 14 inches long, with a single kind of vegetable on each skewer (for zucchini and eggplants, run skewers crosswise from edge to edge

through rounds). Brush vegetables with remaining spiced oil.

When lamb has cooked 10 minutes, place bell pepper, zucchini, and eggplants on grill directly over heat; cook, turning once, until browned and tender when pierced, about 15 minutes. Add tomatoes 20 minutes after starting

meat and cook, turning once, until barely tender when pierced, about **5** minutes. Push vegetables from skewers and arrange around lamb loin roast. Season to taste with **salt** and **pepper.**

Per serving: 230 cal., 82% (189 cal.) from fat; 2.1 g protein; 21 g fat (2.8 g sat.); 11 g carbo (2.5 g fiber); 56 mg sodium; 0 mg chol.

Indirect grilling

■ *If using charcoal briquets,* mound and ignite 60 briquets on the firegrate of a barbecue with a lid. When briquets are dotted with gray ash, in 15 to 20 minutes, push equal amounts to opposite sides of firegrate. Add 5 more briquets to each mound of coals now and after 30 minutes, if grilling takes longer than that.

■ *If using a gas barbecue,* turn all the burners to high, close lid, and heat for 10 minutes. Then adjust burners for indirect cooking (heat on sides of grill, not down center under food) and keep on high.

Set a drip pan on firegrate between coals or burners. Set barbecue grill in place. Set roast in center of grill, not over heat. Cover barbecue; open vents for charcoal. Cook as directed in recipe.

Thai seasonings—fresh ginger, red chili paste, cilantro, mint, and basil—caramelize on turkey thighs roasting over indirect heat on a grill.

Thai-seasoned Turkey Thigh Roast with Fresh Herbs

PREP AND COOK TIME: About 1¼ hours

NOTES: Have the turkey thighs boned and skinned at the meat market. Asian fish sauce and red chili paste are available in well-stocked supermarkets and in Asian grocery stores. You can assemble the roast (through step 2) up to 1 day ahead; cover and chill. If herb mixture sticks to plastic wrap, scrape off and pat back onto roast. Grill chilled roast 1 to 1¼ hours.

MAKES: 4 to 5 servings

- 2 boned, skinned **turkey thighs** (about ¾ lb. each; see notes)
- ¼ cup chopped **fresh basil** leaves
- ¼ cup chopped **fresh cilantro**
- ¼ cup chopped **fresh mint** leaves
- 3 cloves **garlic,** peeled and minced or pressed
- 1 tablespoon firmly packed **brown sugar**
- 1 tablespoon **soy sauce**
- 2 teaspoons minced **fresh ginger**
- 2 teaspoons **Asian fish sauce** (*nuoc mam* or *nam pla*)
- 2 teaspoons **salad oil**
- ½ teaspoon **Asian red chili paste**
   Lime wedges
   Salt

1. Rinse turkey thighs and pat dry.

2. In a bowl, mix basil, cilantro, mint, garlic, brown sugar, soy sauce, ginger, fish sauce, oil, and chili paste. Spread about 2 tablespoons of the mixture evenly over boned side of 1 turkey thigh. Set remaining thigh, boned side down, over herb mixture, aligning with first thigh. Tie thighs together at 1-inch intervals with cotton string to create a cylinder about 3 inches wide and 7 inches long. With your fingers, pat remaining herb mixture evenly all over roast.

3. Prepare barbecue for indirect heat according to instructions in box (above left). Cook roast until a thermometer inserted in center of meat reaches 170°, 40 to 45 minutes.

4. Transfer roast to a platter and, keeping it warm, let rest 5 to 10 minutes. Garnish platter with lime wedges. Cut roast into ½-inch-thick slices to serve. Squeeze juice from lime wedges over portions and add salt to taste.

Per serving: 209 cal., 33% (70 cal.) from fat; 28 g protein; 7.8 g fat (2.2 g sat.); 4.8 g carbo (0.5 g fiber); 400 mg sodium; 102 mg chol.

A turkey breast, pounded thin and rolled around cheese and fresh sage, makes a great summer entrée; grill cooked artichokes and polenta right alongside it on the barbecue.

Prosciutto-wrapped Turkey Breast with Fontina and Sage

PREP AND COOK TIME: About 1¼ hours

NOTES: If the turkey breast is sold unwrapped, have it skinned at the meat market. You can assemble the roast (through step 3) up to 1 day ahead; cover airtight and chill. Grill chilled roast about 40 minutes. Any leftover stuffed turkey breast is delicious sliced and served cool the next day.

MAKES: 4 to 6 servings

- 1 **boned turkey breast half** (about 1¾ lb.), skinned (see notes)
- 1 cup shredded **fontina cheese** (about 4 oz.)
- ¼ cup **grated parmesan cheese**
- 1 tablespoon finely chopped **fresh sage** leaves or 1 teaspoon dried rubbed sage

  Garlic oil (recipe follows)
- 3 ounces **thin-sliced prosciutto**

  Fresh sage sprigs (optional), rinsed

  Salt

1. Rinse turkey and pat dry. Place breast half, skinned side down, between sheets of plastic wrap; with a flat mallet, gently pound to an even ⅜ inch thick. Peel off top sheet of plastic wrap.

2. Sprinkle fontina and parmesan cheeses evenly over pounded turkey breast to within 1½ inches of edges. Scatter sage evenly over cheese. Fold narrow ends of turkey over cheese mixture, then from 1 long side, gently roll turkey, peeling the bottom sheet of plastic wrap away as you go, to enclose filling and form a log about 3 inches wide and 12 inches long. Brush all over with garlic oil.

3. Wrap prosciutto slices crosswise around turkey, overlapping to cover log completely, including ends. Tie roast with cotton string at 2-inch intervals.

4. Prepare barbecue for indirect heat according to instructions in box, page 168. Cook roast until a thermometer inserted in center of meat reaches 160°, 20 to 25 minutes.

5. Transfer roast to a platter and, keeping it warm, let rest 5 to 10 minutes. Garnish with sage sprigs if desired. Cut roast crosswise into ½-inch-thick slices to serve. Add salt to taste.

Per serving: 297 cal., 42% (126 cal.) from fat; 40 g protein; 14 g fat (5.6 g sat.); 1.1 g carbo (0.1 g fiber); 534 mg sodium; 110 mg chol.

Garlic oil. In a small, microwave-safe bowl, mix 2 tablespoons **olive oil**, 1 tablespoon minced **garlic**, and ¼ teaspoon **coarse-ground pepper**. Heat in a microwave oven at full power (100%) until garlic is fragrant, 45 to 60 seconds.

Chipotle- and Maple-glazed Pork Tenderloin

PREP AND COOK TIME: About 40 minutes

NOTES: You can prepare the roast (through step 2) up to 1 day ahead; cover meat and reserved chili–maple syrup mixture separately, both airtight, and chill. Grill the chilled roast about 35 minutes.

MAKES: 4 servings

- 3 tablespoons drained **canned chipotle chilies** plus 1 tablespoon sauce
- ⅔ cup **maple syrup**
- 2 tablespoons **coarse-grain Dijon mustard**
- 1 **pork tenderloin** (1 to 1¼ lb.), fat trimmed

  Salt

1. Wearing gloves, remove and discard seeds and veins from chilies. In a blender, whirl chilies, sauce from chilies, maple syrup, and mustard until smooth.

2. Rinse and dry pork. Trim excess fat and any thin, silvery membrane from tenderloin. Fold thin ends of meat under to make roast uniformly thick and tie cotton string crosswise around each end to secure. Set meat on a rimmed plate; pour about ⅓ cup chipotle–maple syrup mixture over pork and turn to coat completely.

3. Prepare barbecue for indirect heat according to instructions in box, page 168. Place roast on grill and cook until a thermometer inserted in its center reaches 150°, 20 to 25 minutes.

4. Transfer roast to a platter and, keeping it warm, let rest 5 minutes. Cut into thin slices and add salt to taste. Serve with remaining chipotle–maple syrup mixture.

Per serving: 299 cal., 16% (48 cal.) from fat; 22 g protein; 5.3 g fat (1.7 g sat.); 38 g carbo (0.4 g fiber); 363 mg sodium; 69 mg chol. ◆

flavor on a roll

Five great ways to stack a sandwich

By Linda Lau Anusasananan
Photographs by James Carrier

No time to sit down to a three-course meal? That's the predicament that fostered the invention of the sandwich—more than two centuries ago. When the notorious 18th-century British gambler Sir John Montagu, fourth earl of Sandwich, couldn't afford to take time out from a 24-hour marathon to eat, he slapped meat between two slices of bread so he wouldn't miss a hand. It goes without saying that this clever portable meal, dubbed the sandwich, of course, caught on—seems people are just as busy today as the famed earl. And markets and delis offer so many choices of breads and fillings, there's no need to repeat the same combo for months, unless you want to. Start with the five noble sandwiches here, then play inventor yourself.

■ Smoked
Salmon Bagel

Split a **pumpernickel** or plain **bagel** (6 oz.) in half horizontally. Spread cut sides with a total of 2 tablespoons **chive cream cheese**. Over cheese on 1 bagel half, layer ⅓ cup thinly sliced **English cucumber**, 3 ounces **thin-sliced smoked salmon**, 3 thin rings **red onion**, and ½ teaspoon **drained capers.** Set remaining bagel half, cream cheese side down, over filling.

Per sandwich: 680 cal., 23% (153 cal.) from fat; 34 g protein; 17 g fat (7.8 g sat.); 100 g carbo (7.1 g fiber); 2,893 mg sodium; 50 mg chol.

FOOD STYLING BY BASIL FRIEDMAN

■ Prosciutto Panini

Split a 6-inch length of **sweet baguette** (2 in. wide) in half horizontally. Drizzle cut surfaces with about 2 teaspoons **extra-virgin olive oil**. On cut side of baguette bottom, spread 1½ ounces (¼ cup) **chèvre** (goat) **cheese.** Top with ½ cup **arugula**

leaves and 2 to 3 ounces **thin-sliced prosciutto.** If desired, add a squeeze of **lemon juice** and a sprinkle of fresh-ground **pepper.** Set baguette top, cut side down, on filling.

Per sandwich: 534 cal., 54% (288 cal.) from fat; 31 g protein; 32 g fat (12 g sat.); 34 g carbo (1.9 g fiber); 1,647 mg sodium; 80 mg chol.

■ Breakfast Club

Spread about 2 teaspoons **mayonnaise** on 1 side of each of 3 toasted slices **English muffin bread** (4 in. square). Set 1 slice, mayonnaise side up, on a plate. Top with 2 soft-scrambled **large eggs** or 1 large egg fried sunny side up; sprinkle lightly with **salt** and **pepper**. Top with another slice of toast (mayonnaise side up), 1 **butter lettuce** leaf (optional), 1 thick slice **firm-ripe tomato**, 2 slices crisp-cooked **bacon,** and remaining toast (mayonnaise side down). Secure layers with toothpicks and cut sandwich into halves or quarters.

Per sandwich: 547 cal., 49% (270 cal.) from fat; 24 g protein; 30 g fat (8 g sat.); 43 g carbo (1.8 g fiber); 993 mg sodium; 446 mg chol.

■ Niçoise on a Roll

Split a **crusty sourdough** or other **sandwich roll** (3 to 4 oz.) in half horizontally; pull some of the soft interior out of top to accommodate filling. Drizzle cut surfaces with about 1 table-spoon **extra-virgin olive oil**. On cut side of roll bottom, layer 1 thin slice **red onion**, 3 thin slices **firm-ripe tomato**, 6 thin slices **cucumber**, 4 thin slices hard-cooked **large egg**, 3 ounces (⅓ cup) drained **canned tuna** (in oil), 5 pitted **niçoise olives**, and 2 or 3 drained **canned anchovies**. Drizzle evenly with 2 to 3 teaspoons **white wine vinegar**, and sprinkle with **salt** and **pepper** to taste. Set roll top in place, cut side down, and press down gently.

Per sandwich: 614 cal., 43% (261 cal.) from fat; 39 g protein; 29 g fat (5 g sat.); 49 g carbo (3.7 g fiber); 1,214 mg sodium; 126 mg chol.

■ Turkey Chutney Sandwich

On 1 slice (4 by 5 in.) of **whole-grain bread with nuts** or whole-wheat bread, place 1 **butter lettuce** leaf; 2 or 3 slices **smoked gouda**, sharp cheddar, or münster **cheese** (1½ oz. total); 3 ounces **thin-sliced roast turkey breast;** and 4 or 5 thin slices **pear** or apple. Spread evenly with 1 to 1½ table-spoons **mango chutney** such as Major Grey. Add **salt** and **pepper** to taste, and top with another slice of bread.

Per sandwich: 419 cal., 30% (126 cal.) from fat; 29 g protein; 14 g fat (8 g sat.); 44 g carbo (4.5 g fiber); 794 mg sodium; 84 mg chol. ◆

The Low-Fat Cook

Skinny on chicken salads

By Nicole Perzik

■ Some chicken salads drip with rich, creamy dressing—and weigh in with the expected number of calories from fat. Others boast virtuously lean figures but lack taste. Here are two that strike a balance. We start by grilling the leanest part of the bird, the breast (if time is short, you can purchase grilled chicken breast strips), then layer on flavor with a low-fat dairy product or olive oil, vinegar, fruit, and fresh herbs.

Chicken Salad in Pineapple Boats

PREP TIME: About 35 minutes
MAKES: 4 servings

1 **pineapple** (4¼ to 4½ lb.), rinsed

1 pound grilled **boned, skinned chicken breasts** (recipe at right), cool or cold

2 cups **red** or black **seedless grapes** (1 lb.), rinsed and drained

¼ cup **reduced-fat sour cream**

3 tablespoons **lemon juice**

2 tablespoons **dry white wine** (or 1 tablespoon white wine vinegar)

¼ teaspoon **sugar**

3 tablespoons chopped **fresh mint** leaves

Salt and **pepper**

Fresh mint sprigs (optional)

1. Cut unpeeled pineapple lengthwise into quarters. With a small, sharp knife, cut between flesh and peel of each quarter to release fruit in 1 piece; reserve shell. Trim core from fruit and discard. Cut fruit into ½-inch chunks and place in a large bowl.

2. Cut chicken into ¼-inch-thick strips 2 to 3 inches long. Add chicken and grapes to pineapple in bowl.

3. In a small bowl, whisk sour cream, lemon juice, wine, and sugar until smooth. Stir in chopped mint. Pour dressing over fruit and chicken and mix to coat. Add salt and pepper to taste.

4. Set each pineapple shell, cut side up, on a dinner plate. Spoon ¼ of the chicken salad into each shell, letting excess spill onto plate. Garnish with mint sprigs, if desired.

Per serving: 426 cal., 16% (70 cal.) from fat; 38 g protein; 7.8 g fat (2.4 g sat.); 54 g carbo (5.2 g fiber); 101 mg sodium; 101 mg chol.

Chicken and Pear Spinach Salad

PREP AND COOK TIME: About 20 minutes
MAKES: 4 servings

⅓ cup **slivered almonds**

1 pound grilled **boned, skinned chicken breasts** (recipe at right), cool or cold

1 **firm-ripe pear** (¾ lb.)

½ cup **balsamic vinegar**

2 tablespoons **extra-virgin olive oil**

About ½ teaspoon **garlic salt**

¾ pound **baby spinach leaves** (4 qt.), rinsed and crisped

½ cup **dried cranberries**

¼ cup thinly sliced **green onions** (including tops)

⅓ cup **crumbled feta cheese**

Pepper

Spice crisps (recipe follows)

1. In a 6- to 8-inch frying pan over medium heat, stir nuts until golden, about 6 minutes. Let cool.

2. Cut chicken into ¼-inch-thick strips 2 to 3 inches long. Rinse pear and cut lengthwise into quarters. Trim core from each quarter and discard; thinly slice quarters lengthwise.

Grilled Chicken Breasts

PREP AND COOK TIME: About 10 minutes

NOTES: If making up to 1 day ahead, cover and chill.

MAKES: About 1 pound cooked chicken; 4 servings

1. Rinse 4 **boned, skinned chicken breast halves** (about 5 oz. each); pat dry. Trim off and discard any excess fat.

2. Set breasts on an oiled grill 4 to 6 inches above a solid bed of hot coals or high heat on a gas grill (you can hold your hand at grill level only 2 to 3 seconds); close lid on gas grill. Cook chicken, turning once, until no longer pink in center of thickest part (cut to test), 7 to 9 minutes. Serve hot or cold.

Per serving: 187 cal., 20% (37 cal.) from fat; 35 g protein; 4.1 g fat (1.1 g sat.); 0 g carbo (0 g fiber); 84 mg sodium; 96 mg chol.

3. In a large bowl, mix vinegar, olive oil, and ½ teaspoon garlic salt. Add spinach, cranberries, green onions, almonds, chicken, and ¾ of the pear slices. Mix gently to coat.

4. Spoon ¼ of the salad onto each of 4 dinner plates. Top portions equally with remaining pear slices and sprinkle with cheese. Add garlic salt and pepper to taste. Serve with spice crisps.

Per serving: 645 cal., 29% (189 cal.) from fat; 47 g protein; 21 g fat (4.5 g sat.); 71 g carbo (9.5 g fiber); 1,056 mg sodium; 106 mg chol.

Spice Crisps

PREP AND COOK TIME: About 18 minutes

NOTES: If making up to 1 day ahead, cool and store airtight at room temperature.

MAKES: 8 crisps; 4 servings

1. In a small bowl, mix ½ teaspoon *each* **chili powder, ground coriander,** and **garlic salt.**

2. Split 4 (6-in. diameter) **pocket breads** apart to make 8 rounds. Lay rounds, rough side up and slightly apart, on two 12- by 15-inch baking sheets. Brush tops lightly with a total of 1 tablespoon **white wine vinegar;** sprinkle evenly with spice mixture.

3. Bake in a 375° regular or convection oven until rounds are crisp and lightly browned, 8 to 10 minutes. Serve warm or cool.

Per serving: 167 cal., 4.3% (7.2 cal.) from fat; 5.5 g protein; 0.8 g fat (0.1 g sat.); 34 g carbo (1.1 g fiber); 504 mg sodium; 0 mg chol. ◆

Celebrating 'shrooms in Telluride

In Colorado, August is the month to feast on (and learn about) flavorful fungus

By Hal Clifford

They're wild for mushrooms in Telluride. Every August, this southwestern Colorado town pays homage to the delectable 'shroom, and the fungus is celebrated with a parade, in a conference, and on restaurant menus. The chanterelle, oyster, porcini, and tree ear mushrooms are just a few of the treasures from forests that wind up on diners' plates.

Fungophiles hold a four-day gathering each year to forage for, discuss, and consume mushrooms. The Telluride Mushroom Festival (August 23–26 in 2001; $265) is geared to serious amateur mycologists. But anyone can watch the mushroom parade on Saturday or enjoy a mushroom-laced meal in a Telluride cafe (some three-fourths of the restaurants in town get in on the action, serving themed dishes during the festival).

"Truffles go amazingly well with sweets," says Chad Scothorn, who often leads hotel guests on mushroom- and truffle-hunting forays. He's the chef-owner of a fine place to sample mushroom dishes: **Cosmopolitan Restaurant** (300 W. San Juan Ave.; 970/728-1292). Try the six-course, four-wine mushroom festival dinner ($75; reservations required); some special menu items last year were porcini pot stickers and black truffle ice cream.

At **Campagna** (435 W. Pacific Ave.; 728-6190), chef-owner Vincent Esposito says his approach caters to "real mushroom-heads," and he'll have six to eight different species on the menu. "Risotto is a wonderful medium for mushrooms," he says. Or he may simply sauté some prime specimens with olive oil, a touch of fresh garlic, a bit of fresh sage, butter, salt, pepper, and a splash of wine. Other top-drawer restaurants offering mycological menus include **La Marmotte** (150 W. San Juan Ave.; 728-6232) and **221 South Oak** (221 S. Oak St.; 728-9507).

On Saturday the mushroom parade weaves down Telluride's main drag. The procession is usually led by a man who looks like a Tolkien character and carries a staff topped by a carved *Amanita muscaria;* participants dress as their favorite mushrooms. A sign at last year's parade summed up Telluride's sentiments nicely. It read: "Got 'Shrooms?"

For festival details, call (303) 296-9359 or visit www.telluridemm.com/mushroom.html. For lodging or dining information, call Resort Quest International at (800) 538-7754.

Kitchen Cabinet

Readers' recipes tested in *Sunset's* kitchens

By Paula Freschet

Dip shrimp, in the shell or out, in ginger sauce.

Crunchy Salt Shrimp with Ginger Sauce

Jean Patterson, Pasadena

While in Kenting, a fishing village in Taiwan, Jean Patterson was served just-caught shrimp crisp-fried in hot oil; to her delight, the shells were crunchy and edible, and the shrimp the most succulent she had eaten. Back home, she now cooks shrimp in the shell for adventurous guests; those less daring can shell the shrimp before eating them. You can also start with shelled shrimp.

PREP AND COOK TIME: About 40 minutes

MAKES: 4 servings

1 pound (21 to 25 per lb.) **shrimp in shells**

2 tablespoons **sake** or dry sherry

2 tablespoons **cornstarch**

2 tablespoons **soy sauce**

2 tablespoons **rice vinegar**

1 tablespoon minced **fresh ginger**

About 1½ cups **salad oil**

1 tablespoon minced **garlic**

1 teaspoon **kosher** or other coarse **salt**

¼ cup slivered **fresh basil** leaves

1. Devein shrimp in shells by pushing a toothpick perpendicular to each shrimp through a joint on the back shell and about ⅛ inch under the vein; pull up to lift out dark vein. If it breaks, repeat at another shell joint. If using shelled shrimp (see note at left), slit shrimp backs and pull out vein. Rinse shrimp, put in a bowl, and add sake and cornstarch; stir to mix well.

2. In another small bowl, combine soy sauce, vinegar, and ginger.

3. Pour about 1 inch oil into a 14-inch wok or deep, narrow 3- to 4-quart pan over high heat. When oil reaches 375°, add half the shrimp; stir often until they turn pink and shells are crisp, about 2 minutes (about 1 minute for shelled shrimp). With a slotted spoon, transfer shrimp to towels to drain. Repeat to cook remaining shrimp.

4. Drain oil from wok; discard or save for other uses. Set wok over medium heat, add garlic and salt, and stir until pan is hot. Add shrimp; stir until shrimp are coated with garlic mixture and hot, ½ to 1 minute.

5. Pour shrimp onto a platter, sprinkle with basil, and serve with ginger dipping sauce. Eat shells, if desired, or peel shrimp.

Per serving: 366 cal., 71% (261 cal.) from fat; 19 g protein; 29 g fat (3.8 g sat.); 6.8 g carbo (0.3 g fiber); 1,021 mg sodium; 140 mg chol.

Peachy Peach Ice Cream

Patti Devlin, Lafayette, CA

Very ripe peaches are the flavor secret to this simple ice cream. Patti Devlin uses unpeeled peaches because she likes the flavor the skins add. Our tasters preferred the smoother texture that results from peeling the fruit. It's your choice.

PREP AND COOK TIME: About 45 minutes

MAKES: About 4 cups; 4 to 6 servings

1½ pounds **ripe peaches**

1½ tablespoons **lemon juice**

2 teaspoons **vanilla**

About ⅔ cup **sugar**

2 cups **half-and-half** (light cream)

1. Peel peaches if desired (see note above), then pit and slice them. In a food processor or blender, purée ⅔ of the peaches with 1 tablespoon lemon juice, vanilla, and ⅓ cup sugar. Pour into a large bowl, add half-and-half, and nest bowl in ice water; stir often until cold, 10 to 15 minutes. Or cover and chill until cold, about 1 hour.

2. In a bowl, with a potato masher or fork, coarsely mash remaining peaches with ½ tablespoon lemon juice and ⅓ cup sugar. Set container in ice water and stir often until cold, about 5 minutes. Add to half-and-half mixture; taste, and add more sugar if desired.

3. Pour chilled mixture into a 1-quart (or larger) ice cream maker. Freeze according to manufacturer's directions until mixture is firm enough to scoop, dasher is hard to turn, or machine stops.

4. Serve ice cream softly frozen, or package airtight and freeze up to 1 week; let stand at room temperature 10 to 20 minutes to soften for scooping.

Per serving: 232 cal., 36% (84 cal.) from fat; 3 g protein; 9.3 g fat (5.7 g sat.); 36 g carbo (1.4 g fiber); 34 mg sodium; 30 mg chol.

Brunch BLTs with Chilies and Cheese

Mickey Strang, McKinleyville, CA

"We like these for Saturday morning breakfast (while we read the Sunday paper, which comes on Saturday … go figure!), but they also make a good light supper," says Mickey Strang of these hearty sandwiches.

PREP AND COOK TIME: About 50 minutes

MAKES: 4 servings

8 slices **bacon** (about ½ lb.)

8 slices **sourdough bread,** each 4 by 6 inches and ½ inch thick

¼ pound thinly sliced **jack cheese with chilies**

1 can (7 oz.) **whole green chilies,** drained and torn into strips

2 **firm-ripe tomatoes** (4 to 5 oz. each), rinsed, cored, and sliced

Salt

5 **large eggs**

¼ cup **milk**

1 tablespoon **butter** or margarine

4 large leaves **red-leaf lettuce,** rinsed and crisped (optional)

1. In a 10- to 12-inch frying pan over medium heat, cook bacon until brown and crisp, about 15 minutes, turning slices as needed. Drain bacon on towels and discard fat.

2. On each of 4 bread slices, lay 2 bacon slices. Arrange cheese, chilies, and tomatoes equally on bacon; sprinkle lightly with salt. Cover each stack with another slice of bread.

3. In a wide, shallow dish, beat eggs with milk to blend. On a 12-inch nonstick griddle or in a 12-inch nonstick frying pan over medium-high heat, melt half the butter. Meanwhile, one at a time, lay sandwiches in egg mixture; let stand about 15 seconds on each side. Lift out; put on griddle, 2 sandwiches at a time.

4. Brown sandwiches on each side, turning as needed, about 10 minutes. When they are cooked, transfer to a baking sheet and keep warm in a 200° oven. Add remaining butter to pan and cook remaining 2 sandwiches. Set hot sandwiches on plates and tuck a lettuce leaf alongside each.

Per serving: 517 cal., 49% (252 cal.) from fat; 26 g protein; 28 g fat (12 g sat.); 39 g carbo (2.8 g fiber); 1,232 mg sodium; 319 mg chol.

Garden Vegetable Pizza

Marsha Lawhorn, St. George, UT

On an evening too hot for a meat main dish—and too cool for a salad—Marsha Lawhorn used produce from her garden to make this all-vegetable pizza compromise. For a repeat performance, her family demanded she double the recipe—one pizza just wasn't enough for their appreciative appetites.

PREP AND COOK TIME: 40 to 45 minutes

MAKES: 6 to 8 servings

¼ cup **cider vinegar**

3 tablespoons **olive oil**

1 clove **garlic,** peeled and minced or pressed

1 tablespoon minced **shallots**

1 tablespoon chopped **fresh basil** leaves or 1 teaspoon dried basil

1 teaspoon **fresh thyme** leaves or dried thyme

1 teaspoon chopped **fresh rosemary** leaves or ½ teaspoon dried rosemary

2 **thin, baked pizza crusts** (10 oz. each, 12 in. wide)

2 cups thinly sliced **mushrooms**

2 cups thinly sliced **yellow crookneck squash**

1½ cups thinly sliced **Roma tomatoes**

1 cup diced **orange** or red **bell peppers**

1 cup thinly sliced **green onions**

Salt

2 cups **shredded mozzarella cheese** (½ lb.)

½ cup **grated parmesan cheese**

1. In a bowl, mix vinegar, oil, garlic, shallots, basil, thyme, and rosemary.

2. Set pizza crusts in 2 pizza pans (12 in. wide) or on 2 baking sheets (12 by 15 in.). Brush crusts equally with all but 2 tablespoons of the vinegar-oil mixture. Layer mushrooms, squash, tomatoes, peppers, and onions equally over crusts. Sprinkle lightly with salt, then equally with mozzarella and parmesan cheeses.

3. Bake in a 425° regular or convection oven until cheese is lightly browned, 15 to 20 minutes. Drizzle with remaining vinegar-oil mixture. Cut into wedges.

Per serving: 425 cal., 42% (180 cal.) from fat; 11 g protein; 20 g fat (7.1 g sat.); 47 g carbo (4.9 g fiber); 376 mg sodium; 26 mg chol.

Pork Scaloppine with Plum-Port Sauce

Marilou Robinson, Portland

The flavor of this sweet-tart plum-port sauce, which is a wonderful complement to pork, changes depending on the variety of fruit you use; however, heating intensifies the flavor of all plums.

PREP AND COOK TIME: About 50 minutes

MAKES: 6 to 8 servings

¾ pound **firm-ripe red-** or purple-skinned **plums**

2 tablespoons chopped **shallots**

1 clove **garlic,** peeled and chopped

1 tablespoon **sugar**

3 tablespoons **red wine vinegar**

1 cup **port**

½ cup fat-skimmed **chicken broth**

2 **pork tenderloins** (1¾ to 2 lb. total), fat trimmed

1 to 2 tablespoons **olive oil**

1½ tablespoons **butter** or margarine

Salt and **cracked black pepper**

1. Rinse plums, cut in half, and pit. Cut about 1 cup thin slices, cover, and set aside up to 6 hours. Cut remaining fruit into chunks and drop into a blender or food processor; whirl until puréed.

2. In a 10- to 12-inch nonstick frying pan over high heat, boil plum purée, shallots, garlic, sugar, vinegar, port, and broth, stirring often until reduced to 1½ cups, about 10 minutes. Pour into a bowl; cover and let stand at room temperature up to 6 hours. Rinse and dry pan.

3. Meanwhile, rinse pork, pat dry, and cut across the grain into ¾-inch-thick slices. A few slices at a time, place meat between sheets of plastic wrap and, with a flat mallet, pound firmly but gently to an even ¼ inch thick. Roll meat in plastic wrap, put in a plastic bag, seal, and chill up to 6 hours.

4. In the frying pan over high heat, combine 1 tablespoon oil and the butter. When butter is sizzling, peel plastic wrap from meat and fill pan with 1 layer of pork. As pieces shrink, add more meat. Cook, turning to brown on each side, until no longer pink in center (cut to test), about 5 minutes per batch. Add more oil as needed. As scaloppine is cooked, transfer to a platter and keep warm in a 200° oven.

5. Pour port-plum sauce into frying pan and stir over high heat until boiling; pour into a small bowl. Garnish scaloppine with reserved plum slices. Ladle plum sauce over portions; add salt and pepper to taste.

Per serving: 201 cal., 34% (68 cal.) from fat; 22 g protein; 7.5 g fat (2.8 g sat.); 11 g carbo (0.9 g fiber); 79 mg sodium; 70 mg chol. ◆

New take on an old favorite: fresh corn tamale pie topped with spicy chorizo and tender strips of cactus (recipe on page 188).

September

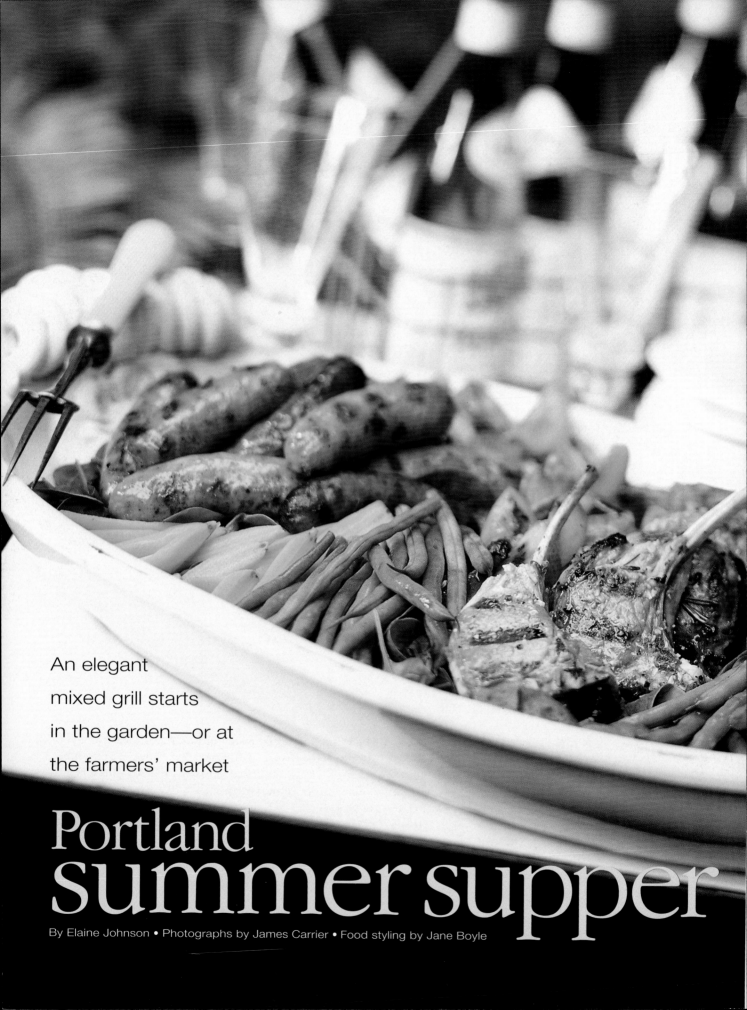

An elegant
mixed grill starts
in the garden—or at
the farmers' market

Portland
summer supper

By Elaine Johnson • Photographs by James Carrier • Food styling by Jane Boyle

summer supper for eight

APPETIZER:
- Rainbow Tomato Bruschetta*
- *Vin d'Orange**

FIRST COURSE:
- Seafood Timbales with Tarragon Beurre Blanc*
- *Chehalem Pinot Gris*

MAIN COURSE:
- Lamb and Sausage Mixed Grill with Molasses-glazed Nectarines*
- Summer Beans and Carrots
- Golden Saffron Rice*
- *Chehalem Pinot Noir*

SALAD:
- Fennel and Greens*

DESSERT:
- Chocolate-Espresso Torte with Raspberry Sauce*
- Lemon Sherbet
- *Clear Creek Distillery Framboise*

*recipe provided

Riches of the Northwest—a verdant backyard, aromatic Pinots, and a platter of local sausages, lamb, and produce.

■ "In summer, my backyard is an intimate outdoor room walled in a tangle of greenery," says Linda Wisner of Portland. The flowers, herbs, and vegetables—including more than a dozen kinds of tomatoes—form a natural backdrop for an alfresco dinner party.

Wisner and her brother, Darryl, harvest the late-summer treasures from that garden for this menu for eight—basil and savory for tomato bruschetta, tarragon for a beurre blanc to set off delicate seafood timbales, nasturtiums for saffron rice, lemon verbena for an icy sherbet. And in keeping with the local-bounty theme, they offer Oregon wines.

But whether you snip the herbs and blooms yourself or fill a basket at a farmers' market, the message of this mixed grill is about the best of the season and the place. (And a good Pinot Noir from anywhere in the West would underline the theme.)

Pile heirloom tomatoes of every stripe on crunchy baguette slices.

(at least 2½ qt.); save fruit for other uses (see notes) or discard. Taste, and add more sugar if desired. Chill until cold, at least 2 hours and up to 1 day.

Per ½ cup: 142 cal., 0% (0 cal.) from fat; 0.2 g protein; 0 g fat; 13 g carbo (0 g fiber); 4.1 mg sodium; 0 mg chol.

Seafood Timbales with Tarragon Beurre Blanc

PREP AND COOK TIME: About 35 minutes

NOTES: Prepare timbales through step 3 up to 1 day ahead; chill airtight. Warm plates in a 200° oven for 10 minutes before serving timbales.

MAKES: 8 servings

- ½ pound **boned, skinned salmon fillet**
- ¼ pound **uncooked shelled, deveined shrimp**
- ¼ pound **bay scallops**
- 2 **large egg** whites
- ½ teaspoon **salt**
- ⅛ teaspoon **cayenne**
- ⅛ teaspoon **ground nutmeg**
- 1½ cups **whipping cream**
  Tarragon Beurre Blanc (recipe follows)
  Fresh chives or fresh tarragon sprigs, rinsed

1. Rinse and drain salmon, shrimp, and scallops. Cut salmon into 1-inch chunks.
2. In a food processor, whirl seafood to a thick paste. Add egg whites, salt, cayenne, and nutmeg; whirl until blended. Then add cream and whirl until very smooth.
3. Butter 8 molds or ramekins (⅓- to ½-cup size). Spoon seafood mixture equally into molds and spread level.

Rainbow Tomato Bruschetta

PREP AND COOK TIME: About 20 minutes

NOTES: Wisner uses a mix of heirloom tomato varieties from her garden; heirlooms are available in many farmers' markets. Toast the baguette slices up to 1 day ahead; cool, wrap airtight, and store at room temperature. Prepare tomatoes up to 1 hour ahead; cover and let stand at room temperature.

MAKES: 8 servings

1. Cut 1 **seeded baguette** (about ¾ lb.) diagonally into ¼-inch-thick slices; arrange in a single layer on two 14- by 17-inch baking sheets. Bake in a 450° regular or convection oven until golden, 4 to 5 minutes. Let cool, then mound in a basket or arrange on a platter.
2. Rinse and core 2⅓ pounds **firm-ripe tomatoes** (red, orange, yellow, and/or green; large and small). For tomatoes larger than 1 inch in diameter, thinly slice crosswise; arrange in a single layer on a rimmed platter. For smaller tomatoes, halve lengthwise and scatter on top. Drizzle 3 tablespoons **extra-virgin olive oil** evenly over tomatoes; sprinkle with 3 tablespoons chopped **fresh herbs** such as chives, basil leaves, and savory leaves. Season to taste with **salt** and **pepper.** Serve with toasted baguette slices. Mound tomatoes on slices to eat.

Per serving: 189 cal., 33% (62 cal.) from fat; 4.8 g protein; 6.9 g fat (1 g sat.); 28 g carbo (2.8 g fiber); 270 mg sodium; 0 mg chol.

Vin d'Orange

PREP TIME: About 15 minutes, plus at least 1 week to steep

NOTES: Start this aperitif at least 1 week or up to 3 weeks ahead (the longer it steeps, the stronger its flavor will be). Wisner chops the fruit strained from the aperitif and cooks it with onion, butter, and curry powder to make a sauce for roasted poultry.

MAKES: About 9 cups

- 2 bottles (750 ml. each) **dry white wine** such as Riesling
- 1¼ cups **brandy**
  About 1 cup **sugar**
- 3 **oranges** (1⅓ lb. total), rinsed and cut into 2-inch chunks
- ½ **lemon** (2½ oz.), rinsed and cut into 2-inch chunks

1. In a 1-gallon jar, stir wine, brandy, 1 cup sugar, oranges, and lemon until sugar is dissolved. Seal airtight (if seal is rubber or synthetic rubber, cover jar top with plastic wrap before screwing on top). Let stand in a cool, dark place at least 1 week or up to 3 weeks, stirring occasionally.
2. Pour mixture through a strainer set over a pitcher

Delicate seafood timbales can be assembled a day ahead of your party.

Lamb chops and sausages paired with molasses-glazed nectarines.
LEFT: Darryl Wisner hosts.

4. Pour ½ inch of boiling water into a 12- by 17-inch baking pan. Set molds in water and cover pan tightly with foil.

5. Bake in a 350° regular or convection oven until a metal skewer inserted in center of timbales comes out clean, about 15 minutes. With a wide spatula, lift timbales from water. If done up to 30 minutes ahead, cover loosely with foil and let stand at room temperature.

6. Spoon Tarragon Beurre Blanc equally onto eight warm plates (see notes). Run a knife between timbales and sides of molds. Invert a mold over sauce on each plate to release timbale; remove mold. Garnish timbales with fresh chives.

Per serving: 393 cal., 85% (333 cal.) from fat; 13 g protein; 37 g fat (21 g sat.); 3.4 g carbo (0 g fiber); 433 mg sodium; 145 mg chol.

Tarragon Beurre Blanc

1. In a 2- to 3-quart pan over high heat, boil ⅓ cup **white wine vinegar,** ⅓ cup **dry vermouth,** 3 tablespoons minced **shallots,** and 1½ tablespoons chopped **fresh tarragon** until reduced to ¼ cup, 5 to 8 minutes. Let stand at room temperature up to 2 hours.

2. Just before serving, set pan over high heat, add ¾ cup (⅜ lb.) **butter,** and stir constantly until it's melted and bubbling, 2 to 3 minutes. Serve warm.

Lamb and Sausage Mixed Grill with Molasses-glazed Nectarines

PREP AND COOK TIME: 40 minutes, plus at least 15 minutes to marinate
NOTES: Arrange hot cooked carrots and green beans such as Kentucky Wonder or Scarlet Runner on platter alongside mixed grill (see photo, page 178); you'll need about 1½ pounds of each. Drizzle vegetables with olive oil and sprinkle with salt and pepper.

MAKES: 8 servings

- 8 **lamb rib chops** (each about ¾ in. thick, 3 to 4 oz.)
- 2 tablespoons **olive oil**
- ⅓ cup **chopped fresh rosemary** leaves or 2 tablespoons dried rosemary
- 3 tablespoons chopped **garlic**
  About ½ teaspoon **salt**
  About ¼ teaspoon **pepper**
- 8 **sausages** (2 lb. total) such as mild or hot Italian
- 2 quarts **baby spinach leaves** (⅔ lb.), rinsed and drained
  Molasses-glazed Nectarines (recipe follows)

1. Rinse lamb chops and pat dry. Trim off and discard excess surface fat. In a bowl, mix chops with olive oil, rosemary, garlic, ½ teaspoon salt, and ¼ teaspoon pepper. Cover and chill at least 15 minutes or up to 2 hours.

2. Lay chops and sausages on a barbecue grill over a solid bed of hot coals or high heat on a gas grill (you can hold your hand at grill level only 2 to 3 seconds); close lid on gas grill. Turn chops and sausages as needed until they're browned on both sides, lamb is still pink in center of thickest part (medium-rare; cut to test), 6 to 8 minutes total (or done to your liking), and sausages are no longer pink in the center (cut to test), 10 to 12 minutes total.

3. Meanwhile, mound spinach leaves on a large rimmed platter. Arrange lamb chops and sausages on spinach and keep warm.

4. With a slotted spoon, lift Molasses-glazed Nectarines from marinade

(reserve marinade) and lay on grill. Turn as needed until quarters are beginning to brown on both sides, about 2 minutes total. Arrange beside meats on platter. Drizzle marinade evenly over nectarines and meats. Add more salt and pepper to taste

Per serving: 464 cal., 56% (261 cal.) from fat; 27 g protein; 29 g fat (9.2 g sat.); 26 g carbo (4.5 g fiber); 862 mg sodium; 89 mg chol.

MOLASSES-GLAZED NECTARINES. In a large bowl, combine 1 tablespoon *each* **molasses, sherry vinegar** or **balsamic vinegar,** and firmly packed **brown sugar.** Rinse, pit, and quarter 5 **firm-ripe nectarines** (½ lb. each). Add to marinade and mix gently. Let stand 15 to 30 minutes.

Golden Saffron Rice

PREP AND COOK TIME: About 20 minutes
NOTES: If making up to 30 minutes ahead, after fluffing with fork, cover pan again and let stand at room temperature. If desired, garnish rice with 1 cup rinsed and drained nasturtium blossoms grown without pesticides.
MAKES: 8 servings

In a 4- to 5-quart pan over high heat, bring 4 cups fat-skimmed **chicken broth,** 2 cups **basmati rice,** ½ teaspoon **salt,** and ⅛ teaspoon **saffron** to a boil. Cover and reduce heat; simmer until liquid is absorbed and rice is tender to bite, about 18 minutes. Remove from heat, stir with a fork to fluff, then spoon into a bowl.

Per serving: 173 cal., 4.2% (7.2 cal.) from fat; 8.9 g protein; 0.8 g fat (0 g sat.); 36 g carbo (0.5 g fiber); 203 mg sodium; 0 mg chol.

(Continued on page 182)

ABOVE: Chocolate torte is flavored with espresso and served with fresh berries. LEFT: Linda Wisner revels in the evening.

C O U N T D O W N

■ **One to two weeks ahead:** **Make** vin d'orange.

■ **One day ahead: Toast** baguette for bruschetta. **Strain** fruit from vin d'orange. **Prepare** seafood timbales through step 3. **Rinse** and **crisp** salad greens. **Make** chocolate-espresso torte and raspberry sauce.

■ **Two hours ahead: Prepare** tarragon beurre blanc through step 1. **Marinate** lamb chops for mixed grill and **make** marinade for nectarines. **Prepare** salad (through step 2).

■ **The last hour: Prepare** tomatoes for bruschetta. **Bake** timbales. **Marinate** nectarines for mixed grill. **Finish** beurre blanc.

■ **Fifteen minutes before serving main course: Grill** chops, sausages, and nectarines for mixed grill; **cook** beans and carrots.

Fennel and Greens

PREP TIME: About 20 minutes

NOTES: Wisner especially likes to use Lollo Rosso lettuce for this salad, but any red-leaf lettuce is attractive. Up to 1 day ahead, rinse lettuce and arugula; wrap in towels, then in plastic bags, and chill. Up to 2 hours ahead, prepare salad through step 2; cover and chill. Mix just before serving.

MAKES: 8 servings

- ½ cup **extra-virgin olive oil**
- 2 tablespoons **lemon juice**
- 1 teaspoon **Dijon mustard**
- 1 head **fennel** (4 to 5 in. wide)
- 9 cups bite-size pieces rinsed and crisped **red-leaf lettuce** leaves (see notes)
- 6 cups lightly packed rinsed and crisped **arugula** (see notes)
  Salt and **pepper**

1. In a wide bowl, mix olive oil, lemon juice, and mustard.

2. Trim stalks from fennel. Rinse feathery green leaves and chop enough to measure ¼ cup; discard remaining leaves and stalks. Trim and discard root end, any bruised areas, and coarse fibers from fennel head; rinse head, thinly slice, and mix with dressing in bowl. Add chopped fennel greens, lettuce, and arugula to bowl.

3. Lift with salad fork and spoon to mix with dressing. Season to taste with salt and pepper.

Per serving: 147 cal., 86% (126 cal.) from fat; 1.8 g protein; 14 g fat (2 g sat.); 5.4 g carbo (1.9 g fiber); 43 mg sodium; 0 mg chol.

Chocolate-Espresso Torte with Raspberry Sauce

PREP AND COOK TIME: About 1 hour, plus at least 1½ hours to chill

NOTES: If you don't have an espresso machine, buy prepared espresso from a coffee shop or use strong brewed coffee: Pour ¾ cup hot (about 195°) water through ⅓ cup ground coffee in a filter cone. If making torte and sauce up to 1 day ahead, chill separately airtight. Serve with scoops of lemon sherbet.

MAKES: 8 to 12 servings

- About 1½ cups (¾ lb.) **butter** or margarine, cut into chunks
- ¾ pound **bittersweet** or semisweet **chocolate,** chopped
- ½ cup **espresso** (see notes)
  About 1 cup **sugar**
- 6 **large eggs**
- 5 cups **raspberries,** rinsed
- 1 cup **marionberries** or blackberries
  Fresh mint sprigs, rinsed

1. Butter and flour an 8-inch cheesecake pan.

2. In a 3- to 4-quart pan over low heat, frequently stir chocolate, 1½ cups butter, espresso, and ¾ cup sugar just until chocolate is melted and mixture is smooth, 12 to 15 minutes.

3. In a bowl, beat eggs to blend. Whisk in chocolate mixture until well blended. Pour into cheesecake pan.

4. Bake torte in a 350° regular or convection oven until center barely jiggles when pan is gently shaken, about 40 minutes. Let cool on a rack for 30 minutes (center of torte will sink), then chill until cold, at least 1½ hours.

5. Meanwhile, in a food processor or blender, whirl 1 quart raspberries until smooth. Rub purée through a fine strainer into a bowl; discard seeds. Stir ¼ cup sugar into raspberry purée; taste, and add more sugar if desired.

6. Spoon raspberry sauce equally onto plates. Run a knife between torte and pan rim; remove rim. Cut torte into wedges. Arrange a wedge on sauce on each plate. Scatter remaining 1 cup raspberries and marionberries over desserts, and garnish with mint sprigs.

Per serving: 475 cal., 68% (324 cal.) from fat; 5.9 g protein; 36 g fat (20 g sat.); 40 g carbo (3.6 g fiber); 266 mg sodium; 168 mg chol. ◆

Shaking up the vines in Lodi

This Central Valley town is famous for growing Zin with zing.
A new wine center, wine trail, and tasting rooms let you sample the fun

By Lisa Taggart

Twenty feet above a Syrah vineyard in Lodi, 35 miles south of Sacramento, I'm riding a tractorlike harvester that's giving the vines a good shaking. The moon rises behind me as the small purple grapes pile up in the container, and a chill wind raises goose bumps on my arms.

That breeze is the secret to success for the more than 600,000 tons of grapes grown in the Lodi appellation each year. Though this midsize Central Valley farming town gets plenty of sunshine, evening winds coming off the delta prevent grapes from overheating here. This combination of warm days and cool nights is great for wine flavor, vintners say.

"We can grow anything here," boasts David Phillips, who owns the vines my harvester is shaking. A fifth-generation Lodi farmer, he runs Phillips Vineyards with his brother, Michael. His family's farm has been growing increasing quantities and varieties of grapes, garnering awards for such unusual varieties as Symphony and Roussanne. "We can grow the best Zinfandel grapes in the world."

"We sure do make good wine here"

Lodi farmers have been growing grapes since 1850. Today they produce more Zinfandel, Cabernet Sauvignon, and Merlot than any other place in California—more than Napa and Sonoma combined—for major winemakers such as Ravenswood, Glen Ellen, and Fetzer. But Lodi has never been known as a wine-tasting center. Locals say that is changing.

Last year, Discover Lodi Wine & Visitor Center opened near downtown. It offers exhibits on grape growing and winemaking as well as a virtual tour of the area—and lets visitors sample from a selection of 60 Lodi wines. The 30-mile Lodi Wine Trail loop leads to 12 tasting rooms and shows off both boutique wineries and large-scale operations as Robert Mondavi.

Despite these new ventures, the idea of wine tasting and wine touring in Lodi may have to grow on some people. Lance Randolph, of Peirano Estate Vineyards, tells the story of an elderly resident who saw a Peirano wine selling for $10 a bottle.

"Who would pay that much for Lodi wine?" she scoffed. He offered to purchase the bottle for her if she'd taste the wine and report back. A few days later she showed up in his tasting room. "We sure make good wine here, don't we?" she said proudly.

"All of a sudden, it was 'we,'" he laughs. "That's what we're doing here—making locals proud."

My tour is finished and I climb down from the machine. It occurs to me that the Phillips family is trying to shake up the wine world just like the harvester was rattling those vines.

Michael Phillips nods as he gazes across the field of hunched leafy shapes: "People keep changing their ideas about what can and can't be done in Lodi."

Lodi Wineries

Lodi is 35 miles south of Sacramento off I-5. For general area information, contact the **Lodi Conference & Visitors Bureau** (2545 W. Turner Rd.; 209/365-1195). All of these wineries lie along the 30-mile Lodi Wine Trail; for a map, visit **Discover Lodi Wine & Visitor Center** in the same building (365-0621).

Area code is 209 unless noted.

Jessie's Grove Winery. This winery and horse farm, run by a fourth-generation farming family, has 112-year-old Zinfandel vines. *11–4 Fri–Sun. 1973 W. Turner, Lodi; 368-0880.*

Lucas Winery. Winemaker David Lucas creates elegant wines out of his Chardonnay and Zinfandel grapes. His traditional operation is set in a barn that's almost 100 years old. *12–5 Thu–Sun. 18196 N. Davis Rd., Lodi; 368-2006.*

Peirano Estate Vineyards. Grows old-vine Zinfandel first planted in the early 1800s, as well as Chardonnay, Cabernet Sauvignon, and Merlot. *10–5 Fri–Sun. 21831 N. State 99, Acampo; 369-9463.*

Phillips Vineyards. Winery includes a produce stand and cafe as well as wine-tasting bar, offering Zinfandel and Chardonnay in addition to many uncommon varietals. *8–5 daily. 4580 W. State 12, Lodi; 368-7384.*

Spenker Winery. Family winery features some of the area's best old-vine Zin. *By appointment. 17303 N. DeVries Rd., Lodi; 367-0467.*

Woodbridge Winery by Robert Mondavi. One of the largest Lodi operations, Woodbridge offers tastes of Cabernet, Chardonnay, Sauvignon Blanc, and Zinfandel. *10:30–4:30 Tue–Sun. 5950 E. Woodbridge Rd., Acampo; 365-2839.* ◆

food guide

By Jerry Anne Di Vecchio   Photographs by James Carrier

It must be the cheese

That favorite
Parisian grilled
sandwich, the
croque
monsieur, is
making a lively
comeback on
menus chic
and plebeian

■ One diners' dictionary on my desk translates *croque monsieur* as "crunch, sir." To the French, it means a toasted ham and cheese sandwich, which (happily) American cooks are taking considerable liberties with. First, James Beard added mustard. District restaurant in New York recently served a version with whole-grain mustard and béchamel sauce on brioche. In Minneapolis, at Brasserie Zinc, the ham is rippled on top of a split baguette and topped with béchamel and a layer of gruyère. In San Francisco, at Baker Street Bistro, the cheese sauce is spread both in the sandwich and over the top; then the bundle is broiled. Personally, I've never met a croque monsieur I didn't like. This one—with a nod to Beard and the Baker Street Bistro—and a green salad make a mighty fine *petit* meal.

Croque Monsieur

PREP AND COOK TIME: 20 to 25 minutes
NOTES: Have ham cut at the deli counter in your supermarket.
MAKES: 4 sandwiches

- 2 tablespoons minced **shallots**
- 2 to 3 tablespoons **butter** or margarine, at room temperature
- 1 tablespoon **all-purpose flour**
- ¼ cup fat-skimmed **chicken broth**
- ¼ cup **milk** or whipping cream
- 6 ounces **gruyère**, Swiss, or fontina **cheese,** shredded (1½ cups)

  About ¹⁄₁₆ teaspoon fresh-grated or ground **nutmeg**
- 8 slices **firm white bread** (each about 4 in. square and ½ in. thick)
- ¼ pound **very thinly sliced cooked ham** (see notes)
- 2 tablespoons **Dijon mustard**

1. In a 10- to 12-inch nonstick frying pan over medium-high heat, stir shallots in 1 tablespoon butter. Stir often until golden, about 3 minutes. Add flour; stir until blended. Remove from heat and add broth and milk; whisk to blend well. Return to heat and whisk until mixture is boiling vigorously. Remove from heat and add cheese and nutmeg; stir until cheese is melted. Pour sauce into a bowl. Rinse and dry pan.

2. Lightly butter one side of each bread slice and lay buttered sides down on a board. Divide half the cheese sauce equally among 4 slices; spread sauce to edges. Lay ham equally over sauce. Spread mustard equally on unbuttered sides of remaining 4 bread slices; invert each onto a slice topped with ham.

3. Put frying pan on medium heat. Lay two sandwiches in pan; cover and cook until well browned on the bottom. Turn with a spatula and brown other sides, about 4 minutes total. Transfer sandwiches to a 10- by 15-inch pan and keep warm, uncovered, in a 200° oven. Repeat to cook remaining sandwiches. Spoon remaining cheese sauce equally over sandwiches; spread slightly over edges.

4. Broil sandwiches about 4 inches from heat until sauce is bubbling and lightly browned, 1 to 1½ minutes.

Per sandwich: 496 cal., 45% (225 cal.) from fat; 26 g protein; 25 g fat (13 g sat.); 38 g carbo (1.7 g fiber); 1,201 mg sodium; 82 mg chol.

Limelight on a leaf

■ If you happen to spot glossy, deep green fresh makrut lime leaves in a well-stocked produce section or Asian market, buy a handful. When cut, rubbed, or crushed, makrut (also called Kieffer) lime leaves exude a marvelous, complex citrus aroma that is at once terribly familiar and—unless you know what it is—unidentifiable. In Thai, Indonesian, Malaysian, and Vietnamese cooking, the leaves play an important role in seasoning soups, curries, salads, and other dishes. John Beardsley, chef at San Francisco's Ponzu restaurant, makes good use of the leaves, following both Southeast Asian traditions and his own creative direction, as in the dressing for this refreshing honeydew and cantaloupe salad.

You can order fresh makrut lime leaves from Uwajimaya (800/889-1928 or bobh@uwajimaya.com). They can be frozen for two to three months.

Melon and Shrimp Salad

PREP AND COOK TIME: About 20 minutes

NOTES: Makrut (Kieffer) lime leaves resemble pairs of wings (see photo below). If fresh leaves aren't available, use ¼ teaspoon *each* grated lime peel and lemon peel and omit heating the sugar, ginger, and water.

MAKES: 4 to 6 servings

- 1 tablespoon **sugar**
- 1 tablespoon minced **fresh ginger**
- 1 **makrut lime leaf** (sections 2½ to 3 in. long; see notes), rinsed
- ¼ cup **lime juice**
- 2 tablespoons **Asian fish sauce** (*nuoc mam* or *nam pla*) or soy sauce
- 1 **cantaloupe** (about 1½ lb., or a 1½-lb. piece)
- 1 **honeydew** (about 1½ lb., or a 1½-lb. piece)
- ½ pound **shelled cooked tiny shrimp**
- 1 **fresh jalapeño chili,** rinsed, stemmed, seeded, and minced

- 1 tablespoon slivered **fresh basil leaves**
- 1 tablespoon finely chopped **fresh cilantro**
- 2 tablespoons finely chopped **salted roasted peanuts**

1. In a microwave-safe bowl, mix sugar, ginger, and 1 tablespoon water. Cut lime leaf crosswise into thin slivers; add to bowl. Heat in a microwave oven on full power (100%) until hot, about 30 seconds. Add lime juice and fish sauce, stir, and let dressing stand.

2. Rinse cantaloupe and honeydew; cut off and discard peel, cut melons in half, and scoop out and discard seeds. Cut each melon into 1-inch-thick slices and arrange on a platter.

3. Place shrimp in a colander and rinse under cold water; lay on towels to drain. Scatter shrimp over melon. Stir minced chili (to taste) into dressing, then spoon dressing over melon and shrimp. Sprinkle basil and cilantro over salad, then top with peanuts. To serve, spoon portions, including dressing, onto plates.

Per serving: 119 cal., 19% (23 cal.) from fat; 10 g protein; 2.6 g fat (0.8 g sat.); 15 g carbo (1.3 g fiber); 307 mg sodium; 74 mg chol.

Little Brussels

■ Whole brussels sprouts are pretty intense. But taken leaf by leaf, they can be light and delicate. Gordon Drysdale, chef-owner of Gordon's House of Fine Eats in San Francisco, prepares them this way in a hot, wilted green salad, a dish in which spinach is the usual principal. The brussels sprouts' mild, cabbagelike flavor and firm texture lend more character, in my opinion.

Brussels Sprouts Salad

PREP AND COOK TIME: About 1 hour

NOTES: Up to one day ahead, prepare brussels sprout leaves (step 1); wrap in a towel, seal in a plastic bag, and chill. To make croutons, bake 1½ cups ½-inch cubes firm white bread in a 10- by 12-inch pan in a 350° oven, stirring often, until lightly toasted, 8 to 10 minutes.

MAKES: 3 or 4 main-dish or 6 to 8 first-course servings

- 1½ pounds **brussels sprouts**
- ½ pound **thick-sliced bacon**
- 5 to 7 tablespoons **extra-virgin olive oil**
- 6 tablespoons **red wine vinegar**
- 2 tablespoons minced **shallots**
- 1 teaspoon minced **garlic**
- ¼ teaspoon minced **fresh thyme** leaves or dried thyme

  About ½ teaspoon **salt**

  About ¼ teaspoon **fresh-ground pepper**
- 1 **red onion** (about 6 oz.)
- 1½ cups **unseasoned croutons** (see notes)
- 1 hard-cooked **large egg,** shelled and coarsely chopped

E. SPENCER TOY

1. Rinse sprouts, drain, and discard discolored leaves. Using a small, sharp knife, trim stem end of each sprout to release a layer of leaves, then pull the leaves from the sprout (save). Continue to trim and discard stem, pulling off (and saving) leaves until only about ½ inch remains of center of sprout; cut this portion in half lengthwise. Repeat to separate leaves on remaining sprouts.

2. Cut bacon into ¼-inch dice. In a 14-inch wok, 14-inch frying pan, or wide 6- to 8-quart pan, stir bacon often over medium-high heat until browned, about 10 minutes; transfer with a slotted spoon to paper towels to drain. Pour bacon drippings from pan and reserve, if desired for dressing.

3. Meanwhile, in a small bowl, mix 5 tablespoons olive oil, 5 tablespoons vinegar, shallots, garlic, thyme, ½ teaspoon salt, and ¼ teaspoon pepper. Peel onion and cut lengthwise into thin slivers.

4. Return 1 tablespoon bacon drippings to pan or add 1 tablespoon olive oil; add sliced onion and 1 tablespoon vinegar. Stir often over medium-high heat until onion is limp and lightly browned, about 8 minutes. Pour into bowl with vinegar and olive oil mixture.

5. Add another tablespoon bacon drippings (discard any remaining) or olive oil to pan over high heat; when hot, add brussels sprout leaves and stir until limp, 3 to 4 minutes. Add croutons, bacon, and oil-and-vinegar mixture to pan; stir until hot and well mixed. Pour into a wide bowl and sprinkle with chopped egg. Add more salt and pepper to taste.

Per serving: 432 cal., 69% (297 cal.) from fat; 13 g protein; 33 g fat (7.5 g sat.); 26 g carbo (9.9 g fiber); 704 mg sodium; 71 mg chol.

Provençal patterns

■ Through the years, I've made no secret of my fondness for Provence in September, where I while away the month with friends over many a memorable meal. Though I don't attempt to cook in Provence style (feeling too laid-back to research recipes while I'm on vacation), I rejoice in the region's ingredients. All month, the fig tree drops soft, ripe fruit. When roasted with tender, mild local lamb, figs and lemons make a wonderful marriage: The heat caramelizes the figs, while thin lemon slices add enough tang to stave off insipid sweetness. By habit I keep notes of my culinary discoveries; they tell me I've repeated this time and again.

Leg of Lamb with Figs and Lemons

PREP AND COOK TIME: About 1¾ hours

MAKES: 8 servings

- 1 **leg of lamb** (5 to 6 lb.), fat trimmed
  Salt
- 1 teaspoon **fresh thyme** leaves or dried thyme
- 4 or **5 rosemary sprigs** (each 5 to 6 in. long), rinsed, or 2 teaspoons dried rosemary
- 12 **ripe black figs** (about 3 oz. each)
- 2 **lemons** (4 oz. each)
  About 1 cup **dry red wine**
- 2 tablespoons **balsamic vinegar**
- 2 tablespoons **sugar**
  About ½ cup fat-skimmed **chicken broth**
- ¼ cup **whipping cream** or crème fraîche

1. Rinse lamb and pat dry. Sprinkle lightly with salt and set in a shallow 10- by 15-inch pan. Pat thyme all over meat; lay rosemary sprigs on the leg.

2. Rinse figs and lemons. Cut figs in half lengthwise through stems and lay, cut side up, around lamb. Trim off and discard ends of lemons, then thinly slice lemons crosswise and discard seeds. Scatter slices over and around figs. Pour about ½ cup wine and the vinegar into pan. Sprinkle fruit with sugar.

3. Bake in a 400° regular or convection oven until a thermometer inserted through thickest part of meat to the bone reaches 130°, about 1½ hours. As liquid evaporates, add more wine to pan to prevent scorching. Occasionally, turn fruit gently. The edges of the pieces should get dark; if fruit starts to scorch, remove from pan.

4. Transfer roast and fruit to a platter and keep warm. Discard rosemary sprigs. Add enough broth to pan to make about ¾ cup juices total, then add cream. Bring to a rolling boil over high heat, stirring to release browned bits. Pour into a small bowl or pitcher.

5. Slice lamb and serve meat and fruit with pan juices. Add salt to taste.

Per serving: 313 cal., 37% (117 cal.) from fat; 40 g protein; 13 g fat (5.2 g sat.); 9.1 g carbo (1.7 g fiber); 103 mg sodium; 130 mg chol. ◆

The Wine Guide
Aromatherapy: The truth about taste
By Karen MacNeil-Fife

■ If you and I—and 10 other people—all had a glass of the same wine in the same place at the same time, chances are we'd generate a dozen different ideas about what the wine tasted like. Moreover, some in the group would probably say they detected only a handful of characteristics, while others might reel off a long list of evocative adjectives. What's going on here? When it comes to wine, why is taste so hard to pin down and seemingly so different for each of us? (One sad outcome of this conundrum is that wine tasting and evaluating intimidate some of us—especially when we find it hard to describe what we taste.)

There's no quick answer. What we refer to simply as "taste" is really an intricate phenomenon involving multiple mechanisms in the mouth and brain. Scientists have discovered that our sensitivity to taste is in fact based on our DNA; some people actually do have the capacity to experience flavors more intensely than others. And a leading taste researcher at Yale University has demonstrated that for women, intensity of taste varies with hormonal cycles.

All this complexity notwithstanding, research and experience also suggest that there are simple ways in

JAMES CARRIER

which you can maximize the flavor of any wine you drink.

Smell well
Much of what we call "taste" is really smell. Research indicates that while many aromas are detected by nerve cells in the nose (and best absorbed by taking lots of quick sniffs while you're drinking), some—and here's the surprising news—are registered at the back of the throat. Conclusion: You need to hold the wine in your mouth for a few seconds and slosh it around a bit to get every smell ("taste").

Taste thoroughly
The sensory organs we call taste buds are contained in onion-shaped structures all over your tongue and

soft palate. And it takes time for flavor molecules to penetrate the opening in the top of these structures (which is why we tell children to swallow fast when they're taking a bad-tasting medicine). The moral of the story? If you drink a wine in down-the-hatch fashion, you simply won't get the full impact of its flavor. Again, you have to hold it in your mouth for several seconds (some evidence suggests up to four).

Master the mechanics
Use large glasses with generously sized bowls to give you room to swirl vigorously—which is the next point: Be sure to swirl every wine more than once. Aerating the wine helps release aromas (and hence flavors). A final corollary to this: Young, tannic reds like Cabernet Sauvignon and Merlot will always taste more profound if you pour them first into a carafe, pitcher, or decanter. Just the act of pouring the wine through the air makes a huge difference.

Skeptical? Try conducting a simple experiment: Taste a wine, intentionally *not* following any of the suggestions above, then try the techniques. You'll be amazed at how much more flavor every glass of wine can yield.

MEET A NEW WINE

Here are some terrific grape varieties on which to try the tasting advice above. Though each of these grapes is beginning to be grown on the West Coast, I've recommended a stellar wine from the grape's ancestral home.

WHITES
■ PINOT GRIGIO (also known as Pinot Gris): This fresh, light, snappy wine can be found all across northern Italy. (Note that Pinot Gris from Alsace, France, is a weightier version.) Try **Alois**

Lageder Pinot Grigio from Alto Adige; the 2000 costs about $15.

■ VIOGNIER: Sensual, rich, wildly aromatic, floral, and perfumed, Viognier (pronounced vee-ohn-*gnay*) is an exotic grape. Its home is Condrieu in the Rhône Valley of France. Try **E. Guigal Condrieu;** the 2000 costs about $35.

REDS
■ GRENACHE: Like a pot of homemade black cherry jam, Grenache is juicy and irre-

sistible. The best in the world is grown in southern France, where it's the dominant grape in Châteauneuf-du-Pape. Try **Château La Nerthe;** the 1998 costs about $37.

■ MOURVÈDRE: Dark, masculine, and brooding, Mourvèdre is a serious red wine. One of the world's best examples is Domaine Tempier from the southern French town of Bandol; the 1999 **Bandol Rouge** costs about $30.

■ SANGIOVESE: This is the great grape of Chianti, with fla-

vors reminiscent of dried leaves, tea, even citrus. Sangiovese has a lot of acidity (unusual for red wine), making it terrific with food. Try **Ruffino Riserva Ducale Chianti Classico Riserva;** the 1997 tan label costs about $21.

■ SYRAH: The most dramatic, meaty, spicy, licorice-flavored Syrahs in the world come from a tiny place in the northern Rhône Valley called Côte-Rôtie. The 1999 **Chapoutier Côte-Rôtie Les Bécasses** costs about $86. ◆

New take on an old favorite: fresh corn pie topped with chorizo and cactus.

Tucson tamale pie

The flavor of fresh corn tamales with a fraction of the work

By Elaine Johnson

High summer yields a special treat in Mexico and the Southwest: green corn tamales, made from mature fresh corn instead of dried masa flour. They're a labor of love—wrapping the bundles is time-consuming. But by turning their components into a pie, you get all the flavor of the traditional dish in much less time. Topped with spicy chorizo sausage and tender strips of cactus, the casserole makes a splendid entrée for supper or brunch.

Green Corn Tamale Pie

PREP AND COOK TIME: About 1¾ hours

NOTES: Canned *nopalitos* (cactus strips) are available in well-stocked supermarkets and in Latino markets. Assemble pie through step 3 and make salsa up to 2 days ahead; chill separately. Bake chilled tamale pie about 1¼ hours.

MAKES: 8 servings

- 7 pounds **corn on the cob** in husks (8 to 10 ears)
- ¾ cup **dehydrated masa flour**
- ⅓ cup **olive oil**
- 2 cups **shredded jack cheese** (½ lb.)
- 1 can (7 oz.) **diced green chilies,** drained

  About 1½ teaspoons **salt**
- 6 ounces **chorizo sausages,** casings removed
- ½ cup canned **cactus strips** (optional, see notes), rinsed and drained

  Chopped **fresh cilantro**

  Green Salsa (recipe follows)

1. With a sharp knife, cut off and discard stem end of each ear of corn down to kernels. Carefully pull off husks without tearing; rinse and cover with damp towels to keep from drying out. Pull off and discard silks from corn; rinse ears. Holding each ear upright, cut off kernels; you need 7 cups (save any extra for other uses). Discard cobs.

2. Working in batches in a blender or food processor (fill blender no more than half full), whirl corn kernels, dehydrated masa flour, and olive oil until corn is finely ground. Scrape mixture into a bowl. Stir in cheese, chilies, and 1½ teaspoons salt.

3. Working with a few at a time, overlap corn husks, concave side down, to line a shallow 3- to 3½-quart casserole, letting ends stick up 3 to 4 inches above rim; drop spoonfuls of the corn mixture onto husks as you go to hold them in place. Discard extra husks. Spoon remaining corn mixture into casserole and spread level. Fold ends of husks over corn mixture. Cover casserole tightly with foil.

4. Bake in a 350° regular or convection oven until corn mixture is steaming and slightly firm to touch in the center (uncover to check), 55 to 60 minutes. Let casserole stand, covered, for 10 minutes.

5. Meanwhile, cut chorizo into ¼-inch-thick slices. In a 10- to 12-inch frying pan over medium-high heat, stir chorizo often until browned, about 5 minutes. Spoon off any fat and discard. Add cactus to pan and stir until hot, about 1 minute.

6. Uncover casserole and unfold husks. Spoon sausage mixture over center of tamale pie and sprinkle cilantro on top. Serve with green salsa. Add salt to taste.

Per serving: 460 cal., 55% (252 cal.) from fat; 18 g protein; 28 g fat (9.6 g sat.); 38 g carbo (6.3 g fiber); 1,177 mg sodium; 49 mg chol.

Green Salsa. Remove and discard husks from ½ pound **fresh tomatillos;** rinse tomatillos well and cut in half (or use a 12-ounce can tomatillos, drained). In a food processor or blender, combine tomatillos; 1 can (7 oz.) **diced green chilies,** drained; ¾ cup lightly packed rinsed **fresh cilantro;** ¼ cup coarsely chopped **green onions** (including tops); and 1 tablespoon **lime juice.** Whirl until mixture is finely chopped. Makes about 1½ cups.

Per serving: 17 cal., 16% (2.7 cal.) from fat; 0.6 g protein; 0.3 g fat (0 g sat.); 3.6 g carbo (1 g fiber); 153 mg sodium; 0 mg chol. ◆

Sweet relief

Vintage soda fountains put some fizz into the dog days of summer

By Sharon Niederman and Nora Burba Trulsson

The sweetness of memory can be more than just a dreamy nostalgia. Especially when the thermometer heads into triple digits, some of the best places to cool off and savor the sweet flavors of bygone days are the old-fashioned ice cream parlors that dot the Southwest, many situated along well-traveled routes. If you know where to look, your next chocolate ice cream soda, made with real carbonated water from a genuine vintage soda fountain, could be waiting for you in that little town just down the road.

Arizona

PHOENIX. MacAlpine's Soda Fountain. Opened in 1928 as a Rexall drug store and soda fountain, MacAlpine's (now sans the drugstore end of the business) still has the original fountain and other fixtures. You can order a sandwich with your phosphate or chocolate shake. Closed for minor renovations, the fountain should reopen by midsummer. *Call for new hours. 2303 N. Seventh St.; (602) 262-5545.*

SCOTTSDALE. Sugar Bowl Ice Cream Parlor/Restaurant. Pink banquettes and candy-striped wallpaper mark this retro favorite, opened in 1958. Try a Camelback soda (any flavor, served with an extra pitcher of soda water), a giant banana split, or a pineapple-mint milk shake. Feeling virtuous? Get a salad or a fruit plate. *11–11 Mon–Thu, 11–12 A.M. Fri–Sat, 11–10 Sun. 4005 N. Scottsdale Rd.; (480) 946-0051.*

TUCSON. Austin's Old Fashion Ice Cream. The original red booths are now covered in mauve, and french fries are more readily available, but otherwise, Austin's retains its 1959 charm. Sit at the original fountain and sip a chocolate soda or a root beer float; banana splits are definitely big enough to split. *11–10 Mon–Thu, 11–11 Fri–Sat, 11–7 Sun. 2920 E. Broadway Blvd.; (520) 327-3892.*

New Mexico

CARRIZOZO. Roy's Ice Cream Parlour. This vintage ice cream parlor still features its original marble-topped 1935 Liquid Carbonic fountain, which makes carbonated water and stores ice cream, toppings, and syrups in gleaming silver chambers. The secret to their memorable chocolate malts? "Lots of loving care," says owner Roy N. Dow. *8:30–6 Mon–Fri, 10:30–4:30 Sat. 1200 Ave. E; (505) 648-2921.*

LAS VEGAS. Murpheys Soda Fountain and Deli. Established in 1893, Murpheys has been putting the fizz in phosphates since ice was delivered by horse and wagon. The green-and-black art deco fountain now in use dates to the early '40s. Cherry-lime soft drinks remain the most popular order under the pressed-tin ceiling. *10–5 Mon–Fri, 10–4 Sat. 600 Douglas Ave.; (505) 425-6811.*

MADRID. Old-Fashioned Soda Fountain. Shining with mirrored black and chrome, one of New Mexico's most venerable soda fountains is the 1934 Liquid Carbonic beauty that remains in its original setting in the Madrid Company Store Building. Where once coal miners came to buy groceries and indulge in chocolate malts, now visitors take a break from gallery hopping in this artists' community to sample ice cream served in homemade waffle cones. *10–5 daily. Madrid Company Store Building on State 14 downtown; (505) 473-3641.*

MAGDALENA. Evett's Cafe & Fountain. With its showcases of memorabilia and its photos of the old days, this is practically a soda fountain museum. Housed in a 1906 brick bank building, Evett's is a ritual road stop for travelers on U.S. 60. Old-fashioned banana splits are the specialty, along with giant Coke floats. The fountain is only 40 years old, but you can take a spin on a stool from the 1930s. *11–9 daily. U.S. 60 downtown; (505) 854-2449.* ◆

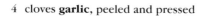

The Quick Cook

Entrées in 30 minutes or less
By Barbara Goldman

Penne pasta and cannellini beans pair up with sausage and fresh arugula in a hearty Italian-style soup.

Pasta and beans

■ Dried pasta and canned beans are pantry partners without peer, ever-ready to pair up in hearty main dishes that satisfy in a hurry. The traditional Italian *pasta e fagioli* (pasta and beans) sets a fine standard. But when you consider the multitude of pasta shapes and the wide selection of canned beans available, the number of possible combinations is staggering. Both pasta and beans absorb liquid as they stand, so if dinner isn't served as promptly as you'd planned, you may need to add a little more broth to these lean, quick main dishes.

Cannellini and Penne Soup

PREP AND COOK TIME: About 30 minutes

MAKES: 6 servings

- 1 pound **low-fat mild turkey Italian sausages,** casings removed
- 1 **onion** (½ lb.), peeled and chopped

- 4 cloves **garlic,** peeled and pressed
- 1 can (14½ oz.) fat-skimmed **chicken broth**
- 1 can (8 oz.) **tomato sauce**
- ½ cup **dry red wine**
- 1 teaspoon **dried oregano**
- 8 ounces **dried penne pasta**
- ¾ pound **arugula** (about 10 cups)
- 2 cans (15 oz. each) **cannellini** (white) **beans,** rinsed and drained

  About ½ cup **shredded parmesan cheese**

  Pepper

1. In a 5- to 6-quart pan over high heat, break meat into chunks with a spoon. Add onion and garlic and stir often until onion is limp, about 5 minutes.

2. Add broth, tomato sauce, wine, oregano, pasta, and 2 cups water. Stirring often, bring to a boil and cook until pasta is just tender to bite, about 10 minutes.

3. Rinse, drain, and coarsely chop arugula. Add arugula and beans to pasta mixture. Stir occasionally until soup is boiling, about 3 minutes.

4. Ladle into bowls and add cheese and pepper to taste.

Per serving: 471 cal., 21% (99 cal.) from fat; 30 g protein; 11 g fat (3.6 g sat.); 59 g carbo (8.4 g fiber); 1,152 mg sodium; 45 mg chol.

Black Beans and Fettuccine with Turkey

PREP AND COOK TIME: About 25 minutes

MAKES: 6 servings

- 1 cup chopped **red bell pepper**
- ½ cup chopped **onion**
- 2 cloves minced **garlic**
- 1 tablespoon **olive oil**
- 3 cups fat-skimmed **chicken broth**
- 1 pound **dried fettuccine**
- 1 package (10 oz.) **frozen corn kernels**
- 2 cans (15 oz. each) **black beans,** rinsed and drained
- 3 cups bite-size pieces boned, skinned **cooked turkey breast** (¾ lb.)
- 2 cups **purchased tomato salsa**
- ½ cup chopped **fresh cilantro**

- ½ cup **lime juice**
- ½ cup **orange juice**

  Salt and **pepper**

1. In an 8- to 10-quart pan over high heat, stir bell pepper, onion, garlic, and oil until onion is limp, about 5 minutes. Add broth, 2 cups water, and fettuccine. Stir often until pasta is just firm to bite, 8 to 10 minutes.

2. Add corn, beans, turkey, and salsa. Stir until soup is simmering, about 3 minutes. Mix in cilantro, lime juice, and orange juice. Ladle into bowls and add salt and pepper to taste.

Per serving: 587 cal., 8.3% (49 cal.) from fat; 41 g protein; 5.4 g fat (0.7 g sat.); 96 g carbo (11 g fiber); 914 mg sodium; 47 mg chol.

White Bean and Orzo Salad with Shrimp

PREP AND COOK TIME: About 25 minutes

MAKES: 4 servings

- ½ pound **dried orzo pasta** (1¼ cups)
- 1½ cups chopped **onions**
- 1 tablespoon **olive oil**
- 1 can (15 oz.) **small white beans,** rinsed and drained
- ½ pound **shelled cooked tiny shrimp,** rinsed and drained
- 2 cups rinsed and halved **cherry tomatoes**
- ¼ cup fat-skimmed **chicken broth**
- ⅓ cup **lemon juice**
- ⅓ cup chopped **fresh mint** leaves
- ¼ cup chopped **parsley**

  Salt

1. In a 6- to 8-quart pan over high heat, bring 2 quarts water to a boil. Add pasta; cook until tender to bite, 9 to 11 minutes. Drain; immerse in cold water. When pasta is cool, in about 3 minutes, drain and pour into a large bowl.

2. Meanwhile, in a 10- to 12-inch frying pan over high heat, stir onions in oil until limp and slightly browned, about 5 minutes. Add to pasta along with beans, shrimp, cherry tomatoes, broth, lemon juice, mint, and parsley. Mix and add salt to taste.

Per serving: 408 cal., 13% (51 cal.) from fat; 27 g protein; 5.7 g fat (0.8 g sat.); 68 g carbo (8.7 g fiber); 520 mg sodium; 111 mg chol. ◆

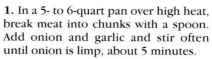 KEVIN CANDLAND; FOOD STYLING: JULIE SMITH

The Low-Fat Cook

Shrimp: Put some swing into lean meals

By Christine Weber Hale

JAMES CARRIER; FOOD STYLING BY: KIM BRENT AND ERIN QUON

Tart ginger-glazed shrimp and grapefruit wedges contrast with the sweetness of rice with coconut milk.

■ Given a choice, would you prefer dinner's main course to be quick, low in fat, easy, or exciting? Why choose? These shrimp dishes offer it all, especially if you use pour-from-the-bag individually frozen shrimp—just rinse with hot tap water to thaw almost at once. The first is sticky-glazed shrimp on rice cooked in reduced-fat coconut milk. The other two are one-pan performers; both the couscous and the pasta cook in distinctly seasoned broths along with the shrimp.

Thai Sticky Shrimp with Coconut Rice

PREP AND COOK TIME: About 25 minutes
MAKES: 4 servings

- 1 can (14 oz.) **reduced-fat coconut milk**
- 1¼ cups **short-grain white rice** such as pearl
- 2 **ruby grapefruit** (about 2 lb. total)
- ½ cup firmly packed **brown sugar**

- 1 tablespoon **cornstarch**
- ¼ cup **soy sauce**
- 2 tablespoons **rice vinegar**
- 2 tablespoons minced **fresh ginger**
- 1 pound thawed **frozen uncooked, shelled, deveined shrimp** (38 to 50 per lb.), rinsed and drained
- ½ pound **Belgian endive**, leaves separated, rinsed, and drained
- ½ cup finely slivered **fresh basil** leaves

1. In a 3- to 4-quart pan over high heat, combine coconut milk, rice, and ¾ cup water. Bring to a boil, reduce heat, cover, and simmer until rice is tender to bite, about 15 minutes.
2. Meanwhile, cut peel and membrane from grapefruit. Cut between fruit and membrane to release segments into a bowl.
3. In a 10- to 12-inch frying pan, mix sugar and cornstarch. Add soy sauce, vinegar, and ginger. Stir on high heat until boiling, about 1 minute. Add shrimp and stir often until opaque but still moist-looking in center of thickest part (cut to test), 3 to 4 minutes.
4. Mound rice equally on warm plates, spoon shrimp mixture equally onto rice, and garnish with grapefruit segments, endive leaves, and basil.

Per serving: 569 cal., 12% (68 cal.) from fat; 31 g protein; 7.5 g fat (3.6 g sat.); 96 g carbo (3 g fiber); 1,238 mg sodium; 173 mg chol.

Shrimp Couscous

PREP AND COOK TIME: About 25 minutes
NOTES: Garam masala can be found in the dried herbs and spices section at most supermarkets; if not available, use curry powder.
MAKES: 4 servings

- 3 cups fat-skimmed **chicken broth**
- ¼ cup **catsup**
- 1 tablespoon minced **fresh ginger**
- 2 teaspoons **mustard seeds**
- 1 teaspoon **chili powder**
- ½ teaspoon **garam masala**
- ½ teaspoon **dried dill weed**
- 1 pound thawed **frozen uncooked, shelled, deveined shrimp** (38 to 50 per lb.), rinsed and drained
- 2 cups **couscous**
- 2 tablespoons finely slivered **fresh mint** leaves
- **Plain nonfat yogurt**
- **Salt**
- **Lime** wedges

1. In a 3- to 4-quart pan, combine broth, catsup, ginger, mustard seeds, chili powder, garam masala, and dill weed. Bring to a boil over high heat; when boiling, add shrimp and cook until opaque but still moist-looking in center of thickest part (cut to test), 3 to 4 minutes.
2. At once, stir couscous into pan, cover, and remove from heat. Let stand 5 minutes. Stir mixture with a fork; there should be some liquid. Spoon shrimp couscous onto plates; sprinkle with mint and add yogurt, salt, and juice from lime wedges.

Per serving: 521 cal., 5.8% (30 cal.) from fat; 42 g protein; 3.3 g fat (0.5 g sat.); 78 g carbo (3.9 g fiber); 419 mg sodium; 173 mg chol.

Lemon and Shrimp Capellini

PREP AND COOK TIME: About 30 minutes
MAKES: 4 servings

- 1 **lemon**
- 2 teaspoons **coriander seeds**
- 1 teaspoon **fennel seeds**
- ½ teaspoon fresh-ground **pepper**
- 6 cups fat-skimmed **chicken broth**
- ½ cup **dry white wine**
- ¾ pound **dried capellini** (angel hair) **pasta**
- 1 pound thawed **frozen uncooked, shelled, deveined shrimp** (38 to 50 per lb.), rinsed and drained
- ½ cup minced **fresh chives** or green onions
- **Lemon** wedges
- **Salt**

1. Rinse lemon; trim and discard thin slices from each end. Thinly slice lemon, saving the juice; discard seeds and finely chop fruit. Put fruit and juice in a 5- to 6-quart pan. Add coriander seeds, fennel seeds, pepper, broth, and wine. Bring to a boil over high heat. Add pasta, stir, then add shrimp; stir often until pasta is tender to bite and shrimp are opaque but still moist-looking in center of thickest part (cut to test), about 5 minutes.
2. Add chives. Using two forks, lift pasta mixture to mix, then transfer equally to wide bowls, adding any remaining broth. Garnish with lemon wedges to squeeze over portions; add salt to taste.

Per serving: 520 cal., 6.2% (32 cal.) from fat; 47 g protein; 3.6 g fat (0.6 g sat.); 69 g carbo (4.1 g fiber); 290 mg sodium; 173 mg chol. ◆

Kitchen Cabinet

Readers' recipes tested in *Sunset's* kitchens

By Andrew Baker and Charity Ferreira

Roasting brings out rich flavor in zucchini and walnuts; mix with orzo for a simple fall entrée.

Roasted Zucchini and Walnut Orzo

Laura Sabo, Portland

This winning combination of vegetables and nuts was improvised by Laura Sabo.

PREP AND COOK TIME: About 30 minutes

MAKES: 4 servings

- 1¼ pounds **zucchini**
- 2 teaspoons **olive oil**
  About ⅛ teaspoon **salt**
  About ⅛ teaspoon **pepper**
- ½ cup **walnut pieces**, coarsely chopped
- 4¾ cups fat-skimmed **chicken broth** or vegetable broth
- 2 cups **dried orzo pasta**
- 2 tablespoons **lemon juice**
- 2 teaspoons **walnut oil**

1. Rinse and dry zucchini; cut each in half lengthwise, then cut crosswise into ¼-inch-thick slices. In a bowl, mix zucchini with olive oil, ⅛ teaspoon salt, and ⅛ teaspoon pepper. Divide mixture equally between two baking sheets, each 12 by 15 inches, and spread zucchini in a single layer.

2. Bake in a 400° regular or convection oven until zucchini is tender when pierced, 8 to 10 minutes. Pour back into bowl. Rinse and dry one baking sheet.

3. Put walnut pieces on clean baking sheet and bake in a 350° oven until pale gold beneath skins, about 5 minutes.

4. Meanwhile, in a 5- to 6-quart pan over high heat, bring broth to a boil. Add orzo, reduce heat, and simmer, stirring occasionally, until orzo is tender to bite and liquid is absorbed, about 10 minutes.

5. Stir zucchini, walnuts, lemon juice, and walnut oil into orzo. Add more salt and pepper to taste.

Per serving: 515 cal., 26% (135 cal.) from fat; 24 g protein; 15 g fat (1.6 g sat.); 71 g carbo (3.5 g fiber); 176 mg sodium; 0 mg chol.

Caramelized Fall Fruit Salad with Chicken

Marilou Robinson, Portland

When East Coast friends were visiting, Marilou Robinson wanted to make a meal that showed off local ingredients. Her combination of fruit, nuts, and cheese with Oregon-raised chicken made a tasty and unusual entrée—proof that what grows together goes together.

PREP AND COOK TIME: About 45 minutes

MAKES: 2 servings

- ¼ cup **hazelnuts**
- 2 **boned, skinned chicken breast halves** (5 to 6 oz. each)
  Salt and **pepper**
- ½ tablespoon **salad oil**
- 1 **firm-ripe pear** such as Bosc or Comice (about 8 oz.)
- 1 **apple** (about 8 oz.)
- ½ tablespoon **butter** or margarine
- 1 tablespoon firmly packed **brown sugar**
- ⅔ cup **rice vinegar**
- ½ cup **orange juice**
- 4 cups **baby salad mix** (4 oz.), rinsed and crisped
- 1 ounce **blue cheese**, crumbled

1. Put hazelnuts in an 8- to 9-inch square baking pan. Bake in a 350° regular or convection oven until nuts are golden beneath skins, 12 to 15 minutes. Pour from pan onto a towel. When cool enough to handle, rub nuts in towel to remove loose skins. Lift nuts from towel and coarsely chop; discard skins.

2. Rinse chicken and pat dry. Place each breast between two sheets of plastic wrap. With a flat mallet, gently pound to about ½ inch thick. Peel off plastic and sprinkle chicken lightly on both sides with salt and pepper.

3. Heat oil in a 10- to 12-inch frying pan over medium-high heat; when hot, add chicken and turn occasionally until pieces are lightly browned on both sides and no longer pink in the center (cut to test), 6 to 8 minutes total. Transfer to a plate and cover with foil to keep warm.

4. Meanwhile, rinse, peel, and core pear and apple; cut each lengthwise into 8 wedges. Add butter and brown sugar to frying pan; stir over medium-high heat until butter is melted and sugar is dissolved, about 1 minute. Add fruit and stir often until beginning to brown, 2 to 3 minutes. Stir in vinegar and orange juice, bring to a boil, and stir often until fruit is tender when pierced and liquid is slightly thickened, 8 to 10 minutes.

5. Divide salad greens equally between two dinner plates and set a chicken breast half on each mound. Spoon hot fruit and liquid over chicken and greens. Sprinkle evenly with toasted hazelnuts and blue cheese. Add more salt and pepper to taste.

Per serving: 533 cal., 37% (198 cal.) from fat; 39 g protein; 22 g fat (6 g sat.); 48 g carbo (6.3 g fiber); 330 mg sodium; 101 mg chol.

Leek and Chard Bisque

Everett C. Caudel, Riverside, CA

This recipe came together one day when the only two things growing in Everett C. Caudel's new garden were leeks and Swiss chard. A few subsequent refinements turned it into a delicate but satisfying soup.

PREP AND COOK TIME: About 45 minutes

MAKES: About 5½ cups; 4 servings

- 1 **leek** (about 1½ in. thick)
- ¾ pound **Swiss chard**
- 3 cups fat-skimmed **chicken broth**
- 1 cup **milk**

  About ¼ teaspoon **white** or black **pepper**
- 1 hard-cooked **large egg,** shelled and finely chopped
- ¼ cup minced **fresh chives**

  Salt

1. Trim and discard stem end and tough green top from leek; peel off and discard outer layer. Cut leek in half lengthwise and hold each half under cold running water, separating layers to rinse well. Coarsely chop.

2. Rinse and drain chard. Trim off discolored stem ends and discard. Thinly slice stems crosswise and coarsely chop leaves.

3. In a 3- to 4-quart pan, mix broth with leek and chard stems and leaves. Bring to a boil over high heat; cover, reduce heat, and simmer until vegetables are

very tender when pierced, about 12 minutes.

4. With a slotted spoon, transfer vegetables to a blender or food processor. Add about ½ cup cooking liquid and whirl until smooth. Pour purée back into pan. Add milk and ¼ teaspoon pepper; stir just until steaming, 3 to 4 minutes.

5. Ladle bisque into wide bowls. Sprinkle equally with chopped egg and chives. Add salt and more pepper to taste.

Per serving: 116 cal., 28% (32 cal.) from fat; 12 g protein; 3.6 g fat (1.7 g sat.); 10 g carbo (1.8 g fiber); 277 mg sodium; 62 mg chol.

Whole-Grain Apple Waffles
Opal Star, Las Vegas

To accommodate her husband's cow's-milk-free diet, Opal Star began experimenting with her favorite apple pancake recipe. In the end, she not only divested it of cow's milk, but she also turned the pancakes into waffles. Star uses barley flour, but we also like the results with whole-wheat. Goat's milk adds a pleasant tang, but regular milk works well too.

PREP AND COOK TIME: About 30 minutes

MAKES: 3 waffles (8 in. square)

- 1½ cups **whole-wheat flour**
- 2 tablespoons **sugar**
- 1 tablespoon **baking powder**
- ¼ teaspoon **salt**
- ⅛ teaspoon **ground nutmeg**
- 2 **large eggs,** beaten to blend
- 1¼ cups **goat's milk** (or regular whole milk; see notes)
- 1 cup **applesauce**
- 2 tablespoons **salad oil**

  Maple syrup

1. In a bowl, mix flour, sugar, baking powder, salt, and nutmeg.

2. In another bowl, mix eggs, milk, applesauce, and oil; add to dry ingredients and stir just until batter is evenly moistened.

3. Turn a waffle iron to high heat and spray both sides with cooking oil spray. When it's hot, add about 1¼ cups batter; close iron and cook until waffle is well browned, about 9 minutes. Remove waffle and serve, or keep warm in a single layer on a baking sheet in a 200° oven up to 15 minutes. Repeat to cook remaining waffles. Serve with maple syrup.

Per serving: 504 cal., 32% (162 cal.) from fat; 17 g protein; 18 g fat (5.3 g sat.); 75 g carbo (8.6 g fiber); 793 mg sodium; 156 mg chol. ◆

Heady days

Summer is the season to pop into a Southwestern brew pub

By Bob Klein

■ There's no time like summer to visit a brew pub. You'll find something special for summer—brews that are light-tasting, not too sweet or too filling, and lower in alcohol than heavier winter beers. Made on-site, these brews are especially fresh and inviting. We checked out a few of the Southwest's best brew pubs to see what was on tap. The menus at these taverns, we found, are as refreshing as the beers.

ARIZONA: Phoenix. *Leinenkugel's at HiTops Café,* set inside a ballpark, is called Leinie's by the locals. On game day, this brew pub scores with baseball patrons. Try a thirst-quenching Bleacher Blonde or the best-selling summer draft beer Hefe-Weizen—made in true Bavarian

style, it has a spicy, citrus character topped with banana and clove notes. It goes down well with the hearty food, like Kansas City–style baby back ribs and creamy beer-based clam chowder. *201 S. Fourth St.; (602) 462-3800.*

Tucson. Each summer, *Thunder Canyon Brewery* offers a Windstorm Wheat, burnished with a sweet, delicate flavor, crisp mouthfeel, and bracing effervescence. It's a good match with the fare, which they've dubbed "pubstantial," including Cajun chicken pasta made with their rich, malty Deep Canyon Amber Ale. *7401 N. La Cholla Blvd., Suite 178; (520) 797-2652.*

NEW MEXICO: Albuquerque. *Il Vicino* is an amiable neighborhood es-

cape from the sometimes frenetic urban buzz of the Nob Hill district. Here, you can feast on wood-fired oven pizza while you slake your thirst with an award-winning Wet Mountain India Pale Ale. This amber brew's trio of hops hints of sweet-and-spicy fruitiness. *3403 Central Ave. NE; (505) 266-7855.*

Near Santa Fe. Sitting alongside the Rio Grande on the route to Taos, *Embudo Station* offers travelers a happy respite. Savor menu selections like rainbow trout roasted on a cedar plank or a turkey-chipotle sausage quesadilla. Wash it down with the zippy, spicy Green Chili Ale, a mouth watering golden beer made with chili peppers. Watch the canoes paddle by and enjoy the breeze in the cottonwoods; you might not want to go back home again. *On State 68, 41 miles north of Santa Fe; (800) 852-4707.* ◆

Brisk autumn days call for satisfying comfort foods, such as our hearty, slow-braised stews (recipes begin on page 196).

October

classic stews made easy

Just stick them in the oven and forget about them—until the smell of slow-braised meat pulls everyone to the kitchen

By Paula Freschet • Photographs by James Carrier • Food styling by Susan Devaty

■ "You need more meat on your bones," Mom used to say. And chefs today seem to understand the hidden comfort in that reproof; they're boldly serving the homiest meat dishes of all—stews on the bone—in the finest places. The slow-braised lamb shanks and short ribs we've tasted in restaurants lately have inspired us to follow suit. But chefs generally have a battery of prep cooks, stock pots, and stovetop burners to enlist in chopping vegetables, browning meats, and straining sauces—to say nothing of a dishwasher to clean up the mess afterward. We've confined the whole process, in most cases, to one pan and one oven, for satisfying flavor that doesn't consign Mom (or Dad) to the kitchen all day.

Beef Short Ribs

Port-braised Short Ribs with Ginger and Star Anise

PREP AND COOK TIME: 2¾ to 3¼ hours
NOTES: Serve these ribs with their flavorful sauce over cooked rice.
MAKES: 4 servings

- 4 pounds **beef short ribs,** cut through the bone into 2½- to 3-inch pieces
  Salt and **pepper**
- 1 cup diced **onion**
- 1 cup diced **carrots**
- 1 cup diced **celery**
- 2 tablespoons minced **fresh ginger**
- 1 teaspoon **black peppercorns**
- 2 **whole star anise** or ½ teaspoon anise seeds
- 1 **cinnamon stick** (1½ to 2 in. long)
- 5 sprigs (about 4 in. long) **fresh rosemary,** rinsed
- 3 cups fat-skimmed **beef broth**
- 1 cup **tangerine** or orange **juice**
- ¾ cup **ruby port**
- 1 **tangerine** (about 5 oz.) or orange, rinsed and thinly sliced crosswise

1. Rinse ribs and pat dry; trim off and discard excess fat. Sprinkle ribs lightly all over with salt and pepper, and place in a single layer, bones down, in a 12- by 17-inch roasting pan. Bake in a 450° regular or convection oven until meat is beginning to brown, 15 to 20 minutes. With tongs, turn ribs. Add onion, carrots, celery, and ginger to pan around ribs, then mix to coat with fat in pan, and spread level. Bake until ribs are well browned and vegetables are beginning to brown, 15 to 20 minutes longer.

2. Meanwhile, wrap peppercorns, star anise, cinnamon stick, and 2 rosemary sprigs in a double layer of cheesecloth, 10 inches square; tie closed with heavy cotton string. To pan, add broth, tangerine juice, port, and spice bundle. Stir gently to mix and scrape browned bits free. Cover pan tightly with foil.

3. Bake in a 325° regular or convection oven until meat is very tender when pierced, 2 to 2½ hours. Uncover pan and discard spice bundle. With tongs, transfer ribs to a rimmed platter; cover and keep warm in a 200° oven. Skim and discard fat from pan juices. Boil over high heat, stirring often, until

reduced to 2½ cups, about 10 minutes. Add tangerine slices and cook just until heated through, about 1 minute.

4. Pour sauce over ribs on platter. Garnish with remaining rosemary sprigs. Add salt and pepper to taste.

Per serving: 434 cal., 39% (171 cal.) from fat; 41 g protein; 19 g fat (8.1 g sat.); 23 g carbo (2.8 g fiber); 216 mg sodium; 110 mg chol.

Ossobuco with Tuscan-style Bean and Fennel Ragout

PREP AND COOK TIME: 3¼ to 3¾ hours
NOTES: Here we combine the classic *ossobuco alla Milanese*—braised veal shanks garnished with *gremolata,* a mixture of chopped parsley, garlic, and lemon peel—with a bean ragout. Buy the veal shanks cut into lengths or have them cut at the meat market.
MAKES: 4 servings

- 4 pounds **veal shanks,** cut into 2- to 3-inch lengths (see notes)
  Salt and **pepper**
- 1 head **fennel** (about 3½ in. wide)
- 1 **onion** (about 8 oz.), peeled and chopped
- ⅔ cup diced **carrots**

Ossobuco with
Tuscan-style
Bean and
Fennel Ragout

⅔ cup diced **celery**

1 tablespoon minced **garlic**

1 tablespoon **olive oil**

2½ cups fat-skimmed **chicken broth**

1 cup **dry white wine**

¼ cup **tomato paste**

1 tablespoon minced **fresh sage**
leaves or ¾ teaspoon dried sage

2 cans (15 oz. each) **cannellini
beans**, rinsed and drained

Gremolata (recipe follows)

Fresh sage sprigs, rinsed

1. Rinse veal shanks and pat dry. Sprinkle lightly all over with salt and pepper, and place in a single layer in a 12- by 17-inch roasting pan. Bake, uncovered, in a 450° regular or convection oven until shanks are beginning to brown, about 15 minutes.

2. Meanwhile, rinse and drain fennel. Trim off stalks; chop enough feathery green leaves to make 1 tablespoon (reserve for gremolata, following) and discard remaining greens and stalks. Trim and discard root end and any bruised areas from fennel head. Cut head lengthwise into quarters, then thinly slice crosswise. In a bowl, mix fennel, onion, carrots, celery, and garlic with olive oil to coat.

3. With tongs, turn shanks. Distribute vegetables around shanks in pan. Bake until shanks are well browned and vegetables are beginning to brown, about 15 minutes longer. Add broth, wine, tomato paste, and sage to pan; stir carefully to mix and scrape browned bits free. Cover pan tightly with foil.

4. Bake in a 325° regular or convection oven until meat is very tender when pierced, 1½ to 2 hours. Increase oven temperature to 400°.

5. Uncover pan and gently stir beans into sauce around shanks. Bake, uncovered, until bean mixture is simmering and slightly thickened, 20 to 30 minutes longer.

6. Spoon equal portions of ossobuco and ragout into four wide, shallow bowls, arranging veal pieces on top of bean mixture. Sprinkle equally with gremolata. Garnish with sage sprigs. Add salt and pepper to taste.

Per serving: 465 cal., 19% (89 cal.) from fat; 52 g protein; 9.9 g fat (2.4 g sat.); 41 g carbo (14 g fiber); 614 mg sodium; 124 mg chol.

Gremolata. In a small bowl, mix 1 tablespoon minced **parsley**, 1 tablespoon minced **fennel greens** (see Ossobuco, preceding), 1 teaspoon grated **lemon** peel, and 1 clove **garlic**, peeled and minced.

Coq au Vin with Crimini Mushrooms

PREP AND COOK TIME: 2½ to 2¾ hours

NOTES: This traditional French stew is proof that red wine and chicken make a great match. Our recipe was inspired by the version served at Absinthe Brasserie and Bar in San Francisco by executive chef Ross Browne. Buy the chicken already cut into pieces or have your butcher cut it. To peel onions easily, trim root ends, cut an X in each, drop into boiling water, and cook just until skins begin to loosen, 5 to 10 seconds. Drain, rinse in cold water until cool enough to handle, then squeeze each onion from its peel. For toast triangles, trim crusts from four slices of firm white bread; toast the slices, then cut in half diagonally.

MAKES: 4 servings

- 1 bottle (750 ml.) **Pinot Noir** or other dry red wine
- 2 ounces **bacon** (2 to 3 slices), diced
- 1 **chicken** (4 to 4½ lb.), cut into 8 pieces (see notes)

  Salt and **pepper**

  About ⅓ cup **all-purpose flour**
- 1½ tablespoons minced **garlic**
- 2 **carrots** (about 6 oz. total), peeled and cut diagonally into ½-inch-thick slices
- 5 ounces **pearl onions** (about 1 in. wide), peeled (see notes), or frozen pearl onions, thawed
- ¼ pound **crimini** or common **mushrooms** (caps about 2 in. wide), rinsed and quartered
- 8 sprigs (about 4 in.) **parsley**, rinsed
- 6 sprigs (3 to 4 in.) **fresh thyme**, rinsed
- 2 **fresh** or dried **bay leaves**
- 8 **black peppercorns**
- 2 tablespoons **cognac** or brandy
- 3 cups fat-skimmed **low-sodium chicken broth**
- 2 tablespoons minced **parsley**
- 8 **toast triangles** (see notes)

1. In a 2- to 3-quart pan over high heat, boil wine, uncovered, until reduced to 1½ cups, 12 to 15 minutes.

2. Meanwhile, in a 12-inch frying pan or 6- to 8-quart pan (with sides at least 3 in. high) over medium-high heat, stir bacon often until browned and crisp, 8 to 10 minutes. With a slotted spoon, transfer to paper towels to drain. Discard all but 2 tablespoons fat in pan.

3. Rinse chicken and pat dry; trim off and discard any excess fat. Sprinkle pieces lightly all over with salt and pepper. Put ⅓ cup flour in a shallow bowl. Press pieces into flour, turning to coat all sides; shake off excess (discard any remaining flour). Add half the

chicken to pan over medium-high heat and turn as needed until well browned on all sides, 4 to 6 minutes total. As chicken is browned, transfer to a large bowl and add remaining chicken to pan to brown.

4. Add 1 tablespoon garlic, carrots, onions, and mushrooms to pan. Stir often until lightly browned, 10 to 12 minutes. While vegetables brown, wrap parsley and thyme sprigs, bay leaves, and peppercorns in a double layer of cheesecloth, 10 inches square; tie closed with heavy cotton string. Add cognac to pan and stir to scrape browned bits free. Return all chicken except breast pieces, plus any accumulated juices, to pan and add reduced wine, bacon, herb bundle, and broth.

5. Bring mixture to a boil over high heat, then reduce heat, cover, and simmer for 20 minutes. Add breast pieces and simmer, turning pieces over in liquid occasionally, until meat is very tender when pierced, 25 to 30 minutes longer. With a slotted spoon, lift chicken and vegetables from pan, and divide equally among four wide, shallow bowls; keep warm in a 200° oven. Skim and discard fat from liquid. Boil over high heat, uncovered, until reduced to about 2 cups, 10 to 12 minutes. Pour

equally over chicken and vegetables.

6. Sprinkle remaining ½ tablespoon garlic and the minced parsley evenly over portions of coq au vin, and set two toast triangles alongside.

Per serving: 914 cal., 54% (495 cal.) from fat; 70 g protein; 55 g fat (16 g sat.); 32 g carbo (2.5 g fiber); 535 mg sodium; 240 mg chol.

Lamb and Artichoke Daube

PREP AND COOK TIME: 3¼ to 3½ hours
NOTES: This is a simplified version of a lamb stew chef Reed Hearon developed at San Francisco's LuLu restaurant. Serve the daube over hot couscous.

MAKES: 4 servings

- 4 **lamb shanks** (about 1 lb. each), bones cracked and fat trimmed

  Salt and **pepper**
- 15 cloves **garlic**, peeled
- 1 **onion** (about 10 oz.), peeled and cut into ½-inch pieces
- 2 **carrots** (about 6 oz. total), peeled and cut into ½-inch pieces
- 1 bottle (750 ml.) **Côtes-du-Rhône** or other dry red wine
- 1 can (about 15 oz.) **crushed** or diced **tomatoes**
- 6 **canned anchovy fillets**, drained and minced

Lamb and Artichoke Daube

Red Wine–braised Oxtails

1 tablespoon minced **fresh thyme** leaves or 1 teaspoon dried thyme

1 tablespoon minced **fresh savory** or 1 teaspoon dried savory

1 teaspoon grated **orange** peel (colored part only)

1 package (8 oz.) **frozen artichoke hearts,** thawed

½ cup **pitted calamata** or niçoise **olives**

1. Rinse shanks and pat dry. Sprinkle lightly all over with salt and pepper, and place in a 12- by 17-inch roasting pan. Bake, uncovered, in a 450° regular or convection oven until meat is beginning to brown, about 20 minutes. With tongs, turn shanks. Add garlic, onion, and carrots to pan around shanks, mix to coat with fat in pan, and spread level. Bake until shanks are well browned and vegetables are beginning to brown, about 20 minutes longer.

2. Add wine, tomatoes and their juices, anchovies, thyme, savory, and orange peel to pan; stir carefully to mix and scrape browned bits free. Cover pan tightly with foil.

3. Bake in a 325° regular or convection oven until meat is very tender when pierced, 2 to 2½ hours.

4. Uncover pan. Spoon off and discard fat from sauce. Gently stir artichoke hearts and olives into sauce around shanks and bake until heated through, about 10 minutes longer.

5. With tongs, transfer shanks to a rimmed platter or plates; pour sauce over lamb. Add salt and pepper to taste.

Per serving: 686 cal., 34% (234 cal.) from fat; 82 g protein; 26 g fat (8.5 g sat.); 29 g carbo (6.8 g fiber); 1,001 mg sodium; 242 mg chol.

Red Wine–braised Oxtails

PREP AND COOK TIME: About 4 hours

NOTES: We first met chef James Ormsby's oxtails at the former Bruno's in San Francisco. Now he has taken the dish across town to Plump-Jack Cafe. Caramelize the root vegetables in the oven while you brown the oxtails; let the vegetables cool and serve at room temperature. Prepare mashed potatoes while oxtails braise.

MAKES: 4 servings

4 pounds **oxtails,** cut at joints
Salt and **pepper**

1 bottle (750 ml.) **Cabernet Sauvignon** or other dry red wine

3 cups fat-skimmed **beef broth** About ¼ cup **balsamic vinegar**

1 tablespoon chopped **fresh rosemary** leaves or 1 teaspoon dried rosemary

1 tablespoon chopped **fresh tarragon** or 1 teaspoon dried tarragon

1 tablespoon chopped **fresh thyme** leaves or 1 teaspoon dried thyme

Yukon Gold Mashed Potatoes (recipe follows; see notes)

Caramelized Root Vegetables (recipe follows; see notes)

1½ tablespoons **cornstarch**

Fresh thyme sprigs, rinsed

1. Rinse oxtails and pat dry; trim off and discard excess fat. Sprinkle lightly all over with salt and pepper, and place in a 12- by 17-inch roasting pan. Bake, uncovered, in a 450° regular or convection oven, turning once with tongs, until oxtails are well browned all over, 30 to 40 minutes total.

2. Add wine, broth, ¼ cup vinegar, rosemary, tarragon, and thyme to pan. Stir gently to mix and scrape browned bits free. Cover pan tightly with foil.

3. Bake in a 325° regular or convection oven until meat is very tender when pierced, 2¼ to 2¾ hours.

4. Mound mashed potatoes equally in the centers of four wide, shallow bowls. With tongs, lift oxtails from braising liquid and arrange equally around mashed potatoes. Scatter caramelized vegetables over meat, cover loosely with foil, and keep warm in a 200° oven.

5. Skim and discard any fat from braising liquid. Boil, uncovered, over high heat, stirring often, until reduced to 3 cups, 12 to 14 minutes. Meanwhile, in a small bowl, mix cornstarch with 2 tablespoons water until smooth. Stir into braising liquid, and stir until mixture boils and thickens. Taste and, if desired, add 1 to 2 more teaspoons vinegar.

6. Ladle sauce over meat and caramelized vegetables; garnish with thyme sprigs. Add salt and pepper to taste.

Per serving: 266 cal., 47% (126 cal.) from fat; 31 g protein; 14 g fat; 4.1 g carbo (0.1 g fiber); saturated fat, sodium, and cholesterol data not available.

Yukon Gold Mashed Potatoes. Peel 2 pounds **Yukon Gold** or russet **potatoes;** cut into 2-inch chunks. Combine potatoes and about 1 quart **water** in a 3- to 4-quart pan. Cover and bring to a boil over high heat; reduce heat and simmer until potatoes mash very easily, about 20 minutes. Drain potatoes and return to pan.

Meanwhile, warm ¾ cup **milk** or half-and-half and 2 tablespoons **butter** or margarine in a microwave-safe container in a microwave oven at full power (100%) until just steaming, or warm in a 1- to 1½-quart pan over medium heat. Add milk mixture to potatoes and mash with an electric mixer on medium speed or a potato masher until smooth. Season to taste with **salt** and **pepper.** Serve, or cover and keep warm in a 200° oven until ready to use. Serve warm or at room temperature.

Caramelized Root Vegetables. Peel 2 **carrots** (about 3 oz. each) or 12 baby carrots (max. ¾ in. thick), 1 **parsnip** (about 6 oz.) or 12 baby parsnips (max. 1 in. thick), 1 **turnip** (about 8 oz.) or 12 baby turnips (max. 1 in. wide), and 1 lb. **pearl onions** or 12 cipollini onions (max. 1½ in. wide; or use 10 oz. frozen pearl onions, thawed). Cut carrots and parsnip crosswise into ½-inch-thick slices and turnip into ¾-inch dice; if using baby vegetables, leave whole. In a 9- by 13-inch pan, mix vegetables with 1½ tablespoons **olive oil** and 1 tablespoon chopped **fresh thyme** leaves. Sprinkle lightly with **pepper.** Bake in a 450° regular or convection oven, turning vegetables occasionally with a wide spatula, until well browned and tender when pierced, about 30 minutes. Add **salt** to taste. Serve warm or at room temperature. ◆

Nutty layers

Pistachio cream and sesame custard make a winning pair

FOOD STYLING: BASIL FRIEDMAN

■ Every year, winemaker Andrew Quady invites pastry professionals to pair their finest desserts with one of his winery's elegant dessert wines. The grand prize goes to the combination that makes the most magic. The contest has a bittersweet side, though: Some stellar desserts are not wine friendly and so fall by the wayside. One memorable example was this cardamom-perfumed pistachio layer cake created by pastry chef James Osborne. He presented the nut-studded beauty, wrapped and filled with softly whipped cream, with a most unusual sesame seed–flavored custard sauce. Although groaning from our indulgent duty, my fellow judges and I gave the cake a rare gesture of praise—we had seconds.

Pistachio Cream Cake

PREP AND COOK TIME: About 50 minutes, plus at least 2½ hours to cool and chill

NOTES: Make the custard sauce up to 1 day ahead or while the frosted cake chills; the cake cuts best when refrigerated at least 2 hours.

MAKES: 12 to 16 servings

About 2 tablespoons **butter** or margarine

About 1½ cups sifted **cake flour**

1¼ cups **sugar**

1 teaspoon **baking powder**

¾ cup coarsely chopped **roasted pistachios** (salted or unsalted)

2 tablespoons **poppy seeds**

1 teaspoon grated **lemon** peel

1 teaspoon grated **orange** peel

½ teaspoon **ground cardamom**

½ cup **milk**

1 teaspoon **vanilla**

3 **large eggs**

Cream Frosting (recipe follows)

Sesame Custard Sauce (recipe follows)

1. Butter and flour two 9-inch round cake pans. Line bottoms with waxed paper cut to fit; butter paper and dust with flour.

2. In a small bowl, mix 1½ cups cake flour, ¼ cup sugar, baking powder, ½ cup chopped pistachios (wrap remaining airtight), poppy seeds, lemon peel, orange peel, and cardamom.

3. In a glass measure or small microwave-safe bowl, melt 2 tablespoons butter in a microwave oven on full power (100%), ½ to 1 minute. Add milk and vanilla.

4. In a deep bowl, with a mixer on high speed, beat eggs with remaining 1 cup sugar until thick enough to hold mounds briefly when you lift the beater, 4 to 5 minutes. Add flour mixture and milk mixture. Stir or mix gently until well blended. Scrape batter equally into prepared pans.

5. Bake cake layers on center rack in a 325° regular or convection oven until edges are browned and begin to pull from pan sides and centers spring back when lightly pressed, 20 to 25 minutes.

6. Cool layers in pans on a rack for about 10 minutes. Invert cakes from pans onto rack and carefully pull off and discard waxed paper.

7. When layers are cool to touch, place one, bottom side up, on a flat plate (10 to 12 in. wide). Mound about 2 cups of the Cream Frosting on cake; with a long, flexible metal spatula, spread frosting level out to cake rim. Place remaining cake layer, bottom side down, on frosting. Scrape remaining frosting on top of cake and, with the spatula, push enough over the sides to frost thickly, then swirl evenly over top of cake. Cover (a large bowl inverted over the cake works best) and chill at least 2 hours or up to 1 day.

8. Uncover cake and sprinkle with remaining ¼ cup pistachios. On each dessert plate, spoon 3 to 4 tablespoons

Sesame Custard Sauce. Cut cake into wedges and set in sauce on plates.

Per serving: 304 cal., 50% (153 cal.) from fat; 5.1 g protein; 17 g fat (8.4 g sat.); 33 g carbo (0.4 g fiber); 106 mg sodium; 102 mg chol.

Cream Frosting. In a chilled large bowl, with a mixer on high speed, beat 1½ cups **whipping cream** until it holds soft, distinct peaks. Add ½ cup **sour cream**, ¼ cup **sugar**, and ½ teaspoon *each* **almond extract** and **vanilla**. Beat on high speed until mixture is thick enough to hold soft, distinct peaks. Use to fill and frost Pistachio Cream Cake (preceding).

Sesame Custard Sauce

PREP AND COOK TIME: **About 25 minutes, plus at least 15 minutes to chill**
NOTES: If making up to 2 days ahead, cover and chill.
MAKES: About 3 cups

- 5 **large egg** yolks
- 1 tablespoon **Asian** (toasted) **sesame oil**
- 3 tablespoons **sesame seeds**
- ¾ cup **sugar**
- 1 cup **whipping cream**
- 1¾ cups **milk**

1. In a large metal bowl, combine egg yolks and sesame oil; whisk just enough to blend.

2. In a 10- to 12-inch frying pan over medium heat, stir and shake sesame seeds until pale golden brown, about 3 minutes. Pour into a blender with the sugar and whirl until seeds are coarsely ground. Return mixture to frying pan; add whipping cream and milk. Stir over medium-high heat until scalding (bubbles form at pan rim but mixture does not boil), about 5 minutes.

3. Whisk cream mixture into egg yolk mixture, then scrape back into frying pan. Stir over medium-low heat with a flexible (silicone or heat-resistant plastic) spatula, scraping pan bottom and sides, until custard is thick enough to coat a metal spoon with a velvety layer, about 15 minutes. Immediately pour mixture back into metal bowl and nest in ice or ice water; stir often until cool, about 15 minutes. Pour custard through a fine strainer into another bowl, pressing moisture from seeds; discard seeds. Serve custard or cover and chill.

Per tablespoon: 44 cal., 59% (26 cal.) from fat; 0.8 g protein; 2.9 g fat (1.4 g sat.); 3.8 g carbo (0.1 g fiber); 6.9 mg sodium; 29 mg chol.

Sweet spirits

■ Our Halloween and Mexico's Day of the Dead, although not quite the same, both celebrate the spirits of the departed. And, according to southern Mexico folk art specialist Angela Villalba, no Day of the Dead (two days really—November 1 and 2) is complete without brightly decorated sugar skulls, whether you use them to enhance a party or—true to tradition—a cemetery. The skulls are easy to make and fun to decorate. Plastic molds for them are sold in many cookware stores ($8 to $10). Villalba sells the molds as well as plain skulls to decorate ($4 to $7.50 each; 626/307-7755 or www.mexicansugarskull.com).

Sugar Skulls

PREP AND COOK TIME: About 1 hour, plus at least 2 hours to dry
MAKES: One or two 4-inch skulls (with front and back portions)

1. In a bowl, combine 3 cups granulated **sugar** and 1 **large egg** white. Blend with your fingers.
2. Pack sugar mixture firmly into front and back halves of a **plastic skull mold**. Scrape tops level with a spatula. Return extra sugar mixture to bowl.
3. With a spoon, gently scoop sugar mixture from the center of each mold to make a shell ½ to ⅝ inch thick.
4. Invert a baking sheet over each mold; holding mold and pan together, invert again. Tap mold gently and lift carefully off sugar skull. If skull breaks, wash and dry mold, then fill again, reusing sugar mixture. (If mixture sticks to mold, dump back into bowl and stir in 2 to 4 tablespoons sugar; if mixture crumbles, return to bowl and mix in more egg white, 1 teaspoon at a time.) Repeat, using remaining sugar mix-

ture, to make a second skull if desired.
5. Bake in a 200° regular or convection oven until skull surface feels hard and solid when lightly pressed, 20 to 30 minutes. Let cool.
6. To join front and back halves of each skull, spread rims with icing (recipe follows) and fit pieces together; rub off any icing that oozes from seam. Let stand until icing is firm, at least 1 hour.
7. Using a pastry bag with plain or decorative tips, pipe icing onto skulls to decorate as desired. Let dry at least 1 hour. To store, wrap airtight.

Icing. In a bowl, with a mixer on high speed, whip 1 **large egg** white and ⅛ teaspoon **cream of tartar** until foamy. Gradually beat in 1½ cups **powdered sugar**. For intense colors, blend in **food coloring paste** as desired. For delicate shades, use liquid **food coloring**. If necessary, beat in more powdered sugar to make icing stiff enough to hold its shape when squeezed through a pastry bag. Makes about ¾ cup, enough to join and decorate one or two skulls.

food guide

The new spice route

■ Exploring an ethnic food market is like digging for treasure. But for those with no time to dig, many of these treasures are making their way into the mainstream. Garam masala, for instance, an Indian spice blend, is now made by Spice Islands and Spice Hunter, both big players at the supermarket. Each version is a unique blend of spices that can make simple meat, fish, poultry, and vegetable dishes quite sophisticated. These flavorful garbanzos, from my Indian friend Ranjan Dey, make an excellent vegetarian main dish.

Garbanzos Masala

PREP AND COOK TIME: 15 to 20 minutes
MAKES: 3 or 4 servings

- 1 **onion** (about 8 oz.), peeled and chopped
- 2 fresh **jalapeño chilies** (2 to 3 oz. total), rinsed, stemmed, seeded, and chopped
- 1 tablespoon minced **fresh ginger**
- 1 tablespoon **salad oil**
- ½ cup finely chopped **fresh cilantro**
- 1 tablespoon **curry powder**
- 1½ teaspoons **garam masala**
- ½ teaspoon **sugar**
- 1 can (15 to 16 oz.) **garbanzos**, drained
- 2 to 3 **firm-ripe tomatoes** (1 lb. total), rinsed, cored, and chopped (including juice)

About 1 cup **plain yogurt**

Salt

1. In a 10- to 12-inch frying pan over medium-high heat, combine onion, chilies, ginger, and oil; stir often until onion is lightly browned, 6 to 8 minutes.

2. Add ¼ cup chopped cilantro, curry powder, garam masala, and sugar; stir until fragrant, about 30 seconds. Stir in garbanzos and all but ½ cup of the tomatoes, then add ½ cup water. Boil over medium-high heat, stirring often, until tomatoes have disintegrated and most of the liquid has boiled away, about 8 minutes. Remove from heat, stir in 1 cup yogurt, and season to taste with salt.

3. Pour into a bowl; top with remaining chopped cilantro, chopped tomatoes, and more yogurt to taste.

Per serving: 192 cal., 31% (59 cal.) from fat; 8.7 g protein; 6.6 g fat (1.1 g sat.); 26 g carbo (5.8 g fiber); 170 mg sodium; 3.4 mg chol.

Go with the grain

■ At Café Terra Cotta in Tucson, chef-owner Donna Nordin fills chiles rellenos with a pilaf made of quinoa (*keen*-wah)—a little grain that sustained the ancient peoples of Peru. I've layered, rather than stuffed, the chilies with the quinoa to make a hearty vegetarian main dish.

Quinoa and Chili Casserole

PREP AND COOK TIME: About 40 minutes
MAKES: 6 servings

- ⅔ cup **pine nuts**
- 4 teaspoons **salad oil**
- 1 cup **quinoa**
- 2 tablespoons coarsely chopped **dried tomatoes**
- 1½ cups **vegetable broth**
- ½ cup chopped **green onions**
- 1 tablespoon chopped **fresh basil** leaves
- 1 tablespoon chopped **fresh cilantro**
- 2 to 3 teaspoons **balsamic vinegar**

Salt

- 2 cans (7 oz. each) **whole green chilies**
- 1 cup shredded **jack cheese with chilies** (4 oz.)

1. In a 4- to 5-quart pan over medium-high heat, stir pine nuts in 1 teaspoon oil until lightly toasted, about 4 minutes. Pour into a bowl.

2. Pour 1 tablespoon oil into pan and add quinoa. Stir over medium-high heat until quinoa smells toasted, about 3 minutes. Add tomatoes and broth; bring to a boil over high heat. Cover, reduce heat, and simmer, stirring occasionally, until quinoa is tender, about 10 minutes. Remove from heat and stir in pine nuts, green onions, basil, and cilantro; season with vinegar and salt. Cover and let stand.

3. Drain chilies and split open lengthwise; discard seeds. Arrange half the chilies in a 2-quart casserole (8 by 12 in.). Scrape quinoa mixture over chilies; spread level. Cover with remaining chilies; sprinkle with cheese.

4. Bake in a 375° oven until casserole is hot in the center and cheese is melted, about 20 minutes.

5. Cut into portions and scoop out with a spoon. Add salt to taste.

Per serving: 325 cal., 53% (171 cal.) from fat; 15 g protein; 19 g fat (5.1 g sat.); 29 g carbo (4.9 g fiber); 560 mg sodium; 20 mg chol. ◆

The Wine Guide

By Karen MacNeil-Fife

Sunset's wine columnist offers a magnum of wisdom

■ Karen MacNeil has voiced her expertise about wine in this column for four years. From aromas to corks to vintages, she has explained wine's enigmas for connoisseurs and novices alike.

Behind the scenes, MacNeil has been writing a comprehensive book on the subject, from growing to making to understanding wines worldwide through history, culture, and food. For once, she got all the space she wanted to bring her passion to the technicalities of wine. *The Wine Bible*—nearly 10 years in the making and more than 900 pages long—will be in stores October 1 (Workman Publishing, New York, 2001; $19.95; 212/254-5900 or www. workman.com). In it, wine is alive—scientific and sensual at once. And drinking it becomes a simple, unpretentious, delightful practice. Below are a few excerpts from MacNeil's pragmatic advice.

—Sara Schneider

On buying wine

If you're trying to describe to the clerk the kinds of wines you like and you're at a loss for words, think about foods. Wines can be big and juicy like a steak; fresh and light like a salad; or spicy and bold like a Mexican sauce. It isn't necessary to use technical wine terms; in fact, they can get in the way. One day, wanting an adventure, I asked a wine clerk to give me a wine like Robin Williams. Amazingly enough, and without a minute's hesitation, he did.

On storing wine

Wine doesn't care if it's stored in a $10,000 custom-built cellar, in a damp basement, or between shoes in the closet, as long as three things are true: (1) The environment is cool. (2) The bottle is lying on its side or upside down (but not standing upright). (3) There is no direct sunlight.

On pairing wine with food

Beginning in the 1980s, wine and food pairing became something of a national sport. Restaurants offered wine and food dinners.... It was all very exciting. But as time went on, what started out as an exploration meant to heighten enjoyment began to border on the neurotic.

The problem with this sort of approach is that it has very little connection—today or historically—to how we actually behave when we cook, eat, and drink.... We sometimes choose wines as much to match the

E. SPENCER TOY

mood as the food.

That said, it's certainly true that extraordinary flavor affinities do exist, and that most of us have had at least a few of those "wow" moments when the wine and food combination was unbelievably good. How do you create those moments?

Ultimately, taste preferences are highly individual. So where does that leave us?... Squarely in the realm of instinct. People who pair wine and food together well don't have a set of rules as much as they have good instincts. And good instincts can be acquired. It's simply a matter of drinking lots of different kinds of wines with different kinds of dishes and paying attention to the principles that emerge. After years of doing precisely that, here's what I've discovered:

• Pair great with great, humble with humble.

• Match delicate to delicate, robust to robust.

• Decide if you want to mirror a given flavor or set up a contrast.

• Think about flexibility.... Though chardonnay is wildly popular, it's one of the least flexible white wines with food.... For maximum flexibility, go with a sauvignon blanc or a dry German or Alsatian riesling.... The most flexible red wines either have good acidity, such as Chianti, red Burgundy, and California and Oregon pinot noir, or they have loads of fruit and not a lot of tannin.

• Saltiness in food is a great contrast to acidity in wine.... Saltiness is also a stunning contrast to sweetness.

• Desserts that are sweeter than the wine they accompany make the wine taste dull and blank.... Wedding cake, for example, can ruin just about anything in a glass, though happily, no one's paying attention anyway.

The price is right

Realize that no price is too little. You don't have to spend a fortune to drink good wine.... Wine professionals often buy very reasonably priced wines. [They] care about what's inside the bottle and the cheaper the price, the better. It's often people who don't know a lot about wine who pay enormous amounts for it, hoping that price will be some sort of assurance. It doesn't really work that way. Unlike cars and stereo systems, there are very good wines at all prices. ◆

Shrimp, asparagus, tomatoes, and even the linguine cook in one pan.

One-pan pastas

■ The two great creators of pasta—the Chinese and the Italians—should get together. Applying Chinese stir-frying techniques to Asian or Italian noodles produces one-pan wonders perfect for quick weeknight suppers.

Asparagus and Shrimp Stir-fry with Noodles

PREP AND COOK TIME: About 30 minutes

MAKES: 3 servings

- ³/₄ pound (41 to 50 per lb.) **frozen shelled, deveined shrimp**
- ³/₄ pound **asparagus**
- 8 to 9 ounces **fresh linguine**
- 1 tablespoon **olive oil**
- 2 cloves **garlic,** peeled and pressed
- 1 cup chopped **tomatoes**
- ³/₄ cup chopped **fresh cilantro**
    About ¹/₂ cup fat-skimmed **chicken** or vegetable **broth**
    Salt and **pepper**

1. Place shrimp in a colander; rinse frequently with cold water until thawed, about 5 minutes. In a covered 5- to 6-quart nonstick pan over high heat, bring 2¹/₂ to 3 quarts water to a boil.

2. Break off and discard tough stem ends from asparagus. Rinse asparagus and cut diagonally into 1¹/₄-inch lengths.

3. Add linguine and shrimp to boiling water; cook, uncovered, until pasta is barely tender to bite and shrimp are opaque but still moist-looking in center of thickest part (cut to test), 2 to 3 minutes. Wash colander; pour pasta and shrimp into it. Rinse with hot water and drain.

4. Rinse pan and return to high heat. When dry, add oil, garlic, and asparagus. Stir often until garlic begins to brown, about 2 minutes. Add tomatoes, cilantro, and ¹/₂ cup broth; bring to a boil, then reduce heat to medium.

5. Pour shrimp mixture into pan. Mix until pasta is hot, 1 to 2 minutes. For a moister dish, add 2 to 4 more tablespoons broth. Pour into a wide bowl. Add salt and pepper to taste.

Per serving: 420 cal., 18% (77 cal.) from fat; 36 g protein; 8.6 g fat (1.3 g sat.); 49 g carbo (3.5 g fiber); 209 mg sodium; 228 mg chol.

Curry Noodles with Chicken

PREP AND COOK TIME: About 30 minutes

NOTES: Thai red curry paste and Asian fish sauce are available in well-stocked supermarkets and Asian grocery stores.

MAKES: 3 servings

- 1 pound **green beans**
- ³/₄ pound **boned, skinned chicken breasts**
- 8 to 9 ounces **fresh fettuccine**
- 1 can (14 oz.) **coconut milk**
- 1 tablespoon **Thai red curry paste**
- 1¹/₂ teaspoons **sugar**
- 1 teaspoon **rice vinegar**
- 1 to 2 tablespoons **Asian fish sauce** (*nuoc mam* or *nam pla*)
    Fresh basil or cilantro **leaves** (optional)

1. In a covered 5- to 6-quart nonstick pan over high heat, bring 2¹/₂ to 3 quarts water to a boil.

2. Meanwhile, rinse green beans; trim and discard ends, then cut beans into 2- to 3-inch lengths. Rinse chicken and pat dry; thinly slice crosswise into ¹/₈-inch-thick strips.

3. Stir fettuccine and beans into boiling water; cook, uncovered, until pasta is barely tender to bite, 2 to 3 minutes. Pour into a colander, rinse with hot water, and drain.

4. Rinse pan and set over medium heat. Stir in ¹/₄ cup coconut milk and curry paste. Add chicken; stir until no longer pink in the center (cut to test), about 3 minutes. Add remaining coconut milk,

¹/₄ cup water, sugar, vinegar, and 1 tablespoon fish sauce; mix.

5. Add pasta and beans to pan; mix until noodles are hot, about 2 minutes. Add more fish sauce if desired. Pour into a wide bowl. Sprinkle with basil leaves.

Per serving: 684 cal., 43% (297 cal.) from fat; 41 g protein; 33 g fat (26 g sat.); 59 g carbo (4 g fiber); 747 mg sodium; 121 mg chol.

Broccoli-Beef Noodles

PREP AND COOK TIME: About 30 minutes

NOTES: Look for black bean sauce and Japanese buckwheat soba noodles in well-stocked supermarkets and Asian grocery stores.

MAKES: 4 servings

- 6 cups **broccoli florets** (1 lb.)
- 1 **onion** (6 oz.)
- 2 cups fat-skimmed **beef broth**
- 2 tablespoons **Chinese black bean and garlic sauce**
- 2 tablespoons **cornstarch**
- ¹/₂ pound **dried spaghetti** or soba noodles
- 1 teaspoon **salad oil**
- ¹/₂ pound **ground lean beef**
    Soy sauce

1. In a covered 5- to 6-quart nonstick pan over high heat, bring 2¹/₂ to 3 quarts water to a boil.

2. Meanwhile, rinse broccoli. Trim stems and cut crosswise into ¹/₄-inch-thick slices, then cut florets lengthwise into 1-inch pieces. Peel onion and cut into thin slivers. In a small bowl, mix broth, black bean sauce, and cornstarch.

3. Add spaghetti to boiling water and cook, uncovered, until barely tender to bite, 6 to 9 minutes. Pour into a colander, rinse with hot water, and drain.

4. Return pan to high heat and pour in oil. Add beef and stir often, breaking up with spoon, until lightly browned and crumbly, 1 to 2 minutes. Add onion and stir until it begins to brown, about 1 minute.

5. Add broccoli and ¹/₂ cup water; cover and stir occasionally until bright green, about 2 minutes. Stir broth mixture, add to pan, and stir until boiling.

6. Add noodles to pan; stir over medium heat until hot and coated with sauce, about 1 minute. Add soy sauce to taste. Pour into bowls.

Per serving: 455 cal., 30% (135 cal.) from fat; 24 g protein; 15 g fat (5.1 g sat.); 56 g carbo (5.6 g fiber); 759 mg sodium; 43 mg chol. ◆

Breakfasts that bite back

Four top Southwestern cafes (and one great recipe)

By Lawrence W. Cheek and Tiffany Armstrong

Enthusiasts of Mexican breakfasts track them down whenever they travel in the Southwest. They cheerily bombard their digestive mills with incendiary chili sauces, peppery chorizo, and pickled jalapeño chilies, not to mention liberal garnishes of garlic and onion—all at 7 A.M.

Hot chilies at dawn may well be addicting. At the very least, they're a surefire wake-up call.

Mexican breakfasts offer plenty of variety. The best breakfasts are frequently found in unpretentious cafes where the vehicles congregated outside include a high percentage of pickups. Hallmarks of a truly great Southwestern breakfast? Fresh, warm flour tortillas, made by hand in the restaurant and served with every meal. And you want a selection of salsas, not just one-flavor-fits-all.

If you can't get to the Southwest's

great breakfast spots, you can satisfy your cravings by cooking your own chili-seasoned breakfast at home.

Chilaquiles are a traditional way for households to use leftover tortillas; restaurants may interpret them in countless permutations involving fried tortilla strips, cheese, beans, chicken, chilies, and more. This chilaquiles recipe is *Sunset's* spin on a Southwestern classic.

Chilaquiles con Pollo y Queso

PREP AND COOK TIME: About 1 hour

NOTES: Look for dried ancho chilies in Latino markets. For a milder sauce, omit the jalapeño chili. If making chicken and sauce up to 1 day ahead, cool, cover, and chill. Reheat chicken, covered, in a microwave oven at half power (50%), stirring once, until warm, about 4 minutes; reheat sauce in a microwave oven on full power (100%), stirring once, until hot, about 2 minutes. If frying tortilla strips up to 1 day ahead, wrap airtight; reheat, uncovered, in a 200° oven until warm, about 5 minutes.

MAKES: 4 servings

- ³⁄₄ cup chopped **onion**
- 2 cloves **garlic,** peeled
- 4 **dried ancho chilies** (sometimes mistakenly labeled pasilla; 1¹⁄₂ ounces total)
- 2 **boned, skinned chicken breast halves** (1 lb. total), rinsed
- 10 **corn tortillas** (6 in. wide)
- 1¹⁄₂ cups **salad oil**
- 2 **Roma tomatoes** (7 oz. total), rinsed
- 1 **jalapeño chili** (1 oz.), rinsed and stemmed (optional)

  Salt

  Softly scrambled **eggs** (optional)
- ¹⁄₄ cup shredded **manchego** or jack **cheese**
- 1 tablespoon finely chopped **fresh cilantro**

  Sour cream

  Lime wedges

Regulate heat level by choice of chilies.

1. In a 3- to 4-quart pan over high heat, combine 1¹⁄₂ quarts water, onion, and garlic. Rinse dried ancho chilies, break off and discard stems, and add chilies to pan. Cover and bring to a boil. Add chicken, cover, and return to a boil. Remove from heat and let stand, covered, until chilies are soft and chicken is no longer pink in center of thickest part (cut to test), 12 to 18 minutes. If chicken is still pink, return it to the hot liquid, cover pan, and let steep a few minutes longer.

2. Meanwhile, cut tortillas into ¹⁄₂-inch-wide strips, then cut strips in half crosswise. Put oil in a 10- to 12-inch frying pan over medium-high heat. When oil is hot, add a fourth of the strips and cook until lightly browned and crisp, 3 to 5 minutes. Remove with a slotted spoon and drain on paper towels. Keep warm in a 200° oven. Repeat to fry remaining strips.

3. Remove cooked chicken from liquid, reserving liquid and vegetables. When chicken is cool enough to handle, in about 10 minutes, tear into shreds.

4. Pour onion-chili mixture into a strainer set over a bowl; reserve liquid and put strained vegetables into a blender or food processor. Purée chili mixture, tomatoes, and jalapeño until smooth. If you prefer a thinner sauce, add 2 to 3 tablespoons reserved liquid (discard remainder). Season to taste with salt.

5. Arrange tortilla strips on a platter or plates; cover with eggs, chicken, chili sauce, cheese, and cilantro. Garnish with sour cream and lime wedges.

Per serving: 498 cal., 43% (216 cal.) from fat; 34 g protein; 24 g fat (4.8 g sat.); 40 g carbo (6.9 g fiber); 226 mg sodium; 73 mg chol. ◆

Rise and shine

Looking for a classic Southwestern breakfast? Each of these four restaurants offers the real thing: morning meals that are hearty, fiery, and deeply satisfying.

ARIZONA

PHOENIX: **Tacos Mexico.** *8 A.M. daily. 2333 N. 16th St.; (602) 253-5163. Other locations also.*

TUCSON: **Teresa's Mosaic Cafe.** *7:30 A.M. daily. 2455 N. Silverbell Rd.; (520) 624-4512.*

NEW MEXICO

SANTA FE: **Cafe Pascual's.** *7 A.M. Mon–Sat, 8 A.M. Sun. 121 Don Gaspar; (505) 983-9340.*

Tia Sophia's. *7 A.M. Mon–Sat. 210 W. San Francisco St.; (505) 983-9880.*

The Low-Fat Cook
Bowlfuls of flavor from Indonesia
By Andrew Baker

A veritable vegetable patch floats in a tangy tamarind broth.

JAMES CARRIER; FOOD STYLING: JULIE SMITH

■ When Evita Prasetya, of Mountain View, California, wants satisfying meals that are low in fat and full of flavor, she turns to traditional dishes of her native Indonesia such as *sayur asam*, a vegetable soup, and *semur ayam*, a chicken stew. Both are easy to make, and neither requires modification to be low-fat—they are naturally lean. In Indonesia, the vegetable soup is made with chunks of corn on the cob, but it's easier to eat if you use corn kernels, fresh or frozen. Imported ingredients give the dishes authenticity, but supermarket alternatives produce convincingly similar results, so out-of-the-way shopping is not needed.

Tamarind Vegetable and Shrimp Soup

PREP AND COOK TIME: About 20 minutes

NOTES: This soup is typically filled with vegetables; for a main dish, we've added shrimp, but you don't have to. Tamarind paste is available in Latino and Asian food markets and in some well-stocked supermarkets; chili sambal and Asian red chili paste are found in the latter two. Serve at once because the acidity of the tamarind makes the green beans lose their bright color quickly.

MAKES: 4 main-dish servings

- ½ cup **tamarind paste with seeds** or 1 cup tamarind concentrate
- 1 **chayote** (about 10 oz.) or ½ to ¾ pound yellow crookneck squash
- 2 cups fresh-cut **corn kernels** or 1 package (10 oz.) frozen corn
- ¼ cup minced **shallots** or onion
- ¼ cup firmly packed **brown sugar**
- 1 clove **garlic**, peeled and minced or pressed
- 6 cups fat-skimmed **chicken broth**
- 1 **fresh Anaheim chili** (about 2 oz.), rinsed
- ¾ pound **shelled, cooked tiny shrimp**
- 2 cups thinly sliced **cabbage**
- 1 package (9 oz.) **frozen French-cut green beans**, thawed
- ¼ cup coarsely chopped **salted roasted peanuts**
- **Salt**
- **Chili sambal**, Asian red chili paste, or hot sauce

1. In a bowl, combine tamarind paste and 1 cup hot water (omit step if using tamarind concentrate). Let stand until paste is soft, about 5 minutes. Rub mixture through a fine strainer into a 5- to 6-quart pan; discard residue.

2. Rinse and peel chayote (or rinse squash and trim ends) and cut into ½-inch chunks (including seeds). Add chayote (or squash) to pan along with corn, shallots, sugar, garlic, and broth. Bring to a boil over high heat; cover, reduce heat, and simmer until the chayote (or squash) pieces are tender when pierced, 5 to 8 minutes.

3. Meanwhile, stem, seed, devein, and finely chop Anaheim chili. Rinse and drain shrimp.

4. When the chayote pieces are tender, stir chili and cabbage into soup; turn heat to high. When soup is boiling, uncover and add shrimp, green beans, and peanuts; stir until shrimp are hot, about 30 seconds. Ladle soup into bowls and add salt and chili sambal to taste.

Per serving: 385 cal., 16% (61 cal.) from fat; 37 g protein; 6.8 g fat (1 g sat.); 47 g carbo (7.7 g fiber); 438 mg sodium; 166 mg chol.

Chicken, Potato, and Tomato Stew

PREP AND COOK TIME: About 45 minutes

NOTES: Sweetened soy sauce is available in Asian food markets, but adding sugar to regular soy sauce creates the same flavor.

MAKES: 4 servings

- 1 pound **thin-skinned potatoes**
- ½ teaspoon **salad oil**
- ¼ cup thinly sliced **shallots** or onion
- ½ pound **Roma tomatoes**, rinsed, cored, and finely chopped
- 3 tablespoons **sweetened soy sauce** *(ketjap manis)* or 1½ tablespoons *each* soy sauce and sugar (see notes)
- 2 cups fat-skimmed **chicken broth**
- 4 **whole cloves**
- 1 pound **boned, skinned chicken breasts**
- ¼ cup chopped **green onions** (including tops) or parsley
- **Salt**

1. Rinse and peel potatoes; cut into ½-inch chunks.

2. In a 3- to 4-quart nonstick pan over high heat, combine oil and shallots. Stir often until shallots are lightly browned, 2 to 3 minutes. Add tomatoes and soy sauce and stir until tomatoes are soft when pressed, about 2 minutes.

3. To pan, add potatoes, broth, and cloves. Bring to a boil; cover, reduce heat, and simmer until potatoes are tender when pierced, about 15 minutes. Uncover and boil over high heat, stirring occasionally, until potatoes are soft enough to mash easily and mixture is reduced to about 3 cups, about 10 minutes.

4. Meanwhile, rinse chicken and pat dry; cut into 1-inch chunks. Add to the stew, cover, and simmer, stirring occasionally, until meat is no longer pink in the center (cut to test), 3 to 4 minutes. If desired, spoon out and discard cloves. Ladle stew into bowls, sprinkle with green onions, and add salt to taste.

Per serving: 270 cal., 7.8% (28 cal.) from fat; 33 g protein; 2.3 g fat (0.5 g sat.); 28 g carbo (2.5 g fiber); 510 mg sodium; 66 mg chol. ◆

Indian dal of Red Chief lentils has nuances of cumin, cardamom, and ginger.

Lentil country

Take advantage of the West's crop of new varieties

By Elaine Johnson • Photographs by James Carrier

The Palouse—a piece of the West cut out of Washington and Idaho—is America's lentil land. The name derives from the French word *pelouse,* meaning *green lawn,* and in spring, the verdant lentil fields validate the label. By late summer the undulating hills are honey-colored, and the ankle-high bushes dry and ready to release their treasure—about 215 million pounds of lentils, more than 70 percent of the country's crop.

Hundreds of combines scoop up millions of thumb-size pods (each holding only two or three lentils), suck them into their inner machinery, shoot the lentils up into a hold, and spew out the chaff.

This harvest is a cook's gold mine: Lentils are inexpensive, versatile, quick-cooking, low in fat, and high in vitamins, protein, and fiber. And now there's a trove of varieties to try—from black to olive green to bright red orange.

Indian Dal

PREP AND COOK TIME: About 35 minutes

NOTES: You can also use Canary or Crimson lentils. Serve this thick stew with hot cooked basmati rice.

MAKES: 5 cups; 5 servings

- 1 tablespoon **salad oil**
- 1 teaspoon **cumin seeds**
- ¼ teaspoon **ground cardamom**
- 1 quart **vegetable** or fat-skimmed chicken **broth**
- 1½ cups **dried Red Chief lentils** (12 oz.; see notes), sorted and rinsed
- 1 cup chopped **onion**

  About ¼ cup chopped **fresh cilantro**
- 2 tablespoons minced **fresh ginger**
- 2 tablespoons minced **fresh jalapeño chilies**
- 1 tablespoon minced **garlic**

- 1 teaspoon **ground dried turmeric**

  Salt

1. In a 5- to 6-quart pan over medium-high heat, frequently stir oil, cumin, and cardamom just until spices are fragrant, 1 to 1½ minutes. Add broth, lentils, onion, ¼ cup cilantro, ginger, chilies, garlic, and turmeric. Bring to a boil over high heat; reduce heat, cover, and simmer, stirring often, until lentils fall apart, about 15 minutes.

2. Ladle dal into bowls, sprinkle with more cilantro, and add salt to taste.

Per serving: 303 cal., 12% (35 cal.) from fat; 20 g protein; 3.9 g fat (0.4 g sat.); 49 g carbo (8.5 g fiber); 67 mg sodium; 0 mg chol.

Sherried Lentil Salad

PREP AND COOK TIME: About 1 hour and 10 minutes, plus about 40 minutes to cool

NOTES: You can also use Eston, Le Puy, or Pardina lentils.

MAKES: 6 servings

- 3 cups fat-skimmed **chicken broth**
- 1½ cups **Beluga lentils** (12 oz.; see notes), sorted and rinsed
- 1 cup minced **onion**
- ¾ cup diced **carrots**
- ½ cup diced **celery**
- 1½ teaspoons **dried thyme**
- 1 cup **dry sherry**
- 1 cup chopped drained **canned peeled roasted red peppers**
- ⅓ cup thinly sliced **green onions** (including tops)
- ¼ cup **extra-virgin olive oil**
- 2 tablespoons **sherry vinegar** or red wine vinegar
- 2 quarts lightly packed **salad mix** (6 oz.), rinsed and crisped

  Salt and **pepper**

1. In a 5- to 6-quart pan over high heat, bring broth, lentils, onion, carrots, celery, and thyme to a boil. Reduce heat, cover, and simmer 25 minutes, stirring occasionally. Add sherry and simmer until lentils are tender to bite, 5 to 10 minutes longer. Drain; reserve liquid.

2. Pour lentil mixture into a bowl and let cool to room temperature, about 40 minutes, stirring occasionally. Meanwhile, return cooking liquid to pan and boil over high heat until reduced to ½ cup, about 5 minutes. Let cool.

3. Stir liquid, chopped red peppers, and green onions into lentil mixture. In a bowl, mix oil and vinegar; stir half the dressing into lentil mixture. Add

LENTIL LEXICON *(vertical side label)*

Grande · LENS-SHAPED · Common brown

Le Puy · Eston

Pardina · Beluga

SMALL, ROUND

Crimson

Red Chief

Canary · DECORTICATED

organic lentils cost $1.25 to $1.75 per lb.), or Zürsun (800/424-8881; $1.50 to $3 per lb.); shipping costs extra.

Basic cooking directions: Sort lentils and remove any debris. Put them in a fine strainer and rinse with cold water. Simmer lentils, covered, in broth or water (3 times their volume if you want to preserve their shape, 4 times if cooking to a purée), stirring occasionally. See cooking times specified for individual types.

■ **LENS-SHAPED:** The most common lentils. If cooked the minimum time required, they get pleasantly mealy inside and soft at the edges; with longer cooking they dissolve into a meaty, putty-colored purée. Cook until tender to bite but not mushy, 25 to 30 minutes, or until they fall apart, about 1 hour.
• **Common brown.** May be Brewer or Richlea variety. Medium size; reddish brown to khaki brown; earthy.
• **Grande.** Also called large, green. An oversize version of common brown lentils; mottled tan and green; earthy.

■ **SMALL, ROUND:** Hold their shape well during cooking and develop a slightly chewy texture; colors lighten. Cook until tender to bite, 25 to 35 minutes.
• **Beluga.** Tiny; black (resembles caviar); mild.
• **Eston.** Small; khaki green; earthy and nutty.
• **Le Puy.** Also called petite French green. Small; mottled green and black; rich and nutty.
• **Pardina.** Also called Spanish brown. Small; reddish brown; nutty.

■ **DECORTICATED:** Because they're hulled, these lentils cook very quickly; colors lighten when the lentils are cooked to a purée. Cook until barely tender to bite, 2 to 7 minutes, or until they fall apart, 10 to 17 minutes.
• **Canary.** Also called Sutter's Gold. Medium size; yellow; split pea flavor.
• **Crimson.** Also called petite crimson. Small; orange; mild, celery-like flavor.
• **Red Chief.** Medium size; orange; rich, herbaceous.

We've divided the most widely available lentil varieties into three basic groups based on their shape, size, color, and cooking properties. Many supermarkets carry several options; look in gourmet food stores for specialty varieties. Or order from Meacham Mills (208/743-0505; 55 cents to 92 cents per lb.), Timeless Specialty Foods (406/278-5770;

---

salad mix to bowl with remaining dressing; mix.

4. Spoon equal amounts of salad mix onto plates. Top equally with lentil mixture. Add salt and pepper to taste.

Per serving: 333 cal., 27% (90 cal.) from fat; 21 g protein; 10 g fat (1.4 g sat.); 43 g carbo (8.1 g fiber); 112 mg sodium; 0 mg chol.

Lentil-Linguisa Soup

PREP AND COOK TIME: About 1½ hours

NOTES: You can also use Beluga, Eston, or Le Puy lentils.

MAKES: 2 quarts; 6 servings

  1 pound **linguisa** (Portuguese) or kielbasa (Polish) **sausages**
     Olive oil (optional)
  2 **onions** (1 lb. total), peeled and thinly sliced

1½ tablespoons minced **garlic**
1½ teaspoons **cumin seeds**
  2 **dried bay leaves**
  3 cups fat-skimmed **reduced-sodium chicken broth**
1½ cups **dried Pardina lentils** (12 oz.; see notes), sorted and rinsed
1¼ cups **dry red wine**
  ⅓ cup chopped **parsley**
  ½ to 1 teaspoon **hot sauce**
     Salt

1. Cut sausages crosswise into ½-inch-thick slices. In a 5- to 6-quart pan over medium-high heat, stir sausages often until browned, 8 to 10 minutes. With a slotted spoon, transfer slices to paper towels to drain. Discard all but 2 table-

spoons of the fat in pan, or, if needed, add olive oil to make this amount.

2. Add onions and garlic to pan. Stir often over medium-high heat until limp, about 8 minutes. Add cumin and bay leaves; stir for 1 minute. Add broth, 1 cup water, sausages, and lentils. Bring to a boil over high heat; reduce heat, cover, and simmer 25 minutes, stirring occasionally.

3. Stir in wine. Simmer, covered, until lentils are tender to bite, 5 to 20 minutes longer. Uncover and boil, stirring often, until soup is reduced to 2 quarts, about 5 minutes. Stir in parsley and hot sauce to taste. Ladle into bowls. Add salt to taste.

Per serving: 471 cal., 40% (189 cal.) from fat; 29 g protein; 21 g fat (7.3 g sat.); 43 g carbo (8 g fiber); 1,148 mg sodium; 51 mg chol. ◆

Kitchen Cabinet

Readers' recipes tested in *Sunset's* kitchens

By Charity Ferreira

Pumpkin Scones

Bonnie Ackerman-Luo, Antioch, CA

Every October, Bonnie Ackerman-Luo makes pumpkin purée and freezes it in measured portions so she can make these scones all year long. We tried the scones with canned pumpkin, which makes a good substitute.

PREP AND COOK TIME: About 45 minutes

MAKES: 6 scones

- About 2½ cups **all-purpose flour**
- ¼ cup firmly packed **brown sugar**
- 1 tablespoon **baking powder**
- ¾ teaspoon **ground cinnamon**
- ½ teaspoon **salt**
- About ½ cup (¼ lb.) **butter** or margarine, cut into chunks
- ¾ cup **canned pumpkin**
- ½ cup plus 1 tablespoon **milk**
- 1 **large egg** yolk
- 1 tablespoon **granulated sugar**

1. In a bowl, mix flour, brown sugar, baking powder, ½ teaspoon cinnamon, and salt. Add ½ cup butter and, with a pastry blender or your fingers, cut or rub in until pea-size crumbs form.

2. In a small bowl, whisk pumpkin and ½ cup milk until well blended. Add to flour mixture and stir just until dough is evenly moistened.

3. Scrape onto a lightly floured board, turn over to coat, and gently knead just until dough comes together, 5 or 6 turns. Pat dough into a 6-inch round 1½ inches thick; cut into 6 equal wedges.

4. Separate wedges and place on a lightly buttered 12- by 15-inch baking sheet. In a small bowl, beat egg yolk and 1 tablespoon milk to blend; brush lightly over tops of scones (discard any remaining egg wash). In another small bowl, mix granulated sugar and remaining ¼ teaspoon cinnamon; sprinkle evenly over scones.

5. Bake in a 375° regular or convection oven until scones are golden brown, 25 to 30 minutes. Transfer to a rack; serve warm or cool.

Per scone: 407 cal., 38% (153 cal.) from fat; 7.1 g protein; 17 g fat (10 g sat.); 56 g carbo (2 g fiber); 610 mg sodium; 80 mg chol.

Wild Rice and Mushroom Pancakes

Pam Norby, Camarillo, CA

Pam Norby created this appetizer as a way of saying thanks to a Minnesota relative for her yearly gift of freshly harvested wild rice. She tops the nutty-tasting pancakes with sour cream and caviar. We've suggested a relatively economical salmon or whitefish roe, but you can skip the caviar altogether and just use sour cream.

PREP AND COOK TIME: About 1 hour

NOTES: Use leftover wild rice or cook purchased rice according to package instructions.

MAKES: About 30 cakes; 6 to 8 appetizer servings

- ½ pound **crimini** or common **mushrooms**
- 2 **large eggs**
- 1 cup cooked **wild rice** (see notes)
- 1 cup shredded **cheddar cheese**
- ½ cup **fine dried bread crumbs**
- ½ cup minced **green onions**, white and pale green parts only
- 2 teaspoons **hot sauce**
- ½ teaspoon **dried thyme**
- ¼ teaspoon **salt**
- ¼ teaspoon **pepper**
- About 2 tablespoons **olive oil**
- ½ cup **sour cream**
- About 2 ounces **salmon** or whitefish **roe** (optional; see notes)

1. Rinse and drain mushrooms. Trim off and discard tough stem ends and any bruised areas; finely chop mushrooms.

2. In a bowl, beat eggs to blend. Add mushrooms, rice, cheese, bread crumbs, green onions, hot sauce, thyme, salt, and pepper; mix until well blended.

3. Heat ½ tablespoon olive oil in a 10- to 12-inch frying pan over medium-high heat. Spoon rice mixture in 1-tablespoon portions, slightly apart, into pan; with back of spoon, flatten into 3-inch rounds. Cook pancakes, turning once, until browned on both sides, 4 to 6 minutes total. With a spatula, transfer to a 12- by 15-inch baking sheet lined with paper towels and keep warm in a 200° oven. Repeat to cook remaining pancakes, adding more oil to pan as needed.

4. Arrange pancakes in a single layer on a platter. Dollop sour cream equally on pancakes. Top each with ½ teaspoon salmon roe if desired.

Per pancake: 52 cal., 60% (31 cal.) from fat; 2.1 g protein; 3.4 g fat (1.5 g sat.); 3.2 g carbo (0.3 g fiber); 74 mg sodium; 20 mg chol.

Orange and Walnut Broccoli

Laura A. Flynn, Littlerock, CA

Laura A. Flynn loved the combined flavors of orange peel and walnuts with spinach in a pork dish. Curious about how those flavors would complement other vegetables, she created this memorable side dish.

PREP AND COOK TIME: About 15 minutes

MAKES: 4 or 5 servings

- 1 **orange** (about 8 oz.)
- 1 tablespoon **salad oil**
- ⅓ cup chopped **walnuts**
- ½ teaspoon minced **fresh ginger**
- 1 tablespoon **soy sauce**
- 5 cups **broccoli florets** (12 oz.), rinsed and drained

1. Rinse and dry orange. With a vegetable peeler or small, sharp knife, pare colored part of peel from orange. Cut peels into very thin slivers. Squeeze juice from orange; measure ¼ cup and save remaining for other uses.

2. Heat oil in a 10- to 12-inch wok or frying pan over medium-high heat. When hot, add orange peel, walnuts, and ginger and stir often just until peel begins to brown slightly at edges, about 2 minutes.

3. Stir in ¼ cup orange juice and soy sauce. Add broccoli and stir occasionally until tender when pierced, about 5 minutes. Pour into a serving bowl.

Per serving: 105 cal., 65% (68 cal.) from fat; 3.8 g protein; 7.6 g fat (0.8 g sat.); 6.1 g carbo (2 g fiber); 227 mg sodium; 0 mg chol. ◆

OCTOBER **209**

Spice-rubbed roast turkey adds new flavor to the traditional Thanksgiving feast. Holiday recipes begin on page 212.

November

holiday
ENTERTAINING

Tradition
with a twist

Southwest chili-rubbed turkey and other fresh dishes
add new flavor to an old-fashioned Thanksgiving feast

By Linda Lau Anusasananan • Photographs by James Carrier • Food styling by Karen Shinto

■ Every year, it's the same old debate: The family traditionalists insist on having Thanksgiving dinner exactly as Grandma always made it; the family modernists want to inject some new life into the menu. This year, we offer a collection of recipes to help you produce a meal that will make both factions happy—on Thanksgiving or any other holiday. Most harbor tradition but are more boldly flavored or lighter than their generations-old counterparts. You can build a whole menu from these choices. But if tradition runs deep in your family, stick with your must-haves and just add a few new touches—who knows, the traditionalists might be fighting for them next year.

Fresh flavors come for dinner: Spices coat the turkey, orange slices lighten sweet potatoes, onion and garlic permeate mashed potatoes, and mustard greens pepper cornbread dressing.

holiday
ENTERTAINING

Artichoke Bisque with
Parsley-Lemon Gremolata

FOR STARTERS

Crimson Spice Champagne Cocktail

PREP AND COOK TIME: About 1¼ hours, plus at least 2 hours to cool and chill syrup

NOTES: For a nonalcoholic alternative, pour 2 tablespoons of the cranberry syrup into an ice-filled glass and fill with chilled lemon-lime or club soda. If making syrup up to 1 week ahead, chill airtight.

MAKES: 16 servings

- 2 quarts **cranberry juice cocktail**
- 8 slices (quarter size and about ⅛ in. thick) peeled **fresh ginger**
- 2 **cinnamon sticks** (about 3 in. long)
- 2 whole **star anise**
- ⅓ cup **cognac** or brandy
- 8 cups **Champagne** or other sparkling wine, chilled
- 32 to 48 **fresh cranberries,** rinsed, or frozen cranberries (optional)

1. In a 3½- to 4-quart pan, combine cranberry juice, ginger, cinnamon sticks, and star anise. Boil over high heat until reduced to 2 cups, about 1 hour. Let cool about 30 minutes, then pour through a fine strainer into a small pitcher. Chill syrup until cold, at least 1½ hours.

2. For each serving, pour 2 tablespoons of the cranberry syrup and 1 teaspoon cognac into a champagne flute (6 to 8 oz.). Add ½ cup (4 oz.) sparkling wine. Garnish with 2 or 3 cranberries if desired.

Per serving: 166 cal., 0.5% (0.9 cal.) from fat; 0.1 g protein; 0.1 g fat (0 g sat.); 19 g carbo (0 g fiber); 8.6 mg sodium; 0 mg chol.

Cranberry Ice Aperitif

PREP TIME: About 20 minutes, plus at least 3 hours to freeze

NOTES: For this festive aperitif, we use cranberry ice from Gerri Gilliland, owner of Lula in Los Angeles. Rather than using it in a drink, you can serve the ice plain as a palate refresher or as a light dessert.

MAKES: 9 to 12 servings

- 1 cup **fresh** or frozen **cranberries**
- ½ cup **sugar**
- 1 teaspoon grated **lemon** peel
- 1 tablespoon **lemon juice**
- 1 bottle (750 ml.) chilled **sparkling wine** such as Champagne or spumante, or sparkling apple cider

  Fresh mint sprigs, rinsed

1. Sort cranberries, discarding any bruised or decayed fruit; rinse and drain berries. In a 1- to 2-quart pan over high heat, bring cranberries and ½ cup water to a boil. Reduce heat and simmer, uncovered, until skins pop on berries, about 10 minutes. Add sugar and stir until dissolved. Remove from heat.

2. Stir in ½ cup cold water, lemon peel, and lemon juice. In a blender, whirl half the mixture at a time until smooth. Pour purée into a 9- by 5-inch loaf pan. Freeze until solid, at least 3 hours, or up to 1 week (cover when solid).

3. Cut cranberry ice into 1-inch cubes. With a wide spatula, lift cubes out of pan and drop three into each Champagne flute or wineglass. Pour ¼ to ⅓ cup wine over cubes. Garnish each glass with a mint sprig and serve immediately.

Per serving: 79 cal., 0% (0 cal.) from fat; 0.1 g protein; 0 g fat; 10 g carbo (0.3 g fiber); 3.6 mg sodium; 0 mg chol.

Artichoke Bisque with Parsley-Lemon Gremolata

PREP AND COOK TIME: About 50 minutes

NOTES: If making bisque through step 3 up to 1 day ahead, cool, cover, and chill; stir often over medium heat until hot.

MAKES: 6 to 8 servings

- 2 tablespoons **butter** or margarine
- 1 **onion** (8 oz.), peeled and chopped
- 3 tablespoons **all-purpose flour**
- 6 cups fat-skimmed **chicken broth** or vegetable broth
- 3 packages (8 oz. each) **frozen artichoke hearts**
- ½ teaspoon **dried tarragon**

  Softly whipped **cream** or sour cream

  Parsley-Lemon Gremolata (recipe follows)

  Salt and **white** or black **pepper**

1. In a 4- to 5-quart pan over medium-high heat, melt butter. Add onion and stir often until golden, 7 to 10 minutes.

2. Add flour and stir to coat onion. Add broth, artichoke hearts, and tarragon; stir until mixture boils and thickens, 15 to 20 minutes.

3. In a blender, holding lid down with a towel, whirl mixture in batches until smooth; pour into a large bowl.

4. Return soup to pan and stir over low heat until hot. Ladle into bowls and garnish with spoonfuls of whipped cream and Parsley-Lemon Gremolata. Add salt and pepper to taste.

Bring in color

Orange or yellow candles in casual glass votives add warm atmosphere to your table.

Per serving: 153 cal., 50% (76 cal.) from fat; 9.1 g protein; 8.4 g fat (2.5 g sat.); 12 g carbo (6 g fiber); 129 mg sodium; 7.8 mg chol.

Parsley-Lemon Gremolata

PREP TIME: About 10 minutes

NOTES: Use this sprightly combination of lemon and parsley to season the artichoke bisque (preceding), or mix with about 2 pounds hot cooked green beans, peas, broccoli, or asparagus for a special holiday vegetable. If making mixture up to 1 day ahead, cover and chill.

MAKES: About ¼ cup

In a food processor, whirl 1 cup coarsely chopped **Italian** or regular **parsley,** 3 tablespoons **olive oil,** 2 teaspoons grated **lemon** peel, 1 peeled clove **garlic,** and ¼ teaspoon **pepper** until finely chopped. (Or with a knife, mince parsley and garlic and put in a bowl; mix with oil, lemon peel, and pepper.) Add **salt** to taste.

Per teaspoon: 48 cal., 94% (30 cal.) from fat; 0.2 g protein; 5.1 g fat (0.7 g sat.); 0.7 g carbo (0.4 g fiber); 3 mg sodium; 0 mg chol.

Spinach and Pear Salad with Sherry and Stilton

PREP AND COOK TIME: About 30 minutes

NOTES: If preparing nuts (step 1) up to 1 day ahead, wrap airtight and store at room temperature.

MAKES: 8 servings

- ¾ cup **hazelnuts**
- ⅓ cup **sherry vinegar** or cider vinegar
- ⅓ cup **hazelnut** or salad **oil**
- 1 tablespoon **Dijon mustard**
- 3 **firm-ripe pears** (8 oz. each.), rinsed
- 4 quarts **baby spinach leaves** (1 lb.), rinsed and crisped
- 1 cup crumbled **Stilton** or gorgonzola **cheese** (6 oz.)
- **Salt** and **pepper**

1. In a 6- to 8-inch frying pan over medium heat, stir hazelnuts often until golden under skins, 5 to 10 minutes. Pour onto a towel and let stand until cool enough to handle. Rub nuts in towel to remove any loose skins. Lift nuts from towel and reserve; discard skins. Coarsely chop nuts.

2. In a large bowl, whisk vinegar, oil, and mustard to blend. Cut pears lengthwise into quarters and core; cut quarters lengthwise into thin slices. Drop slices into bowl and mix to coat with dressing. Add spinach and mix gently. Sprinkle

with cheese and toasted nuts and mix gently. Add salt and pepper to taste.

Per serving: 299 cal., 69% (207 cal.) from fat; 7.5 g protein; 23 g fat (5.7 g sat.); 21 g carbo (6.1 g fiber); 445 mg sodium; 19 mg chol.

Shrimp with Wasabi Mayo

PREP TIME: About 10 minutes

NOTES: Look for wasabi powder in the spice or Asian section of your supermarket or in an Asian grocery store. If making wasabi mayo up to 1 day ahead, cover and chill.

MAKES: 12 to 14 appetizer servings

1. In a small bowl, mix 2 tablespoons **dried wasabi powder** with 2 tablespoons **water** until smooth. In a food processor or blender, whirl 1 cup **regular** or reduced-fat **mayonnaise,** 2 tablespoons **lemon juice,** 2 tablespoons chopped **fresh mint** leaves, and three-fourths of the wasabi mixture until smooth. Taste, and add **salt** and more of the wasabi mixture if desired; save remaining for other uses.

2. Scrape into a bowl and garnish with a **fresh mint** sprig, rinsed. Serve with 1½ pounds (31 to 40 per lb.) **shelled cooked shrimp,** rinsed and drained, to dip into sauce.

Per serving: 163 cal., 72% (117 cal.) from fat; 10 g protein; 13 g fat (2 g sat.); 1 g carbo (0.1 g fiber); 199 mg sodium; 104 mg chol.

THE TURKEY—AAH, HERE'S THE RUB

Spice-rubbed Roast Turkey

PREP AND COOK TIME: 2¼ to 3¼ hours, plus at least 30 minutes to rest. For other turkey sizes, see chart, page 216.

NOTES: If time is short, you can substitute a purchased spice blend for any of the spice mixes at right; many are now available in the spice section of most supermarkets. Rub turkey (step 1) up to 1 day ahead; wrap airtight and chill. Be sure your pan is large enough that turkey doesn't overlap rim.

MAKES: Allow ¾ pound uncooked turkey per person

- 1 **turkey** (14 to 23 lb.)
- ¼ cup **olive** or salad **oil**
- 2 tablespoons **Chinese Five-Spice,** Jamaican Jerk, Provençal, Red Curry, or Southwest Chili **Rub** (recipes at right)
- **Salt** and **pepper**

1. Remove and discard leg truss from turkey. Pull off and discard any lumps

Chinese Five-Spice Rub

In a small bowl, mix 1 tablespoon ground **ginger,** 1½ teaspoons ground **cinnamon,** 1 teaspoon crushed **anise** or fennel seed, and ½ teaspoon **ground cloves.** (Or use 2 tablespoons Chinese five-spice blend.) Makes about 2 tablespoons.

Jamaican Jerk Rub

In a small bowl, mix 1½ teaspoons ground **ginger;** 1 teaspoon *each* ground **allspice, dried thyme, cayenne,** and **pepper;** and ½ teaspoon **onion powder.** (Or use 2 tablespoons Jamaican jerk blend.) Makes about 2 tablespoons.

Provençal Rub

In a small bowl, mix 2 teaspoons *each* crushed dried **rosemary** and dried **thyme** and 1 teaspoon *each* dried rubbed **sage** and dried **lavender** (or more sage). (Or use 2 tablespoons provençal herb blend.) Makes about 2 tablespoons.

Red Curry Rub

In a small bowl, mix 2 teaspoons chili powder; 1 teaspoon *each* ground **coriander,** ground **ginger,** and **cayenne;** ¾ teaspoon ground **cumin;** and ¼ teaspoon ground **turmeric.** (Or use 2 tablespoons red curry powder.) Makes about 2 tablespoons.

Southwest Chili Rub

In a small bowl, mix 1 tablespoon ground **ancho** or California **chili** and 1 teaspoon *each* ground **cumin,** ground **chipotle chili** or cayenne, and dried **oregano.** (Or use chili powder or a Southwest chili blend.) Makes about 2 tablespoons.

Oven-roasted turkey

See Spice-rubbed Roast Turkey (page 215) for directions. Follow this chart for oven temperatures and cooking times.

Turkey weight with giblets	Oven temp.	Internal temp.*	Cooking time**
10–13 lb.	350°	160°	1½–2¼ hr.
14–23 lb.	325°	160°	2–3 hr.
24–27 lb.	325°	160°	3–3¾ hr.
28–30 lb.	325°	160°	3½–4½ hr.

* To measure the internal temperature of the turkey, insert a thermometer through the thickest part of the breast to the bone.

** Times are for unstuffed birds. A stuffed bird may cook at the same rate as an unstuffed one; however, be prepared to allow 30 to 50 minutes more. While turkeys take about the same time to roast in regular and convection heat, a convection oven does a better job of browning the bird all over.

When you remove the turkey legs, if you find that the meat around the thigh joint is still too pink, cut the drumsticks from the thighs and put thighs in a shallow pan in a 450° oven until no longer pink, 10 to 15 minutes.

of fat. Remove giblets and neck; save for Savory Gravy (recipe page 219). Rinse turkey inside and out and pat dry. Rub all over with oil. Rub spice mixture evenly over skin and inside neck and body cavities.

2. Place turkey, breast up, on a V-shaped rack in a 12- by 17-inch roasting pan (see notes).

3. Roast in a 325° regular or convection oven until a thermometer inserted through thickest part of breast to bone registers 160°, 2 to 3 hours.

4. Transfer turkey to a platter. Let rest, uncovered, in a warm place at least 30 minutes, then carve. (See chart above for directions if thigh joints are still pink.) Add salt and pepper to taste.

Per ¼ pound boned cooked turkey with skin, based on percentages of white and dark meat in an average bird: 240 cal., 38% (90 cal.) from fat; 32 g protein; 10 g fat (3 g sat.); 2.9 g carbo (0 g fiber); 376 mg sodium; 93 mg chol.

IN-OR-OUT DRESSINGS

■ If you are stuffing your turkey, just before roasting, fill the neck and body cavities loosely with dressing. When the bird is done, make sure the dressing is heated to a bacteria-safe 160°: Insert a thermometer into the center of it; if the temperature is too low, spoon the dressing into a bowl and heat in a microwave oven at full power (100%), stirring often to distribute heat, until it is 160° throughout.

Cornbread-Pecan Dressing

PREP AND COOK TIME: About 1½ hours

NOTES: The cornbread (homemade or from a 13-oz. mix) can be baked up to 1 day before preparing dressing. If you especially like mustard greens, use two packages. Prepare dressing through step 4 up to 1 day ahead; cover and chill. Heat, covered, in a microwave-safe container in a microwave oven on full power (100%), stirring occasionally, until hot in the center, 5 to 6 minutes. Or bake, covered, as directed in step 5 until hot, 50 to 60 minutes, then uncover to brown as directed.

MAKES: 13 cups; 13 to 17 servings

- 7 to 8 cups ½-inch cubes **cornbread** (see notes)
- 1 cup coarsely chopped **pecans**
- 2 tablespoons **butter** or margarine
- 6 ounces **cooked ham,** cut into ¼-inch dice
- 1 **onion** (12 oz.), peeled and chopped
- 1 cup chopped **celery**
- 1 or 2 bags (1 lb. each) **frozen chopped mustard greens,** thawed (see notes)
- 1 package (1 lb.) **frozen corn kernels**
- 1 tablespoon chopped **fresh sage** leaves or 1 teaspoon dried rubbed sage
- ½ to ¾ cup fat-skimmed **chicken broth**
- **Salt** and **pepper**

1. Spread cornbread cubes in a 12- by 17-inch roasting pan. Bake in a 350° regular or convection oven, stirring occasionally, until edges begin to brown, 25 to 35 minutes. Spread pecans in a 9-inch pie pan and bake in same oven until lightly browned, about 10 minutes.

2. In a 5- to 6-quart pan over medium-high heat, melt butter; add ham, onion, and celery and stir often until onion begins to brown, 7 to 10 minutes.

3. Squeeze excess liquid from mustard greens. Stir greens, corn, and sage into ham mixture. Mix in cornbread and enough broth to moisten lightly. Stir in pecans.

4. Spoon dressing into a shallow 3-quart baking dish and cover tightly.

5. Bake in a 325° regular or convection oven (350° if baking with a turkey at that temperature) until hot in the center, 15 to 25 minutes. Uncover and bake until top is lightly browned, 15 to 25 minutes longer. Add salt and pepper to taste.

Per serving: 211 cal., 43% (90 cal.) from fat; 7 g protein; 10 g fat (2.4 g sat.); 25 g carbo (2.8 g fiber); 431 mg sodium; 29 mg chol.

Nature's decorations

Hazelnuts and almonds in wood containers make simple additions to a Thanksgiving table. Leave nuts in their shells for a harvest feel.

Wild Rice and Squash Dressing

Wild Rice and Squash Dressing

PREP AND COOK TIME: About 1½ hours

NOTES: If making up to 1 day ahead, cool, cover, and chill. Reheat, covered, in a microwave-safe container in a microwave oven at full power (100%), stirring occasionally, until hot, 5 to 6 minutes. Or bake, covered, in a shallow 2½- to 3-quart casserole in a 325° oven (350° if baking with a turkey at that temperature), stirring once or twice, until hot in the center, about 1 hour.

MAKES: 10 cups; 10 to 12 servings

- 1 cup **wild rice**
- 1½ pounds **banana squash**
- 1 pound **mild Italian sausages**
- 1 **onion** (12 oz.), peeled and chopped
- 1 cup **long-grain white rice**
- 2 cups fat-skimmed **chicken broth**
- ⅓ cup **dried currants**
- 1 teaspoon **ground coriander**
- ¼ teaspoon **ground nutmeg**
- 1 **cinnamon stick** (3 in. long)
- 1 package (10 oz.) **frozen chopped spinach,** thawed
  Salt and **pepper**

1. In a 5- to 6-quart pan over high heat, bring 1½ to 2 quarts water to a boil. Rinse and drain wild rice. Add to boiling water, cover, and return to a boil; reduce heat and simmer, covered, until rice is tender to bite and beginning to split, 35 to 45 minutes. Drain.

2. Meanwhile, cut off and discard peel from squash. Cut squash into ½-inch cubes (you should have about 4 cups).

3. Remove casings from sausages and discard. Crumble sausages into a 5- to 6-quart nonstick pan; stir often over medium-high heat until browned, about 5 minutes. Discard all but 2 tablespoons fat in pan. Add onion; stir often until lightly browned, about 5 minutes. Add white rice; stir until beginning to turn opaque, about 3 minutes.

4. Add broth, currants, coriander, nutmeg, and cinnamon to pan. Bring to a boil over high heat; cover, reduce heat, and simmer for 5 minutes. Add squash; cover and simmer over low heat, gently stirring once, until rice and squash are tender to bite, 15 to 20 minutes.

5. Squeeze liquid from spinach. Add spinach and wild rice to pan and mix gently. Cover and cook until hot, about 5 minutes. Add salt and pepper to taste.

Per serving: 257 cal., 33% (84 cal.) from fat; 12 g protein; 9.3 g fat (3.1 g sat.); 32 g carbo (2.8 g fiber); 300 mg sodium; 23 mg chol.

SAVORY SIDE DISHES

Marmalade- and Ginger-glazed Sweet Potatoes

PREP AND COOK TIME: About 1½ hours

NOTES: Prepare through step 3 up to 1 day ahead; cool, cover, and chill. Reheat, covered, in a 325° oven (350° if baking with a turkey at that temperature) until hot in the center, 25 to 35 minutes, then continue with step 4.

MAKES: 8 servings

- 2 pounds **sweet potatoes** or yams (each 2 to 2½ in. wide)
- 1 **orange** (about 2½-in. diameter; 6 oz.), rinsed
- ⅔ cup **orange marmalade**
- ⅓ or ½ cup plus 1 tablespoon **brandy** or orange juice
- 2 tablespoons **butter** or margarine, melted
- ¼ cup finely chopped **crystallized ginger**
  About ½ teaspoon **salt**

1. Peel sweet potatoes and cut crosswise into ¼-inch-thick slices. Cut unpeeled orange in half through stem, then crosswise into ¼-inch-thick slices, discarding end pieces and seeds.

2. In a large bowl, mix ⅓ cup marmalade, ⅓ cup brandy (½ cup if using sweet potatoes), butter, ginger, and ½ teaspoon salt. Add sweet potatoes and mix to coat. Arrange slices in rows in a single layer, overlapping them slightly, in a shallow, 3-quart casserole (such as a 9 by 13 in. baking dish), interspersing the orange slices evenly throughout. Drizzle any of the remaining brandy mixture over the sweet potatoes. Cover tightly with foil.

3. Bake in a 325° regular or convection oven (350° if baking with a turkey at that temperature) until sweet potatoes are tender when pierced, 50 to 60 minutes.

4. In a small bowl, mix remaining ⅓ cup marmalade and 1 tablespoon brandy. Uncover sweet potatoes and brush marmalade mixture evenly over the top. Broil 6 inches from heat until lightly browned, 8 to 10 minutes. Add more salt to taste.

Per serving: 242 cal., 12% (28 cal.) from fat; 1.9 g protein; 3.1 g fat (1.8 g sat.); 55 g carbo (4.7 g fiber); 204 mg sodium; 7.8 mg chol.

Tomato Mashed Potatoes

Italian Mashed Potatoes

PREP AND COOK TIME: About 40 minutes

NOTES: Gemma Sciabica of Modesto, California, uses a fruity olive oil in her mashed potatoes. If making up to 1 day ahead, cool, cover, and chill. Reheat, covered, in a microwave-safe container in a microwave oven on full power (100%), stirring occasionally, until hot, 5 to 7 minutes. Or bake, covered, in a shallow 1½- to 2-quart casserole in a 325° oven (350° if baking with a turkey at that temperature), stirring once after 30 minutes, until hot in the center, 40 to 50 minutes total.

MAKES: 6 to 8 servings

- 3 pounds **thin-skinned potatoes**
  About 1 cup **milk**
- 1 to 2 tablespoons minced **garlic**
- ½ cup **olive oil**
- ½ cup **grated romano cheese**
- ½ cup minced **fresh basil** leaves or parsley
- ⅛ teaspoon **paprika** or cayenne
  Salt and **pepper**

1. In a 5- to 6-quart pan over high heat, bring 1 quart water to a boil.

2. Peel and rinse potatoes; cut into 1-inch chunks. Add potatoes to boiling water; cover and return to a boil, then reduce heat to medium and simmer until potatoes mash easily, 10 to 12 minutes.

3. Meanwhile, in a 1- to 1½-quart pan over medium heat, warm 1 cup milk and garlic until steaming, about 5 minutes. (Or in a 2-cup microwave-safe container, heat milk and garlic in a microwave oven on full power [100%] until steaming, 1 to 2 minutes.)

4. Drain potatoes and return to pan. Add the hot milk mixture, oil, cheese, basil, and paprika. Mash with a potato masher or an electric mixer until potatoes are as lumpy or smooth as you like, adding a little more milk for a softer, creamier texture if desired. Add salt and pepper to taste.

Per serving: 283 cal., 51% (144 cal.) from fat; 5.7 g protein; 16 g fat (3.3 g sat.); 29 g carbo (2.8 g fiber); 87 mg sodium; 9.5 mg chol.

Prosciutto Mashed Potatoes. Follow recipe for **Italian Mashed Potatoes** (preceding), stirring ½ cup finely chopped **prosciutto** (1½ oz.) into mixture in step 4.

Per serving: 297 cal., 52% (153 cal.) from fat; 7.2 g protein; 17 g fat (3.5 g sat.); 30 g carbo (2.8 g fiber); 185 mg sodium; 14 mg chol.

Chive Mashed Potatoes. Follow recipe for **Italian Mashed Potatoes** (preceding), stirring ½ cup thinly sliced **chives** into mixture in step 4.

Per serving: 285 cal., 51% (144 cal.) from fat; 5.8 g protein; 16 g fat (3.3 g sat.); 30 g carbo (2.9 g fiber); 87 mg sodium; 9.5 mg chol.

Tomato Mashed Potatoes. Follow recipe for **Italian Mashed Potatoes** (preceding), stirring ¾ cup chopped drained **oil-packed dried tomatoes** into mixture in step 4.

Per serving: 307 cal., 47% (144 cal.) from fat; 7.2 g protein; 16 g fat (3.3 g sat.); 34 g carbo (4.3 g fiber); 95 mg sodium; 9.5 mg chol.

Creamy Onion and Garlic Mashed Potatoes

PREP AND COOK TIME: About 40 minutes

NOTES: Stu Revak of Livermore, California, seasons fluffy mashed potatoes with sautéed onion and garlic. If making up to 1 day ahead, cool, cover, and chill. Reheat, covered, in a microwave-safe container in a microwave oven on full power (100%), stirring every 2 minutes, until hot, 5 to 7 minutes. Or bake, covered, in a shallow 1½- to 2-quart casserole in a 325° oven (350° if baking with a turkey at that temperature), stirring once after 30 minutes, until hot in the center, 40 to 50 minutes total.

MAKES: 6 or 7 servings

- ⅓ cup chopped **onion**
- 2 tablespoons minced **garlic**
- 2 tablespoons **olive oil**
- 3 pounds **russet potatoes**
- ½ cup **sour cream**
- ¼ cup **mayonnaise**
- ¼ cup **whipping cream**
- 2 tablespoons **butter** or margarine
- 1 to 2 tablespoons **milk** (optional)
  Salt and **pepper**

1. In a 5- to 6-quart pan over medium-high heat, stir onion and garlic in oil until limp, about 5 minutes. Scrape into a small bowl.

2. Pour 1 quart water into the 5- to 6-quart pan (no need to wash pan) and bring to a boil over high heat.

3. Peel and rinse potatoes; cut into 1-inch chunks. Add potatoes to boiling water; cover and return to a boil, then reduce heat to medium and simmer until potatoes mash easily, 8 to 10 minutes. Drain potatoes and return to pan.

4. Add onion mixture, sour cream, mayonnaise, cream, and butter to potatoes. Mash with a potato masher or an electric mixer until mixture is as lumpy or smooth as you like, gradually beating in enough of the milk to reach desired consistency. Add salt and pepper to taste.

Per serving: 328 cal., 55% (180 cal.) from fat; 4.4 g protein; 20 g fat (7.3 g sat.); 34 g carbo (3.1 g fiber); 104 mg sodium; 30 mg chol.

Southwestern Roasted Green Beans

PREP AND COOK TIME: About 25 minutes

NOTES: This dish comes from Barnie Barnick of Colorado Springs.

MAKES: 8 servings

2½ pounds **green beans**

1 tablespoon **olive oil**

⅓ cup **pine nuts** or slivered almonds

1 tablespoon **butter** or margarine

About ¼ teaspoon **cayenne**

Salt

1. Rinse and drain beans; trim and discard stem ends. In each of two 12- by 17-inch baking pans, mix half the beans with half the oil; spread level.

2. Bake in a 450° regular or convection oven until beans are tender when pierced and slightly browned, 15 to 25 minutes; switch pan positions halfway through baking.

3. Stir half the nuts and butter into beans in each pan; continue baking until nuts are golden, 5 to 6 minutes longer. Pour into a bowl, add ¼ teaspoon cayenne, and mix well. Taste, and add more cayenne and salt if desired.

Per serving: 97 cal., 59% (57 cal.) from fat; 3.7 g protein; 6.3 g fat (1.6 g sat.); 9.8 g carbo (2.9 g fiber); 22 mg sodium; 3.9 mg chol.

Asian Sesame Roasted Green Beans. Follow recipe for **Southwest Roasted Green Beans** (preceding), but substitute 2 tablespoons **sesame seeds** for the pine nuts and 1 tablespoon **Asian** (toasted) **sesame oil** for the butter; bake until sesame seeds are golden, about 5 minutes. Omit cayenne and add **soy sauce** to taste.

THE TRIMMINGS

Savory Gravy

PREP AND COOK TIME: About 2½ hours

NOTES: If preparing through step 4 up to 1 day ahead, cover and chill. After turkey roasts, continue with step 5.

MAKES: 1½ to 2 quarts; 10 to 12 servings

Giblets and **neck** from a 14- to 23-pound turkey

2 **onions** (12 oz. total), peeled and quartered

2 **carrots** (8 oz. total), peeled and cut into chunks

¾ cup sliced **celery**

1½ quarts fat-skimmed **chicken broth**

½ teaspoon **pepper**

½ cup **cornstarch**

Spice-rubbed or other **Roast Turkey** (page 215)

Salt

1. Rinse giblets and neck (chill liver airtight to add later, save for other uses, or discard). In a 5- to 6-quart pan, combine giblets, neck, onions, carrots, celery, and 1 cup water. Cover and bring to a boil over high heat; reduce heat and simmer for 15 minutes. Uncover and stir often over high heat until liquid has evaporated and giblets and vegetables are browned and begin to stick to pan, 12 to 15 minutes longer.

2. Add 1 quart broth and pepper; stir to scrape browned bits free. Cover, reduce heat, and simmer until gizzard is tender when pierced, 1 to 1½ hours. If desired, add liver; cook 10 minutes longer.

3. Pour broth through a fine strainer into a bowl. Measure and, if needed, add water to make 1 quart. Discard vegetables. If desired for gravy, pull meat off neck and finely chop, along with giblets and liver; otherwise discard neck, giblets, and liver.

4. In the 5- to 6-quart pan (no need to wash), blend cornstarch with ⅓ cup water until smooth. Add the 1 quart broth, plus the chopped neck meat, giblets, and liver if using. Stir over high heat until boiling, 3 to 5 minutes.

5. When turkey is done, remove rack and bird from pan; skim off and discard fat from pan juices. Add remaining 2 cups broth to roasting pan and stir over low heat, scraping browned bits free. Add mixture to gravy and stir over high heat until boiling. Add salt to taste.

Per ½ cup without giblets and neck meat: 43 cal., 0% (0 cal.) from fat; 4.1 g protein; 0 g fat; 6.1 g carbo (0.4 g fiber); 43 mg sodium; 0 mg chol.

Wine Gravy. Follow recipe for **Savory Gravy** (preceding), but in step 5 replace the last 2 cups broth with 2 cups **Chardonnay** or other dry white wine, tawny port, dry sherry, or dry madeira.

Baked Cranberry-Orange Sauce

PREP AND COOK TIME: About 1¼ hours

NOTES: Serve this sauce as a relish with the turkey or use it on the Cranberry Crown Cheesecake (page 229).

MAKES: About 2 cups; 8 to 12 servings

1. Sort 1 package (12 oz.) **fresh** or thawed frozen **cranberries,** discarding any bruised or decayed fruit. Rinse and drain berries.

2. In an 8- or 9-inch square baking dish, mix cranberries, 1¼ cups **sugar,** ½ cup **orange-flavor liqueur** (or orange juice), and 1 teaspoon grated **orange** peel.

3. Bake, uncovered, in a 350° regular or convection oven, stirring occasionally, until berries are tender when pierced and juices are syrupy, about 1 hour. Serve warm or cool.

Per ¼ cup: 160 cal., 0.6% (0.9 cal.) from fat; 0.2 g protein; 0.1 g fat (0 g sat.); 41 g carbo (1.5 g fiber); 0.7 mg sodium; 0 mg chol.

Warm elegance

Place a piece of soaked florist's foam (cut to size) in a small to medium-size wood bowl. Cut one to two dozen rose stems to 1 to 2 inches long and insert (tightly packed) into foam to create a low mound. Do not leave arrangement in bowl overnight. ◆

Mushroom-Herb Risotto

FOOD STYLING: SUSAN DEVATY

Mushrooms: Earthy delights for the holidays

Wild or cultivated, exotic or common,
mushrooms add a rich note to cool-weather dishes

By Charity Ferreira • Photographs by James Carrier

They're in the market now: knobby chanterelles, hairy hedgehogs, broad-capped portabellas with flaring gills, and smooth, white button mushrooms. More varieties of mushrooms are being cultivated than ever before. And more wild types, gathered by professional foragers, are making their way to market, giving us easy access to a wide selection.

Whatever variety you unearth at the market, mushrooms' rich, assertive quality gives them a natural affinity for hearty, warming dishes. Here we showcase the most widely available mushrooms in appetizers and entrées that would make any holiday occasion special.

Mushroom-Herb Risotto

PREP AND COOK TIME: About 50 minutes

NOTES: Use a combination of two or three types of mushrooms, such as black or yellow chanterelles, crimini, oyster, shiitake, or common. High-quality parmesan cheese is worth the expense in this dish. Garnish servings with curls of the cheese if desired.

MAKES: 8 cups; about 4 main-dish servings

- 2 tablespoons **olive oil**
- 1 cup finely chopped **onion**
- 1½ pounds **fresh mushrooms** (see notes), cleaned (see page 221) and thinly sliced
- 1½ cups **arborio** or medium-grain white **rice**
- ½ cup **dry white wine**

   About 4½ cups fat-skimmed **reduced-sodium chicken broth**
- ½ cup shredded **parmesan cheese** or other dry Italian cheese (see notes)
- 2 tablespoons chopped **parsley**
- 1 tablespoon chopped **fresh sage** leaves
- 1 tablespoon chopped **fresh tarragon**
- 1 tablespoon chopped **fresh thyme** leaves

   Salt and **pepper**

1. Pour oil into a 5- to 6-quart pan over medium-high heat; when hot, add onion and mushrooms and stir often until onion is limp and liquid has evaporated, 5 to 6 minutes. Add rice and stir until opaque, about 3 minutes.

2. Add wine and stir until it's absorbed, 1 to 2 minutes. Add 4½ cups broth and bring to a boil over high heat, stirring often. Reduce heat and, stirring often, simmer until rice is tender to bite, 15 to 20 minutes. If a creamier consistency is desired, stir in about ½ cup more broth. Stir in cheese, parsley, sage, tarragon, and thyme. Add salt and pepper to taste.

Per serving: 423 cal., 23% (99 cal.) from fat; 18g protein; 11 g fat (3.3 g sat.); 62 g carbo (6.3 g fiber); 939 mg sodium; 9.6 mg chol.

Mushroom Pâté

PREP AND COOK TIME: About 45 minutes, plus 1 day to chill

NOTES: Mirka Hodur, a San Francisco Bay Area caterer, got the recipe for this pâté from restaurateur Bob Goldberg. She serves it on thin, toasted slices of bread, topped with chopped calamata olives and fresh thyme leaves. It's also delicious on crackers or plain baguette slices. Make pâté one day before serving.

MAKES: 2 cups

- 1 **onion** (about 4 oz.), peeled and quartered
- 1 clove **garlic,** peeled
- ¾ pound **crimini mushrooms,** cleaned (see page 221) and quartered
- 6 tablespoons **butter**
- ¾ teaspoon **ground thyme**

   About 1 teaspoon **salt**
- 1 cup **almonds**

1. In a food processor, whirl onion and garlic, pulsing on and off, until very finely chopped. Scrape into a bowl. Add half the mushrooms to processor and pulse until finely chopped (take care not to purée); scrape into bowl with onion mixture. Repeat to finely chop remaining mushrooms and scrape into bowl.

2. In a 10- to 12-inch frying pan over medium-high heat, melt butter. Add mushroom-onion mixture, thyme, and 1 teaspoon salt; stir often until liquid has evaporated, about 20 minutes.

3. Meanwhile, spread almonds in an 8-inch square pan. Bake in a 350° regular or convection oven, shaking pan occasionally, until nuts are golden beneath skins, about 10 minutes. Pour into food processor. Whirl until nuts are as finely ground as possible. Stir into warm mushroom mixture.

4. Pack into a small bowl (at least 2½-cup capacity) or two 1-cup ramekins; cover with plastic wrap. Chill overnight to blend flavors. Bring to room temperature and serve in bowl or ramekins.

Per serving: 47 cal., 83% (39 cal.) from fat; 1.1 g protein; 4.3 g fat (1.5 g sat.); 1.6 g carbo (0.6g fiber); 96 mg sodium; 5.8 mg chol.

Crab and Mushroom Strata

PREP AND COOK TIME: About 1½ hours

NOTES: To ensure enough bread slices, be careful not to cut thicker than ½ inch. If assembling strata through step 3 up to 1 day ahead, cover and chill; let chilled strata stand at room temperature for 15 minutes, then bake about 1 hour.

MAKES: 10 to 12 servings

2 tablespoons **olive oil**

1½ pounds **fresh mushrooms,** such as crimini, porcini, shiitake, or common (use one kind or a combination), cleaned (see below) and thinly sliced

2 teaspoons minced or pressed **garlic**

4 teaspoons **sherry vinegar**

2 teaspoons **fresh thyme** leaves

About ¼ teaspoon **salt**

About ⅛ teaspoon **pepper**

6 **large eggs**

3½ cups **milk**

1 loaf (1 lb.) day-old **crusty sourdough bread,** cut diagonally into ½-inch-thick slices (see notes), ends discarded

6 ounces **shelled cooked crab,** any bits of shell removed

⅓ cup chopped **green onions,** white and pale green parts only

2 cups **shredded jack cheese** (about 8 oz.)

1. Pour olive oil into a 12-inch frying pan or 14-inch wok over medium-high heat; when hot, add mushrooms and garlic and stir until mushrooms begin to brown and liquid has evaporated, 3 to 5 minutes. Add vinegar and thyme; cook, stirring often, to blend flavors, 1 to 2 minutes longer. Add salt and pepper to taste.

2. In a bowl, whisk eggs, milk, ¼ teaspoon salt, and ⅛ teaspoon pepper to blend.

3. Cover bottom of a 3-quart baking dish (such as 9 by 13 in., at least 2 in. deep) with bread slices, trimming if necessary to fit in a single layer. Spread half the mushroom mixture evenly over bread; top with all the crab and half the green onions. Sprinkle evenly with 1 cup cheese. Pour half the custard mixture evenly over cheese. Arrange another layer of bread on top (overlap slightly if desired; save any extra bread for other uses), followed by remaining mushroom mixture, green onions, and 1 cup cheese. Spoon remaining custard

FOOD STYLING: SUSAN DEVATY

Crab and Mushroom Strata

mixture evenly over the top. Let strata stand at room temperature about 15 minutes, or cover and chill.

4. Bake, uncovered, in a 350° regular or convection oven until center is set (cut to test) and top is well browned, 45 to 50 minutes. Cut into rectangles or scoop out with a large spoon to serve.

Per serving: 304 cal., 41% (126 cal.) from fat; 18 g protein; 14 g fat (6.2 g sat.); 26 g carbo (1.4 g fiber); 489 mg sodium; 150 mg chol.

Salmon and Chanterelles Baked in Parchment

PREP AND COOK TIME: About 45 minutes

NOTES: To clean leeks, cut in half lengthwise and flip layers under cold running water to flush out grit. Hedgehog and oyster mushrooms also work well in this dish.

MAKES: 4 servings

1 cup thinly sliced **leeks** (about 4 oz.; see notes), white and pale green parts only

4 pieces **boned, skinned salmon fillet** (about 6 oz. each)

½ pound **fresh chanterelle mushrooms** (see notes), cleaned (see left) and sliced

2 teaspoons **olive oil**

¼ cup **dry white wine**

Salt and **pepper**

1. Cut four 13- by 15-inch rectangles of cooking parchment or foil. Fold each rectangle in half crosswise; starting from fold, cut out a half-heart 7 inches wide and 13 inches long. Open each and lay flat. Divide leeks equally among hearts, mounding them on one half of each.

2. Rinse salmon and pat dry. Place one

CARE AND HANDLING

BUYING: Choose blemish-free mushrooms whose surfaces look dry but not dried out.

STORING: If kept dry and covered in the refrigerator, enclosed in a paper bag or in paper towels in a basket, mushrooms should stay fresh for several days. Wait to wash them until just before using.

CLEANING: Trim off tough or discolored bottoms of mushroom stems and any bruised spots or blemishes. (For shiitakes and oysters, remove the entire fibrous stem.) For firm, nonporous mushrooms such as portabellas, wipe dirt off with a damp cloth or place in a colander, rinse thoroughly under cool running water, and pat dry with towels. For delicate mushrooms that have lots of places for dirt to hide, such as chanterelles and hedgehogs, submerge in a bowl of cool water and gently agitate with your hands to loosen any particles. Drain, rinse thoroughly under running water, and gently pat dry with a towel.

piece on each mound of leeks. Top equally with chanterelles. Drizzle each stack with ½ teaspoon olive oil and 1 tablespoon wine; sprinkle generously with salt and pepper.

3. Fold bare half of each parchment heart over fish and vegetable stack so that cut edges meet evenly. Fold and pleat packet edges to seal: Starting at top of heart, fold a ½-inch section of edge up and in; holding this section down, fold next section up and in, slightly overlapping first to form a pleat. Continue folding and pleating edge until you reach bottom of heart; twist point to secure. Transfer packets to a 14- by 16-inch baking sheet.

4. Bake in a 400° regular or convection oven until a thermometer inserted through parchment into center of fish reaches 140°, about 10 minutes.

5. Place each packet on a dinner plate. Open at the table, taking care to avoid steam. Add salt and pepper to taste.

Per serving: 380 cal., 50% (189 cal.) from fat; 37 g protein; 21 g fat (4 g sat.); 7.6 g carbo (1.7 g fiber); 124 mg sodium; 100 mg chol.

Wine Country Beef Stroganoff

PREP AND COOK TIME: About 45 minutes

NOTES: At the Joel Palmer House in Dayton, Oregon, Jack Czarnecki serves this dish topped with sliced white truffles. Oyster sauce is sold in well-stocked supermarkets and in Asian grocery stores.

MAKES: 4 servings

- 12 ounces **wide egg noodles**
- 1 pound **boned beef sirloin,** fat trimmed
- 3 tablespoons **olive oil**
- ¾ cup finely chopped **onion**
- 1½ teaspoons pressed or minced **garlic**
- ¾ pound **fresh shiitake** or mixed **mushrooms,** cleaned (see page 221) and thinly sliced
- ¾ cup **Pinot Noir** or other dry red wine
- 3 tablespoons **cognac**
- 2 tablespoons **prepared oyster sauce**
- 1½ cups **whipping cream**
- 1½ teaspoons **cornstarch**
- 6 tablespoons **sour cream**

FOOD STYLING: SUSAN DEVATY

Chili-painted Portabellas in Puff Pastry

Salt and **pepper**

- 2 tablespoons chopped **parsley** (optional)

1. In a 5- to 6-quart pan over high heat, bring 3 to 4 quarts water to a boil. Add noodles, return to a boil, and cook, stirring occasionally, until barely tender to bite, 5 to 7 minutes. Drain and pour into a large serving bowl.

2. Meanwhile, rinse beef and pat dry. Cut meat across the grain into ⅛-inch-thick slices.

3. Pour 1 tablespoon olive oil into a 12-inch frying pan or 14-inch wok over medium-high heat; when hot, add beef and stir until browned on the edges but still pink in the center (cut to test), 2 to 3 minutes. Pour into another bowl.

4. Add remaining 2 tablespoons olive oil to pan; when hot, add onion and garlic and stir until onion is limp, 3 to 5 minutes. Add mushrooms and stir often until beginning to brown, 3 to 5 minutes.

5. Add wine, cognac, and oyster sauce to mushroom mixture. Bring to a boil over high heat, then reduce heat and simmer to blend flavors, about 5 minutes.

6. Add cream and bring to a simmer. In a small bowl, mix cornstarch with 1 tablespoon cold water until smooth. Add to mushroom mixture and stir until it boils and thickens, about 2 minutes.

7. Add sour cream and beef with any accumulated juices to pan and stir just until heated through, about 1 minute. Add salt and pepper to taste.

8. Pour the beef Stroganoff over hot noodles. Sprinkle with parsley if desired.

Per serving: 975 cal., 47% (459 cal.) from fat; 42 g protein; 51 g fat (24 g sat.); 74 g carbo (3.8 g fiber); 486 mg sodium; 259 mg chol.

Chili-painted Portabellas in Puff Pastry

PREP AND COOK TIME: About 30 minutes

NOTES: This elegant appetizer is from Jack Czarnecki's *A Cook's Book of Mushrooms.* For the puréed chipotle chilies, whirl a 7-ounce can of chipotles with sauce in a blender until smooth. Measure 1 to 2 tablespoons, depending on desired heat; chill or freeze remainder for other uses. If assembling through step 3 up to 4 hours ahead, cover and chill; bake about 13 minutes.

MAKES: 4 first-course servings

- 1 sheet (10 in. square) **frozen puff pastry** (half of a 1-lb. package), thawed
- 2 tablespoons **prepared oyster sauce**
- 1 to 2 tablespoons puréed **canned chipotle chilies** (see notes)
- 4 **portabella mushrooms** (3- to 4-in.-wide caps; 10 to 12 oz. total), cleaned (see page 221), stems trimmed flush with caps
- 1 **large egg**

1. Unfold puff pastry sheet on a lightly floured board; cut into quarters, each 5 inches square. Roll each slightly into a 6-inch square.

2. In a small bowl, mix oyster sauce and puréed chipotle chilies. Brush mixture generously over both sides of mushroom caps, using it all.

3. Center each cap, gill side up, on a puff pastry square. Fold corners of pastry over mushroom to enclose, overlapping slightly; press edges together to seal. Set bundles, seams down and slightly apart, on a 12- by 15-inch baking sheet lined with cooking parchment.

4. In a small bowl, beat egg to blend with 1 tablespoon water. Brush tops and sides of pastry bundles lightly with egg mixture (discard extra). With a small, sharp knife, cut 3 or 4 slits (each about ¼ in. long) through pastry across top of each bundle.

5. Bake in a 425° regular or convection oven until puff pastry is golden brown, about 10 minutes. Serve warm.

Per serving: 370 cal., 56% (207 cal.) from fat; 8.5 g protein; 23 g fat (3.5 g sat.); 33 g carbo (2.1 g fiber); 551 mg sodium; 53 mg chol. ◆

Dressed for dinner

Quick ways to make simple vegetables shine

By Charity Ferreira

Come holiday time, vegetables are often little more than an afterthought. Other dishes simply demand more attention. Luckily, simple is often best when it comes to making vegetables special. Cut them into small pieces to roast or steam quickly, then add a few bright seasonings and common vegetables become uncommonly good.

Roasted Cauliflower with Capers and Bread Crumbs

JAMES CARRIER; FOOD STYLING: BASIL FRIEDMAN

Roasted Cauliflower with Capers and Bread Crumbs

PREP AND COOK TIME: About 30 minutes
MAKES: 4 to 6 servings

  2 heads **cauliflower** (about 3 lb.)
  ¼ cup **olive oil**
     About ¼ teaspoon **salt**
  4 slices (about 3 by 4 in. and ½ in. thick) Italian-style **white bread** such as pane pugliese
  1 clove **garlic,** peeled
  6 **canned anchovy fillets,** drained
  ¼ cup **lemon juice**
  ¼ cup chopped **parsley**
  2 tablespoons drained **capers**
  1 teaspoon **hot chili flakes**

1. Rinse cauliflower; cut into quarters. Cut off and discard leaves and cores; cut quarters into ¼- to ½-inch-thick slices.
2. In a 12- by 17-inch baking pan, mix cauliflower with olive oil and ¼ teaspoon salt. Spoon half the mixture into another 12- by 17-inch pan and spread mixture in both pans level.
3. Roast in a 450° regular or convection oven until cauliflower is browned on the edges and tender when pierced, 15 to 20 minutes.
4. Meanwhile, toast bread slices. Rub one side of each with garlic clove; discard any remaining garlic. Let bread cool, then tear into 1-inch chunks. In a

food processor or blender, whirl to coarse crumbs.
5. In a large bowl, mash anchovies with lemon juice to a coarse paste. Add cauliflower, parsley, capers, hot chili flakes, and bread crumbs, and mix. Add salt to taste.

Per serving: 143 cal., 63% (90 cal.) from fat; 3.9 g protein; 10 g fat (1.4 g sat.); 11 g carbo (2.6 g fiber); 444 mg sodium; 2.2 mg chol.

Roasted Broccoli Rabe and Radicchio with Lemon

PREP AND COOK TIME: About 30 minutes
MAKES: 4 to 6 servings

  1¼ pounds **broccoli rabe**
   1 head **radicchio** (about 8 oz.)
   1 **lemon** (about 5 oz.)
   2 tablespoons **olive oil**
   1 ounce **thin-sliced pancetta** or bacon, chopped
      About ¼ teaspoon **salt**
      Pepper

1. Rinse and drain broccoli rabe; cut diagonally into 2-inch lengths. Rinse and drain radicchio; core and cut head lengthwise into ½-inch-thick slices. Rinse and dry lemon; cut in half lengthwise, then thinly slice crosswise, discarding ends and seeds.
2. In a 12- by 17-inch baking pan, mix broccoli rabe, radicchio, lemon, olive oil, pancetta, and ¼ teaspoon salt. Transfer half the mixture into another 12- by 17-inch baking pan and spread

mixture in both pans level.
3. Roast in a 400° regular or convection oven until broccoli rabe is tender when pierced and radicchio is wilted, about 10 minutes. Add salt and pepper to taste.

Per serving: 96 cal., 70% (67 cal.) from fat; 3.4 g protein; 7.4 g fat (1.6 g sat.); 7.3 g carbo (1.3 g fiber); 153 mg sodium; 3.2 mg chol.

Beets with Orange Vinaigrette

PREP AND COOK TIME: About 30 minutes
MAKES: 4 to 6 servings

  4 pounds **beets** (about 3 bunches)
  1 tablespoon grated **orange** peel
  ¼ cup **orange juice**
  ¼ cup **white wine vinegar**
  2 tablespoons **olive oil**
  1½ tablespoons chopped **fresh tarragon**
     Salt and **pepper**

1. Trim and discard tops and root ends from beets. Rinse beets, peel, and cut crosswise into ⅛- to ¼-inch-thick slices.
2. In a 5- to 6-quart pan over high heat, bring 1 inch of water to a boil. Place beets on a rack over water, cover pan, reduce heat, and steam until beets are tender when pierced, about 15 minutes.
3. Meanwhile, in a bowl, mix orange peel, orange juice, vinegar, olive oil, and tarragon. Remove beets from steaming rack and add to bowl. Mix gently to coat. Add salt and pepper to taste.

Per serving: 137 cal., 31% (43 cal.) from fat; 3.1 g protein; 4.8 g fat (0.6 g sat.); 22 g carbo (2 g fiber); 146 mg sodium; 0 mg chol. ◆

Yogurt Cheese Torta with Pesto

JAMES CARRIER; FOOD STYLING: KAREN SHINTO

Appetizing favorite

Cheese torta goes low-fat

By Linda Lau Anusasananan

One of *Sunset's* most reader-requested appetizers is a cheese torta—a layered spread that food editor Jerry Di Vecchio developed in the mid-1970s to replicate versions she had tasted in Italy made of mascarpone, an ultra-rich (and then hard to find) Italian cream cheese. It was striking, delicious—and high in fat. Now we offer a lighter alternative, a cheese torta with the same stylish good looks but a fraction of the fat. We've replaced the buttery mascarpone with fresh, tangy cheese made from nonfat yogurt. You simply drain the yogurt until what's left is thick and smooth. Yogurt cheese can be used just as you would cream cheese, in these tortas as well as in the festive cheesecake on page 229.

Yogurt Cheese Torta with Pesto

PREP TIME: About 15 minutes, plus at least 1 hour to chill

NOTES: Make the Yogurt Cheese (recipe at right) at least 24 hours before making torta; layer the cheese with pesto at least 1 hour or up to 1 day before serving.

MAKES: 8 to 12 servings

- 1⅓ to 1¾ cups **Yogurt Cheese** (¾ to 1 lb.; see notes)
- ½ to ¾ cup **Cilantro Pesto** or Tomato Tapenade (recipes on page 225)

    Fresh **cilantro** or basil **sprigs** (optional), rinsed

    Thin **baguette** slices

1. Line a wide-mouth, 2- to 3-cup noncorrosive container with two smooth layers of cheesecloth or a clean, dry muslin or linen towel.
2. Press a fourth of the yogurt cheese evenly over bottom of container. Spread a third of the pesto evenly over cheese to edges of container. Repeat steps to layer remaining cheese and pesto, ending with cheese. Fold edges of cloth over cheese and press gently to compact. Cover airtight and chill until firm, at least 1 hour or up to 1 day; occasionally uncover and tilt container to pour off any accumulated liquid.
3. Fold back cloth; invert a plate over torta and then, holding plate and container together, invert torta onto plate. Peel off cloth. Garnish with cilantro sprigs if desired. Serve with baguette slices.

Per serving: 38 cal., 37% (14 cal.) from fat; 3.4 g protein; 1.6 g fat (0.2 g sat.); 2.7 g carbo (0.4 g fiber); 30 mg sodium; 0.5 mg chol.

Mascarpone Torta with Pesto

PREP TIME: About 20 minutes, plus at least 1 hour to chill

NOTES: Look for mascarpone in specialty cheese shops, well-stocked supermarkets, and Italian delis.

MAKES: 8 to 12 servings

Follow recipe for **Yogurt Cheese Torta with Pesto** (preceding), but substitute **mascarpone** or cream cheese, at room temperature, for the yogurt cheese. In a bowl, beat cheese with an electric mixer on medium speed until soft and spreadable before layering with pesto in step 2, but omit pouring off liquid.

Per serving: 142 cal., 89% (126 cal.) from fat; 2.8 g protein; 14 g fat (8.7 g sat.); 1.6 g carbo (0.4 g fiber); 28 mg sodium; 24 mg chol.

Yogurt Cheese

PREP TIME: About 5 minutes, plus 24 hours to 4 days to drain

NOTES: Don't use a brand of yogurt made with gelatin (check the ingredient list on the carton)—it won't drain. Drain the yogurt at least 24 hours before using; the longer you drain it, the thicker and creamier the cheese will be but the less you will get (the volume of cheese also varies with brand of yogurt used). Use this nonfat cheese to make the Yogurt Cheese Torta with Pesto (at left) and the Cranberry Crown Cheesecake (page 229). Chill airtight up to 9 days from when you began draining it; occasionally drain off any whey that accumulates. Discard cheese if moldy or sour-smelling.

MAKES: 1⅓ to 1¾ cups cheese (about ¾ to 1 lb.)

1. Set a strainer or colander over a deep pan or bowl, supporting it so base of strainer is at least 2 inches above pan bottom. Line strainer with two layers of cheesecloth or a clean muslin or linen towel.

2. Scrape 1 quart (2 lb.) **plain nonfat yogurt** (without gelatin; see notes) into cloth. Enclose strainer and pan airtight in plastic wrap.

3. Chill at least 24 hours or up to 4 days (see notes), pouring off liquid (the whey) as it accumulates.

4. Unwrap yogurt cheese and scrape from cloth.

Per tablespoon: 9.4 cal., 0% (0 cal.) from fat; 1.3 g protein; 0 g fat; 1 g carbo (0 g fiber); 7.9 mg sodium; 0.2 mg chol.

Cilantro Pesto

PREP TIME: About 10 minutes

NOTES: Use in one of the cheese tortas (page 224) or mix with 3 tablespoons olive oil and serve as a spread for bread.

MAKES: ½ to ⅔ cup

In a food processor, whirl 1½ cups coarsely chopped **fresh cilantro,** ⅓ cup **salted roasted peanuts,** ¼ to ½ teaspoon **hot chili flakes,** and ½ to 1 teaspoon chopped **garlic.** (Or with a knife, mince cilantro, nuts, chili, and garlic.) Add **salt** and **pepper** to taste.

Per tablespoon: 28 cal., 79% (22 cal.) from fat; 1.3 g protein; 2.4 g fat (0.3 g sat.); 1 g carbo (0.5 g fiber); 21 mg sodium; 0 mg chol.

Tomato Tapenade

PREP AND COOK TIME: About 20 minutes

NOTES: Use in one of the cheese tortas (page 224) or mix with 3 tablespoons olive oil and then serve as a spread for bread.

MAKES: About ¾ cup

1. In a bowl, cover 1 ounce (¾ to 1 cup) **dried tomatoes** with boiling water. Let stand until soft, 10 to 15 minutes.

2. Meanwhile, in a 6- to 8-inch frying pan over medium heat, stir 3 tablespoons **pine nuts** or slivered almonds until golden, about 5 minutes.

3. Drain tomatoes; squeeze out and discard excess liquid. In a food processor, whirl tomatoes, nuts, 3 tablespoons **grated parmesan cheese,** 2 tablespoons chopped **fresh basil** leaves or 1 teaspoon dry basil, and 1 peeled clove **garlic** until finely chopped. (Or with a knife, mince tomatoes, nuts, basil, and garlic; put in a bowl and mix in cheese.) Add **salt** and **pepper** to taste. ◆

Per tablespoon: 26 cal., 54% (14 cal.) from fat; 1.7 g protein; 1.6 g fat (0.5 g sat.); 1.9 g carbo (0.7 g fiber); 31 mg sodium; 1.2 mg chol. ◆

Stuffed Rolled
Flank Steak

FOOD STYLING: BASIL FRIEDMAN

Overnight success

Do the work ahead of time for a special holiday-time meal

By Andrew Baker • Photographs by James Carrier

Layers, fillings, stuffings—these are the elements of impressive party food. But they add steps that take time, which is in short supply for most of us these days, especially this time of year. Fortunately, many dishes that are layered, filled, or stuffed can be assembled a day ahead of the party. In fact, many are *better* that way: The flavors have a chance to get comfortable together. Just heat up a soup and an entrée and put the final garnish on a dessert for a special, stress-free dinner.

Stuffed Rolled Flank Steak

PREP AND COOK TIME: About 1 hour

NOTES: Serve the steak with hot, buttered noodles sprinkled with chopped parsley or penne pasta topped with your favorite marinara sauce.

MAKES: 5 to 6 servings

- 2 teaspoons **pink,** green, or black **peppercorns** (or a combination)
- ½ cup **grated parmesan cheese**
- ¼ cup finely chopped drained **oil-packed dried tomatoes**
- 1 **beef flank steak** (about 1¾ lb.)

1. On a hard, flat surface, with the bottom of a glass (or with a mortar and pestle), coarsely crush peppercorns. Put in a small bowl and mix with parmesan cheese and dried tomatoes.

2. Rinse flank steak and pat it dry; trim off and discard fat. Lay steak flat on a board and spread peppercorn mixture evenly over meat. Starting from one end, roll steak tightly around filling into a neat, compact log. Tie with heavy cotton string at 2-inch intervals. Wrap log tightly in plastic wrap and chill up to 1 day.

3. Place a 10- to 12-inch frying pan with ovenproof handle over high heat. When hot, remove rolled steak from plastic wrap, add steak to pan, and turn to brown evenly on all sides, 3 to 4 minutes total. Transfer pan with steak to a 400° regular or convection oven; bake until a thermometer inserted in center of thickest part of meat registers 135° for medium-rare, 45 to 50 minutes (35 to 40 minutes in convection), or until beef is as done as you like.

(Continued on page 226)

4. Transfer steak to a rimmed cutting board and let rest about 5 minutes. Remove and discard strings. To serve, cut steak crosswise into $\frac{1}{4}$- to $\frac{1}{2}$-inch-thick slices.

Per serving: 273 cal., 49% (135 cal.) from fat; 29 g protein; 15 g fat (6.4 g sat.); 2.9 g carbo (0.7 g fiber); 276 mg sodium; 71 mg chol.

Roasted Green Chili Bisque with Chicken

PREP AND COOK TIME: About 50 minutes

NOTES: Use leftover cooked chicken or buy a roasted chicken from a good deli.

MAKES: 2 quarts; 4 servings

$1\frac{1}{2}$ pounds **fresh poblano chilies** (often mislabeled pasillas)

1 pound **onions**

3 cups fat-skimmed **chicken broth**

2 cups **half-and-half** (light cream)

2 cups shredded skinned **cooked chicken** (see notes)

1 **firm-ripe avocado** (about 8 oz.), pitted, peeled, and chopped

1 **firm-ripe tomato** (about 6 oz.), rinsed, cored, and chopped

$\frac{1}{4}$ cup minced **fresh cilantro**

Salt

1. Rinse and dry chilies; cut in half lengthwise and discard stems and seeds. Peel onions; cut crosswise into $\frac{1}{2}$-inch-thick slices. Arrange chilies (skin up) and onions in a single layer in a 12- by 17-inch pan.

2. Broil 4 to 6 inches from heat until vegetables are soft and slightly charred, 20 to 25 minutes, turning onions as needed to brown evenly. When chilies are cool enough to handle, pull off and discard skins.

3. In a blender or food processor, whirl half the chilies and onions with about $\frac{3}{4}$ cup chicken broth until smooth, scraping container sides as necessary. Rub mixture through a fine strainer set over a bowl; discard residue. Repeat to purée remaining chilies and onions with another $\frac{3}{4}$ cup broth and strain into bowl.

4. Stir in remaining $1\frac{1}{2}$ cups broth, half-and-half, and chicken. Cover and chill up to 1 day.

5. In a 3- to 4-quart pan over medium-high heat, stir bisque often until steaming, about 15 minutes. Place avocado, tomato, and cilantro in separate small bowls.

6. Ladle bisque into wide bowls. Serve

Chocolate-Caramel Trifle with Raspberries

FOOD STYLING: BASIL FRIEDMAN

with avocado, tomato, cilantro, and salt to add to taste.

Per serving: 480 cal., 49% (234 cal.) from fat; 35 g protein; 26 g fat (11 g sat.); 31 g carbo (4.8 g fiber); 185 mg sodium; 107 mg chol.

Chocolate-Caramel Trifle with Raspberries

PREP AND COOK TIME: About $1\frac{1}{4}$ hours, plus at least 2 hours to chill

NOTES: Make and cool pastry cream while cake bakes and cools. For a non-alcoholic version, substitute a hazelnut- or raspberry-flavor syrup (such as Torani, available in most well-stocked supermarkets) for the liqueur; the trifle will be somewhat sweeter.

MAKES: 8 to 10 servings

About $\frac{1}{2}$ cup ($\frac{1}{4}$ lb.) **butter** or margarine, at room temperature

About $1\frac{1}{2}$ cups **all-purpose flour**

4 ounces **semisweet chocolate**

1 cup **sugar**

2 **large eggs**

1 teaspoon **vanilla**

$\frac{3}{4}$ teaspoon **baking soda**

$\frac{1}{2}$ teaspoon **salt**

$\frac{3}{4}$ cup **milk**

$\frac{3}{4}$ cup **hazelnut-** or coffee-**flavor liqueur** (see notes)

Caramel Pastry Cream (recipe follows)

$1\frac{1}{2}$ cups **fresh raspberries** (6 oz.), rinsed and drained

1. Butter and flour a 9-inch square baking pan.

2. Coarsely chop 3 ounces of the chocolate and place in a microwave-safe bowl. Heat in a microwave oven on full power (100%), stirring every 30 seconds, until melted and smooth, about $1\frac{1}{2}$ minutes total.

3. In a large bowl, with a mixer on medium-high speed, beat $\frac{1}{2}$ cup butter and the sugar until fluffy. Add eggs and vanilla and beat until well blended. Stir in melted chocolate.

4. In another bowl, mix $1\frac{1}{2}$ cups flour, baking soda, and salt. Add flour mixture and milk to butter mixture, stir to combine, then beat until well blended. Scrape batter into prepared pan and spread level.

5. Bake in a 350° regular or convection oven until cake begins to pull from pan sides, 40 to 50 minutes. Let cake cool to room temperature in pan on a rack, about $1\frac{1}{2}$ hours.

6. Run a thin knife between cake and pan sides and invert onto a board to release. Cut cake into 1- to $1\frac{1}{2}$-inch cubes. Layer a third of the cubes in the bottom of a 3- to $3\frac{1}{2}$-quart trifle bowl or other straight-sided glass bowl.

Drizzle ¼ cup liqueur evenly over cake. Spoon a third of the Caramel Pastry Cream over cake and spread level. Repeat to make two more layers each of cake, liqueur, and pastry cream, ending with pastry cream. Cover and chill at least 2 hours or up to 1 day.

7. Finely chop remaining 1 ounce chocolate or scrape into curls. Arrange raspberries on trifle and sprinkle chocolate evenly over berries. Scoop onto dessert plates to serve.

Per serving: 669 cal., 40% (270 cal.) from fat; 8.6 g protein; 30 g fat (18 g sat.); 88 g carbo (2 g fiber); 379 mg sodium; 205 mg chol.

Caramel Pastry Cream

PREP AND COOK TIME: 45 to 50 minutes, plus 30 minutes to chill

MAKES: About 5 cups

1½ cups **sugar**

2⅔ cups **milk**

4 **large egg** yolks

¼ cup **cornstarch**

1½ cups **whipping cream**

1. In a 10- to 12-inch nonstick frying pan over medium-high heat, tilt and stir sugar until melted and amber-colored, 8 to 10 minutes. Pour onto a sheet of foil (about 12 by 18 in.) and let cool to room temperature, about 20 minutes. Peel off foil and break caramel into chunks; put in a food processor or blender and whirl into a fine powder.

2. Combine milk and caramel powder in a 1½- to 2-quart pan; stir over medium heat just until caramel is dissolved (it will form lumps, then melt; do not boil), 9 to 10 minutes.

3. In a small bowl, beat egg yolks to blend. Add cornstarch and whisk until smooth. Pour about ½ cup of the hot milk mixture into yolks and whisk until blended, then whisk yolk mixture into pan and stir over medium-high heat just until mixture boils and thickens, 3 to 4 minutes.

4. Rub pastry cream through a fine strainer set over a bowl; discard residue. Cover pastry cream and chill about 1 hour, or nest bowl in ice water and stir until cool, about 30 minutes.

5. In a large bowl, with a mixer on high speed, beat whipping cream until it holds soft peaks. Gently stir the whipped cream into the cool pastry cream.

Per ½ cup: 296 cal., 46% (135 cal.) from fat; 4 g protein; 15 g fat (8.9 g sat.); 37 g carbo (0 g fiber); 48 mg sodium; 134 mg chol.

Coconut-Curry Seafood Crêpes

PREP AND COOK TIME: About 1¾ hours

NOTES: Curried crêpes can be made up to 3 days before filling. If not assembling crêpes a day ahead in step 5, put directly in the oven in step 6 and bake 15 to 20 minutes.

MAKES: 5 to 6 servings

3½ cups fat-skimmed **reduced-sodium chicken broth**

½ pound (26 to 30 per lb.) **shelled, deveined shrimp**, rinsed

½ pound **boned, skinned salmon fillet**, rinsed

About ¼ cup (⅛ lb.) **butter** or margarine

1 **onion** (about 8 oz.), peeled and minced

6 tablespoons **all-purpose flour**

1½ cups **coconut milk**

Salt and **pepper**

½ pound **shelled cooked crab**

Curried Crêpes (recipe follows)

1 tablespoon minced **fresh cilantro**

1. In a 2- to 3-quart pan over high heat, bring broth to a boil. Add shrimp, cover pan, and remove from heat. Let stand until shrimp are barely opaque but still moist-looking in center of thickest part (cut to test), 1 to 2 minutes. With a slotted spoon, transfer shrimp to a board.

2. Return pan with broth to high heat. When boiling again, add salmon, cover, and remove from heat. Let stand until fish is barely opaque but still moist-looking in center of thickest part (cut to test), 8 to 9 minutes. With slotted spoon, transfer to board. Pour broth into a 1-quart glass measure or a bowl; rinse and dry pan.

3. Set pan over medium-high heat and add ¼ cup butter; when melted, add onion and stir often until limp, 10 to 15 minutes. Sprinkle flour over onion and stir for 1 minute. Remove from heat and whisk in reserved broth and the coconut milk, then whisk over medium-high heat until mixture boils and thickens, 8 to 10 minutes. Remove from heat. Add salt and pepper to taste.

4. Meanwhile, remove any bits of shell from the crab; put crab into a bowl. When shrimp and salmon are cool enough to handle, cut shrimp into ½-inch chunks and with a fork, flake salmon; put these into bowl with crab. Mix in 1½ cups coconut sauce.

5. Lay one crêpe flat in a lightly buttered 9- by 13-inch pan. Spoon about ⅓ cup of the seafood mixture onto half the crêpe, spreading to within 1 inch of edge; fold bare half of crêpe over filling, then fold in half again to form a triangle. Repeat to fill remaining crêpes, slightly overlapping in a single layer in pan. Cover and chill up to 1 day.

6. Uncover and bake in a 350° regular or convection oven until crêpes are hot in the center, 35 to 40 minutes.

7. Spoon remaining coconut sauce evenly onto dinner plates. With a wide spatula, transfer crêpes to plates, setting in sauce. Sprinkle cilantro evenly over crêpes. Add more salt and pepper to taste.

Per serving: 537 cal., 52% (279 cal.) from fat; 34 g protein; 31 g fat (19 g sat.); 30 g carbo (1.5 g fiber); 706 mg sodium; 256 mg chol.

Curried Crêpes

PREP AND COOK TIME: About 30 minutes

MAKES: About 10 crêpes

1¼ cups **milk**

3 **large eggs**

1 cup **all-purpose flour**

1½ teaspoons **curry powder**

About 2½ teaspoons **butter** or margarine

1. In a blender or food processor, whirl milk, eggs, flour, and curry powder until smooth, scraping container sides as necessary. (Or in a bowl, whisk mixture until smooth.)

2. Place a 10-inch nonstick frying pan (7½ to 8 in. across bottom) or crêpe pan over medium-high heat. When pan is hot, add about ¼ teaspoon butter and swirl until melted. All at once, add about ¼ cup batter and tilt pan in a circular motion to coat bottom evenly. Cook until crêpe is dry-looking on top and browned on the bottom, ¾ to 1 minute. Turn with a wide spatula and cook until other side is lightly speckled with brown, 20 to 30 seconds. Slide crêpe from pan onto a plate. Repeat to cook remaining crêpes, stacking on first (if making crêpes up to 3 days ahead, stack between sheets of waxed paper, wrap airtight, and chill; freeze to store longer).

Per crêpe: 96 cal., 33% (32 cal.) from fat; 4.2 g protein; 11 g fat (1.7 g sat.); 11 g carbo (0.4 g fiber); 44 mg sodium; 71 mg chol. ◆

New endings

Mix and match holiday flavors
for stylish desserts

By Linda Lau Anusasananan
Photographs by James Carrier

Classic holiday ingredients aren't following the rules this year. Pumpkin escapes the ubiquitous pie and tangles with caramel, chocolate, and candied nuts in an elegant frozen torte. Apples mingle with dried cherries and apricots under a crumbly hazelnut streusel in a multiple-harvest pie. And cranberries have moved from the relish tray to the top of a cheesecake (a wonderful light, tangy yogurt version). Any of these desserts would end your feast on a delicious new note.

Pumpkin Ice Cream Torte
with Ginger Crust

FOOD STYLING: BASIL FRIEDMAN

Pumpkin Ice Cream Torte with Ginger Crust

PREP AND COOK TIME: About 1 hour, plus 5 hours to freeze

NOTES: For the smoothest texture, use a rich, full-fat ice cream. To soften slightly, heat it in the carton in a microwave oven at half power (50%) for 15 to 30 seconds.

MAKES: 12 servings

- 8 ounces **crisp gingersnap cookies**
- 2 tablespoons **sugar**
- 3 tablespoons **butter** or margarine, melted
- 1 can (15 oz.) **pumpkin,** chilled
- 2 teaspoons **pumpkin pie spice**

  About 1¼ cups **caramel ice cream topping**
- 1 quart **vanilla ice cream,** softened (see notes)

  About 1 cup **hot fudge sauce** or chocolate ice cream topping

  Candied Walnuts (recipe follows)

1. Place about a third of the cookies in a zip-lock plastic bag, seal bag, and roll with a rolling pin until cookies are finely crushed; pour into a 9-inch cheesecake pan with removable rim (at least 2 in. tall). Repeat to crush remaining cookies (you need 1¾ cups total) and pour into pan. Add sugar and butter and mix. Press cookie mixture over bottom and about 1 inch up sides of pan.

2. Bake crust in a 325° regular or convection oven until lightly browned, 10 to 12 minutes. Let cool about 5 minutes, then chill or freeze until cold, 5 to 10 minutes.

3. In a chilled large bowl, mix pumpkin, pumpkin pie spice, and ¼ cup of the caramel topping until smooth. Add ice cream and mix until blended.

4. Working quickly, spoon about a third of the ice cream mixture into the cold crust. Drizzle with 2 tablespoons caramel topping and 2 tablespoons fudge sauce (if fudge sauce is too stiff, warm slightly in a microwave oven at 100% power, stirring once, just until fluid, 15 to 30 seconds); sprinkle half the Candied Walnuts on top. Repeat with two more layers, omitting nuts on the top layer. Freeze until solid, about 5 hours, then cover and freeze up to 1 week.

5. About 15 minutes before serving, remove sides from pan, set torte on a serving plate, and let stand in refrigerator to soften slightly. Cut into wedges. Serve with additional caramel topping and fudge sauce (warm and stir again if too stiff) to add to taste.

Per serving: 495 cal., 38% (189 cal.) from fat; 5.9 g protein; 21 g fat (9.1 g sat.); 77 g carbo (1.3 g fiber); 339 mg sodium; 38 mg chol.

Candied Walnuts

PREP AND COOK TIME: About 5 minutes, plus about 7 minutes to cool

NOTES: Use these sweet nuts in the Pumpkin Ice Cream Torte (preceding) or sprinkle on salads or ice cream. If making candied walnuts up to 2 days ahead, store airtight at room temperature.

MAKES: About 1 cup

In a heavy, 8- to 10-inch frying pan, combine 6 tablespoons **sugar** and ⅔ cup **walnut** or pecan **pieces** (about ½ in.). Shake and stir often over medium-high heat until sugar is melted and amber-colored, about 5 minutes. Pour onto a piece of foil and spread into a thin layer. Let cool until hard, about 7 minutes. Break into small pieces.

Per 2 tablespoons: 101 cal., 55% (56 cal.) from fat; 1.4 g protein; 6.2 g fat (0.6 g sat.); 11 g carbo (0.5 g fiber); 1.1 mg sodium; 0 mg chol.

Harvest Apple Pie with Hazelnut Streusel

PREP AND COOK TIME: About 2 hours, plus at least 1½ hours to cool

NOTES: If desired, substitute a home-made pastry for the purchased one. To save time, you can slice the apples (peeled, cored, and quartered) in a food processor. If making pie up to 1 day ahead, cool, cover, and chill. If desired, reheat, uncovered, in a 325° oven 20 to 25 minutes.

MAKES: About 8 servings

- ½ cup chopped **dried apricots**
- ½ cup chopped **dried cherries**
- ¼ cup **rum** or orange juice
- ⅓ cup **granulated sugar**
- 2 tablespoons **cornstarch**
- 1 teaspoon **ground coriander**
- ¾ teaspoon **ground ginger**
- ¾ teaspoon **ground cinnamon**
- 6 cups thinly sliced peeled **Granny Smith apples** (about 2 lb.; see notes)
- 1 **refrigerated purchased pastry** for a 9-inch single-crust pie (half of a 15-oz. package), at room temperature

  About 1 cup **all-purpose flour**
- ½ cup firmly packed **brown sugar**
- 6 tablespoons cold **butter** or margarine, cut into chunks
- ½ cup chopped **hazelnuts**

1. In a bowl, mix apricots, cherries, and rum; let stand until fruit is slightly softened, 6 to 8 minutes.

2. Meanwhile, in a large bowl, mix granulated sugar, cornstarch, coriander, ginger, cinnamon, and apples. Stir in dried-fruit mixture.

3. Ease pastry gently into a 9-inch pie pan, fold edge under itself flush with rim, and flute decoratively. Mound apple mixture in crust.

4. In a food processor or bowl, whirl or stir 1 cup flour and the brown sugar until well blended. Add butter and whirl or rub in with your fingers until mixture forms coarse crumbs. Stir in nuts and whirl until coarsely chopped, or chop nuts with a knife and stir into flour mixture. Squeeze handfuls of the streusel until it sticks together, then crumble into chunks evenly over apple mixture. Set pie on a foil-lined rimmed baking pan.

5. Bake on the bottom rack of a 350° regular or convection oven until filling is bubbling around edges, about 1¼ hours. If pie becomes brown too quickly, cover its dark portions loosely with foil. Cool on a rack at least 1½ hours.

Per serving: 490 cal., 37% (180 cal.) from fat; 3.1 g protein; 20 g fat (8.6 g sat.); 77 g carbo (3.8 g fiber); 190 mg sodium; 28 mg chol.

Cranberry Crown Cheesecake

FOOD STYLING: BASIL FRIEDMAN

Cranberry Crown Cheesecake

PREP AND COOK TIME: About 1¼ hours, plus at least 2½ hours to cool

NOTES: For the yogurt cheese, drain 2½ to 3 quarts nonfat yogurt at least 24 hours. If using cream cheese, omit the gelatin and step 3; in step 4, beat in the liqueur and vanilla until smooth, then beat in eggs.

MAKES: 12 servings

- 1 cup **graham cracker crumbs**
- 2 tablespoons **butter** or margarine, melted
- 1½ teaspoons **unflavored gelatin**
- 2 tablespoons **orange-flavor liqueur** or orange juice
- 2 teaspoons **vanilla**
- 3 cups **Yogurt Cheese** (recipe page 224; see notes) or cream cheese
- 1 cup **sugar**
- 4 **large eggs**
- 1½ to 2 cups cool **Baked Cranberry-Orange Sauce** (recipe page 219)

1. In a 9-inch cheesecake pan with removable rim (at least 1¾ in. tall), mix graham cracker crumbs and butter. Pat mixture evenly over bottom and about ½ inch up sides of pan.

2. Bake crust in a 350° regular or convection oven until slightly browner, 8 to 10 minutes.

3. In a 1- to 1½-quart pan, mix gelatin with 2 tablespoons cold water; let stand until softened, about 1 minute. Stir over medium heat until gelatin is dissolved, about 45 seconds. Remove from heat and stir in liqueur and vanilla.

4. In a large bowl, with an electric mixer on medium speed, beat cheese, sugar, and gelatin mixture until smooth. Beat in eggs, one at a time, until smoothly blended. Pour mixture into hot or cool crust.

5. Bake cheesecake in a 325° regular or 300° convection oven until center jiggles only slightly when pan is gently shaken, 30 to 35 minutes. Cool cake on a rack for about 30 minutes, then chill, uncovered, until cold, at least 2 hours. Serve, or cover airtight and chill up to 1 day.

6. Just before serving, lightly blot any moisture from surface of cake with a paper towel. Spread cranberry sauce evenly over cake. Remove pan rim and cut cake into wedges.

Per serving with yogurt cheese: 259 cal., 15% (39 cal.) from fat; 7.9 g protein; 4.3 g fat (1.8 g sat.); 48 g carbo (1 g fiber); 116 mg sodium; 77 mg chol.

Per serving with cream cheese: 419 cal., 52% (216 cal.) from fat; 6.9 g protein; 24 g fat (14 g sat.); 45 g carbo (1 g fiber); 251 mg sodium; 138 mg chol. ◆

Crusty

A round of
Garden
Tomato Bread
and a batard
of Leek and
Walnut.

With tips from a master baker and fresh ingredients from the garden, you can make rustic, artisan-style bread at home

Lou Preston

loaves
from your oven

By Charity Ferreira • Photographs by James Carrier • Food styling by Tiffany Armstrong

Mornings often find Lou Preston, owner and winemaker of Preston Vineyards near Healdsburg, California, mixing bread dough, not cuvées, and deftly loading his brick oven with dozens of uniform loaves. Heavy wood farmhouse tables cohabit equally with gleaming stainless steel equipment in the winery's commercial bakery, an arrangement echoed by the way Preston keeps track of the recipes for his artisan breads—on a floury Palm Pilot in his pocket.

Much of what grows on the winery grounds—vegetables, herbs, olives, even the grapes themselves—makes its way into Preston's crusty loaves. It makes sense that a passion for baking bread would coincide with a passion for making wine. Both depend on warm weather to ripen the harvest that imbues them with the character of the place where they were made; both develop the best flavor from a long, cool fermentation; and for both, a successful blend of flavors depends on no one element overwhelming the rest.

Combinations like leek and walnut and tomato and herb inspired us to adapt Preston's recipes and techniques for the home kitchen. We offer them here, along with tips and shortcuts, in the cause of making artisans of us all.

Preston Vineyards' tasting room is open daily, 11:00–4:30 (holiday hours vary); 9282 W. Dry Creek Rd., Healdsburg; (707) 433-3372.

Leek and Walnut Bread

PREP AND COOK TIME: About $1\frac{1}{2}$ hours, plus at least 15 hours to chill biga and let dough rise
NOTES: See "Terms & Tips" on page 232 for an explanation of the techniques here. Mix biga 1 day before baking bread.
MAKES: 2 loaves, $1\frac{3}{4}$ pounds each

$\frac{3}{4}$ teaspoon **active dry yeast**
   Biga (recipe follows), at room temperature
   About 5 cups **bread flour**
$\frac{3}{4}$ cup **whole-wheat flour**
$3\frac{1}{2}$ teaspoons **salt**
$1\frac{1}{2}$ cups (about 6 oz.) chopped **leeks** (white and pale green parts only)
$\frac{3}{4}$ cup chopped **walnuts** (about 4 oz.)
   2 tablespoons chopped **fresh oregano** leaves
   About $\frac{1}{4}$ cup **cornmeal**

1. In the bowl of a standing mixer or another large bowl, sprinkle yeast over 1 cup warm (100° to 110°) water; let stand until foamy, about 10 minutes.

2. Add $1\frac{1}{4}$ cups cold water, biga, 3 cups bread flour, whole-wheat flour, and salt to yeast mixture. Beat with paddle attachment on low speed, or stir with a heavy spoon, until well blended. Gradually beat or stir in 2 more cups bread flour, $\frac{1}{2}$ cup at a time, until mixture forms a soft dough.

3. Switch to a dough hook and beat on medium speed until dough is smooth and elastic and pulls cleanly from sides of bowl but is still slightly sticky, 6 to 8 minutes; or scrape dough onto a lightly floured board and knead by hand until smooth and elastic but still slightly sticky, 7 to 10 minutes.

4. Add leeks, nuts, and oregano and beat in with dough hook or knead in by hand just until incorporated (after mixing in by hand, place dough in a bowl).

5. Cover bowl with plastic wrap; let dough rise at room temperature until doubled, 2 to $2\frac{1}{2}$ hours. Punch down with your hand to expel air.

6. Re-cover dough with plastic wrap and let rise again until doubled, 1 to $1\frac{1}{2}$ hours. Or for a slow rise, chill at least 8 and up to 12 hours. Let come to room temperature, about 3 hours.

7. Scrape dough onto a well-floured board and knead briefly to expel air. Divide in half. With lightly floured hands, gather halves, one at a time, into a ball, then stretch and tuck edges under to shape into smooth ovals with slightly tapered ends (about 8 in. long and 4 in. wide in the center). Place loaves on a well-floured surface, dust lightly with flour, cover loosely with plastic wrap, and let rise at room temperature until they're slightly puffy and hold the imprint of a finger when lightly pressed, about $1\frac{1}{2}$ hours.

8. Sprinkle a 13- by 17-inch baking sheet generously with cornmeal. Transfer loaves, one at a time, to sheet, spacing 2 to 3 inches apart. With a sharp knife, make three diagonal slashes 1 inch deep and 1 to 2 inches apart across loaf tops. Place sheet on rack in lower third of a 450° regular or convection oven.

Or, if using a baking stone, gently slide edge of cornmeal-covered baking sheet under one loaf and lift it onto end of sheet. Slash as directed above, then gently slide loaf onto one side of stone in oven, leaving room for second loaf. Repeat to slash and transfer second loaf.

Spray 3 to 4 squirts of water on floor or sides of oven, taking care not to spray near heating element or lightbulb, then quickly close door.

9. Bake bread, spraying twice more at 5-minute intervals during the first 10 minutes of baking, until crust is well browned, 35 to 45 minutes total.

10. Transfer loaves to a rack to cool for at least 1 hour. Store in paper bags at room temperature up to 2 days. To recrisp the crust, place loaves directly on a rack in a 400°

SHORTCUT LOAVES

Using a bread machine: You can give bakery character to bread by using artisan techniques for baking and shaping after a machine has mixed and kneaded the dough.

Leek and Walnut Bread. Add 3 cups **bread flour**, ½ cup **whole-wheat flour**, 1½ cups **water**, 1 tablespoon chopped **fresh oregano** leaves, 1 teaspoon **salt**, and 1½ teaspoons **active dry yeast** to bread machine according to manufacturer's directions. Select dough cycle. At end of cycle, scrape dough onto a lightly floured board. Knead in ½ cup finely chopped **leeks** and ⅓ cup chopped **walnuts**. Follow step 7 of Leek and Walnut Bread (page 231) to shape into a loaf, letting it rise about 30 minutes. Follow steps 8 through 10 to slash, bake, and cool loaf. Makes one 1½-pound loaf.

Per ounce: 85 cal., 15% (13 cal.) from fat; 2.8 g protein; 1.4 g fat (0.1 g sat.); 15 g carbo (0.9 g fiber); 98 mg sodium; 0 mg chol.

---

oven and bake for about 5 minutes.

Per ounce: 82 cal., 17% (14 cal.) from fat; 2.6 g protein; 1.6 g fat (0.1 g sat.); 14 g carbo (0.7 g fiber); 147 mg sodium; 0 mg chol.

BIGA. In a bowl, sprinkle ¼ teaspoon **active dry yeast** over ¼ cup warm (100° to 110°) **water.** Let stand until foamy, about 5 minutes. Add ½ cup cold water. With a wood spoon, stir in 1½ cups **bread flour** until mixture forms a soft dough. Cover with plastic wrap and chill 12 to 24 hours. Let come to room temperature before using, about 1 hour.

Garden Tomato Bread

PREP AND COOK TIME: About 1½ hours, plus at least 15 hours to chill biga and let dough rise

NOTES: It's important to use ripe, juicy tomatoes in this bread.

MAKES: 2 loaves, 1¾ pounds each

- ¾ teaspoon **active dry yeast**
- 1½ pounds **ripe tomatoes** (see notes)
   Biga (preceding), at room temperature
- 2 tablespoons **tomato paste**
- ¼ cup chopped **parsley**
- 2 tablespoons chopped **fresh sage** leaves
- 1 tablespoon minced **garlic**
- 1 tablespoon **fresh thyme** leaves
- ½ teaspoon fresh-ground **black pepper**
- 3½ cups **whole-wheat flour** About 3½ cups **bread flour**
- 3½ teaspoons **salt**
- ¼ cup raw **pumpkin seeds**
- ¼ cup raw **sunflower seeds** About ¼ cup **cornmeal**

1. In the bowl of a standing mixer or another large bowl, sprinkle yeast over ¼ cup warm (100° to 110°) water. Let stand until foamy, about 10 minutes.

2. Meanwhile, rinse and core tomatoes; cut each in half crosswise. Squeeze juice and seeds into a bowl; cut tomatoes into ½-inch chunks. You need ¼ cup juice with seeds (if you have less than ¼ cup, add water to make up the difference; if you have more, discard extra) and 3½ cups tomato chunks.

3. Add biga, tomatoes and juice, tomato paste, parsley, sage, garlic, thyme, pepper, whole-wheat flour, 2 cups bread flour, and salt to yeast mixture. Beat with paddle attachment

---

TERMS & TIPS
Artisan steps

BIGA: A yeast-based starter in which a portion of the dough is mixed first and allowed to ferment, giving the finished loaf some of the characteristics of bread made with a sourdough starter.

Shortcut: Without the biga, our recipes still produce great loaves. In the basic recipe, just increase the yeast by 1¼ teaspoons, the bread flour by 1½ cups, and the water by ¾ cup.

MIXING: Because of many variables that affect the dough's consistency, the amounts of flour we call for are somewhat approximate. The dough should be soft, malleable, and slightly sticky. If the mixer is laboring or the dough feels stiff, add water, a tablespoon at a time, and continue kneading until it's soft and elastic. If dough sticks to the sides of the bowl or is too sticky to knead by hand, add more flour, 2 tablespoons at a time, until it pulls cleanly from the sides or feels only slightly sticky.

SLOW RISE: When bread rises slowly at a cool temperature, it develops more flavor than when it rises quickly in a warm place.

PROOFING: Once the loaves are shaped, they need to rise again before they are baked. To tell whether they've proofed long enough, press one gently; your finger should leave a distinct imprint that fills in slowly. Underproofed loaves feel tight and spring back quickly; overproofed loaves feel flabby and offer little resistance when you press them.

SLASHING: This gives the loaf a place to grow during its last burst of expansion in the oven.

BAKING STONE: A stone distributes the heat more evenly and makes a crisper crust. At least 30 minutes before baking, set the stone on a rack in the lower third of the oven and heat oven to 450°.

STEAM: Prevents the crust from forming before loaf has fully expanded and contributes to the final thick, hard crust. You can create steam in your oven by using a spray bottle filled with clean water.

on low speed, or stir with a heavy spoon, until well blended. Gradually beat or stir in 1½ more cups bread flour, ¼ cup at a time, until mixture forms a soft dough.

4. Switch to a dough hook and beat on medium speed until dough is smooth and elastic and pulls cleanly from sides of bowl but is still slightly sticky, 6 to 8 minutes; or scrape dough onto a lightly floured board and knead by hand until smooth and elastic but still slightly sticky, 7 to 10 minutes. Add pumpkin and sunflower seeds and beat in with dough hook or knead in by hand just until incorporated (after mixing in by hand, place dough in a bowl).

Follow steps 5 through 10 of Leek and Walnut Bread. In step 7, shape dough into two round loaves. In step 8, slash a 1-inch-deep X on top of each loaf.

Per ounce: 82 cal., 7.7% (6.3 cal.) from fat; 2.9 g protein; 0.7 g fat (0.1 g sat.); 16 g carbo (1.5 g fiber); 152 mg sodium; 0 mg chol.

Zucchini Bread with Moroccan Spices

PREP AND COOK TIME: About 1½ hours, plus at least 15 hours to chill biga and let dough rise

NOTES: To toast cumin seeds, shake in a frying pan over medium heat until aromatic, 2 to 3 minutes. Let cool, then coarsely grind in a mortar and pestle or coarsely chop with a knife.

MAKES: 2 loaves, 1¾ pounds each

- ¾ teaspoon **active dry yeast**
  Biga (preceding), at room temperature
- 1 cup grated **zucchini** (about 4 oz.)
  About 4½ cups **bread flour**
- 1½ cups **whole-wheat flour**
- 3½ teaspoons **salt**
- ½ cup chopped **parsley**
- ½ cup diced **red bell pepper**
- ½ cup finely chopped **unsalted roasted pistachios**
- 1 tablespoon **cumin seeds,** toasted and coarsely ground (see notes)
- 1½ teaspoons **hot chili flakes**
  About ¼ cup **cornmeal**

1. In the bowl of a standing mixer or another large bowl, sprinkle yeast over 1 cup warm (100° to 110°) water; let stand until foamy, about 10 minutes.

2. Add ¾ cup cold water, biga, zucchini, 3 cups bread flour, whole-wheat flour, and salt to yeast mixture. Beat with paddle attachment on low speed, or stir with a heavy spoon, until well blended. Gradually beat or stir in 1½ more cups bread flour, ¼ cup at a time, until mixture forms a soft dough.

3. Switch to a dough hook and beat on medium speed until dough is smooth and elastic and pulls cleanly from sides of bowl but is still slightly sticky, 6 to 8 minutes; or scrape dough onto a lightly floured board and knead by hand until smooth and elastic but still slightly sticky, 7 to 10 minutes.

4. Add parsley, bell pepper, pistachios, cumin, and chili flakes and beat in with dough hook or knead in by hand just until incorporated (after mixing in by hand, place dough in a bowl).

Follow steps 5 through 10 of Leek and Walnut Bread.

Per ounce: 76 cal., 11% (8.1 cal.) from fat; 2.6 g protein; 0.9 g fat (0.1 g sat.); 14 g carbo (1 g fiber); 147 mg sodium; 0 mg chol. ◆

Spicy slices flecked with cumin, chilies, pistachios, and red peppers.

Cozy blanquette

■ One of my favorite old-fashioned French classics is among the retro dishes appearing on the most chic restaurant menus across the country: *blanquette de veau.* A delicate, satisfying stew made of veal shoulder, it's quite easy to make—the simple process will bring some sanity into your kitchen during this busy month. You needn't brown the meat (so no spatters); just simmer it gently with a few herbs and spices in broth until it's tender. Then boil the juices briefly to concentrate their flavor, polish them off with a modest splash of cream, thicken them a little, and combine them with vegetables—mushrooms and onions—that have been glazed separately in a little butter to retain their form. The French serve blanquette de veau with almost anything that captures the good sauce, such as rice, mashed potatoes, or pasta. They might draw the line at soft polenta, but I don't.

JAMES CARRIER; FOOD STYLING: BASIL FRIEDMAN

Blanquette de Veau

PREP AND COOK TIME: About 1¾ hours

NOTES: To use a 4- to 6-quart electric slow cooker, combine ingredients for step 1, cover, and cook on high setting until meat is very tender when pierced, about 3 hours. Transfer meat and seasonings to the cooked mushrooms and pour juices into a 4- to 5-quart pan, then complete steps 3 and 4 on the stove.

MAKES: 6 servings

3 pounds **boned veal shoulder,** cut into 1- to 2-inch chunks

2 cups fat-skimmed **chicken broth**

2 **carrots** (3 to 4 oz. each), peeled and cut into ¼-inch dice

3 or 4 **whole cloves**

2 **dried bay leaves** (3 to 4 in. long)

½ teaspoon **white** or black **peppercorns**

1 pound **mushrooms** (about 1-in.-wide caps)

2 tablespoons **butter** or margarine

1 package (10 oz.) **frozen cooked small onions** (about 1 in. wide)

½ teaspoon grated **lemon** peel

½ cup **whipping cream**

½ cup chopped **parsley**

2 tablespoons **cornstarch**

1 tablespoon **lemon juice**

Salt

1. Rinse meat and place in a 5- to 6-quart pan. Add broth, carrots, cloves, bay leaves, and peppercorns. Bring to a boil over high heat, cover, and simmer gently until meat is very tender when pierced, 1 to 1¼ hours.

2. Meanwhile, rinse mushrooms; trim off and discard discolored stem ends. In a 10- to 12-inch frying pan over medium heat, melt butter; add mushrooms and onions, mix, cover, and cook, shaking pan or stirring often, until mushroom juices have evaporated and vegetables are beginning to brown, about 15 minutes. Remove from heat.

3. When veal is tender, transfer meat and seasonings with a slotted spoon to the pan with the mushrooms and onions (mounding, if necessary); discard cloves and bay leaves if desired. Add lemon peel and cream to the broth in the 5- to 6-quart pan and boil, uncovered, over high heat until reduced to 3 cups, 10 to 15 minutes. Stir in parsley.

4. In a small bowl, blend cornstarch with 2 tablespoons water until smooth; stir into boiling veal juices. Add lemon juice and the meat and vegetables; stir gently until meat is hot, 2 to 3 minutes. Add salt to taste and ladle stew into wide bowls.

Per serving: 453 cal., 44% (198 cal.) from fat; 49 g protein; 22 g fat (11 g sat.); 13 g carbo (2.3 g fiber); 292 mg sodium; 230 mg chol.

Specialized spatula

■ Like knives, spatulas come in a great variety of shapes and sizes geared for special tasks. Thin metal ones—long or short—are for spreading, flexible plastic (or silicone) ones are for scraping, and wide ones are for lifting and turning. But in that last department, there's a sub-category: Wide, slotted, slightly curved, and flexible spatulas, like the one at right, slide easily under fragile foods. My chef friends tell me they're indispensable for getting sautéed sole fillets, sand dabs, and the like out of the pan in one piece. Various sizes are sold in cookware stores and catalogs. This model costs about $20.

Sole Meunière

PREP AND COOK TIME: About 20 minutes

MAKES: 4 servings

- 1 **lemon**
- 1 pound **boned, skinned sole fillets**
- **Salt**
- About ¼ cup **all-purpose flour**
- 4 to 5 tablespoons **butter** or margarine
- 2 tablespoons drained **capers**
- 3 tablespoons **lemon juice**
- ¼ cup minced **parsley**
- Fresh-ground **white pepper**

1. Rinse lemon, and with a small, sharp knife, cut off and discard peel and white membrane. Thinly slice lemon crosswise, discarding seeds and ends.

2. Rinse sole and pat dry. If fillets are longer than 6 to 7 inches, cut in half crosswise so they'll be less likely to break when you turn them. Sprinkle each fillet lightly with salt. Coat on all sides with flour, shake off excess, and lay pieces side by side on a sheet of plastic wrap.

3. In a 12- to 14-inch frying pan over high heat, melt 2 tablespoons butter; when hot, lay as many pieces as will fit side by side in pan without crowding and cook until browned on the bottom, 1½ to 2 minutes. Turn with a thin, flexible metal spatula (such as the one above) and brown remaining side, 1 to 2 minutes longer (if butter begins to scorch, reduce heat to medium-high). With spatula, transfer fillets to an ovenproof platter, laying pieces side by side, and keep warm in a 200° oven. Melt 1 more tablespoon butter in frying pan; repeat step to cook remaining sole fillets, transfer to platter, and keep warm in the oven.

4. With a paper towel, wipe frying pan clean and return to high heat. Add 1 to 2 more tablespoons butter and the capers; stir until butter is melted. Add lemon juice, remove from heat, and stir in about 3 tablespoons of the parsley. At once, scrape butter mixture over hot fish fillets. Garnish with lemon slices and remaining parsley and sprinkle generously with pepper. With spatula, transfer fillets to plates. Season to taste with more salt.

Per serving: 237 cal., 49% (117 cal.) from fat; 23 g protein; 13 g fat (7.5 g sat.); 8.5 g carbo (1.5 g fiber); 404 mg sodium; 86 mg chol.

Wild luxury tamed

■ White sturgeon is farmed in the Sacramento Valley for at least three reasons: One, in the wild, many sturgeon species are under stress from overfishing or water pollution. Two, the fish make excellent eating. And three, salted sturgeon eggs (roe) make the only true caviar (all other caviars must be labeled with the name of the fish they came from). • At Stolt Sea Farm California, it takes 8 to 12 years for farmed sturgeon to produce roe for the company's Sterling caviar, which connoisseurs praise for texture, size, and flavor. Stolt offers four grades of white sturgeon caviar—currently 7,000 pounds a year total—ranging from $30 to $45 an ounce, plus shipping. Refrigerated unopened, it keeps its quality for four weeks. Call (800) 525-0333 or go to www.sterlingcaviar.com. • Serve the caviar well chilled, nested in ice. For simple luxury, scoop the plump, glossy beads onto thin slices of white toast and top with a dab of sour cream and a smidgen of minced green onion. For absurd indulgence, mound the caviar onto open-faced egg salad sandwiches. ◆

E. SPENCER TOY

Entertaining with wine

By Karen MacNeil-Fife

When I was a young woman, I once decided not to have a holiday dinner party simply because I didn't have matching wineglasses. I can't imagine feeling that way today. The rules of entertaining—if they can be called rules at all now—have changed completely. Creativity is what counts, not cut crystal. Moreover, in our high-tech, time-pressed world, having friends over for dinner takes on even greater importance. And, for entertaining, wine has no substitute. Since ancient times, it has been a communal beverage—a drink meant to share. (There's a reason wine doesn't come in single-serving containers!) There are practical questions, however, about sharing wine in the most inviting, convivial way.

1. How do you choose wines to match your menu?

Easy. Despite all the hoopla, putting wines and foods together is not a sci-

ence; you aren't graded. Think about the best wine experience of your life; chances are, the wine in question wasn't matched to a food, it was matched to a mood.

Still, if you've cooked something wonderful, you want to serve a wine that tastes delicious with it. My favorite technique is this: Think of the wine not as a wine but as a flavor, and then use your instinct. For example, let's say you plan to serve a roast leg of lamb. Before your dinner party, you go to a wine store and buy a few wines to try. One white wine smells and tastes perfumey, like flowers; another white is woody and vanilla-flavored; one red tastes like candied apples; and another red is earthy and gamy. Which flavor (and therefore wine) would taste good next to the lamb? Instinct says, the earthy-gamy one. Then that's the wine to buy.

My example of roast lamb was easy. But what if you're having a Mexican-inspired turkey, rubbed with ancho chilies? The flavor of the turkey is not the point; the ancho chilies are. It's the dominant flavor in the dish you need to think about.

If you don't have the time (or the means) to do a few wine-tasting experiments, a good wine store is indispensable. Take your first-course and main-dish recipes to the best wine shop in town. Ask who among the sales clerks is the best cook. Show that person the recipes and ask him or her to recommend a few wines and describe the flavor of each. Your question is then exactly the same: Which flavors do you imagine would taste good next to your dishes?

I should say here that I almost never serve only one wine with the main dish. I love to hear what other people think tastes good, so I always serve two wines. Serving two also makes the food and wine experience more playful, and I like that.

But let's start at the beginning. In many cases, guests will arrive well before you actually sit down to the table, so you'll need an aperitif. Ask the wine clerk to recommend something fresh, sassy, light in alcohol, and fun to drink while standing around in the kitchen (which is where most people gravitate). My two favorites are Austrian Rieslings and Alsatian Muscats. Both are just becoming fashionable here—you can introduce your friends to a new trend. The latter, while dry, is fruity and exotic—not quite like any other wine on the planet.

2. How do you serve all those wines smoothly?

An aperitif, one wine with the first course, and two with the main event—won't that mean a lot of juggling of wines and glasses? Not necessarily. For years, my solution has been to assign someone the role of "wine buddy." The job is to open wines, pour them, and make sure everyone has refills—freeing me up to give the sauce a final whisk.

As for glasses, if you serve two wines with the main dish, every place will be set with two wine glasses. Don't worry about having fresh ones for every course or washing glasses between courses. A tiny drop of the previous wine (especially if it was white) makes no difference in the wine to come.

3. What should you do if a guest brings a wine?

You may have decided that the lamb will be terrific with a Châteauneuf-du-Pape, but if a guest arrives with an interesting red from Morocco, open it too. This will make your guest feel good and add to the overall festivity of the evening. The only time I don't open wine from guests brings is when they tell me specifically they've brought something for my cellar.

In the end, far from being something to worry about, wine might just save the day: Unlike the roast beef, you can't burn the wine. ◆

Kitchen Cabinet

Readers' recipes tested in *Sunset's* kitchens

By Charity Ferreira • Photographs by Kevin Candland

Apples add unexpected sweetness to golden, spiced butternut squash soup.

FOOD STYLING: BASIL FRIEDMAN

Brie's Butternut Squash Bisque

Brie Tennis, Big Bear Lake, CA

After one of her favorite restaurants refused to divulge the recipe for its velvety butternut squash and apple soup, Brie Tennis came pretty close with her own version.

PREP AND COOK TIME: About 1¼ hours
MAKES: 2 quarts; 4 servings

- 2½ pounds **butternut squash**
- 3 **sweet apples,** such as Golden Delicious (about 1¼ lb. total)
- 3 cups fat-skimmed **chicken broth**
- ½ cup **dry white wine**
- ¼ teaspoon **ground cinnamon**
- ¼ teaspoon **ground nutmeg**
- ¼ teaspoon **ground ginger**
- ⅛ teaspoon **hot chili flakes**

Salt and **pepper**

3 tablespoons minced **fresh chives**

1. Rinse squash; cut in half lengthwise and scoop out seeds. Place halves cut side down in a 12- by 17-inch baking pan. Peel, halve, and core apples; add to pan, along with ¼ cup water.

2. Bake in a 400° regular or convection oven until squash and apples are tender when pierced, about 45 minutes. When cool enough to handle, scoop flesh of squash from peels; discard peels.

3. In a blender or food processor, in batches if necessary, whirl squash, apples, and broth until smooth. Pour purée into a 3- to 4-quart pan. Add wine, cinnamon, nutmeg, ginger, and chili flakes. Bring to a simmer over medium-high heat; reduce heat and simmer, stirring occasionally, to blend flavors, about 15 minutes. Add salt and pepper to taste.

4. Ladle soup into wide bowls and garnish with chives.

Per serving: 224 cal., 2.8% (6.3 cal.) from fat; 8.6 g protein; 0.7 g fat (0.1 g sat.); 46 g carbo (6.7 g fiber); 67 mg sodium; 0 mg chol.

Warm Turkey and Bacon Salad

Carmela Meely, Walnut Creek, CA

This main-dish salad created by Carmela Meely is a great way to use leftover Thanksgiving turkey (avoid using thin-sliced deli meat).

PREP AND COOK TIME: About 45 minutes
MAKES: 4 servings

- ½ pound **sliced bacon,** cut into 1-inch pieces
- 1 pound **mushrooms**
- 1 pound **cooked turkey breast** (see note above), chopped or torn into 1-inch pieces (about 2 cups)
- ½ cup **balsamic vinegar**
- 10 cups bite-size pieces rinsed and crisped **romaine lettuce** leaves (about 10 oz. total)
- 2 cups **watercress** sprigs (about 2 oz.), rinsed and crisped
- 1 cup thinly sliced **red onion**

Salt and **pepper**

- 4 ounces **blue cheese,** crumbled (optional)

1. In a 10- to 12-inch nonstick frying pan over medium-high heat, stir bacon often until browned and crisp, 3 to 5 minutes. With a slotted spoon, transfer to paper towels to drain. Spoon out and discard all but 1 tablespoon fat from pan.

2. Meanwhile, rinse and drain mushrooms. Trim off and discard stem ends and any bruised areas; thinly slice mushrooms. Add to pan and stir often until browned, about 5 minutes. Add turkey and cooked bacon and stir until hot, 1 to 2 minutes. Remove from heat and stir in vinegar.

3. In a large bowl, combine lettuce, watercress, and onion. Add turkey mixture and mix well. Add salt and pepper to taste. Divide salad equally among four dinner plates. Sprinkle evenly with blue cheese if desired.

Per serving: 329 cal., 33% (108 cal.) from fat; 43 g protein; 12 g fat (3.9 g sat.); 12 g carbo (3.6 g fiber); 350 mg sodium; 110 mg chol. ◆

Best holiday cookies in the West: Celebrate the season with winning contest recipes from our readers (see page 246).

December

Celebrate the holidays with party menus from around the West

By Linda Lau Anusasananan
Photographs By James Carrier
Food Styling By Basil Friedman

Regional Christmas: The Southwest

a tree-trimming fiesta

Fresh classics from the Southwest to help fill your home with spirit

Fragrant piñon fires and foods shaped by Mexican, Spanish, Native American, and European roots make for spirited holiday gatherings in the Southwest. We've borrowed some regional favorites—the stacked enchilada, bizcochitos, and Mexican hot chocolate—to inject that spirit into a tree-decorating party. If you put so much time into ornaments that you have little left for food, buy the cookies; bizcochitos are available in many supermarkets and in Latino grocery stores. For a fast version of the hot chocolate, buy Mexican chocolate tablets and blend them with hot milk, or simply add cinnamon to your favorite hot chocolate recipe.

Southwest Fiesta

Tortilla Chips with
Salsa and Guacamole

Spinach Salad with Apple Slices
and Pomegranate Seeds

Stacked Enchilada Pie*

Sangria or Beer

Orange-scented Bizcochitos*

Mexican Hot Chocolate*

Recipe provided

Stacked Enchilada Pie

PREP AND COOK TIME: About $1\frac{1}{2}$ hours

NOTES: For a nonvegetarian pie, substitute $2\frac{1}{4}$ cups shredded cooked chicken for the black beans. If cheese-cake pan rim is less than 3 inches tall, fold a 36- by 12-inch strip of foil in half twice lengthwise and oil one side. Line rim with strip, oiled side in and edge extending above rim. If preparing through step 2 up to 1 day ahead, cover and chill pie, remaining chili sauce, and cheese separately. Bake chilled pie, covered, for 1 hour; uncover and continue baking until hot in the center, 40 to 50 minutes longer.

MAKES: 8 servings

1 **onion** (about 8 oz.), peeled and chopped

2 **red bell peppers** (about 1 lb. total), rinsed, stemmed, seeded, and chopped

2 cloves **garlic,** peeled and pressed or minced

2 teaspoons **cumin seeds**

About 1 teaspoon **salad oil**

1 package (1 lb.) **frozen corn kernels,** thawed

2 cans (about 15 oz. each) **black beans,** rinsed and drained (see notes)

$\frac{1}{2}$ cup chopped **fresh cilantro**

1 can (19 oz.) **red chili** (enchilada) **sauce**

8 **flour tortillas** (10 in.)

3 cups shredded **pepper jack** or plain jack **cheese** (about 9 oz.)

$1\frac{1}{2}$ cups crumbled **cotija** or feta **cheese** (about 8 oz.)

1 **firm-ripe avocado** (about 6 oz.)

Fresh cilantro sprigs, rinsed

Stacked Enchilada Pie

1. In a 5- to 6-quart nonstick pan over high heat, frequently stir onion, bell peppers, garlic, and cumin seeds in 1 teaspoon oil until the onion is limp, 5 to 7 minutes. Stir in corn, beans, and chopped cilantro and remove pan from heat.

2. Pour all of the chili sauce into a 12-inch rimmed pizza pan or 10-inch pie pan. Dip one tortilla in chili sauce to coat both sides lightly; lift tortilla out, letting excess sauce drip back into

Orange-scented Bizcochitos

pan. Set tortilla in an oiled 10-inch cheesecake pan with removable rim at least 3 inches tall (see notes). Spread ¹⁄₇ (about 1 cup) of the vegetable filling level over tortilla. Sprinkle evenly with ¹⁄₃ cup jack cheese and 3 tablespoons cotija cheese. Repeat layers, making a total of seven; top with remaining tortilla. Reserve any leftover chili sauce and remaining jack and cotija cheese. Cover pan with an oiled piece of foil, oiled side down. Set pan in a rimmed 10- by 15-inch baking pan.

3. Bake enchilada pie in a 350° regular or 325° convection oven for 30 minutes. Uncover and continue baking until hot (160°) in the center, 30 to 40 minutes longer.

4. Shortly before serving, in a microwave-safe bowl, in a microwave oven on full power (100%), heat remaining chili sauce until hot, 20 to 30 seconds. Pit, peel, and slice avocado.

5. Run a knife between pie and pan rim to loosen. Remove rim and set pie on a platter. Drizzle chili sauce over hot enchilada pie. Arrange avocado slices

in a ring on pie, sprinkle with remaining jack and cotija cheeses, and garnish with cilantro sprigs. Cut into wedges to serve.

Per serving: 597 cal., 41% (243 cal.) from fat; 27 g protein; 27 g fat (12 g sat.); 66 g carbo (7.2 g fiber); 1,784 mg sodium; 56 mg chol.

Orange-scented Bizcochitos

PREP AND COOK TIME: About 1¼ hours

NOTES: Orange adds fresh appeal to these old-time favorite Southwest cookies. Lard gives them an authentic texture, but some people prefer them made with butter. To make them sparkle, lightly sprinkle coarse-ground white sugar over unbaked cookies on pan; press the sugar lightly into surface. If making cookies up to 3 days ahead, cool completely and store airtight at room temperature; freeze to store longer.

MAKES: About 3 dozen

About 3 cups **all-purpose flour**

1½ teaspoons **baking powder**

½ teaspoon **salt**

1 cup (¼ lb.) **lard** or butter, at room temperature (see notes)

¾ cup plus 2 tablespoons **sugar**

1 teaspoon **anise seeds**

1 teaspoon grated **orange** peel

1 **large egg**

¼ cup **orange juice**

½ teaspoon **ground cinnamon**

1. In a bowl, mix 3 cups flour, baking powder, and salt.

2. In a large bowl, with a mixer on high speed, beat lard, ¾ cup sugar, anise seeds, and orange peel until fluffy. Beat in egg and orange juice. Turn mixer to low and beat in dry ingredients, then beat on medium speed until dough is well blended and sticks together. Divide in half and press each half into a ball.

3. On a shallow, rimmed plate, mix remaining 2 tablespoons sugar and the cinnamon.

4. On a well-floured board, roll one ball of dough to ¼ inch thick. With a flour-dusted cookie cutter (2 to 3 in. wide), cut dough into shapes. Lightly press one side of each cookie into

cinnamon sugar. Set cookies, sugar side up, about ½ inch apart on 12- by 15-inch baking sheets (you'll need a total of five or six; bake in sequence). Gather scraps into a ball, roll out, and cut out remaining cookies. Repeat with second ball of dough.

5. Bake cookies in a 325° regular or convection oven until bottoms are golden, 8 to 10 minutes; if baking two sheets in one oven, switch their positions after 5 minutes. With a wide spatula, transfer cookies to racks to cool. Serve warm or cool.

Per cookie: 90 cal., 34% (31 cal.) from fat; 1.3 g protein; 3.4 g fat (1.3 g sat.); 13 g carbo (0.3 g fiber); 54 mg sodium; 8.9 mg chol.

Mexican Hot Chocolate

PREP AND COOK TIME: About 30 minutes

NOTES: If preparing hot chocolate through step 2 up to 1 day ahead, cool, cover, and chill; stir often in a 5- to 6-quart pan over low heat until warm, then continue with step 3.

MAKES: 8 servings

²⁄₃ cup **slivered almonds**

2 quarts **milk**

8 ounces **unsweetened chocolate**, coarsely chopped

1 cup **sugar**

1 tablespoon **vanilla**

2 teaspoons **ground cinnamon**

8 **cinnamon sticks** (each 4 to 5 in. long), optional

1. In a 5- to 6-quart pan over medium heat, stir almonds until golden, 5 to 7 minutes.

2. Add milk and chocolate to pan and stir occasionally over medium heat just until chocolate is melted (flecks are okay) and milk is hot (do not boil), 12 to 15 minutes. Add sugar, vanilla, and ground cinnamon and stir just until sugar is dissolved, about 1 minute.

3. Pour about a third of the hot milk mixture into a blender. Holding lid down with a towel, whirl until very smooth and frothy; pour into a pitcher. Repeat twice to purée remaining mixture and add to pitcher. To serve, pour hot chocolate into cups (8 to 12 oz.) and garnish with cinnamon sticks.

Per serving: 466 cal., 58% (270 cal.) from fat; 13 g protein; 30 g fat (15 g sat.); 47 g carbo (4.9 g fiber); 125 mg sodium; 34 mg chol.

christmas eve crab feed

Celebrate with ease, in coastal style, with cracked crab and artichokes

Christmas Eve can suffer from holiday excess—too many last-minute presents to wrap, two pies to bake for dessert tomorrow.... It needs a meal that accepts all that, yet turns the evening into an event in its own right, effortlessly. Northern California has the answer: crab and artichokes.

Buy the crab cooked, cleaned, and cracked and just arrange it on a platter. Boil the artichokes with pungent spices for a compatible partner. Three make-ahead sauces serve as dips for both. Long breadsticks made from baguettes add drama to the table, but if time is short, serve the skinny loaves plain. End with purchased madeleines and shell-shaped chocolate truffles to carry the theme.

Cracked Crab Platter

menu

Coastal Crab Feed

Cracked Crab Platter*

Seasoned Artichokes*

Cilantro-Lime Sauce,* Spicy Red Pepper Sauce,* and Béarnaise Cream*

Herbed Baguette Breadsticks*

Chardonnay

Chocolate Truffle Shells and Madeleines

Recipe provided

Cracked Crab Platter

PREP TIME: About 5 minutes

NOTES: Have the crabs cleaned and cracked at the market; ask for the whole back shells to garnish the platter. If assembling up to 4 hours ahead, cover platter with plastic wrap and chill. Provide crab crackers or nut crackers to break shells further, containers to hold discarded shells, and damp towels or bowls of water to clean dirty hands at the table.

MAKES: 8 servings

Rinse 6 to 8 **cooked Dungeness crabs in the shell** (about 2 lb. each; see notes) under cool running water to remove loose bits of shell; pat dry. Arrange on a large platter and lay back shells on top. Garnish with **lemon wedges**.

Per serving: 222 cal., 15% (34 cal.) from fat; 44 g protein; 3.8 g fat (0.5 g sat.); 0 g carbo; 606 mg sodium; 217 mg chol.

Seasoned Artichokes

PREP AND COOK TIME: About 1 hour

NOTES: If you don't have a 12- to 14-quart pan, cook half the artichokes at a time in a 6- to 8-quart pan. If making up to 1 day ahead, chill airtight. Arrange on a platter up to 4 hours ahead; cover with plastic wrap and chill or let stand at room temperature.

MAKES: 8 servings

3 tablespoons **white wine vinegar**

1 tablespoon **olive oil**

1 teaspoon **black peppercorns**

2 **dried bay leaves**

Cilantro-Lime Sauce is one of three sauces that do double dipping duty—for artichokes *and* crab.

8 **whole allspice**

8 **artichokes** (each 3 to 3½ in. wide and about ¾ lb.)

1. In a 12- to 14-quart pan (see notes), combine about 6 quarts water, vinegar, olive oil, peppercorns, bay leaves, and allspice. Cover and bring to a boil over high heat.

2. Meanwhile, rinse artichokes well. Slice off and discard about 1 inch from tops; trim off stems. With scissors, cut off and discard remaining thorny tips from outer leaves.

3. Add artichokes to boiling water. Return to a boil, cover, and simmer until bottoms are tender when pierced with a fork, 25 to 30 minutes. Drain and let cool. Serve cool or cold.

Per artichoke: 68 cal., 7.9% (5.4 cal.) from fat; 4.5 g protein; 0.6 g fat (0.1 g sat.); 14 g carbo (7.1 g fiber); 128 mg sodium; 0 mg chol.

Cilantro-Lime Sauce

PREP TIME: **About 10 minutes**

NOTES: If making up to 1 day ahead, chill airtight.

MAKES: About 1¼ cups

In a blender or food processor, whirl ⅓ cup **regular** or reduced-fat **mayonnaise,** 1 cup coarsely chopped **fresh cilantro,** 2 tablespoons sliced **green onion,** 1 tablespoon chopped peeled **fresh ginger,** 1 teaspoon grated **lime peel,** and 2 tablespoons **lime juice** until smooth. Pour into a bowl and whisk in ⅔ cup more mayonnaise and **salt** to taste.

Per tablespoon: 27 cal., 96% (26 cal.) from fat; 0.1 g protein; 2.9 g fat (0.4 g sat.); 0.3 g carbo (0.1 g fiber); 21 mg sodium; 2.1 mg chol.

Spicy Red Pepper Sauce

PREP TIME: **About 5 minutes**

NOTES: If making up to 1 day ahead, chill airtight.

MAKES: About 1 cup

In a blender or food processor, whirl ½ cup drained **canned peeled roasted red peppers,** ½ cup **plain nonfat yogurt,** ½ teaspoon **hot chili flakes,** and 1 peeled clove **garlic** until smooth. Scrape into a bowl and whisk in ¼ cup **regular** or reduced-fat **mayonnaise** and **salt** to taste.

Per tablespoon: 31 cal., 77% (24 cal.) from fat; 0.4 g protein; 2.7 g fat (0.4 g sat.); 1.2 g carbo (0 g fiber); 33 mg sodium; 2.2 mg chol.

Béarnaise Cream

PREP AND COOK TIME: About 15 minutes

MAKES: About 1¼ cups

1. In a 1- to 1½-quart pan over medium heat, stir ½ cup minced **shallots,** 3 tablespoons **white wine vinegar,** and 1 tablespoon finely chopped **fresh tarragon** or 1 teaspoon dried tarragon until liquid has evaporated, 3 to 4 minutes. Scrape into a bowl. Let cool to room temperature, 3 to 5 minutes.

2. Add 1 cup **reduced-fat** or regular **sour cream,** 2 tablespoons **Dijon mustard,** and 1 tablespoon **white wine vinegar** to shallot mixture and mix well. Add **salt** to taste.

Per tablespoon: 25 cal., 56% (14 cal.) from fat; 0.9 g protein; 1.6 g fat (0.8 g sat.); 1.6 g carbo (0 g fiber); 43 mg sodium; 4 mg chol.

Herbed Baguette Breadsticks

PREP AND COOK TIME: About 30 minutes

NOTES: If slender baguettes aren't available, buy thicker ones; cut them in half lengthwise, then cut each half lengthwise into 1-inch-thick wedges.

MAKES: 12 breadsticks; 8 to 12 servings

3 **baguettes** (each 20 to 24 in. long, 2 in. wide, and ½ lb.)

½ cup (¼ lb.) **butter** or margarine, melted

¼ cup chopped **parsley**

1 teaspoon **Italian dried herb blend** (or use ¼ teaspoon *each* dried thyme, dried basil, dried oregano, and dried rosemary)

2 cloves **garlic,** peeled and pressed or minced

1. Cut two 18- by 22-inch sheets of heavy-duty foil; lay each on a 14- by 17-inch baking sheet (the foil will extend well beyond the edges of the sheets).

2. With a serrated knife, cut baguettes lengthwise into quarters. In a small bowl, mix butter, parsley, herb blend, and garlic. Brush mixture lightly over cut surfaces of bread. Lay breadsticks slightly apart on foil-lined sheets (bread will extend beyond edges of sheets).

3. Bake in a 400° regular or convection oven until the breadsticks are lightly browned, 8 to 12 minutes. Serve them warm.

Per breadstick: 173 cal., 46% (79 cal.) from fat; 3.5 g protein; 8.8 g fat (5 g sat.); 20 g carbo (1.1 g fiber); 310 mg sodium; 21 mg chol.

Regional Christmas: **Rocky Mountains**

christmas in the mountains

Take tradition to new heights this year with a rib roast and all the trimmings

When you find yourself in a place where you don't have to dream of a white Christmas, tradition seems just right for dinner: Snow-shrouded mountains make a fitting backdrop for the table-top drama of a grand rib roast. We've crusted ours with lemon and pepper, and we roasted small potatoes and shallots on the side. Surround the main course with the traditional colors of Christmas—salmon caviar on sour cream to set the mood, greens with cranberries to start the meal, green beans with cherry tomatoes to set off the roast, and an elegant *bûche de Noël* to end the feast.

Lemon- and Pepper-crusted Prime Rib Roast with Root Vegetables

menu

Mile-High Christmas Dinner

Salmon Caviar on Cream*

Sparkling Wine or Champagne

Mixed Greens with
Cranberries and Pine Nuts*

Lemon- and Pepper-crusted
Prime Rib Roast with Root Vegetables*

Green Beans
with Sautéed Cherry Tomatoes*

Dinner Rolls

Cabernet Sauvignon

Bûche de Noël
or your favorite festive dessert

* Recipe provided

Salmon Caviar on Cream

PREP TIME: About 10 minutes

NOTES: Look for fresh salmon caviar *(ikura)* at Japanese markets and specialty food stores. Or use canned salmon caviar.

MAKES: 8 to 10 servings

1. Gently rinse ½ pound **fresh salmon caviar** in a fine wire strainer under cold water; drain thoroughly.

2. Spread ¾ cup **sour cream** in the bottom of a small, shallow bowl. Mound caviar over cream and sprinkle with 1 tablespoon thinly sliced **fresh chives.** Nestle dish in a bowl of ice.

3. To eat, spoon caviar and sour cream onto toasted thin **white bread** slices, cut diagonally into quarters to make triangles (you'll need about 40 total, from 10 slices of bread) or onto Belgian endive leaves (about 40 total), separated, rinsed, and crisped.

Per serving: 131 cal., 56% (74 cal.) from fat; 7.5 g protein; 8.2 g fat (2.3 g sat.); 9.3 g carbo (0 g fiber); 440 mg sodium; 141 mg chol.

Mixed Greens with Cranberries and Pine Nuts

PREP AND COOK TIME: About 15 minutes

NOTES: If toasting nuts (step 1) up to 1 day ahead, cool and wrap airtight; mix dried cranberries into salad with nuts in step 3.

MAKES: 8 to 10 servings

½ cup **pine nuts**

½ cup **dried cranberries**

6 tablespoons **white wine vinegar**

3 tablespoons **salad oil**

¾ teaspoon **vanilla**

¼ teaspoon fresh-grated or -ground **nutmeg**

4 quarts **salad mix** (1¼ lb.), rinsed and crisped

Salt and **pepper**

1. In an 8- to 10-inch frying pan over medium heat, stir or shake pine nuts until pale gold, 3 to 5 minutes. Remove from heat and stir in dried cranberries.

2. In a large bowl, mix vinegar, oil, vanilla, and nutmeg.

3. Add salad mix and pine nut–cranberry mixture to bowl. Lift with two spoons to mix with dressing. Add salt and pepper to taste.

Per serving: 109 cal., 64% (70 cal.) from fat; 2.3 g protein; 7.8 g fat (1.1 g sat.); 8.2 g carbo (1.8 g fiber); 13 mg sodium; 0 mg chol.

Lemon- and Pepper-crusted Prime Rib Roast with Root Vegetables

PREP AND COOK TIME: About 3 hours

NOTES: Consider a buffalo prime rib roast as an alternative to beef. It looks and tastes much the same but the meat is much leaner. For juicy results, don't roast buffalo past medium-rare. For a half-roast, which weighs about 6 pounds and makes 6 to 8 servings, start checking for doneness after about 1½ hours of roasting. See box at right for a source.

MAKES: 8 to 10 servings

2½ pounds **red thin-skinned potatoes** (1½ in. wide), scrubbed

1 pound **shallots** (1 in. wide), rinsed

1 tablespoon **olive oil**

1 **center-cut bone-in beef rib roast** (about 8 lb.; see notes)

About 2 tablespoons **coarse-ground pepper**

1 tablespoon grated **lemon** peel

2 teaspoons **dried thyme**

About ½ teaspoon **salt**

3 cloves **garlic**, peeled and minced or pressed

½ cup **tequila** or fat-skimmed beef broth

1½ cups fat-skimmed **beef broth**

1 tablespoon chopped **parsley**

1. In a 12- by 17-inch roasting pan (at least 2 in. deep), mix potatoes and shallots (unpeeled) with olive oil to coat. Push vegetables to edge of pan and set a V-shaped rack (or flat rack about 10 in. square) in the center; mound vegetables if necessary.

2. Rinse beef and pat dry; trim layer of fat to ¼ inch thick.

3. In a small bowl, mix 2 tablespoons pepper, lemon peel, thyme, ½ teaspoon salt, and garlic. Rub mixture all over beef. Set roast, fat side up, on rack in pan.

4. Roast in a 325° regular or convection oven until a thermometer inserted in center of thickest part of meat registers 135° for medium-rare, about 2¼ hours. For medium-well, roast meat until it reaches 145°, about 2½ hours.

5. Transfer roast to a board or platter. With a slotted spoon, lift vegetables

Where buffalo still roam

You need to order a buffalo roast at least 3 days ahead of time. A whole, bone-in prime rib roast (also called an export rib) weighs 12 to 15 pounds; a half-roast weighs about 6 pounds. The latter costs about $150—pricey, but it makes a memorable dinner. **Native Game Company,** 308 Walnut St., Brighton, CO, 80601; www.nativegame.bigstep.com.

from pan and mound in a bowl or arrange alongside beef. Keeping meat and vegetables warm, let rest 5 to 10 minutes.

6. Meanwhile, tilt roasting pan to skim fat off drippings and discard. Add tequila to pan and set over medium heat. When tequila is warm, remove from heat (and away from any vent, fan, or flammables) and ignite with a match. When flames subside, add broth to pan and bring to a boil over high heat, scraping browned bits free. Pour into a bowl.

7. Sprinkle vegetables with parsley. Carve roast. Serve with pan drippings to spoon over meat and vegetables. Add salt and pepper to taste.

Per serving: 1,035 cal., 64% (666 cal.) from fat; 56 g protein; 74 g fat (30 g sat.); 28 g carbo (2.6 g fiber); 287 mg sodium; 201 mg chol.

Green Beans with Sautéed Cherry Tomatoes

PREP AND COOK TIME: About 40 minutes

NOTES: Rinse and trim beans and tomatoes up to 1 day ahead; cover and chill. Start heating water about 10 minutes before meat is done; cook beans and tomatoes while beef rests.

MAKES: 8 to 10 servings

1. Rinse 2 pounds **green beans;** remove and discard ends and any strings. In a 6- to 8-quart pan over high heat, bring about 3 quarts water to a boil. Add beans, cover, and cook until tender-crisp to bite, 4 to 5 minutes. Drain beans, pour into a serving dish, and keep warm. Dry pan.

2. Meanwhile, rinse 2 cups **cherry tomatoes;** remove and discard stems. Set pan over high heat and add 2 tablespoons **olive oil;** 1 clove **garlic,** peeled and pressed or minced; tomatoes; and 1 teaspoon **dried basil.** Stir until tomatoes are hot, about 3 minutes. Pour over beans. Add **salt** and **pepper** to taste.

Per serving: 54 cal., 48% (26 cal.) from fat; 1.7 g protein; 2.9 g fat (0.4 g sat.); 6.8 g carbo (1.7 g fiber); 6.7 mg sodium; 0 mg chol. ◆

a Western cookie

For countless families worldwide, cookies define holiday tradition. We wanted to know which ones are an indispensable part of holiday celebrations here in the West, so last year we asked. Readers responded from every part of the West, sending us hundreds of their favorite recipes—cookies that they, relatives, or friends had created.

They gave us cookies as diverse as the West itself, reflecting influences from Europe, Asia, and Central and South America. One reader remembers making bizcochitos with her mother in Santa Fe; another had obtained a recipe for Chinese almond cookies from her husband's shipmate in World War II. But in true Western fashion, some of the recipes we received weren't old family traditions at all but thoroughly modern innovations.

Awarding the prizes we had offered for the best of the lot was daunting. But we assembled a crack team of cookie tasters and rated from our hearts. We offer you 20 of our favorites here, hoping they'll become part of your own holiday tradition.

GRAND PRIZE WINNER

Coconut-Cranberry Chews
Nancy Jamison, Woodside, CA

Nancy Jamison was right when she wrote us that these cookies are addictive. We loved their combination of coconut, cranberries, and orange. In fact, these straightforward, tasty rounds are everything a holiday cookie should be. The mixture will look dry until it comes together as a dough. If it's too crumbly to form into balls, the dough needs to be mixed longer; it should be a smooth, homogenous mass.

PREP AND COOK TIME: About 1 hour

MAKES: About 6 dozen cookies

> About 1½ cups (¾ lb.) **butter** or margarine, at room temperature
> 2 cups **sugar**
> 1 tablespoon grated **orange** peel
> 2 teaspoons **vanilla**
> 3¼ cups **all-purpose flour**
> 1 teaspoon **baking powder**
> ¼ teaspoon **salt**
> 1½ cups **dried cranberries**
> 1½ cups **sweetened flaked dried coconut**

1. In a large bowl, with a mixer on medium speed, beat 1½ cups butter, sugar, orange peel, and vanilla until smooth.

2. In a medium bowl, mix flour, baking powder, and salt. Add to butter mixture, stir to mix, then beat on low speed until dough comes together, about 5 minutes (see note at left). Mix in cranberries and coconut.

3. Shape dough into 1-inch balls and place about 2 inches apart on buttered 12- by 15-inch baking sheets.

4. Bake in a 350° regular or convection oven until cookie edges just begin to brown, 8 to 11 minutes (shorter baking time will yield a chewier cookie; longer baking time will yield a crisper cookie). If baking two sheets at once in one oven, switch their positions halfway through baking. Let cookies cool on sheets for 5 minutes, then use a wide spatula to transfer to racks to cool completely.

Per cookie: 92 cal., 45% (41 cal.) from fat; 0.7 g protein; 4.5 g fat (2.8 g sat.); 12 g carbo (0.4 g fiber); 58 mg sodium; 10 mg chol.

RUNNERS-UP

Louisiana Pecan Balls
Heather Allen, Aptos, CA

Heather Allen's parents made these tender, melt-in-your-mouth cookies every year; now she makes them with her children. We thought they were the best of their kind.

PREP AND COOK TIME: About 45 minutes

MAKES: About 28 cookies

> About 1 cup (½ lb.) **butter**, at room temperature
> 2 cups **powdered sugar**
> 2 teaspoons **vanilla**
> 2 cups **all-purpose flour**
> ¼ teaspoon **baking powder**
> 1 cup chopped **pecans** (about 4 oz.)

1. In a large bowl, with a mixer on medium speed, beat 1 cup butter, ½ cup powdered sugar, and vanilla until smooth.

2. In a medium bowl, mix flour and baking powder. Add to butter mixture, stir to mix, then beat until well blended. Stir in pecans.

3. Shape dough into 1-inch balls and place about 1 inch apart on buttered 12- by 15-inch baking sheets.

4. Bake in a 300° regular or convection oven until cookies are pale golden brown, about 25 minutes. If baking two sheets at once in one oven, switch their positions halfway through baking. Let cookies stand on sheets until cool enough to handle.

5. Place remaining 1½ cups powdered sugar in a shallow bowl. Roll warm

collection

Twenty original recipes

that affirm our region's

rich tradition and

innovation, baking

and otherwise

By Charity Ferreira

Photographs by
James Carrier

Food styling by
Karen Shinto

Apricot Buttons
p. 254

Gingerbread
Cookies
p. 252

Chocolate–
Macadamia
Nut Clusters
p. 252

Cranberry
Rugelach
p. 249

Napoleon's
Hats, below

Pfeffernüsse,
below

Louisiana
Pecan Balls
p. 246

About ½ cup (¼ lb.) **butter** or margarine, at room temperature

2 cups firmly packed **brown sugar**

2 **large eggs**

1½ teaspoons **baking soda**

3¼ cups **all-purpose flour**

½ teaspoon **ground cinnamon**

½ teaspoon **ground nutmeg**

½ teaspoon **ground cloves**

¼ teaspoon **ground ginger**

½ teaspoon **salt**

1½ cups chopped **pecans** (6 oz.)

¼ cup finely chopped **candied citron**

1. In a large bowl, with a mixer on medium speed, beat ½ cup butter and the brown sugar until well blended. Add eggs and beat until smooth. In a small bowl, stir baking soda in 1 tablespoon hot water until dissolved; beat into butter mixture.

2. In a medium bowl, mix flour, cinnamon, nutmeg, cloves, ginger, and salt. Add to butter mixture, stir to mix, then beat until well blended. Stir in pecans and citron.

3. Divide dough in half and shape each portion into a log about 11 inches long and 1½ inches in diameter. Wrap logs separately in waxed paper and freeze until firm enough to slice, at least 1 hour.

4. Unwrap dough. Cut logs crosswise into ¼-inch-thick rounds and place about 1 inch apart on buttered 12- by 15-inch baking sheets.

5. Bake cookies in a 350° regular or convection oven until lightly browned, 8 to 12 minutes; if baking two sheets at once in one oven, switch their positions halfway through baking. Let cookies cool on sheets for 5 minutes, then use a wide spatula to transfer to racks to cool completely.

Per cookie: 76 cal., 37% (28 cal.) from fat; 0.9 g protein; 3.1 g fat (1 g sat.); 11 g carbo (0.3 g fiber); 63 mg sodium; 9.5 mg chol.

Alfajores de Dulce de Leche (Caramel Sandwich Cookies)

Paula Austin, Portland

Paula Austin made these flaky, caramel-filled Argentine sandwich cookies for her sister-in-law's wedding brunch; they drew rave reviews. Dulce de leche, a thick, rich caramel made with sweetened milk, is sold in Mexican markets and some well-stocked supermarkets. If it's unavailable, use a thick caramel sauce or ice cream topping.

PREP AND COOK TIME: About 1½ hours, plus at least 30 minutes to chill

MAKES: 18 to 25 sandwiches

---

cookies in powdered sugar to coat all over; discard remaining sugar. Set cookies on racks to cool completely.

Per cookie: 143 cal., 59% (85 cal.) from fat; 1.3 g protein; 9.4 g fat (4.4 g sat.); 14 g carbo (0.5 g fiber); 73 mg sodium; 18 mg chol.

Napoleon's Hats

Ellen Taylor, Rathdrum, ID

These almond-filled pastries are shaped like three-cornered hats—thus the name. The smell of them baking always reminds Ellen Taylor of Christmas and her grandmother, who always filled the house with aromas of German baked goods.

PREP AND COOK TIME: About 1½ hours

MAKES: About 3½ dozen cookies

About ¾ cup (⅜ lb.) **butter** or margarine, at room temperature

⅓ cup **granulated sugar**

1 **large egg**

About 2 cups **all-purpose flour**

1 cup **powdered sugar**

⅜ cup **almond paste** (3½ oz.)

2 **large egg** whites

1. In a large bowl, with a mixer on medium speed, beat ¾ cup butter and granulated sugar until smooth. Add egg and beat until well blended. Stir in 2 cups flour, then beat just until dough comes together.

2. In a food processor, whirl powdered sugar and almond paste until blended. In a deep bowl, with a mixer on high speed, beat egg whites until they hold soft peaks. Gently stir in almond mixture until well blended.

3. On a lightly floured surface, with a floured rolling pin, roll about half the dough at a time to about 1/16 inch thick. With a floured, 2- to 3-inch round cutter, cut out cookies. Place about 1 inch apart on buttered 12- by 15-inch baking sheets. Place about 1 teaspoon almond mixture in the center of each round, then fold edges over filling toward the center to form a three-cornered hat shape. With your fingers, pinch corners to seal. Gather excess dough into a ball, reroll, and cut out more cookies; fill and fold. Repeat to roll remaining dough and fill and shape cookies.

4. Bake cookies in a 325° regular or convection oven until golden brown, 18 to 20 minutes. If baking two sheets at once in one oven, switch their positions halfway through baking. Let cookies cool on sheets for 5 minutes, then use a wide spatula to transfer to racks to cool completely.

Per cookie: 83 cal., 46% (38 cal.) from fat; 1.2 g protein; 4.2 g fat (2.2 g sat.); 10 g carbo (0.2 g fiber); 39 mg sodium; 14 mg chol.

Pfeffernüsse

Suzanne Fossett, Albuquerque

Suzanne Fossett's German grandmother never wrote down the recipe for her favorite spice cookies; it took Suzanne and her mother years to re-create the cookie they remembered.

PREP AND COOK TIME: About 1 hour, plus at least 1 hour to chill

MAKES: About 6 dozen cookies

About 1 cup (1/2 lb.) **butter** or margarine, at room temperature

2/3 cup **sugar**

2 **large egg** yolks

1 **large egg**

3 tablespoons **dark rum**

1 teaspoon **vanilla**

About 2 cups **all-purpose flour**

1 cup **cornstarch**

1 teaspoon **baking powder**

About 1 3/4 cups **dulce de leche** or caramel sauce (see note preceding)

About 1 cup **sweetened flaked dried coconut**

1. In a large bowl, with a mixer on medium speed, beat 1 cup butter and sugar until smooth. Add egg yolks, whole egg, rum, and vanilla and beat until well blended.

2. In a medium bowl, mix 2 cups flour, cornstarch, and baking powder. Stir into butter mixture, then beat until well blended. Divide dough in half, press each half into a disk, wrap in plastic wrap, and freeze until firm, about 30 minutes.

3. Unwrap dough. On a lightly floured surface, with a floured rolling pin, roll one disk at a time to about 1/8 inch thick. With a floured, 2- to 3-inch round cutter, cut out cookies. Place about 1 inch apart on buttered 12- by 15-inch baking sheets. Gather excess dough into a ball, reroll, and cut out remaining cookies.

4. Bake in a 350° regular or convection oven until cookie edges just begin to brown, about 10 minutes. If baking two sheets at once in one oven, switch their positions halfway through baking. Let the cookies cool on sheets for 5 minutes, then use a wide spatula to transfer them to racks to cool completely.

5. Turn half the cookies bottom side up and spread each with about 1 tablespoon dulce de leche. Top with remaining cookies, bottom side down. Place coconut in a shallow bowl. Gently squeeze each sandwich until filling begins to ooze out sides, then roll edges in coconut.

Per sandwich: 229 cal., 36% (83 cal.) from fat; 2.1 g protein; 9.2 g fat (5.7 g sat.); 35 g carbo (0.5 g fiber); 188 mg sodium; 46 mg chol.

Chocolate Therapy Cookies

Debbie Dahlin, Hilmar, CA

Debbie Dahlin writes that the salubrious benefits promised by the name of these ultrarich chocolate–chocolate chip cookies come not just from eating them but also from baking them.

PREP AND COOK TIME: About 30 minutes
MAKES: About 2 1/2 dozen cookies

8 ounces **semisweet chocolate,** chopped

About 6 tablespoons **butter** or margarine

3/4 cup **sugar**

1 **large egg**

2 teaspoons **vanilla**

2/3 cup **all-purpose flour**

1/2 teaspoon **baking soda**

1/2 teaspoon **baking powder**

1/4 teaspoon **salt**

1 cup **semisweet chocolate chips** (6 oz.)

1. In a large bowl set over (but not touching) barely simmering water, stir chopped semisweet chocolate and butter often until chocolate is melted and mixture is smooth, about 5 minutes. Remove bowl from over water and, with a whisk or a mixer on medium speed, beat in the sugar, egg, and vanilla until well blended.

2. In a medium bowl, mix flour, baking soda, baking powder, and salt. Add to chocolate mixture and stir until well blended. Stir in chocolate chips.

3. Drop dough in 1-tablespoon portions 3 inches apart onto buttered 12- by 15-inch baking sheets.

4. Bake in a 350° regular or convection oven just until cookies are set on the edges but still slightly soft in the center, 7 to 10 minutes; if baking two sheets at once in one oven, switch their positions halfway through baking. Let cookies cool for 5 minutes, then use a wide spatula to transfer to racks to cool completely.

Per cookie: 118 cal., 50% (59 cal.) from fat; 1 g protein; 6.6 g fat (3.9 g sat.); 16 g carbo (0.8 g fiber); 76 mg sodium; 14 mg chol.

■ HONORABLE MENTION

Cranberry Rugelach

Jeannie Lee, Marin County, CA

A trip to New York inspired Jeannie Lee to develop this cranberry-filled variation on the favorite flaky pastry. Use any leftover cranberry filling as you would a cranberry relish or jam.

PREP AND COOK TIME: About 2 1/2 hours, plus at least 45 minutes to chill
MAKES: 4 dozen cookies

About 1 cup (1/2 lb.) **butter,** at room temperature

6 ounces **cream cheese,** at room temperature

2 teaspoons **vanilla**

2/3 cup **granulated sugar**

1/4 cup firmly packed **brown sugar**

About 2 1/4 cups **all-purpose flour**

2 teaspoons **ground cinnamon**

1/2 teaspoon **ground cloves**

Cranberry Filling (recipe follows)

1/3 cup chopped **white chocolate** (2 oz.)

1/3 cup chopped **walnuts**

1 **large egg** yolk

1 tablespoon **milk**

1. In a large bowl, with a mixer on medium speed, beat 1 cup butter, cream cheese, and vanilla until smooth. Add 1/3 cup granulated sugar and the brown sugar and beat until very smooth.

2. In a medium bowl, mix 2 1/4 cups flour, 1 teaspoon cinnamon, and cloves. Add to butter mixture, stir to mix, then beat until well blended. Divide dough into thirds and flatten each into a disk. Wrap each in plastic wrap and freeze until firm, about 45 minutes.

3. With a floured rolling pin, on a lightly floured surface, roll one disk at a time into a 1/8-inch-thick round about 12 inches in diameter. Spread each evenly with about 1/2 cup Cranberry Filling, then sprinkle with a third of the chopped white chocolate and a third of the walnuts. Cut each round into 16 wedges. Starting at the wide end, roll each wedge around filling; bend each roll slightly into a crescent. Place cookies about 1 inch apart on buttered 12- by 15-inch baking sheets.

4. In a small bowl, beat egg yolk and milk to blend. In another small bowl, mix remaining 1/3 cup granulated sugar and 1 teaspoon cinnamon. Brush cookies lightly with egg mixture and sprinkle with cinnamon sugar; discard any remaining egg mixture and save cinnamon sugar for other uses.

5. Bake cookies in a 350° regular or convection oven until golden brown, 20 to 25 minutes; if baking two sheets at once in one oven, switch their positions halfway through baking. Let cookies cool on sheets for 5 minutes, then use a wide spatula to transfer to racks to cool completely.

Per cookie: 111 cal., 50% (55 cal.) from fat; 1.2 g protein; 6.1 g fat (3.6 g sat.); 13 g carbo (0.4 g fiber); 53 mg sodium; 19 mg chol.

CRANBERRY FILLING. In a food processor, whirl 2 1/2 cups **fresh cranberries** (sorted and rinsed) or thawed frozen cranberries, 3 tablespoons minced **fresh ginger,** and 1 **orange,** rinsed and

Chinese Almond
Cookies, below

Chocolate Chip
Meringues, below

PREP AND COOK TIME: About 1 hour
MAKES: About 3½ dozen meringues

- 2 **large egg** whites
- ¼ teaspoon **cream of tartar**
- ⅔ cup **sugar**
- ¼ teaspoon **almond extract**
- 1 cup finely chopped **semisweet chocolate** (6 oz.) or miniature semisweet chocolate chips

1. In a large bowl, with a mixer on high speed, beat egg whites with cream of tartar until thick and foamy. Gradually add sugar and continue to beat until mixture holds stiff, shiny peaks.

2. With a spatula, gently stir in almond extract and chopped chocolate. Spoon ½-tablespoon portions into 1-inch-wide mounds (or with a pastry bag fitted with a ½-inch plain or star tip, pipe 1-inch-wide mounds) about 1 inch apart onto cooking parchment–lined 12- by 15-inch baking sheets.

3. Bake meringues in a 275° regular or convection oven until dry and firm to touch on the outside and almost dry inside (break one open to test), 30 to 35 minutes; if baking two sheets at once in one oven, switch their positions halfway through baking. Let cool for 5 minutes on sheets, then slide a spatula underneath meringues and transfer to racks to cool completely.

Per meringue: 33 cal., 33% (11 cal.) from fat; 0.3 g protein; 1.2 g fat (0.7 g sat.); 5.8 g carbo (0.2 g fiber); 3.1 mg sodium; 0 mg chol.

Orange-Anise Bizcochitos

Mary Castañeda Balzer, Santa Cruz, CA

These crisp sugar cookies are Mary Castañeda Balzer's version of ones her mother made every Christmas in New Mexico. Lightly crush the anise seeds with a mortar and pestle or chop roughly with a knife. Use 2- to 2½-inch cookie cutters.

PREP AND COOK TIME: About 1 hour, plus at least 30 minutes to chill
MAKES: 7 to 8 dozen cookies

- ¾ cup **solid vegetable shortening**, at room temperature
- 1 cup **sugar**
- 1 **large egg**
- 1 tablespoon grated **orange** peel
- ¼ cup **orange juice**
  - About 2½ cups **all-purpose flour**
- 1½ tablespoons **anise seeds**, crushed (see note preceding)
- 1 teaspoon **baking powder**
- ¼ teaspoon **salt**
- 1 teaspoon **ground cinnamon**

quartered (seeds discarded), until smooth. Scrape into a 3- to 4-quart pan and add ½ cup **sugar**; stir often over medium heat until sugar is dissolved and mixture is reduced to about 2 cups, about 10 minutes. Chill until cool, about 30 minutes.

Chinese Almond Cookies

Louise Pariani, Novato, CA

The recipe for these crisp almond cookies was given to Louise Pariani nearly 50 years ago by Ah Lee Wong of Chicago, who was a Navy shipmate of her husband's during World War II.

PREP AND COOK TIME: About 45 minutes
MAKES: About 4 dozen

- About 1 cup (½ lb.) **butter** or margarine, at room temperature
- 1 cup **sugar**
- 1 **large egg**
- ½ teaspoon **almond extract**
- 2½ cups **all-purpose flour**
- 1 teaspoon **baking powder**
- 1 **large egg** yolk
- 1 tablespoon **milk**
- ⅓ cup **blanched whole almonds**
- 2 tablespoons **sesame seeds**

1. In a large bowl, with a mixer on medium speed, beat 1 cup butter and

sugar until smooth. Add whole egg and almond extract and beat until well blended. Add flour and baking powder; stir to mix, then beat until well blended.

2. Shape dough into 1-inch balls, flatten each slightly, and place about 1 inch apart on buttered 12- by 15-inch baking sheets.

3. In a small bowl, beat egg yolk with milk to blend. Brush cookies lightly with egg mixture; discard any remaining. Press an almond into the center of each cookie and sprinkle with about ⅛ teaspoon sesame seeds.

4. Bake cookies in a 325° regular or convection oven until lightly browned, 15 to 20 minutes; if baking two sheets at once in one oven, switch their positions halfway through baking. Let cookies cool on sheets for 5 minutes, then use a wide spatula to transfer to racks to cool completely.

Per cookie: 86 cal., 51% (44 cal.) from fat; 1.2 g protein; 4.9 g fat (2.6 g sat.); 9.4 g carbo (0.3 g fiber); 52 mg sodium; 19 mg chol.

Chocolate Chip Meringues

Patricia Buckholz, Sun City West, AZ

Patricia Buckholz calls these ethereal cookies "forgotten meringues" because she turns off her oven and leaves them there to cool overnight.

White Chocolate–
Raspberry Slices
p. 252

Alfajores de Dulce de Leche (Caramel Sandwich Cookies) p. 248

Mocha-Marmalade
Shortbread Bars,
at right

Royal Raspberry
Bars, below

2. Bake crust in a 325° regular or convection oven until edges begin to brown, 15 to 18 minutes. Let cool about 5 minutes, then spread jam evenly over warm crust.

3. In a large bowl, with a mixer on high speed, whip egg whites and cream of tartar until thick and foamy. Gradually add ²⁄₃ cup sugar and continue to whip until mixture holds soft, shiny peaks. With a spatula, spread meringue evenly over jam.

4. Bake until meringue is lightly browned, about 20 minutes. Let cool 5 minutes, then cut into 24 bars. Let cool completely, then use a wide spatula to remove bars from pan.

Per bar: 158 cal., 39% (61 cal.) from fat; 2 g protein; 6.8 g fat (4.3 g sat.); 23 g carbo (0.9 g fiber); 124 mg sodium; 16 mg chol.

Mocha-Marmalade Shortbread Bars

Jonniepat Mobley, Los Osos, CA

We loved the combination of chocolate, orange, and coffee in this bar from Jonniepat Mobley, who came up with the cookie when she wanted to make something special for holiday guests.

PREP AND COOK TIME: About ½ hour, plus ½ hour to chill

MAKES: 2 dozen bars

- ½ cup (¼ lb.) **butter** or margarine, at room temperature
- ¾ cup **sugar**
- 1 **large egg** yolk
- 1 cup **all-purpose flour**
- 1½ tablespoons **finely ground coffee**
- ½ teaspoon **baking powder**
- ¼ teaspoon **salt**
- ¾ cup **orange marmalade**
- 6 ounces **semisweet chocolate,** chopped, or 1 cup semisweet chocolate chips
- 3 tablespoons **whipping cream**

1. In a large bowl, with a mixer on medium speed, beat butter and sugar until smooth. Add egg yolk and beat until well blended.

2. In a medium bowl, mix flour, ground coffee, baking powder, and salt. Stir into butter mixture, then beat until well blended. Press dough level in bottom of a 9- by 13-inch baking pan.

3. Bake crust in a 325° regular or convection oven until lightly browned, 15 to 18 minutes. Spread the warm crust with marmalade, then let cool completely.

1. In a large bowl, with a mixer on medium speed, beat shortening and ¾ cup sugar until smooth. Add egg, orange peel, and orange juice and beat just until combined.

2. In a medium bowl, mix 2½ cups flour, anise seeds, baking powder, and salt. Add to shortening mixture, stir to mix, then beat until well blended. Divide dough in half and flatten each half into a disk. Wrap each disk tightly in plastic wrap and freeze until firm, about 30 minutes.

3. Unwrap dough. On a lightly floured surface, with a floured rolling pin, roll one disk at a time to about ⅛ inch thick. With floured cookie cutters, cut dough into shapes and place about 1 inch apart on buttered 12- by 15-inch baking sheets. Gather excess dough into a ball, reroll, and cut out remaining cookies.

4. In a small bowl, mix remaining ¼ cup sugar and the cinnamon. Sprinkle about ⅛ teaspoon of the mixture over each cookie; save any remaining cinnamon sugar for other uses.

5. Bake cookies in a 350° regular or convection oven just until edges are golden, 10 to 12 minutes; if baking two sheets at once in one oven, switch their positions halfway through baking. Let cookies cool on sheets for 5 minutes,

then use a wide spatula to transfer to racks to cool completely.

Per cookie: 37 cal., 41% (15 cal.) from fat; 0.4 g protein; 1.7 g fat (0.4 g sat.); 4.8 g carbo (0.1 g fiber); 12 mg sodium; 2.3 mg chol.

Royal Raspberry Bars

Phyllis Ciardo, Albany, CA

Phyllis Ciardo developed her own rich and chewy version of the meringue-topped bars she remembers her mother baking every Christmas.

PREP AND COOK TIME: About 1 hour

MAKES: 2 dozen bars

- 1¼ cup **rolled oats**
- 1¼ cups **all-purpose flour**
- ¾ cup **sweetened flaked dried coconut**
- ¼ cup plus ²⁄₃ cup **sugar**
- ½ teaspoon **salt**
- ¾ cup (⅜ lb.) **butter** or margarine, melted
- ¾ cup **raspberry jam**
- 3 **large egg** whites
- ¼ teaspoon **cream of tartar**

1. In a bowl, mix oats, flour, coconut, ¼ cup sugar, and salt. Add melted butter and stir until well blended. Press dough level in bottom of a 9- by 13-inch baking pan.

4. Meanwhile, in a heatproof bowl set over (but not touching) barely simmering water in a pan, stir chocolate and cream often until chocolate is melted and mixture is smooth. Spread evenly over marmalade and chill until chocolate mixture is firm to touch, about 30 minutes. Cut into 24 bars.

Per bar: 144 cal., 42% (61 cal.) from fat; 1 g protein; 6.8 g fat (4.1 g sat.); 21 g carbo (0.6 g fiber); 80 mg sodium; 21 mg chol.

White Chocolate–Raspberry Slices

Cynthia Monroe, Manchester, CA

Cynthia Monroe won a blue ribbon at the Mendocino County fair for these very pretty but easy-to-make cookies.

PREP AND COOK TIME: About 45 minutes, plus about 1 hour to cool
MAKES: 3 dozen cookies

About 1/2 cup (1/4 lb.) **butter** or margarine, at room temperature
1/4 cup **sugar**
1 teaspoon **vanilla**
About 1 1/4 cups **all-purpose flour**
1/4 cup **raspberry jam**
2 ounces **white chocolate**, chopped

1. In a large bowl, with a mixer on medium speed, beat 1/2 cup butter, sugar, and vanilla until smooth. Stir in 1 1/4 cups flour, then beat until dough comes together.

2. Divide dough into thirds. On a lightly floured surface, with the palms of your hands, roll each portion into a 9-inch-long rope about 1 inch thick. Place ropes 3 inches apart on a buttered 12- by 15-inch baking sheet. Press your finger into dough to make 1/2-inch-wide indentations at about 1-inch intervals along each rope. Spoon about 1/4 teaspoon jam into each indentation.

3. Bake ropes in a 350° regular or convection oven until edges are lightly browned, 12 to 15 minutes. Let cool on baking sheet.

4. Place white chocolate in a plastic sandwich bag, pushing to one corner; secure bag just above chocolate with a twist-tie or knot. Immerse corner of bag in a cup of hot water until chocolate is melted. Dry outside of bag, then, with scissors, cut off the tip of the corner. Squeeze bag to drizzle white chocolate decoratively across ropes. Chill until chocolate is firm to touch, about 1 hour, then cut each rope diagonally into 12 slices.

Per cookie: 59 cal., 49% (29 cal.) from fat; 0.6 g protein; 3.2 g fat (2 g sat.); 7.1 g carbo (0.1 g fiber); 30 mg sodium; 7.4 mg chol.

Nutmeg Sugar Cookies

Elaine Doubleday, Soquel, CA

Elaine Doubleday is famous among her family and friends for making these unusually crisp, delicately flavored sugar cookies.

PREP AND COOK TIME: About 45 minutes, plus at least 1 hour to chill
MAKES: About 3 dozen cookies

About 1/2 cup (1/4 lb.) **butter** or margarine, at room temperature
1/2 cup **granulated sugar**
1/2 cup **powdered sugar**
1/2 cup **salad oil**
1 **large egg**
1/2 teaspoon **vanilla**
About 2 cups **all-purpose flour**
1/2 teaspoon **baking soda**
1/2 teaspoon **ground nutmeg**
1/4 teaspoon **salt**

1. In a large bowl, with a mixer on medium speed, beat 1/2 cup butter, granulated sugar, and powdered sugar until smooth. Add oil, egg, and vanilla and beat until well blended.

2. In a medium bowl, mix 2 cups flour, baking soda, nutmeg, and salt. Stir into butter mixture, then beat until well blended. Cover bowl with plastic wrap and freeze until dough is firm, about 1 hour.

3. Shape dough into 1-inch balls and place about 2 inches apart on buttered 12- by 15-inch baking sheets. Press each cookie with the lightly floured tines of a fork to flatten slightly.

4. Bake cookies in a 350° regular or convection oven until edges are lightly browned, 8 to 10 minutes; if baking two sheets at once in one oven, switch their positions halfway through baking. Let cookies cool on sheets for 5 minutes, then use a wide spatula to transfer to racks to cool completely.

Per cookie: 96 cal., 55% (53 cal.) from fat; 0.9 g protein; 5.9 g fat (2.1 g sat.); 9.9 g carbo (0.2 g fiber); 62 mg sodium; 13 mg chol.

Gingerbread Cookies

Janet De Fusco, Fountain Valley, CA

For Janet De Fusco's family, gingerbread cookies are as much a part of Christmas as decorating the tree. The gingerbread aficionados on our panel were drawn to these because they're slightly softer than typical crisp gingerbread cookies.

PREP AND COOK TIME: About 1 1/2 hours, plus at least 1 hour to chill
MAKES: About 3 dozen 3- to 4-inch cookies

3/4 cup **molasses**
1/2 cup **salad oil**
1/3 cup firmly packed **brown sugar**
1 **large egg**
About 2 3/4 cups **all-purpose flour**
1/2 teaspoon **salt**
1 tablespoon **baking powder**
1 tablespoon **ground cinnamon**
1 tablespoon **ground ginger**
1/2 teaspoon **ground cloves**
Powdered Sugar Icing (recipe follows; optional)

1. In a large bowl, with a mixer on medium speed, beat molasses, oil, brown sugar, and egg until well blended.

2. In a medium bowl, mix 2 3/4 cups flour, salt, baking powder, cinnamon, ginger, and cloves. Stir into molasses mixture, then beat until well blended. Divide dough in half, gather each half into a ball, then flatten into a disk. Wrap each disk in plastic wrap and freeze until firm, about 1 hour.

3. Unwrap dough. On a lightly floured surface, with a floured rolling pin, roll one disk at a time to about 1/4 inch thick. With floured 3- to 4-inch cutters, cut out cookies. Place about 1 inch apart on buttered 12- by 15-inch baking sheets. Gather excess dough into a ball, reroll, and cut out remaining cookies.

4. Bake cookies in a 350° regular or convection oven until edges begin to brown slightly, 8 to 10 minutes; if baking two sheets at once in one oven, switch their positions halfway through baking. Let cookies cool on sheets for 5 minutes, then use a wide spatula to transfer to racks to cool completely. Decorate with Powdered Sugar Icing if desired.

Per cookie: 93 cal., 32% (30 cal.) from fat; 1.2 g protein; 3.3 g fat (0.5 g sat.); 15 g carbo (0.3 g fiber); 79 mg sodium; 6.2 mg chol.

POWDERED SUGAR ICING. In a bowl, stir 2 cups **powdered sugar**, 1 1/2 tablespoons **water**, and 1/2 teaspoon **vanilla** until smooth. Tint to desired color by stirring in **food coloring**, a drop or two at a time. If icing is too thick to work with, stir in more water, a few drops at a time; if too thin, stir in more powdered sugar. Makes 2/3 cup.

Chocolate–Macadamia Nut Clusters

Elsie Chan, Leucadia, CA

These rich drop cookies taste amazingly like chocolate-covered macadamia nut candies, which is the effect Elsie Chan was after. Take care

Amaretto
Butter Cookies,
at right

not to overbake them; their centers should remain soft and chewy.

PREP AND COOK TIME: About 45 minutes
MAKES: About 3½ dozen cookies

- 8 ounces **bittersweet** or semisweet **chocolate,** chopped
  About ¼ cup (⅛ lb.) **butter** or margarine
- 1 cup **sugar**
- 2 **large eggs**
- 1½ teaspoons **vanilla**
- 3 tablespoons **all-purpose flour**
- ¼ teaspoon **baking powder**
- 1½ cups **unsalted macadamia nuts**
- 1 cup **semisweet chocolate chips**
- 1 cup **sweetened flaked dried coconut** (4 oz.)

1. In a heatproof bowl set over (but not touching) barely simmering water in a pan, stir bittersweet chocolate and ¼ cup butter often until mixture is melted and smooth.

2. In a large bowl, with a mixer on high speed, beat sugar, eggs, and vanilla until smooth. Add chocolate mixture and beat until well blended. Stir in flour and baking powder, then beat just until moistened. Stir in macadamia nuts, chocolate chips, and coconut.

3. Drop dough in 1-tablespoon portions about 2 inches apart on buttered 12- by 15-inch baking sheets.

4. Bake cookies in a 350° regular or convection oven just until firm on the edges but still soft when pressed in the middle, 8 to 10 minutes; if baking two sheets at once in one oven, switch their positions halfway through baking. Let cookies cool on sheets for 5 minutes,

then use a wide spatula to transfer to racks to cool completely.

Per cookie: 132 cal., 67% (88 cal.) from fat; 1.5 g protein; 9.6 g fat (4.6 g sat.); 12 g carbo (0.5 g fiber); 20 mg sodium; 13 mg chol.

Oatmeal Cookie Sandwiches

Jane Shapton, Tustin, CA

Jane Shapton suggests sandwiching these thin, crisp oatmeal cookies around chocolate or peppermint frozen yogurt; we thought they were excellent filled with a chocolate-mint ganache. The filling is easiest to spread when slightly warm. If making it up to 3 days ahead, cover and chill, then stir gently in a bowl set over a pan of barely simmering water to rewarm. Fill cookies the day you serve them.

PREP AND COOK TIME: About 1 hour, plus at least 15 minutes to cool
MAKES: About 3 dozen sandwiches

- About ½ cup (¼ lb.) **butter** or margarine
- ¾ cup firmly packed **brown sugar**
- 1½ cups **quick-cooking rolled oats**
- 1 tablespoon **all-purpose flour**
- 1 teaspoon **baking powder**
- ¼ teaspoon **salt**
- 1 **large egg**
- 1 tablespoon **vanilla**
  Chocolate-Mint Ganache (recipe follows)

1. In a 2- to 3-quart pan over medium heat, stir ½ cup butter and the brown sugar frequently until butter is melted and mixture is smooth, about 3 minutes.

2. Meanwhile, in a large bowl, mix oats, flour, baking powder, and salt. Add butter mixture; stir until well blended.

3. Add egg and vanilla to oat mixture and stir until well blended.

4. Drop dough in 1-teaspoon portions about 2 inches apart onto cooking parchment–lined or buttered and floured 12- by 15-inch baking sheets.

5. Bake cookies in a 350° regular or convection oven until browned, 8 to 10 minutes; if baking two sheets at once in one oven, switch their positions halfway through baking. Let cookies cool on sheets for 5 minutes, then use a wide spatula to transfer to racks to cool completely.

6. Spread the bottom of each of half the cookies with about 1 tablespoon Chocolate-Mint Ganache. Top each with a second cookie, bottom toward filling, and press gently to squeeze filling to edges of sandwich.

Per sandwich: 130 cal., 53% (69 cal.) from fat; 1.4 g protein; 7.7 g fat (4.5 g sat.); 16 g carbo (1.2 g fiber); 61 mg sodium; 15 mg chol.

CHOCOLATE-MINT GANACHE. In a heat-proof bowl set over (but not touching) barely simmering water in a pan, occasionally stir 3 cups chopped **semisweet chocolate** (18 oz.) and ¼ cup **whipping cream** until chocolate is melted and mixture is smooth. Remove from heat and stir in ¾ teaspoon **peppermint extract.** Let cool until thick but not firm, about 15 minutes, and use immediately (see note at left).

Amaretto Butter Cookies

Gary Connor, Spokane

Every Christmas at Gary Connor's house, lucky family and friends received 10 or 15 homemade sweets, including these buttery cookies, which are decorated with sliced almonds and flavored with orange peel and almond-flavor liqueur.

PREP AND COOK TIME: About 1 hour, plus at least 30 minutes to chill
MAKES: About 3 dozen cookies

- About 1 cup (½ lb.) **butter** or margarine, at room temperature
- 1 cup **sugar**
- 1 **large egg,** separated
- 3 tablespoons **almond-flavor liqueur,** such as amaretto, or 1 tablespoon almond extract
- 2 teaspoons grated **orange** peel
  About 2 cups **all-purpose flour**
- ½ teaspoon **baking powder**
- ¼ teaspoon **salt**
- 1¼ cups **sliced almonds**

1. In a large bowl, with a mixer on medium speed, beat 1 cup butter and the sugar until smooth. Add egg yolk, liqueur, and orange peel and beat until well blended.

2. In another bowl, mix 2 cups flour, baking powder, and salt. Add to butter mixture; stir to mix, then beat until well blended. Gather dough into a ball, divide in half, and flatten each portion into a disk; wrap each tightly in plastic wrap and freeze until firm enough to roll without sticking, about 30 minutes.

3. Unwrap dough. On a lightly floured surface, with a floured rolling pin, roll one disk at a time to about ¼ inch thick. With a floured, 2-inch round cutter, cut out cookies. Place about 2 inches apart on buttered 12- by 15-inch baking sheets. Gather excess dough into a ball, reroll, and cut out remaining cookies.

4. In a small bowl, beat egg white with 1 teaspoon water to blend. Brush cookies with mixture and sprinkle or arrange about ¹⁄₂ teaspoon sliced almonds on each.

5. Bake cookies in a 325° regular or convection oven until lightly browned, about 15 minutes; if baking two sheets at once in one oven, switch their positions halfway through cooking. Let cookies cool on sheets for 5 minutes, then use a wide spatula to transfer to racks to cool completely.

Per cookie: 119 cal., 54% (64 cal.) from fat; 1.6 g protein; 7.1 g fat (3.5 g sat.); 12 g carbo (0.3 g fiber); 78 mg sodium; 20 mg chol.

Apricot Buttons
Tita Owre, Pecos, NM

Tita Owre writes that her mother's apricot buttons were more than just a Christmas cookie—they were an essential part of every family celebration. Whirl the walnuts in a food processor until very finely ground, or chop very finely with a knife. The buttons are also great filled with raspberry jam.

PREP AND COOK TIME: About 1 hour
MAKES: About 3 dozen cookies

About 1 cup (¹⁄₂ lb.) **butter** or margarine, at room temperature
³⁄₄ cup **sugar**
2 **large eggs,** separated
1 teaspoon **vanilla**

2 cups **all-purpose flour**
¹⁄₂ teaspoon **salt**
1¹⁄₂ cups finely ground **walnuts** (see note preceding)
¹⁄₂ cup **apricot jam**

1. In a large bowl, with a mixer on medium speed, beat 1 cup butter and the sugar until smooth. Add egg yolks and vanilla and beat until well blended. Stir in flour and salt and beat just until dough comes together.

2. In a small bowl, beat egg whites to blend. Place walnuts in another small bowl. Shape dough into 1-inch balls. Dip each in egg whites, turning to coat completely, then roll in walnuts to coat. Place about 1 inch apart on buttered 12- by 15-inch baking sheets. Press your thumb gently into the center of each cookie to make an imprint.

3. Bake cookies in a 325° regular or convection oven until lightly browned, 18 to 20 minutes; if baking two sheets at once in one oven, switch their positions halfway through baking. Let cookies cool on sheets for 5 minutes, then use a wide spatula to transfer to racks to cool completely.

4. Spoon about ¹⁄₂ teaspoon jam into the center of each cool cookie.

Per cookie: 135 cal., 57% (77 cal.) from fat; 1.8 g protein; 8.6 g fat (3.6 g sat.); 13 g carbo (0.5 g fiber); 91 mg sodium; 26 mg chol.

Peppermint Molasses Cookies
Cheryl Zakhar, Coto De Caza, CA

Of the many cookies her grand-mother made at Christmastime, these frosted molasses ones were Cheryl Zakhar's favorite.

PREP AND COOK TIME: About 45 minutes, plus at least 45 minutes to chill
MAKES: About 4 dozen cookies

About ²⁄₃ cup **butter** or margarine, at room temperature
¹⁄₄ cup **granulated sugar**
¹⁄₄ cup firmly packed **brown sugar**
1 **large egg**
¹⁄₄ cup **molasses**
1¹⁄₂ cups **all-purpose flour**
1 teaspoon **ground cinnamon**
1 teaspoon **ground ginger**
¹⁄₂ teaspoon **ground cloves**
¹⁄₂ teaspoon **baking soda**
¹⁄₄ teaspoon **salt**
¹⁄₂ cup crushed **hard peppermint candy** such as candy canes
Peppermint Icing (recipe follows)

1. In a large bowl, with a mixer on medium speed, beat ²⁄₃ cup butter, granulated sugar, and brown sugar until smooth. Add egg and molasses and beat until well blended.

2. In a medium bowl, mix flour, cinnamon, ginger, cloves, baking soda, and salt. Stir into butter mixture, then beat just until dough comes together. Stir in peppermint candy. Cover bowl with plastic wrap and freeze until dough is firm, about 45 minutes.

3. Shape dough into 1-inch balls and place about 2 inches apart on buttered 12- by 15-inch baking sheets.

4. Bake cookies in a 350° regular or convection oven until lightly browned, 12 to 15 minutes; if baking two sheets at once in one oven, switch their positions halfway through baking. Immediately, with a wide spatula, transfer cookies to racks to cool. When cool, drizzle with Peppermint Icing; save any remaining icing for other uses.

Per cookie: 73 cal., 34% (25 cal.) from fat; 0.6 g protein; 2.8 g fat (1.7 g sat.); 11 g carbo (0.1 g fiber); 56 mg sodium; 11 mg chol.

PEPPERMINT ICING. In a bowl, mix 1 cup **powdered sugar,** 2 tablespoons **milk,** and ¹⁄₄ teaspoon **vanilla** until well blended. If too thick to drizzle, mix in more milk, ¹⁄₂ tablespoon at a time, until thin enough. Stir in 1 tablespoon finely crushed **hard peppermint candy** and 1 to 2 drops **red food coloring** if desired. Makes ¹⁄₂ cup. ◆

Peppermint Molasses Cookies, at right

The Quick Cook

A sauce in the freezer is worth two meals on the table

By Elaine Johnson

Couscous makes an easy, savory accompaniment to pan-browned lamb chops with cherry-wine sauce.

JAMES CARRIER; FOOD STYLING: BASIL FRIEDMAN

■ It's 6:30 P.M. and you've just gotten home. Guests are due at 7. You open the refrigerator to retrieve the lamb chops you had the foresight to buy over the weekend. All the picture needs is a great sauce waiting in the freezer. Voilà—here are two: a mushroom-caper sauce and a cherry-wine sauce. The latter would be perfect for that lamb. Zap it in the microwave, pan-brown the chops, and an elegant entrée is served.

Each sauce complements more than one meat or fish, and the recipe serves eight; divide the batch in half to freeze, and you'll have two very different dinners for four on hand.

Mushroom-Caper Sauce

PREP AND COOK TIME: About 25 minutes

MAKES: 3½ cups; 8 servings

- 1 **onion** (¾ lb.), peeled
- 1 pound **mushrooms**, rinsed, drained, and thinly sliced
- 3 tablespoons **butter** or margarine
- 2 tablespoons **all-purpose flour**

About 1¼ cups fat-skimmed **chicken broth**

- 1 cup **dry white wine**
- 3 tablespoons drained **capers**

1. Cut onion in half lengthwise, then thinly slice crosswise. In a 12- to 14-inch frying pan or 5- to 6-quart pan over medium-high heat, stir mushrooms and onion in butter until lightly browned, about 15 minutes. Sprinkle flour over vegetables; stir 1 minute longer.

2. Add 1¼ cups broth, wine, and capers. Stir over high heat until boiling, 3 to 4 minutes.

3. Let sauce cool to room temperature, about 20 minutes. Spoon equal portions into two microwave-safe freezer containers, each 2- to 3-cup size. Seal, and freeze up to 3 months.

4. To thaw, uncover one container of sauce. Cook in a microwave oven at full power (100%), stirring occasionally, until thawed, 2 to 3 minutes.

Pan-browned Chicken or Snapper with Mushroom-Caper Sauce. Buy 4 **boned, skinned chicken breast halves** (⅓ lb. each) or 4 snapper fillets (each ½ in. thick and ⅓ lb.). Rinse and pat dry. Trim excess fat from chicken and discard. Heat 1 tablespoon **olive oil** in a 12- to 14-inch nonstick frying pan over medium-high heat; add chicken or fish and cook, turning once, until chicken is no longer pink in center of thickest part (cut to test), 10 to 12 minutes, or fish is opaque but still moist-looking in center of thickest part (cut to test), about 6 minutes. (Or cook half at a time in a 10-inch frying pan.) Arrange on plates and keep warm. Pour **Mushroom-Caper Sauce** (preceding) into pan and stir over high heat, scraping up browned bits, until boiling, about 5 minutes. If desired, thin with more **chicken broth**. Spoon sauce over chicken or fish. Season to taste with **salt** and **pepper**. Makes 4 servings.

Per serving with chicken: 297 cal., 30% (89 cal.) from fat; 38 g protein; 9.9 g fat (3.7 g sat.); 8.1 g carbo (1.4 g fiber); 301 mg sodium; 99 mg chol.
Per serving with fish: 282 cal., 32% (90 cal.) from fat; 34 g protein; 10 g fat (3.6 g sat.); 8.1 g carbo (1.4 g fiber); 300 mg sodium; 67 mg chol.

Cherry-Wine Sauce

PREP AND COOK TIME: About 15 minutes

MAKES: 2 cups; 8 servings

- 1½ cups **dry red wine**
- 1½ cups **cherry jam** (15 oz.)
- ½ cup **raspberry vinegar**
- 2 tablespoons chopped **fresh rosemary** leaves, or 2 teaspoons dried rosemary, crumbled
- ¾ teaspoon fresh-ground **pepper**
- ¼ cup thinly sliced **green onions** (including tops)

1. In a 10- to 12-inch frying pan over high heat, bring wine, jam, vinegar, rosemary, and pepper to a boil; stir often until reduced to 2 cups, 8 to 10 minutes. Stir in green onions.

2. Let sauce cool to room temperature, about 20 minutes. Scrape equal portions into two microwave-safe freezer containers, each 1- to 2-cup size. Seal, and freeze up to 3 months.

3. To thaw, loosen lid on one container of sauce but leave in place. Cook in a microwave oven at full power (100%), stirring occasionally, until thawed, 2 to 3 minutes.

Pan-browned Lamb Chops or Pork Tenderloin with Cherry-Wine Sauce. Buy 8 single-rib **lamb chops** (each ½ in. thick, 1⅔ lb. total) with bones trimmed, or 2 pork tenderloins (1 lb. total). Rinse meat and pat dry; trim and discard excess fat. Slice pork crosswise ½ inch thick. Pour 2 teaspoons **olive oil** into a 12- to 14-inch nonstick frying pan over medium-high heat. When pan is hot, add lamb chops or pork slices in a single layer and cook, turning once, until browned on both sides and as done as you like in the center (cut to test), 5 to 7 minutes for medium-rare lamb or medium pork. (Or cook a few at a time in a 10-inch frying pan.) Arrange lamb chops or pork slices equally on plates and keep warm; discard fat from pan. Pour **Cherry-Wine Sauce** (preceding) into pan and stir over high heat, scraping up browned bits, until heated through and as thick as desired, 1 to 3 minutes. Spoon equally over or around meat. Season to taste with **salt**. Makes 4 servings.

Per serving with lamb: 334 cal., 38% (126 cal.) from fat; 17 g protein; 14 g fat (3.6 g sat.); 36 g carbo (0.8 g fiber); 83 mg sodium; 54 mg chol.
Per serving with pork: 261 cal., 13% (33 cal.) from fat; 22 g protein; 3.7 g fat (1.2 g sat.); 36 g carbo (0.8 g fiber); 76 mg sodium; 68 mg chol. ◆

A soft spot for caramel

Surrender to the gooey, dentist-be-darned texture
and deep, toasted-sugar flavor of these
shamelessly sweet dishes

By Elaine Johnson • Photographs by James Carrier

As far as meanings go, the word *caramel* is rich. It's three things: a flavor, a color, and a process—to caramelize means to heat sugar until it melts and develops the bittersweet flavor and amber brown color we associate with the candy. The sugar can be caramelized alone, in which case it hardens to amber glass as it cools. Or it can be mixed with cream before or during the process to create thick, sticky sauces that scream for ice cream, and candylike mixtures perfect for filling apple dumplings or cloaking sumptuous tortes.

Rich caramel cloaks dense, chocolate-filled hazelnut cake.

Caramel-Cloaked Chocolate-Hazelnut Torte

PREP AND COOK TIME: About 2¾ hours, plus about 2½ hours for the ganache to cool

NOTES: Make chocolate ganache first; let it cool while you bake the cake. Prepare cake through step 5 before starting caramel cloak. An accurate candy or instant-read thermometer that registers high temperatures is crucial to making the caramel; to coat cake evenly, it must cool just enough to be thick but still pourable, about 150°. Assemble torte through step 5 up to 1 day ahead and chill filled cake airtight; pour caramel over cold cake. Or complete entire recipe up to 1 day ahead and chill airtight; bring cake to room temperature to serve, about 1 hour, and warm sauce as directed in step 7, about 2 minutes.

MAKES: 8 to 10 servings

- 2 cups **hazelnuts** (10 oz.)
- 6 **large eggs,** separated
- ½ cup **sugar**
- 3 tablespoons **fine dried bread crumbs**
- 1 tablespoon **vanilla**
  Chocolate Ganache (recipe follows; see notes)
  Caramel Cloak (recipe follows; see notes)

1. Place nuts in a 10- by 15-inch baking pan. Bake in a 350° regular or convection oven, shaking pan occasionally, until nuts are golden beneath skins, 10 to 12 minutes. Pour nuts into a towel and rub to remove loose skins. Let cool at least 15 minutes. Set aside 8 to 10 completely skinned nuts. Whirl remaining nuts in a food processor until finely ground.

2. In a bowl, with a mixer on high speed, beat egg yolks and ¼ cup sugar until very thick and light-colored, about 4 minutes, scraping bowl occasionally. Stir in ground nuts, bread crumbs, and vanilla.

3. In a large bowl, with clean beaters, beat egg whites on high speed until they hold soft peaks. Gradually add remaining ¼ cup sugar and continue to beat until egg whites hold short, distinct peaks, about 3 minutes total. Add half the whites to nut mixture and stir to blend well. Gently fold in remaining whites. Spread batter level in a buttered and floured 9-inch cheesecake pan with removable rim.

4. Bake in a 350° regular oven or 325° convection oven until cake is golden brown and springs back in the center when lightly pressed, 25 to 30 minutes. Let cool in pan for 10 minutes. Run a knife between cake and pan rim, then remove rim. Let cake cool on a rack about 45 minutes.

5. With a long, serrated knife, split the cake in half horizontally. Gently slide a baking sheet under the top cake layer and lift it off. Spread the bottom cake layer evenly with ganache. Slide top layer, cut side down, back in place over ganache.

6. Set cake on rack in a 12- by 17-inch pan. Pour about 1½ cups warm (see notes) Caramel Cloak over cake enough to coat it—starting at the center and spiraling to edges, letting caramel drip down sides to cover completely. Arrange reserved hazelnuts evenly around top edge of cake. Let stand until caramel stops dripping and is firm enough to cut, about 30 minutes.

7. Scrape caramel drips from pan back into the measuring cup containing Caramel Cloak. Cook, uncovered, in a microwave oven at 30% power until warm and fluid, stirring occasionally, about 2 minutes. Pour into a bowl.

8. Place cake on a plate. Cut into wedges with a sharp knife. Offer remaining Caramel Cloak to spoon over portions.

Per serving: 787 cal., 61% (477 cal.) from fat; 10 g protein; 53 g fat (22 g sat.); 77 g carbo (2.9 g fiber); 218 mg sodium; 206 mg chol.

Chocolate Ganache. In a 2- to 3-quart pan over low heat, stir 8 ounces chopped **bittersweet** or semisweet chocolate (1½ cups) and 1 cup **whipping cream** until melted and smoothly blended, 8 to 10 minutes. Let cool, stirring occasionally, until ganache no longer flows when pan is tilted, 2 to 2½ hours.

Caramel Cloak. In a 3- to 4-quart pan, combine 1 cup *each* firmly packed **brown sugar, light corn syrup,** and **whipping cream;** ½ cup (¼ lb.) **butter** or margarine; and ¼ teaspoon **salt.** Bring to a boil over medium-high heat and stir occasionally until mixture reaches 240°, 12 to 14 minutes. Pour into a 1-quart glass measure and stir occasionally until mixture cools to 150°, about 25 minutes. Stir in 1 teaspoon **vanilla**. Pour over cake immediately.

Double-Caramel Apple Dumplings

PREP AND COOK TIME: About 1¼ hours

NOTES: Make the Caramel Sauce without the rum; if desired, stir rum into sauce after using ¼ cup in step 1 be-

Crisp, golden pastry wraps a caramel-filled apple.

low. Prepare dumplings through step 4 up to 1 day ahead; chill sauce, dumplings, and egg mixture separately airtight. Bake chilled dumplings as directed.

MAKES: 4 servings

- ⅔ cup **pecan halves**
- **Caramel Sauce** (recipe follows; see notes)
- 4 **Golden Delicious apples** (4 to 6 oz. each)
- 1 tablespoon **lemon juice**
- 1 sheet **frozen puff pastry** (half of a 17.3-oz. package), thawed
- 1 **large egg**, beaten to blend with 1 tablespoon water
- **Vanilla ice cream** (optional)

1. Set aside four pecan halves; chop remaining nuts. In a bowl, mix chopped nuts with ¼ cup Caramel Sauce.

2. Peel apples; core each, creating a 1-inch-wide hollow from top to bottom. Place apples in a bowl and coat with lemon juice.

3. On a lightly floured board, roll puff pastry into a 12-inch square. Cut into four equal squares and center an apple upright on each. Push nut and caramel mixture equally into apple hollows.

4. Brush a ½-inch-wide border around each pastry with egg mixture; reserve remaining mixture. To wrap each dumpling, with floured fingers bring two opposite corners of pastry up over apple and pinch tips together. Repeat with remaining two corners. Firmly pinch all tips together; pinch each seam, then fold over about ⅛ inch along the seam and pinch again, leaving no holes. Space dumplings evenly on a buttered 12- by 15-inch baking sheet.

5. Bake in a 375° regular or convection oven for 20 minutes. Dip reserved pecan halves in egg mixture (save remaining egg for other uses or discard); press a nut half on top of each dumpling. Bake until pastry is deep golden, 10 to 15 minutes longer in a regular oven, about 5 minutes in a convection oven.

6. With a wide spatula, transfer dumplings to plates. Accompany with remaining caramel sauce and ice cream, if desired.

Per serving: 868 cal., 59% (513 cal.) from fat; 9.4 g protein; 57 g fat (16 g sat.); 85 g carbo (4.1 g fiber); 196 mg sodium; 119 mg chol.

Caramel Sauce

PREP AND COOK TIME: About 20 minutes

NOTES: This rich sauce is excellent over ice cream. If making up to 3 weeks ahead, chill airtight. To heat, place in a microwave-safe container and cook, uncovered, in a microwave oven at 30% power, stirring occasionally, until warm and fluid, about 2 minutes.

MAKES: About 1 cup

1. In a 2- to 3-quart pan over medium heat, tilt and swirl ⅔ cup **sugar** often until melted and amber-colored, 5 to 7 minutes. Stir in 1 cup **whipping cream**; mixture will bubble and sugar will harden. Stir until sugar melts again and sauce boils, 6 to 8 minutes.

2. At once, pour sauce into a bowl. Stir in 1 teaspoon **vanilla**.

3. Let sauce cool for 10 minutes, then, if desired, stir in 3 tablespoons **rum**. Serve warm or cool.

Per tablespoon: 77 cal., 53% (41 cal.) from fat; 0.3 g protein; 4.6 g fat (2.9 g sat.); 8.8 g carbo (0 g fiber); 5.2 mg sodium; 17 mg chol.

Caramel Pudding

PREP AND COOK TIME: About 10 minutes

MAKES: 2 cups; 4 servings

- 2 cups **whole milk**
- 2 tablespoons **cornstarch**
- 1 **large egg**
- ⅔ cup **sugar**
- 2 teaspoons **vanilla**

1. In a bowl, whisk ½ cup milk, cornstarch, and egg until well blended.

2. In a 2- to 3-quart pan over medium-high heat, tilt and swirl sugar until melted and deep amber, about 4 minutes. Stir in remaining 1½ cups milk; mixture will bubble and sugar will harden. Stir until sugar melts again, about 2 minutes.

3. Whisk about ½ cup of the caramelized sugar mixture into cornstarch mixture, then return all to pan. Stir over medium-high heat until pudding thickens and begins to bubble, 3 to 5 minutes. Remove from heat and stir in vanilla.

4. Pour into bowls and serve warm. Or let cool, chill airtight up to 2 days, and serve cold.

Per serving: 244 cal., 20% (48 cal.) from fat; 5.6 g protein; 5.3 g fat (2.9 g sat.); 43 g carbo (0 g fiber); 76 mg sodium; 70 mg chol.

Caramel Caffe Latte

PREP AND COOK TIME: About 5 minutes

NOTES: Make Caramel Sauce with or without rum. In step 1, if using chilled sauce, combine with coffee in a microwave-safe glass or mug and cook in a microwave oven at full power (100%) until steaming, about 1 minute; stir.

MAKES: 1 serving

1. Pour ¼ cup **Caramel Sauce** (at left; see notes) and 1 cup hot **coffee** into a heatproof glass or mug (at least 12 oz.). Stir until caramel is dissolved.

2. Pour ½ cup **whole** or low-fat **milk** into a 1-cup glass measure. Heat in a microwave oven at full power (100%) until steaming, about 50 seconds. Pour into a blender and whirl until frothy, about 1 minute. Pour over coffee.

Per serving: 386 cal., 54% (207 cal.) from fat; 5.5 g protein; 23 g fat (14 g sat.); 42 g carbo (0 g fiber); 85 mg sodium; 83 mg chol. ◆

food guide

By Jerry Anne Di Vecchio

Crowning glory

Regal ribs for the holidays

■ Behind the fanfare of its form, a spectacular-looking crown roast is like any other roast—you just stick it in the oven. Moreover, it's as easy as a boned one to carve. A crown is made from two or more loin roasts, from the choice muscle that's tucked alongside the backbone and back ribs. The backbone is sawed off to make the roasts flexible enough to curve and tie together—a task a professional at the meat market can take care of. To serve the crown, you just cut between the ribs.

A traditional crown roast of pork is grand in scale, but two lamb rib racks, joined, are enough for a table of eight or fewer, depending on how many rib chops you consider a serving. Lamb racks vary in size, so order by weight. Some markets include ruffled paper or foil cuffs to slip on the rib bone tips while the roast rests for carving. You can also buy the cuffs in well-stocked meat or food markets and in cookware stores.

JAMES CARRIER; FOOD STYLING: BASIL FRIEDMAN

Crown Lamb Rack with Green Herb Couscous

PREP AND COOK TIME: About 1 hour

NOTES: It's wise to order the roast a few days ahead. You can toast the pine nuts (step 4) up to 1 day ahead; cover and store at room temperature. You can also prepare the couscous (step 5), but don't add the peas; cool, cover, and chill. While the roast rests (step 7), in a microwave-safe bowl, mix peas with the cold couscous and heat in a microwave oven on full power (100%), stirring occasionally, until steaming, 3 to 4 minutes total. Mix the chopped herbs with the hot couscous and use more fresh herbs for garnish.

MAKES: 8 servings, 2 chops each

2 **lamb rib racks**, 8 ribs each (4½ to 5 lb. total)

½ teaspoon **ground cumin**

About ½ teaspoon *each* **salt** and **pepper**

¼ cup **pine nuts**

1 **onion** (8 oz.), peeled and finely chopped

2 **pork Italian sausages** (about 8 oz. total), casings removed

2 cups fat-skimmed **chicken broth**

1 cup **frozen petite peas**

1 cup **couscous**

½ cup *each* coarsely chopped **parsley, fresh mint** leaves (or 2 tablespoons dried mint), and **fresh dill** (or 2 tablespoons dried dill)

1. Have your butcher trim the fat from the lamb rib racks, trim the bone ends, cut off the backbone for easy carving between ribs, and tie racks together to make a crown roast.

2. Rinse lamb roast, pat dry, and set on a rack in a shallow pan (at least 10 in. square). Mix ground cumin and ½ teaspoon *each* salt and pepper; rub onto roast, inside and out.

3. Bake lamb in a 450° regular or convection oven until a thermometer inserted horizontally through roast into center of thickest part reads 145° to 150° for rare, 35 to 40 minutes, or 155° for medium-rare, 40 to 45 minutes. If bone tips start to scorch, drape them with foil.

4. Meanwhile, in a 10- to 12-inch frying pan over medium-high heat, shake pine nuts frequently until lightly browned, about 3 minutes; pour into a small bowl.

5. To pan, add onion and sausages; stir often over high heat, breaking meat into small pieces, until lightly browned, about 10 minutes. Add broth and cover; when boiling, stir in peas and cover. When boiling again, stir in couscous, cover, and remove from heat. Let stand in a warm place 10 to 20 minutes.

6. As lamb roasts, in a food processor or with a knife, finely chop parsley, mint, and dill (or crumble dried herbs).

7. Transfer roast to a platter; keeping it warm, let rest 5 to 10 minutes. Stir herb mixture into hot couscous; fill center of roast with some of the couscous and spoon remainder around the meat. Sprinkle couscous with pine nuts. Cut lamb between ribs and serve chops with couscous. Add more salt and pepper to taste.

Per serving: 455 cal., 45% (207 cal.) from fat; 35 g protein; 23 g fat (7.8 g sat.); 25 g carbo (3.6 g fiber); 482 mg sodium; 100 mg chol.

Foie gras—
fact and fancy

■ Once a rarity, foie gras is now on every prestigious—or evenly moderately upscale—menu. And ducks are now being reared in this country for their fat, oversized livers (*foie gras de canard,* in French). Prepared at home, foie gras is a relative bargain. A whole duck foie gras weighs 1 to 1½ pounds, and 3 ounces makes a generous first-course serving. Polarica in San Francisco (800/426-3872 or www.polarica.com) ships whole livers (grade A, $35 to $38 per lb.; grade B, about $30 per lb.—both are fine for sautéing). At an upscale meat market, fancy food store, or supermarket, the price is higher, but you can usually buy a portion of a liver.

A whole liver has two lobes. To clean, gently pull them apart and pull or trim out any veins. To sauté foie gras, keep it cold until ready to cook, cut it into fairly thick slices, and then sear it quickly over high heat to lightly brown.

Foie gras is so lavishly rich, it tastes best with powerful partners, such as an intensely sweet, high-acid French Sauternes or a late-harvest white wine.

Seared Foie Gras
with Ginger Cream

PREP AND COOK TIME: About 30 minutes

NOTES: Order fresh duck foie gras at least 1 week ahead. To assemble this dish easily, slice the foie gras up to 1 day ahead; arrange in a single layer on a plate and chill airtight. Also make sauce up to 1 day ahead; cover and chill, then reheat to use, whisking in a little more whipping cream if too thick.

MAKES: 4 to 6 first-course servings

1½ tablespoons chopped **crystallized ginger**

1 tablespoon finely chopped **fresh ginger**

2 tablespoons firmly packed **brown sugar**

¼ cup **sherry vinegar**

About ¾ cup **whipping cream**

4 to 6 toasted slices **firm-textured egg** or white **bread** (each about ½ in. thick and 3½ in. square), crusts trimmed and discarded

1 piece (⅔ to 1 lb.) chilled **fresh duck foie gras,** rinsed and patted dry (see notes)

Coarse salt and fresh-ground **pepper**

8 to 12 **fresh chive** spears, rinsed

1. In a blender, whirl crystallized ginger, fresh ginger, brown sugar, and vinegar until ginger is minced. Pour into a 2- to 3-quart pan and add ¾ cup cream. Stir over high heat until boiling, then stir often until reduced to about ¾ cup, 8 to 10 minutes; keep warm.

2. On each salad plate, lay a slice of toast; keep warm up to 10 minutes in a 150° to 200° regular or convection oven.

3. With a hot, thin-bladed sharp knife (heat in hot water or over a burner), cut foie gras across narrow dimension into ½-inch-thick slices; wipe knife clean after each cut and heat again. Sprinkle slices lightly with salt and pepper.

4. Place a 10- to 12-inch nonstick frying pan over high heat; when it's hot enough for a drop of water to bounce off the surface, quickly lay foie gras slices in pan, filling it without crowding. Cook foie gras just until lightly browned on the bottom, 15 to 45 seconds, then turn slices and brown other sides (interiors will be warm, not hot), 15 to 45 seconds. Remove pan from heat, and with a wide spatula, quickly transfer equal portions of foie gras to toast; spoon fat in pan evenly over toast. Ladle ginger sauce equally around portions and garnish with chive spears.

Nutritional data is not available.

The cutting edge

■ A good knife is the making of a cook; a *beautiful* knife is a cook's joy. The culinary knives handcrafted by Corey Milligan and Michael Merriman, of New West KnifeWorks, take an aesthetic step beyond the making of a cook. The blades are keen-edged, high-carbon, surgical stainless steel. The handles, however, are not standard black but layered with colors—hardwood veneers, vacuum-impregnated with wood hues or vivid dyes, then bound for strength and durability under heat and intense pressure.

The selection from New West includes 6- and 8-inch chef's knives ($69 and $95, respectively), a 10-inch bread knife ($85), a cleaver ($125), a paring knife ($37.50), and carving ($179) and steak knives ($245 for a six-piece set). The handles come in eight different color combinations; holders are also available (877/258-0100 or www.newwestknifeworks.com).

Sweet roll for drop-ins

■ In December, the doorbell rings often—a little refreshment on hand to offer is in order. My friend Gigi showed me how to make this lovely, spiraled nut roll, from a recipe her mother brought from Hungary. Chilled airtight, it stays fresh up to a week and makes a delectable alternative to cookies.

Gigi's Hungarian Almond Roll

PREP AND COOK TIME: 2¾ hours, plus at least 1 hour to cool

MAKES: One 2-pound loaf

    1   package **active dry yeast**
    ¼   cup **sugar**
    2   **large egg** yolks
        About 6 tablespoons **butter** or margarine
        About 1½ cups **all-purpose flour**
        Almond Filling (recipe follows)
    1   tablespoon **milk** or water

1. In a bowl, sprinkle yeast over 6 tablespoons warm (about 110°) water; let stand until soft, about 5 minutes. Add sugar, 1 egg yolk, 6 tablespoons butter (cut into small pieces), and 1½ cups flour; stir until evenly moistened.

2. *To knead with a dough hook,* beat at medium speed until dough pulls cleanly from bowl, about 5 minutes. *To knead by hand,* scrape dough onto a lightly floured board and knead until smooth, about 10 minutes, adding flour (as little as possible) if necessary to prevent sticking; return to bowl.

3. Cover dough with plastic wrap and let rise in a warm place until it's puffy enough to hold an impression when pressed with a finger (dough won't double in volume), about 1 hour.

4. With dough hook or your hands, punch air out of dough; lift dough from bowl and shape into a smooth ball. Set on the center of a floured pastry cloth or clean, smooth-textured dish towel. Pat dough flat; with a floured rolling pin, roll into a 14- to 15-inch square. Spread or evenly dot Almond Filling over dough to within 1 inch of edges. Lift cloth from one side to roll dough into a compact loaf. Gently lift loaf and lay seam down on a buttered 12- by 17-inch baking sheet. Pinch ends to seal, then fold under. Cover loosely with plastic wrap and let stand in a warm place until dough is slightly puffy, about 45 minutes.

5. In a small bowl, mix remaining egg yolk with milk. Brush loaf with yolk mixture; discard any remaining mixture.

6. Bake loaf on the center rack in a 325° regular or convection oven until rich golden brown, about 45 minutes. Transfer to a rack and let cool at least 1 hour. Serve at room temperature. Cut crosswise into ¼-inch-thick slices.

Per ounce: 109 cal., 41% (45 cal.) from fat; 2 g protein; 5 g fat (1.9 g sat.); 15 g carbo (0.9 g fiber); 28 mg sodium; 20 mg chol.

Almond Filling. In a food processor, whirl 1 cup **unblanched almonds** to fine meal. In a 10- to 12-inch nonstick frying pan, combine almonds, ¾ cup **raisins**, ¾ cup **sugar**, ¾ cup **milk**, and 1 teaspoon grated **lemon** peel. Stir over high heat until mixture is thick enough to hold a clean trail for a few seconds when you draw a spoon across pan bottom. Stir in ½ teaspoon **vanilla**. Let cool at least 30 minutes.

The mysteries of food

■ Seeking a low-calorie, mysterious gift for a foodie friend? Buy a culinary mystery. Diane Mott Davidson has made the best-seller lists with *Tough Cookie,* one of a series featuring Goldy Schulz, a high-altitude caterer in Colorado. Phyllis C. Richman, retired food critic for the *Washington Post,* weaves plots for her fictitious D.C. food critic in *The Butter Did It* and *Murder on the Gravy Train.* Mary Daheim follows the sleuthing of Northwest bed-and-breakfast proprietor Judith McMonigle Flynn and her cousin Renie in *Creeps Suzette, Just Desserts, Fowl Prey,* and more. Rex Stout's Nero Wolfe is preoccupied with the efforts of his chef, Fritz. Peter King's English ex-chef is identified only as a gourmet detective in *Dying on the Vine.* Susan Wittig Albert's crime-solving heroine, China Bayles, runs an herb shop, where she cavorts in the pages of *Thyme of Death* and *Chile Death.* In *The Debt to Pleasure: A Novel,* by John Lanchester, the supercilious narrator and general gourmand is a suspiciously nasty fellow. Among other authors who blend food and crime: Anthony Bruno, Camilla T. Crespi, Martin Harry Greenberg, Cathie John, Katherine Hall Page, and Kathleen Taylor. For more, check www.amazon.com or your local bookstore. Most are light reading, all easily digested. ◆

The Wine Guide

Champagne and sparkling wine: Truce for the holidays

By Karen MacNeil-Fife

■ As far as I can tell, there are two kinds of people in the world: those who drink sparkling wine pretty much all the time because there's nothing else quite as refreshing and snappy, and those who drink it now—at holiday time—because it's simply more festive, more celebratory than anything else.

The division between camp #1 and camp #2 has very little to do with money, by the way. It's just not true that bubbles always cost a lot. Indeed, one of the more remarkable facts about wine prices these days is that in a single store you can find dozens of mediocre Chardonnays priced at $20 or more sitting next to terrific sparklers that cost less than $15, even though the latter is infinitely harder to make than the former. But that's another story. This time of year, what matters most is that we're all on the same side of the fence—Champagne is a state of mind we can all share.

You've probably noticed that I've gone back and forth between the terms sparkling wine and Champagne. Technically, they're not quite the same thing. A sparkling wine is any wine, from anywhere in the world (including Champagne, France), that has bubbles in it; Champagne is a sparkling wine from the Champagne district. Sparklers are divided into two broad groups: (a) those made by the painstaking process developed in Champagne, and (b) wines that have gotten bubbles by being carbonated (à la cola).

Forget the carbonated stuff right off the bat. It's dirt cheap, but the bad news is that it tastes even cheaper than it is.

Sparkling wines made by the traditional Champagne method (*méthode*

JAMES CARRIER

Champenoise)—including Champagne itself—are entirely different. The process took centuries to refine and would take pages to explain. The important point is this: The bubbles weren't created; they occurred naturally over time (as much as six years) inside each bottle. That's why, unlike cola's florid fizz, a great sparkler's bubbles are tiny, elegant, and gloriously persistent.

Champagne is singled out from other quality sparklers because it comes from a place that's truly unique. Standing on the craterlike region's white, chalky soil, you can almost imagine you're on Mars rather than about 90 miles northeast of Paris. This soil and the area's mostly cold, forbidding climate give the wine a contrapuntal tension: It seems sharp and creamy at the same time.

The top California sparklers, by comparison, aren't quite as counterintuitive; they're more hedonistic,

Q: **How many of those tiny bubbles are there in a bottle of Champagne?**

A: None—until you open the bottle. Popping the cork releases the pressure inside, at which point the gas erupts into bubbles—about 56 million or so, according to the Champagne firm of Bollinger, which has conducted extensive research on the subject.

A FEW STARS

The prices below are suggested retail, but shop around—many wine stores have big discounts on bubblies for the holidays.

■**Mirabelle Brut nonvintage (North Coast, CA),** $16. Crisp, clean, and fresh, with a hint of toastiness.

■**Iron Horse Wedding Cuvée Blanc de Noirs 1998 (Green Valley, Sonoma County),** $28. Originally created for the wedding of one of the owners, this exotic but elegant fruity sparkler is irresistibly creamy.

■**Schramsberg Blanc de Blancs Brut 1998 (Napa, Sonoma, Mendocino, and Monterey Counties),** $31. With its utterly rich mouthfeel and sophisticated flavors, this is one of the most refined and complex sparklers made in California.

■**Delamotte Blanc de Blancs Brut nonvintage (Champagne),** $35. One of France's best-kept secrets—rich but full of finesse, creamy yet incisively crisp. Packed with light lemon tart, vanilla crème anglaise, and ginger flavors.

■**Bollinger Special Cuvée Brut nonvintage (Champagne),** $45. Dramatic and sleek, with such an elegant citrus aroma you'll feel as though you've just drifted into a lemon grove. Beautifully classic.

more generous—like the state's climate itself.

Neither is better than the other. In fact, as a teacher, I set up many blind sparkling-wine tastings for my students (all of whom are adult professionals), and no one has ever been able to distinguish all the California wines from the Champagnes. I'm quite sure I couldn't do this myself—even though (I'll admit now) I belong to camp #1. Taste, in the end, is highly personal. Isn't that worth celebrating? ◆

Kitchen Cabinet

Readers' recipes tested in *Sunset's* kitchens

By Charity Ferreira • Photographs by James Carrier

Poached pears and cranberries do double holiday duty—as a side dish or dessert.

FOOD STYLING: BASIL FRIEDMAN (2)

Holiday Pears

Beth Cann, Temecula, CA

This recipe for oven-poached pears has been in Beth Cann's family for more than 40 years. She serves them as a side dish with turkey or ham. Spooned over vanilla ice cream or frozen yogurt, they also make a great dessert.

PREP AND COOK TIME: About 1¼ hours

MAKES: 4 servings

- 1 cup **fresh** or thawed frozen **cranberries**
- 4 **firm-ripe pears** such as d'Anjou or Bosc (about 2½ lb. total)
- ½ rinsed **lemon** (about 2 oz. total), thinly sliced (ends discarded)
- 1 cup **sugar**
- 2 tablespoons **cider vinegar**
- ¼ teaspoon **ground ginger**
- ¼ teaspoon **ground cinnamon**
- ⅛ teaspoon **ground cloves**

1. Sort cranberries and discard stems and any bruised or decayed fruit. Rinse and drain berries. Peel pears; cut in half and core. In a 2- to 2½-quart baking dish, combine cranberries, pears, and lemon slices.

2. In a 1- to 2-quart pan over medium-high heat, stir sugar, vinegar, ginger, cinnamon, cloves, and ½ cup water until mixture boils and sugar is dissolved. Pour over fruit. Cover dish tightly with foil.

3. Bake in a 350° regular or convection oven until pears are tender when pierced, 45 minutes to 1 hour. Serve warm or at room temperature.

Per serving: 368 cal., 3% (11 cal.) from fat; 1.4 g protein; 1.2 g fat (0.1 g sat.); 96 g carbo (8.4 g fiber); 1.8 mg sodium; 0 mg chol.

Lentil and Sweet Potato Curry

Christine Mac Ritchie, San Diego

Not many kindergartners name lentils among their favorite foods, but Christine Mac Ritchie's daughter does, thanks to this easy, nutritious dish. Serve it with hot basmati rice and plain yogurt or sour cream.

PREP AND COOK TIME: About 1 hour

MAKES: 10 cups; 6 servings

- 1 **onion** (8 oz.), peeled and chopped
- 2 teaspoons minced **garlic**
- 1 tablespoon **salad oil**
- 2 cups **dried lentils** (about 13 oz.)
- 2 pounds **sweet potatoes** or yams, peeled and diced (¼ in.)
- 2 tablespoons **curry powder**
- 1 tablespoon **ground cumin**
- About 1 teaspoon **salt**
- About ¼ teaspoon **pepper**
- 1½ quarts **vegetable broth** or fat-skimmed chicken broth
- Chopped **fresh mint** leaves

1. In a 5- to 6-quart pan over medium heat, stir onion and garlic in oil often until onion is limp, about 5 minutes.

2. Meanwhile, sort lentils and discard debris, then rinse and drain lentils. Add lentils, sweet potatoes, curry powder, cumin, 1 teaspoon salt, ¼ teaspoon pepper, and broth to onion mixture. Bring to a boil over high heat; reduce heat, cover, and simmer until lentils are tender to bite and sweet potatoes are tender when pierced, 25 to 30 minutes. Add more salt and pepper to taste. Garnish with chopped mint.

Per serving: 401 cal., 9.2% (37 cal.) from fat; 21 g protein; 4.1 g fat (0.4 g sat.); 73 g carbo (12 g fiber); 484 mg sodium; 0 mg chol.

Chocolate Banana Bread

Teresa Sizemore, Catheys Valley, CA

This variation on traditional banana bread has become a favorite snack for Teresa Sizemore's children.

PREP AND COOK TIME: About 1¼ hours, plus about 1 hour to cool

MAKES: 1 loaf (about 2 lb.); 8 to 10 servings

About ½ cup (¼ lb.) **butter** or margarine, at room temperature

About 1½ cups **all-purpose flour**

1 cup **sugar**

2 **large eggs,** at room temperature

1½ cups mashed **ripe bananas**

⅓ cup **Dutch-process unsweetened cocoa**

1 tablespoon **baking powder**

½ teaspoon **salt**

1 cup chopped **pecans** (optional)

1. Butter and flour a 9- by 5-inch loaf pan (8-cup capacity).

2. In a bowl, with a mixer on high speed, beat ½ cup butter and the sugar until fluffy, about 3 minutes, scraping bowl occasionally. Add eggs and beat until well blended. Stir in bananas.

3. In a small bowl, mix 1½ cups flour, cocoa, baking powder, and salt; add to banana mixture and mix just until evenly moistened. Stir in pecans if using. Pour batter into prepared pan.

4. Bake in a 350° regular or convection oven until a thin wood skewer inserted in center of loaf comes out clean, 45 to 55 minutes. Cool in pan on a rack for 10 minutes, then invert loaf from pan and cool completely on rack, about 1 hour.

Per serving: 287 cal., 34% (99 cal.) from fat; 4.2 g protein; 11 g fat (6.7 g sat.); 45 g carbo (1.1 g fiber); 394 mg sodium; 68 mg chol.

Port-braised Lamb Shanks

Mickey Strang, McKinleyville, CA

Mickey Strang describes this dish as "elegant comfort food." Serve it over mashed potatoes or polenta.

PREP AND COOK TIME: About 3 hours

MAKES: 3 servings

Cold-weather comfort: Lamb shanks braised with orange slices and port, served over creamy mashed potatoes.

2 **leeks** (about 1¼ lb. total)

1 tablespoon **olive oil**

2 teaspoons minced or pressed **garlic**

3 **lamb shanks** (about 3½ lb. total), bones cracked and fat trimmed

1 pound **oranges,** rinsed and thinly sliced crosswise (ends discarded)

⅔ cup **port**

¼ cup **Cointreau** or other orange-flavor liqueur (optional)

About ½ teaspoon **salt**

About ½ teaspoon **pepper**

1. Trim root ends, coarse tops, and outer layers from leeks; cut leeks in half lengthwise. Rinse under running water, flipping layers to flush out grit. Coarsely chop.

2. Pour oil into a 6- to 8-quart Dutch oven or ovenproof pan over medium-high heat. When hot, add leeks and garlic; stir often until leeks are limp, about 10 minutes.

3. Meanwhile, rinse lamb shanks and pat dry. Add lamb, 1 cup water, orange slices, port, Cointreau, ½ teaspoon salt, and ½ teaspoon pepper to pan. Cover and bring to a simmer.

4. Transfer pan to a 325° regular or convection oven and bake until lamb is very tender when pierced, 2 to 2½ hours. Check occasionally; if pan gets too dry, add water, ¼ cup at a time, as needed. Uncover and bake until meat is well browned, 10 to 20 minutes longer.

5. Serve from pan, or spoon into a wide, shallow bowl. Add more salt and pepper to taste.

Per serving: 636 cal., 28% (180 cal.) from fat; 79 g protein; 20 g fat (6.2 g sat.); 41 g carbo (3.9 g fiber); 634 mg sodium; 234 mg chol.

Quick Winter Tomato Relish

Jim Hardeman, Long Beach, CA

This sweet-tart relish is one for the history books—at least in Jim Hardeman's family. It came from his Aunt Dede (so called because he couldn't pronounce her name, Edith), who was born in 1894. The relish tastes great with baked beans, on sandwiches, and with hot or cold roasted meats.

PREP AND COOK TIME: About 35 minutes

MAKES: About 5 cups

1½ pounds **onions,** peeled and thinly sliced

1 tablespoon **butter** or margarine

1 can (28 oz.) **tomatoes**

1 cup firmly packed **brown sugar**

1 cup **cider vinegar**

1 teaspoon **pepper**

½ teaspoon *each* **ground allspice, ground cinnamon,** and **ground cloves**

Salt

1. In a 3- to 4-quart pan over medium-high heat, stir onions in butter until limp, about 6 minutes.

2. Add tomatoes and their liquid, brown sugar, vinegar, pepper, allspice, cinnamon, and cloves; boil over high heat, stirring often, until mixture is reduced to 5 cups, 25 to 30 minutes. Add salt to taste.

3. Serve sauce hot, warm, or cool. Or chill airtight up to 1 week.

Per ¼ cup: 68 cal., 9.3% (6.3 cal.) from fat; 0.7 g protein; 0.7 g fat (0.4 g sat.); 16 g carbo (0.8 g fiber); 76 mg sodium; 1.6 mg chol. ◆

The Low-Fat Cook

Start with a flavor-infused stock for satisfying lean entrées

By Jerry Anne Di Vecchio

■ The art of adding rich flavor without many calories depends on adept seasonings. One method is to infuse fat-skimmed chicken broth with the essence of zingy ginger, aromatic thyme, and mellow mushrooms. You can use this make-ahead stock—packed with flavor—as the foundation for easy, lean casseroles, such as the handsome chicken and sole dishes here.

Ginger for zip, mushrooms for earthiness, and thyme for depth—a formidable flavor trio for low-fat dishes.

Chicken Breast and Mushroom Casserole

PREP AND COOK TIME: 35 to 40 minutes

NOTES: Bake the chicken while the potatoes cook; keep it warm for a few minutes while you mash the potatoes and make the sauce.

MAKES: 4 servings

> **Mushroom Essence** (recipe at right)
> 1 pound **boned, skinned chicken breast halves,** rinsed
> ¾ cup chopped **green onions**
> 2 tablespoons drained **capers**
> 2 tablespoons **cream sherry**
> 1 tablespoon **soy sauce**
> 1 teaspoon minced peeled **fresh ginger**
> 1½ pounds **thin-skinned potatoes,** rinsed, peeled, and cut into ½-inch cubes
> ½ teaspoon **dried tarragon**
> 2 teaspoons **cornstarch**
> About ½ cup **low-fat (1%) milk**
> ¼ cup shredded **gruyère** or Swiss **cheese**
> **Salt** and **pepper**

1. Pour one recipe's worth of Mushroom Essence through a fine strainer into a 4- to 5-quart pan; discard the ginger. Put mushrooms in a shallow 10- to 11-inch oval casserole dish (about 2½ qt.). Cut each chicken breast in half horizontally into two thinner pieces. Add chicken, ½ cup green onions, capers, sherry, soy sauce, and ginger to mushrooms; mix and spread level. Cover casserole tightly with foil.

2. Bake chicken in a 375° oven until meat is no longer pink in center of thickest part (cut to test), about 15 minutes; keep warm.

3. While chicken bakes, add potatoes and tarragon to mushroom broth. Bring to a boil over high heat; cover and simmer until potatoes are soft enough to mash easily, about 15 minutes. Drain potatoes in a strainer over a bowl. Pour liquid back into pan and put potatoes in the bowl.

4. Uncover chicken and drain juices into pan. Boil liquid over high heat until reduced to about ¾ cup, 4 to 5 minutes. In a small bowl, blend cornstarch with 1 tablespoon water and stir into boiling liquid; stir until boiling again, and remove from heat. Turn oven to broil.

5. Meanwhile, with a potato masher or a mixer, mash potatoes until smooth, adding enough milk for desired texture. Push chicken and mushrooms toward center of casserole to leave a 1-inch space around edge. Spoon potatoes (or pipe through a pastry bag with a large plain or star tip) into space. Pour sauce over chicken mixture. Sprinkle potatoes with cheese.

6. Broil about 4 inches from heat until cheese is very lightly browned, about 4 minutes. Sprinkle with remaining ¼ cup green onions. Add salt and pepper to taste.

Per serving: 376 cal., 11% (42 cal.) from fat; 43 g protein; 4.7 g fat (2 g sat.); 40 g carbo (4.4 g fiber); 655 mg sodium; 75 mg chol.

Sole and Mushroom Casserole. Follow directions for Chicken Breast and Mushroom Casserole (preceding), but omit chicken and instead use 1 pound **boned, skinned sole fillets,** rinsed. In step 1, mix seasonings with mushrooms in casserole, then lay fillets evenly over mixture, overlapping if necessary. In step 2, bake until fillets are opaque but still moist-looking in center of thickest part, about 15 minutes. Then complete through step 6.

Per serving: 354 cal., 12% (42 cal.) from fat; 39 g protein; 4.7 g fat (2 g sat.); 40 g carbo (4.4 g fiber); 673 mg sodium; 63 mg chol.

Mushroom Essence

PREP AND COOK TIME: 35 to 40 minutes

NOTES: For quick-start low-fat meals, make several batches of this flavorful stock and freeze; thaw in a microwave oven.

MAKES: 4 cups

1. Rinse 1 pound **mushrooms;** trim and discard discolored stem ends, then thinly slice mushrooms. In a 4- to 6-quart pan, mix mushrooms with 1 tablespoon **lemon juice,** then add ½ cup **dry white wine,** 6 slices (quarter-size) **fresh ginger,** and ½ teaspoon **dried thyme.** Cover and place over medium-high heat; stir occasionally until mushrooms are juicy, about 5 minutes. Uncover and stir occasionally over high heat until liquid is evaporated, 15 to 20 minutes.

2. Add 4 cups fat-skimmed **chicken broth** to pan. Cover and simmer to blend flavors, about 15 minutes. Measure mushrooms and liquid. If there's more than 4 cups, return to pan and boil, uncovered, until reduced to 4 cups; if there's less, add water.

Per cup: 67 cal., 6.7% (4.5 cal.) from fat; 10 g protein; 0.5 g fat (0.1 g sat.); 6.2 g carbo (1.5 g fiber); 82 mg sodium; 0 mg chol. ◆

Articles Index

All-American barbecue, 132
Appetizing favorite, 224
Avocado green, 78

Bay Area picnics, 103
Berry sweet endings, 90
Bold hand with ginger, 30
Breakfasts that bite back, 205
Brick chicks, 147
Brunch for Mom, 94
Burgers on the beach, 151

Caffeine castles in the Southwest, 33
Celebrating 'shrooms in Telluride, 173
Christmas Eve crab feed, 242
Christmas in the mountains, 244
Classic stews made easy, 196
Cool bowlfuls, 150
Coolest sandwiches, 120
Craving for crab, 20
Crêpe craze, 42
Crusty loaves from your oven, 230

Driving the berry trail, 145

Flavor of lime, 138
Flavor on a roll, 170
Food Guide
  April, 82
  August, 163

Food Guide (cont'd.)
  December, 258
  February, 46
  January, 26
  July, 141
  June, 123
  March, 62
  May, 99
  November, 234
  October, 200
  September, 184
Frank Sinatra ate here: classic
  eateries of L.A., 127

Grand old pot pies, 58

Heady days: Southwestern brew
  pubs, 193

In mint condition, 116
Inn-spiration, 50

Kitchen Cabinet
  April, 86
  August, 174
  December, 262
  February, 52
  January, 32
  July, 152
  June, 128
  March, 70
  May, 106
  November, 247

Kitchen Cabinet (cont'd.)
  October, 209
  September, 192

Lentil country, 207
Little roast, big taste, 166
Low-Fat Cook
  chicken salads, 172
  frozen shrimp, 191
  Indonesian soups, 206
  make ahead stock, 264
  Mexican popsicles, 149
  saucy ravioli, 105
  showtime snacks, 69

Mushrooms: earthy delights, 220

New endings, 228
New takes on tea, 87
Northern California's artisan cheese
  factories, 67

Oregon wine tasting detour, 104
Over easy on the coast, 55
Overnight success, 225

Perfect roast chicken, 36
Pies à la road, 156
Portland summer supper, 178

Quick Cook
  falafel, 102
  lower the heat on fish, 81
  one-pan pastas, 204
  pasta and beans, 190
  sauces for the freezer, 255

Quick Cook (cont'd.)
  savory skewers, 126
  sole, 41
  world wraps, 148

Renowned main-dish salads, 110

Shaking up the vines in Lodi, 183
Soft spot for caramel, 256
Spring lamb feast, 74
Sweet heat, 65
Sweet relief: vintage soda fountains, 189

Tequila time, 53
Tradition with a twist, 212
Tree-trimming fiesta, 240
Tucson tamale pie, 188
Two-tone rice, 98

Vegetables, dressed for dinner, 223

Weeknight wisdom, 8
Western cookie collection, 246
Wine Guide
  aroma and taste, 187
  champagne and sparkling, 261
  discover these "bests", 66
  entertaining tips, 236
  Jancis Robinson interview, 49
  jug and inexpensive wines, 29
  port, 85
  rosé, 144
  salad solutions, 122
  uncorking a new trend, 165
  The Wine Bible, 203

Index of Recipe Titles

All-time favorite guacamole, 78
Amaretto butter cookies, 253
Apple-mint salad, 50
Apple tart with mustard custard and
  cheese streusel, 65
Apple-yam soup, 53
Apricot buttons, 254
Apricots with brandy, lemon, and
  honey, 129
Arizona tortilla soup, 138
Artichoke, fennel, and tricolor
  tomato salad, 135
Artichoke and red pepper
  bruschetta, 152
Artichoke bisque with parsley-lemon
  gremolata, 214
Asian sesame roasted green beans, 219
Asparagus, potato, and papaya
  salad with green onion
  dressing, 106
Asparagus and shrimp stir-fry with
  noodles, 204
Asparagus sole rolls, 41
Avocado, red onion, and prosciutto
  sandwiches, 80
Avocado and grapefruit salad with
  mint dressing, 80
Avocado-shrimp cocktail, 79

Bacon–ginger sandwiches, 31
Baked bacon, 141
Baked cranberry-orange sauce, 219
Banana paletas, 149
Béarnaise cream, 243
Béchamel sauce, 27
Beehive smoked-trout rillettes, 101
Beets sumac, 71

Beets with orange vinaigrette, 223
Berry–Muscat wine goblets, 93
Black bean–mango salsa, 128
Black beans and fettuccine with
  turkey, 190
Blackberry paletas, 149
Blanquette de veau, 234
Blueberries with oranges, 97
Blueberry-lemon squares, 70
Blue corn pancakes, 123
Braised chicken in coconut milk, 14
Braised chicken with vegetables, 14
Breakfast club, 171
Brick-grilled chicken, 147
Brie and chutney crêpe triangles, 43
Brie's butternut squash bisque, 237
Broccoli-beef noodles, 204
Broiled salmon with corn relish, 17
Brownie-mint ice cream stacks, 121
Brunch BLTs with chilies and
  cheese, 174
Brussels sprouts salad, 185
Butter crusts, 140
Butter lettuce and cilantro salad, 76
Butter pastry, 65

Cambozola fondue, 142
Candied walnuts, 228
Cannellini and penne soup, 190
Caramel caffe latte, 257
Caramel-cloaked chocolate-
  hazelnut torte, 256
Caramel pastry cream, 227
Caramel pudding, 257
Caramel sandwich cookies (*Alfa-
  jores de dulce de leche*), 248
Caramel sauce, 257

Caramelized fall fruit salad with
  chicken, 192
Cardamom sour cream cake in a
  flowerpot, 97
Cheese streusel, 65
Cherry-chocolate strudel, 153
Cherry-wine sauce, 255
Chicken, potato, and tomato stew, 206
Chicken and pear spinach salad, 172
Chicken breast and mushroom
  casserole, 264
Chicken-lamb kebabs, 126
Chicken pot pie, 58
Chicken salad in pineapple boats, 172
Chilaquiles con pollo y queso, 205
Chili-cheese steak with avocado, 80
Chili glaze, 124
Chili-orange dressing, 129
Chili-painted portabellas in puff
  pastry, 222
Chinese almond cookies, 250
Chinese five-spice rub, 215
Chipotle- and maple-glazed pork
  tenderloin, 169
Chipotle-pepper rub, 125
Chive mashed potatoes, 218
Chocolate amaretto cheesecake, 107
Chocolate banana bread, 263
Chocolate-caramel trifle with
  raspberries, 226
Chocolate chip meringues, 250
Chocolate-espresso torte with
  raspberry sauce, 182
Chocolate-hazelnut soufflé crêpes, 45
Chocolate-macadamia nut clusters, 252

Chocolate tart with nut crust, 51
Chocolate therapy cookies, 249
Cilantro-lime sauce, 243
Cilantro pesto, 225
Citrus-scented port flan, 77
Citrus sugar, 27
Classic margarita rocks, 54
Classic mint julep, 117
Classic vichyssoise, 150
Classic Western burgers, 134
Cobb salad, 113
Coconut-cranberry chews, 246
Coconut-curry seafood crêpes, 227
Coq au vin with crimini mushrooms, 197
Cornbread-pecan dressing, 216
Corn chowder with red peppers and
  pancetta, 152
Crab and mushroom risotto, 24
Crab and mushroom strata, 221
Crab chawan mushi, 25
Crab salad in avocado boats, 79
Crab-wise seafood cakes, 22
Cracked crab platter, 242
Cracked crab with tamarind sauce, 24
Crackle crêpes with shrimp, 148
Cranberry crown cheesecake, 229
Cranberry ice aperitif, 214
Cranberry rugelach, 249
Cream cheese pastry, 61
Creamy crab and caviar parfaits, 22
Creamy onion and garlic mashed
  potatoes, 218
Creamy wasabi dressing, 22
Crêpes Milanese, 44
Crêpes Suzette, 44
Crimson spice champagne cocktail, 214
Crisp "dirty" rice, 69
Croque monsieur, 184

Low-Fat Recipes

General Index